R. Gupta's®

IIT-JAM
Joint Admission Test for M.Sc.

Mathematics
Previous Years' Papers
& Practice Test Papers

(Solved with Explanations)

by
RPH Editorial Board

2020
EDITION

Ramesh Publishing House, NEW DELHI

Published by
O.P. Gupta *for* Ramesh Publishing House

Admin. Office
12-H, New Daryaganj Road, Opp. Officers' Mess,
New Delhi-110002 ☏ 23261567, 23275224, 23275124

E-mail: info@rameshpublishinghouse.com
Website: www.rameshpublishinghouse.com

Showroom
● Balaji Market, Nai Sarak, Delhi-6 ☏ 23253720, 23282525
● 4457, Nai Sarak, Delhi-6, ☏ 23918938

Book Code: R-1273

ISBN: 978-93-5012-130-6

HSN Code: 49011010

Contents

IIT-JAM

JOINT ADMISSION TEST FOR M.SC. (MATHEMATICS), 2019

Section-A : Multiple Choice Questions (MCQ)

Q. (1–10) carry one mark each.

1. Let $a_1 = b_1 = 0$, and for each $n \geq 2$, let a_n and b_n be real numbers given by

$$a_n = \sum_{m=2}^{n} \frac{(-1)^m m}{(\log(m))^m} \text{ and } b_n = \sum_{m=2}^{n} \frac{1}{(\log(m))^m}.$$

Then which one of the following is TRUE about the sequences $\{a_n\}$ and $\{b_n\}$?
A. Both $\{a_n\}$ and $\{b_n\}$ are divergent
B. $\{a_n\}$ is convergent and $\{b_n\}$ is divergent
C. $\{a_n\}$ is divergent and $\{b_n\}$ is convergent
D. Both $\{a_n\}$ and $\{b_n\}$ are convergent

2. Let $T \in M_{m \times n}(\mathbb{R})$. Let V be the subspace of $M_{n \times p}(\mathbb{R})$ defined by

$$V = \{X \in M_{n \times p}(\mathbb{R}) : TX = 0\}.$$

Then the dimension of V is
A. $pn - \text{rank}(T)$
B. $mn - p\,\text{rank}(T)$
C. $p(m - \text{rank}(T))$
D. $p(n - \text{rank}(T))$

3. Let $g : \mathbb{R} \to \mathbb{R}$ be a twice differentiable function. Define $f : \mathbb{R}^3 \to \mathbb{R}$ by

$$f(x,\, y,\, z) = g(x^2 + y^2 - 2z^2).$$

Then $\dfrac{\partial^2 f}{\partial x^2} + \dfrac{\partial^2 f}{\partial y^2} + \dfrac{\partial^2 f}{\partial z^2}$ is equal to

A. $4(x^2 + y^2 - 4z^2)\, g''(x^2 + y^2 - 2z^2)$
B. $4(x^2 + y^2 + 4z^2)\, g''(x^2 + y^2 - 2z^2)$
C. $4(x^2 + y^2 - 2z^2)\, g''(x^2 + y^2 - 2z^2)$
D. $4(x^2 + y^2 + 4z^2)\, g''(x^2 + y^2 - 2z^2) + 8g'(x^2 + y^2 - 2z^2)$

4. Let $\{a_n\}_{n=0}^{\infty}$ and $\{b_n\}_{n=0}^{\infty}$ be sequences of positive real numbers such that $na_n < b_n <$

$n^2 a_n$ for all $n \geq 2$. If the radius of convergence of the power series $\sum_{n=0}^{\infty} a_n x^n$ is 4, then the power series $\sum_{n=0}^{\infty} b_n x^n$
A. converges for all x with $|x| < 2$
B. converges for all x with $|x| > 2$
C. does not converge for any x with $|x| > 2$
D. does not converge for any x with $|x| < 2$

5. Let S be the set of all limit points of the set

$$\left\{ \frac{n}{\sqrt{2}} + \frac{\sqrt{2}}{n} : n \in \mathbb{N} \right\}.$$ Let $\mathbb{Q}_+$ be the set of all positive rational numbers. Then
A. $\mathbb{Q}_+ \subseteq S$
B. $S \subseteq \mathbb{Q}_+$
C. $S \cap (\mathbb{R} \backslash \mathbb{Q}_+) \neq \varnothing$
D. $S \cap \mathbb{Q}_+ \neq \varnothing$

6. If $x^h y^k$ is an integrating factor of the differential equation

$$y(1 + xy)\, dx + x(1 - xy)dy = 0,$$

then the ordered pair $(h,\, k)$ is equal to:
A. $(-2, -2)$
B. $(-2, -1)$
C. $(-1, -2)$
D. $(-1, -1)$

7. If $y(x) = \lambda e^{2x} + e^{\beta x}$, $\beta \neq 2$, is a solution of the differential equation

$$\frac{d^2 y}{dx^2} + \frac{dy}{dx} - 6y = 0$$

satisfying $\dfrac{dy}{dx}(0) = 5$, then $y(0)$ is equal to
A. 1
B. 4
C. 5
D. 9

8. The equation of the tangent plane to the surface $x^2 z + \sqrt{8 - x^2 - y^4} = 6$ at the point $(2, 0, 1)$ is:

A. $2x + z = 5$ B. $3x + 4z = 10$
C. $3x - z = 10$ D. $7x - 4z = 10$

9. The value of the integral

$$\int_{y=0}^{1} \int_{x=0}^{1-y^2} y\sin(\pi(1-x)^2)\,dx\,dy$$

is

A. $\dfrac{1}{2\pi}$ B. 2π

C. $\dfrac{\pi}{2}$ D. $\dfrac{2}{\pi}$

10. The area of the surface generated by rotating the curve $x = y^3$, $0 \le y \le 1$, about the y-axis, is

A. $\dfrac{\pi}{27}10^{3/2}$ B. $\dfrac{4\pi}{3}(10^{3/2} - 1)$

C. $\dfrac{\pi}{27}(10^{3/2} - 1)$ D. $\dfrac{4\pi}{3}10^{3/2}$

Q. (11–30) carry two marks each.

11. Let H and K be subgroups of $\mathbb{Z}_{144}$. If the order of H is 24 and the order of K is 36, then the order of the subgroup $H \cap K$ is:
A. 3   B. 4
C. 6   D. 12

12. Let P be a 4×4 matrix with entries from the set of rational numbers. If $\sqrt{2}+i$, with $i = \sqrt{-1}$, is a root of the characteristic polynomial of P and I is the 4×4 identity matrix, then
A. $P^4 = 4P^2 + 9I$ B. $P^4 = 4P^2 - 9I$
C. $P^4 = 2P^2 - 9I$ D. $P^4 = 2P^2 + 9I$

13. The set $\left\{\dfrac{x}{1+x} : -1 < x < 1\right\}$, as a subset of $\mathbb{R}$, is:
A. connected and compact
B. connected but not compact
C. not connected but compact
D. neither connected nor compact

14. The set $\left\{\dfrac{1}{m}+\dfrac{1}{n} : m, n \in \mathbb{N}\right\} \cup \{0\}$, as a subset of $\mathbb{R}$, is:

A. compact and open
B. compact but not open
C. not compact but open
D. neither compact nor open

15. For $-1 < x < 1$, the sum of the power series $1+\sum_{n=2}^{\infty}(-1)^{n-1}n^2 x^{n-1}$ is:

A. $\dfrac{1-x}{(1+x)^3}$ B. $\dfrac{1+x^2}{(1+x)^4}$

C. $\dfrac{1-x}{(1+x)^2}$ D. $\dfrac{1+x^2}{(1+x)^3}$

16. Let $f(x) = (\ln x)^2$, $x > 0$. Then

A. $\displaystyle\lim_{x\to\infty} \dfrac{f(x)}{x}$ does not exist

B. $\displaystyle\lim_{x\to\infty} f'(x) = 2$

C. $\displaystyle\lim_{x\to\infty} \left(f(x+1) - f(x)\right) = 0$

D. $\displaystyle\lim_{x\to\infty} \left(f(x+1) - f(x)\right)$ does not exist

17. Let $f : \mathbb{R} \to \mathbb{R}$ be a differentiable function such that $f'(x) > f(x)$ for all $x \in \mathbb{R}$, and $f(0) = 1$. Then $f(1)$ lies in the interval:
A. $(0,\ e^{-1})$ B. $\left(e^{-1}, \sqrt{e}\right)$
C. $\left(\sqrt{e}, e\right)$ D. (e, ∞)

18. For which one of the following values of k, the equation
$$2x^3 + 3x^2 - 12x - k = 0$$
has three distinct real roots?
A. 16   B. 20
C. 26   D. 31

19. Which one of the following series is divergent?

A. $\displaystyle\sum_{n=1}^{\infty} \dfrac{1}{n}\sin^2\dfrac{1}{n}$ B. $\displaystyle\sum_{n=1}^{\infty} \dfrac{1}{n}\log n$

C. $\displaystyle\sum_{n=1}^{\infty} \dfrac{1}{n^2}\sin\dfrac{1}{n}$ D. $\displaystyle\sum_{n=1}^{\infty} \dfrac{1}{n}\tan\dfrac{1}{n}$

20. Let S be the family of orthogonal trajectories of the family of curves
$$2x^2 + y^2 = k, \text{ for } k \in \mathbb{R} \text{ and } k > 0.$$
If $C \in S$ and C passes through the point $(1, 2)$, then C also passes through

A. $\left(4,-\sqrt{2}\right)$ B. $(2,-4)$

C. $\left(2,2\sqrt{2}\right)$ D. $\left(4,2\sqrt{2}\right)$

21. Let x, $x + e^x$ and $1 + x + e^x$ be solutions of a linear second order ordinary differential equation with constant coefficients. If $y(x)$ is the solution of the same equation satisfying $y(0) = 3$ and $y'(0) = 4$, then $y(1)$ is equal to:

A. $e + 1$ B. $2e + 3$

C. $3e + 2$ D. $3e + 1$

22. The function
$$f(x,\ y) = x^3 + 2xy + y^3$$
has a saddle point at

A. $(0,\ 0)$ B. $\left(-\dfrac{2}{3},-\dfrac{2}{3}\right)$

C. $\left(-\dfrac{3}{2},-\dfrac{3}{2}\right)$ D. $(-1,\ -1)$

23. The area of the part of the surface of the paraboloid $x^2 + y^2 + z = 8$ lying inside the cylinder $x^2 + y^2 = 4$ is:

A. $\dfrac{\pi}{2}(17^{3/2} - 1)$ B. $\pi(17^{3/2} - 1)$

C. $\dfrac{\pi}{6}(17^{3/2} - 1)$ D. $\dfrac{\pi}{3}(17^{3/2} - 1)$

24. Let C be the circle $(x-1)^2 + y^2 = 1$, oriented counter clockwise. Then the value of the line integral
$$\oint_C -\frac{4}{3}xy^3\,dx + x^4\,dy$$
is

A. 6π B. 8π

C. 12π D. 14π

25. Let $\vec{F}(x, y, z) = 2y\hat{i} + x^2\hat{j} + xy\hat{k}$ and let C be the curve of intersection of the plane $x + y + z = 1$ and the cylinder $x^2 + y^2 = 1$. Then the value of
$$\left|\oint_C \vec{F}\cdot d\vec{r}\right|$$
is

A. π B. $\dfrac{3\pi}{2}$

C. 2π D. 3π

26. The tangent line to the curve of intersection of the surface $x^2 + y^2 - z = 0$ and the plane $x + z = 3$ at the point $(1, 1, 2)$ passes through

A. $(-1, -2, 4)$ B. $(-1, 4, 4)$

C. $(3, 4, 4)$ D. $(-1, 4, 0)$

27. The set of eigenvalues of which one of the following matrices is NOT equal to the set of eigenvalues of $\begin{pmatrix} 1 & 2 \\ 4 & 3 \end{pmatrix}$?

A. $\begin{pmatrix} 1 & 4 \\ 2 & 3 \end{pmatrix}$ B. $\begin{pmatrix} 3 & 2 \\ 4 & 1 \end{pmatrix}$

C. $\begin{pmatrix} 3 & 4 \\ 2 & 1 \end{pmatrix}$ D. $\begin{pmatrix} 2 & 3 \\ 1 & 4 \end{pmatrix}$

28. Let $\{a_n\}$ be a sequence of positive real numbers. The series $\sum_{n=1}^{\infty} a_n$ converges if the series

A. $\sum_{n=1}^{\infty} a_n^2$ converges

B. $\sum_{n=1}^{\infty} \dfrac{a_n}{2^n}$ converges

C. $\sum_{n=1}^{\infty} \dfrac{a_{n+1}}{a_n}$ converges

D. $\sum_{n=1}^{\infty} \dfrac{a_n}{a_{n+1}}$ converges

29. For $\beta \in \mathbb{R}$, define
$$f(x,y) = \begin{cases} \dfrac{x^2\,|x|^\beta\,y}{x^4 + y^2}, & x \neq 0, \\[2mm] 0, & x = 0. \end{cases}$$
Then, at $(0, 0)$, the function f is

A. continuous for $\beta = 0$

B. continuous for $\beta > 0$

C. not differentiable for any β

D. continuous for $\beta < 0$

30. Let $\{a_n\}$ be a sequence of positive real numbers such that
$$a_1 = 1,\ a_{n+1}^2 - 2a_n a_{n+1} - a_n = 0 \text{ for all } n \geq 1.$$
Then the sum of the series $\sum_{n=1}^{\infty} \dfrac{a_n}{3^n}$ lies in the interval

A. $(1, 2]$ B. $(2, 3]$

C. $(3, 4]$ D. $(4, 5]$

Section-B : Multiple Select Questions (MSQ)

Q. (31–40) carry two marks each.

31. Let G be a noncyclic group of order 4. Consider the statements I and II:
I. There is NO injective (one-one) homomorphism from G to $\mathbb{Z}_8$
II. There is NO surjective (onto) homomorphism from $\mathbb{Z}_8$ to G
Then
A. I is true
B. I is false
C. II is true
D. II is false

32. Let G be a nonabelian group, $y \in G$, and let the maps f, g, h from G to itself be defined by $f(x) = yxy^{-1}$, $g(x) = x^{-1}$ and $h = g \circ g$.
Then
A. g and h are homomorphisms and f is not a homomorphism
B. h is a homomorphism and g is not a homomorphism
C. f is a homomorphism and g is not a homomorphism
D. f, g and h are homomorphisms

33. Let S and T be linear transformations from a finite dimensional vector space V to itself such that

$S(T(v)) = 0$ for all $v \in V$. Then
A. rank(T) $\geq$ nullity(S)
B. rank(S) $\geq$ nullity(T)
C. rank(T) $\leq$ nullity(S)
D. rank(S) $\leq$ nullity(T)

34. Let $\vec{F}$ and $\vec{G}$ be differentiable vector fields and let g be a differentiable scalar function.
Then
A. $\nabla \cdot (\vec{F} \times \vec{G}) = \vec{G} \cdot \nabla \times \vec{F} - \vec{F} \cdot \nabla \times \vec{G}$
B. $\nabla \cdot (\vec{F} \times \vec{G}) = \vec{G} \cdot \nabla \times \vec{F} + \vec{F} \cdot \nabla \times \vec{G}$
C. $\nabla \cdot (g\vec{F}) = g\nabla \cdot \vec{F} - \nabla g \cdot \vec{F}$
D. $\nabla \cdot (g\vec{F}) = g\nabla \cdot \vec{F} + \nabla g \cdot \vec{F}$

35. Consider the intervals S = (0, 2] and T = [1, 3). Let S° and T° be the sets of interior points of S and T, respectively. Then the set of interior points of S\T is equal to:

A. S\T°
B. S\T
C. S°\T°
D. S°\T

36. Let $\{a_n\}$ be the sequence given by:

$$a_n = \max\left\{\sin\left(\frac{n\pi}{3}\right), \cos\left(\frac{n\pi}{3}\right)\right\}, \ n \geq 1.$$

Then which of the following statements is/are TRUE about the subsequences $\{a_{6n-1}\}$ and $\{a_{6n+4}\}$?
A. Both the subsequences are convergent
B. Only one of the subsequences is convergent
C. $\{a_{6n-1}\}$ converges to $-\dfrac{1}{2}$
D. $\{a_{6n+4}\}$ converges to $\dfrac{1}{2}$

37. Let
$f(x) = \cos(|\pi - x|) + (x - \pi)\sin|x|$ and $g(x) = x^2$ for $x \in \mathbb{R}$.
If $h(x) = f(g(x))$, then
A. h is not differentiable at $x = 0$
B. $h'\left(\sqrt{\pi}\right) = 0$
C. $h''(x) = 0$ has a solution in $(-\pi, \pi)$
D. there exists $x_0 \in (-\pi, \pi)$ such that $h(x_0) = x_0$

38. Let $f: \left(0, \dfrac{\pi}{2}\right) \to \mathbb{R}$ be given by
$$f(x) = (\sin x)^\pi - \pi \sin x + \pi.$$

Then which of the following statements is/are TRUE?
A. f is an increasing function
B. f is a decreasing function
C. $f(x) > 0$ for all $x \in \left(0, \dfrac{\pi}{2}\right)$
D. $f(x) < 0$ for some $x \in \left(0, \dfrac{\pi}{2}\right)$

39. Let

$$f(x, y) = \begin{cases} \dfrac{|x|}{|x| + |y|}\sqrt{x^4 + y^2}, & (x, y) \neq (0, 0) \\ 0, & (x, y) = (0, 0) \end{cases}$$

Then at $(0, 0)$,

A. f is continuous

B. $\dfrac{\partial f}{\partial x} = 0$ and $\dfrac{\partial f}{\partial y}$ does not exist

C. $\dfrac{\partial f}{\partial x}$ does not exist and $\dfrac{\partial f}{\partial y} = 0$

D. $\dfrac{\partial f}{\partial x} = 0$ and $\dfrac{\partial f}{\partial y} = 0$

40. Let $\{a_n\}$ be the sequence of real numbers such that

$a_1 = 1$ and $a_{n+1} = a_n + a_n^2$ for all $n \geq 1$.

Then

A. $a_4 = a_1(1 + a_1)(1 + a_2)(1 + a_3)$

B. $\displaystyle\lim_{n\to\infty} \dfrac{1}{a_n} = 0$

C. $\displaystyle\lim_{n\to\infty} \dfrac{1}{a_n} = 1$

D. $\displaystyle\lim_{n\to\infty} a_n = 0$

Section-C : Numerical Answer Type (NAT)

Q. (41–50) carry one mark each.

41. Let x be the 100-cycle $(1, 2, 3, \dots 100)$ and let y be the transposition $(49, 50)$ in the permutation group S_{100}. Then the order of xy is __________ .

42. Let W_1 and W_2 be subspaces of the real vector space $\mathbb{R}^{100}$ defined by

$W_1 = \{(x_1, x_2, \dots, x_{100}) : x_i = 0$ if i is divisible by 4$\}$,

$W_2 = \{(x_1, x_2, \dots, x_{100}) : x_i = 0$ if i is divisible by 5$\}$.

Then the dimension of $W_1 \cap W_2$ is _______

43. Consider the following system of three linear equations in four unknowns x_1, x_2, x_3 and x_4

$$x_1 + x_2 + x_3 + x_4 = 4$$
$$x_1 + 2x_2 + 3x_3 + 4x_4 = 5$$
$$x_1 + 3x_2 + 5x_3 + kx_4 = 5$$

If the system has no solutions, then $k =$ _____

44. Let $\vec{F}(x, y) = -y\hat{i} + x\hat{j}$ and let C be the ellipse

$$\dfrac{x^2}{16} + \dfrac{y^2}{9} = 1$$

oriented counter clockwise. Then the value of $\displaystyle\oint_C \vec{F}\cdot d\vec{r}$ (round off to 2 decimal places) is

____

45. The co-efficient of $\left(x - \dfrac{\pi}{2}\right)$ in the Taylor series expansion of the function

$$f(x) = \begin{cases} \dfrac{4(1 - \sin x)}{2x - \pi}, & x \neq \dfrac{\pi}{2} \\[2mm] 0, & x = \dfrac{\pi}{2} \end{cases}$$

about $x = \dfrac{\pi}{2}$, is _________

46. Let $f : [0, 1] \to \mathbb{R}$ be given by

$$f(x) = \dfrac{\left(1 + x^{1/3}\right)^3 + \left(1 - x^{1/3}\right)^3}{8(1 + x)}$$

Then

$\max\{f(x) : x \in [0,1]\} - \min\{f(x) : x \in [0,1]\}$ is __________

47. If

$$g(x) = \int_{x(x-2)}^{4x-5} f(t)\,dt, \text{ where } f(x) = \sqrt{1 + 3x^4} \text{ for }$$

$x \in \mathbb{R}$

then $g'(1) =$ _______

48. Let

$$f(x, y) = \begin{cases} \dfrac{x^3 + y^3}{x^2 - y^2}, & x^2 - y^2 \neq 0 \\[2mm] 0, & x^2 - y^2 = 0. \end{cases}$$

Then the directional derivative of f at $(0, 0)$ in the direction of $\dfrac{4}{5}\hat{i} + \dfrac{3}{5}\hat{j}$ is __________

49. The value of the integral

$$\int_{-1}^{1}\int_{-1}^{1}|x+y|\,dx\,dy$$

(round off to 2 decimal places) is _______

50. The volume of the solid bounded by the surfaces $x = 1 - y^2$ and $x = y^2 - 1$, and the planes $z = 0$ and $z = 2$ (round off to 2 decimal places) is __________

Q. (51–60) carry two marks each.

51. The volume of the solid of revolution of the loop of the curve $y^2 = x^4(x + 2)$ about the x-axis (round off to 2 decimal places) is ______

52. The greatest lower bound of the set

$$\left\{\left(e^n + 2^n\right)^{1/n} : n \in \mathbb{N}\right\},$$

(round off to 2 decimal places) is _______

53. Let $G = \{n \in \mathbb{N} : n \le 55, \gcd(n, 55) = 1\}$ be the group under multiplication modulo 55. Let $x \in G$ be such that $x^2 = 26$ and $x > 30$. Then x is equal to _______

54. The number of critical points of the function
$$f(x, y) = (x^2 + 3y^2)e^{-(x^2 + y^2)}$$
is _______

55. The number of elements in the set $\{x \in S_3 : x^4 = e\}$, where e is the identity element of the permutation group S_3, is _______

56. If $\begin{pmatrix} 2 \\ y \\ z \end{pmatrix}$, $y, z \in \mathbb{R}$, is an eigenvector corresponding to a real eigenvalue of the matrix $\begin{pmatrix} 0 & 0 & 2 \\ 1 & 0 & -4 \\ 0 & 1 & 3 \end{pmatrix}$, then $z - y$ is equal to _______

57. Let M and N be any two 4×4 matrices with integer entries satisfying

$$MN = 2\begin{pmatrix} 1 & 0 & 0 & 1 \\ 0 & 1 & 1 & 0 \\ 0 & 0 & 1 & 0 \\ 0 & 0 & 0 & 1 \end{pmatrix}.$$

Then the maximum value of $\det(M) + \det(N)$ is _______

58. Let M be a 3×3 matrix with real entries such that $M^2 = M + 2I$, where I denotes the 3×3 identity matrix. If α, β and γ are eigenvalues of M such that $\alpha\beta\gamma = -4$, then $\alpha + \beta + \gamma$ is equal to _______

59. Let $y(x) = xv(x)$ be a solution of the differential equation

$$x^2\frac{d^2 y}{dx^2} - 3x\frac{dy}{dx} + 3y = 0.$$

If $v(0) = 0$ and $v(1) = 1$, then $v(-2)$ is equal to __________

60. If $y(x)$ is the solution of the initial value problem

$$\frac{d^2 y}{dx^2} + 4\frac{dy}{dx} + 4y = 0, \quad y(0) = 2, \frac{dy}{dx}(0) = 0,$$

then $y(\ln 2)$ is (round off to 2 decimal places) equal to _____________

ANSWERS

Section A : Multiple Choice Questions (MCQ)

1	2	3	4	5	6	7	8	9	10
D	D	B	A	B	A		B	A	C

11	12	13	14	15	16	17	18	19	20
D	C	B	B	A	C	D	A	B	C

21	22	23	24	25	26	27	28	29	30
D	A	C	B	C	B	D	C	B	A

Section-B : Multiple Select Questions (MSQ)

31	32	33	34	35
A, C	B, C	C, D	A, D	B, D

36	37	38	39	40
A	B, C, D	B, C	A, D	A, B

Section-C : Numerical Answer Type (NAT)

41	42	43	44	45
99	60	7	75.35 to 75.45	1

46	47	48	49	50
0.25	8	2.6	2.60 to 2.70	5.30 to 5.50

51	52	53	54	55
6.60 to 6.80	2.69 to 2.74	31 or 46	5	4

56	57	58	59	60
3	17	3	4	1.12 to 1.25

EXPLANATORY ANSWERS

SECTION-A

1. We have,

$$a_n = \sum_{m=2}^{n} \frac{(-1)^m m}{(\log(m))^m} \quad \text{and} \quad b_n = \sum_{m=2}^{n} \frac{1}{(\log(m))^m}$$

Let,
$$X_m = \sum \frac{(-1)^m}{(\log m)^m}$$

$$\lim_{m \to \infty} \left| X_m \right|^{1/m} = \lim_{m \to \infty} \frac{-1\, m^{1/m}}{(\log m)}$$

$$= \lim_{m \to \infty} \frac{1}{\log m} = 0$$

So, a_n is converging

Again, Let $Y_m = \sum \frac{1}{(\log m)^m}$

$$\lim_{m \to \infty} \left| Y_m \right|^{1/m} = \lim_{m \to \infty} \frac{1}{\log m} = 0$$

So, b_n is also converging.

2. $T \in M_{m \times n}(\mathbb{R})$, $T : \mathbb{R}^n \to \mathbb{R}^m$

$$\text{rank (T)} + \text{Nullity (T)} = n \qquad \text{...(}i\text{)}$$

$$V = \{X \in M_{n \times p}(\mathbb{R}) : T_{mn}X_{np} = 0_{m \times p}\}$$

$$S = M_{n \times p}(\mathbb{R}) \to M_{n \times p}(\mathbb{R}), \ S(X) = TX$$

$$V = \text{Ker}(S) = P.N(T)$$

$$\dim V = N(S) = p \times n(T)$$

From equation (*i*), nullity (T) = n – Rank (T)

$\therefore$ dim V = N(S) = p (n – Rank (T)).

3. $f(x, y, z) = g(x^2 + y^2 - 2z^2)$

$$\frac{\partial f}{\partial x} = f_x = g'(x^2 + y^2 - 2z^2).2x$$

$$\frac{\partial^2 f}{\partial x^2} = f_{xx} = 2g'(x^2 + y^2 - 2z^2) +$$

$$g''(x^2 + y^2 - 2z^2).4x^2 \quad \text{...(}i\text{)}$$

$$\frac{\partial^2 y}{\partial y^2} = f_{yy} = 2g'(x^2 + y^2 - 2z^2) +$$
$$g''(x^2 + y^2 - 2z^2).4y^2 \quad ...(ii)$$
$$\frac{\partial f}{\partial z} = f_z = g'(x^2 + y^2 - 2z^2).(-4z)$$
$$\frac{\partial^2 f}{\partial z^2} = f_{zz} = -4g'(x^2 + y^2 - 2z^2) +$$
$$g''(x^2 + y^2 - 2z^2)16z^2 \quad ...(iii)$$

Now, $\dfrac{\partial^2 f}{\partial x^2} + \dfrac{\partial^2 f}{\partial y^2} + \dfrac{\partial^2 f}{\partial z^2} = (i) + (ii) + (iii)$

$$= 0 + 4(x^2 + y^2 + 4z^2)g''(x^2 + y^2 - 2z^2)$$

Hence, correct option is (B).

4. From question, we have
$$na_n < b_n < n^2 a_n \ \forall \ n \geq 2$$

Now, power series $\sum\limits_{n=0}^{\infty} a_n \cdot x^n = 4.$ {Radius of convergence}

$$\lim_{n \to \infty} |a_n|^{1/n} = \frac{1}{4}$$

From given range $na_n < b_n < n^2.a_n$

$$n^{1/n} \cdot a_n^{1/n} < b_n^{1/n} < n^{2/n} a_n^{1/n}$$
$$-\frac{1}{4} < \lim_{n \to \infty} b_n^{1/n} < \frac{1}{4} n$$

Hence, $\sum\limits_{n=0}^{\infty} b_n$ is converges for all x with $|x| < 2.$

5. $a_n = \dfrac{n}{\sqrt{2}} + \dfrac{\sqrt{2}}{n} = \dfrac{n^2 + 2}{\sqrt{2} \cdot n} \ \forall n \in \mathbb{N}$

$$a_1 = \frac{1}{\sqrt{2}} + \sqrt{2} = \frac{1+2}{\sqrt{2}} = \frac{3}{\sqrt{2}}$$
$$a_2 = \frac{2^2 + 2}{\sqrt{2} \cdot 2} = \frac{4+2}{2\sqrt{2}} = \frac{3}{\sqrt{2}}$$
$$a_3 = \frac{3^2 + 2}{\sqrt{2} \cdot 3} = \frac{11}{3\sqrt{2}}$$
$$a_4 = \frac{4^2 + 2}{\sqrt{2} \cdot 4} = \frac{18}{4\sqrt{2}} \ .....$$

So, $\lim\limits_{n \to \infty} a_n = \infty, \quad$ Here $S = \phi$

Hence, only option (B) $S \subseteq \mathbb{Q}_+$ is correct.

6. Given differential equation
$$y(1 + xy) \, dx + x(1 - xy)dy = 0$$
This is in the form of
$$y\text{M}.dx + \text{N}.dy = 0$$

$$\text{I.F.} = \frac{1}{\text{M}x - \text{N}y} = \frac{1}{xy(1 + xy) - yx(1 - xy)}$$
$$= \frac{1}{xy + x^2 y^2 - xy + x^2 y^2} = \frac{1}{2x^2 y^2}$$
$$= \frac{1}{2} x^{-2} y^{-2}$$

Thus, $\qquad x^h.y^k = \dfrac{1}{2} x^{-2} y^{-2}$

$\therefore \qquad (h, k) = (-2, -2).$

7. $y(x) = \lambda e^{2x} + e^{\beta x}, \ \beta \neq 2$

Given differential equation: $\dfrac{d^2 y}{dx^2} + \dfrac{dy}{dx} - 6y = 0$

Characteristic equation: $m^2 + m - 6 = 0$
$$m^2 + 3m - 2m - 6 = 0$$
$$(m + 3)(m - 2) = 0$$
$\therefore \qquad\qquad m = 2, -3$
$$y(x) = C_1 e^{2x} + C_2 e^{-3x}$$
Now, $y(x) = \lambda e^{2x} + e^{\beta x} = C_1 e^{2x} + C_2 e^{-3x}$
$\therefore \qquad C_1 = \lambda$ and $C_2 = 1, \ \beta = -3$
$$y'(x) = 2\lambda e^{2x} + \beta e^{\beta x}$$
$$y'(0) = 2\lambda + \beta = 5 \Rightarrow 2\lambda - 3 = 5$$
$\Rightarrow \qquad\qquad \lambda = 4$
$\therefore \qquad y(x) = 4e^{2x} + e^{-3x}$
$$y(0) = 4(1) + (1) = 5.$$

8. Given equation of surface :
$$x^2 z + \sqrt{8 - x^2 - y^4} = 6$$

and given point $= (2, 0, 1)$

Equation of tangent : $z - z_0 = z_x(x - x_0) +$
$$z_y(y - y_0)$$

Given equation: $x^2 z + \sqrt{8 - x^2 - y^4} = 6$

On differentiation w.r.t. x

$$2xz + x^2 z_x - \frac{x}{\sqrt{8 - x^2 - y^4}} = 0$$

$\therefore \quad 2(2)1 + (2)^2 z_x - \dfrac{2}{\sqrt{8 - z^2 - 0}} = 0$

$4 + 4z_x - \dfrac{2}{2} = 0 \implies z_x = -\dfrac{3}{4}$

On differentiation w.r.t. y, we have

$x^2 . z_y - \dfrac{2y^3}{\sqrt{8 - x^2 - y^4}} = 0$

$2^2 . z_y - 0 = 0 \implies z_y = 0$

Now, equation of tangent

$z - z_0 = z_x(x - x_0) + z_y(z - z_0)$

$z - 1 = -\dfrac{3}{4}(x - 2) + 0$

$4z - 4 = -3x + 6$

$3x + 4z = 10.$

9. $I = \displaystyle\int_{y=0}^{1} \int_{x=0}^{1-y^2} y \sin(\pi(1-x)^2)\, dx\, dy$

Here $x = 1 - y^2$. This is the equation of parabola.

Here x varies from $x = 0$ to $1 - y^2$ and y varies from $y = 0$ to 1.

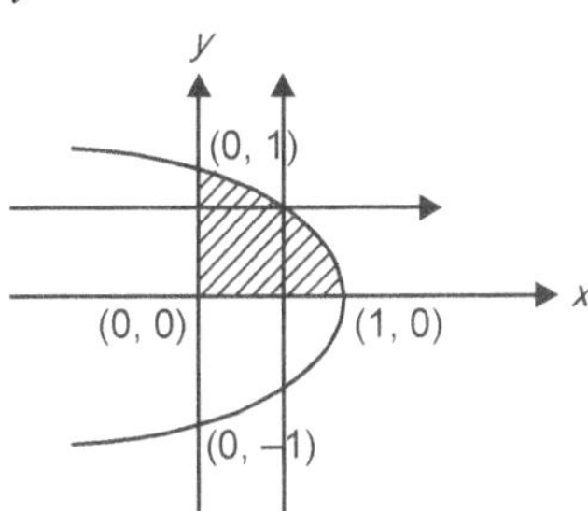

By changing the variables

$I = \displaystyle\int_{0}^{1}\left(\int_{0}^{\sqrt{1-x}} y \sin\left(\pi(1-x)^2\right) dy \right) dx$

$\because x = 1 - y^2 \qquad \therefore y = \sqrt{1-x}$

$= \displaystyle\int_{0}^{1}\left(\dfrac{y^2}{2} \sin \pi(1-x)^2 \Big|_{0}^{\sqrt{1-x}} \right) dx$

$= \displaystyle\int_{0}^{1} \dfrac{1-x}{2} \sin \pi(1-x)^2\, dx$

Let $\pi(1-x)^2 = t \implies dt = -2\pi(1-x)dx$

$\qquad\qquad (1-x)dx = \dfrac{-1}{2\pi} dt$

Now, $\displaystyle\int_{0}^{1} \dfrac{1-x}{2} \sin \pi(1-x)^2\, dx$

$= -\dfrac{1}{2\pi} \displaystyle\int_{0}^{\pi} \dfrac{1}{2} \sin t\, dt$

$= \dfrac{-1}{4\pi}[\cos t]_{0}^{\pi}$

$= \dfrac{-1}{4\pi}[-1 - 1] = \dfrac{1}{2\pi}.$

10. The curve equation $x = y^3$

for $0 \le y \le 1$

The graph of the equation $x = y^3$

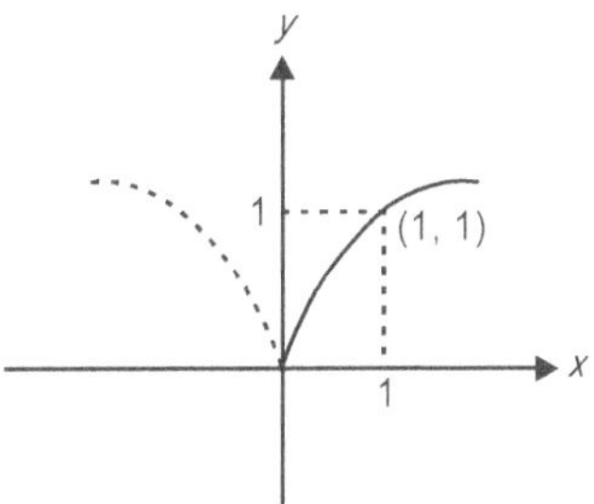

We know the area enclosed by the curve when the curve is rotated about y-axis

$S = \displaystyle\int_{0}^{1} 2\pi y^3 \sqrt{1 + \left(\dfrac{dx}{dy}\right)^2}\, dy$

$= \displaystyle\int_{0}^{1} 2\pi y^3 \sqrt{1 + (3y^2)^2}\, dy$

$= \displaystyle\int_{0}^{1} 2\pi y^3 \sqrt{1 + 9y^4}\, dy$

$\left\{ \text{Here } x = y^3, \dfrac{dx}{dy} = 3y^2 \right\}$

Let, $1 + 9y^4 = t \qquad$ Now change of limit

$36y^3 dy = dt \qquad$ when $y = 0$, $t = 1 + 0 = 1$

$y^3 dy = \dfrac{dt}{36} \qquad$ when $y = 1$,

$\qquad\qquad\qquad t = 1 + 9(1)^4 = 10$

$\therefore \qquad S = 2\pi \displaystyle\int_{1}^{10} \sqrt{t}\, \dfrac{dt}{36}$

$$= \frac{2\pi}{36}\left[\frac{(t)^{3/2}}{\frac{3}{2}}\right]_1^{10}$$

$$= \frac{\pi}{27}\left[(10)^{3/2} - 1\right].$$

11. Order of H, O(H) = 24

Order of K, O(K) = 36

Order of HK, O(HK) = LCM of (O(H), O(K))

$$= \text{LCM } (24, 36) = 72$$

Now, $\qquad$ O(HK) = $\dfrac{O(H)O(K)}{O(H \cap K)}$

$\Rightarrow \qquad$ O(H $\cap$ K) = $\dfrac{O(H)O(K)}{O(HK)}$

$$\text{O(H} \cap \text{K)} = \frac{24 \times 36}{72} = 12.$$

12. From question P is a 4×4 matrix with one root $\lambda = \sqrt{2} + i$

$$\lambda^2 = \left(\sqrt{2} + i\right)^2$$

$$\lambda^2 = 2 - 1 + 2\sqrt{2}i = 1 + 2\sqrt{2}i$$

$$\lambda^4 = \left(1 + 2\sqrt{2}i\right)^2$$

$$= 1 - 8 + 4\sqrt{2}i = -7 + 4\sqrt{2}i$$

$$= 2\left(2\sqrt{2}i + 1\right) - 9$$

$\therefore \qquad$ $P^4 = 2(P^2) - 9I$

Hence, correct option is (C).

13. $f(x) = \dfrac{x}{1+x}$: $-1 < x < 1$

Range of $f(x) = \dfrac{x}{1+x} = \left(-\infty, \dfrac{1}{2}\right)$, which is not compact but this is connected.

14. $f(m, n) = \dfrac{1}{m} + \dfrac{1}{n}$: $m, n \in \mathbb{N} \cup \{0\}$ as a subset of $\mathbb{R}$

Limit point $\left\{\dfrac{1}{m} : m \in \mathbb{N}\right\} \cup \left\{\dfrac{1}{n} : n \in \mathbb{N}\right\} \cup \{0\}$

this is not open, no point has n.b.d.

$\because$ {0} is in the set

Each limit point in the set, so it is compact.

15. Power series S = $1 + \underset{\underset{S_1}{\downarrow}}{\underbrace{\sum_{n=2}^{\infty} (-1)^{n-1} n^2 x^{n-1}}_{\underset{S_2}{\downarrow}}}$

$$S_2 = \sum_{n=2}^{\infty} (-1)^{n-1} n^2 x^{n-1}$$

$$S_2 = \frac{d}{dx}\left(\sum_{n=2}^{\infty} (-1)^{n-1} n(x)^n\right)$$

Now, $\displaystyle\sum_{n=2}^{\infty} (-1)^{n-1} nx^n = -2x^2 + 3x^3 - 4x^4 \ ....$

$$= \frac{x^3}{(1+x)^2}$$

$$S_1 + S_2 = 1 + \frac{d}{dx}\left(\frac{x^3}{(1+x)^2}\right)$$

$$1 + \frac{(1+x)^2 \cdot 3x^2 - x^3 \cdot 2(1+x)}{(1+x)^4}$$

$$1 + \frac{x^2(1+x)\{3(1+x) - 2x\}}{(1+x)^4} = 1 + \frac{x^2(3+x)}{(1+x)^3}$$

$$= \frac{1-x}{(1+x)^3}$$

16. $\qquad f(x) = (\ln(x))^2$

$$\lim_{x \to \infty} \frac{f(x)}{x} = \frac{(\log x)^2}{x} = 0$$

$$\lim_{x \to \infty} f'(x) = \lim_{x \to \infty} \frac{2\log x}{x} = 0$$

$\therefore \ \displaystyle\lim_{x \to \infty} \left(f(x+1) - f(x)\right) = 0.$

17. Given function: $f'(x) > f(x)$

Let, $\qquad f(x) = e^{kx}$, then $f'(x) = K \cdot e^{kx}$

Here, $\qquad f'(x) > f(x)$

$\therefore \qquad$ $K \cdot e^{kx} > e^{kx}$, This is valid for $k > 1$

$\therefore \qquad f(1) = e^k$ for $k \in (1, \infty)$

$\therefore \ f(1)$ lies between (e, ∞).

18. Given equation : $2x^3 + 3x^2 - 12x - k = 0$

$2x^3 + 3x^2 - 12x = k$

Now, $\qquad f(x) = 2x^3 + 3x^2 - 12x$

$$= x(2x^2 + 3x - 12)$$

Root of $2x^2 + 3x - 12 = 0$ are

$$\frac{-3 \pm \sqrt{9 + 96}}{4} = \frac{-3 \pm \sqrt{105}}{4}$$

From graph:

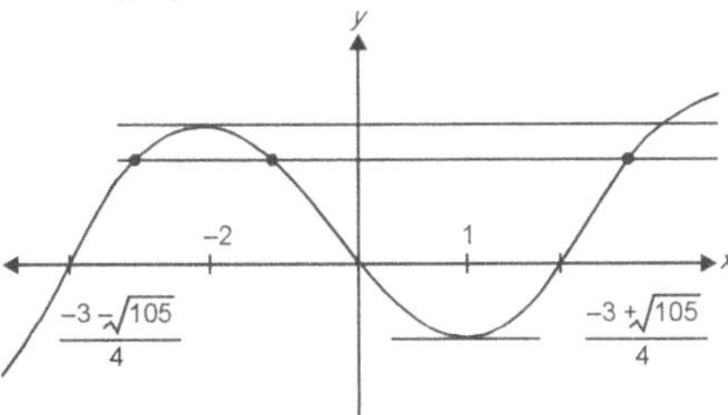

Again $\quad f(x) = 2x^3 + 3x^2 - 12x$

$$f'(x) = 6x^2 + 6x - 12$$
$$= 6(x^2 + x - 2)$$
$$= 6(x + 2)(x - 1)$$

Now, $\quad f(-2) = 2(-2)^2 + 3(-2)^2 - 12(-2) = k$

$$= -16 + 12 + 24 = k$$
$$k = 20$$

Now, for three distinct real roots,

$$k < 20$$

and from option, $k = 16 < 20$.

19. B. Going through options

A. $u_n = \displaystyle\sum_{n=1}^{\infty} \frac{1}{n} \sin^2 \frac{1}{n}$

and $V_n = \dfrac{1}{n^3}$

Now, $\displaystyle\lim_{n \to \infty} \frac{u_n}{V_n} = \lim_{n \to \infty} \frac{\sin^2 \frac{1}{n}}{\frac{1}{n^2}}$

$$= \lim_{n \to \infty} \left(\frac{\sin \frac{1}{n}}{\frac{1}{n}} \right)^2 = 1 \ne 0$$

u_n is finite

$\therefore u_n$ is converges

C. $u_n = \displaystyle\sum_{n=1}^{\infty} \frac{1}{n^2} \sin \frac{1}{n}$ and $V_n = \dfrac{1}{n^3}$

$\displaystyle\lim_{n \to \infty} \frac{u_n}{V_n} = \lim_{n \to \infty} \frac{\sin \frac{1}{n}}{\frac{1}{n}} = 1 \ne 0$, so converges.

D. $u_n = \displaystyle\sum_{n=1}^{\infty} \frac{1}{n} \tan \frac{1}{n}$ and $V_n = \dfrac{1}{n^2}$

$\displaystyle\lim_{n \to \infty} \frac{u_n}{V_n} = \lim_{n \to \infty} \frac{\frac{1}{n} \left(\tan \frac{1}{n} \right)}{\frac{1}{n^2}}$

$$= \lim_{n \to \infty} \frac{\sin \left(\frac{1}{n} \right)}{\cos \left(\frac{1}{n} \right) \left(\frac{1}{n} \right)}$$

$$= \lim_{n \to \infty} \frac{1}{\cos \left(\frac{1}{n} \right)} = \frac{1}{1} = 1 \ne 0$$

So, it is converges

Hence, $\displaystyle\sum_{n=1}^{\infty} \frac{1}{n} \log(n)$ is diverges.

20. Given curve: $2x^2 + y^2 = k$

Differentiating both sides, we have

$$\frac{d}{dx}(2x^2 + y^2) = \frac{d}{dx}(k)$$

$$4x + 2y \frac{dy}{dx} = 0 \quad \Rightarrow \quad \frac{dy}{dx} = -\frac{2x}{y}$$

$\therefore$ Slope of orthogonal trajectories

$$\frac{-dx}{dy} = \frac{-2x}{y}$$

$$\frac{dx}{x} = \frac{2\,dy}{y}$$

On integrating both sides,

$$\int \frac{dx}{x} = 2 \int \frac{dy}{y}$$

$$\ln(x) + \ln(c) = \ln y^2$$

$$\text{where } \ln C = \text{constant}$$

$$y^2 = c.x$$

As this goes to the point $(1, 2)$

$\therefore \qquad (2)^2 = C(1) \Rightarrow C = 4$

Hence, the curve is $y^2 = 4x$

For point $\left(4, -\sqrt{2}\right) : \left(-\sqrt{2}\right)^2 = 4 \times 4 \Rightarrow 2 \ne 16$

For point $(2, -4) : (-4)^2 \ne 4 \times 2 \Rightarrow 16 \ne 8$

For point $\left(2, 2\sqrt{2}\right) : \left(2\sqrt{2}\right)^2 = 4 \times 2 \Rightarrow 8 = 8$

For point $\left(4, 2\sqrt{2}\right) : \left(2\sqrt{2}\right)^2 = 4 \times 4 \Rightarrow 8 \ne 16$.

21. Linear second order ordinary differential equation: $ay'' + by' + c = f(x)$

General solution: $y(x) = C_1 e^{\alpha x} + C_2 e^{\beta x} + p(x)$

Given roots of the equations are x, $x + e^x$ and $1 + x + e^x$

$$y_1 = 1 = e^{0.x}$$
$$y_2 = e^x = e^{1.x}$$

and $\qquad p(x) = x$

$\therefore \qquad y(x) = C_1 + C_2 e^x + x \qquad ...(i)$
$$y(0) = C_1 + C_2 = 3 \qquad ...(ii)$$

From (i)

$$y'(x) = C_2 e^x + 1$$
$$y'(0) = C_2 + 1 = 4$$
$$C_2 = 3$$

From (ii)

$$C_1 + 3 = 3 \Rightarrow C_1 = 0$$
$\therefore \qquad y(x) = C_1 + C_2 e^x + x$
$$= 0 + 3e^x + x$$
$$y(1) = 3e + 1 .$$

22. Given function,

$$f(x, y) = x^3 + 2xy + y^3$$
$$f_x = 3x^2 + 2y = 0$$
$$\Rightarrow \qquad y = \frac{-3}{2}x^2$$
$$f_y = 2x + 3y^2 = 0$$
$$\Rightarrow \quad 2x + 3\left(\frac{-3}{2}x^2\right)^2 = 0$$
$$x(8 + 27x^3) = 0$$
$\therefore \quad x = 0 \ \text{ or } \ 8 + 27x^3 = 0$
$$x = \left(\frac{-8}{27}\right)^{1/3} = \frac{-2}{3}$$

Now, when $\quad x = \dfrac{-2}{3}$

$$y = \frac{-3}{2} \times \left(\frac{-2}{3}\right)^2 = \frac{-2}{3}$$

and at $x = 0$, $y = 0$

Hence, point are $(0, 0)$ and $\left(\dfrac{-2}{3}, \dfrac{-2}{3}\right)$.

Now, $f_{xx} = 6x$, $f_{xy} = 2$ and $f_{yy} = 6y$

At $(0, 0)$: $f_{xx} \cdot f_{yy} - f_{xy}^2 = 0 - 4 = -4$

At $\left(\dfrac{-2}{3}, \dfrac{-2}{3}\right)$: $6x.6y - (2)^2$

$$= 36\left(\frac{-2}{3}\right)\left(\frac{-2}{3}\right) - 4 = 12$$

Hence, the function has a saddle point at $(0, 0)$.

23. Parabola equation: $x^2 + y^2 + z = 8$

and circle : $x^2 + y^2 = 4$

$$\text{Area} = \iint_R \sqrt{1 + \left(\frac{\partial z}{\partial x}\right)^2 + \left(\frac{\partial z}{\partial y}\right)^2} \, dx \, dy$$

From equation, $x^2 + y^2 + z = 8$

$\therefore \qquad z = 8 - x^2 - y^2$

$$\frac{\partial z}{\partial x} = -2x, \quad \frac{\partial z}{\partial y} = -2y$$

$\therefore \ \text{ Area (A)} = \iint_R \sqrt{1 + (-2x)^2 + (-2y)^2} \, dx \, dy$

$$= \iint_R \sqrt{1 + 4(x^2 + y^2)} \, dx \, dy$$

Circle : $x^2 + y^2 = 4$

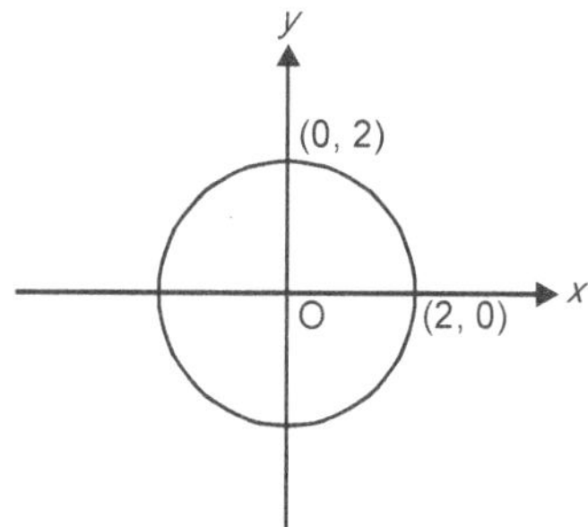

Polar form :

Let $x = r \cos \theta$, $y = r \sin \theta$

$$dx \cdot dy = rd\theta \, dr$$
$$x^2 + y^2 = r^2 \cos^2\theta + r^2 \sin^2\theta = r^2$$

Now, $\quad A = \iint_R \sqrt{1 + 4(x^2 + y^2)} \, dx \, dy$

$$= 4 \int_0^{1/2} \int_0^2 (1 + 4r^2)^{1/2} \, rd\theta \, dr$$

$$= 4 \left[\int_0^{1/2} d\theta\right]\left[\int_0^2 (1 + 4r^2)^{1/2} \, r \, dr\right]$$

Let $(1 + 4r^2) = t \Rightarrow dt = 8r\,dr \Rightarrow rdr = \dfrac{dt}{8}$

$\therefore\ A = 4 \times \dfrac{\pi}{2} \times \displaystyle\int_1^{17} t^{1/2} \cdot \dfrac{dt}{8} \quad \left\{ \begin{array}{l} \because \text{ when } r = 0,\ t = 1 \\ \quad\ \text{when } r = 2,\ t = 17 \end{array} \right\}$

$= 4 \times \dfrac{\pi}{2 \times 8} \times \dfrac{(t)^{3/2}}{\frac{3}{2}}\Bigg|_1^{17} = \dfrac{\pi}{6}\left[(17)^{3/2} - 1\right].$

24. Circle equation is $(x - 1)^2 + y^2 = 1$

Let $x = 1 + \cos t$ and $y = \sin t$

$dx = -\sin t\,dt$ and $dy = \cos t\,dt$

Now, $\ I = \displaystyle\oint_C -\dfrac{4}{3}xy^3 dx + x^4 dy$

$= \displaystyle\int_0^{2\pi} -\dfrac{4}{3}(1 + \cos t)\sin^3 t(-\sin t)dt +$

$\qquad\qquad\qquad \displaystyle\int_0^{2\pi} (1 + \cos t)^4 \cos t\,dt$

$= \dfrac{4}{3}\displaystyle\int_0^{2\pi} \sin^4 t(1 + \cos t)dt +$

$\displaystyle\int_0^{2\pi} (1 + \cos^4 t + 4\cos^2 t + 2\cos^2 t + 4\cos^3 t + 4\cos t)\cos t\,dt$

{Here, $(1 + \cos t)^4 = 1 + \cos^4 t + 4\cos^2 t + 2\cos^2 t + 4\cos^3 t + 4\cos t$}

We know that

$\displaystyle\int_0^{2\pi} \cos^n x\,dx = 0,$ for all n is odd.

So, second integral will reduce to

$\displaystyle\int_0^{2\pi} (\cos t + \cos^5 t + 2\cos^3 t + 4\cos^4 t + 4\cos^2 t)dt$

$= \displaystyle\int_0^{2\pi} (0 + 0 + 0 + 4\cos^4 t + 4\cos^2 t)dt$

and first integral will be reduce to

$\displaystyle\int_0^{2\pi} \sin^4 t + \sin^4 t \cdot \cot t\,dt = \displaystyle\int_0^{2\pi} \sin^4 t\,dt$

So, $I = \dfrac{4}{3}\displaystyle\int_0^{2\pi} \sin^4 t\,dt + 4\displaystyle\int_0^{2\pi} \cos^4 t\,dt + 4\displaystyle\int_0^{2\pi} \cos^2 t\,dt$

and for $\displaystyle\int_0^{2\pi} \sin^m x\,dx = \displaystyle\int_0^{2\pi} \cos^m x\,dx$

$\therefore\ \dfrac{4}{3}\displaystyle\int_0^{2\pi} \sin^4 t\,dt + 4\displaystyle\int_0^{2\pi} \sin^4 t\,dt + 4\displaystyle\int_0^{2\pi} \cos^2 t\,dt$

$= \dfrac{16}{3}\displaystyle\int_0^{2\pi} \sin^4 t\,dt + 4\displaystyle\int_0^{2\pi} \cos^2 t\,dt$

$= \dfrac{16}{3} \times 4\displaystyle\int_0^{\pi/2} \sin^4 t\,dt + 4\displaystyle\int_0^{2\pi} \left(\dfrac{1 + \cos 2t}{2}\right) dt$

$= \dfrac{64}{3}\displaystyle\int_0^{\pi/2} \sin^4 t\,(\cos t)^0 dt + 4\pi$

Now, for $\displaystyle\int_0^{\pi/2} \sin^m x \cos^n x\,dx = \dfrac{\left|\underline{\dfrac{m+1}{2}} \cdot \right|\underline{\dfrac{n+1}{2}}}{2\left|\underline{\dfrac{m+n+2}{2}}\right.}$

Here $m = 4,\ n = 0$

$\therefore\ \dfrac{64}{3}\displaystyle\int_0^{\pi/2} \sin^4 t\,dt = \left(\dfrac{\left|\underline{\dfrac{4+1}{2}} \cdot \right|\underline{\dfrac{0+1}{2}}}{2\left|\underline{\dfrac{4+0+2}{2}}\right.}\right)\dfrac{64}{3}$

$= \dfrac{\dfrac{64}{3} \times \dfrac{3}{2} \times \dfrac{\pi}{2}}{4} = 4\pi$

$\therefore\qquad\qquad I = 4\pi + 4\pi = 8\pi.$

25. $\vec{F}(x, y, z) = 2y\hat{i} + x^2\hat{j} + xy\hat{k}$

Let, $x = \cos t,\ y = \sin t$ and $z = t$

$dx = -\sin t.dt,\ dy = \cos t.dt$ and $dz = dt$

Work done $= \displaystyle\oint \vec{F}\overrightarrow{dr},$

where $\overrightarrow{dr} = dx\hat{i} + dy\hat{j} + dz\hat{k}$

In term of t,

$\displaystyle\int \vec{F}\overrightarrow{dr} = \displaystyle\int (2\sin t\hat{i} + \cos^2 t\hat{j} + \cos t\sin t\hat{k})$

$\qquad\qquad\qquad\qquad (dx\hat{i} + dy\hat{j} + dz\hat{k})$

$\displaystyle\int \vec{F}\overrightarrow{dr} = \displaystyle\int (2\sin t\hat{i} + \cos^2 t\hat{j} + \cos t\sin t\hat{k})$

$\qquad\qquad\qquad\qquad (-\sin t\,dt\hat{i} + \cos t\,dt\hat{j} + dt\hat{k})$

$$= \int -2\sin^2 t\, dt + (1 - \sin^2 t)\cos t\, dt + \cos t \sin t\, dt$$

$$= \int (\cos 2t - 1)dt + \cos t\, dt - \sin^2 t \cos t\, dt + \cos t \sin t\, dt$$

$$\int_0^{2\pi} \vec{F} \vec{dr} = \left[\frac{\sin 2t}{2} - t + \sin t - \frac{\sin^3 t}{3} + \frac{\sin^2 t}{2} \right]_0^{2\pi}$$

$$= -2\pi$$

$\therefore$ Absolute value of $\left| \oint_R \vec{F} \vec{dr} \right| = |-2\pi| = 2\pi$.

26. Given surface $f : (x^2 + y^2 - z) = 0$

$$\nabla f = (2x, 2y, -1)|_{(1,\,1,\,2)} = (2, 2, -1)$$

$$\vec{N}_1 = \left(2\hat{i} + 2\hat{j} - \hat{k} \right)$$

Given point P : $(x + 2) = 3$, $\vec{N}_2 = \hat{i} + \hat{k}$

$$N = \vec{N}_1 \times \vec{N}_2 = \begin{vmatrix} \hat{i} & \hat{j} & \hat{k} \\ 2 & 2 & -1 \\ 1 & 0 & 1 \end{vmatrix}$$

$$= 2\hat{i} + (-1 - 2)\hat{j} + (0 - 2)\hat{k}$$

$$= 2\hat{i} - 3\hat{j} - 2\hat{k}$$

and given point $(1, 1, 2)$

Tangent line to the curve: $\dfrac{x-1}{2} = \dfrac{y-1}{-3} = \dfrac{z-2}{-2}$

From option,

A. $(-1, -2, 4)$: $\dfrac{-1-1}{2} \neq \dfrac{-2-1}{-3} \neq \dfrac{4-2}{-2}$

B. $(-1, 4, 4)$: $\dfrac{-1-1}{2} = \dfrac{4-1}{-3} = \dfrac{4-2}{-2}$

$$= -1 = -1 = -1.$$

Hence, tangent line passes through point $(-1, 4, 4)$.

27. Given matrix: $A = \begin{bmatrix} 1 & 2 \\ 4 & 3 \end{bmatrix}$

Eigenvalues of $A = |A\lambda - I| = 0$

$$= \begin{vmatrix} 1-\lambda & 2 \\ 4 & 3-\lambda \end{vmatrix} = 0$$

$$(1 - \lambda)(3 - \lambda) - 8 = 0$$

$$\lambda^2 - 4\lambda - 5 = 0$$

$$\lambda^2 - 5\lambda + \lambda - 5 = 0$$

$$(\lambda - 5)(\lambda + 1) = 0 \implies \lambda = 5 \text{ and } -1$$

Now, going through the options

A. Eigenvalues of $\begin{pmatrix} 1 & 4 \\ 2 & 3 \end{pmatrix}$

$$\begin{vmatrix} 1-\lambda & 4 \\ 2 & 3-\lambda \end{vmatrix} = 0$$

$$(1 - \lambda)(3 - \lambda) - 8 = 0$$

$$\lambda^2 - 4\lambda - 5 = 0 \implies \lambda = -1 \text{ and } 5$$

B. Eigenvalue of $\begin{pmatrix} 3 & 2 \\ 4 & 1 \end{pmatrix}$:

$$\begin{vmatrix} 3-\lambda & 2 \\ 4 & 1-\lambda \end{vmatrix} = 0$$

$$(3 - \lambda)(1 - \lambda) - 8 = 0$$

$$\lambda^2 - 4\lambda - 5 = 0 \implies \lambda = -1 \text{ and } 5$$

C. Eigenvalue of $\begin{pmatrix} 3 & 4 \\ 2 & 1 \end{pmatrix}$:

$$\begin{vmatrix} 3-\lambda & 4 \\ 2 & 1-\lambda \end{vmatrix} = 0$$

$$(3 - \lambda)(1 - \lambda) - 8 = 0$$

$$\lambda^2 - 4\lambda - 5 = 0 \implies \lambda = -1 \text{ and } 5$$

D. Eigenvalue of $\begin{pmatrix} 2 & 3 \\ 1 & 4 \end{pmatrix}$:

$$\begin{vmatrix} 2-\lambda & 3 \\ 1 & 4-\lambda \end{vmatrix} = 0$$

$$\implies (2 - \lambda)(4 - \lambda) - 3 = 0$$

$$\implies \lambda^2 - 6\lambda + 5 = 0$$

$$\implies (\lambda - 5)(\lambda - 1) = 0 \implies \lambda = 5 \text{ and } 1$$

Hence, correct option is (D).

28. Let $\displaystyle\sum_{n=1}^{\infty} \frac{a_{n+1}}{a_n}$ is converges

Considering the nth term $\displaystyle\lim_{n\to\infty} \frac{a_{n+1}}{a_n} = 0 < 1$

$\therefore$ By ratio test Σa_n converges.

29. $f(x, y) = \begin{cases} \dfrac{x^2 |x|^\beta\, y}{x^4 + y^2}, & x \neq 0, \\ 0, & x = 0. \end{cases}$

Consider the limit at point $(0, 0)$

$$\lim_{(x,y)\to(0,0)} \frac{x^2 |x|^\beta \, y}{x^4 + y^2}$$

Let $y = mx^2$, then $\lim_{x\to 0} \dfrac{x^2 |x|^\beta \, mx^2}{x^4 + (mx^2)^2}$

$$= \lim_{x\to 0} |x|^\beta \frac{m}{1 + m^2}$$

This is continuous for $\beta > 0$.

32. Let G be a nonabelian group

and $f(x) = y.xy'$, $g(x) = x^{-1}$ and $h = g \circ g$

$$f(x_1 \times x_2) = f(x_1) \times f(x_2)$$
$$f(x_1 x_2) = f(x_1) \cdot f(x_2) = y x_1 y' \cdot y x_2 y'$$
$$\downarrow$$
$$y x_1 \cdot x_2 y' = y x_1 \cdot y' y x_2 y' = f(x_1) f(x_2)$$

Hence, $f(x)$ is homomorphism

Again, $g(x_1 x_2) = g(x_1) \cdot g(x_2) = x_1^{-1} . x_2^{-1}$

$$\downarrow$$

$$(x_1 \cdot x_2)^{-1} = x_1^{-1} . x_2^{-1} = x_2^{-1} . x_1^{-1} \pm x_1^{-1} . x_2^{-1}$$

Hence, $g(x)$ is abelian $\Leftrightarrow f : G \to G$

$g(x)$ is not homomorphism.

Again, $h(x) = g(g(x)) = g(x^{-1}) = (x^{-1})^{-1} = x$

$$h(x_1 x_2) = h(x_1) \cdot h(x_2) = x_1 \cdot x_2$$
$$\downarrow$$
$$x_1 \cdot x_2 = x_1 \cdot x_2 = h(x_1) \cdot h(x_2)$$

Hence, $h(x)$ is also homomorphism.

33. dim $V = n$

$$S : v \to V, \quad T : v \to V$$

$\therefore \quad$ rank(S) + Nullity(S) = n,

$\quad$ rank(T) + Nullity(T) = n

$$\forall \; v \in V, \; S(T(v)) = 0$$

$T(v) \in$ Ker (S) $\forall \; V \in V$

Range (T) $\leq$ Ker(S) $\Rightarrow$ rank (T) $\leq$ Nullity(S)

$$\text{... option (C).}$$

Again,

rank(S) + Nullity(S) = Rank(T) + Nullity(T)

rank(S) – Nullity(T) = Rank(T) – Nullity(S) ≤ 0

rank(S) $\leq$ Nullity(T) $\quad\quad$ .... option (D).

35. Given intervals

$$S = (0, 2] \text{ and } T = [1, 3)$$

$\therefore \quad$ $S^\circ = (0, 2)$ and $T^\circ = (1, 3)$

Now, $S \backslash T = (0, 2] \backslash [1, 3) = (0, 1)$ ...option (B)

Line is :

goes through the options

A. $S \backslash T^\circ = (0, 2] \backslash (1, 3) = (0, 1]$ — False.

C. $S^\circ \backslash T^\circ = (0, 2] \backslash (1, 3) = (0, 1]$ — False.

D. $S^\circ \backslash T = (0, 2] \backslash [1, 3) = (0, 1]$ — True.

Hence, correct option is (B and D).

36. Given that

$$a_n = \max\left\{ \sin\left(\frac{n\pi}{3}\right), \cos\left(\frac{n\pi}{3}\right) \right\} \; n \geq 1$$

$$a_{(6n-1)} = \max\left\{ \sin\frac{(6n-1)\pi}{3}, \cos\frac{(6n-1)\pi}{3} \right\}$$

$$= \max\left\{ \sin\left(2n\pi - \frac{\pi}{3}\right), \cos\left(2n\pi - \frac{\pi}{3}\right) \right\}$$

$$= \max\left\{ -\sin\frac{\pi}{3}, \cos\frac{\pi}{3} \right\}$$

$$= \max\left\{ \frac{-\sqrt{3}}{2}, \frac{1}{2} \right\} = \frac{1}{2}$$

$\therefore \quad a_{(6n-1)}$ is converges.

Now,

$$a_{(6n+4)} = \max\left\{ \sin(6n+4)\frac{\pi}{3}, \cos(6n+4)\frac{\pi}{3} \right\}$$

$$= \max\left\{ \sin\left(2n\pi + \frac{4\pi}{3}\right), \cos\left(2n\pi + \frac{4\pi}{3}\right) \right\}$$

$$= \max\left\{ \sin\frac{4\pi}{3}, \cos\frac{4\pi}{3} \right\}$$

$$= \max\left\{ -\sin\frac{\pi}{3}, -\cos\frac{\pi}{3} \right\}$$

$$= \max\left\{ \frac{-\sqrt{3}}{2}, \frac{-1}{2} \right\} = \frac{-1}{2}$$

Hence, $a_{(6n+4)}$ is also converges.

38. Let $f : \left(0, \dfrac{\pi}{2}\right) \to$ R be given by

$$f(x) = (\sin x)^\pi - \pi \cdot \sin x + \pi$$

$$f'(x) = \pi(\sin x)^{\pi - 1} \cdot \cos x - \pi \cos x$$
$$= \pi \cos x \left((\sin x)^{\pi - 1} - 1\right)$$

Now, in $\left(0, \dfrac{\pi}{2}\right)$, $0 < \sin x < 1$

and in $\left(0, \dfrac{\pi}{2}\right)$, $0 < \cos x < 1$

So, $f'(x) = \pi \cos\{(\sin x)^{\pi - 1} - 1\} \leq 0$

Hence, $f(x)$ is strictly decreasing function

Now, from graph
$$f(x) = (\sin x)^{\pi} - \pi \sin x + \pi$$

At $x = 0$, $f(0) = (\sin 0)^{\pi} - \pi \sin 0 + \pi = \pi$

At $x = \dfrac{\pi}{2}$, $f\left(\dfrac{\pi}{2}\right) = \left(\sin \dfrac{\pi}{2}\right)^{\pi} - \pi \sin \dfrac{\pi}{2} + \pi = 1$

Again, $f(x)$ is a decreasing function

From $\left(0, \dfrac{\pi}{2}\right)$. So graph will be

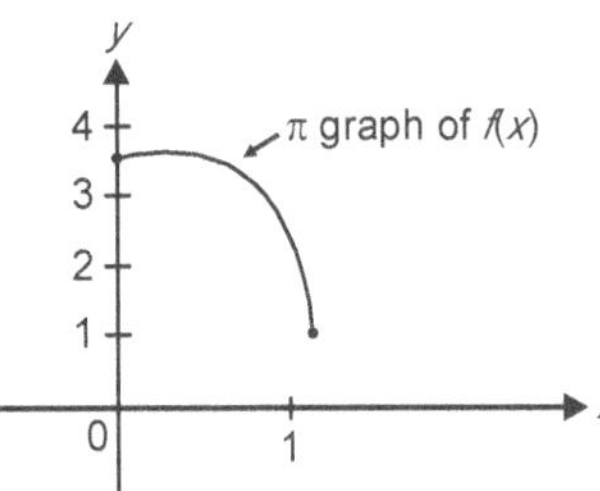

Thus, $f(x) > 0$ for all $x \in \left(0, \dfrac{\pi}{2}\right)$.

39. $f(x, y) = \begin{cases} \dfrac{|x|}{|x| + |y|}\sqrt{x^2 + y^2} & : (x, y) \neq (0, 0) \\ 0 & : (x, y) = (0, 0) \end{cases}$

Let $x = r \cos \theta$, $y = r \sin \theta$

then At $(0, 0)$, $(x, y) \to (0, 0) \Rightarrow r = 0$

$$\lim_{r \to 0} \frac{r|\cos\theta| \cdot r}{r(|\cos\theta| + |\sin\theta|)} \sqrt{r^2 \cos^4\theta + \sin^2\theta}$$

$$\lim_{r \to 0} r\left(\frac{|\cos\theta|}{|\cos\theta| + |\sin\theta|} \sqrt{r^2 \cos^4\theta + \sin^2\theta}\right) = 0$$

$$f_x(0, 0) = \lim_{h \to 0} \frac{f(h, 0) - f(0, 0)}{h}$$

$$= \lim_{h \to 0} \frac{1}{h} \frac{|h|}{(|h| + |0|)} \sqrt{h^4} = \lim_{h \to 0} \frac{h^2}{h} = 0$$

$$f_y(0, 0) = \lim_{k \to 0} \frac{f(0, k) - f(0, 0)}{k}$$

$$= \lim_{k \to 0} \frac{0 - 0}{k} = 0$$

Hence, function f is continuous at point $(0, 0)$

and also $\dfrac{\partial f}{\partial x} = 0$ and $\dfrac{\partial f}{\partial y} = 0$.

40. Given that $a_{n+1} = a_n + a_n^2$ and $a_1 = 1$

Now, $a_1 = 1$

$a_2 = a_1 + a_1^2 = 1 + 1 = 2$

$a_3 = a_2 + a_2^2 = 2 + 2^2 = 2 + 4 = 6$

$a_4 = a_3 + a_3^2 = 6 + 6^2 = 42$

and $a_4 = a_3 + a_3^2 = a_3(1 + a_3)$

$= a_2(1 + a_2)(1 + a_3)$

$= a_1(1 + a_1)(1 + a_2)(1 + a_3)$

$= 1(1 + 1)(1 + 2)(1 + 6)$

$= 1 \times 2 \times 3 \times 7 = 42$

Again, $\lim\limits_{n \to \infty} a_n = \infty$

$\therefore \quad \lim\limits_{n \to \infty} \dfrac{1}{a_n} = 0$.

41. $x = (1, 2, 3, \ldots 100) \Rightarrow O(x) = 100$

$y = (49, 50) \Rightarrow O(y) = 2$

$O(xy) = $ LCM of $(O(x), O(y))$

$= $ LCM of $(100, 2) = 100$

and order of $O(x \cap y) = 1$

$\therefore \quad O(xy) = 100 - 1 = 99$.

42. $W_1 = \{(x_1, x_2, x_3 \ldots x_{100})| x_i = 0$, if i is divisible by 4$\}$

$W_2 = \{(x_1, x_2, x_3 \ldots x_{100})| x_i = 0$, if i is divisible by 5$\}$

$\dim (W_1 \cap W_2) = ?$

Now,

$n(W_1) = 25$ {they are $x_4, x_8, x_{12} \ldots x_{100}$}

$n(W_2) = 20$ {they are $x_5, x_{10}, x_{15} \ldots x_{100}$}

$n(W_1 \cap W_2) = 5$ {they are $x_{20}, x_{40}, x_{60}, x_{80}$ and x_{100}}

Now,

$n(W_1 \cup W_2) = 25 + 20 - 5 = 40$

$\therefore \quad \dim(W_1 \cap W_2) = 100 - 40 = 60$.

43. Given equation are

$$\begin{bmatrix} 1 & 1 & 1 & 1 & | & 4 \\ 1 & 2 & 3 & 4 & | & 5 \\ 1 & 3 & 5 & k & | & 5 \end{bmatrix} =$$

$$= \begin{bmatrix} 1 & 1 & 1 & 1 & | & 4 \\ 0 & 1 & 2 & 3 & | & 1 \\ 0 & 2 & 4 & k-1 & | & 1 \end{bmatrix}$$

{Applying $R_2 \to R_2 - R_1,\ R_3 \to R_3 - R_1$}

$$= \begin{bmatrix} 1 & 1 & 1 & 1 & | & 4 \\ 0 & 1 & 2 & 3 & | & 1 \\ 0 & 0 & 0 & k-7 & | & -1 \end{bmatrix}$$

{Applying $R_3 \to R_3 - 2R_2$}

$\therefore$ Rank (A/B) = 3

From question, system has no solution

$\therefore\ k - 7 = 0 \Rightarrow k = 7.$

44. $\vec{F}(x, y) = -y\hat{i} + x\hat{j}$

and ellipse : $\dfrac{x^2}{16} + \dfrac{y^2}{9} = 1$

For $\dfrac{x^2}{a^2} + \dfrac{y^2}{b^2} = 1$ Area $dA : \pi.a.b$

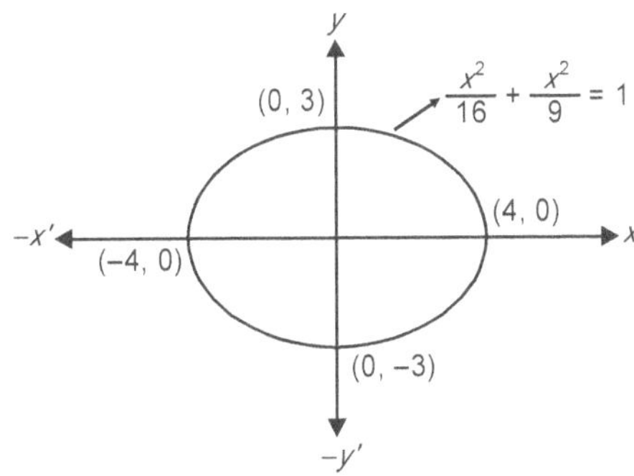

Now, $\qquad \vec{F} = -y\hat{i} + x\hat{j}$

$$\text{curl } \vec{F} = \left(\frac{\partial N}{\partial x} - \frac{\partial M}{\partial y} \right) \hat{k}$$

$$= \left(\frac{\partial x}{\partial x} - \left(\frac{-\partial y}{\partial y} \right) \right) \hat{k} = 2\hat{k}$$

$$\oint \vec{F} \cdot \vec{dl} = \iint_D (\text{curl } \vec{F})\hat{k} \cdot dA$$

$$= \iint_D 2\hat{k} \cdot dA$$

$$= 2\pi(4 \times 3) = 75.36.$$

45. $f(x) = \begin{cases} \dfrac{4(1 - \sin x)}{2x - \pi}, & x \neq \dfrac{\pi}{2} \\ 0, & x = \dfrac{\pi}{2} \end{cases}$

Now, $\quad f(x) = \dfrac{4\left(1 - \cos\left(\dfrac{\pi}{2} - x \right) \right)}{2\left(x - \dfrac{\pi}{2} \right)}$

$$= \dfrac{2}{\left(x - \dfrac{\pi}{2} \right)} \left[1 - \cos\left(x - \dfrac{\pi}{2} \right) \right]$$

$$= \dfrac{2}{\left(x - \dfrac{\pi}{2} \right)} \left[1 - \left\{ 1 - \dfrac{\left(x - \dfrac{\pi}{2} \right)^2}{2!} + \dfrac{\left(x - \dfrac{\pi}{2} \right)^4}{4!} + ... \right\} \right]$$

$$= \dfrac{2}{2!}\left(x - \dfrac{\pi}{2} \right) = \dfrac{2\left(x - \dfrac{\pi}{2} \right)^3}{4!} + ...$$

Now co-efficient of $\left(x - \dfrac{\pi}{2} \right) = \dfrac{2}{2!} = 1.$

47. $g(x) = \displaystyle\int_{x(x-2)}^{(4x-5)} f(t)dt$

$g'(x) = f(4x - 5)4 - f(x(x - 2))(2x - 2)$

$g'(1) = f(-1)4 - f(-1)0$

$\qquad = 4f(-1) = 4\sqrt{1+3} = 8.$

48. Given function,

$$f(x, y) = \begin{cases} \dfrac{x^3 + y^3}{x^2 - y^2} & , x^2 - y^2 \neq 0 \\ 0 & , x^2 - y^2 = 0 \end{cases}$$

At point (0, 0) $\vec{V} = \dfrac{4}{5}\hat{i} + \dfrac{3}{5}\hat{j}$

$$= u_1\hat{i} + u_2\hat{j}$$

Now,

$$D_{\hat{k}}f\big|_{(0,0)} = \lim_{\rho \to 0} \frac{f(0+3u_1, 0+3u_2) - f(0,0)}{3}$$

$$= \lim_{\rho \to 0} \frac{1}{3} \cdot \frac{(3u_1)^3 + (3u_2)^3}{(3u_1)^2 - (3u_2)^2}$$

$$= \lim_{\rho \to 0} \frac{(u_1)^3 + (u_2)^3}{(u_1)^2 - (u_2)^2}$$

$$= \frac{\left(\dfrac{4}{5}\right)^3 + \left(\dfrac{3}{5}\right)^3}{\left(\dfrac{4}{5}\right)^2 - \left(\dfrac{3}{5}\right)^2} = \frac{\dfrac{64+27}{125}}{\dfrac{16-9}{25}}$$

$$= \frac{91 \times 25}{7 \times 125} = \frac{91}{35} = 2.6.$$

49. $I = \displaystyle\int_{-1}^{1}\int_{-1}^{1} |x+y|\, dx\, dy$

Graph of $|x+y| = 0$

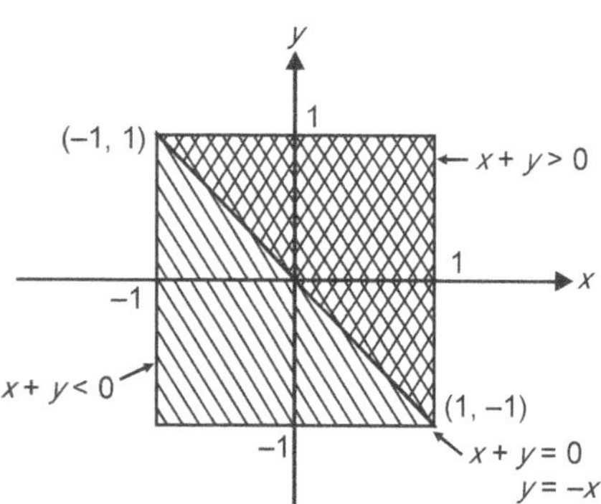

Now, $\quad I = \displaystyle\int_{-1}^{1}\int_{-1}^{1} |x+y|\, dx\, dy$

$$= 2\int_{-1}^{1}\left(\int_{-y}^{1}(x+y)dx\right)dy$$

$$= 2\int_{-1}^{1}\left|\frac{x^2}{2} + yx\right|_{-y}^{1} dy$$

$$= 2\int_{-1}^{1}\left(\frac{1}{2} + \frac{y^2}{2}\right)dy$$

$$= 2(2)\int_{0}^{1}\left(\frac{1}{2} + \frac{y^2}{2}\right)dy$$

$$= 4\left(\frac{y}{2} + \frac{y^3}{6}\right)_{0}^{1}$$

$$= 4\left(\frac{1}{2} + \frac{1}{6}\right) = 2.64.$$

50. Given curve:

$x = 1 - y^2 \implies y^2 = 1 - x$

$x = y^2 - 1 \implies y^2 = 1 + x$

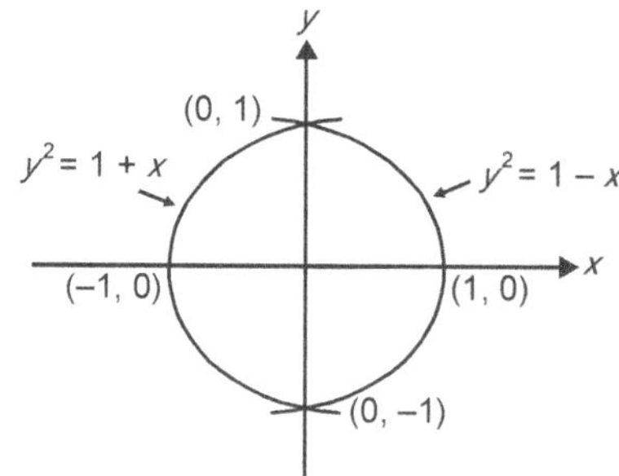

Now, volume

$$V = \int_{0}^{2}\int_{-1}^{1}\int_{1-y^2}^{y^2-1} dx\, dy\, dz$$

$$V = \int_{0}^{2}\int_{-1}^{1}(y^2 - 1 - 1 + y^2)\, dy\, dz$$

$$= \int_{0}^{2}\int_{-1}^{1} 2(y^2 - 1)\, dy\, dz$$

$$= \int_{0}^{2}\left[2\left(\frac{y^3}{3} - y\right)\right]_{-1}^{1} dz$$

$$= \int_{0}^{2} 2\left(\frac{1+1}{3} - (1+1)\right) dz$$

$$= 2\int_{0}^{2} -\frac{4}{3}\, dz = \frac{-16}{3} = -5.33$$

Taking absolute value V = 5.33.

51. Given curve $y^2 = x^4(x + 2)$

When $y = 0$, $x^4(x + 2) = 0$

$x = 0$ and -2

Now the graph of $y^2 = x^4(x + 2)$

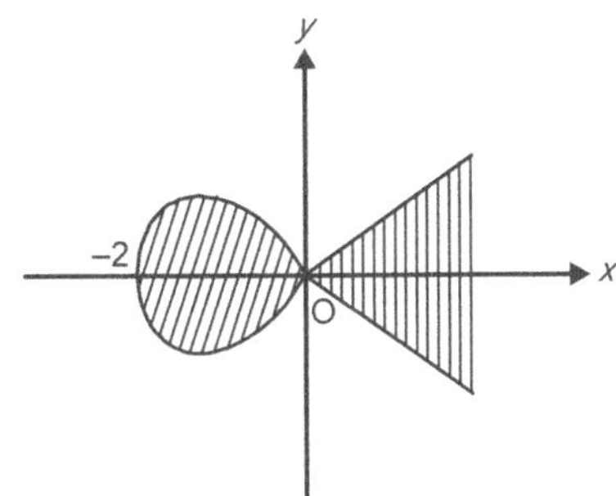

$$\text{Volume} \quad V = \int_{-2}^{0} \pi y^2 \, dx = \int_{-2}^{0} \pi x^4 (x+2) \, dx$$

$$= \int_{-2}^{0} \pi (x^5 + 2x^4) \, dx$$

$$= \pi \int_{-2}^{0} (x^5 + 2x^4) \, dx$$

$$= \pi \left[\frac{x^6}{6} + \frac{2x^5}{5} \right]_{-2}^{0}$$

$$= \pi \left[\frac{0 - (-2)^6}{6} + \frac{2(0) - 2(-2)^5}{5} \right]$$

$$= \pi \left[\frac{-64}{6} + \frac{64}{5} \right]$$

$$= \frac{64}{30} \pi = \frac{32 \times 3.14}{15}$$

$$= 6.698 \approx 6.7.$$

52.
$$a_n = \left(e^n + 2^n \right)^{1/n} : n \in \mathbb{N}$$

$$= e \left(1 + \left(\frac{2}{e} \right)^n \right)^{1/n}$$

$$\lim_{n \to \infty} a_n = e \left[\lim_{n \to \infty} \left[1 + \left(\frac{2}{e} \right)^n \right] \right]^{1/n}$$

Now, $\dfrac{2}{e} < 1$, so, $\lim_{n \to \infty} \left(\dfrac{2}{e} \right)^n \to 0$

$\therefore \quad \lim_{n \to \infty} a_n = e.1 = e = 2.72.$

53. $G = \{ n \in N : n \le 55, \, gcd\,(n, 55) = 1 \}$
For $x^2 = 26$, then $x^2 - 26 = $ identify $= 55.I$,
where $I = $ Integer

$$I = \frac{x^2 - 26}{55}$$

to get I integer, $(x^2 - 26)$ must be a multiple of 55.

Possible value of $x(30 \le x \le 55) = 31, 46$

For $x = 31$, $I = \dfrac{31 \times 31 - 26}{55} = 17$

For $x = 46$, $II = \dfrac{46 \times 46 - 26}{55} = 38$

Hence, $x = 31$ and 46.

54. $f(x, y) = (x^2 + 3y^2) \cdot e^{-(x^2 + y^2)}$

$$f_x = 2x \cdot e^{-(x^2 + y^2)} + (x^2 + 3y^2) e^{-(x^2 + y^2)} (-2x)$$

$$= e^{-(x^2 + y^2)} 2x[1 - x^2 - 3y^2] = 0 \quad ...(i)$$

$$f_y = 6y \cdot e^{-(x^2 + y^2)} + (x^2 + 3y^2) e^{-(x^2 + y^2)} (-2y)$$

$$= e^{-(x^2 + y^2)} \cdot 2y(3 - (x^2 + 3y^2)) = 0 \quad ...(ii)$$

From (i)
$x(1 - (x^2 + 3y^2)) = 0 \Rightarrow x = 0$ or $x^2 + 3y^2 = 1$
and from (ii)
$y\{3 - (x^2 + 3y^2)\} = 0 \Rightarrow y = 0$ or $3y^2 = 3$
$$\Rightarrow y = 0, \, y = \pm 1$$
So points are $(0, 0)$, $(0, 1)$, $(0, -1)$
Now, $y(3 - 1) = 0 \Rightarrow 2y = 0 \Rightarrow y = 0$
and $x^2 = 1$, $x = \pm 1 \Rightarrow$ So, points $= (1, 0)$, $(-1, 0)$
Hence, 5 critical points are $(0, 0)$, $(0, 1)$, $(0, -1)$, $(1, 0)$ and $(-1, 0)$.

55. Given set $\{ x \in S_3 : x^4 = e \}$
For $\qquad x^4 = e$
$\therefore$ Order of the set $O(x)$ must be divided by 4.
$O(x) = 1, 2, 4$, but 4 can not be lies in S_3.
$\qquad$ Element $= \{(1, 2), (1, 3), (2, 3)\}$ and $\{e\}$
Hence, number of elements in the set $= 4$.

56. Given matrix:

$$\begin{vmatrix} 0 & 0 & 2 \\ 1 & 0 & -4 \\ 0 & 1 & 3 \end{vmatrix}$$

The characteristic poly is $|A - \lambda I| = 0 \Rightarrow$

$$\begin{vmatrix} -\lambda & 0 & 2 \\ 1 & -\lambda & -4 \\ 0 & 1 & 3-\lambda \end{vmatrix} = 0$$

$$-\lambda(\lambda(-3 + \lambda) + 4) - 1(0 - 2) = 0$$
$$\lambda(\lambda^2 - 3\lambda + 4) - 2 = 0$$
$$\lambda^3 - 3\lambda^2 + 4\lambda - 2 = 0$$
$$(\lambda - 1)(\lambda^2 - 2\lambda + 2) = 0$$

Root of $(\lambda^2 - 2\lambda + 2)$ is no complex

$\because (-2)^2 - 4 \times 2 < 0$

$\therefore$ Only real eigenvalue $\lambda = 1$

Now,
$$\begin{vmatrix} 0 & 0 & 2 \\ 1 & 0 & -4 \\ 0 & 1 & 3 \end{vmatrix}\begin{vmatrix} 2 \\ y \\ z \end{vmatrix} = 1\begin{vmatrix} 2 \\ y \\ z \end{vmatrix}$$

$$\begin{vmatrix} 2z \\ 2-4z \\ y+3z \end{vmatrix} = \begin{vmatrix} 2 \\ y \\ z \end{vmatrix}$$

$\therefore \quad z = 1,\ y = 2 - 4z$

$\qquad y = 2 - 4 = -2$

$\therefore \quad z = 1$ and $y = -2$

$\therefore \quad z - y = 1 - (-2) = 3.$

57. $MN = 2\begin{pmatrix} 1 & 0 & 0 & 1 \\ 0 & 1 & 1 & 0 \\ 0 & 0 & 1 & 0 \\ 0 & 0 & 0 & 1 \end{pmatrix}$

Now Let $\det(M) = x$ and $\det(N) = y$

$\det(MN) = \det(M).\det(N) = 2^4 \times 1 = 16$

$\therefore \qquad x.y = 16$

For $\max(x + y)$, $x = 16$ or 1 and $y = 1$ or 16.

$\therefore \qquad x + y = 16 + 1 = 17.$

58. M is a 3×3 matrix

Such that $\qquad M^2 = M + 2I$

$\qquad M^2 - M - 2I = 0$

Characteristics equation $\lambda^2 - \lambda - 2 = 0$

$\Rightarrow \qquad (\lambda - 2)(\lambda + 1) = 0$

$\therefore \qquad \lambda_1 = -1$ and $\lambda_2 = 2$

For $\alpha.\beta.\gamma = -4$, $\alpha = \beta = 2$ and $\gamma = -1$

$\qquad 2 \times 2 \times -1 = -4$

$\therefore \qquad \alpha + \beta + \gamma = 2 + 2 - 1 = 3.$

59. Given differential equation

$$x^2\frac{d^2y}{dx^2} - 3x\frac{dy}{dx} + 3y = 0$$

$$\frac{x\,dy}{dx} = D.y, \quad \frac{x^2 d^2 y}{dx^2} = D(D-1)y$$

where $D = \dfrac{d}{dx}$

$\therefore$ Above equation becomes

$$D(D - 1)y - 3Dy + 3y = 0$$
$$(D(D - 1) - 3D + 3)y = 0$$
$$(D^2 - D - 3D + 3)y = 0$$
$$(D^2 - 4D + 3)y = 0$$

A.E. $\qquad m^2 - 4m + 3 = 0$

$\qquad m^2 - 3m - m + 3 = 0$

$\qquad (m - 3)(m - 1) = 0$

$\Rightarrow \qquad m = 1, 3$

General equation:

$$y = C_1 e^z + C_2 e^{3z}$$
$$y = C_1 x + C_2 x^3 - x(C_1 + C_2 x^2)$$
$$y(x) = xv(x)$$
$$v(x) = C_1 + C_2 x^2$$
$$v(0) = C_1 = 0$$
$$v(1) = C_1 + C_2 = 1 \Rightarrow C_2 = 1$$

$\therefore \qquad v(x) = x^2$

$$v(-2) = (-2)^2 = 4.$$

60. Given differential equation:

$$\frac{d^2y}{dx^2} + 4\frac{dy}{dx} + 4y = 0$$

Characteristics equation: $m^2 + 4m + 4 = 0$

$\qquad (m + 2)^2 = 0$

$\qquad m = -2, -2$

$\therefore \qquad y(x) = (C_1 + C_2 x)e^{-2x}$

$\qquad y(0) = 2 = (C_1 + 0) \Rightarrow C_1 = 2$

$\qquad y'(x) = C_2 e^{-2x} + (C_1 + C_2 x)(-2e^{-2x})$

$\qquad y'(0) = C_2 + C_1(-2)$

$\qquad 0 = C_2 + 2(-2) \Rightarrow C_2 = 4$

$\therefore \qquad y(x) = (2 + 4x)e^{-2x}$

$$y(\ln(2)) = 2 + 4\ln(2)e^{-2\ln(2)}$$

$$= (2 + 4\ln(2))\frac{1}{4} = 1.19.$$

Previous Paper (Solved)

IIT–JAM

JOINT ADMISSION TEST FOR M.SC. (MATHEMATICS), 2018

| Section-A : Multiple Choice Questions (MCQ) |

Q. (1–10) carry one mark each.

1.

$$\mathbb{Z}_n \qquad\qquad n$$
$$\mathbb{Z}_n$$

2. $\quad a_n = \dfrac{b_{n+}}{b_n} \qquad b \qquad b$

$$b_n \quad b_n \quad b_n \quad n \in \mathbb{N} \qquad \underset{n\to\infty}{} a_n$$

$$\dfrac{\sqrt{\;}}{+\sqrt{\;}} \qquad\qquad \dfrac{\sqrt{\;}}{+\sqrt{\;}}$$

3. $\quad v \quad v \quad v$

$$\mathbb{R}$$

$$v \quad v \quad v \quad v \quad v \quad v \quad v \quad v$$
$$v \quad v \quad v \quad v \quad v \quad v$$
$$v \quad v \quad v \quad v \quad v \quad v \quad v \quad v \quad v$$
$$v \quad v \quad v$$
$$v \quad v \quad v \quad v \quad v \quad v$$

4. $\quad a \qquad\qquad\qquad f$

$$a \quad a \qquad \int_a^a \frac{f(x)}{+e^x}\,dx$$

$$\int^a f(x)\,dx \qquad\qquad \int \frac{f(x)}{+e^x}\,dx$$

$$\int^a f \not\;\; dx \qquad\qquad a\int^a \frac{f(x)}{+e^x}\,dx$$

5. $\qquad\qquad z = \sqrt{x + y}$

$$(\;)$$
$$x \quad y \quad z \qquad\qquad x \quad y \quad z$$
$$x \quad y \quad z \qquad\qquad x \quad y \quad z$$

6. $\quad \mathbb{R}$

$$x \quad y \quad z \qquad\qquad z \quad x$$
$$y \quad (\;)$$

$$\dfrac{\sqrt{\;}}{\sqrt{\;}} \qquad\qquad \dfrac{\sqrt{\;}}{\sqrt{\;}}$$

7. $\quad f \;\; \mathbb{R} \to \mathbb{R} \qquad\qquad \vec{v} \;\; \mathbb{R} \to \mathbb{R}$

$$\vec{a} \in \mathbb{R}$$
$$\vec{r}$$
$$xi + yj + zk$$

$$curl(f\;\vec{v}) = grad(f) \times \vec{v} + f\,curl(\vec{v})$$

$$div(grad(f)) = \left(\frac{\partial}{\partial x} + \frac{\partial}{\partial y} + \frac{\partial}{\partial z}\right) f$$

$$curl(\vec{a} \times \vec{r}) = \quad \vec{a}\;\vec{r}$$

$$div\left(\frac{\vec{r}}{\vec{r}}\right) = \qquad \vec{r} \neq \vec{}$$

8. $\mathbb{R}$

x y a

x y c x y c

x y c x y c

9. $\mathbb{R}$

$\mathbb{R}$ $\to$

$(\quad f)(x)\quad f(x)\quad x f'(x)$

10. $s_n = +\dfrac{}{}+\dfrac{}{}+\ +\dfrac{}{n}\qquad n \in \mathbb{N}$

$s_n\ {}_{n=}^{\infty}$

$s_n\ {}_{n=}^{\infty}\qquad\qquad \mathbb{Q}$

$s_n\ {}_{n=}^{\infty}$

$\mathbb{Q}$

$s_k n\ {}_{n=}^{\infty}$

$\mathbb{R}\qquad\qquad k$

$s_n\ {}_{n=}^{\infty}$

Q. (11–30) carry two marks each.

11. $a_n = \begin{cases} +\dfrac{0\ \ \frac{n}{}}{n} & n \\ \\ +\dfrac{}{n} & n \end{cases}\qquad n \in \mathbb{N}$

$a_n\ n \in \mathbb{N}\qquad\qquad a_n\ n \in \mathbb{N}$

$(\quad a_n)\ (\quad a_n)\quad -$

$a_n\ n \in \mathbb{N}\qquad\qquad a_n\ n \in \mathbb{N}$

$(\quad a_n)\ (\quad a_n)$

12. $a\ b\ c \in \mathbb{R}$

$a\ b\ c$

$$\sum_{n=}^{\infty} \frac{a^n}{n^b(\ \ )_e n^{\,c}}$$

$a\qquad b \in \mathbb{R}\ c \in \mathbb{R}$

$a\qquad b\qquad c \in \mathbb{R}$

$a\qquad b \geq\quad c$

$a\qquad b \geq\quad c$

13. $a_n = n + \dfrac{}{n}\quad n \in \mathbb{N}$

$$\sum_{n=}^{\infty} 0\quad {}^{n+}\ \frac{a_{n+}}{n}$$

$e\qquad\qquad\qquad\qquad e$

$\quad e\qquad\qquad\qquad\qquad e$

14. $a_n = \dfrac{(\ )^{\,n}}{\sqrt{\ +n}}\qquad c_n = \sum_{k=}^{n} a_{n\ k}a_k$

$n \in \mathbb{N} \cup$

$\displaystyle\sum_{n=}^{\infty} a_n\qquad\qquad \sum_{n=}^{\infty} c_n$

$\displaystyle\sum_{n=}^{\infty} a_n\qquad\qquad \sum_{n=}^{\infty} c_n$

$\displaystyle\sum_{n=}^{\infty} c_n\qquad\qquad \sum_{n=}^{\infty} a_n$

$\displaystyle\sum_{n=}^{\infty} a_n\qquad\qquad \sum_{n=}^{\infty} c_n$

15. $f\ g\quad \mathbb{R} \to \mathbb{R}$

f

$g\qquad\qquad\qquad\qquad p(x)\quad f(g(x))$

$q(x)\quad g(f(x))\ \forall x \in \mathbb{R}\qquad\qquad t$

$$\int^{t} p'(x)(q'(x)\ )\ dx$$

t

$f\qquad g$

16. $x \in \mathbb{R}$ $\qquad f(x) = \begin{cases} x & \left(\dfrac{}{x}\right) & x \neq \\ & & x = \end{cases}$

$$\lim_{x \to} \frac{f(x)}{x} =$$

$$\lim_{x \to} \frac{f(x)}{x} =$$

$$\frac{f(x)}{x}$$

$$()$$

$$\frac{f(x)}{x} \qquad x$$

$$x$$

17. $f(x, y) = \begin{cases} \dfrac{xy}{(x + y)^\alpha} & (x, y) \neq () \\ & (x, y) = () \end{cases}$

$f()$

$\qquad \alpha \qquad f$

$\qquad \alpha \quad - \quad f$

$\qquad \alpha \quad - \quad f$

$\qquad \alpha \quad - \quad f$

18. $a, b \in \mathbb{R}$ $\qquad f \ \mathbb{R} \to \mathbb{R}$

$\qquad \qquad z \quad e^u f(v)$

$u \quad ax \quad by \qquad v \quad ax \quad by$

$b \ z_{xx} \quad a \ z_{yy} \qquad a \ b \ e^u f'(v)$

$b \ z_{xx} \quad a \ z_{yy} \qquad e^u f'(v)$

$bz_x \quad az_y \quad abz$

$bz_x \quad az_y \quad abz$

19. $\qquad \qquad \qquad yz$

$$y = - \qquad \qquad y \quad z$$

$$y \geq$$

$z \qquad \mathbb{R}$

$$\frac{\pi}{\sqrt{\ }} \qquad \qquad \frac{\pi}{\sqrt{\ }}$$

$$\frac{\pi\sqrt{\ }}{\ } \qquad \qquad \pi\sqrt{\ }$$

20. $(\ x)y \in \ (y \ i +) \ y \quad xy \ j \ (\ x \ y)$

$\in \mathbb{R} \qquad \oint \vec{\ } \, d\vec{r}$

$x \qquad y \qquad x \quad y$

$-$

21.

$\qquad \qquad \qquad \to \qquad \qquad \to$

$\qquad \qquad \to$

$0\ 0\ 0$

$0\ 0\ 0$

$\qquad \qquad \qquad \qquad \neq$

22. $y(x)$

$$\frac{dy}{dx} + y = f(x) \qquad x \geq \quad y()$$

$$f(x) = \begin{cases} & \leq x < \\ & x \geq \end{cases} \qquad y(x)$$

$(\quad e^{x}) \quad \le x \; (\quad e) \; e^{x}$
$\quad x \ge$

$(\quad e^{x}) \quad \le x \qquad x \ge$

$(\quad e^{x}) \quad \le x \; (\quad e) e^{x}$
$\quad x \ge$

$(\quad e^{x}) \quad \le x \qquad e^{\;x}$
$\quad x \ge$

23.

$$\left(y + -y\; +-x \right)dx + -(x+xy)\,dy =$$

x

$_e x$

x

$_e x$

24.

$$y'' + \; y' + \; y = e^{e^{x}}$$

$e^{e^{x}} e^{\;x} \qquad\qquad e^{e^{x}} e^{\;x}$

$e^{e^{x}} e^{\;x} \qquad\qquad e^{e^{x}} e^{x}$

25.

$f \qquad \to \mathbb{Z}$
$f(g) \qquad \forall g \in$

$\mathbb{Z} \qquad\qquad \mathbb{Z}$
$\mathbb{Z} \qquad\qquad \mathbb{Z}$

26. $\hspace{4cm} \mathbb{Q}\; \mathbb{Z}$

27.

$$\pm\sqrt{\dfrac{\pm\sqrt{\;\;}}{\;\;}}$$

28. $\hspace{3cm} \mathbb{Z}\;(\quad a\; b)\quad a\; b \in \mathbb{Z}$

$\hspace{5cm} \mathbb{Z}$

$(\quad a\; b) \in \mathbb{Z} \quad ab$
$(\quad a\; b) \in \mathbb{Z} \quad a \qquad b$
$(\quad a\; b) \in \mathbb{Z} \qquad\qquad ab$
$(\quad a\; b) \in \mathbb{Z} \qquad\qquad a \hspace{4cm} b$

29. $\quad f \quad \mathbb{R} \to \mathbb{R}$

$\hspace{6cm} \mathbb{R}$

$(\quad f) \hspace{2cm} f(x)\; x \in \hspace{2cm} f(x)\; x \in$

$(\quad f\quad) \le (\quad f\quad) \hspace{3cm} \subset$

$\quad f \hspace{7cm} \supset$

$\supset \qquad \supset{}_n \supset \hspace{4cm} n \to \infty$

$\quad{}_n$

$\underset{n\to\infty}{(\quad)}\; f{}_n =$

$\quad f \hspace{7cm} a \in$

$(\quad f) \quad \ne$

$\quad f \hspace{7cm} a \in$

$\hspace{3cm} \varepsilon$

$\subset (\hspace{3cm} f) \hspace{2cm} \in$

30. $\quad x > \!\!-\!\!- \hspace{1.5cm} f(x) = \dfrac{x}{\;+\;x} \quad f(x)$

$_e(\quad x) \quad f(x) \quad x$

$f(x)\; f(x)\; f(x) \hspace{2cm} x \quad \dfrac{\sqrt{\;\;}}{\;\;}$

$f(x)\; f(x)\; f(x) \quad x$

$f(x)\; f(x) \quad \dfrac{f(x)}{\;\;} \hspace{1.5cm} x \quad \dfrac{\sqrt{\;\;}}{\;\;}$

$f(x)\; f(x)\; f(x) \hspace{2cm} x$

Section-B : Multiple Select Questions (MSQ)

Q. (31–40) carry two marks each.

31. $f \mathbb{R} \rightarrow \mathbb{R}$ $\qquad$ $f(x) = x + \dfrac{}{x}$

( )

f

$(\quad \infty)$ $\qquad$ ( )

( ) $\qquad$ $(\quad \infty)$

32. ( )

$$\frac{dy}{dx} = (\ ) \quad x \quad y \qquad y()\ ()$$

$y(x)$

$$y(x) = \sqrt{\dfrac{}{}} \quad x$$

$$y(x) = \sqrt{\dfrac{}{}} \quad x$$

$$y(x) = \sqrt{\dfrac{}{}} \quad x$$

33. $\qquad$ $f \quad g \quad h$
$\alpha \ \beta \ \gamma \ \delta$

f	α	β	γ	δ
g	β	γ	α	δ
h	γ	δ	α	β

( ) $\qquad \alpha \qquad \delta$ ( ) $\qquad \beta \qquad \gamma$

$f \circ g \circ h \circ g \circ f \qquad g \circ h \circ f \circ h \circ g$

$g \circ f \circ h \circ f \circ g \qquad h \circ g \circ f \circ g \circ h$

34.

$\mathbb{R}$ ( )

$\cup$

$\cup$

$\cup$

$\cup$

35. $\mathbb{C} \qquad \mathbb{C}$

$\qquad n \qquad z \in \mathbb{C} \quad z^n \qquad n \in \mathbb{N}$

( ) ( )

$\mathbb{C}$

$\displaystyle\bigcup_{n=} \ _n \qquad\qquad \bigcup_{n=}^{\infty} \ _n$

$\displaystyle\bigcup_{n=}^{\infty} \ _n \qquad\qquad \bigcup_{n=}^{\infty} \ _n$

36. $\qquad \alpha \ \beta \ \gamma \in \mathbb{R}$

$x \quad y \quad z \quad \alpha x \quad \beta y \quad z \quad \gamma \ x \quad y \quad \alpha \qquad \beta$

( )

α	γ
β	$\gamma \quad \alpha$
$\beta \neq$	α
γ	α

37. $\qquad m \quad n \in \mathbb{N} \quad m \quad n \qquad \in \ _{n \ m}(\mathbb{R})$
$\in \ _{m \ n}(\mathbb{R})$

( )

( ) $\qquad\qquad n$

( ) $\qquad\qquad m$

( ) $\qquad\qquad m$

( ) $\qquad\qquad \left\lceil \dfrac{m+n}{} \right\rceil$

$\dfrac{m+n}{}$

38. $(\vec{\ } \ x \ y \ z (= \ x) + \ (z \ i +) \ xz \ (\ y \ j) + \ xy + \ z \ k$

$(\quad x \quad y \quad z) \in \mathbb{R}$

( )

$\nabla \times \vec{\ } = \vec{\ }$

$\displaystyle\oint_C \vec{\ } \ d\vec{r} =$

$$\phi\ \mathbb{R}\ \to\ \mathbb{R}$$

$$\nabla\ \vec{}\ =\phi_{xx}+\phi_{yy}+\phi_{zz}$$

$$\nabla\times\ \vec{}\ =$$

39. $\mathbb{R}\,()$

$x\in\mathbb{R}\quad x\quad x$

$x\in\mathbb{R}\quad x\quad x$

$x\in\mathbb{R}\quad x\quad\quad x$

$x\in\mathbb{R}\quad x\quad\quad x$

40. $\mathbb{R}$

$()$

$y\in\quad y\neq$

y

$z\in\qquad z$

Section-C : Numerical Answer Type (MAT)

Q. (41–50) carry one mark each.

41. $(\ )(\ )$

$()$

42. $\phi\,(x\ y\ z)\quad y\quad yz\,(\quad x\ y\ z)\in\mathbb{R}$

$$\phi$$

$$\frac{x}{\quad}=\frac{y}{\quad}=\frac{z}{\quad}\ ()$$

43. $f(x)=\sum_{n=}^{\infty}0\ \ {}^{k}(x)x^{\ n}\qquad x$

$$f\left(\frac{\pi}{\quad}\right)$$

44. $f\ \mathbb{R}\ \to\ \mathbb{R}$

$$f(x\ y)=\begin{cases}\dfrac{x\ y(x\quad y)}{x\ +y} & (x\ y\ \neq)\\[2ex] & (\ x)\,y\ (=)\end{cases}$$

$$\frac{\partial}{\partial x}\left(\frac{\partial f}{\partial y}\right)\quad\frac{\partial}{\partial y}\left(\frac{\partial f}{\partial x}\right)()$$

45. $f(x\ y)=\sqrt{x\ y}\ \left[\dfrac{\pi}{\quad}e^{\left(\frac{y}{x}\right)}\right]+xy\ \left[\dfrac{\pi}{\quad}e^{\left(\frac{x}{y}\right)}\right]$

$(\quad x\ y)\in\mathbb{R}\quad x\qquad y$

$f_x()\qquad f_y()$

46. $f\quad\infty)\to\quad\infty)\qquad\qquad\infty)$

$(\qquad\qquad\qquad\infty)$

$$f(x)=\int^{x}\sqrt{f(t)}\,dt\qquad f()$$

47. $$a_n=\frac{(\ +0)\ {}^{n}(\ 0\ +)\ {}^{n}}{n}+\frac{}{n}$$

$$\sum_{n=}^{\infty}a_n x^n\qquad x$$

48.

49.

50. $$e^{\ x}\qquad x$$

$()$

Q. (51–60) carry two marks each.

51. $a_k()\quad {}^{k}\quad s_n\quad a\quad a\qquad a_n$

$\sigma_n(\quad s\quad s\qquad s_n)\,n\qquad k\ n\in\mathbb{N}$

$$\lim_{n\to\infty}\sigma_n\ (\quad)$$

52. $f\ \mathbb{R} \to \mathbb{R}$ f''
$\mathbb{R}$ $f()$ $f'()$ $f''()$

$$\lim_{x \to \infty}\left(f\left(\sqrt{\dfrac{}{x}}\right) \right)^{x} \quad ($$

$)$

53. $x\ y\ z$
x y z

       xyz —

54. $\mathbb{R}$

x x y y z y z
α π α

55. $\alpha = \displaystyle\int_{\pi}^{\pi} \dfrac{t + \quad t}{\sqrt{\quad t}}\, dt$

$$\left(\quad \dfrac{\alpha}{} + \quad \right)$$

56. $\displaystyle\int \int_{x} y\ e^{xy}\, dy\, dx$

$($
$)$

---

57. $\in$ $(\ \mathbb{R})$
       $(\mathbb{R}) \to$ $(\ \mathbb{R})$
$()$

58.

$((\qquad\qquad u) \quad v\ (\qquad\qquad u) \quad v$

$u) \in \mathbb{R} \qquad \le u \le \dfrac{\pi}{} \qquad \le v \le \dfrac{\pi}{}$

$()$

59. $x(t)$

$$\dfrac{dx}{dt} = x\ t\ + xt \qquad t \qquad\qquad x()$$

$$x\left(\sqrt{\ }\right)\ ($$

$)$

60. $y(x)$ $v(x)$ x

$y''\ ($ $x)\ y'$ y $\dfrac{\pi}{} < x < \dfrac{\pi}{}$

          $y()$ $y'()\ = \sqrt{\ }$

$v\left(\dfrac{\pi}{\sqrt{\ }} \right)$ $($
$)$

ANSWERS

Section : Multiple Choice Questions (MCQ)

1	2	3	4	5	6	7	8	9	10
11	12	13	14	15	16	17	18	19	20
21	22	23	24	25	26	27	28	29	30

Section-B : Multiple Select Questions (MSQ)

31	32	33	34	35
36	37	38	39	40

Section-C : Numerical Answer Type (NAT)

41	42	43	44	45
46	47	48	49	50
51	52	53	54	55
56	57	58	59	60

EXPLANATORY ANSWERS

SECTION-A

1. $\mathbb{Z}_n$ $n.$

$\mathbb{Z}_n$

$\therefore ()$

$l \quad \dfrac{\pm\sqrt{}}{}$

$l \quad \dfrac{+\sqrt{}}{}$

$()$

2. $a_n \quad \dfrac{b_{n+}}{b_n} \qquad b \qquad b$

$b_n \qquad b_n \quad b_n \qquad n \in \mathbb{N}$

$a_n \quad \dfrac{b_{n+}}{b_n} \quad a_n \quad \dfrac{b_{n+}}{b_{n+}}$

$a_n \quad \dfrac{b_{n+} \quad b_n}{b_n} = \dfrac{b_{n+}}{b_n}$

$a_n \quad \dfrac{b_{n+}}{b_{n+}} \dfrac{b_{n+}}{b_n}$

$a_n \quad a_n \quad a_n$

$\underset{n\to\infty}{} a_n \quad \underset{n\to\infty}{} a_{n+} \quad \underset{n\to\infty}{} a_n$

$l \quad l\,l$

$\Rightarrow l \quad l$

$l \quad \dfrac{\pm\sqrt{}+}{}$

3.

$\alpha(v \quad v) \quad \beta(v \qquad v) \quad \gamma(v \qquad v)$

$\Rightarrow (\alpha \quad \gamma)v \ (\quad \alpha \quad \beta)v \ (\quad \beta \quad \gamma)v$

$\qquad\qquad\qquad v \quad v \quad v$

$\alpha \quad \gamma$

$\alpha \quad \beta$

$\beta \quad \gamma$

$\alpha \quad \beta \quad \gamma$

$v \quad v \ v \quad v \ v \quad v$

$()$

4. $\displaystyle\int_a^a \dfrac{f(x)}{+e^x}\,dx$

$\displaystyle\int_a^a \dfrac{f(x)}{+e^x} + \dfrac{f(\ x)}{+e^{-x}}\,dx \qquad (\because f(\ x) \ f(x))$

$$\int\limits^{a} \frac{f(x)}{+e^x} + \frac{e^x f(x)}{+e^x}\, dx$$

$$\int\limits^{a} \frac{f(x)}{+e^x} + e^x\, dx$$

$$\int\limits^{a} f(x)\, dx$$

$$\therefore\ (\ )$$

5.
$$z \quad \sqrt{x\ +\ y}$$
$$z\ (\ x \qquad y\ ) \qquad\qquad (\ i)$$

$$x\ \to\ xx \quad y\ \to\ yy \quad z\ \to\ zz$$

$$x \to \frac{x+x}{} \quad y \to \frac{y+y}{} \quad z \to \frac{z+z}{}$$

$$(\qquad\qquad i)$$
$$zz \quad xx \quad yy$$
$$(\ )$$

$$z \quad x \quad y$$
$$\Rightarrow \quad x \quad y \quad z$$
$$0$$

6.
$$f \quad x \quad y \quad z$$
$$f \quad z \quad x \quad y$$
$$x\ (\ )$$

$$\nabla f \qquad xi +\ yj +\ zk$$

$$\nabla f \qquad xi \quad yj + k$$

$$x\ (\ )$$

$$\nabla f \qquad i +\ j +\ k$$
$$\nabla f \qquad i \quad j + k$$

$$\because \quad \eta \qquad \frac{\nabla f}{\nabla f} = \frac{i +\ j +\ k}{\sqrt{+\ +}}$$

$$\frac{i +\ j +\ k}{}$$

$$\eta \qquad \frac{\nabla f}{\nabla f} = \frac{i \quad j + k}{\sqrt{+\ +}}$$

$$\frac{i \qquad j + k}{\sqrt{}}$$
$$\theta \quad \eta \quad \eta$$

$$\frac{(\ i +\ j +)\ (k}{} \qquad \frac{i)\quad j + k}{\sqrt{}}$$

$$\frac{+}{\times \sqrt{}} = \frac{}{\sqrt{}}$$

$$\overline{\sqrt{\ }}$$

7. $\quad f \quad \mathbb{R}^3 \to \mathbb{R}$

$$\vec{v} \quad \mathbb{R} \quad \to \mathbb{R}$$

$$\vec{a} \in \mathbb{R}$$

$$\vec{r} \qquad xi + yj + zk$$

$$0 \quad (\quad) f\ \vec{v} \qquad \nabla \times (f\ \vec{v})$$

$$\sum i \frac{\partial}{\partial x} \times \left(f\ \vec{v} \right)$$

$$\sum i \frac{\partial}{\partial x} f \times \vec{v} + f \sum i \frac{\partial}{\partial x} \times \vec{v}$$

$$\nabla f \times \vec{v} + f\ \nabla \times \vec{v}$$

$$f \times \vec{v} + f \qquad \vec{v}$$

$$\Rightarrow \quad (\quad) f\ \vec{v} \qquad f \times \vec{v} + f \qquad \vec{v}$$

$$0 \quad ((\qquad f)) \quad \nabla(\ \nabla)$$

$$\sum i \frac{\partial}{\partial x} \left(\sum i \frac{\partial f}{\partial x} \right)$$

$$\sum \frac{\partial\ f}{\partial x}$$

$$\frac{\partial\ f}{\partial x} + \frac{\partial\ f}{\partial y} + \frac{\partial\ f}{\partial z}$$

$$\Rightarrow \quad (\qquad f) \quad \left(\frac{\partial}{\partial x} + \frac{\partial}{\partial y} + \frac{\partial}{\partial z} \right) f$$

0   ($\vec{a}) \times \vec{r}$ $\nabla \times (\vec{a} \times \vec{r})$

$\vec{a}(\nabla \cdot \vec{r}) + (\vec{r} \cdot \nabla)\vec{a} \quad \vec{r}(\nabla \cdot \vec{a}) \quad (\vec{a} \cdot \nabla)\vec{r}$

a $\qquad\qquad a$

a

() $\quad div\left(\dfrac{\vec{r}}{\vec{r}}\right)$

$\nabla \cdot \left(\dfrac{\vec{r}}{\vec{r}}\right)$

$\sum i \dfrac{\partial}{\partial x}\left(\dfrac{xi + yj + zk}{(x + y + z)}\right)$

$\sum \dfrac{\partial}{\partial x}\left(\dfrac{x}{(x + y + z)}\right)$

$\dfrac{(x + y + z) \quad (x + y + z \quad)x}{(x + y + z)}$

$+ \dfrac{(x + y + z) \quad (x + y + z \quad)y}{(x + y + z)}$

$+ \dfrac{(x + y + z) \quad (x + y + z \quad)z}{(x + y + z)}$

$\dfrac{(x + y + z)}{(x + y + z)} \; (y \quad z \quad x \quad x \quad z$

$\qquad\qquad\qquad y \quad x \quad y \quad z)$

()

8.

$x + y \qquad a$

$\qquad\qquad x$

$\Rightarrow \quad -x \quad + -y \quad y'$

$\Rightarrow \qquad\qquad y' \quad \dfrac{-x}{-y} = \dfrac{y}{x}$

$\qquad\qquad y' \quad \dfrac{x}{y}$

$\Rightarrow \qquad\qquad y \; dy \quad x \; dx$

$\qquad\qquad -y \qquad -x \quad + -d$

$\Rightarrow \qquad x \qquad y \qquad c$

$\therefore ()$

9. $\qquad\qquad \rightarrow$

$(\quad f)(x) \quad f(x) \quad xf'(x)$

$\qquad\qquad x \quad x \quad x$

$() \qquad\qquad\qquad x \quad x \quad x$

$(\quad x) \quad x \quad x$

$\qquad\qquad\qquad x \quad x \quad x$

$(\quad x) \quad x \quad x(\quad x)$

$\qquad\qquad x \quad x$

$\qquad\qquad x$

$\qquad\qquad\qquad x \quad x \quad x$

$(\quad x) \quad x \quad x(\quad x)$

$\qquad\qquad x \quad x$

$\qquad\qquad x$

$\qquad\qquad\qquad x \quad x \quad x$

$\Rightarrow$

$\therefore$

10.

$$S_n \quad + \!-\! + \!-\! + \!-\! + \quad + \quad \frac{}{n}$$

$$n \quad + \!-\! + \!-\! + \!-\! + \quad + \quad \frac{}{(\ n)} + \frac{}{n+}$$

$$n \quad \le - \ _n \ \forall \, n \ge$$

$$-$$

$$\therefore \ ()$$

15. $\quad f(x) \quad x$

$$\mathbb{R}$$

$$g(x) \quad x$$

$$\mathbb{R}$$

$$\therefore \quad p(x) \quad f(g(x))$$
$$f(\ x)$$
$$(\quad x)$$
$$x$$
$$x$$
$$q(x) \quad g(f(x))$$
$$g(\ x)$$
$$(\quad x)$$
$$x$$
$$x$$

$$\int p'(x)(q'(x)\ )\ dx$$

$$\int () \quad dx$$

$$\int \quad dx$$

$$t$$
$$t$$

$$\therefore \ ()$$

16. $f(x) \quad \begin{cases} x\ (\ )\ x & x \ne \\ & x = \end{cases}$

$$0 \qquad \lim_{x \to} \frac{f(x)}{x} \qquad \lim_{x \to} \frac{x\ (\ )\ x}{x}$$

$$\lim_{x \to} \frac{(x\ )}{} \quad x$$

$$(\quad x)$$

$$()$$

$$0 \qquad \lim_{x \to} \frac{f(x)}{x} \qquad \lim_{x \to}(\ x) \qquad x =$$

$$()$$

$$0 \qquad \frac{f(x)}{x} \qquad \frac{x\ (\ )\ x}{x} = x \qquad \frac{}{x}$$

$$()\,()$$

$$0 \qquad \frac{f(x)}{x} \qquad \frac{x\ (\ )\ x}{x}$$

$$\frac{(\ )\ x}{x} \qquad g(x)$$

$$\Rightarrow \qquad \lim_{x \to} \frac{f(x)}{x} \qquad \lim_{x \to} \frac{(\ )\ x}{x}$$

$$()$$
$$()$$

17. $\qquad f(x\ y) = \begin{cases} \dfrac{xy}{(x\ +y\ )^{\alpha}} & (\ x\ y\ \ne\ ) \\[2mm] & (\ x)y\ \in\ ) \end{cases}$

$$f(a\ h\ b\ k)\quad f(a\ h)$$

$$h+\ k+\sqrt{h\ +k\ +\phi(h\ k)}$$

$$\phi(h\ k) \to$$

$$\lim_{(h\ k)\to()}(\ \phi)h\ k =$$

h k $f(x\ y)$
$(a\ b)$

$$f(x\ y)\quad \frac{xy}{(x^2+y^2)^\alpha}$$

$y\quad mx\quad x\to$

$$f(x\ mx)\quad {}_{x\to}\ \frac{mx}{x^\alpha(\ +m)}\ \to$$

$$\alpha\Rightarrow\qquad \alpha\Rightarrow\alpha$$

α

$$_{(x\ y)\to(a\ b)}(\ f\ )x\ y(\ =)a\ b$$

$$\to$$

$()$ $\qquad \alpha\quad -$

$$f(x\ y)\quad \frac{xy}{\sqrt{x^2+y^2}}$$

$f()$

$$_{(x\ y)\to()}(\ f\ )x\ y\qquad _{(x\ y)\to()}\ \frac{xy}{\sqrt{x^2+y^2}}=$$

$$f(x\ y)\quad \frac{xy}{(x^2+y^2)^\alpha}$$

$$f(h\ k)\quad f()\quad \frac{hk}{(h^2+k^2)^\alpha}$$

$$h^2+\ k^2+\sqrt{h^2+k^2}\quad \frac{hk}{(h^2+k^2)^{a+}}$$

$$\phi(h\ k)\quad \frac{hk}{(h^2+k^2)^{a+}}\qquad (\ i)$$

$$\alpha\quad -$$

$$\phi(h\ k)\quad \frac{hk}{(h^2+k^2)}$$

$h\quad mk$

$$\phi(h\ k)\quad {}_{k\to}\ \frac{mk^2}{m^2\ k^2+k^2}=\frac{m}{\ +m^2}$$

$\phi(h\ k)$

$\quad f(x\ y)$

$()$ $\qquad \alpha\quad -$

$($ $\qquad i)$

$$\phi(h\ k)\quad \frac{hk}{(h^2+k^2)^{\ +}}$$

$$\frac{hk}{(h^2+k^2)}$$

$$\phi(h\ k)\quad \frac{hk}{(h^2+k^2)}$$

$h\to mk$

$$\phi(h\ k)\quad \frac{mk^2}{k^2(\ +m^2)}\ \to$$

$f(x\ y)$ $\qquad\qquad \alpha=-$

$f(x\ y)$

$()$ $\qquad \alpha\quad -$

$($ $\qquad i)$

$$\phi(h\ k)\quad \frac{hk}{(h^2+k^2)^{\ +}}$$

$$\frac{hk}{(h^2+k^2)}$$

$h\quad mk$

$$\phi(h\ k)\quad {}_{k\to}\ \frac{mk^2}{k^2(\ +m^2)}$$

$()$

18.

$$z = e^u f(v)$$
$$u = ax + by, \quad v = ax - by$$
$$\Rightarrow \quad u_x = a, \ u_y = b, \ v_x = a, \ v_y = -b$$
$$\Rightarrow \quad u_{xx} = u_{yy} = v_{xx} = v_{yy} = 0$$
$$\therefore \ z_x = e^u f'(v)v_x + e^u . u_x . f(v)$$
$$= ae^u f'(v) + ae^u f(v)$$
$$= ae^u (f'(v) + f(v))$$
$$z_{xx} = ae^u (f''(v) + f'(v))v_x + ae^u . u_x (f'(v) + f(v))$$
$$= a^2 e^u (f''(v) + f'(v)) + a^2 e^u (f'(v) + f(v))$$
$$= a^2 e^u (f''(v) + 2f'(v) + f(v))$$

$$z_y = e^u f'(v)v_y + e^u . u_y f(v)$$
$$= -be^u f'(v) + be^u f(v)$$
$$= be^u (f(v) - f'(v))$$
$$z_{yy} = be^u (f'(v) - f''(v))v_y + be^u . u_y (f(v) - f'(v))$$
$$= -b^2 e^u (f'(v) - f''(v)) + b^2 e^u (f(v) - f'(v))$$
$$= b^2 e^u (f''(v) - 2f'(v) + f(v))$$

$$\therefore \ b^2 z_{xx} - a^2 z_{yy}$$
$$= a^2 b^2 e^u (f''(v) + 2f'(v) + f(v)) - a^2 b^2 e^u (f''(v) - 2f'(v) + f(v))$$
$$= 4a^2 b^2 e^u f'(v)$$
$$\therefore ()$$

20.

$$\vec{F} = (x - y)i + (y - xy)j$$

$$x, y \qquad x, y$$

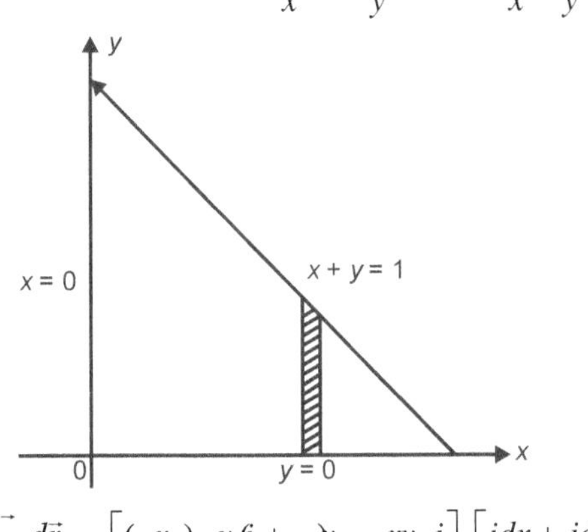

$$\vec{F} \cdot d\vec{r} = \left[(x - y)i + (y - xy)j \right] \cdot \left[i\,dx + j\,dy \right]$$
$$= (x - y)\,dx + (y - xy)\,dy$$

$$\therefore \ \int_C \vec{F} \cdot d\vec{r} = \int (x - y)\,dx + (y - xy)\,dy$$

$$= \int M\,dx + N\,dy$$
$$(M = x - y)(N = y - xy)$$

$$\Rightarrow \quad \frac{\partial M}{\partial y} =$$

$$\frac{\partial N}{\partial x} = -y$$

$$\int M\,dx + N\,dy$$

$$= \iint \left(\frac{\partial N}{\partial x} - \frac{\partial M}{\partial y} \right) dx\,dy$$

$$= \int \int_0^x (-y) + dx\,dy$$

$$= \int \int_0^x (-y) + dy\,dx$$

$$= \int \left[-y + y \right]_0^x dx$$

$$= \int \left[() + (\ ) + x\,dx \right]$$

$$= \int (x -)x + dx$$

$$= \left[x - x + x \right]$$

22.

$$\frac{dy}{dx} + y = f(x)$$

$$\leq x \qquad f(x)$$

$$\Rightarrow \quad \frac{dy}{dx} + y$$

$$\therefore \qquad e^{\int dx} = e^x$$

$$y(x)\,e^x \qquad \int e^x\,dx +$$

$$\Rightarrow \qquad y(x)\,e^x \qquad e^x$$

$$y()$$

$$\Rightarrow \qquad\qquad\qquad \Rightarrow$$

$$\therefore \qquad y(x)e^x \qquad e^x$$

$$\Rightarrow \qquad y(x) \qquad e^{\,x}$$

$$\Rightarrow \qquad y(x)\,(\qquad e^{\,x})$$

$$x \ge \qquad f(x)$$

$$\Rightarrow \qquad \frac{dy}{dx} + y$$

$$\Rightarrow \qquad () \qquad y$$

$$\Rightarrow \qquad y(x) \qquad e^{\,x}$$

$$y() \qquad \Rightarrow$$

$$y(x)$$

23.

$$\left(y + - y \ + - x\ \right)dx + -\left(x + xy\ \right)dy =$$

$$() \quad x$$

$$x$$

$$x\left(y + - y\ + - x\ \right)dx + \frac{x}{\quad}\left(x + xy\ \right)dy =$$

$$x\ y + - x\ y\ + - x$$

$$\frac{x}{\quad} + \frac{x\ y}{\quad}$$

$$\frac{\partial}{\partial y} \qquad x \qquad x\ y$$

$$\frac{\partial}{\partial x} \qquad \frac{x}{\quad} + \frac{x\ y}{\quad}$$

$$\Rightarrow \qquad \frac{\partial}{\partial y} \neq \frac{\partial}{\partial x}$$

$$x$$

$$() \qquad e^x$$

$$e^x$$

$$_e\,x\left(y + - y\ + - x\ \right)dx + \frac{e^{\,x}}{\quad}\left(x + xy\ \right)dy =$$

$$_e\,(y +) \qquad _e\,x\ y\,(+) \qquad _e\,x\ x$$

$$\frac{x}{\quad} \qquad _e\,x + - xy \qquad _e\,x$$

$$\frac{\partial}{\partial y} \qquad _e\,x \qquad y \qquad _e\,x$$

$$\frac{\partial}{\partial x} \qquad - \qquad _e\,x + - x\ \frac{-}{x} + - y \qquad _e\,x + - xy \qquad \frac{-}{x}$$

$$- \qquad _e\,x + - + - y \qquad _e\,x + - y$$

$$\Rightarrow \qquad \frac{\partial}{\partial y} \neq \frac{\partial}{\partial x}$$

$$() \quad x$$

$$x$$

$$x\left(y + - y\ + - x\ \right)dx + \frac{x}{\quad}\left(x + xy\ \right)dy =$$

$$x\ y + - x\ y\ + - x$$

$$\frac{x}{\quad} + \frac{x\ y}{\quad}$$

$$\frac{\partial}{\partial y} \qquad x \qquad x\ y$$

$$\frac{\partial}{\partial x} \qquad x \qquad x\ y$$

$$\Rightarrow \qquad \frac{\partial}{\partial y} \qquad \frac{\partial}{\partial x}$$

$$x$$

$$()$$

24.

$$y'' \qquad y' \qquad y \qquad e^{e^x}$$

$$\Rightarrow \qquad (y\ )(\ \ y) \qquad \qquad e^{e^x}$$

$$\therefore$$

$$\overline{(\ \ )(\ )}\, e^{e^x}$$

$$\overline{(\ \ )}\, e^{-x}\int e^x e^{e^x}\, dx$$

$$\overline{(\ \ )}\, e^{-x}\int e^{e^x +}\, dx$$

$$\overline{(\ \ )}\, e^{-x} e^{e^x}$$

$$e^{-x}\int e^{-x} e^{-x} e^{e^x}\, dx$$

$$e^{-x}\int e^{e^x}\, dx$$

$$e^{-x} e^{e^x}$$

$$\therefore\ (\ )$$

25. $f \qquad \to \mathbb{Z}$

$\Rightarrow f(g) \qquad \forall g \in$

$\therefore \qquad\qquad \mathbb{Z} \quad \mathbb{Z} \quad \mathbb{Z} \quad \mathbb{Z}$

$$\mathbb{Z}_n \to \mathbb{Z}_m$$

$$\mathbb{Z}_n \qquad \mathbb{Z}_m$$

$$\gcd(n\ m)$$

$$\gcd(n\ )$$

$$\Rightarrow \gcd(\ )$$

$$\Rightarrow \gcd(\ ) \qquad\qquad \neq$$

$$\Rightarrow \gcd(\ ) \qquad\qquad \neq$$

$$\Rightarrow \gcd(\ ) \qquad\qquad \neq$$

$$\mathbb{Z}$$

26. $\qquad\qquad \mathbb{Z} \subseteq \mathbb{R}\ \mathbb{Z} \cong \quad \subset \mathbb{C}$

$\Rightarrow$

$\therefore\ (\ )$

27.

$$\pm\sqrt{\ \ \frac{\ \pm\sqrt{\ }}{\ }}$$

$$\Rightarrow \qquad\qquad\qquad \frac{\pm\sqrt{\ }}{\ }$$

$$\Rightarrow \qquad\qquad\qquad \pm\sqrt{\ }$$

$$\Rightarrow \qquad\qquad\qquad \pm\sqrt{\ }$$

$$\Rightarrow \qquad (\quad)$$

$$\Rightarrow$$

$$\Rightarrow$$

$$\Rightarrow$$

$$\Rightarrow$$

$$\Rightarrow \qquad\qquad (\qquad\quad)$$

$$\Rightarrow$$

$$\Rightarrow$$

$$\Rightarrow$$

28.

$\mathbb{Z}\ (\ \ a\ b)\ \ a\ b\in\mathbb{Z} \qquad \mathbb{Z}\quad \mathbb{Z}$

$\quad (a\ b)(\ c\ d)\ (\ a\ c\ b\ d)$

$()(\ \ a\ b)\in\mathbb{Z} \qquad ab$

$$\subset$$

$a\ b\in \quad \Rightarrow a\ b\in (\ ab\ \in)$

$\quad ()() \qquad\qquad \in\mathbb{Z}^2$

$()()() \qquad\qquad\qquad \notin$

$\qquad\qquad ()\qquad\qquad \neq$

$0 \qquad\qquad a\qquad b$

$\qquad\qquad ()\qquad\qquad\qquad\qquad \in$

$\qquad\qquad ()\qquad\qquad\qquad\qquad \in$

$()()(\ )$

$\qquad\qquad ()\qquad\qquad \notin$

$\quad ()()\qquad\qquad\qquad \neq$

$\qquad\qquad\qquad \nless$

$0 \qquad\qquad\qquad ab$

$(a\ b)\in (\ c\ d)\in$

$\Rightarrow \ ab \quad cd$

$(a\ b)(\ c\ d)(\ a\ c\ b\ d) \in$
$\Rightarrow (\ a\ c)(b\ d)$
$\Rightarrow (\ ab\ cd\ ad\ bc)$

$()(\ a\ b) \in\ \Rightarrow a\ b$

$(a\ b)(\ c\ d)(\ a\ c\ b\ d) \in$

$\because\ a\ c \Rightarrow a\ c$
$b\ d \Rightarrow b\ d$

$()$

32. $\dfrac{dy}{dx}\ (\quad x)y\qquad y()$

$\Rightarrow\ \dfrac{dy}{y}\qquad x\ dx$

$\Rightarrow\ \dfrac{y}{\quad}\quad \dfrac{x}{\quad}+c$

$y()$

$-+c \Rightarrow c\ -$

$\therefore$

$\dfrac{y}{\quad}\quad -\quad x+-$

$\Rightarrow\ y\quad -(\ )\quad x$

$\Rightarrow\ \dfrac{y}{\quad}\quad -\quad x$

$y\quad -\quad x$

$y\quad -\quad \times\ x$

$y\quad \pm\sqrt{-}\quad x$

$()()$

$y(x)$

$y()$

$()$

33.

$f(\ \alpha\ \beta)$
$g(\ \beta\ \gamma)$
$h(\ \gamma\ \delta)$

$\qquad \alpha\ \beta\ \gamma\ \delta$

$0\quad f \circ g \circ h \circ g \circ f$
$(\ \alpha\ \beta)(\ \beta\ \gamma)(\ \gamma\ \delta)(\ \beta\ \gamma)(\ \alpha\ \beta)$
$(\ \alpha\ \delta)(\ \beta)(\ \gamma)(\ \ \alpha\ \delta)$

$0\quad g \circ h \circ f \circ h \circ g$
$(\ \beta\ \gamma)(\ \gamma\ \delta)(\ \alpha\ \beta)(\ \gamma\ \delta)(\ \beta\ \gamma)$
$(\ \beta)(\ \gamma\ \delta)$

$0\quad g \circ f \circ h \circ f \circ g$
$(\ \beta\ \gamma)(\ \alpha\ \beta)(\ \gamma\ \delta)(\ \alpha\ \beta)(\ \beta\ \gamma)$
$(\ \beta\ \delta)$

$0\quad h \circ g \circ f \circ g \circ h$
$= (\gamma\ \delta)(\ \beta\ \gamma)(\ \alpha\ \beta)(\ \beta\ \gamma)(\ \gamma\ \delta)$
$(\ \gamma)(\ \delta\ \alpha)(\ \beta)$

$()()$

35. $\mathbb{C}\quad \mathbb{C}$

$n\qquad z \in \mathbb{C}\ \ z^n\qquad n \in \mathbb{N}$

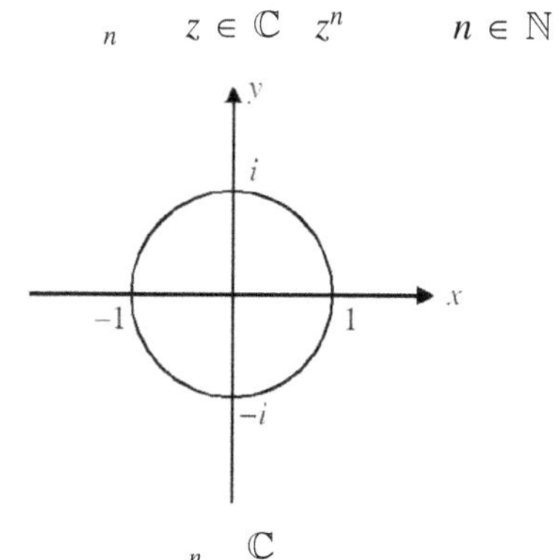

$n\qquad \mathbb{C}$

$w\quad w\ w$
$i\quad i$

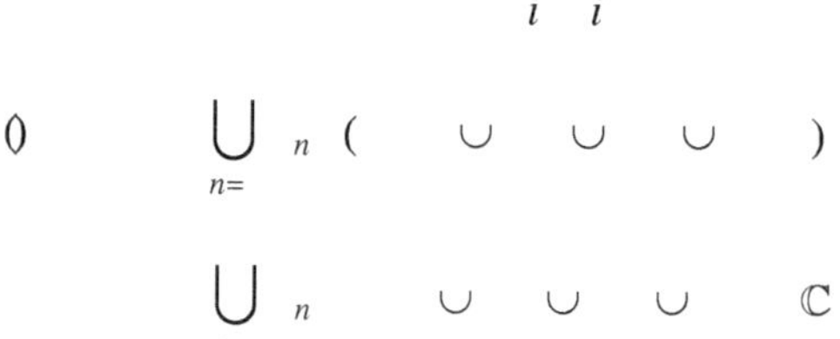

$0\quad \bigcup_{n=}\ n\ (\quad \cup\quad \cup\quad \cup\quad)$

$\bigcup_{r=}\ n\qquad \cup\quad \cup\quad \cup\quad \mathbb{C}$

$$w, i \Rightarrow w\, i \notin \bigcup_{n=} {}_n \nleq \mathbb{C}$$

$$x \in \qquad \in \qquad xy \notin \bigcup_{n=} {}_n$$

$$()$$

$$() \bigcup_{n=}^{\infty} {}_n$$

$$\mathbb{Z}^{n}$$

$$\Rightarrow \qquad\qquad 0 \quad {}^{n}$$

$$\bigcup_{n=}^{\infty} {}_n \quad \mathbb{C}$$

$$z \quad z \in \bigcup_{n=}^{\infty} {}_n \;(\quad z\, z \;\in)$$

$$z^{i}$$

$$z^{i}$$

$$\Rightarrow \qquad z^{i} z^{i}$$

$$i \quad j \quad k$$

$$\left(z\, z\right)^{k}$$

$$\Rightarrow \qquad z\, z \;\in$$
$$i \neq j \;\; i \quad j \quad i \quad j$$

$$\left(z\, z\right)^{i}$$

$$\because \qquad z^{i} z^{i}$$

$$\Rightarrow z^{0} \quad {}^{0} \quad z \qquad\qquad \left(z\, z^{i\,i}\right)^{i} =$$

$$\Rightarrow \qquad z\, z \;\in$$

$$i$$

$$\bigcup_{n=}^{\infty} {}_n \quad \mathbb{C}$$

$$0 \qquad \bigcup_{n=}^{\infty} {}_n \quad \mathbb{C}$$

$$0 \qquad \bigcup_{n=}^{\infty} {}_n \quad \mathbb{C}$$

$$()()()$$

36.

$$\begin{array}{cccc} x & y & z & \alpha \\ x & \beta y & z & \gamma \\ x & y & \alpha z & \beta \end{array}$$

$$\begin{bmatrix} & & & \alpha \\ \beta & & & \gamma \\ & \alpha & & \beta \end{bmatrix}$$

$$\begin{bmatrix} & & & & \\ \beta & & & & \gamma \\ & & \alpha & & \beta \end{bmatrix}$$

$$\therefore$$

$$\begin{array}{c} \alpha \\ \beta \qquad \gamma \end{array}$$

$$\therefore ()$$

$$\beta \qquad \alpha \quad \gamma \quad i.e,\; \alpha \quad \gamma.$$

$$\therefore ()$$

37. $\qquad m \qquad n$

$$\begin{bmatrix} \; \\ \; \\ \; \end{bmatrix}_{\times} \in (\;_{n\times m}\; \mathbb{R}$$

$$\begin{bmatrix} \; \\ \; \\ \; \end{bmatrix}_{\times} \in \;_{m}(\,_{n}\;)\mathbb{R}$$

$$\therefore \qquad \begin{bmatrix} \; \\ \; \\ \; \end{bmatrix}_{\times} \begin{bmatrix} \; \\ \; \\ \; \end{bmatrix}_{\times}$$

$$\begin{bmatrix} \; \\ \; \\ \; \end{bmatrix}_{\times}$$

$$\therefore () \qquad\qquad m \neq n$$
$$()$$

$$\begin{bmatrix} & \\ & \end{bmatrix}_\times \begin{bmatrix} & \\ & \end{bmatrix}_\times$$

$$\begin{bmatrix} & \\ & \end{bmatrix}_\times$$

$\therefore ()$ $\qquad m \neq n$

$()$

41. $()()()$

$$\begin{pmatrix} & \\ & \end{pmatrix}\begin{pmatrix} & \\ & \end{pmatrix}\begin{pmatrix} & \\ & \end{pmatrix}$$

$$\begin{pmatrix} & \\ & \end{pmatrix}\begin{pmatrix} & \\ & \end{pmatrix}$$

$$\begin{pmatrix} & \\ & \end{pmatrix}\begin{pmatrix} & \\ & \end{pmatrix}\begin{pmatrix} & \\ & \end{pmatrix}$$

$()()$

$()$

$()$

$()$

$(\qquad)$

42. $\phi(x\ y\ z)\quad y\quad yz$

$$\frac{x}{\quad}\quad \frac{y}{\quad}=\frac{z}{\quad}$$

$\vec{a}\quad ai+bj+ck=\ i\quad j\quad k$

$$a\qquad \frac{\vec{a}}{\vec{a}}=\frac{i\quad j\quad k}{\sqrt{\ +\ +}}$$

$$i\quad j\quad k$$

$$\phi$$

$$\frac{x}{\quad}\quad \frac{y}{\quad}=\frac{z}{\quad}$$

$\nabla\phi\ a$

$$\left(\frac{\partial\phi}{\partial x}i+\frac{\partial\phi}{\partial y}j+\frac{\partial\phi}{\partial z}k\right)\left(\frac{i\quad j\quad k}{\quad}\right)$$

$$\left(-\frac{\partial}{\partial x}\quad -\frac{\partial}{\partial y}\quad -\frac{\partial}{\partial z}\right)\phi$$

$$\left(-\frac{\partial}{\partial x}\quad -\frac{\partial}{\partial y}\quad -\frac{\partial}{\partial z}\right)\ y\ +\ yz$$

$$(-\ y)+(z\ )\ -\ y$$

$$y\quad z\quad y$$
$$y\quad z$$

$()$

$\Rightarrow\quad \nabla\phi\ a\big|_{()}\qquad ()$

44. $\quad f\ \ \mathbb{R}\ \to\ \mathbb{R}$

$$f(x\ y)\quad \begin{cases} \dfrac{x\ y(x\quad y)}{x\ +y} & (x\ y\ \neq) \\[2mm] & (\ x)\ y\ (=) \end{cases}$$

$$\frac{\partial}{\partial x}\left(\frac{\partial f}{\partial y}\right)\quad \frac{\partial}{\partial y}\left(\frac{\partial f}{\partial x}\right)\quad \frac{\partial\ f}{\partial x\partial y}\quad \frac{\partial\ f}{\partial y\partial x}$$

$$\frac{\partial\ f}{\partial x\partial y}\bigg|_{(a\ b)}\quad \lim_{h\to}\ \frac{f_y(a+h\ b)\quad f_y\ a)b}{h}$$

$$\frac{\partial\ f}{\partial x\partial y}\bigg|_{()}\quad \lim_{h\to}\ \frac{f_y(h)\quad (f_y}{h}\qquad (\ i)$$

$$f_y(h)\quad \lim_{k\to}\ \frac{f(h\ k)\quad (f\ )h}{k}$$

$$\lim_{k\to}\ \frac{h\ k(h\quad k}{k(h\ +k\ )}$$

$$f_y(h)$$

$$f_y() \qquad _{k\to} \quad \frac{f(\ )k\ (\ )f}{k}$$

$$\frac{\partial\ f}{\partial x \partial y} \qquad _{h\to} \quad \frac{h}{h} \ =$$

$$\left.\frac{\partial\ f}{\partial y \partial x}\right|_{(a\ b)} \qquad _{k\to} \quad \frac{f_x(a\ b+k)\quad f_x\ a)b}{k}$$

$$\left.\frac{\partial\ f}{\partial y \partial x}\right|_{()} \qquad _{k\to} \quad \frac{f_x(\ )k\quad (\ )f_x}{k} \qquad (\ ii)$$

$$f_x(\quad k) \qquad _{h\to} \quad \frac{f(h\ k)\quad (f)\ k}{h}$$

$$f_x(\quad k) \qquad _{h\to} \quad \frac{\dfrac{h\ k(h\quad k}{h(h\ +k\ )\quad +k}}{h}$$

$$f_x() \qquad _{h\to} \quad \frac{f(h)\quad (\ )f}{h}$$

$$f_x()$$

$$\frac{\partial\ f}{\partial x \partial y} \quad \frac{\partial\ f}{\partial y \partial x}$$

$$\frac{\partial\ f}{\partial x \partial y} \quad \frac{\partial\ f}{\partial y \partial x}$$

45.

$$f(x\ y) \quad \sqrt{x\ y}\left(\frac{\pi}{\ }e^{\left(\frac{y}{x}\right)}\right)+xy\left(\frac{\pi}{\ }e^{\left(\frac{x}{y}\right)}\right)$$

$$(\quad x\ y)\in\mathbb{R}\quad x \qquad y$$

$$\therefore f_x(x\ y) \quad \sqrt{x\ y}\left(\frac{\pi}{\ }e^{\left(\frac{y}{x}\right)}\right)\frac{\pi}{\ }e^{\left(\frac{x}{y}\right)}\left(\ \frac{y}{x}\right)$$

$$+-(x\ y)\quad x\ y\quad \left(\frac{\pi}{\ }e^{\left(\frac{y}{x}\right)}\right)$$

$$+xy\left(\left(\frac{\pi}{\ }e^{\left(\frac{x}{y}\right)}\right)\right)\frac{\pi}{\ }e^{\left(\frac{x}{y}\right)}\left(\frac{\ }{y}\right)$$

$$+y\quad \left(\frac{\pi}{\ }e^{\left(\frac{x}{y}\right)}\right)$$

$$\frac{\pi}{\ }\frac{y}{x}\sqrt{x\ y}e^{\left(\frac{y}{x}\right)}\quad \left(\frac{\pi}{\ }e^{\left(\frac{y}{x}\right)}\right)$$

$$+-x\ y(x\ y)\quad \left(\frac{\pi}{\ }e^{\left(\frac{y}{x}\right)}\right)$$

$$\frac{\pi}{\ }xe^{\left(\frac{x}{y}\right)}\quad \left(\frac{\pi}{\ }e^{\left(\frac{x}{y}\right)}\right)$$

$$+y\quad \left(\frac{\pi}{\ }e^{\left(\frac{x}{y}\right)}\right)$$

$$\therefore f_x() \qquad +-\ \frac{\pi}{\ }\times\frac{\sqrt{\ }}{\ }+-\qquad \frac{\pi\sqrt{\ }}{\ }$$

$$f_y(x\ y)\quad \sqrt{x\ y}\quad \left(\frac{\pi}{\ }e^{\left(\frac{y}{x}\right)}\right)\frac{\pi}{\ }e^{\left(\frac{y}{x}\right)}\left(\ \frac{\ }{x}\right)$$

$$+-(x\ y)\quad x\quad \left(\frac{\pi}{\ }e^{\left(\frac{y}{x}\right)}\right)$$

$$+xy\left(\left(\frac{\pi}{\ }e^{\left(\frac{x}{y}\right)}\right)\right)\frac{\pi}{\ }e^{\left(\frac{x}{y}\right)}\left(\ \frac{x}{y}\right)$$

$$+x\quad \left(\frac{\pi}{\ }e^{\left(\frac{x}{y}\right)}\right)$$

$$\frac{\pi}{x}\sqrt{x\,y}\,e^{\left(\frac{y}{x}\right)} \quad \left(\frac{\pi}{}e^{\left(\frac{y}{x}\right)}\right)$$

$$+-x\,(x\,y)\quad\left(\frac{\pi}{}e^{\left(\frac{y}{x}\right)}\right)$$

$$+\frac{\pi}{}\frac{x}{y}e^{\left(\frac{x}{y}\right)}\quad\left(\frac{\pi}{}e^{\left(\frac{x}{y}\right)}\right)$$

$$+x\quad\left(\frac{\pi}{}e^{\left(\frac{x}{y}\right)}\right)$$

$$\therefore f_y()\qquad -+\frac{\pi}{}\sqrt{\ }+-$$

$$+\frac{\pi\sqrt{\ }}{}$$

$$\therefore f_x()\qquad f_y()$$

$$\frac{\pi\sqrt{\ }}{}+\ +\frac{\pi\sqrt{\ }}{}$$

46. $\quad f\qquad \infty)\to\quad \infty)\qquad\qquad \infty)$
$\quad (\qquad\qquad\qquad\qquad \infty)$

$$f(x)\quad\int^{x}\sqrt{f(t)}\,dt$$

$$\Rightarrow\qquad f'(x)\quad\sqrt{f(x)}$$

$$\int\frac{f'(x)}{\sqrt{f(x)}}\,dx\quad\int\ dx$$

$$\Rightarrow\quad\begin{array}{c}f(x)\quad t\\ f'(x)\,dx\quad dt\end{array}$$

$$\Rightarrow\qquad\int\frac{dt}{\sqrt{t}}\quad\int\ dx$$

$$\Rightarrow\qquad\sqrt{t}\quad x$$

$$\Rightarrow\qquad t\quad \frac{x}{}$$

$$\therefore\qquad f(x)\quad \frac{x}{}$$

$$f0\quad\frac{()}{}=\ =$$

$$f0$$

47. $\qquad a_n\quad\frac{(\ +0\ )^{n}}{n}+\frac{(\ 0\ +)^{n}}{n}$

$$a_n\quad\begin{cases}\overline{\ }n & n\\[4pt] \overline{\ }n & n\end{cases}$$

n

$$\Rightarrow\qquad \underset{n\to\infty}{\ }\left(\frac{\ }{n}\right)^{n}$$

$$\underset{n\to\infty}{\ }\frac{\ }{}^{n}$$

$$\Rightarrow\qquad \ -\ $$

n

$$\Rightarrow\qquad \underset{n\to\infty}{\ }\left(\frac{\ }{n}\right)^{n}=\ -$$

$$\Rightarrow\qquad \ \left(-\ -\ \right)$$

$$\left(-\ -\right)$$

$$\Rightarrow\qquad \ -\ -$$

48.

$$\sigma \in \quad \sigma$$

$$\therefore \ \sigma \in$$

$$(\qquad \sigma)$$
$$(\ ) \qquad \rightarrow$$
$$(\,)(\,) \qquad \rightarrow$$

50. $\quad f(x) \quad e^{\,x}$

$\Rightarrow \quad f'(x) \quad e^{\,x} \quad x$

$\qquad x\,e^{\,x}$

$\Rightarrow \quad f''(x) \quad x\,e^{\,x} \quad x(\quad x)\,e^{\,x}$

$\qquad x\,e^{\,x} \qquad x\,e^{\,x}$

$\Rightarrow \quad f'''(x) \quad x\,e^{\,x} \quad x \qquad x$

$\qquad (\quad x)\,e^{\,x} \qquad x\,e^{\,x} \quad x$

$\qquad x\,e^{\,x}$

$\qquad x\,e^{\,x} \qquad x \quad x\,e^{\,x}$

$\qquad x \quad x\,e^{\,x} \qquad x\,e^{\,x}$

$\qquad x\,e^{\,x} \qquad x\,e^{\,x}$

$$-\qquad x\,e^{\,x}$$

$$x\,e^{\,x}$$

$$x\,e^{\,x} - \quad x\,e^{\,x}$$

$$x\,e^{\,x}$$

$\Rightarrow \quad f^{(iv)}(x) \quad x\,e^{\,x} \quad x \qquad x$

$\qquad (\quad x)\,e^{\,x}$

$$-\quad x\,e^{\,x} \quad x$$

$$-\quad x \quad e^{\,x}$$

$$x\,e^{\,x} \quad x$$
$$(\quad x)\,e^{\,x}$$
$$x\,e^{\,x} \qquad x \quad x\,e^{\,x}$$

$$-\quad x \quad x\,e^{\,x}$$

$$x\,e^{\,x}$$
$$x\,e^{\,x} \qquad x\,e^{\,x}$$

$$\therefore \qquad\qquad x$$

$$-f^{(iv)}(\,)$$

$$-(\,)$$

$$-\ =\ -$$

52.

$$f(x) \qquad \frac{x}{\quad}$$

$$f(\,0\,)$$
$$f'(x) \qquad x$$
$$\Rightarrow \quad f'(\,0\,)$$
$$f''(x)$$
$$\Rightarrow \quad f''(\,0\,)$$

$$\therefore \ \lim_{x\to\infty}\left(f\left(\sqrt{\frac{\ }{x}}\right)\right)^{x}$$

$$\lim_{x\to\infty}\left[\frac{\left(\sqrt{\frac{\ }{x}}\right)}{\qquad} \right]^{x}$$

$$\lim_{x\to\infty}\left(\frac{\ }{x}\right)^{x}$$

$$\frac{\ }{e}$$

55.

$$\alpha \qquad \int_{\pi}^{\pi} \frac{t+\quad t}{\sqrt{\quad t}}\,dt$$

$$\int_{\pi}^{\pi} \frac{t+\quad t}{\sqrt{\quad +\quad t\quad t}}\,dt$$

$$\int_{\pi}^{\pi} \frac{t + t}{\sqrt{t \qquad t + t \quad t}}\,dt$$

$$\int_{\pi}^{\pi} \frac{t + t}{\sqrt{(\ )\,t \quad t}}\,dt$$

$$u \qquad t \qquad t$$
$$\Rightarrow du\ (\qquad t \qquad t)\,dt$$

$$\int_{\pi}^{\pi} \frac{du}{\sqrt{\ u}} = \Big[\qquad u \Big]_{\pi}^{\pi}$$

$$\Big[\ (\ )\ t \qquad t \Big]_{\pi}^{\pi}$$

$$\left[\frac{\sqrt{\ }}{} - \right] \qquad \left(- \frac{\sqrt{\ }}{} \right)$$

$$\left(\frac{\sqrt{\ }}{} \right) + \qquad \left(\frac{\sqrt{\ }}{} \right)$$

$$\left(\frac{\sqrt{\ }}{} \right)$$

$$\Rightarrow \alpha \qquad \left(\frac{\sqrt{\ }}{} \right)$$

$$\left(\frac{\alpha}{} + \right)$$

$$\left(\ \ \left(\ \left(\frac{\sqrt{\ }}{} \right) \right) + \right)$$

$$\left(\left(\frac{\sqrt{\ }}{} \right) + \right)$$

$$\left(\sqrt{\ } + \right)$$

$$\left(\sqrt{\ } \right) =$$

57.

$$(\mathbb{R})$$

$$\therefore$$

$$\times$$

$$\therefore$$

58.

$$((\qquad u)\quad v(\qquad u)\quad v\quad u)$$

$$\in \mathbb{R} \qquad \leq u \leq \frac{\pi}{} \qquad \leq v \leq \frac{\pi}{}$$

$$(\quad u\ v)\ (\qquad u)\quad v$$
$$(\quad u\ v)\ (\qquad u)\quad v$$
$$(\quad u\ v)\qquad u$$

$$\left(\frac{\partial}{\partial u}\right)\ +\left(\frac{\partial}{\partial u}\right)\ +\left(\frac{\partial}{\partial u}\right)$$

$$u\qquad v\qquad u\qquad v\qquad u$$
$$u(\qquad v\qquad v)\qquad u$$
$$u\qquad u$$

$$\Rightarrow$$

$$\frac{\partial}{\partial u}\ \frac{\partial}{\partial v}+\frac{\partial}{\partial u}\ \frac{\partial}{\partial v}+\frac{\partial}{\partial u}\ \frac{\partial}{\partial v}$$

$$(\qquad u\qquad v)\ (\qquad v(\qquad u))$$
$$(\qquad u\qquad v)((\qquad u)(\qquad v))$$

$$\begin{vmatrix} u & v & v & u & u & v & v \\ & & & u & & v & v \\ & & u & v & u & & v \end{vmatrix}$$

$\Rightarrow$

$$\left(\frac{\partial}{\partial v}\right)^2 + \left(\frac{\partial}{\partial v}\right)^2 + \left(\frac{\partial}{\partial v}\right)^2$$

$$(\quad u)\quad v$$

$$(\quad u)\quad v$$

$$(\quad u)\,(\quad v\quad v)$$

$$(\quad u)$$

$\Rightarrow (\quad u)$

$\therefore \quad (\quad u)$

$$(\quad u)$$

$$\iint\limits_{S} \sqrt{(\ )}\ du\,dv$$

$$\int\limits_{\frac{\pi}{}}^{\frac{\pi}{}} \int \sqrt{(\ +)\ u}\ du\,dv$$

$$\frac{\pi}{}\int^{\frac{\pi}{}}(\ +)\ u\ du$$

$$\frac{\pi}{}\Big[\ u + \ u\Big]^{\pi}$$

$$\frac{\pi}{}\ \pi +$$

IIT–JAM

JOINT ADMISSION TEST FOR M.Sc. (MATHEMATICS), 2017

Section-A : Multiple Choice Questions

Q. 1 – Q. 10 carry one mark each.

1. $f(x, y)$ x y

x π $y \in \mathbb{R}$

$f(x, y)$

2. $\varphi \ \mathbb{R} \to \mathbb{R}$

φ'

$\varphi'\,()$ α β

$\varphi(x)$

β $\varphi()$ α $\varphi()$

β $\varphi()$ α $\varphi()$

3. $\mathbb{Z}$

4. $\displaystyle \lim_{n \to \infty} \frac{\pi}{n} \sum_{k=}^{n} \left(\frac{\pi}{} + \frac{\pi}{} \cdot \frac{k}{n} \right) =$

$\dfrac{\pi}{}$

$-$

$-$ $\dfrac{\pi}{}$

5. $f \ \mathbb{R} \to \mathbb{R}$

$g(u, v) \quad f(u \ - v)$ $\qquad \dfrac{\partial\, g}{\partial u} + \dfrac{\partial\, g}{\partial v} =$

$(\quad u \quad v\,) f\,''\,(u \quad v\,)$

$(\quad u \quad v\,) f\,''\,(u \quad v\,)$

$f\,'\,(u \quad v\,)(\quad u \quad v\,) f\,''(u \quad v\,)$

$(\quad u \quad v\,)\ f\,''(u \quad v\,)$

6. $\displaystyle \int \int_{x} (\quad) y \quad dy\,dx =$

$\underline{\quad + \quad}$

$\underline{\quad - \quad}$

7. $f(x)\ f(x)\ g(x)\ g(x)$

$\mathbb{R}\,(\qquad x\,) \quad \begin{vmatrix} f(x) & f(x) \\ g(x) & g(x) \end{vmatrix}$

$\begin{bmatrix} f(x) & f(x) \\ g(x) & g(x) \end{bmatrix}$

$'(x)$

$\begin{vmatrix} f\,'(x) & f\,'(x) \\ g(x) & g(x) \end{vmatrix} + \begin{vmatrix} f(x) & g\,'(x) \\ f\,'(x) & g(x) \end{vmatrix}$

$\begin{vmatrix} f\,'(x) & f\,'(x) \\ g(x) & g(x) \end{vmatrix} + \begin{vmatrix} f(x) & g\,'(x) \\ f(x) & g\,'(x) \end{vmatrix}$

$\begin{vmatrix} f\,'(x) & f\,'(x) \\ g(x) & g(x) \end{vmatrix} - \begin{vmatrix} f(x) & g\,'(x) \\ f(x) & g\,'(x) \end{vmatrix}$

$\begin{vmatrix} f\,'(x) & f\,'(x) \\ g\,'(x) & g\,'(x) \end{vmatrix}$

8. $f(x) = \dfrac{x + x(\quad +)x}{x} \qquad \left(\dfrac{\ }{x}\right) \qquad x \neq$

Write $L = \lim_{x \to} f(x)$ $\qquad x \to f(x)$

9. $\quad _{\to\infty} \displaystyle\int e^{-x}\,dx = \dfrac{\sqrt{\pi}}{\ }$

$\quad _{T\to\infty}\displaystyle\int x\,e^{-x}\,dx =$

$\qquad \dfrac{\sqrt{\pi}}{\ } \qquad\qquad\qquad \dfrac{\sqrt{\pi}}{\ }$

$\qquad \sqrt{\ }\,\pi \qquad\qquad\qquad \sqrt{\ }\pi$

10. $f(x) \begin{cases} +x & x < \\ (\ -)(\ px+ y) & x \geq \end{cases}$

$(p\ q)$
$()\qquad\qquad\qquad ()$
$()\qquad\qquad\qquad ()$

Q. 11 – Q. 30 carry two marks each.

11.

$\vec{\ } = \left(\ \pi x + \dfrac{x\ y}{\pi}\right)i + \left(\ \pi xy - \dfrac{y}{\pi}\right)j$

$x \qquad y$
$\quad \pi \qquad\qquad\qquad \pi$
$\quad \pi \qquad\qquad\qquad \pi$

12. $\mathcal{M}$

$\qquad\qquad\qquad \in \mathcal{M}$

$n\,() \qquad n\,()$

$\left|\ _{\in\mathcal{M}}()n \quad ()-n \quad \right| =$

13. $\begin{bmatrix} - & - \\ & \end{bmatrix} \qquad x \qquad \begin{bmatrix} \ \\ \ \end{bmatrix}$

$_{n\to\infty}\ ^{n}x$

$\begin{bmatrix} \ \\ \ \end{bmatrix}$

$\begin{bmatrix} \ \\ \ \end{bmatrix} \qquad\qquad \begin{bmatrix} \ \\ \ \end{bmatrix}$

14. $\vec{\ } \ (\ +)\,xy(i + x \ + y\ j$

$\vec{r}(t) = e^{t}\ t\,i + e^{t}\ t\,j \qquad \leq t \leq \pi$

$\displaystyle\int \vec{\ }\cdot d\vec{r} =$

$e\ ^{\pi} \qquad\qquad\qquad e\ ^{\pi}$
$e\ ^{\pi} \qquad\qquad\qquad e\ ^{\pi}$

15.

$\vec{\ } = zx\,i + xy\,j + yz\,k$

$()()$
$()$
$(\ )$

$\dfrac{\ }{\ }$

$\_$

16. $\qquad\qquad z \quad \dfrac{xy}{\ }$

$\qquad x \qquad y \leq$
$(\quad \pi \quad \pi \qquad\qquad (\quad \pi \quad \pi$
$(\quad \pi \quad \pi \qquad\qquad (\quad \pi \quad \pi$

17. $\quad a \qquad b \qquad \vec{\ }\ \dfrac{xj - yi}{b\ x\ + a^{2}y}$

$(\qquad\qquad\qquad\qquad x\ y) \in \mathbb{R} \quad x$
$y \quad a \quad b$

$\displaystyle\oint \vec{\ }\cdot d\vec{r} =$

$\dfrac{\pi}{ab} \qquad\qquad\qquad \pi$

πab

18. $\vec{} = y\,i - x\,j + z\,k$
norm al, across the surface of the solid $\{\,(x\ y$
$z)\ \in\ \mathbb{R}\qquad \le x \le \qquad \le y \le \qquad \le z \le$

$$\sqrt{\ -x\ -y\ }$$

— —

— —

19. $f\ \mathbb{R} \to \mathbb{R}$
$f()\qquad\quad f(x)\ f(y) \le (\ x\quad y)$
$x \in \mathbb{R}\ \ y \in \mathbb{R}\qquad g(x)\qquad x\ f(x)$
$g'()$

—

20. $f\ \mathbb{R} \to \quad \infty)$

$x \in \mathbb{R}\qquad\qquad f(x)$

$$\overline{f()\ +\text{\o}}$$

$x \in \mathbb{R}\qquad\qquad f(x)$

$$\sqrt{f(-)\ \text{\o}}$$

$x \in \mathbb{R}\qquad\qquad f(x)$

$$\int_{\_}\ f(t)\,dt$$

$x \in \mathbb{R}\qquad f(x)\quad \int\ f(t)\,dt$

21.

$$\sum_{n=}^{\infty} \frac{(\ x)-\ ^n}{(-)^{\,n+}\ \ n\ +}$$

$—\le x < —\qquad\qquad —\le x < —$

$—\le x \le —\qquad\qquad —\le x \le —$

22. $\mathcal{P}$

$\mathcal{P} \to \mathcal{P}$

$(\qquad\qquad p(x))\quad p''\,(x)\quad p(x)$

23. $f(x,\ y)\quad \dfrac{x\ y}{x\ +y}\quad (\ x\ y) \ne ()$

$\dfrac{\partial f}{\partial x}\qquad f$

$\dfrac{\partial f}{\partial x}\qquad\qquad\qquad f$

$\dfrac{\partial f}{\partial x}\qquad\qquad\qquad f$

$\dfrac{\partial f}{\partial x}\qquad f$

24. $\qquad\qquad\qquad\qquad \mathbb{R}$

$\alpha \qquad\qquad\qquad \alpha \in$

S

25. $\displaystyle\sum_{n=}^{\infty}\ \frac{-}{n}\ =$

$\dfrac{\pi}{}\qquad\qquad\qquad \dfrac{\pi}{}$

$\dfrac{\pi}{}\qquad\qquad\qquad \pi$

26. $\qquad a\qquad b\qquad n \ge \qquad a_n$

$\sqrt{a_n b_n}\qquad b_n\qquad \dfrac{a_n + b_n}{}$

$a_n\qquad b_n$

$a_n\qquad b_n$

27. $\displaystyle\lim_{n\to\infty} \frac{b_n}{a_n}\,\frac{1}{\sqrt{n}}\left(\frac{1}{\sqrt{\ }+\sqrt{\ }}+\frac{1}{\sqrt{\ }+\sqrt{\ }}+\ +\frac{1}{\sqrt{n}+\sqrt{\ n+\ }}\right)=$

$$+\sqrt{\quad}\qquad\sqrt{\quad}$$

$$\overline{\sqrt{\quad}}\qquad\qquad \overline{\ +\sqrt{\quad}}$$

28.

$$n$$

$$\left\{ n\quad -\frac{}{n}\right\}$$

29.

$$\frac{d\ y}{dx}-\frac{dy}{dx}=e^{\ x}\qquad x$$

$$\frac{e^{\ x}}{}(\qquad x\qquad x)$$

$$-\frac{e^{\ x}}{}(\qquad x\qquad x)$$

$$-\frac{e^{\ x}}{}(\qquad x\qquad x)$$

$$\frac{e^{\ x}}{}(\qquad x\qquad x)$$

30. $\quad y(x)$

$$(\qquad xy\quad y\quad e^{\ x})dx\ (\quad x\quad e^{\ x})dy$$
$$y()\qquad\qquad y()$$

$$\frac{e}{e-}\qquad\qquad\qquad \frac{e}{e-}$$
$$\frac{}{\dfrac{e}{-e}}$$

Section-B : Multiple Select Questions

Q. 31 – Q. 40 carry two marks each.

31. $\alpha\ \beta\in\mathbb{R}$ $\qquad\varphi_{\alpha,\beta}\ \mathbb{R}\to\mathbb{R}$
$\varphi_{\alpha,\beta}(x)\ \alpha x\ \beta\qquad \varphi_{\alpha,\beta}(\ \alpha\ \beta)\in$
$\mathbb{R}\quad f,g\in G,\qquad g\circ f\in G\ (\quad g\circ f)(x)$
$g(f(x))$

$$\circ$$
$$\circ$$

$(\qquad\alpha\ \beta)\in\mathbb{R}\quad \alpha\neq$
$(a\ b)\in\mathbb{R}\qquad\qquad \varphi_{\alpha,\beta}\circ\varphi_{a,b}\quad \varphi$
$(\quad\circ)$

32.

$$\left\{(x\ y\ z\in\mathbb{R}\quad \le x\le\qquad \le y\le\frac{}{x}\right.$$

$$\left.\le z\le x\right\}$$

$$\int\int^{\ x}\int^{\ x}dz\,dy\,dx$$

$$\int\int^{x}\int^{\ x}dy\,dz\,dx$$

$$\int\int^{z}\int^{\ x}dy\,dx\,dz$$

$$\int\int_{\ z}\int^{\ x}dy\,dx\,dz$$

33. $f\ \mathbb{R}\to\mathbb{R}$

$f\ (\ )$

$\qquad\qquad\qquad f\ ()$
$\qquad\qquad\qquad\qquad\qquad f$
$()\qquad\qquad f\ ()$
$\qquad\qquad\qquad\qquad\qquad f$
$()\qquad\qquad f\ ()$

$$\frac{\partial f}{\partial x}\qquad \frac{\partial f}{\partial y}$$

$()\qquad\qquad f\ ()$

34. $\qquad n\quad n$

$$\mathbb{R}^n$$

λ $\lambda \in \mathbb{R}$

35.

36. x_n x_n

x_n $n \geq$

   x $-$ x_n

   x $-$ x_n

   x $-$ x_n

   x $-$ x_n

37.
 $()$

   $\mathbb{R}$

    $\mathbb{R}$

        $\mathbb{R}$

     $x \in ()$

38. n n

    $=$ $v \neq v$

    $v.$

   n

   n

39. $y(x)$

$$\frac{dy}{dx} \ (\ \ y\ )(\ \ y\ )$$

        $y()$

      $y(x)$

      $y(x)$

$$\lim_{x \to +\infty} (\ \ y\ )\, x\ =$$

$$\lim_{x \to -\infty} (\ \ y\ )\, x\ =$$

40. $k,\ \ell \in \mathbb{R}$

$$\frac{d\ y}{dx} + \ k\frac{dy}{dx} + \ell y =$$

$$\lim_{x \to \infty} (\ \ y\ )\, x\ =$$

     k ℓ k

     k ℓ k

     k $\ell \leq$ k

     k ℓ k ℓ

Section-C : Numerical Answer Type

Q. 41 – Q. 50 carry one mark each.

41.

    x y c c

y $c\, x^{\alpha},\, c \ \in \mathbb{R}$ α

42. $(\mathbb{R})$

$$\begin{bmatrix} \ \ \end{bmatrix} \quad \begin{bmatrix} -\ \\ -\ \end{bmatrix}$$

43. σ

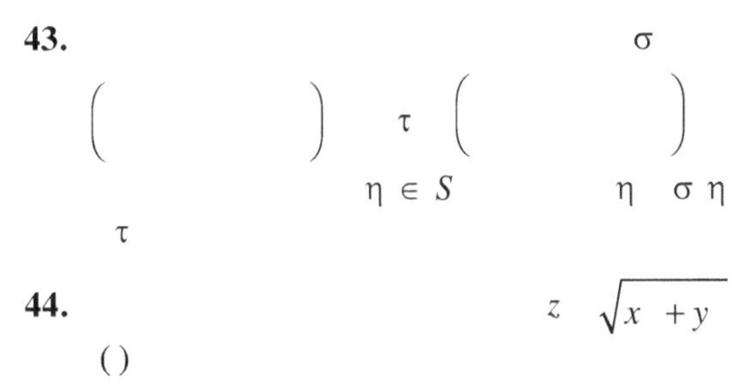

$$\begin{pmatrix} \ \ \end{pmatrix} \ \tau \ \begin{pmatrix} \ \ \end{pmatrix}$$

        $\eta \in S$ η $\sigma\,\eta$

  τ

44. z $\sqrt{x + y}$

 $()$

45. $\left(\int x\,(\,-x\,)\,dx\right)^{-} =$

46. v $\begin{bmatrix} \\ \end{bmatrix}$ v $\begin{bmatrix} \\ \end{bmatrix}$

v v v v

v v

x

47. $-\dfrac{1}{\pi}\left(\dfrac{\pi}{} - \dfrac{\pi}{} + \dfrac{\pi}{(\ )(\ )} - + \dfrac{(-)^{\,n-}\,\pi^{\,n+}}{n- \quad n+} + \right) =$

48.

$a \in \mathbb{R}$

aa

49. x $\qquad$ x

$x.$

$$\lim_{x \to \,^+} x\left(\left[\dfrac{}{x}\right] + \left[\dfrac{}{x}\right] + \ + \left[\dfrac{}{x}\right]\right) =$$

50. $\mathbb{Z}$ $\mathbb{Z}$

Q. 51 – Q. 60 carry two marks each.

51. $y(x)$ x

$$x\,\dfrac{d\,y}{dx} + x\dfrac{dy}{dx} + y =$$

$y(\ )$

$y'(\ )$ $\qquad$ $e\,y(e)$

52.

$$t\,i + \quad t\,j + \dfrac{t}{\sqrt{\ }}\,k$$

t $\qquad\qquad$ t

$$\vec{\ } = xj - yi$$

---

53. $f(x)$ $\dfrac{\pi x}{\pi \quad x}$ $x \in (\ )\pi$ $\qquad x \in$

$(\ \pi)$ $\qquad f\,'(x)$

$\left(f(x)\right)\left(\nmid \pi \nmid \quad x\right) =$

54. σ

55. a_n $\sqrt{n}$ $n \ge$ $\qquad n$ a a

$a_n.$

$$\lim_{n \to \infty}\left(\dfrac{a_n \quad n}{-(\quad -a)_n \quad n}\right) =$$

56. $x,$ $\qquad x$

$x.$

$$\int \int \int (x + y) + z \ dx\,dy\,dz =$$

57. x

$$f(x) \quad \int^{x}\left(\sqrt{\ }\,t -- \quad \sqrt{t}\right)dt$$

y $f(x)$

x y

58. $\alpha, \beta, \gamma, \delta$

$$\begin{bmatrix} & & & - \\ & & & \end{bmatrix}$$

α β γ δ

59.

$$\sum^{\infty} n\,x^{n}$$

60. $y(x)$ $\displaystyle\int_{\sqrt{x}}^{x}\dfrac{e^{t}}{t}\,dt$ $x >$ $\qquad y'(\ )$

SECTION-A

1. $f(x\ y)$ $x\ y$

$\dfrac{\partial f}{\partial x}$ x

$\dfrac{\partial f}{\partial y}$ y

$\dfrac{\partial f}{\partial x}$ $\dfrac{\partial f}{\partial y}$

$x\ (\quad n)$ $\dfrac{\pi}{\ } = \dfrac{\pi}{\ }\ \dfrac{\pi}{\ }$

y

$\left(\dfrac{\pi}{\ }\right)\left(\dfrac{\pi}{\ }\right)$

r $\dfrac{\partial\ f}{\partial x} = $ x

s $\dfrac{\partial\ f}{\partial x \partial y}$

t $\quad \dfrac{\partial f}{\partial y}$

$rt \quad s \qquad x \geq \qquad x \leq \pi$

$\pi \quad x \leq \quad \pi$

$\left(\dfrac{\pi}{}\ \right) f \qquad\qquad \left(\dfrac{\pi}{}\ \right)$

2.

$\phi(3)$

$\phi(2)$

$\phi(1)$

$1 \quad 2 \quad 3$

$x \longrightarrow$

$\alpha \quad \phi()$

$\beta \quad \phi()$

3. $\qquad\qquad \mathbb{Z} \qquad \phi()$

$\phi() \qquad \phi(\ \cdot\ )$

$$\left(--\right)\left(--\right)$$

$$\times - \times - =$$

4. $\displaystyle\sum_{k=}^{n}\left(\dfrac{\pi}{}+\dfrac{\pi}{}\cdot\dfrac{k}{n}\right) \qquad \sum_{k=}^{n}\left(\dfrac{\pi}{}\cdot\dfrac{k}{n}\right)$

$a(\quad a \quad d)(\quad a \quad d)$

$(\quad a(\ n\ )\quad d)$

$$\dfrac{\left(a+n-\dfrac{d}{}\right)\ nd}{d}$$

$$\sum_{k=}^{n}\left(\dfrac{\pi}{}\dfrac{k}{n}\right) \quad \dfrac{\left(n\cdot\dfrac{\pi}{n}\right)(\ )\left(n+\dfrac{\pi}{n}\right)}{\dfrac{\pi}{n}}$$

$$\dfrac{\dfrac{\pi}{}\cdot\left(\dfrac{n}{n}\dfrac{\pi}{}\right)-\dfrac{\pi}{n}}{\dfrac{\pi}{n}}$$

$$\dfrac{-\left(\left(\dfrac{\pi}{}+\dfrac{\pi}{n}\right)+\dfrac{\pi}{n}\right)-\dfrac{\pi}{n}}{\dfrac{\pi}{n}}$$

$$\dfrac{-\left(\left(\dfrac{\pi}{}+\dfrac{\pi}{n}\right)-\dfrac{\pi}{n}\right)}{\dfrac{\pi}{n}}$$

$$\dfrac{-\left(\dfrac{\pi}{}+\dfrac{\pi}{n}\right)}{\dfrac{\pi}{n}} \ --$$

$$\dfrac{\pi}{n}\cdot\sum_{k=}^{n}\left(\dfrac{\pi k}{n}\right) \quad \dfrac{-\dfrac{\pi}{n}}{\dfrac{\pi}{n}}\cdot\dfrac{\pi}{n}-\dfrac{\pi}{n}$$

$n \to \infty \qquad \displaystyle\lim_{n\to\infty}\dfrac{\pi}{n}\sum_{k=}^{n}\left(\dfrac{\pi k}{n}\right)$

$$\lim_{n\to\infty}\ -\ \dfrac{\pi}{n}\cdot\dfrac{\dfrac{\pi}{n}}{\dfrac{\pi}{n}}-\lim_{x\to\infty}\dfrac{\pi}{n}\ -$$

5. $\qquad g(u\ v)\quad f(u\quad v)$

$$\dfrac{\partial g}{\partial u} \qquad u f'(u\quad v)$$

$$\dfrac{\partial g}{\partial v} = (\quad v)\, f'(u\quad v)$$

$$\dfrac{\partial\ g}{\partial u} \qquad f'(u\quad v)\quad u\, f''(u\quad v)$$

$$\dfrac{\partial\ g}{\partial v} = \quad f'(u\quad v)\quad v\, f''(u\quad v)$$

$$\dfrac{\partial\ g}{\partial u}+\dfrac{\partial\ g}{\partial v} \quad (\quad u\quad v)\, f''(u\quad v)$$

6.

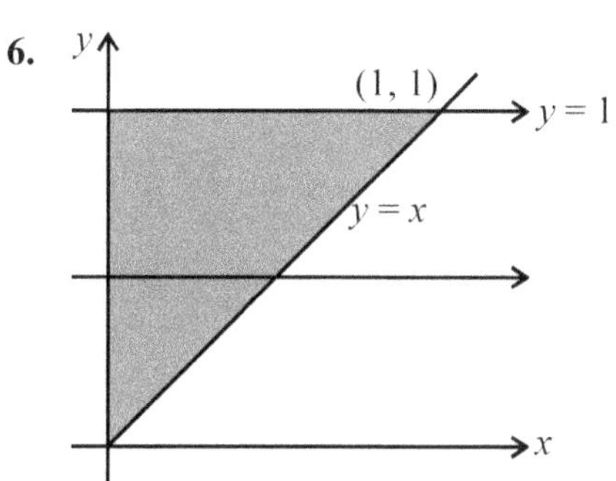

$$\iint_x y\,dy\,dx \qquad \iint^y y\,dx\,dy$$

$$\iint y \quad y\,dy = -\int \quad t\,dt$$

$$(t \quad y)$$

$$-[-\quad t]\ (\ -)\ -$$

7. $(x) \begin{vmatrix} f(x) & f(x) \\ g(x) & g(x) \end{vmatrix}$

$$'(x) \quad \begin{vmatrix} f'(x) & f'(x) \\ g(x) & g(x) \end{vmatrix} + \begin{vmatrix} f(x) & f(x) \\ g'(x) & g'(x) \end{vmatrix}$$

$$\begin{vmatrix} f'(x) & f'(x) \\ g(x) & g(x) \end{vmatrix} + \begin{vmatrix} f(x) & g'(x) \\ f(x) & g'(x) \end{vmatrix}$$

8. $f(x) \quad \dfrac{x + x(\quad)x}{x} \quad \left(\dfrac{}{x}\right)$

$$\lim_{x\to^+} (\ f\ x \quad \lim_{h\to} \dfrac{h + h(\ + h}{h} \quad \left(\dfrac{}{h}\right)$$

$$\lim_{h\to} (\quad) + h \quad \left(\dfrac{}{h}\right)$$

$$\lim_{h\to} \quad \left(\dfrac{}{h}\right)$$

9. $\displaystyle\lim_{\to\infty}\int x\,e^{-x}\,dx \quad \int^\infty x\,e^{-x}\,dx = -\int^\infty \sqrt{t}\cdot e^{-t}\,dt$

$$(\quad x \quad t \quad x\,dx \quad dt)$$

$$-\int^\infty t^{--}\,e^{-t}\,dt$$

$$-\left\lceil\quad\right. = -\cdot-\left\lceil\quad\right. = \dfrac{\sqrt{\pi}}{}$$

10. $f(x)$
$f(x)$

$f(x) \qquad x$

$$\lim_{x\to^-} (\ f\ x \qquad \lim_{x\to^+} (\ f\ x$$

$$\Rightarrow \qquad q$$
$$\Rightarrow \qquad q$$

$f(x) \qquad x$

$$\lim_{x\to^-} (f\ x \qquad \lim_{x\to^+} (f\ x$$

$$\Rightarrow \qquad \lim_{x\to^+}(\ - px) + q(+p)\ - x$$

$$p \quad q$$

$$p \quad q$$
$$\Rightarrow \qquad p$$
$$(\ p,\ q)\ ()$$

11.

$$x \qquad y$$

$$\oint_S \vec{}\cdot n\,d \qquad \oint_S \vec{}\cdot n\,d + \oint_S \vec{}\cdot n\,d + \oint_S \vec{}\cdot n\,d$$

At the top of the right column:

$$\lim_{x\to^-} (\ f\ x \qquad \lim_{h\to}\dfrac{(-h) + -h(\ \to h}{-h} \quad \left(\dfrac{}{-h}\right)$$

$$\lim_{h\to}\dfrac{-h + h(\ -h}{h} \quad \dfrac{}{h}$$

$$\lim_{h\to}(\ )-h \quad \dfrac{}{h} =$$

$$\int \nabla \cdot \vec{}\, d\tau \qquad\qquad \int \vec{}\cdot nd$$

$$\left(\quad \vec{}\cdot n = \qquad\qquad \right)$$

$$\Rightarrow \quad \int \vec{}\cdot nd \quad \int\left(\pi + \frac{xy}{\pi} + \pi x - \frac{}{\pi} \right) d\tau$$

$$\iiint\left(\pi - \frac{}{\pi} \right) + x\left(\frac{y}{\pi} + \pi \right) dz\,dx\,dy$$

$$\left(\pi - \frac{}{\pi} \right) \iint dx\,dy + \int \int_{\underline{\sqrt{-x}}}^{\overline{\sqrt{-x}}} \left(\frac{y}{\pi} + \pi \right) x\,dx\,dy$$

$$\left(\pi - \frac{}{\pi} \right) \cdot \pi \cdot \ \cdot -(= \ \pi) \ -$$

12.

$$\rightarrow \quad (\ )\, n \quad (\ ) - n \qquad =$$

13.

$$\lambda \quad -$$

$$\left(\ -- \ \right)$$

$$\lim_{n \to \infty}$$

$$\lim_{x \to \infty}$$

14. $\vec{}$ $\quad (+)xy\, i (+ x -) y\ i$

$$\int \vec{F} \cdot \overrightarrow{dr}$$

$$\int \vec{F} \cdot \overrightarrow{dr} \quad \int (+)xy\, dx (+ x -) y\ dy$$

$$x + x\ y - y \Big|_0^{(\quad -e)^{\pi}}$$

$$e^{\pi}$$

15.

$$x \quad y \quad z$$

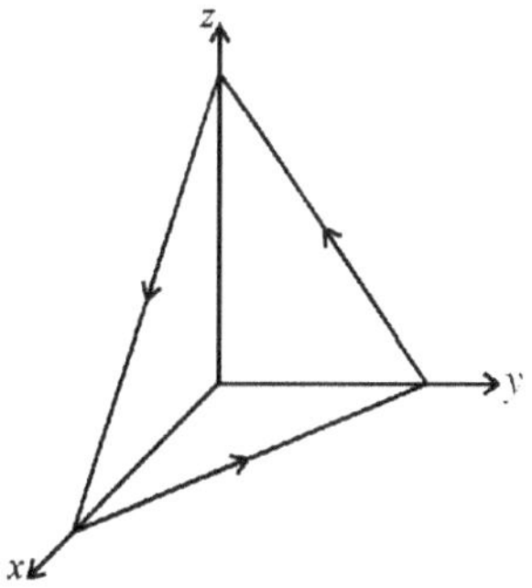

$$\nabla \times \vec{} \quad \begin{vmatrix} i & j & k \\ \dfrac{\partial}{\partial x} & \dfrac{\partial}{\partial y} & \dfrac{\partial}{\partial z} \\ zx & xy & yz \end{vmatrix}$$

$$zi + xj + yk$$

$$n \quad \frac{i + j + k}{\sqrt{\ }}$$

$$\oint \vec{} \cdot \overrightarrow{dr} \quad \int \nabla \times \vec{} \cdot nd$$

$$\frac{1}{\sqrt{\ }} \int (x + y + z)\, d$$

$$\frac{1}{\sqrt{\ }} \int d$$

$$\frac{1}{\sqrt{\ }} \cdot \frac{\sqrt{\ }}{\sqrt{\ }} \times (\sqrt{\ }) = -$$

18. $\quad \oint \vec{F} \cdot n\, dS \quad \int \nabla \cdot \vec{F}\, d\tau$

$$\int z\, d\tau$$

$$\iint \int^{\sqrt{-x\ -y}} z\, dz\, dx\, dy$$

$$\iint z\ dx\, dy \Big|^{\sqrt{-x\ -y}}$$

$$\iint (- x\ - y)\ dx\, dy$$

$$\int \left. x - \frac{x}{\ } - xy \right| dy$$

$$\int \left(- - - y\ \right) dy$$

$$\int \left(- - y\ \right) dy$$

$$\left. \left(-y - \frac{y}{\ } \right) \right| = -$$

19. $\quad \dfrac{f(x) - f(y)}{x - y} \leq \quad x - y \ /$

$$f'(x) \quad \frac{f(x) - f(y)}{x - y} \leq \quad (y \to x)$$

$$f'(x) \qquad f'(x)$$

$$g(x) \quad x\, f(x)$$

$$g'(x) \quad x\, f'(x) \qquad x\, f(x) \qquad x\, f(x)$$

$$g'() \qquad f()$$

21. $\quad f(x) \quad \displaystyle\sum_{n=}^{\infty} \frac{(^n\ x) - ^n}{(-)^{n+}\ n\ +}$

$$g(x) \quad \sum_{n=}^{\infty} \frac{n}{(-)^{n+}\ n\ +} x^n$$

$$\overline{\lim_{n\to\infty} a_n^{\,/n}}$$

$$a_n^{\,/n} = \left[\left(--\right)^n \cdot -- \cdot \frac{}{n\,+}\right]^{/n}$$

$$\lim_{n\to\infty} a_n^{\,/n}$$

$$\lim_{n\to\infty}\left|\frac{\left(--\right)^n \cdot -- \cdot \dfrac{}{n\,+}}{\left(--\right)^{n+} \cdot -- \cdot \dfrac{}{(n+)\;+}}\right|$$

$$= \lim_{n\to\infty} \frac{(\,n\,)\;+}{n\,+}$$

$$= \lim_{n\to\infty} \frac{\left(-+\;\right)+\dfrac{}{n}}{+\dfrac{}{n}}$$

$$-$$

$f(x)$

$$-\quad x < \;+-$$

$$-< x < --$$

$g(x)\quad x\quad -$

$$g\left(-\right)\quad \sum_{n=}^{\infty}\frac{}{(-)^{\,n+}}\cdot\frac{n}{n\,+}\left(-\right)^n$$

$$\sum_{n=}^{\infty}\frac{(-)^{\,n}}{(\,n\,)}$$

$$\lim_{n\to\infty} u_n$$

$$u_n \;\le u_n$$

$g\left(-\right)\qquad\qquad f(x)$

$$-$$

$$g\left(--\right)\quad \sum_{n=}^{\infty}\frac{n}{(-)^{\,n+}}\cdot\frac{n}{n\,+}\cdot\left(--\right)^n$$

$$\sum_{n=}^{\infty}\frac{}{(\,n\,)}$$

$g\left(--\right)\qquad\qquad f(x)$

$x\quad -$

$f(x)\qquad\qquad -\le x \le -$

22. $\mathcal{P}\;\to\;\mathcal{P}$

$$(\,p(x))$$
$$\Rightarrow\quad p''(x)\quad p(x)$$
$$p(x)$$

$$\mathcal{P}\;\to\;\mathcal{P}$$

23. $f(x\;y)\quad \dfrac{x\;y}{x\,+y} = \dfrac{r\quad\theta\quad\theta}{r}$

$$r\quad\theta\quad\theta$$
$$\infty\quad r\to\infty$$

$$\frac{\partial f}{\partial x}\quad \frac{x(y\;x\,+y)\;-\;x\;y}{(x\,+y)}$$

$$\frac{xy}{(x\,+y)} = \frac{r\quad\theta\quad\theta}{r}$$

$$\theta\quad\theta$$
$$x\qquad y$$

25. $\displaystyle\sum_{n=}^{\infty} \quad -\frac{}{n} \quad \frac{\pi}{} \quad ()$

27. $\displaystyle\lim_{n\to\infty} \frac{}{\sqrt{n}}\left(\frac{}{\sqrt{}+\sqrt{}}+\frac{}{\sqrt{}+\sqrt{}}+\ +\frac{}{\sqrt{n}+\sqrt{n+}}\right)$

$\displaystyle\lim_{n\to\infty}\frac{-}{\sqrt{n}}\left[\left(\sqrt{}-\sqrt{}\right)+\left(\sqrt{}-\sqrt{}\right)+\right.$

$\left.+\left(\sqrt{n}-\sqrt{n+}\right)\right]$

$\displaystyle\lim_{n\to\infty}\frac{\sqrt{n+}-\sqrt{}}{\sqrt{n}} \qquad \sqrt{}$

29. $(\quad)\quad y\quad e^{x}\quad x$

$$\frac{}{(\ )} e^{x}\quad x$$

$$e^{x}\frac{}{(\ )\ (-)\ +}\quad x$$

$$e^{x}\frac{}{+}\quad x$$

$$e^{x}\frac{}{(\ )-}\quad x$$

$$e^{x}\frac{(\ )+}{(\ )-}\quad x$$

$$\frac{-e^{x}}{}(\quad x)+\quad x$$

30. $(xy\quad y\quad e^{x})dx\ (\quad x\quad e^{x})dy$

$\displaystyle\Rightarrow \frac{dy}{dx}+\frac{(x+)\ y+e^{-x}}{(x+e^{-x})}$

$\displaystyle\Rightarrow \frac{dy}{dx}+\frac{(x+)\ e^{x}}{(xe^{x}+)}y \qquad -\frac{}{xe^{x}+}$

$$e^{\int \frac{(x+)\ e^{x}}{xe^{x}+}}$$

$$e^{(\quad xe)^{x}+}$$

$$(\quad xe^{x})$$

$$(xe^{x})\quad y\quad -\int\ dx+c$$

$(xe^{x})\qquad y=-x\quad c$

$x\qquad y\qquad \Rightarrow\ c$

$y\qquad \dfrac{-x+}{xe^{x}+}$

$y()\qquad \dfrac{}{-e^{-}}=\dfrac{e}{e-}$

32. $\displaystyle\int\int_{x}^{/x}\int^{x} dz\,dy\,dx$

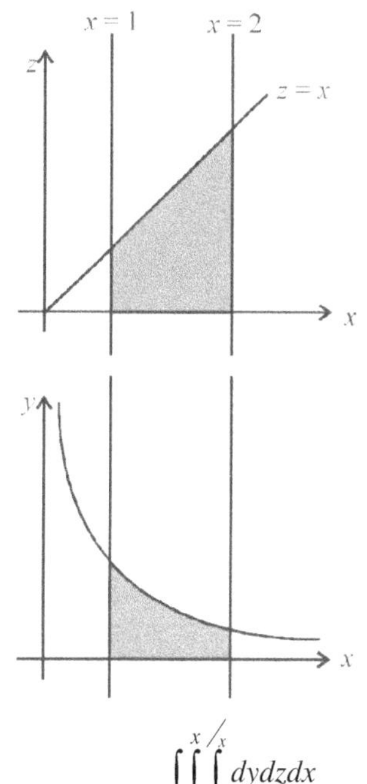

$\displaystyle\int\int_{x}^{x/x}\int dy\,dz\,dx$

$\displaystyle\int_{(\ )}\int_{z}\int^{/x} dy\,dx\,dz$

36. $\qquad x_{n}\qquad \dfrac{x_{n}+}{}$

$x\qquad -$

$x\qquad \dfrac{-+}{}=\dfrac{}{}$

$x_n \to \qquad n \to \infty$

$x \qquad -$

$x \qquad \dfrac{-\quad+}{\qquad} = - \ =$

$x \qquad \dfrac{0 \qquad +}{\qquad} =$

$n \to \infty \quad x_n \to$

SECTION-C

41. $\qquad x \qquad y \qquad c$

$\Rightarrow \qquad x + \ y\dfrac{dy}{dx}$

$\left(\dfrac{dy}{dx}\right) \qquad -\dfrac{x}{y}$

$\qquad y \quad c \ x^{\alpha}$

$\Rightarrow \qquad \left(\dfrac{dy}{dx}\right) \qquad c \ \alpha x^{\alpha}$

$\left(\dfrac{dy}{dx}\right)\left(\dfrac{dy}{dx}\right)$

$\Rightarrow \quad -\dfrac{x}{y} c \ \alpha \cdot x^{\alpha-}$

$\Rightarrow \qquad \dfrac{c \ \alpha \ x^{\alpha}}{c \ x^{\alpha}}$

$\Rightarrow \qquad \dfrac{\alpha}{}$

$\qquad \alpha$

42. $\quad \begin{bmatrix} - \\ - \end{bmatrix} = \begin{bmatrix} - \\ - \end{bmatrix}\begin{bmatrix} - \\ - \end{bmatrix} = \begin{bmatrix} - \\ - \end{bmatrix}$

$\begin{bmatrix} - \\ - \end{bmatrix} = \begin{bmatrix} - \\ - \end{bmatrix}\begin{bmatrix} - \\ - \end{bmatrix} = \begin{bmatrix} - \\ - \end{bmatrix}$

$\begin{bmatrix} \\ \end{bmatrix}$

44.

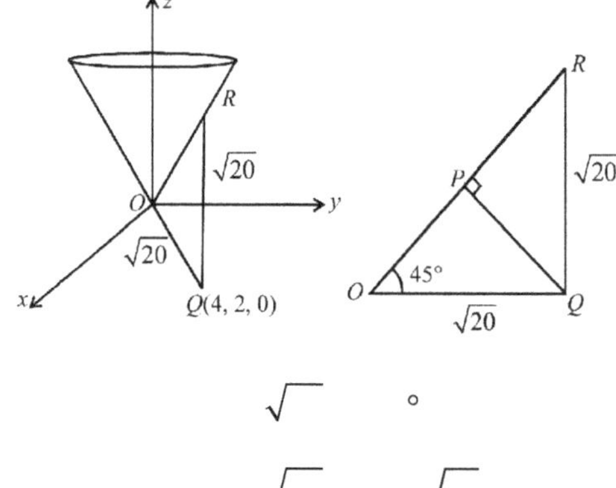

$\sqrt{\qquad} \qquad \circ$

$\sqrt{\qquad} \cdot \dfrac{}{\sqrt{\ }} = \sqrt{\qquad}$

45. $\displaystyle\int x \ (\ -\!x \quad dx \qquad \int x^{\ -} \ (\ -\!x\ )^{\ -} \ dx$

$\beta() \qquad \dfrac{\lceil\ \rceil}{\lceil\ }$

$\dfrac{\cdots\cdot\lceil}{\cdots\cdot\lceil}$

$\left(\displaystyle\int x \ (\ -\!x \quad dx\right)^{-}$

47. $\qquad x \qquad x - \dfrac{x}{} + \dfrac{x}{} - \dfrac{x}{} +$

$\displaystyle\int_{}^{\pi} x \qquad x\,dx \quad \int_{}^{\pi} x\left(x - \dfrac{x}{} + \dfrac{x}{} - \quad\right) dx$

$\Rightarrow -x \qquad x + \quad x\big|^{\pi} \quad \displaystyle\int_{}^{\pi}\left(x \quad -\dfrac{x}{} + \dfrac{x}{} - \quad\right) dx$

$\Rightarrow \qquad\qquad \pi \quad \dfrac{\pi}{} - \dfrac{\pi}{} + \dfrac{\pi}{}$

$\dfrac{}{\pi}\left(\dfrac{\pi}{} - \dfrac{\pi}{} + \dfrac{\pi}{}\right)$

49.

$$\lim_{x\to\ ^+} x\left[\left(\frac{}{x}\right)+\left(\frac{}{x}\right)+\ +\left(\frac{}{x}\right)\right]$$

$$\lim_{x\to\ ^+} x\left[\frac{}{x}+\frac{}{x}+\ +\frac{}{x}-\left(\left\{\frac{}{x}\right\}+\left\{\frac{}{x}\right\}+\ \left\{\frac{}{x}\right\}\right)\right]$$

$$\lim_{x\to\ ^+}\left[\frac{\times}{}-x\left(\left\{\frac{}{x}\right\}+\left\{\frac{}{x}\right\}+\ \left\{\frac{}{x}\right\}\right)\right]$$

51.

$$\frac{d}{dz}=x\frac{d}{dx}=x$$

$$(x\qquad x)\qquad y$$
$$(\ (\ )\qquad\ )\quad y$$
$$(\qquad\ )\quad y$$
$$y\quad (c\quad c\ z)e^{\ z}$$

$$(\ c\quad c\qquad x)\frac{}{x}$$

$$y()\qquad\Rightarrow\ c$$

$$y'\quad -\frac{}{x}(c +c\quad)\ x +\frac{c}{x}$$

$$y'()$$
$$\Rightarrow\qquad\qquad c$$
$$c$$

$$y\ (\qquad\qquad x)\frac{}{x}$$

$$y(e)\ ()\qquad\frac{}{e}$$
$$e\ y(e)$$

52.

$$\vec{r}\qquad t i+\quad t j+\frac{t}{\sqrt{}}k$$

$$\vec{}\qquad -yi +xj$$
$$-\quad t i+\quad t j$$

$$\vec{dr}\quad \left(-\quad t i+\quad t j+\frac{}{\sqrt{}}k\right)dt$$

$$\vec{}\cdot\vec{dr}\qquad dt$$

$$\int\vec{}\cdot\vec{dr}\qquad\int dt =$$

$$\frac{\vec{dr}}{dt}\quad -\quad t i+\quad t j+\frac{}{\sqrt{}}k$$
$$t$$

$$\frac{\vec{dr}}{dt}\qquad j+\frac{}{\sqrt{}}k$$
$$t$$

$$\frac{\vec{dr}}{dt}\quad -\quad i+\qquad j+\frac{}{\sqrt{}}k$$

$$\left(\frac{\vec{dr}}{dt}\right)_{t=}\cdot\left(\frac{\vec{dr}}{dt}\right)_{t=}$$

$$\Rightarrow\qquad\qquad -$$

$$\qquad\qquad --$$

$$\Rightarrow\qquad\qquad\frac{\pi}{}$$

53.

$$f(x)\qquad\frac{\pi x}{\pi\quad x}$$

$$f'(x)\qquad\frac{\pi\quad x\quad \pi x-\quad \pi x\quad x}{\pi\quad x}$$

$$f'(x)$$
$$\Rightarrow\qquad \pi x\quad \pi\quad x$$
$$x\qquad\qquad\qquad\qquad\qquad \pi x\quad \pi\quad x$$
$$\pi x\quad \pi\quad x$$

$$f(x\ )\qquad\frac{\pi x}{\pi\quad x}$$

$$\pi x\qquad\frac{\pi\quad x}{\sqrt{}\ +\pi\quad x}$$

$$(f(x\ ))\qquad\frac{\pi x}{\pi\qquad x}$$

$$\frac{\dfrac{\pi \qquad x}{\pi \left(+\pi \quad x \right) \quad x}}{\left(+\pi \quad x \right) \quad x}$$

$$\frac{}{x +\pi \quad x}$$

$$\frac{}{+\pi + \quad x}$$

$$\left(f(x) \right) \left(+\pi + \quad x \right) =$$

55.

$$\frac{n}{a_n} \qquad \frac{\sqrt{n}}{\sqrt{}+\sqrt{}+ +\sqrt{n}}$$

$$\frac{n}{a_n} \qquad \frac{\sqrt{}+\sqrt{}+ +\sqrt{n}}{\sqrt{n}}$$

$$\frac{\sqrt{n}+\sqrt{n}+ +\sqrt{n}}{n}$$

$$\lim_{n\to\infty} \left(\frac{n}{a_n} \right) \quad \infty$$

$$\left(-\frac{a_n}{n} \right) \quad -\left(\frac{a_n}{n} \right) --\left(\frac{a_n}{n} \right) \quad --\left(\frac{a_n}{n} \right)$$

$$\frac{-\quad\left(-\dfrac{a_n}{n} \right)}{\left(\dfrac{a_n}{n} \right)} \qquad +-\lim_{n\to\infty}\left(\frac{a_n}{n} \right)+-\lim_{n\to\infty}\left(\frac{a_n}{n} \right) +$$

56. $\iiint (x + y)+ z \quad dx\, dy\, dz$

$$\iiint dxdydz =$$

58. $\qquad \alpha + \beta + \gamma + \delta$

$$\lambda$$

$$\begin{vmatrix} -\lambda & & & \\ & -\lambda & & - \\ & & -\lambda & \\ & & & -\lambda \end{vmatrix} (\quad \lambda) \begin{vmatrix} -\lambda & & & - \\ & -\lambda & & \\ & & & -\lambda \end{vmatrix}$$

$$\lambda(\lambda \quad \lambda \quad \lambda)$$
$$\lambda(\lambda \quad \lambda \quad \lambda \quad \lambda \quad \lambda)$$
$$\lambda(\lambda)(\quad \lambda \quad \lambda)$$
$$\lambda(\lambda)(\quad \lambda)(\quad \lambda)$$

$$\alpha \quad \beta \quad \gamma \quad \delta$$

59.

$$f(x) \quad \sum n \ x^n$$

$$\lim_{n\to\infty} ( ) \left| n \quad {}^{/n} \right|$$

$$\lim_{n\to\infty} \frac{(n)^{/n}}{((n+))^{/n}}$$

$$\lim_{n\to\infty} \overline{(n+)^{/n}} =$$

IIT-JAM

Joint Admission Test for M.Sc. (Mathematics), 2016

Section-A : Multiple Choice Questions

Q. 1 – Q. 10 carry one mark each.

1.

$$s_n = \dfrac{\dfrac{\pi}{}}{} + \dfrac{\dfrac{\pi}{}}{} + \quad + \dfrac{\dfrac{\pi}{n}}{n\,(n+\ )}$$

2. $(\qquad \mathbb{R})$

$$\leq$$

$$\to$$

$$(\ a \quad a\,x \quad a\,x \quad a\,x\ ) \quad a \quad a\,x \quad a\,x$$
$$a\,x$$

$$x \quad x \quad x$$

3. $f \qquad \to \mathbb{R}$

$$\int^{\pi} x\,f(\ )\,x\,dx$$

$$\dfrac{\pi}{}\int^{\pi} f(\ )\,x\,dx \qquad \dfrac{\pi}{}\int^{\pi} f(\ )\,x\,dx$$

$$\pi\int^{\pi} f(\ )\,x\,dx \qquad \pi\int^{\pi} f(\ )\,x\,dx$$

4. σ

$$\sigma$$

5. f

$$a \quad b$$

$$f(a) \quad a \qquad f(b) \quad b$$

$$c \in (\,a \quad b\,)$$
$$f(c) \quad c$$

$$c \quad c \in (\,a \quad b\,)$$
$$f(c_i) \quad c_i \ i$$
$$c \in (\,a \quad b\,)$$
$$f(c) \quad c$$

$$c \in (\,a \quad b\,)$$
$$f(c) \quad c$$

6.

$$\lim_{(x\ y)\to(\ -\ )} \dfrac{\sqrt{(x-y)}-}{x-y-}$$

$$-$$

$$- \qquad\qquad -$$

7. $\vec{r} = \left(x\,i + y\,j + z\,k\right) \qquad r = |\vec{r}| \quad f(r) \qquad r$

$$g(r) = \dfrac{}{r} \quad r \neq \qquad \nabla f + (h\,)\,r\ \nabla g = \vec{}$$

$$h(r)$$

$$r \qquad\qquad \dfrac{}{r}$$

$$r \qquad\qquad \dfrac{}{r}$$

8. n

$(\ xy\quad n\ x\ y)dx\ (\quad nx\quad x\ y)dy\qquad x\ne$

9.

$(y\quad x)dx\ (\quad x\quad y)dy$

$y(\ )$

$(\ )\qquad\qquad(\ )$

$(\ )\qquad\qquad(\ )$

10. $\mathbb{R}$

$\mathbb{R}\qquad\cap\quad\ne\phi$

$\cap$

Q. 11 – Q. 30 carry two marks each.

11.

$$\sum_{k=}^{\infty}\frac{1}{(\ k-\ )^{(\ k-\ )}}$$

$$\sum_{k=}^{\infty}\left(\frac{k-}{k+}\right)^{(k+)}$$

12. a_n

$$\frac{1}{a_{n+}}=\frac{1}{a_n}+\frac{a_n}{}\qquad n\ge\quad a$$

$$\left[-\ -\right]$$

13. $\begin{bmatrix}\ \ \end{bmatrix}$

14.

$$\frac{(\ n)}{^n(n\ )}\int_{-}(\ -x\ )^n dx\quad n\in\mathbb{N}$$

$$\overline{(\ n+\ )}\qquad\qquad\frac{n}{(\ n+\ )}$$

$$\frac{(n\ )}{n+}\qquad\qquad\frac{(n+\ )}{n+}$$

15.

$x\quad y\quad z\qquad x\qquad y\qquad z$

$$\int\int^{\lambda(x)}\int^{\mu(x\ y)}dz\ dy\ dx$$

$\lambda(x)\qquad\mu(x\ y)$

$x\quad y\qquad\qquad x\quad y$

$x\qquad\qquad\qquad y$

16.

$y\quad z\qquad\qquad\qquad x\quad y$

$$\frac{\sqrt{\ }}{}\pi\qquad\qquad\frac{\sqrt{\ }}{}\pi$$

$$\frac{\sqrt{\ }}{}\pi\qquad\qquad\frac{\sqrt{\ }}{}\pi$$

17. $f\ \mathbb{R}\ \to\mathbb{R}$

$$f(x\ y)\quad\begin{cases}\dfrac{xy}{x+y} & x+y\ne\\[2mm] & x+y=\end{cases}$$

$$\left(\frac{\partial\ f}{\partial x\partial y}+\frac{\partial\ f}{\partial y\partial x}\right)$$

$(\ )$

18. $f(x\ y)$ $x\ y$ y x y

     ()   ()
     ()   ()

19. $\vec{F} = r^{\beta}\left(yi - xj\right)$

  $\beta \in \mathbb{R}$ $\vec{r} = xi + yj$ $r = |\vec{r}|$

$$\oint_c \vec{}\, d\vec{r}$$

        x y a

  () π β

20. $z = \sqrt{x\ + y}$

      z z

       $\rightarrow$

$$\nabla \times \vec{} = -xi - yj$$

$$\oint_c \vec{}\, d\vec{r} \qquad \vec{r} = xi + yj + zk$$

   $r = |\vec{r}|$

           π

    π π

21. $y(x)$

$$\frac{d}{dx}\left(x\frac{dy}{dx}\right) = x \quad y(\ ) = \quad \left.\frac{dy}{dx}\right|_{x=} =$$

 ()

   $\dfrac{3}{\ }+-$ $\dfrac{3}{\ }--$

   $\dfrac{3}{\ }+$ $\dfrac{3}{\ }-$

22.

$$\frac{d\ y}{dx} + b\frac{dy}{dx} + cy =$$

          $x \rightarrow \infty$

   b c
   b c
     b c
     b c

23. $\subset \mathbb{R}$ ∂ x

   $\mathbb{R}$ x

                     $-$

   ∂ $\mathbb{R}$

   $\partial(\mathbb{R}\ )$ ∂ $\subset \mathbb{R}$

   $\partial(\ \cup)$ $\partial\ \cup \partial$ $\subset \mathbb{R}$

     $\cap$ $\neq \phi$

   $\partial\ = \overline{} \cap (\overline{\mathbb{R}})$ $\subset \mathbb{R}$

24.

$$\sum_{n=}^{\infty} \frac{(-\ )^n}{n\ + n -}$$

   $-$ $--$ $-$ $--$

   $-$ $--$ $-$ $--$

25. $f(x)$ $\dfrac{}{\ +|x|} + \dfrac{}{\ +|x-\ |}$ $x \in$

             $f(x)$ $-$

             $f(x)$ $-$

          $f(x)$ x $-$

          $f(x)$ x

26.

$$\begin{bmatrix} \alpha & & \alpha \\ i\ & \alpha & i\ & \alpha \end{bmatrix}$$

     α

   $(\ n+\ )\dfrac{\pi}{\ }\ n \in \mathbb{Z}$ $(\ n+\ )\dfrac{\pi}{\ }\ n \in \mathbb{Z}$

   $(\ n+\ )\dfrac{\pi}{\ }\ n \in \mathbb{Z}$ $(\ n+\ )\dfrac{\pi}{\ }\ n \in \mathbb{Z}$

27.

$$\begin{bmatrix} & & - \\ - & & \alpha \\ & -\alpha & \end{bmatrix} \quad \alpha \in \mathbb{R} \qquad b$$

$x \in \mathbb{R}$
α

$x \quad b$
$x \quad b$
α

28.

$\mathbb{Z}$ $\mathbb{Z}$

29.

$_n(n \geq)$

30. $f \quad \mathbb{R} \to \mathbb{R}$

$$f(x) \quad \begin{cases} x(+ x^q( )) & x \\ & x = \end{cases}$$

x f

α
α

α

α

Section-B : Multiple Select Questions

Q. 31 – Q. 40 carry two marks each.

31. s_n

$$s_{n+} = s_n + - \quad n \geq$$

α β

$x - x + - = \quad \alpha \quad s \quad \beta$

$()()$

s_n
s_n

$n \to \infty \ s_n \quad \alpha$
$n \to \infty \ s_n \quad \beta$

32. $()$

$$\int_{-\pi}^{\pi} |x| \quad nx\, dx \quad n \geq$$

$()$

n
n

$-\dfrac{}{n} \qquad n$

$-\dfrac{}{n} \qquad n$

33. $f \ \mathbb{R} \ \to \mathbb{R}$

$$f(x\ y) = \begin{cases} \dfrac{xy}{|x|} & x \neq \end{cases}$$

$()$
$()()$
f
f
f

f

34.
$$\vec{} = xi + yj$$

$\subset \mathbb{R}$

$()()$

$\to$

$\to$

$\to$

$\to$

35.

$$x\frac{dy}{dx} = y + \qquad x \ y\left(\frac{\pi}{}\right) = -\sqrt{}$$

$0 0$

$x \to$

$x \to \dfrac{\pi}{}$

$x \to$

$x \to \dfrac{\pi}{}$

36. $()\ ()$

$\mathbb{R}$

$\mathbb{R}$

$\mathbb{R}$

$\mathbb{R}$

37. $(\ )\ x = \left(-\right)^x + \left(-\right)^x -$ $\qquad x \in$

$0 0$

$(\qquad\qquad x)$
$\qquad \mathbb{R}$
$(\quad x)$ $\qquad\qquad x \in \mathbb{R}$
$(\qquad\qquad x)$
$\qquad \mathbb{R}$
$(\quad x)$ $\qquad\qquad x \in \mathbb{R}$

38. $\qquad\qquad\qquad o()$

$()$

$()$

$\qquad\qquad o()\quad pq \qquad p \quad q$

$\overline{(\ \ )}$

$()$

$\qquad\qquad o()\quad p \qquad p$

39.

$$= \left\{ \begin{bmatrix} x \\ y \\ z \end{bmatrix} \in \mathbb{R} \ \middle|\ \alpha x + \beta y + z = \gamma \quad \alpha\ \beta\ \gamma\ \in \mathbb{R} \right\}$$

$()$
$\qquad\qquad\qquad\qquad\qquad\qquad\qquad \mathbb{R}$

$\mathbb{R}$

α	β	γ
α	β	γ
α	β	γ
α	β	γ

40. $\qquad = \left\{ \dfrac{}{n} + \dfrac{}{m} \ \middle|\ n\ m \in \mathbb{N} \right\}$

$()\,()$

Section-C : Numerical Answer Type (NAT)

Q. 41 – Q. 50 carry one mark each.

41. $\qquad s_n$

$$s_n = \frac{(-)^n}{}\left(- \frac{}{n} \right)\ \frac{n\pi}{}\qquad n \in \mathbb{N}$$

s_n

42.

$\qquad s_k \quad k^{\alpha k} \quad k \ge \qquad \alpha$

$\left(\underset{n\to\infty}{\quad} s\ s \right)\ s_n{}^{\,n}$

43. $\qquad x = \begin{bmatrix} x \\ x \\ x \end{bmatrix} \in \mathbb{R}$

$$= \frac{x\,x}{x\ x}$$

$\left\{ y \in \mathbb{R} \ \middle|\ \ y = 0 \right\} \qquad \mathbb{R}$

44. f

$$f(x\ y)=\left(x\ y\ e^{\frac{y}{x}}\right)\quad x>\quad y>$$

$$x\frac{\partial f}{\partial x}+y\frac{\partial f}{\partial y}$$

$(x\ y)\qquad x\qquad y$

45. $\quad \vec{}=\sqrt{x}\,i+(\ x+y)\ j$

$(\ x\ y)\qquad x\geq\qquad \vec{r}=xi+yj$

$$\int \vec{}\ d\vec{r}\ ()$$

$0\qquad\qquad x\quad t\quad y\quad t\quad \leq t\leq$

46. $f(\qquad \infty)\to\mathbb{R}\qquad f(x)=\dfrac{x}{+x}$

$$f(x)=-+-(x-)\ +\frac{(\ c\ x)-}{(\ +\xi)}$$

$\xi\qquad\qquad x$

c

47. $\quad y\ (x)\quad y\ (x)\qquad y\ (x)$

$$\frac{d\ y}{dx}-\frac{d\ y}{dx}+\frac{dy}{dx}-\ y=$$

$(\qquad\qquad y\ y\ y\ )$

$ke^{bx}\qquad\qquad k\qquad\qquad\qquad b$

48.

$$\sum_{n=}^{\infty}\frac{(-\ )^{n}}{n(n+\ )}(x+\ )^{\ n}$$

49. $\quad f(\quad \infty)\to\mathbb{R}$

$$\int_{}^{x}f(t)\,dt=-\ +\frac{x}{}+\ x\qquad x+\qquad x$$

$$\frac{}{\pi}f\left(\frac{\pi}{}\right)$$

50.

Q. 51 – Q. 60 carry two marks each.

51.

$$\lim_{n\to\infty}\left(n-\frac{}{n}\right)^{\frac{(-\ )^{n}}{n}}$$

52. $\qquad\qquad\qquad\qquad x\qquad y\geq$

$x\qquad y\ \leq$

$$\iint|xy|\,dx\,dy$$

53. $\begin{bmatrix}\alpha & & \\ & \beta & \\ & & \gamma\end{bmatrix}\ \alpha\beta\gamma=\ \alpha\ \beta\ \gamma\in\mathbb{R}$

$$x=\begin{bmatrix}x\\ x\\ x\end{bmatrix}\in\mathbb{R}\qquad\qquad x$$

$()$

54.

$y\quad x\quad y\quad x\qquad\qquad x$

$$\oint(xy-y\ )dx-x\ dy$$

55. $\qquad\qquad\qquad\qquad\qquad x\qquad y$

$z\qquad z$

$$\nabla\vec{}=\ y+z+$$

$$\frac{}{\pi}\iint\vec{}\ n\,ds$$

n

56. $y(x)$

$$\frac{d\,y}{dx} + \frac{dy}{dx} + y = \qquad y() \qquad \left.\frac{dy}{dx}\right|_{x=} = - $$

$$y(x) \qquad\qquad x$$

57.

$$\int_{\pi}^{x}\int \frac{y}{\pi - y}\,dy\,dx$$

58.

$$\mathbb{Z}$$

59. $\quad = \begin{bmatrix} - \end{bmatrix} = \begin{bmatrix} - \end{bmatrix} ()$

$$() $$
$$() \qquad\qquad \cap ()$$
$$\mathbb{R}$$

60. $\quad f(x\ y)\quad x \qquad y$
$$\qquad\quad y\quad x$$

ANSWERS

SECTION-A : (MCQ) Multiple Choice Questions

1	2	3	4	5	6	7	8	9	10
11	12	13	14	15	16	17	18	19	20
21	22	23	24	25	26	27	28	29	30

SECTION-B : (MSQ) Multiple Select Questions

31	32	33	34	35
36	37	38	39	40

SECTION-C : (NAT) Numerical Answer Type

41	42	43	44	45
46	47	48	49	50
51	52	53	54	55
56	57	58	59	60

EXPLANATORY ANSWERS

SECTION-A

1.

$$t_n \qquad n \qquad n$$

$$\frac{\dfrac{\pi}{n+}}{(n+)(\ n+)} >$$

$$n$$

$$n \qquad \frac{\dfrac{\pi}{}}{} + \frac{\dfrac{\pi}{}}{} + \ + \frac{\dfrac{\pi}{n}}{(\ \ )n\ n+}$$

$$< \frac{}{} + \frac{}{} + \ + \frac{}{(\ \ )n\ n+}$$

$$\left(\ \ -\right) + \left(-\ \ -\right) + \ \left(\frac{}{n}\ \ \frac{}{n+}\right)$$

$$\overline{n+}$$

$$\frac{n}{n+} < \quad \forall n \in$$

2.

$$x\ x\ x$$

$$0 \qquad x$$

$$\Rightarrow \quad 0 \qquad \begin{bmatrix} \\ \\ \\ \end{bmatrix}$$

$$(x) \quad x$$

$$\Rightarrow \quad (x) \qquad \begin{bmatrix} \\ \\ \\ \end{bmatrix}$$

$$(x) \quad x$$

$$\Rightarrow \quad (x) \qquad \begin{bmatrix} \\ \\ \\ \end{bmatrix}$$

$$(x)$$

$$\Rightarrow \quad (x) \qquad \begin{bmatrix} \\ \\ \\ \end{bmatrix}$$

$$\begin{bmatrix} \\ \\ \\ \\ \end{bmatrix}$$

$$(a\ a)$$

3.

$$\int^{\pi} x f(\ ) x\ dx$$

$$\int^{\pi} (\pi + \ ) x\ f\left(\ \ \pi + \ x\ \right) dx$$

$$\left(\ \int^{a} (f) x\ dx = \int^{a} (f\ a)\ x\ dx \right)$$

$$\int^{\pi} (\pi \ ) x\ f(\ \ )\pi \ x\ dx)$$

$$\int^{\pi} (\pi \ ) x\ f\ )\ x\ dx$$

$$\pi \int^{\pi} f(\ ) x\ dx$$

$$\frac{\pi}{} \int^{\pi} f(\ ) x\ dx$$

4. $\sigma(\ a\ a\ a\ )(a\ a\ )$

5.

$$g(x)\quad f(x)\quad x$$
$$g(a)\qquad x\quad a$$
$$g(b)\qquad x\quad b$$

$f(x)$

$$b\quad a\ f(b)\quad f(a)$$

$$g(x)$$
$$x\qquad\qquad x\quad a$$
$x\quad b\ ($
$)$

6. $\displaystyle\lim_{(x,y)\to(\ )}\frac{\sqrt{(x\ y\ )}}{x\ y}$

$$\lim_{(x,y)\to(\ )}\frac{\left(\sqrt{(x\ y\ )}\ \right)\left(\sqrt{x\ y}+\ \right)}{(x\ y)\ \left(\sqrt{x\ y}+\ \right)}$$

$$\lim_{(x,y)\to(\ )}\frac{}{\sqrt{x\ y}+\ }=\ -$$

7. $\qquad f\quad \nabla f=\Sigma i\,\dfrac{\partial f}{\partial x}$

$$\Sigma i\,\frac{\partial}{\partial x}(\ )\ r$$

$$\Sigma i\ \frac{x}{r}\ \frac{}{r}$$

$$\frac{}{r}\vec r$$

$$g\quad \frac{}{r}\quad \nabla g=\Sigma i\,\frac{\partial}{\partial x}\left(\frac{}{r}\right)$$

$$\Sigma i\ \frac{x}{r}\ \frac{}{r}=\ \frac{\vec r}{r}$$

$\nabla f\quad h\nabla g$

$$\Rightarrow\quad \frac{\vec r}{r}\quad \frac{h\vec r}{r}$$

$$\Rightarrow\qquad h\quad r.$$

8.

$$dx\qquad dy$$

$$\frac{\partial}{\partial y}\qquad \frac{\partial}{\partial x}$$

$$\Rightarrow\qquad xy\quad n\ x\qquad nx\qquad xy$$
$$n\qquad n\Rightarrow n$$

9.

$$(y\quad x)dx\ (\quad x\quad y)dy$$
$$(ydx\quad xdy)\quad xdx\quad ydy$$

$$xy\quad \frac{x}{}+\frac{y}{}$$

$$x\qquad y$$

$$-$$

$$xy\quad \frac{x}{}+\frac{y}{}\quad -$$

$$\Rightarrow\qquad xy\quad x\quad y$$
$()$
$()$

10. $\cap\qquad \subseteq$

$$\cap$$
$$\cap$$

$$\cap$$
$$\cap$$

11. $\qquad n\quad (\ n)\qquad {}^{n}<\frac{}{n}=\ n$

n

$$\left(\frac{k}{k+}\right)^{k+}$$

$$\left(\frac{}{k+}\right)^{k+-}$$

$$\left[\left(+\dfrac{}{k}\right)^{\frac{k}{}}\right]^{-}\quad\left(\dfrac{}{k+}\right)^{-}$$

$$\to\infty$$

$$\left(\dfrac{k}{k+}\right)^{\frac{k+}{}}\to e^{-}$$

12. a

n

$$\dfrac{}{a}\quad-+-=-$$

$$a\quad-$$

$$\dfrac{}{a}\quad\dfrac{}{a}+\dfrac{a}{}\approx-\times\ +-\times-$$

$$\dfrac{}{a}\quad-+--$$

$$\Rightarrow\quad a\approx-$$

$$n\to\infty\ a_n\quad a_n\ \to k$$

$$\dfrac{}{k}\quad\dfrac{}{k}+\dfrac{k}{}$$

$$\Rightarrow\quad\dfrac{}{k}\quad\dfrac{k}{}$$

$$k$$

$$\Rightarrow\quad k$$

$$[\,]$$

13.

$$\lambda$$

$$\to\ +\ +$$

$$(\,)\quad=$$

$$\lambda\ \lambda\ \lambda\ (\,)$$
$$\lambda\quad\lambda\quad\lambda$$
$$\lambda\quad\lambda\quad\lambda$$
$$\lambda\quad\lambda$$

14.

$$\dfrac{(\ )}{(\ )}\int(\ \ )x^{\ n}\,dx$$

$$\dfrac{(\ )}{(\ )}\int(\ )x^{\ n}\,dx$$

$$x\quad y\Rightarrow x\quad\sqrt{y}$$

$$dx\quad\dfrac{}{\sqrt{y}}\,dy$$

$$\dfrac{(\ )}{(\ )}\ -\int y(\ )\ y^{\ n}\,dy$$

$$\dfrac{(\ )}{(\ )}\ \left(-n+\right)$$

$$\dfrac{(\ )}{(\ )}\quad\dfrac{\sqrt{\ }\overline{(n+)}}{\overline{n+-}}$$

$$\frac{(\text{ }n\text{ }\sqrt{}/\,n}{^n\,n\left(n+-\right)\left(n\ -\right)\left(n\ -\right)\ -\sqrt{}/}$$

$$\frac{(\text{ }n\text{ })^{n+}}{(\ n)(+\ )\ n}$$

$$\frac{(\ )(\ n\ )\ n}{(\ n)(+\ )\ n}^{n+}$$

$$\frac{^{n}\ ^{n+}\,n\,(\ )\ n}{(\ n+} = \frac{n}{n+}$$

15.

$$\int\int^{\lambda(x)}\int^{\mu(x\ y)} dz\,dy\,dx$$

$$\int\int^{x}\int^{x\ y} dz\,dy\,dx$$

$$\mu(x\ y) \qquad x \quad y$$
$$\lambda(x) \qquad x$$
$$\lambda(x) \quad \mu(x\ y) \qquad x \qquad x \quad y \quad y$$

16.

$$\iint \sqrt{+\left(\frac{\partial z}{\partial x}\right) + \left(\frac{\partial z}{\partial y}\right)}\,dx\,dy$$

$$\iint \sqrt{+-}\,dx\,dy$$

$$\frac{\sqrt{}}{}\iint dx\,dy = \frac{\sqrt{}}{}\times \pi(\sqrt{})$$

$$\frac{\sqrt{}}{}\pi$$

17.

$$(x\ y)\ ()$$

$$f'(xy) \quad \lim_{h\to} \frac{fy(h)\ (fy}{h} = \frac{}{h} =$$

$$f'(yx) \quad \lim_{k\to} \frac{fx(\ )k\ (fx}{k}$$

$$\lim_{k\to} \frac{k}{k} =$$

$$f'(y)_0 \quad \lim_{k\to} \frac{f(\ )k\ ()f}{k} = \frac{}{k} =$$

$$f'(x)_0 \quad \lim_{h\to} \frac{f(h)\ ()f}{h} = \frac{}{h} =$$

$$f'(y)_{(h)} \quad \lim_{k\to} \frac{f(h\ k)\ (f\ )h}{k}$$

$$\lim_{k\to} \frac{hk}{h+k} =$$

$$f'(x)_{(\ k)} \quad \lim_{h\to} \frac{f(h\ k)\ (f\ )\ k}{h}$$

$$\lim_{h\to} \frac{k}{h+k} = k$$

$$\left(\frac{\partial\ f}{\partial x\partial y} + \frac{\partial\ f}{\partial y\partial x}\right)()$$

18.
$$f'(x) \qquad xy \qquad x$$
$$f'(y) \qquad x \qquad y \qquad y$$
$$r \quad f''(x)$$
$$t \quad f''(y) \qquad y$$
$$s \quad f''(xy) \qquad x$$
$$rt \quad s\ (\qquad y\ ) \qquad x$$
$$(\qquad y\ ) \qquad x\ ()$$

19.

$$\rightarrow \qquad r^{\beta}\left(yi \quad xj\right)$$

$$r^{\beta}\,r\left(\quad \theta i \qquad \theta j\right)$$

$$\oint \overrightarrow{}\,\overrightarrow{dr} \quad \int r^{(\beta+)}\,e_{\theta}\,\overrightarrow{dr}$$

$$\oint r^{(\beta+)}\,dl = \oint r^{\beta+}\,r\,d\theta$$

$$\int r^{(\beta+)}\,d\theta$$

$$a^{(\beta+)}\int_{}^{\pi} d\theta = \pi a^{\beta+} = \pi$$

β

20.

$$\oint \vec{}\cdot \vec{dr} \qquad \int \nabla\times\vec{}\cdot n\,d$$

$$\int (\ xi\ )yj\ n\,d$$

$$\int (re_r)\cdot n\,d$$

$$\int_{}^{\pi}\int r\ rdr\,d\theta$$

$$(\ e_r\cdot n = \quad d\ \Rightarrow rdr\,d\theta$$
$$\pi$$

$$\left(\oint \vec{}\cdot\vec{dr}\right)\qquad \pi$$

21.

$$\frac{d}{dx}\left(x\frac{dy}{dx}\right)\quad x$$

$$x\frac{dy}{dx}\quad \frac{x}{}+c$$

$$\frac{dy}{dx}\quad \frac{x}{}+\frac{c}{x}$$

$$x\qquad \frac{dy}{dx}=$$

$$-+c \Rightarrow c = \frac{1}{}$$

$$\frac{dy}{dx}\quad \frac{x}{x}$$

$$y\quad \frac{x}{}- \quad x+c$$

<hr>

$$\begin{array}{cc} x & y \end{array}$$

$$-\ -\quad +c$$

$$\Rightarrow \qquad c\quad -$$

$$y\quad \frac{x}{}-\quad x\ -$$

$$y()\qquad -\ -$$

22. $(\quad b\quad c)y$

$$\frac{b\pm\sqrt{b\quad c}}{}$$

$$b\qquad\qquad c$$

23.

$$()$$
$$\partial$$
$$()$$
$$\partial$$
$$\cup\ ()$$
$$\partial(\ \cup)$$
$$\partial\ \cup\ \partial$$
$$\partial(\ \cup)\qquad \partial\ \cup\ \partial$$

24.

$$\sum_{n=}^{\infty}\frac{0\quad^{n}}{n\ +n}$$

$$\sum_{n=}^{\infty}\frac{0\quad^{n}}{(n+)(\ n)}$$

$$-\sum_{n=}^{\infty}0\quad^{n}\left[\frac{}{n}\quad \frac{}{n+}\right]$$

$$-\left[\sum_{n=}^{\infty}\left(\frac{}{n}\quad \frac{}{n+}\right)\quad \sum_{n=}^{\infty}\left(\frac{}{n}\quad \frac{}{n+}\right)\right]$$

$$-\left[\sum_{n=}^{\infty}\left(\frac{}{n}\quad \frac{}{n+}\right)\quad \sum_{n=}^{\infty}\left(\frac{}{n+}\quad \frac{}{n+}\right)\right]$$

$$-\left[\left(\ -+-\ -\ \right)\left(-\ -+-\ -+-\ -+\ \right)\right]$$

$$-\left[\ \left(\ -+-\ -+\ \right)-\right]$$

$$-\quad\ -$$

25.

$$f(x)\quad \frac{}{+\ x}+\frac{}{+\ x}$$

$$\frac{}{x}+\frac{}{x}\qquad \le x \le$$

$$\le x \le$$

$$f(x)\quad \frac{}{+\ x}+\frac{}{x}$$

$$f'(x)\quad \frac{}{(\ +\ x)}+\frac{}{(\ )\ x}=$$

$$\Rightarrow (\quad x)\ (\quad x)$$

$$\Rightarrow \quad x\ -$$

$$f''(x)\quad \frac{}{(\ +\ x)}+\frac{}{(\ )\ x}>\qquad x=-$$

$$f(x)\qquad x\ -$$

$$f\left(-\right)\quad \frac{}{+-}+\frac{}{-}$$

$$f\left(-\right)\quad -+-=-$$

$$x$$

$$f(x)\quad -+\ =-$$

26.

$$x$$

$$f(x)\quad -+-=-$$

$$-$$

$$\Rightarrow$$

$$\Rightarrow\quad \begin{bmatrix}\ \alpha & i & \alpha\end{bmatrix}\begin{bmatrix}\alpha \\ i \quad \alpha\end{bmatrix}$$

$$\Rightarrow\quad \alpha \quad \alpha \quad \alpha \quad \alpha$$

$$\alpha$$

$$\alpha \quad n\pi$$

$$\alpha \quad \frac{n\pi}{}$$

27.

$$b$$

$$b$$

$$\Rightarrow\quad b$$

28. $\mathbb{Z}$

$\mathbb{Z}$ $(\ )$

29.

are contained in A_n $\subset\ _n$

$$_n$$

$$\sigma \in\ _n$$

$$\sigma$$

$$(\quad)(\quad)(\ _k\quad _k)$$

with k k

$$\sigma$$

$$(\ a\ b)(\ c\ d)$$

Case 1 : $a \quad b \qquad c \quad d$

Case 2 : $(a\ b)\ (\quad c\ d)$

$$(\ )(\ )(\ )$$

$$(x \ y)(y \ z) \ (\ x \ y \ z)$$
$$x \ y \ z$$

Case 3 : $a \ b \ c \quad d$
$$(\ a \ b)(c \ d) \ (\ a \ b \ c)(b \ c \ d)$$
$$= \mathbb{A}_n$$
$$n$$

30.
$$f(x) \quad x \quad x^{\alpha} \quad (\quad x \ ) \quad x \neq$$
$$\alpha$$
$$\alpha$$

SECTION-B

31.

$$x \qquad x + -$$

$$\Rightarrow \quad x \quad x$$
$$\Rightarrow \quad x \quad x \quad x$$
$$\Rightarrow x(\ x \ ) (\qquad x \ )$$
$$\Rightarrow \quad (\ x \ )(\qquad x \ )$$

$$\Rightarrow \qquad\qquad x \quad - \ -$$

$$\alpha \quad -$$

$$\beta \quad -$$

$$s$$

$$s \quad s \ + -$$

$$s \quad - < s$$

$$s \quad s \ + - = - + - = -$$

$$s \quad - - < s$$

$$s_n$$
$$\alpha$$

32.

$$\int_{\pi}^{\pi} x \qquad nx \, dx$$

$$\int^{\pi} x \qquad nx \, dx$$

$$\int^{\pi} x \qquad nx \, dx$$

$$f(x)$$

$$\left[\frac{x}{n} \quad nx \ - \int \quad nx \, dx \right]$$

$$\left[\frac{x}{n} \quad nx + \frac{}{n} \quad nx \right]^{\pi}$$

$$\frac{}{n^2}(\quad)n\pi$$

$$n$$

$$\frac{}{n} \qquad n$$

33.

$$f(x \ y) \begin{cases} y & x > \\ y & x < \\ & x = \end{cases}$$

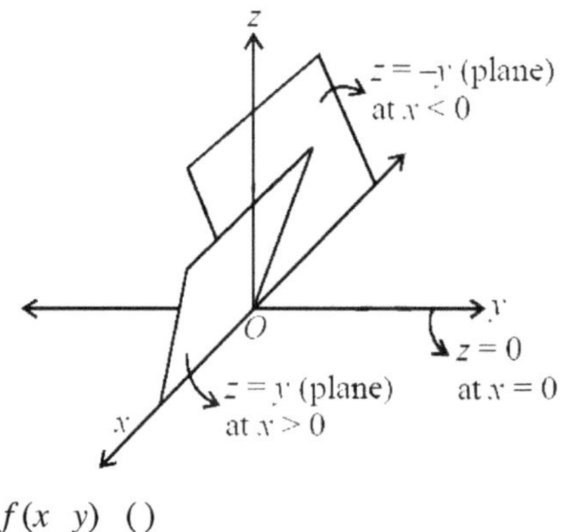

$$f(x \ y) \ (\ )$$

$$f$$

34.

35.

$$x\frac{dy}{dx} \qquad y \qquad x$$

$$\frac{dy}{dx} \quad \underline{\qquad}\, y \qquad \underline{\qquad}$$

$$e^{\int \frac{\quad}{x \quad x}dx} \qquad e^{\int \quad x\,dx}$$

$$e^{-\quad x}$$

$$y \, \underline{\quad}_x \qquad \int \underline{\quad}_x \, \underline{\quad}_x \, dx + c$$

$$\underline{\quad}_x + c$$

$$y \qquad x \quad c \qquad x$$

$$x \qquad \frac{\pi}{\quad}$$

$$y \qquad \sqrt{\quad}$$

$$\Rightarrow \qquad \sqrt{\quad} \qquad \sqrt{\quad} + c$$

$$c$$

$$y \qquad x \qquad x$$

$$x \to \qquad y \to$$

$$\lim_{x \to \frac{\pi}{\quad}}(\quad) \, x \qquad x \qquad \lim_{x \to \frac{\pi}{\quad}} \frac{x}{x}$$

$$\left(-\quad\right)$$

$$\lim_{x \to \frac{\pi}{\quad}}\frac{x}{(\;)\,x} =$$

$$y \qquad\qquad x \to$$

$$x \to \frac{\pi}{\quad}$$

36.
$$n \qquad \left[\frac{\quad}{n}\right]$$

$$\bigcup_{n=}^{\infty} \quad n \; ($$

$$\mathbb{R}$$

$$(a \quad b) \qquad\qquad \mathbb{R}$$

37.
$$x$$

$${}'(x) \qquad \left(-\quad\right)^{x} \qquad \left(-\quad\right) + \left(-\quad\right)^{x} \qquad -\; <$$

$$(\; x)$$

$$\underline{\quad} \qquad \theta$$

$$\underline{\quad} \qquad \theta$$

$$\Rightarrow \quad \frac{(\; x)}{x} \quad {}^{x}\,\theta \qquad {}^{x}\,\theta$$

39.
$$\mathbb{R}$$

40.
$$\in \quad nbd$$

$$-\;+\;- \qquad -$$

SECTION-C

41.

42. n

a_n n

$\lim_{n\to\infty} (a_n)^n$ $\quad \lim_{n\to\infty} \dfrac{a_{n+}}{a_n}$

$\lim_{n\to\infty} s_{n+}$

$\lim_{n\to\infty} (\quad)n+ \quad^{\alpha\ n+}$

43. $=\dfrac{xx}{x\ x}$

44.

$f(x\ y)\qquad x\ y\ e^{y/x}\quad u()$

$x\ y\ e^{y/x}\quad e^u\quad v()$

$v\quad x\ y\ e^{y/x}$

$x\left(\dfrac{y}{x}e^{y\ x}\right)$

$x\dfrac{\partial v}{\partial x}+y\dfrac{\partial y}{\partial y}\qquad v$

$\Rightarrow\ x\,e^u\quad -\dfrac{\partial u}{\partial x}+y\,e^u\quad -\dfrac{du}{dy}\qquad e^u$

$x\dfrac{\partial u}{\partial x}+y\dfrac{\partial u}{\partial y}$

45. $\quad c\qquad x\quad t$

$\Rightarrow\qquad dx\quad t\,dt$

$\qquad y\quad t$

$\Rightarrow\qquad dy\quad t\ dt$

$\vec{dr}\qquad \sqrt{x}\,dx+(x+y\ )dy$

$t\ t\,dt\,(+\ t\ +t)\quad t\ dt$

$\int \vec{dr}\quad \int (\ t\ +\ t\ +)t\quad dt$

$-t\ +-t\ +\dfrac{t}{\ }\Big|$

$-+-+-$

$-\ =$

46. $f(x)\quad f((\quad x))$

$f()\ +f'()(\quad)x\quad (+)x(\ )\quad f''\ \xi$

$f(x)\qquad \dfrac{x}{+x}=\overline{(\ x+)}$

$x\qquad\qquad f()\qquad\quad -\ =\ -$

$f'(x)\qquad \overline{(\ +x)}$

$\Rightarrow\qquad f'()\quad -$

$f''(x)\qquad \overline{(\ +x)}$

$f''(\xi)\qquad \overline{(\ +\xi)}$

$f(x)\quad -+-(x\ )\quad \dfrac{(\ )x}{(\ +\xi)}$

c

47.

$$\begin{vmatrix} y & y & y \\ y^0 & y & y \\ y^0 & y & y \end{vmatrix}$$

$$\begin{vmatrix} e^x & e^x & e^x \\ e^x & e^x & e^x \\ e^x & e^x & e^x \end{vmatrix}$$

$$\begin{vmatrix} & & \\ & e^x \; e^x \; e^x \end{vmatrix}$$

$$ke^x$$

$$b$$

48.

$$\left| \lim_{n\to\infty} a_n \right|^n$$

$$\left[\left| \lim_{n\to\infty} \frac{a_n}{a_{n+}} \right| \right]$$

$$\left[\left| \lim_{n\to\infty} \frac{()^n (\; n(+ \;)n+}{n(n+)} \frac{}{()^{n+}} \right| \right]$$

$$\left(- \right) = - =$$

49.

$$\int^x f(t)\,dt \qquad + \frac{x}{} + \; x \qquad x + \qquad x$$

$$x$$

$$f(x) \quad x+ \qquad x+ \; x \qquad x \qquad x$$

$$x \quad \frac{\pi}{}$$

$$f\left(\frac{\pi}{} \right) \quad \frac{\pi}{} + \; +$$

$$\frac{\pi}{}$$

$$\frac{}{\pi} \int \left(\frac{\pi}{} \right) \quad - =$$

50.

51. $\lim_{n\to\infty} u_n{}^n \qquad \lim_{n\to\infty} \dfrac{u_{n+}}{u_n}$

$$u_n \quad \left(n \; - \frac{}{n} \right)^0{}^{\,n}$$

$$\frac{u_{n+}}{u_n} \quad \frac{\left((n + \dfrac{}{n+} \right)^{/n+}}{\left(n \; - \dfrac{}{n} \right)^{/n}}$$

$$\frac{{}^{/n}(\; n) + {}^{/n+} \left(\dfrac{}{(n + } \right)^{/n+}}{{}^{/n} \; n^{/n} \left(\dfrac{}{n} \right)^{/n}}$$

$$\lim_{n\to\infty} \frac{u_{n+}}{u_n}$$

$$\frac{{}^{/n+}(\; n + {}^{/n+} \left(\dfrac{}{(n + } \right)^{/n+}}{{}^{/n} \; n^{/n} \left(\dfrac{}{n} \right)^{/n}}$$

52. $x \quad y \leq$
$\Rightarrow \quad x \quad y$

$y \quad \sqrt{\quad x}$
$x \quad y \geq$
$\Rightarrow \quad x \quad y$

$y \quad \dfrac{\sqrt{\quad x}}{x}$

n

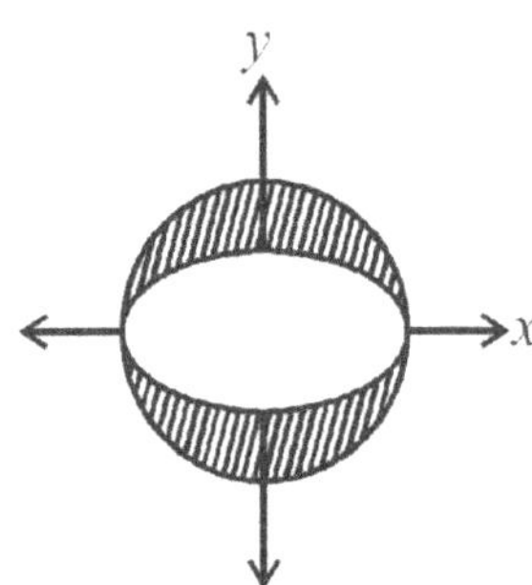

xy

$\displaystyle\int_{x}^{x}\int_{y}^{y} xy\,dx\,dy \qquad \int \int_{\sqrt{\ x}}^{\sqrt{\ x}} xy\,dy\,dx$

$\displaystyle\int \dfrac{x}{\quad}--(\quad)x \quad dx$

$-\displaystyle\int (x \quad x)\,dx$

$-\displaystyle\int\left(-\ -\ -\right)$

$-\times \underline{\quad\quad}$

$\underline{\quad}$

$\displaystyle\iint (xy)\,dx\,dy \qquad \times -\!\!-$

$-$

53.

$\alpha \quad \beta \quad \gamma$
$(\ )$

54.

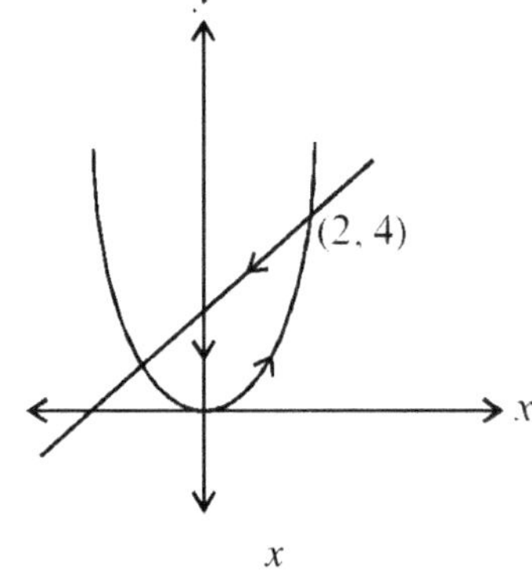

x

x

x

$\displaystyle\oint (xy \quad y)\,dx \quad x\,dy$

$\displaystyle\iint\left(\dfrac{\partial}{\partial x} \quad \dfrac{\partial}{\partial y}\right)dx\,dy$

$\displaystyle\int\int_{x}^{x+} (\quad x \quad x) + \quad y\,dx\,dy$

$\displaystyle\int \quad x \ y \quad xy + y \ \Big|_{x}^{x+}\ dx$

$\displaystyle\int \ (x \quad x+)\ (x \quad x)x + \quad x^2$

$+(x + \ x + \ )x \quad dx$

$$\int (x \quad x \quad x)+ x+ \; dx$$

$$\left[\frac{x}{} \quad \frac{x}{} \quad \frac{x}{}+\frac{x}{}+ \; x \right]$$

$$\frac{}{} \qquad + +$$

55.

$$\oint \vec{} \, n\,ds \quad \int \nabla \; ds$$

$$\iiint (\; y+z+ \;)\; dz\,dx\,dy$$

$$\iint \; yz+\frac{z}{}+z \bigg| \; dx\,dy$$

$$\iint (\; y)+ \quad dx\,dy$$

$$\pi$$

$$\pi$$

$$\frac{}{\pi}\int \vec{} \, n\,ds$$

56. ( ) y

$y \qquad e^{\;x} \qquad e^{\;x}$

$y' \qquad e^{\;x} \qquad e^{\;x}$

x

y'

$\Rightarrow$

x

y

$\Rightarrow$

$y \qquad e^{\;x} \; e^{\;x}$

$y' \qquad e^{\;x} \qquad e^{\;x}$

$$\Rightarrow \qquad e^{x} \quad -$$

$$\Rightarrow \qquad x \qquad \left(-\right)$$

$y'' \qquad e^{-x} \qquad e^{\;x}$

$$\times\frac{}{} \qquad \times\frac{}{}$$

$$\frac{}{} \quad \frac{}{}=$$

$y(x)$

$x \;()$

57.

$y \qquad y \quad x\;x \qquad x \quad \pi$

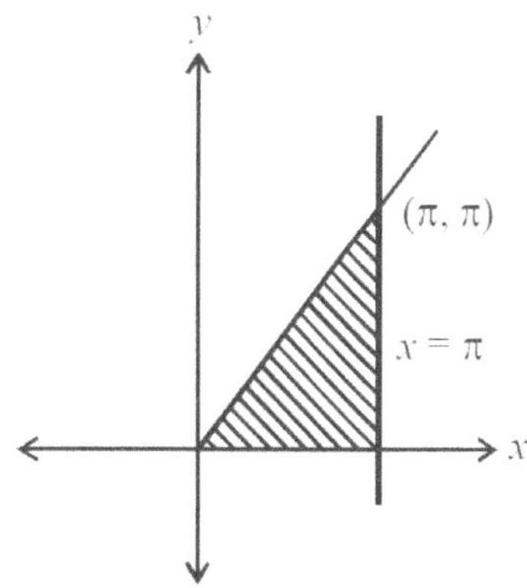

$$\int_{y}^{\pi}\int_{}^{\pi}\frac{y}{\pi \; y}\,dx\,dy \qquad \int_{}^{\pi}\frac{y}{\pi \; y}\; x\Big|_{y}^{\pi}dy$$

$$\int_{}^{\pi} \; y\,dy$$

$$y\Big|^{\pi} =$$

58.

$$\begin{bmatrix} & \end{bmatrix}$$

$$\begin{bmatrix} & \end{bmatrix}\begin{bmatrix} & \end{bmatrix}\begin{bmatrix} & \end{bmatrix}$$

$$\begin{bmatrix} & \end{bmatrix}\begin{bmatrix} & \end{bmatrix}\begin{bmatrix} & \end{bmatrix}$$

$$\begin{bmatrix} & \end{bmatrix} =$$

59.

$()$ $\cap ()$

60.

$f(x\ y)\quad x\quad y$

$y\quad x$

$\Rightarrow\quad y\quad x$

$f(x\ y)\quad x\ (\quad x\ )$

$x\quad x$

$g(x)$

$g'(x)\quad x\quad x$

$\Rightarrow\quad x(\ x\ )$

$\Rightarrow\quad x\quad \pm\dfrac{\sqrt{\ }}{}$

$g''(x)\quad x$

x

$g(x)$

x

IIT–JAM—Joint Admission Test for M.Sc. (Mathematics)~2015

SECTION A : MULTIPLE CHOICE QUESTIONS

1.

2. $y(x)$ $u(x)$ x $v(x)$ x
y y x
$u(x)$
x x
x x

3. a b c d
a b c d

$$\begin{bmatrix} a & b \\ c & d \\ & - \end{bmatrix}$$

a c $\qquad$ a b
a b $\qquad$ b d

4. $\mathbb{R}$

$\notin$

$\notin$

$\in$ $\qquad$ $\in$

$\in$ $\qquad$ $\in$

$\in$ $\qquad$ $\in$

5. x_n

x π $\sqrt{}$ x_n $\pi + \sqrt{x_n - \pi}$

n _

π $\qquad$ $\pi + \sqrt{}$
π $\qquad$ $\pi + \sqrt{\pi}$

6.

x y _
z x y
xy

π $\qquad$ π
π $\qquad$ π

7. f $\mathbb{R} \to \mathbb{R}$
$f()$ $\qquad$ $x \in \mathbb{R}$ $\qquad$ $f(x)$

$($ $\qquad$ $\infty)$
f
f
f
f

8.

$$(y - x)\frac{dy}{dx} = \;()(\qquad \alpha)$$
α

e $\qquad$ e
e $\qquad$ e

9.

$$\frac{dy}{dx} = \frac{xy + y}{x - y}$$

$\overline{y}$ $\qquad$ $\overline{y}$
y $\qquad$ y

10. $\mathbb{R}$ ()

()

11.

$\oplus$

12.

$y \qquad x$

$x \qquad y \qquad\qquad x \qquad y$

$x \qquad y \qquad\qquad x \qquad y$

13. $\alpha \in$

$\beta \in$

$\alpha\beta$

$k \qquad k \ge$

14.

$x \qquad y \qquad\qquad z$

$z \qquad x$

$$\iint z\, d\sigma$$

$$\int^{\pi} (\,+\,)\ \theta\ d\theta$$

$$\int^{\pi} \theta\ )\theta + \theta\ d\theta$$

$$\int^{\pi} (\,+\,)\ \theta\ d\theta$$

$$\int^{\pi} \theta\ )\theta + \theta\ d\theta$$

15.

$z \qquad w$

$x \qquad y$

$f(x\ y\ z\ w) \qquad g(x\ y\ z\ w)$

$f_z g_w \qquad f_w g_z$

$z_x \quad f_w g_x \quad f_x g_w \qquad\qquad z_x \quad f_x g_w \quad f_w g_x$

$z_x \quad f_z g_x \quad f_x g_z \qquad\qquad z_x \quad f_z g_w \quad f_z g_x$

16. $= \begin{bmatrix} & 1-i \\ -1-i & i \end{bmatrix} \qquad = \quad -$

17. $$\lim_{x \to +} \frac{}{x} \int_{\frac{x}{}}^{x} {}^{-}\ t\, dt$$

$-$

$- \qquad\qquad -$

18. $(\mathbb{R})$

x

$(\mathbb{R})$

$(\mathbb{R})$

$\to \quad (\mathbb{R}) \qquad\qquad (\ \mathbf{y} = \begin{bmatrix} f0 & -\phi \\ & \phi \end{bmatrix}$

$() \qquad\qquad \left\{ \begin{bmatrix} \ \end{bmatrix} \begin{bmatrix} - \end{bmatrix} \right\}$

$() \qquad\qquad x \qquad x \qquad x$

19. $(\ )(\ ) \qquad\qquad (\ )$

$() \qquad\qquad \mathbb{R} \qquad \mathbb{R} \to$

$\mathbb{R}$

$\begin{bmatrix} - \end{bmatrix} ()$

$() \qquad\qquad ()$

$() \qquad\qquad ()$

20. $\quad \bigcap_{n=}^{\infty} \left(\left[\dfrac{}{n+} \right] \cup \left[\dfrac{}{n} \right] \right)$

$$a_n \qquad b_n$$
$$\bigcup_{n=}^{\infty} (a_n \ b_n)$$

21. $\quad f \quad \mathbb{R} \rightarrow \mathbb{R}$

$$a_n$$
$$f(a_n)$$

22.

$$\sum_{n=}^{\infty} (-)^{n} \frac{(\mathit{N})}{n^{n}}$$

23. $\quad \left\{ \left[- \ - \left(-\dfrac{n}{} \right)^{n} \right] \right\}$

24. $\quad y(t)$

$$y \quad y \quad e^{t} \qquad \underset{t \to \infty}{\quad} e^{(t}y \ t$$

$$\underline{\quad} \qquad \underline{\quad}$$

$$\underline{\quad} \qquad \underline{\quad}$$

25. $\qquad\qquad x \qquad y$

$$\int_{x}^{y} (\ -t-t)\ dt$$

$$x \qquad y$$
$$x \qquad y$$
$$x \qquad y$$
$$x \qquad y$$

26.

$$x \qquad y \qquad\qquad x \qquad y$$

$$\dfrac{\sqrt{\ }}{} \qquad\qquad\qquad \dfrac{\sqrt{\ }}{}$$

$$\dfrac{\sqrt{\ }}{} \qquad\qquad\qquad \sqrt{\ }$$

27. $\quad n \ \_ \qquad f_n \quad \mathbb{R} \rightarrow \mathbb{R} \qquad\qquad f_n(x)$
$x^n \quad x \qquad\qquad x \qquad f_n$

$$n$$
$$n$$
$$n$$
$$n$$

28. $\quad m \quad n \in \mathbb{N}$

$$f_{m\ n}(x) = \begin{cases} x^m \quad \left(\dfrac{}{x^n} \right) & x \neq \\[2mm] & x = \end{cases}$$

$$\begin{array}{ll} m \ n & m \quad n \\ m,\ n & m \quad n \\ & m,\ n \end{array}$$

$$m \quad n \qquad\qquad\qquad m,\ n$$

$$m \quad n$$

29. $\qquad\qquad\qquad\qquad\qquad \mathbb{R}$

$$\cup$$

$$\cap \qquad \varnothing$$
$$\cap \qquad \varnothing$$
$$\cap \qquad \neq \varnothing$$
$$\cap \qquad \neq \varnothing$$

30. $\quad f(\ x \ y) \in \mathbb{R} \quad x \qquad y \qquad \rightarrow \mathbb{R}$

$$f(x\ y) = x^{-}\ y^{--} \quad - \left(\dfrac{y}{x} \right) + \dfrac{}{\sqrt{x\ +y}}$$

$$g(x,y) = \frac{xf_x(x,y) + yf_y(x,y)}{f(x,y)}$$

changes with x y y x x y x y

SECTION B : MULTIPLE SELECT QUESTIONS

1. $f : \mathbb{R} \to \mathbb{R}$

$f(x) \quad \int_-^x (t-)\,dt$

$()$ f

2. $()$

$\mathbb{Z} \oplus \mathbb{Z}$ $\mathbb{Z}$

$\mathbb{Z} \oplus \mathbb{Z}$ $\mathbb{Z}$

$\mathbb{Z} \oplus \mathbb{Z}$ $\mathbb{Z}$

$\mathbb{Z} \oplus \mathbb{Z} \oplus \mathbb{Z}$ $\mathbb{Z}$

3.

$()$ x_n

ε $n \in \mathbb{N}$

$n\ \_\ n \quad x_n \quad x_n \quad \varepsilon$

ε $n \in \mathbb{N}$

$n\ \_\ n \quad \overline{(n+)^2} \quad x_n \quad x_n \quad \varepsilon$

ε $n \in \mathbb{N}$

$n\ \_\ n\ (\ n\ ) \quad x_n \quad x_n \quad \varepsilon$

ε $n \in \mathbb{N}$

$m, n \quad m \quad n\ \_\ n \quad x_m \quad x_n \quad \varepsilon$

4.

$\vec{(\ x\ y)}\,z = -yi + xyj + z\,k\ (\quad x\ y\ z)\in \mathbb{R}$

$x \quad y \qquad y \quad z$

$()$ $\left| \int \vec{\ } \cdot d\vec{r} \right|$

$\int_^\pi \int (+ \dot{r}) \quad \theta\, r\, dr d\theta$

$\int_^\pi \left(-+-\quad \theta \right) d\theta$

$\int_^\pi \int (+ \dot{r}) \quad \theta\, dr d\theta$

$\int_^\pi (+) \quad \theta\, d\theta$

5.

$$\begin{bmatrix} a & a \\ a & a \end{bmatrix}$$

$a \quad a$

$a \quad \overline{a} =$

$()$

$\mathbb{C}$
$\mathbb{C}$
$\mathbb{R}$
$\mathbb{R}$

6. $y = \sqrt{y}\ \ y() = \alpha$

$\alpha \geq$

     α

α

α

α

7. $()$

$$\left(\frac{\pi}{} \right)$$

$x(<) \qquad x$

$x < x$

$\sqrt{+x} < +\dfrac{x}{}-\dfrac{x}{}$

$\dfrac{-x}{} < (\ \ )+x$

8. $f : \mathbb{R} \to \mathbb{R}$

$$f(x,y) = \begin{cases} xy\dfrac{x-y}{x+y} & (x,y) \neq () \\[2mm] & (x,y) () \end{cases}$$

()

  f

  f f_x f_y

  f

  f_x f_y f

9. f g $\to ($ $f)$

 ($g)$ f g

 ()

    $f(x) \_ g(x)$ $x \in ($ $f)$

  $\_ ($ $g)$

   $f(x) \_ g(x)$ $x \in$

(f) $\_ ($ $g)$

  $f(x) \_ g(y)$ $x, y \in$

($f) \_ ($ $g)$

  $f(x) \_ g(y)$ $x, y \in$

($f) \_ ($ $g)$

10. f ( ) $\to \mathbb{R}$

  $f(x)$ $x\, e^{(\quad x\,)}$

  f ( )

  f ( )

  $f(x)$ ( )

  $f(x)$ ( )

SECTION C : NUMERICAL ANSWER TYPE

1.

 (π) $Q\left(\dfrac{\pi}{\quad} \right)$ xy

$$\int_C e^x (\quad y\,dx - \ )\, y\,dy$$

2.

  $z = \sqrt{\ \ -x}$ x

 x y y

3.

4. f $\mathbb{R}$ $\to \mathbb{R}$

$$f(x\ y) = \begin{cases} \left(\quad + \dfrac{x}{y} \right) & y \neq \\ & y = \end{cases}$$

           $f()$

        $\alpha i + \quad \alpha j$

 $\alpha \neq$ α

5. f $\mathbb{R}$ $\to \mathbb{R}$

$$f(x\ y\ z) = \quad x + e^{\frac{y}{\quad}} + z$$

        f $\left(\dfrac{\pi}{\quad} \right)$

6.

$$\sum_{n=}^{\infty} \frac{n}{n^n} x^{\,n}$$

  x c x c

  c

7. $\equiv n(\ )$ $n \in$

          n

8.

$$\left\{ \begin{bmatrix} x & -x \\ - & \end{bmatrix} \begin{bmatrix} & - \\ x & x \end{bmatrix} \begin{bmatrix} & - \\ & \end{bmatrix} \right\}$$

               x

9. f $\mathbb{R}$ $\to \mathbb{R}$

$$f(x) = \begin{cases} x - & x \in \mathbb{Q} \\ - x & x \notin \mathbb{Q} \end{cases}$$

         f

10. f ( ) $\to \mathbb{R}$

          f

 ( ) f

          $y \in \mathbb{R}$

         $f(x)$ y

 ()

11.
$$\oint x(\ -y)\,dx + (\ x\ -y)\,dy$$

12. $\sigma, \tau \in$

$(\qquad \sigma)\ (\qquad \tau)$

$\sigma \quad \tau$

13.
$$\lim_{n\to\infty}\sum_{k=}^{n}\frac{1}{k\ -k}$$

14. $(\mathbb{R})$

$(\mathbb{R})$

$$\left\{ (\ \ni\quad \mathbb{R}\quad \begin{bmatrix} \ \end{bmatrix} = \begin{bmatrix} \ \end{bmatrix} \right\}$$

15. $f\ \mathbb{R}\ \to\ \mathbb{R}$

$$f(x\ y) = \begin{cases} \dfrac{y}{y} & y \neq \\ & y = \end{cases}$$

$$\frac{1}{\pi}\int_{x=}\int_{y=\ -x}^{\frac{\pi}{}} f(x\ y)\,dy\,dx$$

16.
$$f(x) = \quad x\ \left(x + \frac{\pi}{}\right)\ \left(x - \frac{\pi}{}\right)\ x \in \mathbb{R}$$

$$\frac{\pi}{}$$

17.
$$\int^{x}(e^{-t}\ +\ )\ t\ dt$$

$$\sum_{n=}^{\infty} a_n x^n \qquad a$$

18. l

$x\quad x(y) \qquad\qquad y \qquad y$

$x(y)$

$$\frac{dx}{dy} = \frac{\sqrt{\ +y\ +y}}{y}\quad x()$$

$$l$$

19.
$$\lim_{x\to\ +}\frac{1}{x}\left(\frac{}{\ -x} - \frac{1}{x}\right)$$

20.
$$()$$
$$0\ ()$$

ANSWERS

SECTION A : MCQ

1	2	3	4	5	6	7	8	9	10
11	12	13	14	15	16	17	18	19	20
21	22	23	24	25	26	27	28	29	30

SECTION B : MSQ

1	2	3	4	5	6	7	8	9	10

SECTION C : NAT (Numerical Answer Type Questions)

1	2	3	4	5
6	7	8	9	10
11	12	13	14	15
16	17	18	19	20

SOME SELECTED EXPLANATORY ANSWERS

SECTION A

2. $y + y = ( )\ x$

$()$

$(\quad i)$

$(\quad i)$

$$\overline{()\ (\ )(+i)}\ \overline{-i} = -\frac{1}{i}\left[\frac{}{-i} - \frac{}{+i}\right]$$

$$\frac{}{-i}\ x \quad e^{ix}\int e^{-ix}\cdot\ x\cdot dx$$

$$e^{ix}\int \frac{(\ x -)i\ x}{x}\cdot dx$$

$$e^{ix}\left[x + i\cdot\ x\right]$$

$(\ x\ i\ x)\ x + i\ x$

$x\cdot\ x - x\cdot\ x +$

$\qquad i(x\cdot\ x +)\ x\cdot\ x$

$$\frac{}{+i}\ x$$

$\left(x\cdot\ x - x\cdot\ x\right) - i(x\cdot\ x + x$

$x)$

$\therefore$

$$\frac{}{()}\ x$$

$$-\frac{1}{i}\left[\frac{}{-i}\ x - \frac{}{+i}\ x\right]$$

$$-\frac{1}{i}\left[(\ x\cdot\ x +)\ x\cdot\ x\right]$$

$x\ x\ x\cdot\ x$

$\therefore\quad u(x)\ x\ c$

3.

$$\begin{bmatrix} a-\lambda & b & \\ c & d-\lambda & \\ & - & -\lambda \end{bmatrix} = \lambda$$

$(a\ \lambda)(\ d\ \lambda)(\ \lambda)\qquad b\quad c\lambda$

$\qquad\qquad\qquad \lambda\ c\ d$

$(a\ \lambda)(d\ \lambda)(\ \lambda)\ (\ a\ \lambda)\ b\ bc\lambda$

$\qquad\qquad\qquad \lambda\ c\ d$

$bc\ ad\ (\ a\ d)\lambda\ \lambda$

$\qquad\qquad\qquad a\ b\ c\ d$

$\lambda\ (\ a\ d)\lambda\ ad\ bc$

$\qquad \lambda$

$$\lambda\quad \frac{(a+d)\pm\sqrt{(a+d)\ -(\ ad-bc)}}{}$$

$$\frac{(a+d)\pm\sqrt{(a-d)\ +\ bc}}{}$$

$$\frac{(a+d)\pm\sqrt{(b-c)\ +\ bc}}{}$$

$$\frac{(a+d)\pm\sqrt{(b+c)}}{}$$

$$\frac{(a+d)\pm(b+c)}{}$$

$$\lambda \quad \frac{(a+d)+(b+c)}{a} \quad \frac{(a+b)+(a+b)}{b}$$

9. $\dfrac{dy}{dx} = \dfrac{xy + y}{x - y}$

$\Rightarrow (\ xy \quad y)\, dx \ (\ x \quad y \ )\, dy$

$(\qquad xy \quad y) \ (\qquad y \quad x)$

$$\frac{\dfrac{\partial}{\partial} - \dfrac{\partial}{\partial x} \ (\ \dfrac{\partial}{\partial y} \ xy) + y(\ - \dfrac{\partial}{\partial x})y \ - x}{(\ y \ - x)}$$

$$\frac{(\ xy) \ +}{(\ y \ - x)}$$

$$\frac{(\ xy) +}{(\ y \ - x)}$$

$$\frac{\dfrac{\partial}{\partial y} - \dfrac{\partial}{\partial x}}{(y \ x)y +} = \frac{(\ xy) +}{\ } = \frac{-}{y}$$

$$e^{-\int \frac{-}{y} \cdot dy} \qquad e^{- \quad y}$$

$$\overline{y}$$

12. $\qquad y \qquad x$

$$\frac{dy}{dx} = \qquad \cdot x$$

$$\frac{dy}{dx} \qquad\qquad \frac{dx}{dy}$$

$$-\frac{dx}{dy} = \qquad \cdot x$$

$$-\frac{dx}{dy} = \left(\frac{y}{x} \right) \cdot x \ = \frac{y}{x}$$

$$x\, dx \qquad y\, dy$$

$$-\frac{x}{x} = \frac{y}{y} +$$

$$x \qquad y$$

16. $= \begin{bmatrix} & -i \\ - \ -i & i \end{bmatrix} \qquad = \begin{bmatrix} - & -i \\ -i & i \end{bmatrix}$

$$- = \begin{bmatrix} & +i \\ - \ +i & -i \end{bmatrix}$$

$$B = \quad \cdot - = \begin{bmatrix} - & -i \\ -i & i \end{bmatrix}\begin{bmatrix} & +i \\ - \ +i & -i \end{bmatrix}$$

$$= \begin{bmatrix} (\ ) & (-) i \\ 0 \ +) & -i \end{bmatrix}$$

$$\begin{bmatrix} & + \\ + & \end{bmatrix} = \begin{bmatrix} & \\ & \end{bmatrix}$$

$$\lambda \qquad \begin{bmatrix} \lambda - & \\ & \lambda - \end{bmatrix} =$$

$$\lambda(\lambda \ )$$

$$\lambda \qquad \lambda$$

$$\lambda \qquad \frac{\pm \sqrt{}}{}$$

22.

$$\frac{u_n}{u_{n+}} = \frac{(-) \ \dfrac{n}{(n)^{\ n}}}{\dfrac{(\ n) }{(n+)^{\ (\ n)}}}$$

$$\Rightarrow \frac{u_n}{u_{n+}} = - \frac{(n+)^{\ n+}}{(\ n)(\ )n+ \ \cdot n^{\ n}}$$

$$\frac{u_n}{u_{n+}} = -\left(\frac{n+}{n} \right)^{n} \cdot \frac{(\ n)}{(\ n)(\ )n+}$$

$$-\left(\frac{n+}{n}\right)^{n}\cdot\frac{\left(n+\right)}{\left(\,n+\right)}$$

$$\lim_{n\to\infty}\left(\frac{u_{n}}{u_{n+}}\right)=-\lim_{n\to\infty}\frac{(n+)}{(\,n)+}\cdot\left(\frac{n+}{n}\right)^{n}$$

$$\frac{e}{}$$

$$\lim_{n\to\infty}|u_{n}|>\quad i.e.\qquad u_{n}$$

$$\therefore$$

26.

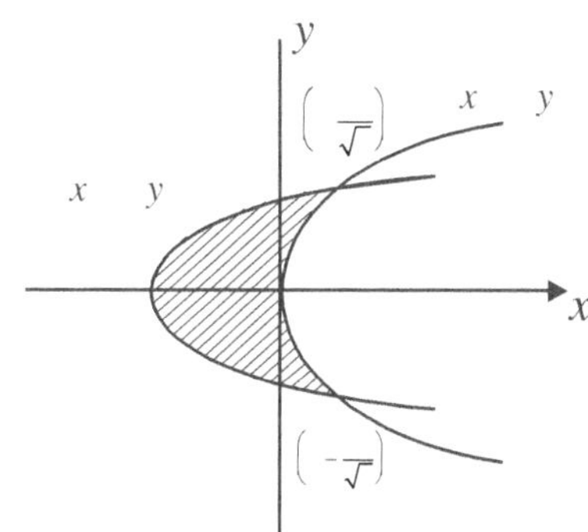

$$\begin{array}{ll}x\quad y & \qquad x\quad y\\ y\quad y\end{array}$$

$$\Rightarrow\quad y$$

$$y\quad\pm\frac{}{\sqrt{}}\qquad x$$

$$\left|\int_{-\sqrt{}}^{\sqrt{}}\{(\,y\,+\,(-\,)\,y\,\}\cdot dy\right|$$

$$\left|\int^{\sqrt{}}(\,y\,+\,\cdot dy\right|$$

$$\left|\left[\frac{y}{}-\,y\right]^{\sqrt{}}\right|$$

$$\left|\left[\frac{}{\times\sqrt{}}-\frac{}{\sqrt{}}\right]\right|$$

$$\left|\left[\frac{\sqrt{}}{}-\sqrt{}\right]\right|$$

$$\frac{\sqrt{}}{}$$

28. $f()\,=\lim_{h\to}\dfrac{f(\,+h\,-f)}{h}$

$$\lim_{h\to}h^{m}\cdot\left(\frac{}{h^{n}}\right)$$

$$\lim_{h\to}h^{(m-n)}\cdot\frac{\left(\dfrac{}{h^{n}}\right)}{\left(\dfrac{}{h^{n}}\right)}$$

$$\begin{array}{ll}m & n\\ m & n\end{array}$$

SECTION B

1. $f(x)=\displaystyle\int_{-}^{x}(t-)\,\cdot dt$

$$\left[\frac{t}{}-\,t-t\,-\frac{t}{}\right]_{-}^{x}$$

$$\frac{x}{}-x-x\,-\,-x\,-\,-\frac{}{}\,-\,-\,+\frac{}{}$$

$$f(x)\qquad\frac{x}{}-x\,-\,-x\,-x-\frac{}{}$$

$$\frac{x\,-\,x\,-\,x\,-\,x-}{}$$

$$f(x)$$
$$x\qquad x\qquad x\qquad x$$

4. $\displaystyle\int\vec{}\cdot\vec{dr}=\iint\nabla\vec{}\cdot r\cdot dr\cdot d\theta$

$$\nabla\vec{}\quad\begin{vmatrix}i & j & k\\[2pt] \dfrac{\partial}{\partial x} & \dfrac{\partial}{\partial y} & \dfrac{\partial}{\partial z}\\[4pt] -y & xy & z\end{vmatrix}\qquad (\,y+\,)\,k$$

$$\int \vec{\ } \cdot \overrightarrow{dr} = \iint (\ \ )\ +\ \ \vec{k}\cdot\overrightarrow{dr} \qquad (\ i)$$

$$x \quad r \quad \theta \quad y \quad r \quad \theta$$
$$z \qquad r \quad \theta \qquad \theta$$
$$\pi$$
$$r$$

$$(\qquad i)$$

$$\int\int_{0}^{\pi} (\ r\ \ )\theta + \ \cdot r\cdot dr \cdot d\theta$$

$$\int\int^{\pi} (\ r\ \cdot\ \ \ \theta + r\ \ dr\cdot d\theta$$

$$\int^{\pi}\left[\frac{r}{\ \ }\cdot\ \ \theta + \frac{r}{\ }\right]\cdot d\theta$$

$$\int^{\pi}\left[-\ \ \theta + -\right]\cdot d\theta$$

$$(\ )\ (\ )$$

6. $\quad y = \sqrt{y} \quad \Rightarrow \quad \dfrac{dy}{dx} = \sqrt{y}$

$$\frac{dy}{\sqrt{y}} = dx$$

$$\sqrt{y} = x +$$

$$x \qquad y \quad \alpha$$

$$\therefore \quad \sqrt{\alpha} = \ +\ \qquad \Rightarrow \ = \sqrt{\alpha}$$

$$\sqrt{y} = x + \ \sqrt{\alpha}$$

$$\alpha \qquad \Rightarrow x \qquad y$$

$$\alpha$$

7. $\quad (\ \ ) + x \quad (\ (\ +)) + x$

$$(\ +)\ -\frac{(\ +)\ }{\ }+\frac{(\ +)x\ (\ \ )+x}{\ }-\frac{}{\ }$$

$$(\ +)\ \left(\frac{-\ -x}{\ }\right)(\ \ )+x\ (\ )\ +x}{\ }-\frac{}{\ }+$$

$$\frac{(\ +)(\ \ )x\ (\ \ )+x\ (\ )\ +x}{\ }+\frac{}{\ }-\frac{}{\ }$$

$$\frac{(\ -)x}{\ }+\frac{(\ +)x}{\ }\ (\ \ )+x}{\ } \qquad \left(\frac{-x}{\ }\right)$$

8. $\quad f_{x}(\ )\ =\lim_{h\to}\dfrac{f(\ +h\ )-f\ }{h}$

$$=\lim_{h\to}\frac{-}{h}=$$

$$f_{y}(\ )\qquad \lim_{k\to}\frac{f(\ )+k\ -f}{k}$$

$$\frac{-}{k}=$$

$$f_{x}(\ )\ =(\ )\ f_{y}\ (\ )=f\ \ =$$
$$f$$

10. $\qquad f(x)\quad x\ e^{(\ -x)}$

$$f(x)\qquad x\cdot e^{(\ -x)}+x\ \cdot e^{(\ -x)}\ (-\ )$$

$$x\cdot e^{(\ -x)}\ (\ -\ )$$

$$f(x)$$

i.e. $\quad x\cdot e^{\ -x}\ (\ -\ )\ =$

$$x \qquad\qquad -$$

$$f(\ x)\qquad x(\ \ x\ \ x\ \ \ x\ )\ e^{\ -x}$$

$$f(\ x)\qquad\qquad x\qquad -$$

$$f(x)\qquad\qquad x\qquad -$$
$$x$$

i.e. $f(x)(\ )$
$(\ )$

$$f(x)$$

$$x\ \cdot e^{\ -x}\ =$$

$$e^{\ -x}\ =\frac{}{x}$$

$$x \qquad\qquad x$$

SECTION C

5. $f(x, y, z) = x + e^{\frac{y}{z}} + z$

$$\frac{\partial f}{\partial x} = \frac{\partial}{\partial x}\left(x + e^{\frac{y}{z}} + z \right) = \quad x$$

$$\frac{\partial f}{\partial x}\bigg|_{\left(x=\frac{\pi}{}\right)} = \left(\frac{\pi}{}\right) = \frac{}{\sqrt{}}$$

$$\frac{\partial f}{\partial y} = \frac{\partial}{\partial y}\left(x + e^{\frac{y}{z}} + z \right) = e^{\frac{y}{}}$$

$$\frac{\partial f}{\partial y}\bigg|_{(y=\ )} = e^{} =$$

$$\frac{\partial f}{\partial z} = \frac{\partial\left(x + e^{\frac{y}{}} + z \right)}{\partial z} = \quad z$$

$$\frac{\partial f}{\partial z}\bigg|_{(z=)} =$$

$$\frac{f}{\sqrt{\left(\frac{\partial f}{\partial x}\right) + \left(\frac{\partial f}{\partial y}\right) + \left(\frac{\partial f}{\partial z}\right)}}$$

$$\frac{}{\sqrt{\left(\frac{}{\sqrt{}}\right) + (\ ) + (\ )}}$$

6. $\dfrac{u_n}{u_{n+}} = \dfrac{\dfrac{n}{(n)^n}(x)^n}{\dfrac{(n+)}{(n+)^{n+}}(x)^{(\ n)}}$

$$= \frac{n}{(n+)} \quad (n+) \cdot \left(\frac{(n+)}{n}\right)^n \cdot x^{-}$$

$$\frac{(n)}{(n+)} \cdot \left(+\frac{}{n}\right)^n \cdot x^{-} \qquad \left(+\frac{}{n}\right)^n \cdot x^{-}$$

$$\lim_{n\to\infty}\left(+\frac{}{n}\right)^n \cdot x^{-}$$

$$e \cdot x^{-}$$

diveres at $|x| \qquad\qquad x$

$$e \cdot (c)^{-}$$
$$\qquad c \qquad e$$
$$\therefore \qquad\qquad c = \sqrt{e}$$

7.

$$\equiv (\ )$$
$$(\quad)$$
$$\equiv (\ )$$
$$(\qquad n\ )$$

11. $\oint x(\ -y)\cdot dx + (\ x\ -y)\ dy$

$$\iint \left\{ \frac{\partial}{\partial x}(x(\ -y)) - \frac{\partial}{\partial y}(\ x\ -y) \right\} \cdot dx \cdot dy$$

$$\iint \{(\ -y + \ y\} dx \cdot dy$$

$$\int dx \int (\ +y)\cdot dy$$

$$x \left[y + \frac{y}{} \right]$$

$$(\ ) \quad \left(+\frac{}{}\right) =$$

13. $\displaystyle\lim_{n\to\infty}\sum_{k=}^{n} \frac{}{(k\ -k)}$

$$\lim_{n\to\infty}\left(\frac{}{(\ )} + \frac{}{(\ )-(\ )} + \frac{}{\ -(\ +\ )} + \frac{}{n\ -n} \right)$$

$$\lim_{n\to\infty}\left(\frac{}{\cdot\ \cdot} + \frac{}{\cdot\ \cdot} + \frac{}{(\ \cdot)} + \frac{}{(\ n)-\ \cdot n\ n+} \right)$$

$$\lim_{n\to\infty} \ -\left\{ -\left(---\right) + -\left(---\right) + -\left(---\right) + \right.$$

$$\frac{}{n}\left(\frac{}{n-}-\frac{}{n+}\right)\Big\}$$

$$\lim_{n\to\infty}\left\{-\frac{}{\times}+\frac{}{\times}-\frac{}{\times}+\frac{}{\times}+\right.$$

$$\left.\frac{}{n(n+}\right\}$$

$$\lim_{n\to\infty}\left\{--\frac{}{(n\ n)+}\right\}$$

$$-=$$

16. $f(x)$ $x=\dfrac{\pi}{}$

$f(x)$

x $\dfrac{\pi}{}$

$$f(x)=f\left(\frac{\pi}{}\right)+\left(x-\frac{\pi}{}\right)\cdot f'\left(\frac{\pi}{}\right)+$$

$$\frac{\left(x-\dfrac{\pi}{}\right)}{}f''\left(\frac{\pi}{}\right)+\frac{\left(x-\dfrac{\pi}{}\right)}{}f'''\left(\frac{\pi}{}\right)+$$

$$\left(x-\frac{\pi}{}\right)$$

$$\frac{f\ \left(\dfrac{\pi}{}\right)}{}$$

$f(x)$ $x\cdot$ $\left(x+\dfrac{\pi}{}\right)$

$$-\left[\ \left(x+\frac{\pi}{}\right)-\ \left(\frac{\pi}{}\right)\right]$$

$f'(x)$ $-\cdot$ $\left(x+\dfrac{\pi}{}\right)\cdot$ $\left(x+\dfrac{\pi}{}\right)$

$f''(x)$ $-\cdot$ $\left(x+\dfrac{\pi}{}\right)$

$f(x)$ $-\cdot$ $\left(x+\dfrac{\pi}{}\right)$

$f\left(\dfrac{\pi}{}\right)$ $-\cdot$ $\left(\dfrac{\pi}{}+\dfrac{\pi}{}\right)$

$$\left(-\frac{}{\sqrt{\ }}\right)\ \sqrt{\ }$$

$$\left(x-\frac{\pi}{}\right)$$

$$\frac{\sqrt{\ }}{}\ \sqrt{\ }$$

19. (x) $x-\dfrac{x}{}+\dfrac{x}{}-\dfrac{x}{}$

$$\lim_{x\to\ ^+}\left(\frac{}{\ x}-\frac{}{x}\right)\quad \lim_{x\to\ ^+}\frac{}{x}\left(\frac{x-\ ^-\ x}{x\cdot\ ^-\ x}\right)$$

$$\lim_{x\to\ ^+}\frac{\left(x-x+\dfrac{x}{}-\dfrac{x}{}+\dfrac{x}{}\right)}{x\ \cdot\left(x-\dfrac{x}{}+\dfrac{x}{}-\dfrac{x}{}\right)}$$

$$\lim_{x\to\ ^+}\ x\ \frac{\left(--\dfrac{x}{}+\dfrac{x}{}\right)}{x\left(-\dfrac{x}{}+\dfrac{x}{}\right)}$$

$\times-$

20.

$()$ $\_\ ()$

f

$()$ $\_\ ()$

IIT–JAM–Joint Admission Test for M.Sc. (Mathematics)-2014

PART-I : OBJECTIVE QUESTIONS

1. $f(x)$ x $x \in \mathbb{R}$

     $\mathbb{R}$ f

( )

2. (x)

     $f(x)$ $xe^{x}(\,x \in \mathbb{R})$

  x

   $\dfrac{e}{}$ e

   $\dfrac{e}{}$ e

3. $f(x\,y) = \displaystyle\sum_{k=}(x\quad y)^{\,k}$ ($x\,y) \in \mathbb{R}$

($x\,y) \in \mathbb{R}$

$x\dfrac{\partial f}{\partial x}(x\,y)\quad y\dfrac{\partial f}{\partial y}(\;x)\,y =$

$x\dfrac{\partial f}{\partial x}(x\,y) + y\dfrac{\partial f}{\partial y}(\;x)\,y =$

$y\dfrac{\partial f}{\partial x}(x\,y)\quad x\dfrac{\partial f}{\partial y}(\;x)\,y =$

$y\dfrac{\partial f}{\partial x}(x\,y) + x\dfrac{\partial f}{\partial y}(\;x)\,y =$

4. $a\;b\;c \in \mathbb{R}$

$(ax\quad bxy\quad y\,)dx\,(\quad x\quad cxy\quad y\,)dy$

    b c a b c

    b c b a c

5. $f(x\;y\;z)$ $x\,y$ $y\,z$ $z\,x$ ($x\;y\;z)$

$\in \mathbb{R}$ $\nabla = \dfrac{\partial}{\partial x}\mathbf{i} + \dfrac{\partial}{\partial y}\mathbf{j} + \dfrac{\partial}{\partial z}\mathbf{k}$

$\nabla\,(\quad \nabla\quad \nabla f)\quad \nabla\,(\quad \nabla f)\,(\;)$

6.

$\displaystyle\sum_{n=}^{\infty}\; ^{n}x^{n}$

$-$

7.

8.

           $\mathbb{R}$

$\{(x\;y\;z) \in \mathbb{R}\quad x+\;y=\quad x+\;z=\;\}$

$\{(x\;y\;z) \in \mathbb{R}\quad x+\;y+\;z-\;=\quad z=\;\}$

$\{(x\;y\;z) \in \mathbb{R}\quad x\geq\quad y\geq\;\}$

$\{(x\;y\;z) \in \mathbb{R}\quad x-\;=\quad y=\;\}$

9. $\mathbb{R} \to \mathbb{R}$

($x\;y\;z)\,(\quad x\quad y\;y\quad z\;z\quad x)$

($x\;y\;z) \in \mathbb{R}$

( ) ( )

( ) ( )

( ) ( )

( ) ( )

10. f $\mathbb{R} \to \mathbb{R}$

$$x + \int_0^x f(t)\,dt = e^x \qquad x \in \mathbb{R}$$

$$x \in \mathbb{R} \qquad \le f(x) \le$$

e $\qquad$ e

e

11.

x $\quad y$ $\quad z$ $\quad b$
x $\quad y$ $\quad z$ $\quad b$
$\quad y$ $\quad z$ $\quad b$
$($ $\qquad\qquad$ b $\quad b$ $\quad b$ $)$

$(\ )$ $\qquad$ $(\ )$
$(\ )$ $\qquad$ $(\ )$

12. $= \begin{bmatrix} a \\ & b \end{bmatrix}$

$a \qquad b$

13. $($ $\qquad\qquad$ x $\quad x$ $\qquad x$ $)$

$\in \mathbb{R}$ $\quad x_n$ $\quad x_n$ $\qquad x_n$ $\qquad \le n \le$

$\mathbb{R}$

14. $y\ (x)$ $\qquad y\ (x)$

$x\ y''(x)$ $\quad xy'(x)$ $\quad y(x)$ $\qquad x \in$
$($ $\qquad\qquad x)$ $\quad y\ (x)y'\ (x)$
$y\ (x)y'\ (x)()()()$

15.

$\left(\dfrac{\pi}{} \quad \right)$ $\qquad\qquad \dfrac{(\ )\ x}{x} \quad \dfrac{y}{x}$

$($ $\qquad x \quad y)$ $\qquad x \ne$

$x\ y + (\ )\quad x = \dfrac{\pi}{}$

$x\ y + (\ )\ x = \dfrac{\pi}{}$

$x\ y\ (\ )\quad x = \dfrac{\pi}{}$

$x\ y + (\ )\ x = \dfrac{\pi}{} +$

16. $\qquad \alpha \in \mathbb{R}$ $\qquad\qquad x$

αy $\qquad y \quad x$

$\underline{\qquad}$

$\underline{\qquad}$

17. $x_n = \ ^n\left(\qquad \left(\dfrac{}{n} \right) \right) \qquad n \in \mathbb{N}$

x_n

$\underline{\qquad}$

$\underline{\qquad}$

18. x_n

$\left(\lim_{n \to \infty} x_{n+} \right) x_n = c \qquad\qquad c$

$\left\{ \dfrac{x_n}{n} \right\}$

c

19. $\displaystyle\sum_{n=}^{\infty} a_n \qquad \sum_{n=}^{\infty} b_n$

$$a_n = \frac{0 \quad^{n} n}{n} \qquad b_n = \frac{0 \qquad^{n}}{(\quad)n+} \qquad\qquad n \in \mathbb{N}$$

$$\sum_{n=}^{\infty} a_n \qquad \sum_{n=}^{\infty} b_n$$

$$\sum_{n=}^{\infty} a_n \qquad\qquad\qquad \sum_{n=}^{\infty} b_n$$

$$\sum_{n=}^{\infty} a_n$$
$$\sum_{n=}^{\infty} b_n$$

$$\sum_{n=}^{\infty} a_n \qquad \sum_{n=}^{\infty} b_n$$

20. $\displaystyle\left\{ \frac{x}{+x} \quad x \in \mathbb{R} \right\}$

$\mathbb{R}$
$\mathbb{R}$
$\mathbb{R}$
$\mathbb{R}$

21.

$\displaystyle\left\{ \frac{}{x+} \quad x \in () \right\} \qquad \mathbb{R}$

$\infty) \qquad\qquad (\qquad \infty)$
$\qquad\qquad\qquad \infty)$

22. $\qquad\qquad \cup) \qquad\qquad f \quad \to \mathbb{R}$

$$f(x) = \begin{cases} x & x \in \\ - x & x \in \end{cases}$$

$f(x) \quad x \in$
$f \qquad \to$

23. $\quad f(x) \quad x \quad x \qquad g(x) \quad x \quad x \qquad\qquad x$
$\in \mathbb{R} \quad f$
f
$g \circ f$

$$\text{—} \qquad\qquad\qquad \text{—}$$

$$\text{—} \qquad\qquad\qquad \text{—}$$

24. $\quad (\qquad x \quad y) \in \mathbb{R}$

$$f(x \ y) = \begin{cases} x & y = \\ x \quad y(\ ) \quad y & y \neq \end{cases}$$

$()$
f
f

$\dfrac{\partial f}{\partial x} \qquad\qquad \dfrac{\partial f}{\partial y}$
f

25. $\quad (\qquad x \quad y) \in \mathbb{R}$

$$f(x \ y) = \begin{cases} \dfrac{x}{x}\sqrt{x +y} & x \neq \\ & x = \end{cases}$$

$\dfrac{\partial f}{\partial x}( ) \quad +\dfrac{\partial f}{\partial y}$

26. $\quad f \quad \mathbb{R} \to \mathbb{R}$

$$f(\sqrt{\ }) =$$

$$f(x) \quad \underset{t \to}{} \quad \frac{}{t}\int_{x-t}^{x+t} (f)' s \ ds \qquad\qquad x \in \mathbb{R}$$

$f()$
$\sqrt{\ } \qquad\qquad\qquad \sqrt{\ }$
$\sqrt{\ }$

27. $$\int\limits_{x=}^{x}\int\limits_{y=}^{x}\int\limits_{z=}^{y}(y+ z)\,dz\,dy\,dx$$

———

———

——

——

28. $\mathbb{R}$ ( )

() $\int(\ xy+z)\ dx$

$(x\ +\ z)dy\ +\ (y\ +\ 2xz)dz$

29. $x, y\ \in \mathbb{R}\qquad \le y \le\qquad \le x \le\ -y$

$$\oint\limits_{C} y\,dx + 2x\,dy \text{ is}$$

$\dfrac{-4}{3}$ $\dfrac{-2}{3}$

$\dfrac{2}{3}$ $\dfrac{4}{3}$

30.

31. n

n

n

n

$()\ ($ $n)$

n

32. $x\ +\ y\ +\ z$

$\mathbf{n}$

$\mathbf{F}(x,\ y,\ z)\quad x\mathbf{i}\quad y\mathbf{j}\quad z\mathbf{k}$

$$\iint\limits_{S} \mathbf{F.n}\ d\mathrm{S}$$

$\dfrac{\pi}{3}$

2π

$\dfrac{4\pi}{3}$

4π

33. $f(\quad \infty) \to \mathbb{R}$

$f'(x\ )\qquad x\qquad\qquad x$

$f()\qquad\qquad f()$

$\dfrac{-47}{5}$

$\dfrac{-47}{10}$

$\dfrac{-16}{5}$

$\dfrac{-8}{5}$

34.

p p

$f\qquad \to$

$f(x)\quad x\qquad x \in$

35. $x \in \mathbb{R}\quad x\quad x\ \le 100$

$x\quad x\quad x \in (0, \infty)\qquad\qquad \cap$

$\mathbb{R}$

$\mathbb{R}$

$\mathbb{R}$

$\mathbb{R}$

PART-II : DESCRIPTIVE QUESTIONS

36.

$f \; \mathbb{R} \to \mathbb{R} \qquad f(x, y) \quad x \quad xy \quad y$

$(\quad x \; y) \in \mathbb{R}$

f

37.

P $\quad y' + \; y = e^x y \quad y()$

Q $\quad y'' + \; y' + \alpha y =$

α

Q

38. $\quad f \; \mathbb{R} \to \mathbb{R}$

$$f\left(\frac{1}{2^n}\right) = 0 \qquad n \in \mathbb{N}$$

$f'() \qquad f''()$

39. $\qquad n \quad n$

$n \times n$

40.

$$\iint\limits_{S} \frac{xy}{\sqrt{1+2x^2}} \, dS,$$

$(\quad x, y, x \quad y) \in \mathbb{R} \qquad \le x \le y, \; x + y$

$\le$

41. $\quad f : () \quad \to \mathbb{R}$

$f'(x) \mid \le \qquad x \in ()$

$$\left\{ f\left(\frac{1}{n+1}\right) \right\} \qquad \mathbb{R}$$

42. $\quad (\qquad\qquad\qquad \mathbb{R})$

$\cap$

43. $\qquad\qquad\qquad\qquad \mathbb{R}$

$x \quad y \quad x \in \quad y \in$

$\mathbb{R}$

ANSWERS

1	2	3	4	5	6	7	8	9	10
11	12	13	14	15	16	17	18	19	20
21	22	23	24	25	26	27	28	29	30
31	32	33	34	35					

SOME SELECTED EXPLANATORY ANSWERS

2.

$f(x) \qquad\qquad x \quad a$

$$f(x) \quad f(a) + f'(a)(x-a) + \frac{f''(a)}{}(x-a)$$

$$+ \frac{f'''(a)}{}(x-a) +$$

a

$(\qquad\qquad\qquad x\;) \qquad\qquad \dfrac{f''()}{}$

$f(x) \quad x.e^x$

$f'(x) \quad e^x(\quad x)$

$f''(x) \quad e^x(\quad x)$

$\dfrac{f''()}{} \quad \dfrac{e(\;+\;)}{} = \dfrac{e}{}$

4.

$$dx \qquad dy$$

$$\frac{d}{dy} \qquad \frac{d}{dx}$$

$$\frac{d}{dy}(ax + bxy + y) \qquad \frac{d}{dx}(x + cxy + y)$$

$$bx \quad y \quad x \quad cy$$

$(b) \quad x (\quad c)y$

$\therefore \qquad b \qquad \Rightarrow b$

$$c \quad \Rightarrow c$$

5. $\qquad \nabla . f \quad \dfrac{\partial f}{\partial x}i + \dfrac{\partial f}{\partial y}j + \dfrac{\partial f}{\partial z}k$

$$xyi + yzj + zxk$$

$$\nabla(\nabla f) \quad yi + zj + xk$$

$\nabla(\nabla f)$ ()

$$\nabla \quad \nabla f \quad \begin{vmatrix} i & j & k \\ \dfrac{\partial}{\partial x} & \dfrac{\partial}{\partial y} & \dfrac{\partial}{\partial z} \\ xy & yz & zx \end{vmatrix}$$

$$- yi - zj - xk$$

$\nabla(\nabla \quad \nabla f)$

$\therefore \nabla(\nabla \quad \nabla f) \quad \nabla (\nabla f)$

9. $x \quad y \qquad y \quad z \qquad x \quad z$

$$\begin{vmatrix} & \\ & \end{vmatrix}$$

10.

$$x \quad f(x) \quad e^x$$

$$f(x) \quad e^x \qquad x$$

$$x \in \quad f(x)$$

$i.e.,$

$$\leq e^x \quad \leq$$

$$\leq e^x \leq$$

$$\leq x \leq$$

$$x$$

11.

$$\Delta_x \neq \Delta_y \neq \Delta \neq \qquad \Delta$$

$$\Delta_x \quad b \quad b \quad b \ ()$$

$$\Delta_x \quad \begin{vmatrix} & - & \\ & & - \\ & & - \end{vmatrix}$$

$$()()()$$

$$\neq$$

12.

$$\lambda \quad \begin{vmatrix} a-\lambda & - & \\ & b-\lambda & \\ & & -\lambda \end{vmatrix} =$$

$$(\quad a \quad \lambda)(b \quad \lambda)(\quad \lambda)$$

$\therefore \qquad \lambda \quad a \quad b$

$$a \quad b \qquad \Rightarrow a \quad b$$

$$a\,b \qquad \Rightarrow ab$$

$$(a \quad b) \quad \sqrt{(a+b) - ab}$$

$$\sqrt{\quad - \times}$$

$$\sqrt{} =$$

$$a \quad b \qquad a \quad b$$
$$a \qquad b$$
$$\therefore \quad a \quad b \;(\,) \qquad (\,)$$

14.

$$x \quad z$$

$$x\frac{d}{dx} \quad \frac{d}{dz} =$$

$$x\frac{d}{dx} \qquad (\quad)$$

$$x \quad y''(x) \quad xy'(x) \quad y(x)$$
$$(\quad (\quad)\,(\qquad))\ y$$
$$(\qquad)\ y$$
$$(\quad)(\qquad)\ y$$

$$y\,(x) \quad c\ e^{\,z} \qquad y\,(x) \quad c\ e^{\,z}$$
$$c\ e^{\,x} \qquad y\,(x) \quad c\ e^{\,x}$$

$$y\,(x) \quad \frac{c}{x} \qquad y\,(x) \quad c\,(x)$$

$$(\qquad x)\ \begin{vmatrix} y\,(x) & y\,(x) \\ y\,(x) & y\,(x) \end{vmatrix}$$

$$\begin{vmatrix} \dfrac{c}{x} & c\ x \\[2mm] -\dfrac{c}{x} & c\ x \end{vmatrix}$$

$$c\ c\ x \qquad c\ c\ x$$
$$(\quad x) \quad c\ c\ x$$
$$x\ (\,)$$

$$c\ c \;\Rightarrow\; c\ c \qquad -$$

$$\therefore \qquad (\quad x)\quad x$$
$$(\,)\,(\,)\,(\,) \qquad (\,)$$

15.

$$\frac{dy}{dx} \qquad \frac{x}{x} - \frac{y}{x}$$

$$\frac{dy}{dx} + \frac{y}{x} \qquad \frac{x}{x}$$

$$\frac{}{x} \qquad \frac{x}{x}$$

$$e^{\int \; dx}$$

$$e^{\int \frac{-}{x} dx} = e^{\int \; x\,dx} = x$$

$$y(\,) \qquad \int (\,) \qquad dx$$

$$y\ x \qquad \int x \quad \frac{x}{x}\ dx = \int \quad x\ dx$$

$$y\,x \qquad x \quad c$$

$$x \quad \frac{\pi}{} \quad y$$

$$\frac{\pi}{} \qquad c$$

$$\Rightarrow \qquad c \quad \frac{\pi}{}$$

$$\therefore \qquad y\,x \quad - \quad x + \frac{\pi}{}$$

$$y\,x \qquad x \quad \frac{\pi}{}$$

16. $x \quad \alpha y \qquad y \quad x$

$$x$$

$$x + \quad \alpha\ y\ \frac{dy}{dx} \qquad \frac{dy}{dx} = \quad x$$

$$\left(\dfrac{-x}{\alpha\,y}\right)(\ )x$$

$$\dfrac{x}{\alpha y}$$

$$\alpha \quad \dfrac{x}{y}$$

$$y \quad x$$

$$\dfrac{x}{y}$$

$$\therefore \quad \alpha$$

$$\alpha$$

17. $x_n \quad n\left\{ - \left(\dfrac{}{n}\right)\right\}$

$$n\left\{ \left(\dfrac{}{n+}\right)\right\}$$

$$n+ \quad \left(\dfrac{}{n+}\right)$$

$$\lim_{n\to\infty}\dfrac{u_{n+}}{u_n} \qquad \lim_{n\to\infty} - \; (n+) \quad \left\{\dfrac{}{n+}\right\}$$

$$\lim_{n\to\infty} - \dfrac{\left(\dfrac{}{n+}\right)}{\left(\dfrac{}{n+}\right)} = -$$

21. $y \quad \dfrac{}{x+}$

$$x \quad \dfrac{}{y}$$

$$x \quad \dfrac{}{y}-- = \dfrac{-y}{y}$$

$$x \in (\ )$$

$$\dfrac{-y}{y} \leq$$

$$y \qquad y \leq y$$

$$y \leq y$$

$$y \geq$$

$$y \qquad \infty)$$

22. $f'(x) \quad \dfrac{x}{} \quad x \in [\quad -]$

$$-\dfrac{x}{} \quad x \in [\quad)$$

25. $\left.\dfrac{\partial f}{\partial x}\right|_{()} \quad \lim_{h\to}\dfrac{f(h) \;-(f)}{h}$

$$\lim_{h\to}\dfrac{f(-h) \;-(f)}{-h} =$$

$$\left.\dfrac{\partial f}{\partial y}\right|_{()} \quad \lim_{h\to}\dfrac{f(\ )h \;-(f)}{h}$$

$$\lim_{h\to}\dfrac{f(\ -)h \;-(f)}{-h}$$

$$\lim_{h\to}\dfrac{\sqrt{\ +h}}{h} =$$

$$\therefore \left.\dfrac{\partial f}{\partial x}\right|_{()} + \left.\dfrac{\partial f}{\partial y}\right|_{()} \; = \; + \; =$$

27. $\displaystyle\int_{x=}\ \int_{y=}^{x}\ \int_{z=}^{y}\ (y+z)\ dz\ dy\ dx$

$$=\int_{x=}\ \int_{y=}^{x}\ (yz+z)^{y}\ dy\ dx$$

$$=\int_{x=}\ \int_{y=}^{x}\ y\ dy\ dx \Rightarrow \int_{x=}\ -\left(y\right)^{x}\ dx$$

$$=-\int_{x=}\ x\ dx$$

$$=-\times\left[\dfrac{x}{}\right]\ =-$$

28. $\int(\ xy+z)\ dx+(\ x\ +z)\ dy+(\ y+)\ xz\ dz$

$$\int\vec{}\ \overrightarrow{dr}$$

$$\vec{}\ (\ xy+z)\ i+(\ x\ +z)\ j+(\ y+)xz\ k$$

$$\nabla\times\vec{}\quad \begin{vmatrix} i & j & k \\[4pt] \dfrac{\partial}{\partial x} & \dfrac{\partial}{\partial y} & \dfrac{\partial}{\partial z} \\[8pt] (\ xy+z) & (\ x\ +z) & (\ y+)xz \end{vmatrix}$$

$$(\ +)\ i+(\ z)-(\ j+)\ x-\ x\ k$$

$$\overrightarrow{}$$

$$\phi$$

$$\overrightarrow{}\ \nabla\phi$$

$$\phi\quad x\ y\quad yz\quad xz$$

$$\overrightarrow{}\ \overrightarrow{dr}\quad \int\nabla\phi\ \overrightarrow{dr}=\int d\phi=[\phi]$$

$$\left[\,x\ y+yz+xz\,\right]_{-}^{-}$$

29. $\displaystyle\oint y\ dx+\ xdy$

$$=\iint\left(\dfrac{\partial}{\partial x}-\dfrac{\partial}{\partial y}\right)\ dx\ dy$$

$$=\int_{-}\ \int^{-y}\ (\ +)\ dx\ dy$$

$$=\int_{-}(\ -y)\ dy$$

$$=\int_{-}(\ -y)\ dy=\left[y-\dfrac{y}{}\right]$$

$$=\ \times-=-$$

32. $\displaystyle\iint\ n\ ds\quad \int\nabla\vec{}\ d\tau$

$$\times\dfrac{\pi}{}\ =\pi$$

33. $\qquad f'(x)\qquad x$

$$(\ x)^{-}$$

$$x\qquad y$$

$$f'(y)\quad (\ y)^{-}$$

$$f(y)\quad y--(y)^{-}+c$$

$$y\qquad f()$$

$$-- + c$$

$$\Rightarrow \qquad c \quad --$$

$$f(y) \quad y--(y)^{-} \, --$$

$$f() \qquad -+) \, ^{-} \, --$$

$$--$$

36. $\qquad f(x \ y) \quad x \quad xy \quad y$

$$\frac{\partial f}{\partial x} \quad x \quad y$$

$$y \qquad x \qquad \qquad (\ i)$$

$$\frac{\partial f}{\partial y} \quad y \quad x$$

$$x \quad y \qquad \qquad (\ ii)$$

$(\quad i) \ (\quad ii)$

$$x \ (\qquad x \ )$$
$$x \qquad x$$
$$x \quad x$$
$$x(\ x \ )$$

$$x \qquad --$$

$$x \qquad y$$

$$x \quad -- \quad y \quad - \left(--\right) = --$$

$$() \qquad\qquad \left(-- \ --\right)$$

$$r \qquad \frac{\partial\ f}{\partial x} = \ x$$

$$s \qquad \frac{\partial\ f}{\partial x\ \partial y} =$$

$$t \qquad \frac{\partial\ f}{\partial y} = \ y$$

$$r.t \quad s \qquad xy \qquad \left(-- \ --\right)$$

$$r \qquad\qquad \left(-- \ --\right)$$

$$f \qquad\qquad \left(-- \ --\right)$$

37. $\qquad y' \quad y \quad e^{x}\, y$

$$(y\ )y'\ (\quad y\ )\ e^{x} \qquad\qquad (\ i)$$
$$y \qquad v$$

$$\frac{dv}{dx} \qquad --\!\!- \quad \frac{dy}{dx}$$

$$(\qquad i)$$

$$\frac{-dv}{dx} + \ v \quad e^{x}$$

$$\frac{dv}{dx} - \ v \quad e^{x}$$

$$e^{\int -\ dx} = e^{-\ x}$$

$$v\, e^{\ x} \qquad \int e^{-\ x}(-e^{x})\ dx$$

$$\frac{e^{-\ x}}{y} \qquad -\int e^{-x}\ dx$$

$$\frac{e^{-\ x}}{y} \qquad e^{\ x} \quad c$$

$$x \qquad y$$

$$\therefore \qquad\qquad c$$

$$\Rightarrow \qquad\qquad c$$

$$\frac{e^{-x}}{y} \qquad e^{x}$$

$$\Rightarrow \qquad y \quad e^{x}$$

$$y' \quad e^{x}$$

$$y'' \quad e^{x}$$

$$e^{x}(\quad e^{x}) \quad \alpha \quad e^{x}$$

$$e^{x} \quad e^{x} \quad \alpha \quad e^{x}$$

$$e^{x} \quad \alpha \quad e^{x}$$

$$\therefore \qquad\qquad \alpha$$

$$y'' \quad y' \quad y$$

$$m \qquad m$$

$$(m\ )(\quad m\ )$$

$$m$$

$$y \quad c\ e^{x} \quad c \quad e^{x}$$

38.

$$f(x) \qquad\qquad x \in$$

$$f'(x) \qquad\qquad \forall x \in$$

$$f'(a) \qquad f'(b)$$

$$c \in\ a\ b$$

$$f'c$$

$$f'(a) \quad f'(c) \quad f'(b)$$

$$c \qquad f'() \qquad f''()$$

39.

$$n \quad n$$

$$\Rightarrow$$

$$\Rightarrow \qquad\qquad \lambda \quad \lambda$$

$$\Rightarrow \lambda$$

$$0\ 0\ 0$$

$$(\ )\ ()$$

40. $\leq x \leq y \qquad x \quad y \leq$

$$\leq x \leq\ -$$

$$\leq y \leq$$

$$\int \int \frac{xy}{\sqrt{\ +\ x}}\ dx\ dy$$

$$x \quad z$$

$$x\ dx \quad z\ dz$$

$$\Rightarrow \qquad x\ dx \quad \frac{z\ dz}{}$$

$$\int\int (y) \frac{z\ dz}{z}\ dy$$

$$-\int y\,dy\ z$$

$$z \quad \sqrt{\ +\ x}$$

$$-$$

$$-\int y\ dy\ \left(\sqrt{\ +\ x}\right)$$

$$-\left(\sqrt{\ -\ -}\ \right)\left[\frac{y}{}\right]$$

$$-\left(\sqrt{\ -\ -}\ \right)(\ -\ -\ )$$

$$-\left(\sqrt{\ -\ -}\ \right)$$

42.

of all its elements. Let $a \in$ a e

a e a $a \in$ $a \; i$

$\neq e$ a

$a^r \quad a^s \qquad r \quad s$ a

$a^{s\,r} \quad e \quad s \quad r$ **43. Hint :**

$a \quad e$

$s \quad r \qquad b$

$a^{s\,r} \qquad a$

$a \quad b \quad a^{s\,r} \quad e \; b$

a

$a \in \qquad a$

x

$x \quad \phi \qquad x \quad x \quad x$

IIT–JAM
JOINT ADMISSION TEST FOR
M.SC. (MATHEMATICS)-2013

1. $A = \begin{pmatrix} & \\ & \\ & \end{pmatrix}$ V

$X \in \mathbb{R}$ AX (V)

2. n

$$\vec{F} = \frac{\vec{r}}{|\vec{r}|^n} \quad \vec{r}$$

$= xi + yj + zk \quad \vec{r} \ne$

3. A B $\mathbb{R}$
NOT

$\left(A \cap B\right)^{\circ} \subseteq A^{\circ} \cap B^{\circ}$

$A^{\circ} \cup B^{\circ} \subseteq \left(A \cup B\right)^{\circ}$

$\overline{A} \cup \overline{B} \subseteq \overline{A \cup B}$

$\overline{A} \cap \overline{B} \subseteq \overline{A \cap B}$

4. x

x α

$$f(x) = \begin{cases} \dfrac{x}{x} & x \ne \\ \alpha & x = \end{cases}$$

x

()

5. $f(x)$

$$f(x) = \begin{cases} e^{x} & x \\ e^{\ x} & x \end{cases}$$

x ()

f ()

f ()

f ()

f ()

6.

$$\iint\limits_{D} \sqrt{x + y}\; dxdy$$

$D = \left\{ (x \ y) \in \mathbb{R} \quad x \le x + y \le x \right\}$

—

—   —

7.

$$x_n = \left(- \right)\left(- \right)\left(- \right) \left[\frac{}{n(n+)} \right]$$

$n \ge$ $\lim\limits_{n \to \infty} x_n$

—   —

—

8. p G

$$\mathbb{Z}_p$$

G

$(\ p\ )\quad p(p\ )\qquad\qquad p\ (p\ )$
$p\qquad\qquad\qquad\qquad p\ (p\ )\qquad p$

9. V

$$\mathbb{R}$$

$$W = \left\{ \begin{pmatrix} a & a \\ c & d \end{pmatrix} \; a\ c\ d \in \mathbb{R} \right\}$$

$$W = \left\{ \begin{pmatrix} a & b \\ a & d \end{pmatrix} \; a\ b\ d \in \mathbb{R} \right\}$$

$m(\qquad W \cap W)\qquad n(\qquad W\quad W)$
$(\qquad\qquad m\ n)$
$()\qquad\qquad\qquad\qquad ()$
$()\qquad\qquad\qquad\qquad ()$

10. $\wp_n$

$$n$$

$D\ \ \wp_n \to \wp_n\qquad T\ \ \wp_n \to \wp_n$

$D(a\quad a\,x\quad a\,x\qquad\quad a_n x^n)\quad a\quad a\,x$
$\qquad na_n x^n$

$T(a\quad a\,x\quad a\,x\qquad\quad a_n x^n)\quad a\,x\quad a\,x$
$a\,x\qquad\quad a_n x^n$

$$A$$

$DT - TD\quad \wp_n \to \wp_n$
$\qquad\qquad\quad \wp_n$

A

$n\qquad\qquad\qquad\qquad n$
$n\qquad\qquad\qquad\quad (\quad n\ )$

11. $y\dfrac{dy}{dx}$

$(\ y\ )\quad x\quad y$

12. f

$$\int^{x} f(t)\,dt = e^{\ x}\qquad\qquad x \in (\quad)$$

$$f'(\pi)$$

13. $u = \dfrac{y\quad x}{x\ y}\quad v = \dfrac{z\quad y}{y\ z}\qquad x \neq\quad y \neq$

$z \neq\qquad w\ \ f(\,u\ v)\qquad\qquad f$

$$\mathbb{R}$$

$$x\,\frac{\partial w}{\partial x} + y\,\frac{\partial w}{\partial y} + z\,\frac{\partial w}{\partial z}\quad ()$$

14.

$f(x\ y)\quad x\quad y\quad x\quad y\ (\quad x\ y) \in \mathbb{R}$

15. C

$$y\qquad\qquad x\quad x$$
$$y$$

$$\oint_c (xy\ dx\quad x\ y\,dy)$$

16. $f(x) = \begin{cases} \qquad \le x \le \\ x \qquad < x \le \end{cases}$

$$f(x) = \sum_{k=}^{n} \frac{f^{(k)}()}{k}\,x^k + \frac{f^{(n+)}(\xi)}{(\ n+)}\,x^{n+}$$

$$f\qquad\qquad x$$
$$n$$

$\xi \qquad\qquad x \le$

17. $\vec{F} = \ zi + \ xj + \ yk\qquad\qquad C$

$$z\quad x$$
$$x\quad y$$

$$\oint_C \vec{F}\ d\vec{r}$$

18. $f\qquad g\qquad\qquad\qquad\qquad \mathbb{R}$

$\mathbb{R}\qquad\qquad f(x) = -\dfrac{}{x}\qquad g(x) = \dfrac{x}{x}$

$x \in \mathbb{R}$
$\mathbb{R}\qquad\qquad \mathbb{R}\qquad\qquad f\quad g$

19.

$$\frac{x}{}+ y\ = c$$

$()$

20.

$$\sum_{n=}^{\infty} 0\quad {}^{n+}\ n\ x^{\ n}$$

21. $a \leq$ $s = \dfrac{a}{}$ $n \in \mathbb{N}$

$s_{n+} = -\left(s_n + a\right)$

s_n

22. $\displaystyle \int \int_{\sqrt{x\ x}}^{\sqrt{x}} \dfrac{x\quad y}{x}\,dy\,dx$

23.

$x\ \dfrac{d\ y}{dx} + x\dfrac{d\ y}{dx}\quad \dfrac{dy}{dx} + \dfrac{y}{x} = \dfrac{x\quad x+}{x}\quad x>$

24. S $x\quad y\quad z$

z S $x\quad y \leq$

xy

$$\iint\limits_{S} \vec{F}\,d\vec{S}$$

$\vec{F} = z\ xi + \left(\dfrac{y}{} + \quad z\right) f + x\ z +)y\quad k$

$S\quad S \cup S$ $\displaystyle \iint\limits_{S} \vec{F}\,d\vec{S}$

25. $f(x\ y) = \begin{cases} \dfrac{\left(x\ +y\ \right)}{x\ +\ y} & (x\ y) \neq () \\[2mm] (& x)y\ \in) \end{cases}$

f $x\quad y\ ()$

$f\ ()$

26. A $n\quad n$

$($ $x\quad a)^p\ (\ x\quad b)^q$

$a\quad b$

V $n\quad n$

B $AB\quad BA$

V

27. A $n\quad n$

n

P $AP\quad PD$ D

28. K $\mathbb{R}$

K $a\ b$

$a\ b\quad \cup\ I_n$ I_n

K

29. $f\quad a\ b\ \rightarrow \mathbb{R}$

$f\quad ($ $a\ c)$

$(c\ b)\quad a\quad c\quad b$

$\displaystyle\lim_{x\to c}(\ f)\ x$ f

c $f(c) = \lim_{x\to c}(\ f\ x$

30. G φ

G $\varphi(x)\quad x$

$x\quad e$ e

G

$g \in G$

$g\quad x\ \varphi(x)$ $x \in G$

$\varphi(\varphi(x))\quad x$ $x \in G$

G

ANSWERS

1	2	3	4	5	6	7	8	9	10

()

1.

$$A = \begin{pmatrix} & \\ & \\ & \end{pmatrix}$$

$$= \begin{bmatrix} & \\ & \end{bmatrix}$$

$$= \frac{\quad}{\quad}$$

$$= \begin{bmatrix} & - \\ & \end{bmatrix}$$

$$= \begin{bmatrix} & - \\ & \end{bmatrix}$$

A

$(\qquad V)$

AX

$n \quad r$

$n \qquad\qquad A \quad r$

A

2. $\qquad \vec{F} = \dfrac{\vec{r}}{r^{n}} \quad \vec{r} = xi + yj + zk \quad \vec{r} \ne$

$\because \ \vec{r} = \sqrt{x^2 + y^2 + z^2}$

$\Rightarrow r^2 = x^2 + y^2 + z^2$

$\therefore div\vec{F} \qquad div\left\{ \dfrac{\vec{r}}{(x^2+y^2+z^2)^n} \right\}$

$(x^2+y^2+z^2)^n \ div\vec{r} + grad(x^2+y^2+z^2)^n \ \vec{r}$

$(x^2+y^2+z^2)^n \quad + \left\{ \sum (- x^2+y^2+z^2)^{\frac{n}{2}} \ xi \right\} \vec{r}$

$(x^2+y^2+z^2)^n \ (- x^2+y^2+z^2)^{\frac{n}{2}} \ (\ \sum xi \ \vec{r}$

$(x^2+y^2+z^2)^n \ (n \ x^2+y^2+z^2)^{\frac{n}{2}} \ (\ \vec{r} \ \vec{r}$

$(x^2+y^2+z^2)^n \ (n \ x^2+y^2+z^2)^{\frac{n}{2}} \ r$

$(x^2+y^2+z^2)^n \ (n \ x^2+y^2+z^2)^{\frac{n}{2}} \ (\ x^2+y^2+z^2$

$(x^2+y^2+z^2)^n \ (n \ x^2+y^2+z^2)^n$

$(\ )(n \ x^2+y^2+z^2)^n$

$(\ )(n \ r^2)^n$

$(\ )n \ \vec{r}^n$

$\qquad\qquad \vec{F}$

$(\qquad\qquad n)$

$\Rightarrow n$

3. $0 \ \because \qquad \cap \ \subseteq \ \Rightarrow (\ \cap) \ \subseteq$

$\qquad\qquad \cap \ \subseteq \ \Rightarrow (\ \cap) \ \subseteq$

$\Rightarrow \qquad (\ \cap) \ \subseteq \ \cap \quad (\quad i)$

$\qquad\qquad\qquad \subseteq \qquad\qquad \subseteq$

$\Rightarrow \qquad \cap \ \subseteq \ \cap$

$\Rightarrow \qquad (\ \cap) \ \subseteq (\ \cap) \ (\quad ii)$

$\qquad\qquad\qquad\qquad ()$

$\cap ()$

$\Rightarrow \qquad (\ \cap) \qquad\qquad \cap \ (\quad iii)$

$\qquad\qquad \because$

$(\qquad\qquad ii) \ (\quad iii)$

$$\cap \quad \subseteq (\quad \cap \quad)$$

$$0 \quad \because \quad \subseteq (\quad \cup \quad) \Rightarrow \quad \subseteq (\quad \cup \quad)$$

$$\subseteq (\quad \cup \quad) \Rightarrow \quad \subseteq (\quad \cup \quad)$$

$$\Rightarrow \quad (\quad \cup \quad) \subseteq (\quad \cup \quad)$$

$$0 \quad \because \quad \subseteq \quad \cup \quad \Rightarrow \quad \nsubseteq \quad)\cup$$

$$\subseteq \quad \cup \quad \Rightarrow \quad \nsubseteq \quad)\cup$$

$$\Rightarrow \quad (\quad \psi \quad \subseteq (\quad \psi \qquad (\ i)$$

$$\subseteq \qquad \subseteq$$

$$\Rightarrow \quad \cup \quad \subseteq \quad \cup$$

$$\Rightarrow \quad (\quad \psi \quad \subseteq (\quad \psi \qquad (\ ii)$$

$$\Rightarrow \quad \cup \quad ()$$

$$\Rightarrow \quad (\quad \psi \quad (\quad \psi \qquad (\ iii)$$

$$\because \quad ($$

$$ii) (\quad iii)$$

$$(\quad \psi \quad \subseteq (\quad \psi$$

$$0 \quad \because \quad \cap \quad \subseteq \quad \Rightarrow (\quad \cap \quad \subseteq$$

$$\cap \quad \subseteq \quad \Rightarrow (\quad \cap \quad \subseteq$$

$$\Rightarrow \quad (\quad \cap \quad \subseteq \quad \cap$$

4.

$$f(x) = \begin{cases} \dfrac{x}{x} & x \neq \\ \alpha & x = \end{cases}$$

$$\because \quad f() \quad \alpha$$

$$f() \qquad \lim_{h \to} (\ f) \quad h$$

$$\lim_{h \to} \dfrac{h}{h}$$

$$\because \quad h \ ()$$

$$\lim_{h \to} \dfrac{0}{0}$$

$$()$$

$$f() \qquad \lim_{h \to} (\ f \ ) + h$$

$$\lim_{h \to} \dfrac{h}{h}$$

$$\lim_{h \to} \dfrac{0}{0}$$

$$()$$

$$\because \quad f(x) \qquad x$$

$$\therefore \quad f()$$

$$\Rightarrow \alpha \ () \ ()$$

5.

$$f(x) = \begin{cases} e^x & x \\ e^{\ x} & x \end{cases}$$

$$()$$

$$\Rightarrow \qquad e^x \quad e^{\ x}$$

$$\Rightarrow \qquad x \qquad x$$

$$\Rightarrow \qquad x$$

$$\Rightarrow \qquad x \qquad -$$

$$f(x) \qquad x \quad - \qquad f$$

$$()$$

8.
$$p$$
$$\mathbb{Z}_p \quad \mathbb{Z}_z$$

$$\left\{ \begin{bmatrix} \ \end{bmatrix} \begin{bmatrix} \ \end{bmatrix} \begin{bmatrix} \ \end{bmatrix} \right\}$$

$$\therefore \ ()$$

Option (A) : $\qquad p$

$$(p \ ) \qquad p (p \ )$$

$$( )( ) \qquad\qquad \neq$$

$$\therefore \ ()$$

Option (B) : $\qquad p$

$$p \ (p \ )$$

$$( ) \qquad\qquad \neq 3$$

$$\therefore \ ()$$

Option (C) : $\qquad p$

$$p \qquad\qquad \neq$$

$$\therefore \ ()$$

Option (D) : p

$p\ (p\ )\qquad p$

$(\ )$

$\therefore\ (\ )$

$(\ )$

9. $\quad V$

$\mathbb{R}$

$$W = \left\{ \begin{pmatrix} a & a \\ c & d \end{pmatrix}\ a\ c\ d \in \mathbb{R} \right\}$$

$$W = \left\{ \begin{pmatrix} a & b \\ a & d \end{pmatrix}\ a\ b\ d \in \mathbb{R} \right\}$$

$W \qquad\qquad W$

$\leq (\quad W \cap W) \leq$

$(\quad W \quad W)$

$\qquad W \qquad W\ (\quad W \cap W)$

$(\qquad W \cap W)$

$(\qquad W \cap W)$

Case-I : $(\qquad W \cap W)$

$(\qquad W \quad W)$

$(\quad m\ n)\ (\ )$

Case-II : $(\qquad W \cap W)$

$(\quad W \quad W)$

$(\quad m\ n)\ (\ )$

Case-III : $(\qquad W \cap W)$

$(\quad W \quad W)$

$(\quad m\ n)\ (\ )$

Case-IV : $(\qquad W \cap W)$

$(\quad W \quad W)$

$(\quad m\ n)\ (\ )$

10. $\quad \wp_n$

$\qquad\qquad n$

$D\ \wp_n \to \wp_n \qquad T\ \wp_n \to \wp_n$

$(\ a \quad a\,x \quad a\,x \qquad a_n x^n)$

$a \qquad a\,x \qquad na_n x^n$

$(\ a \quad a\,x \quad a\,x \qquad a_n x^n)$

$a\,x \quad a\,x \quad a\,x \qquad a_n x^n$

$(\quad a \quad a\,x \quad a\,x \qquad a_n x^n)$

$(\quad a \quad a\,x \quad a\,x \qquad a_n x^n)$

$(\quad a\,x \quad a\,x \quad a\,x \qquad a_n x^n\ )$

$a \qquad a\,x \quad a\,x\ (\qquad n\ )\quad a_n x^n$

$(\quad a \quad a\,x \quad a\,x \qquad a_n x^n)$

$(\quad a \quad a\,x \quad a\,x \qquad a_n x^n)$

$(\ a \qquad a\,x \qquad na_n x^{n-1})$

$a\,x \quad a\,x \qquad na_n x^n$

$$\wp_n \to \wp_n$$

$(\ )(\qquad a \quad a\,x \quad a\,x \qquad a_n x^n)$

$(\quad a \quad a\,x \quad a\,x \qquad a_n x^n)$

$(\quad a \quad a\,x \quad a\,x \qquad a_n x^n)$

$(a \quad a\,x \quad a\,x\ (\qquad n\ )\quad a_n x^n)$

$(a\,x \quad a\,x \qquad na_n x^n)$

$a \quad a\,x \quad a\,x \quad a\,x \qquad a_n x^n$

$x\ x \qquad x^n$

$$\wp_n$$

$(\ )(\ )$

$(\ )(\qquad x)\quad x$

$(\ )(\qquad x\ )\quad x$

$(\ )(\qquad x\ )\quad x$

$(\ )(\qquad x^n)\quad x^n$

$($

$)\qquad \wp_n \to \wp_n$

$$A = \begin{bmatrix} \\ \\ \\ \end{bmatrix}$$

$()$ $($ $n)$

n

11. $\qquad y\dfrac{dy}{dx}$ $(y)\ x\quad y$

$\Rightarrow \qquad \dfrac{dy}{dx}\qquad y\ x\ y\ y$

$\Rightarrow \qquad \dfrac{dx}{dy}\quad y\quad x\ y\ y$

$\Rightarrow \quad y\quad y\dfrac{dy}{dx}\quad y\quad x$

$\qquad\qquad v\qquad y$

$\qquad\qquad \dfrac{dv}{dx}\qquad y\quad y\dfrac{dy}{dx}$

$\therefore \qquad \dfrac{dv}{dx}\quad v\quad x$

$\qquad\qquad e^{\int\ dx}\quad e^{-x}$

$\therefore$

$\qquad\qquad v\,e^{x}\quad \int e^{x}\,x\,dx+c$

$\Rightarrow \qquad v\,e^{x}\quad x\,e^{x}\ e^{x}\ c$

$\Rightarrow \qquad\quad v\quad x\quad ce^{x}$

$\Rightarrow \qquad\quad y\ (\ x)\qquad ce^{x}.$

12. $\qquad \displaystyle\int\limits^{x} f(t)\,dt = e^{\ x}$

$\qquad\qquad x$

$f(\ x)\ x\quad f()\qquad e^{\ x}(\ )\ x\quad x$

$x(f\ )x\ =\quad x\quad x\,e^{\ x}$

$f(\ x)\ =\ -\quad x\,e^{\ x}$

$\qquad\qquad x$

$f'(\ x)\ x\quad -\Big\{\ x\quad x\,e^{\ x}$

$\qquad\qquad\qquad x\quad x\,e^{\ x}\Big\}$

$\Rightarrow \qquad f'(\ x)\quad \dfrac{}{x}\,e^{\ x}\ x\big\{\ x\qquad x\big\}$

$\Rightarrow \qquad f'(\ x)\quad -e^{\ x}\big\{\ x\qquad x\big\}$

$\left(x=\sqrt{\dfrac{\pi}{}}\right)$

$\Rightarrow \qquad f'(\pi)\quad -e^{\ x}\left\{\dfrac{\pi}{}\qquad \left(\dfrac{\pi}{}\right)\right\}$

$\Rightarrow \qquad f'(\pi)\quad -e\,\{\,0\qquad \}$

$\Rightarrow \qquad f'(\pi)\quad -\quad \{\qquad \}=-$

13. $\qquad u\quad \dfrac{y\quad x}{x\ y}$

$\qquad\qquad v\quad \dfrac{z\quad y}{x\ z}\qquad \forall\ \neq\quad y\neq\quad z\neq$

$\dfrac{\partial u}{\partial x}\quad \dfrac{(x\ y)(\ )x(\ y)(x\ )\ xy}{(x\ y)}$

$\qquad =\ \dfrac{x\ y\quad xy\ +\ x\ y}{x\ y}$

$\qquad =\ \dfrac{}{x}$

$\dfrac{\partial u}{\partial y}\quad \dfrac{(x\ y)(\ y)(\ y\ )(x\ )\ x\ y}{(x\ y)}$

$\qquad =\ \dfrac{x\ y\quad x\ y\ +\ x\ y}{x\ y}$

$\qquad =\ \dfrac{}{y}$

$\dfrac{\partial u}{\partial z}$

$\dfrac{\partial v}{\partial x}$

$$\frac{\partial v}{\partial y} = \frac{(y\ z\ )(\ )\,\mathrm{x}(\ z\ )(y\ )\ yz}{(y\ z\ )}$$

$$= \frac{y\ z\ \ yz\ +\ y\ z}{y\ z}$$

$$=\ \frac{}{y}$$

$$\frac{\partial v}{\partial z} = \frac{(y\ z\ )(\ \mathrm{x}(\ z\ )(y\ )\ y\ z}{(y\ z\ )}$$

$$= \frac{y\ z\ \ y\ z\ +\ y\ z}{y\ z}$$

$$=\ \frac{}{z}$$

$w\ f(u\ v)\qquad f$

$$\mathbb{R}$$

$$\frac{\partial w}{\partial x}\ \frac{\partial f}{\partial u}\frac{\partial u}{\partial x}+\frac{\partial f}{\partial v}\frac{\partial v}{\partial x}$$

$$\frac{\partial f}{\partial u}\left(\ \frac{}{x}\ \right)+\frac{\partial f}{\partial v}()$$

$$\ \frac{}{x}\frac{\partial f}{\partial u}$$

$$\frac{\partial w}{\partial y}\ \frac{\partial f}{\partial u}\frac{\partial u}{\partial y}+\frac{\partial f}{\partial v}\frac{\partial v}{\partial y}$$

$$\frac{\partial f}{\partial u}\left(\frac{}{y}\right)+\frac{\partial f}{\partial v}\left(\ \frac{}{y}\ \right)$$

$$\ \frac{}{y}\frac{\partial f}{\partial u}\ \ \frac{}{y}\frac{\partial f}{\partial v}$$

$$\frac{\partial w}{\partial z}\ \frac{\partial f}{\partial u}\frac{\partial u}{\partial z}+\frac{\partial f}{\partial v}\frac{\partial v}{\partial z}$$

$$\frac{\partial f}{\partial u}()\ \ +\frac{\partial f}{\partial v}\left(\frac{}{z}\right)$$

$$\ \frac{}{z}\frac{\partial f}{\partial v}$$

$$x\ \frac{\partial w}{\partial x}+y\ \frac{\partial w}{\partial y}+z\ \frac{\partial w}{\partial z}$$

$$x\ \left(\ \frac{}{x}\frac{\partial f}{\partial u}\right)+y\ \left[\ \frac{}{y}\frac{\partial f}{\partial u}\ \ \frac{}{y}\frac{\partial f}{\partial v}\right]$$

$$+z\ \left(\ \frac{}{z}\frac{\partial f}{\partial v}\right)$$

$$\frac{\partial f}{\partial u}+\ \frac{\partial f}{\partial u}\ \ \frac{\partial f}{\partial v}+\ \frac{\partial f}{\partial v}$$

$$x\ \frac{\partial w}{\partial x}+y\ \frac{\partial w}{\partial y}+z\ \frac{\partial w}{\partial z}\ (\ )$$

14. $f(x\ y)\quad x\quad y\quad x\quad y$

$p\quad \dfrac{\partial f(x\ y)}{\partial x}\qquad x\quad x$

$q\quad \dfrac{\partial f(x\ y)}{\partial y}\qquad y\quad y$

$r\quad \dfrac{\partial\ f}{\partial x}\qquad x$

$s\quad \dfrac{\partial\ f}{\partial x\partial y}$

$t\quad \dfrac{\partial\ f}{\partial y}\qquad y$

$$f(x\ y)$$

$$\frac{\partial f}{\partial x}=\frac{\partial f}{\partial y}=$$

$$\Rightarrow\quad x\quad x\qquad \Rightarrow x(\ x\ )$$

$$\Rightarrow x\qquad \pm\frac{}{\sqrt{}}$$

$$y\quad y\qquad \Rightarrow y(\ y\ )$$

$$\Rightarrow y\qquad \pm\frac{}{\sqrt{}}$$

$$\therefore$$

$$(\ )\ (\qquad \pm\frac{}{\sqrt{}}\quad \pm\frac{}{\sqrt{}}\ )$$

$(\quad)$

$$r \quad ()$$
$$s$$
$$t \quad ()$$

$rt \quad s \quad () \, ()$

$\therefore \; rt \quad s \qquad r$

$f(x \quad y) \; ()$

$$\left(\pm \dfrac{}{\sqrt{\quad}} \quad \pm \dfrac{}{\sqrt{y}} \right)$$

$r \qquad \left(\pm \dfrac{}{\sqrt{\quad}} \right) \quad = \quad \times - \quad = \quad = \; >$

s

$t \qquad \left(\pm \dfrac{}{\sqrt{\quad}} \right) \quad = \quad \times - \quad = \quad = \; >$

$rt \quad s \quad () \, () \, ()$

$\therefore \; rt \quad s \qquad r$

$f(x \quad y) \qquad \left(\pm \dfrac{}{\sqrt{\quad}} \quad \pm \dfrac{}{\sqrt{\quad}} \right)$

15.

$$y \qquad x \quad x$$
$$y$$

$$\oint_C xy \, dx \quad x \, y \, dy$$

$$\int x(\;\;)x \quad dx \; (x \;)(\;)x \qquad x \, dx$$

$$\int \left[x \quad x + x + \quad x \quad x \right] dx$$

$$\int \left[x \quad x \right] dx$$

$$\left[\dfrac{x}{} \quad \dfrac{x}{} \right] = - \quad - = - = -$$

16. Hint:

Theorem:

$f^{(n)} \quad (x)$

$$a \quad h$$

$f(a \quad h) \quad f(a) \quad h.f'(a) \qquad h \quad f''(a)$
$h \quad f^{()} \,(a) \qquad h^n \,.\, f^{(n)}(a) \quad n$
$h^n \qquad f^{(n)} \,(c) \,(\; n\;)$

$$c \qquad a \qquad a \quad h$$

Proof:

$$r$$

$f(a \quad h) \quad f(a) \quad h \; f'(a) \qquad h \quad f''(a)$
$h \quad f^{()} \,(a) \qquad h^n \quad f^{(n)}(a) \quad n$
$$h^n \qquad r \,(\; n\;)$$
$$a \qquad h \quad x$$
$$r \quad f^{(n)} \,(\xi) \qquad \xi$$
$a \qquad a \quad h$

$g(x) \quad f(a \quad x) \; (\quad f(a) \quad x \; f'(a)$
$\quad x \; f''(a) \qquad x \; f^{()} \,(a)$
$\quad x^n \; f^{(n)}(a) \quad n \quad x^n \quad r(\; n\;))$
$$n$$
$g'(x) \quad f'(a \quad x) \; (\quad f'(a) \quad x \; f''(a)$
$\quad x^n \quad f^{(n)}(a) \;(\; n\;) \qquad x^n \quad r \, n)$
$g''(x) \quad f''(a \quad x) \; (\quad f''(a) \qquad x^n \quad f^{(n)}(a)$
$(\; n\;) \qquad x^n \quad r(\; n\;))$

$g^{(n)} \,(x) \quad f^{(n)}(a \quad x) \; (\quad f^{(n)}(a) \quad x \, r)$
$g^{(n)} \,(x) \quad f^{(n)} \,(a \quad x) \quad r$
$$f \qquad f^{(n)}$$
$$a$$
$g(x)$

$g() \quad g(h) \Rightarrow \qquad \xi \qquad\qquad h$
$g(\xi)$

$g'() \quad g'(\xi) \Rightarrow \qquad \xi$
$h \qquad g''(\xi)$

$g^{(n)}() \qquad g^{(n)}(\xi_n) \Rightarrow \qquad \xi_n$
$\qquad h \qquad\qquad g^{(n)} \,(\xi_n)$

$$f^{(n)} \,(a \quad \xi_n) \quad r$$
$\Leftrightarrow \; f^{(n)} \,(\xi) \quad r \qquad\qquad \xi \qquad a$
$$a \quad h$$
$h^{(n)} \,(\xi)(\; n\;)$

17.

$$x \qquad t \quad y \qquad t \quad z \qquad\qquad t$$
$$t \qquad\qquad z$$
$$C$$
$$\overline{r} \qquad xi + yj + zk$$
$$t \, i \qquad t \, j(\qquad t \;) \quad k$$

$$\therefore \quad \frac{d\bar{r}}{dt} \qquad t\,i \qquad t\,j \qquad t\,k$$

$$\int_{t=}^{z} \big[(\ )+ \ i+ \ t\,j+ \ t\,k\big]$$

$$\big[\ t\,i+ \ t\,j \ t\,k\big]dt$$

$$\int_{}^{z} (\ t\ )t+ \ t \ t\,dt$$

$$\int_{}^{z} (\ t+ + \ )\ t+ + \ t\,dt$$

$$\int_{}^{z} (\ +)\ t\,dt$$

$$\big[\ t \qquad t\big]^{z}$$

$$\pi \qquad t$$
$$\pi$$
$$\pi.$$

18. $\qquad f\ u \to v$

$u \qquad v$

(i) f

(ii) f

$$u \qquad v$$

$$u \cong v$$

$$f(x) \ \frac{-}{x} \qquad g(x) \ \frac{x-}{x}$$

$$x \in$$

$$f(g(x)) \ \overline{g(x)}$$

$$f\!\left(\frac{x-}{x}\right) \ \frac{x}{x-}$$

19.

$$\frac{x}{} + y = c$$

<hr>

$$x$$

$$\Rightarrow \qquad \frac{x}{} + \ y\,\frac{dy}{dx}$$

$$\Rightarrow \qquad x+ \ y\,\frac{dy}{dx}$$

$$\left(\frac{dy}{dx} = \frac{}{dy\ dx}\right)$$

$$\therefore \quad x+ \ y\left\{\frac{}{dy\ dx}\right\}$$

$$\Rightarrow \qquad x \quad y\,\frac{dx}{dy}$$

$$\Rightarrow \qquad x \qquad y\,\frac{dx}{dy}$$

$$\Rightarrow \qquad \int \frac{dy}{y} \quad \int \frac{dx}{x}$$

$$\Rightarrow \qquad y \qquad x \qquad c$$
$$\Rightarrow \qquad y \quad x\ c$$
$$(\ )$$
$$\Rightarrow \qquad c \Rightarrow c$$
$$\therefore$$
$$\Rightarrow \qquad y \qquad x$$

20.

$$\sum_{n=}^{\infty} (-)^{\,n+} \cdot n(\ )x^{\,n-}$$

i.e.,
$$u_n \ ()^{\,n} \quad n \ (\ x)^{\,n}$$
$$u_n \ ()^{\,n} \quad (\ n)(\ x)^{(\ n)}$$
$$()^{\,n} \ (\ n)(\ x)^{\,n}$$

$$\frac{u_n}{u_{n+}} \quad -\,\frac{n\cdot (x)^{\,n-}}{(n+)\,(\ )x^{\,n}}$$

$$-\,\frac{n\cdot}{(n+)\,(\ )x}$$

$$-\,\frac{n}{(n+)}\cdot\frac{}{x}$$

$$\lim_{n\to\infty}\frac{u_n}{u_{n+}} \qquad \lim_{n\to\infty}\left(-\frac{n}{(n+)}\cdot\frac{}{x}\right)$$

$$f(x) \ \frac{-}{x}$$

21.

$$a \leq s \quad \frac{a}{}$$

$$n \in \mathbb{N}$$

$$s_n \quad -\left(s_n + a\right)$$

$$s \quad \frac{a}{}$$

$$s \quad -\left(s + a\right)$$

$$-\left(\frac{a}{} + a\right)$$

$$\frac{a}{} + \frac{a}{}$$

$$s$$

$$s_k \qquad s_k$$

$$s_{k+} > s_k$$

$$s_{k+} + a > s_k + a$$

$$-\left(s_{k+} + a\right) > -\left(s_k + a\right)$$

$$s_k \qquad s_k$$

$$\forall n \qquad s_n \qquad \qquad s_n \qquad s_n$$

$$s_n$$

$$s \quad \frac{a}{}$$

$$\leq \quad (\because \quad a \leq)$$

$$s_n \leq$$

$$s_n \leq$$

$$s_n \quad a \leq \qquad a$$

$$-(s_n + a) \leq -(+ a)$$

$$\leq \quad (\because \quad a \leq)$$

$$s_n \leq \quad \forall n$$

$$s_n \leq \quad \forall$$

$$n \qquad s_n$$

$$s_n$$

$$s_n$$

$$\lim_{n \to \infty} s_n = l \qquad \lim_{n \to \infty} s_{n+} = l$$

$$s_n \qquad \frac{1}{}\left(s_n + a\right)$$

$$n \to \infty$$

$$l \qquad \frac{1}{}(l + a)$$

$$l \qquad l \qquad a$$

$$\Rightarrow \qquad l \qquad \frac{\pm\sqrt{\quad} \ a}{}$$

$$\frac{\pm\sqrt{\quad} \ a}{}$$

$$l \leq$$

$$l \qquad \sqrt{\quad} \ a$$

22.

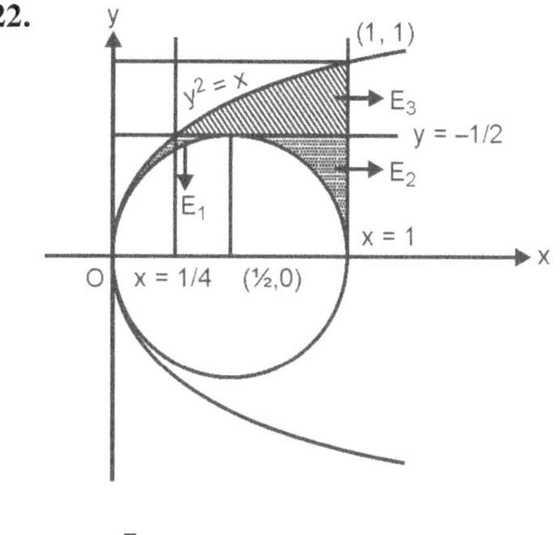

$$\int \quad \int_{\sqrt{x} \ x}^{\sqrt{x}} \frac{x \quad y}{x} \, dy \, dx$$

$$x = -$$

$$y \qquad \qquad x$$

$$y \qquad x$$

$$x \qquad y \qquad x$$

$$x \qquad\qquad y$$

$$y \quad x \Rightarrow x \quad y$$
$$y \quad x \quad x \Rightarrow x \quad x \quad y$$

$$\Rightarrow x \quad \frac{\pm\sqrt{\quad y}}{\qquad}$$

$$\int \int_{\sqrt{x\ x}}^{\sqrt{x}} \frac{x \quad y}{x}\, dy\,dx$$

$$\int dy \int_{y}^{\sqrt{\quad y}} \frac{x \quad y}{x}\, dx +$$

$$\int dy \int_{+\sqrt{\quad y}} \frac{x \quad y}{x}\, dx +$$

$$\int dy \int_{y} \frac{x \quad y}{x}\, dx$$

23. $\quad x\ \dfrac{d\ y}{dx} + x\ \dfrac{d\ y}{dx} \quad \dfrac{dy}{dx} + \dfrac{y}{x} = \dfrac{x \quad x+}{x}$

$$\Rightarrow x\ \frac{d\ y}{dx} + x\ \frac{d\ y}{dx} \quad x\frac{dy}{dx} + \quad y = \frac{x \quad x+}{x}$$

$$x \quad e^{z} \Rightarrow z \qquad x$$
$$\Rightarrow \quad '(\ ')(\quad '\ z) \quad '(\ ') \qquad '$$

$$y \quad \frac{z\,e^{z} +}{e^{z}}$$

$$\Rightarrow \quad ' \quad ' \quad ' \quad ' \quad ' \quad ' \quad y$$
$$z \quad e^{-z}$$
$$\Rightarrow (\ ' \quad ' \quad ')\quad y\ z\ e^{z}$$

$$m \quad m \quad m$$
$$m\,(\ m) \qquad m(\ m)(\qquad m)$$
$$\Rightarrow (m\ )(\quad m\quad m\ )$$
$$\Rightarrow (m\ )\quad m\quad m\quad m$$

$$\Rightarrow (m\ )(\quad m\ )(\quad m)$$
$$\Rightarrow m$$
$$\therefore \qquad c\ e \qquad c\ e^{z} \quad c\ e^{z}$$

$$\frac{c}{x} + c\ x + c\ x$$

$$\frac{z + e^{\ z}}{(\ )(\ )(\ ) \qquad\qquad +}$$

$$\frac{e^{\ z}}{(\ )(\ )(\ ) \qquad\qquad +}$$

$$-\left\{ \quad + \frac{\rule{3cm}{0pt}}{} \right\}\ z$$

$$\frac{e^{\ z}}{} + -\left\{ \quad + - \right\}\ z$$

$$\frac{e^{\ z}}{} + -\left\{ z + - \right\}$$

$$\frac{}{x} + -\left(\qquad x + - \right)$$

$$\therefore \quad y$$

$$\frac{c}{x} + c\ x + c\ x \quad + \frac{}{x} + -\left(\qquad x + - \right)$$

24. Gauss's Divergence Theorem

$$\vec{\ } \quad z\ x i + \left(\frac{y}{} + \quad z \right) j (+ \ x\ z +) y\ k$$

$$\iint_{S} \vec{F}\, d\vec{S}$$

$$\iint_{S} \left[z\ x \cdot dy \cdot dz + \left(\frac{y}{} + \quad z \right) dz \cdot dx (+ \ x\ z +) y \ \cdot dx\,dy \right]$$

$$\iiint_{v} \left[\frac{\partial}{\partial x}(z\ x) + \frac{\partial}{\partial y}\left(\frac{y}{} + \quad \right) + \frac{\partial}{\partial z}(\ x\ z +) y \ \right] dx \cdot dy \cdot dz$$

$$\iiint_{v} (z\ + y\ + x\ ) \cdot dx \cdot dy \cdot dz$$

$$\iiint_{v} \quad \cdot dx \cdot dy \cdot dz$$

$$\int \int_0^\pi \int_0^\pi r \cdot \quad \theta \cdot d\phi \cdot d\theta \cdot dr$$

$(\because \quad)$

$$\int r \cdot dr \int_0^\pi \quad \theta \cdot d\theta \int_0^\pi d\phi$$

$$\left[\frac{r}{3}\right] \times [-\quad \theta]_0^\pi \times [\phi]_0^\pi \quad -\pi$$

25.

$$f(x\ y) = \begin{cases} \dfrac{\left(x\ +y\ \right)}{x\ +\ y} & (x\ y\ \neq) \\[2mm] & (\ x)\ y\ (=) \end{cases}$$

$$f_x() \quad \lim_{h\to} \frac{\left[f(\ +h)\ ()\ f\quad \right]}{h}$$

$$\lim_{h\to} \frac{f(h)}{h}$$

$$\lim_{h\to} \frac{\left(\dfrac{h}{h}\right)}{h}$$

$$\lim_{h\to}$$

$$f_y() \quad \lim_{k\to} \frac{\left[f(\ )+k\ ()\ f\quad \right]}{k}$$

$$\lim_{k\to} \frac{f(\ )k}{k}$$

$$\lim_{k\to} \frac{\left(\dfrac{k}{k}\right)}{k}$$

$$\lim_{k\to} k$$

$$\qquad\qquad x\qquad y\ () \qquad f$$

$$(\qquad\qquad x\ y)\to()$$

$$y = \quad \frac{x}{\quad} + mx$$

$$f(\ x\quad x\quad mx\ ) \quad \frac{\left[x\ +\left(\dfrac{x}{\quad}+mx\right)\right]}{x\ +\ \left[\dfrac{x}{\quad}+mx\right]}$$

$$\frac{x\ \left[\ +\left(\dfrac{x}{\quad}+mx\right)\right]}{\quad mx}$$

$$\lim_{x\to} f\left(x\ \frac{x}{\quad}+mx\right) = \frac{}{m}$$

$$\qquad\qquad\qquad\qquad m$$

$$\lim_{(x\ y)\to()} (\ f\ )x\ y$$

$()$

26.

$\qquad u\ \to\ v\qquad\qquad v$

$\qquad\qquad\qquad\qquad\qquad n$

$\qquad\qquad\qquad n\qquad n$

$\qquad\qquad\qquad\qquad\qquad\qquad\qquad v$

$\qquad\qquad \alpha\quad \alpha\qquad \alpha_n \qquad\qquad\qquad v$

$\qquad\qquad\quad \lambda\quad \lambda\quad \lambda\quad \lambda_n$

$\alpha\qquad \lambda\ \alpha\qquad \lambda\ \alpha\qquad \alpha\qquad \alpha\qquad \alpha_n$

$\alpha\qquad \lambda\ \alpha\qquad \alpha\quad \lambda\ \alpha\qquad \alpha_n$

$\vdots$

$\alpha_n\qquad \lambda_n\alpha_n\qquad \alpha\qquad \alpha\qquad \lambda_n\alpha_n$

i.e.,

$$\begin{bmatrix} \lambda & & & & \cdots & \\ & \lambda & & & \cdots & \\ \cdots & \cdots & \cdots & \cdots & \cdots \\ \cdots & \cdots & \cdots & \cdots & \cdots \\ \cdots & \cdots & \cdots & & \lambda_n \end{bmatrix}$$

i.e.,

,

27. n n

n $\quad$ λ λ λ_n $\quad$ x x

x_n

x x x_n

x x x_n

x x x_n

x λx x λx x_n $\lambda_n x_n$

λx λx $\lambda_n x_n$

x x x_n $\begin{bmatrix} \lambda & & & & \\ & \lambda & & & \\ & & \lambda & & \\ & & & & \\ & & & & \lambda_n \end{bmatrix}$

$\begin{bmatrix} \lambda & & & & \\ & \lambda & & & \\ & & \lambda & & \\ & & & & \\ & & & & \lambda_n \end{bmatrix}$

29. Hints:

$f(x)$

x c

$\lim_{h\to} \dfrac{f(c+h)-f(c)}{h}$

$f(x)$ $\qquad x \quad c$

$f'(c) \quad \lim_{x \to c} (\,f\,)\, x$

$f(x) \quad x \quad c \qquad f'(c)$

$f'(c) \quad \lim_{h\to} \dfrac{f(c+h)-f(c)}{h}$

h

$f(x) \quad x$

$c \qquad f'(c)$

$f'(c) \quad \lim_{h\to} \dfrac{f(c-h)-f(c)}{-h} \quad h$

$x \quad c \quad f'(c) \qquad f'(c)$

$x \quad c$

30. $\qquad g(x) \quad x \quad \varphi(x)$

x

$x \quad \varphi(x)$

$g(x)$

$g(x)$

$($

$)$ $\qquad g(x)$

$g(c) \quad g(b) \Rightarrow c \quad b$

$c \qquad b$

$g(c) \quad g(b) \qquad\qquad c \quad b$

$g(c) \quad g(b)$

$c \quad \varphi(c) \quad b \quad \varphi(b)$

$b \; c \quad \varphi(b) \quad \varphi(c)$

$\varphi(\,)$

$b \; c \quad \varphi(b\; c\;)$

φ

$b \; c \quad e$

$c \quad b$

h

$x \quad \varphi(x)$

$c \ b \qquad\qquad cb$

$($

$)$

$c \quad d \quad \varphi(d)$
$b \quad e \quad \varphi(e)$
$cb \quad g \quad \varphi(g)$

$d, \ e \qquad g$

$cb \quad g \quad \varphi(g)$

$(d \quad \varphi(d)) \ (\ e \quad \varphi(e)) \quad g \quad \varphi(g)$

φ

$(\ d \quad \varphi(d)) \ (\ e \quad \varphi(e) \quad g \quad \varphi(g)$
$(e \quad \varphi(e)) \ (\ d \quad \varphi(d)) \quad \varphi(g) \quad g$
$(\varphi(e) \quad e) \ (\quad \varphi(d) \quad d) \quad \varphi(g) \quad g$
$(\varphi(e \ ) \quad e) \ (\quad \varphi(d \ ) \quad d) \quad \varphi(g \ ) \quad g$

φ
$\varphi(\varphi(g)) \quad g$
$\varphi(\varphi(e)) \quad e \qquad \varphi(\varphi(d)) \quad d$

$(\varphi(e \ ) \quad \varphi(\varphi(e)) \ (\quad \varphi(d \ ) \quad \varphi(\varphi(d))$
$\varphi(g \ ) \quad \varphi(\varphi(g))$

φ

$(\qquad\qquad\qquad \varphi(a) \quad \varphi(b) \quad \varphi(ab))$
$(\varphi(e \ ) \quad \varphi(\varphi(e))) \ (\quad \varphi(d \ ) \quad \varphi(\varphi(d)))$
$\varphi(g \ ) \quad \varphi(g))$

$(\varphi(e \quad \varphi(e)) \ (\quad \varphi(d \quad \varphi(d)) \quad \varphi(g \quad \varphi(g))$

$c \quad d \quad \varphi(d)$
$b \quad e \quad \varphi(e)$
$cb \quad g \quad \varphi(g)$

$\varphi(b) \quad \varphi(c) \quad \varphi(cb)$
$\varphi(bc) \quad \varphi(cb)$
$\varphi \qquad\qquad\qquad\qquad \varphi$
φ
φ

$bc \quad cb$

Previous Paper (Solved)

IIT–JAM

JOINT ADMISSION TEST FOR
M.SC. (MATHEMATICS)-2012

1. x_n

$$\sqrt{\quad}+\sqrt{\quad}\quad\sqrt{\quad}+\sqrt{\quad}\quad\sqrt{\quad}\quad+\sqrt{\quad}\quad\sqrt{\quad}+\sqrt{\quad}$$

$$y_n = \frac{x + x + \ \cdots + x_n}{n} \qquad n \in \mathbb{N}$$

y_n

2.
$$x \cdot x \quad x \quad x \quad x$$

3. $f \ \mathbb{R} \ \to \mathbb{R}$

$$f(x\ y) = \begin{cases} \dfrac{x}{x\ + y} & (\ x)y \ (\neq) \\[2ex] & (\ x)y \ (=) \end{cases}$$

$f_x()\qquad f_y()$
$f_x()\qquad f_y()$
$f_x()\qquad f_y()$
$f_x()\qquad f_y()$

4.
$$\int\limits_{z=}^{z}\int\limits_{y=}^{y}\int\limits_{x=}^{y} x\ y\ z\ dx\,dy\,dz$$

— —

— —

5. $(\qquad\qquad x\ y\quad \alpha x\ y\ )\ dx$
$(\quad x\ y\quad x\ y)\ dy \qquad\qquad \alpha$

— —

6.
$$(\qquad xy \quad x\ y \quad y\ )\,dx(\quad x \qquad y\ )\,dy$$

$x \qquad\qquad\qquad y$
$e^{\ x} \qquad\qquad\qquad e^{\ y}$

7. $c \qquad ai + bj + ck$

$$\left(\ \sqrt{\quad}\ \right) \qquad\qquad z \quad \sqrt{x\ + y}$$

$a \quad b \quad c$
$a \quad b \quad c$
$a \quad b \quad c$
$a \quad b \quad c$

8. $\mathbb{Q}\ \mathbb{Z}$

$$-+\mathbb{Z} \qquad \mathbb{Q}\ \mathbb{Z}$$

9. $\mathbb{Z}$

$\mathbb{Z}$

$$(\mathbb{Z}\ \ \mathbb{Z})\times\ \mathbb{Z}$$

$$\mathbb{Z}\times\ \mathbb{Z}$$

10. W $\mathbb{R}$

$T\ \mathbb{R}\ \to W$
$S \quad Te\ Te\ Te \qquad W$

$S \qquad\qquad W$
$T(\mathbb{R}\ ) \neq W$
$Te\ Te\ Te \qquad W$
(T)

$()$

11. $\mathbb{R}$

$$\{(x\ y\ z)\in\mathbb{R}\quad x+\ y+z=$$
$$x+\ y\quad z=\quad x+y\quad z=\ \}$$

W

12. P

P

13. $\displaystyle\sum_{n=}^{\infty}a_n x^n$ $\qquad x$

$$\sum_{n=}^{\infty}a_n x^n$$

x

x

x

x

14. $Y=\left\{\dfrac{x}{+\ x}\,\middle|\,x\in\mathbb{R}\right\}$

Y

$()$ $\qquad\qquad ($

15. C $\qquad\qquad\mathbb{R}\ ()$

$()$

$$\int_C(\ xy+z)\,dx+(z+x\ )\,dy+(x+y)\,dz$$

16. $()$

$$\sum_{n=}^{\infty}\frac{n}{(\ )\quad n}$$ **(6)**

$()$ $\qquad Z$

$*\qquad m*n\quad m+n$

$m,\ n\in Z$

(9)

17. $()$

$$\lim_{x\to}\frac{\displaystyle\int^{x}\sqrt{\ +t}\ dt}{x}$$ **(6)**

$()$ $\qquad f\ \mathbb{R}\to\mathbb{R}$

a

18. $()\ ()$

$u\quad v\quad f''$

f

$f'(a)\neq$ $\qquad a\ \delta$

$a\quad\delta\quad x\quad a\quad\delta\ (\quad x_n)_{n\in N}$

a **(9)**

$u\quad v$

$f\ \mathbb{R}\ \to\mathbb{R}$

$f(x,y)\quad x\quad x\ y\quad y\qquad (x\ y)\in\mathbb{R}$ **(6)**

$f\ \mathbb{R}\ \to\mathbb{R}\qquad f(x\ y)\quad x\quad y\quad x$

$y\qquad\qquad (x\ y)\in\mathbb{R}$

f

(9)

19. $()$

$$\int_{x=}\int_{y=\sqrt{\ x}}(e^{y})\,dy\,dx$$ **(6)**

$()$

$\mathbb{R}$

$$z=\ +\sqrt{\ x\quad y}$$
$$z=\sqrt{x\ +y}$$

(9)

20.

$x\quad y\quad z$

z **(15)**

21. $y(x)$

$$\frac{d\ y}{dx}\quad y=\qquad\qquad y()$$

$y'()\quad\alpha\qquad\qquad\alpha\in)$

$$\{y(x)\ x\in\mathbb{R}\}$$

(15)

22. $()$ $\qquad y(x)\quad x\quad y(x)\quad x$

$$x\ \frac{d\ y}{dx}\quad x\frac{dy}{dx}+\ y=$$

$$x\ \frac{d\ y}{dx}\qquad x\frac{dy}{dx}+\ y=x \qquad\textbf{(6)}$$

$$()\qquad \frac{dy}{dx}+\frac{}{x}\qquad y=x \qquad y$$

$$\textbf{(9)}$$

23. ()   ∪   **R** $u($

) $v\ ()$

     ∪

($u, v)$ ∪   **(6)**

()

   $u\ ()$ $u\ ()$ $u\ ()$

(9)

24. () G

               $g \in G$

      $h \in G$ g h **(6)**

() A

        B

     C

            A B C

(9)

25. () I R

$$A=\left\{r \in R\ \ r^{n} \in I \qquad n \in \mathbb{N}\right\}$$

     A $R.$ **(6)**

()   **R**

   ()()(

)   **R**   ()

    () ()

(9)

---

26. () P, D A

           P D

      D PAP A^{n}

$n \in \mathbb{N}$ A **(6)**

()   **R** →

R ($x, y, z)(\ x + y, y - z)$

()()()

()()   **(9)**

27. ()   →

($x, y, z)(\ x + y, y + z, z - x)$

(6)

() v v v **R**

   $v\ ()$ $v\ ()$ $v\ ($

)   →

($v\ )()(\ $ $v\ )$

()($v\ )()$

(9)

28. () $f\ \mathbb{R} \to \mathbb{R}$

   $f(x)$ x $x \in \mathbb{R}$

(6)

() $n \in \mathbb{N}$ $f_{n}\ \mathbb{R} \to \mathbb{R}$

     f_{n} $\mathbb{R}$

     $f\ \mathbb{R} \to \mathbb{R}$ f

(9)

29. () A

      $a \in$ a

($a)$ $a\beta$ a $x\ x \in$ **(6)**

() f →

        $x_{n\ n}$ $y_{n\ n}$

   x_{n} $y_{n\ n}$

$f(x_{n})$ $f(y_{n})$ $_{n}$ **(9)**

ANSWERS

1	2	3	4	5	6	7	8	9	10

11	12	13	14	15

3. $\left.\dfrac{\partial f}{\partial x}\right|_{(\ )}$ $\displaystyle\lim_{h\to}\ \dfrac{\dfrac{h}{h+}}{h}$

$\left.\dfrac{\partial f}{\partial y}\right|_{(\ )}$ $\displaystyle\lim_{h\to}\ \dfrac{+h}{h}$

$f_x()$ $\qquad$ $f_y()$

4. $\displaystyle\int_{z=}^{z}\int_{y=}^{y}\int_{x=}^{} x\,y\,z\ dx\,dy\,dz$

$\displaystyle\int_{z=}^{z}\int_{y=}^{} y\,z\,dy\,dz\left[\int_{x=}^{y} x\,dx\right]$

$\displaystyle\int_{z=}^{z}\int_{y=}^{} y\,z\,dy\,dz\left[\dfrac{x}{\ }\right]^{y}$

$\displaystyle\int_{z=}^{z} z\,dz\int_{y=}^{} y\,\dfrac{y}{\ }\,dy$

$\displaystyle\int_{z=}^{z} z\,dz\left[\dfrac{y}{\times}\right]^{z}$

$\displaystyle\int_{z=}^{} \dfrac{z\,z}{\ }\,dz$

$\displaystyle\int_{z=}^{} \dfrac{z}{\ }\,dz$

$\left[\dfrac{z}{\times}\right]\quad -$

5. $(\ x\,y\ \ \alpha x\,y\ )\,dx(\ \ x\,y\ \ x\,y)\,dy$

$x\,y\ \ \alpha x\,y$

$x\,y\ \ x\,y$

$\dfrac{\partial M}{\partial y}\qquad x\,y\qquad \alpha x\,y$

$\dfrac{\partial N}{\partial x}\qquad x\,y\qquad x\,y$

$\dfrac{\partial M}{\partial y}\qquad \dfrac{\partial N}{\partial x}$

$x\,y\qquad \alpha x\,y\qquad x\,y\qquad x\,y$
α

$\alpha\qquad -$

6. $(\ xy\quad x\,y\quad y\ )\,dx(\ x\quad y\ )\,dy$

$M\qquad xy\quad x\,y\quad y$

$N\qquad x\quad y$

$\dfrac{\partial M}{\partial y}\qquad x\quad x\quad y$

$\dfrac{\partial N}{\partial x}\qquad x$

$\dfrac{\dfrac{\partial M}{\partial y}\quad \dfrac{\partial N}{\partial x}}{N}$

$e^{\int\ dx}\quad e^{\ x}$

7. $f(x\ y\ z)\quad x\quad y\quad z$

$\nabla f\qquad x\vec{i}+\ y\vec{j}\quad z\vec{k}$

$\nabla f|_{(\ \sqrt{\ })}\qquad 0\ \vec{i}0+\quad \vec{j}\quad (\sqrt{\ })\vec{k}$

$\vec{i}+\ \vec{j}\quad \sqrt{\ }\,\vec{k}$

$\dfrac{\vec{i}+\ \vec{j}\quad \sqrt{\ }\,\vec{k}}{\sqrt{(\ )\ +(\ )\ +(\ \sqrt{\ })}}$

$\dfrac{\vec{i}+\ \vec{j}\quad \sqrt{\ }\,\vec{k}}{\ }$

$\dfrac{\vec{i}+\ \vec{j}\quad \sqrt{\ }\,\vec{k}}{\ }\qquad a\vec{i}+b\vec{j}+c\vec{k}$

$\vec{i}\quad \vec{j}\qquad \vec{k}$

$a\quad -\qquad\qquad b\quad -\qquad\qquad c\quad \sqrt{\ }$

$a\quad b\quad c\qquad\qquad a\quad b\quad c$

11. W

$\begin{vmatrix} & & \\ & & \end{vmatrix}$

$(\quad\quad \rightarrow \quad)$

$(\quad\quad \rightarrow \quad)$

$(\quad\quad \rightarrow \quad)$

W

12. P

$$P \quad \begin{vmatrix} a & a & a & a \\ a & a & a & a \\ a & a & a & a \\ a & a & a & a \end{vmatrix}$$

$$P \quad \begin{vmatrix} a & a & a & a \\ a & a & a & a \\ a & a & a & a \\ a & a & a & a \end{vmatrix}$$

$()$

13. $\displaystyle\sum_{n=}^{\infty} a_n x^n$ converges for $x = 3$.

We know $\displaystyle\sum_{n=}^{\infty} a_n x^n$

$x \quad x$

$x \quad x \qquad x \quad x$

x

14. $y \quad \left\{ \dfrac{x}{+x} \,\middle|\, x \in \mathbb{R} \right\}$

$y \quad \dfrac{x}{+x} \quad x \geq \quad \Rightarrow \quad x \quad \dfrac{y}{y}$

$$\dfrac{x}{x} \quad x \qquad \Rightarrow \qquad x \quad \dfrac{y}{+y}$$

$$x \geq \quad \dfrac{x}{+x} \qquad y$$

$$x \qquad \dfrac{x}{x} \qquad y$$

$()$

15. $\nabla \quad A \quad \begin{vmatrix} \vec{i} & \vec{j} & \vec{k} \\ \dfrac{\partial}{\partial x} & \dfrac{\partial}{\partial y} & \dfrac{\partial}{\partial z} \\ (xy+z) & (z+x) & (x+y) \end{vmatrix}$

$\vec{i}\,() \quad (\ )\vec{j} \quad (\ )\vec{k} \quad x \quad x$

$$\iiint () \; dx\,dy\,dz$$

16. (a) $U_n \quad \dfrac{n}{(\ ) \quad n}$

$$\dfrac{n(\ ) \quad n}{(\ )(\ ) \quad n \qquad n}$$

$$\dfrac{n(n)^{n}}{(\ )} \qquad \dfrac{(n)^{n}}{(\ )}$$

$$U_n \quad \dfrac{((n+)\ )^{n+}}{\{(\ n\ )\ \}}$$

$$\dfrac{U_{n+}}{U_n} \quad \dfrac{\{(n+)\ \}^{n+}}{\{(\ n\ )\ \}} \quad \dfrac{(\ )}{(n)^{n}}$$

$$\dfrac{U_{n+}}{U_n} \quad \dfrac{(n+)}{(\ n)(\ )n+}$$

$$\dfrac{U_{n+}}{U_n} \quad \dfrac{(n+)}{(\ n)}$$

$$\lim_{n\to\infty} \dfrac{U_{n+}}{U_n} \quad \lim_{n\to\infty} \dfrac{n+}{(\ n)} \quad -$$

16. ()

$$m * n \qquad m + n$$

$$e \qquad m$$

$$m * e \qquad m + e \quad \Rightarrow e$$

i.e., m' $\qquad m$

$$m * m'$$

$$\Rightarrow \qquad m + m'$$

$$\Rightarrow \qquad m' \qquad m$$

i.e.,

17. (a)
$$\lim_{x \to} \frac{\int^x \sqrt{+t}\, dt}{x}$$

$$\lim_{x \to} \frac{+x}{x} \qquad\qquad -$$

$$x$$

$$\lim_{x \to} \frac{x}{x}$$

17. () $\qquad f \qquad u\ v$

$$f' \qquad u\ v$$

$$u \quad a \quad v \quad f'(a) \neq \qquad \mu \quad x$$

$$a \quad \mu$$

$$g \quad a \quad \mu \ a + \mu \to \mathbb{R} \quad x \to x \quad \frac{f(x)}{f'(x)}$$

$$f$$

$$f'(x) \neq$$

$$a \quad \mu \ a \quad \mu$$

$$g(a) \quad a$$

$$g(x) = \frac{(f(x)) \quad (f)\ x (f)\ x}{(f(x))}$$

$$g'(a)$$

$$g' \qquad \qquad \delta \qquad \delta$$

$$\leq \mu \qquad g() \ <- \qquad a \quad \delta \quad x \quad a$$

$$\delta$$

$$x$$

$$g(x) \quad a \qquad g(x) \ g(a) \qquad g(a) \quad a$$

$$g'(c) \quad x \quad a$$

$$a\delta \quad c \quad a \quad \delta$$

$$\leq -\delta$$

$$\delta$$

$$f(x) \in \quad a \quad \delta \ a \quad \delta$$

$$g$$

$$a \quad \delta \ a \quad \delta \to a \quad \delta \ a \quad \delta$$

$$a \quad \delta \quad x_n \quad a \quad \delta \qquad \qquad x_n$$

$$(x_n)_{n \in \mathbb{N}} \qquad x \in a \quad \delta \ a$$

$$\delta \qquad x_n \qquad g(x_n) \qquad n \in \mathbb{N}$$

$$x \quad y \in a \quad \delta \ a \quad \delta$$

$$g(x) \quad g(y) \qquad g'(c) \quad x \quad y$$

$$x \quad c \quad y$$

$$\leq - \quad x \quad y \qquad x\ y \in a \quad \delta \ a \quad \delta$$

$$x_{n+} \quad x_{n+}$$

$$g(x_{n+}) \quad (g\ x)_n \quad \leq - \quad x_{n+} \quad x_n$$

$$j \in \mathbb{N},$$

$$x_{n+k} \quad x_n \ \leq \sum_{j=}^{k} x_{n+j+} \quad x_{n+j}$$

$$\sum_{j=}^{k} \left(-\right)^{j} \quad x_{n+} \quad x_n$$

$$\frac{\left(-\right)^{k}}{-} \quad x_{n+} \quad x_n$$

$$x_{n+} \quad x_n$$

$$\left(-\right) \quad x \quad x$$

$$()$$

$$\left(-\right)^{n} \quad g(x) \quad x$$

$$g(x) \quad x \qquad f(x)$$

$$x \quad a$$

$$g(x) \quad x \quad \neq$$

$(x_n)_{n \in \mathbb{N}}$

$g(b) \qquad g\left(\lim_{n \to \infty} x_n\right)$

$\lim_{n \to \infty}(\ g) x_n$

g

$\lim_{n \to \infty} x_{n+}$

b

$g(b) \quad b \quad f b) \qquad\qquad b \quad a$

18. $()\quad f(x\ y)\qquad x\quad x\ y\ y$

$f(x\ y)$

$f_x \qquad \Rightarrow \quad x \quad xy \qquad (\quad i)$

$f_y \qquad \Rightarrow \quad x \quad y \qquad (\quad ii)$

$(\qquad i)(\quad ii)$

$y \qquad x$

$x \quad x(\ x\ )$

x

x

y

$i.e.,()$

$f_{xx} \qquad x \quad y$

$f_{xy} \qquad x$

f_{yy}

$f(x,\ y)$

$f_{xx}\ f_{yy}\ f_{xy}$

$(\quad x\quad y)\quad x$

$x\quad y\quad x$

$x\quad x\quad y$

$()\ ($

$)$

18. (b) $f(x\ y)\quad x\quad y\quad x\qquad y$

$f_x \quad x \qquad f_x \qquad \Rightarrow x \quad \pm$

$f_y \quad y \qquad f_y \qquad \Rightarrow y \quad \pm$

$()()()$

$()$

$f_{xx} \qquad x \qquad f_{yy} \qquad y \quad f_{xy}$

$f_{xx} f_{yy}(\ f_{xy}) \qquad (\ x)(\ y)$

xy

$0 \qquad f_{xx}\ f_{yy}(\ f_{xy})$

$f_{xx}()$

$f(x\ y)()$

$f_{xx} f_{yy}\ \left(f_{xy}\right)\Big|_{()}$

$f_{xx}\Big|_{()}$

$f(x\ y)()$

$f(x\ y)\big|_{0} \qquad ()$

$f(x\ y)\big|_{(} \qquad 0$

19. $()\quad \displaystyle\int_{x=}\int_{y=\sqrt{\ x}} (e^y)\ dy\,dx$

$\displaystyle\int_{x=}\int_{y=\sqrt{\ x}} e^{\ y}\,dy\,dx$

$\displaystyle\int_{x=} \left[\frac{e^{\ y}}{\ }\right]_{\sqrt{\ x}} dx\,dx$

$\displaystyle\int_{x=} \left(\frac{e}{\ } \quad \frac{e^{\sqrt{\ x}}}{\ }\right) dx$

$\displaystyle\int_{x=} \frac{e}{\ }\,dx \quad -\int e^{\sqrt{\ x}}\,dx$

$\dfrac{e}{\ } \quad -\int e(\quad)x\,dz \qquad\qquad x = z$

$\dfrac{e}{\ } + -\int z\,e^{\ z}\,dz$

$\dfrac{e}{\ } + -\left[\dfrac{z\,e^{\ z}}{\ } \quad \dfrac{e^{\ z}}{\ }\right]$

$$\frac{e}{} + \left[\frac{e^{\sqrt{x}}}{}\left(\sqrt{x} - \right)\right]$$

$$\frac{e}{} + -\left(- \right) - e + \frac{}{} e$$

$$\frac{}{} e -$$

$$\frac{}{}(\ \theta)$$

19. (b) $z + \sqrt{x \ y} \qquad z \ \sqrt{x + y}$

$$+\sqrt{x \ y} \qquad \sqrt{x + y}$$

$$\sqrt{x + y} \quad \sqrt{x + y}$$

$$() \quad \left\{\sqrt{x + y} \quad \sqrt{x \ y}\right\}$$

$$x + y + x \ y(\ \sqrt{x})(+ y \ x \ y)$$

$$\frac{(\sqrt{x} +)(y \ )x \ y}{(\sqrt{x} +)(x) \ y}$$

$$x \ y$$
$$x \ y$$
$$x \ y$$

$$x \ y$$

$$x \ y$$
$$x \ y$$

$$x \quad \pm\sqrt{}$$
$$x$$
$$x \ y$$
$$y \qquad x$$

$$y \quad \pm\sqrt{x}$$

$$y \qquad \sqrt{x} \quad \sqrt{x}$$

20.
$$z$$

$$z \qquad z$$

$$x \quad y$$

$$z = \sqrt{x \ y} \ (\qquad\qquad \geq)$$

$$\frac{\partial z}{\partial x} = \frac{x}{\sqrt{x \ y}}$$

$$\frac{\partial z}{\partial y} = \frac{y}{\sqrt{x \ y}}$$

$$\iint_{x+y\le} \sqrt{+\left(\frac{\partial z}{\partial x}\right) +\left(\frac{\partial z}{\partial y}\right)}\, dxdy$$

$$\iint_{x+y\le} \sqrt{+\frac{x}{x \ y} +\frac{y}{x \ y}}\, dxdy$$

$$\iint_{x+y\le} \sqrt{+\frac{x}{x \ y} +\frac{y}{x \ y}}\, dxdy$$

$$\int^{\pi}\int^{\sqrt{}} \sqrt{+\frac{r \ (\ )\theta}{r} +\frac{(\ )\theta}{r}}\, r\,dr\,d\theta$$

$$\int^{\pi}\int^{\sqrt{}} \sqrt{+\frac{r}{r}}\, r\,dr\,d\theta$$

$$\int^{\pi}\int^{\sqrt{}} \sqrt{\frac{}{r}}\, r\,dr\,d\theta$$

$$\int^{\pi}\int^{\sqrt{}} \frac{r}{\sqrt{r}}\, dr\,d\theta$$

$$\int^{\pi} (\ )\ r \ \Big|_{r=}^{\sqrt{}}\, d\theta$$

$$\int^{\pi} (\ )+ \ d\theta$$

$$\pi$$

$$\pi$$

21.
$$\frac{d\ y}{dx} \qquad y$$

$$m$$

$$\Rightarrow \quad m \quad \pm$$
$$y \quad c\,e^x \quad c\,e^x$$
$$y \quad \underline{\qquad}()$$
$$m$$
$$y \quad c\,e^x \quad c\,e^{-x}$$
$$\Rightarrow \quad y \quad c\,e^x \quad c\,e^{-x}$$
$$y() \qquad \Rightarrow c \quad c \qquad (\ i)$$
$$y() \quad \alpha \Rightarrow c \quad c \quad \alpha\ (\ ii)$$
$$(\ i)(\ ii)$$
$$c \qquad \alpha\ c \qquad \alpha$$
$$y \quad (\ \alpha)e^x(\ \alpha)e^{-x}$$
$$\alpha \in)$$

22. ()

$$x\,\frac{d\ y}{dx} \quad x\,\frac{dy}{dx} + \ y$$
$$\frac{}{x}\,\frac{d\ y}{dx} \quad \frac{}{x}\,\frac{dy}{dx} + \frac{y}{x} \qquad (\ i)$$
$$x \quad x$$

$$y \quad x \quad x$$
$$x$$

$$x \quad x \qquad (\ ii)$$
$$y \quad x \quad x$$
$$y \qquad x$$
$$y \qquad x \quad x$$

()

$$\frac{}{x}\Big[\ +\ x\ +\ x\Big]\ \frac{}{x}\Big[\ +\ x\ \Big]$$
$$+\frac{}{x}\Big[Ax + Bx\ \Big] = \phi$$
$$\frac{}{x} + \frac{}{x} = b \qquad (\ iii)$$
$$(\ ii)(\ iii)$$
$$\Rightarrow \qquad \frac{}{x} \quad \phi \quad \Rightarrow \frac{d}{dx} \quad \frac{\phi}{}\ x$$
$$\frac{x}{} + c$$
$$x + (\ x)$$
$$\frac{x}{} + c$$

$$0$$
$$y \qquad x \quad x$$
$$c\ x + c\ x \qquad \frac{x}{} + \frac{x}{}$$
$$c\ x + c\ x\ +\frac{x}{}$$

22. ()

$$\frac{dy}{dx} + \frac{}{x}\cdot \quad y \quad x \quad y$$
$$y\frac{dy}{dx} + \frac{}{x} \quad y \quad x$$
$$v \qquad y \qquad \frac{dv}{dx} \qquad y\frac{dy}{dx}$$
$$\frac{dv}{dx} + \frac{}{x}\cdot v \quad x$$

$$e^{\int \frac{-\,dx}{x}} \quad x$$

$$\Rightarrow \qquad v\ x \quad \frac{x}{}$$
$$y \quad \frac{x}{}$$

23. () $\quad u\ i.e.$

$$u \quad \frac{u}{\|u\|} \quad \frac{()}{\sqrt{}} \quad \left(\frac{}{\sqrt{}}\ \frac{}{\sqrt{}}\ \frac{}{\sqrt{}}\right)$$

$$w \quad v \quad v\ u \quad u$$

$$(\ ) - \frac{}{\sqrt{}}\left(\frac{}{\sqrt{}}\ \frac{}{\sqrt{}}\ \frac{}{\sqrt{}}\right)0$$
$$\left(\frac{}{} - \frac{}{} - \frac{}{}\right)$$
$$\left(\frac{}{} - \frac{}{} - \frac{}{}\right)$$

$i.e.$

$$w \quad \frac{w}{\|w\|} \quad \frac{\left(\frac{}{} - \frac{}{} - \frac{}{}\right)}{\sqrt{}} \quad \left(\frac{}{\sqrt{}}\ \frac{}{\sqrt{}}\ \frac{}{\sqrt{}}\right)$$

$i.e.$

$$\left\{\left(\frac{}{\sqrt{}}\ \frac{}{\sqrt{}}\ \frac{}{\sqrt{}}\right)\left(\frac{}{\sqrt{}}\ \frac{}{\sqrt{}}\ \frac{}{\sqrt{}}\right)\right\}$$

23. () u *i.e.*

$$v \quad \frac{u}{\|u\|} \quad \frac{0}{\sqrt{\;+}} \quad \frac{}{\sqrt{}}0$$

$w \quad u \quad u$

$v \quad v \quad () \qquad -\frac{}{\sqrt{}}0\frac{}{\sqrt{}}$

$$() \quad 0 - - \quad = \left(- - \frac{-}{}\right)$$

w *i.e.*

$$v \quad \frac{w}{\|w\|} \quad \frac{\left(- - \dfrac{-}{}\right)}{\sqrt{}} \quad -(\; - \;)$$

$w \quad u (\; u \; v)v (\; u \; v)v$

$\Rightarrow \quad w \quad 0 \qquad \sqrt{\;}\cdot\frac{}{\sqrt{}}0$

$\qquad 0$

$\qquad w \; 0$

i.e.

$$\left\{\frac{}{\sqrt{}}0 \quad (\;)0 \quad - \quad \right\}$$

24. 0 $\qquad G \qquad G$
$\qquad G \qquad G$
$\qquad G$

G
g
$\qquad \in G$
$\qquad h$
$(h) \quad g$
$\qquad h \in G$

24. () $\qquad A$

$B \quad A$

$\qquad A \qquad \in A$
$B \qquad \in A$
$($
$) \qquad\qquad A$
$\qquad a \in A \; a \neq \qquad n \geq \quad n\text{-}$
$\qquad a \quad na \qquad na \neq$

$\qquad n \geq \qquad a \quad \infty \quad A$
$a \neq \qquad\qquad A$

A

$\qquad B$

$() \qquad \neq ()$
$\qquad B$
$B \qquad\qquad A$

25. 0

$\qquad R. \qquad\qquad x \; y$
$\qquad xa \qquad ya(\qquad x \; y)a \; xa$
$ya \qquad\qquad I$
$\qquad\qquad a$
$\qquad x \; I \qquad\qquad xa)$
$(x)a \qquad\qquad x \; I$

$\qquad\qquad R$
$\qquad r \; R \quad x \; I$
$(\quad rx)a \; r(xa) \; r$
$rx \; xr \; I \qquad\qquad I$

25. () $\qquad\qquad \mathbf{R}$

$\qquad)()($
$()()()$
$\qquad\qquad i.e.()$
$\quad 0 \; 0$

$u \quad \frac{0}{\|0\;\|} \quad \frac{}{\sqrt{}}()$

$$\left(\frac{}{\sqrt{}} \; \frac{}{\sqrt{}} \; \frac{}{\sqrt{}}\right)$$

$w \quad v \qquad u \; v \quad u$

$()$

$\qquad w \quad \frac{w}{\|w\|} \quad \frac{()-}{\sqrt{}}$

$\frac{}{\sqrt{}}()-$

$$\left\{\frac{}{\sqrt{}}0 \quad (\;)\; - \quad \right\}$$

26. () P

n

$\qquad\qquad\qquad\qquad\qquad\qquad x_j$

$\qquad\qquad\qquad\qquad y_j \qquad\qquad X \quad PY$

$Y \quad P \quad X$

$\qquad\qquad\qquad\qquad\qquad Q(X) \quad X \quad AX$

$(Y^l P^l)\, A\,(PY) \quad Y(P\,AP)\,Y$

$D \quad P\,AP \qquad A \quad D$

$A \qquad D \qquad\qquad\qquad\qquad\qquad A$

$\qquad\qquad\qquad D$

$\qquad\qquad\qquad\qquad\qquad A \quad D$

$\qquad\qquad\qquad\qquad\qquad\qquad D \quad PAP$

$\qquad\qquad\qquad\qquad P \quad A \quad D$

$\qquad\qquad\qquad\qquad\qquad\qquad\qquad D$

$A \quad PDP \qquad P$

$\qquad\qquad P \qquad P$

26. ()

$\qquad(x, y, z) \quad (x + y, y - z)$

$0 \; 000$

$\qquad 0 \; 000$

$\qquad\qquad 0 \; 000$

$$\begin{bmatrix} & - \\ & \end{bmatrix}$$

27. ()

$\qquad(x, y, z) \quad (x + y, y + z, z - x)$

i.e.   () ()

$\qquad$ () ()

$\qquad$ () ()

() ()()

$\qquad\qquad u \quad \dfrac{0}{\sqrt{}} \qquad \dfrac{}{\sqrt{}} 0$

$\qquad w \quad v \qquad v \quad u \quad u$

$\qquad\qquad 0 \qquad -\dfrac{}{\sqrt{}} 0 \sqrt{}$

$$\left(\dfrac{-}{} - \right)$$

$$u \quad \dfrac{\left\langle \dfrac{-}{}\,-\,- \right\rangle}{\left\| \left\langle \dfrac{-}{}\,-\,- \right\rangle \right\|} \qquad \left(\dfrac{-}{\sqrt{}}\ \dfrac{}{\sqrt{}}\ \dfrac{}{\sqrt{}} \right)$$

27. () () $\qquad\qquad av \quad bv \quad cv$

$\qquad()\qquad\qquad a(\ ) \qquad b(\ )$

$\qquad\qquad\qquad\qquad\qquad\qquad c\,(\ )$

$\qquad() \quad (\qquad a + b + c,\ a + b,\ a)$

$\qquad\qquad\qquad a \qquad a + b$

$\Rightarrow \qquad\qquad b$

$\qquad a + b + c$

$\Rightarrow \qquad\qquad c$

i.e.   ()$\qquad\qquad v \quad v \quad v$

$\qquad \tau(\ )\ (\qquad v\,)(\quad v\,)(\quad v\,)$

$\qquad\qquad\qquad\qquad 00()$

$\qquad\qquad\qquad\qquad 00()$

$\qquad\qquad\qquad\qquad ()$

28. () $\qquad\qquad\qquad\qquad\qquad R$

$\forall x\ \in R\,\forall\varepsilon >\quad \exists\delta >\quad \forall x \in R$

$\left[x \quad x \ <\delta \Rightarrow x \quad x \ <\varepsilon \right]$

$\qquad\qquad x \qquad a \quad x \qquad\qquad \delta$

$(\quad \varepsilon \quad a)(\qquad\qquad \delta \qquad\qquad x \qquad a$

$)\qquad\qquad x \in R \qquad\qquad x \quad x \qquad \delta$

$\qquad x \quad x \qquad x \quad x \qquad a \quad x\, x \quad a$

$x \quad x \ (= x +)\quad x \quad x$

$$\leq\ a\ x\ \ x\ <\ a\delta\leq\ a\frac{\varepsilon}{a}=\varepsilon$$

R *i.e.,*

$$\exists\varepsilon>\ \ \forall\delta>\ \ \exists x\ \in R\ \exists x\in R$$

$$\Big[\ x\ \ x\ \ <\delta\quad\ \ x\ \ x\ \geq\varepsilon\Big]$$

$$\varepsilon\qquad\qquad\delta\qquad\quad x\qquad\quad\delta$$
$$x\ \ x\ \ \delta/2\qquad\quad x\ \ x\ \ \delta\qquad\delta$$

$$x\ \ x\ \ =\left|\left(\frac{}{\delta}+\frac{\delta}{}\right)\ \ \left(\frac{}{\delta}\right)\right|$$

$$=\ +\frac{\delta}{}\ >\ \ =\varepsilon$$

$$(\qquad\qquad\qquad x\qquad\qquad\delta$$

28. () $\qquad\quad f_n\ f\ R\rightarrow($ $\qquad\quad R.\rho)($ $\qquad,$

$d)$ $\qquad\qquad\qquad\qquad\qquad f_n\rightarrow f$

$$f_n$$
$$\in\qquad\qquad N\qquad\quad n$$
$$N\qquad\quad d(f(x)\ f_n(x))\quad\in\qquad x$$
$$N\qquad\quad f_n$$
$$x$$
$$\delta\qquad\qquad\qquad\rho(\ x\ x\ )\quad\delta$$
$$d(f_n(x)\ f_n(x\ ))\quad\in\qquad\qquad x$$
$$\in\qquad\qquad\delta$$
$$\rho(\ x\ x\ )\quad\delta\Rightarrow d(f(x)\ f(x\ ))\quad d\ (f(x)$$
$$f_n(x))\quad d(f_n(x)\ f_n(x\ ))\quad d(f_n(x\ )\ f(x\ ))\quad\in$$
$$f$$
$$x$$

$$R$$
$$d(f_n(x)\ f(x))\quad\in\qquad\quad x\qquad\quad x\in f_{n-1}$$
$$(\ \in(\ f_n(x\ )))\subseteq f\ \ (\ \in(f(x\ )))\qquad f$$
$$(\ \in(f(x\ )))\qquad\qquad x$$
$$\in(y)\qquad\qquad\qquad\qquad\in$$
$$y$$

29. () $\qquad\beta\qquad\quad A\qquad\quad\beta\leq x\qquad\ x\in A$
$$a\beta\leq ax\qquad\quad x\in A$$
$$a\beta\qquad\qquad\quad aA\qquad\qquad\quad w$$
$$aA\qquad\qquad\quad w\leq ax$$
$$\Rightarrow\frac{w}{a}\leq x\qquad\quad x\in A\qquad\qquad\frac{w}{a}$$

$$A\qquad\qquad\qquad\qquad\frac{w}{a}\leq\beta\Rightarrow w$$
$$\leq a\beta\qquad\quad a\beta$$
$$aA$$

29. () $\qquad\qquad\qquad\qquad f(x)$
$$x_n\quad y_{n}\ n$$
$$f(x_n)\ \ f(y_n)\ _n$$

$$f(x_n)\ \ f(y_n)\ _n\qquad\qquad\qquad\qquad\text{\textit{i.e.,}}$$
$$\in\qquad\qquad\qquad N\in\mathbb{N}$$
$$n\quad N\qquad\qquad f(x_n)\quad f(y_n)$$
$$f(x_n)\quad f(y_n)\quad\in$$
$$\in\mathbb{N}\qquad\qquad n\quad N$$
$$f(\ x_{n_i})\ \ (f\ y)_{n_i}\ >\in$$
$$N\quad n\qquad\qquad n\quad N$$
$$f(\ x_{n_i})\ \ (f\ y)_{n_i}\ >\in$$
$$n\ \ \rightarrow\infty$$
$$f(\ x_{n_i})\ \ (f\ y)_{n_i}\ >\in\qquad\quad n_i$$
$$x_n\quad y_{n}\ n$$
$$\{x_{n_i}\quad y_{n_i}\}_n$$

$$f(x)$$
$$\in\qquad\qquad\qquad\delta$$
$$f(s)\ \ f(t)\quad\in\qquad\qquad s\ \ t\quad\delta$$
$$f(\ x_{n_i})\ \ (f\ y)_{n_i}\ <\in$$
$$x_{n_i}\quad y_{n_i}\ <\delta\qquad\quad n_i\qquad\qquad\qquad{}_x\in\mathbb{N}$$

$$f(x_n)\quad f(y_n)\ _n$$

$$x_n\quad y_{n}\ n$$
$$f(x_n)\ \ f(y_n)\ _n$$
$$f(x)$$

$$f(x)$$
$$\in$$
$$\delta\qquad\qquad s\ t\qquad\qquad s\ t\quad\delta$$
$$f(s)\ \ f(t)\quad\in$$
$$\delta_i\qquad\qquad\delta_i\rightarrow$$
$$\delta_i\qquad\qquad\qquad x_i\ \ y_i$$
$$x_i\ \ y_i\quad\delta_i\qquad f(x_i)\ \ f(y_i)\quad\delta$$
$$\delta_i\qquad\qquad\quad x_i\ \ y_i$$
$$f(x_i)\ \ f(y_i)$$

$$f(x)$$

()

IIT–JAM
Joint Admission Test for
M.Sc. (MATHEMATICS)-2011

1. $\quad a_n \quad \displaystyle\sum_{k=}^{n} \frac{n}{n+k} \qquad n \in \mathbb{N}$

a_n

∞

2.

$x \quad x$

3. $\qquad \displaystyle\lim_{n\to\infty}\sum_{k=}^{n} \frac{}{\sqrt{n+kn}}$

$\left(\sqrt{\ }-\right) \qquad\qquad \sqrt{\ }-$

$-\sqrt{\ } \qquad\qquad -\left(\sqrt{\ }-\right)$

4. $\quad V$

$x \quad x \quad y \quad z \qquad y \quad z$

$$\iiint_V y\, dx\, dy\, dz$$

$- \qquad\qquad -$

$-$

5. $\qquad y(x)$

$\dfrac{d\,y}{dx}+\dfrac{dy}{dx}+ \ y=$

$y(\ )= \quad \dfrac{dy}{dx}(\ )=$

$e^{\,x} \qquad\qquad (\ x)\ e^{\,x}$

$e^{-2x} \quad x \qquad\qquad e^{\,x} \quad xe^{\,x}$

6. $\quad y^a$

$xy\, dx\, (\quad x \quad y)\, dy$

a

7. $\quad \vec{F}=ayi+zj+xk \qquad C$

$x \quad y$

$z \qquad \displaystyle\oint_C \vec{F}\ \vec{dr}=\pi \qquad\qquad a$

$-$

8. $\qquad\qquad \vec{F}=\left(ax+y+a\right)i+j$

$-(x+y)k \qquad a \qquad\qquad \vec{F}$

$\vec{F}= \qquad\qquad a$

$-$

9. $\quad G$

$\mathbb{R} \quad H \quad A \in$

$G(\quad A) \qquad H \quad A \in G \quad A$

$H \qquad\qquad G$

$H \qquad\qquad G$

$P \quad Q$

$P \qquad Q$

$P \qquad Q$

$P \quad Q$

10. $\quad n \in \mathbb{N} \quad n\mathbb{Z} \quad nk \quad k \in \mathbb{Z}$

$\mathbb{Z} \quad \mathbb{Z} \qquad \mathbb{Z} \quad \mathbb{Z}$

()

$()$

11. A (A)
(A) A

A I

(i)(i)
(i)(i)
(i)(i)
(i)(i)

12. T $\mathbb{R}^n \to \mathbb{R}^n$

$n \geq$ $k \leq n$

E v v $v_k \subseteq \mathbb{R}^n$ F Tv Tv_2 Tv_k

E F

F E

E F

F E

13. $n \neq m$ T $\mathbb{R}^n \to \mathbb{R}^m$ $\mathbb{R}^m \to \mathbb{R}^n$
T T

(T) n (T) m
(T) m (T) n
(T) n (T) n
(T) m (T) m

14. x

$$\sum_{n=}^{\infty} \frac{n}{(\,n+\,)}(x-\,)^n$$

)

)

15. $\mathbb{R}$

$$E = \left\{ \frac{n}{n+} \ \ n \in \mathbb{N} \right\} \quad F \quad \left\{ \frac{}{-x} \ \ \leq x < \right\}$$

E F

E F

E F

E F

16. a_n

$$\sum_{n=}^{\infty} a_n$$

k_n

$$\sum_{n=}^{\infty} a_{k_n}$$

f $\to \mathbb{R}$
$f'(x) \leq$ $x \in ()$ $f()$
$f()$ $f(x)$ x $x \in$

17. f

I

$x \in I$ a $b \subset I$ $f'(a)$ $f'(b)$
$c \in (a\ b)$

$f(c)$ $\underset{a \leq x \leq b}{} f(x)$

$f(\ a\ b) \to \mathbb{R}$
f'

($a\ b$)

$$\lim_{h\to} \frac{f(x+h)-\ f(x)+f(x-h)}{h} = f''(x)$$

$x \in (a\ b)$

18.

$u(x\ y)$ x y x y $xy(\,x, y) \in \mathbb{R}$

19. φ $a\ b \to \mathbb{R}$
$c\ d$ $\varphi(x)$ $a \leq x \leq b$ f $c\ d$
$\to \mathbb{R}$ g $a\ b \to \mathbb{R}$

$$g(x) \quad \int_{c}^{\varphi(x)} f(t)\,dt \quad x \in a\ b$$

g $g'(x)$
$f(\varphi(x))\ \varphi'(x)$ $x \in a\ b$

f $\to \mathbb{R}$ $\int^{x} f(t)\,dt = \frac{\sqrt{}}{} x$

$x \in \mathbb{R}$ $f\left(-\right)$

20.

$$z = -\sqrt{x + y}$$

$$z \qquad x \qquad y$$

21.

$$y - x\frac{dy}{dx} = \frac{dy}{dx} y\ e^{y}$$

$$\frac{dy}{dx} = \frac{x + y +}{x + y +}$$

22. $\qquad\qquad b$

$$x\ \frac{d\ y}{dx} + x\frac{dy}{dx} + y = \qquad < x < b$$

$$y() \qquad\qquad y(b)$$

$$v(x) \qquad\qquad y(x) \qquad e^{x}\ v(x)$$

$$\frac{d\ y}{dx} - \frac{dy}{dx} + \ y = \left(\ x + \ x\ + \ x\ \right)e^{x}$$

23.

$$\int_{-} \left(\int_{-x}^{-x} f(x\ y)\,dy\right) dx$$

$$\vec{F} = \left(x\ - xy\ \right)i + y\ j$$

$$\int_{C} \vec{F}\ \vec{dr}$$

$$C$$

$$x$$

$$y \quad \sqrt{\ - x}$$

24.

$$\vec{F} = \left(x\ + y - \ \right)i + \ xy\,j + \left(\ xz + z\ \right)k$$

$$\iint_{S}\left(\nabla \times \vec{F}\right) n\,dS \qquad S$$

$$z \qquad -\sqrt{x + y} \qquad\qquad xy$$

$$n \qquad\qquad S$$

$$k$$

$$\sum_{n=}^{\infty} \frac{x}{\sqrt{n}\left(\ + n^{p}x\ \right)}$$

$$\mathbb{R} \qquad p$$

25. $\qquad\qquad c$

$$\begin{matrix} x & y & z \\ x & y & cz \\ x & cy & z \end{matrix}$$

$$V$$

$$n \geq \qquad\qquad\qquad\qquad V^{n}$$

$$\mathbb{R} \quad \mathbb{R}$$

$$W = \left\{ p \in V\ \int p(x)\,dx + \ \right\}$$

$$W \qquad\qquad\qquad V$$

$$(W) \quad n$$

26. $\quad A \quad (\qquad\qquad\qquad\qquad A)$
$\quad (\qquad\qquad\qquad A)$
$\quad v \qquad v \qquad\qquad\qquad \mathbb{R}^{n}\ n \geq$
$\qquad\qquad v$
v

$$T\ \mathbb{R}^{n} \to \mathbb{R}^{n} \qquad\qquad T$$

$$T\ Tv_{1} = v_{2} \qquad T$$

27. $\quad E \qquad\qquad \mathbb{R}$

$$E$$

$$f(\ a\ b) \to \mathbb{R}$$

$$f$$

$$g \quad a\ b$$

$$\to \mathbb{R} \qquad g(x) \quad f(x) \qquad x \in (a\ b)$$

28. $\quad \mathbb{R}$

$$(\qquad\qquad x,\ y\ t)(\ x'\ y'\ t') \quad \mathbb{R}$$

$$(x\ y\ t)(\ x'\ y'\ t') \quad \left(x + x'\ y + y'\ t + t + -\left(x'y - xy'\right)\right)$$

$$(\qquad\qquad \mathbb{R}\ )$$

$$k \in \mathbb{N} \qquad k\mathbb{Z} \qquad kn \quad n \in \mathbb{Z}$$

$$m\ n \in \mathbb{N} \qquad\qquad I \quad m\mathbb{Z} \bigcap n\mathbb{Z}$$

$$\mathbb{Z} \qquad\qquad\qquad\qquad\qquad I$$

29. $\quad G \qquad\qquad\qquad\qquad p \qquad\qquad p$

$$x \in G \qquad\qquad y \in G$$

$$xy \quad yx \quad G$$

ANSWERS

1	**2**	**3**	**4**	**5**	**6**	**7**	**8**	**9**	**10**
11	**12**	**13**	**14**	**15**					

SOME SELECTED EXPLANATORY ANSWERS

1. $\quad a_n \quad \dfrac{n}{n+}+\dfrac{n}{n+}+\quad \dfrac{n}{n+n}$

$\dfrac{n}{n}+\dfrac{n}{n}+\quad \dfrac{n}{n}=\dfrac{n\,n}{n}\quad \forall\ n\in$

$\Rightarrow a_n \qquad n\in$

i.e.

$\qquad a_n\to \qquad n\to\infty.$

2.

$\quad x\quad x \qquad\qquad f() \qquad\qquad f()$

$\Rightarrow$

$\qquad f'(x)\quad x \qquad\qquad \forall\ x$

i.e. $\qquad\qquad\qquad\qquad\qquad x$

3. $\qquad\qquad \displaystyle\lim_{n\to\infty}\sum_{k=}^{n}\frac{}{\sqrt{n^{}+kn}}$

$\qquad\qquad \displaystyle\lim_{n\to\infty}\sum_{k=}^{n}\frac{}{\sqrt{\ +\dfrac{k}{n}}}\times\frac{}{n}$

$\qquad\qquad \displaystyle\int \frac{}{\sqrt{\ +x}}\,dx \qquad \sqrt{\ +x}\Big|$

$\qquad\qquad \sqrt{\ }- \qquad \left(\sqrt{\ }-\ \right)$

4. $\displaystyle\iiint_{V} y\,dx\,dy\,dz \qquad \int_{x=}\int_{y=}\int_{z=}^{-y} y\,dz\,dy\,dx$

$\qquad \displaystyle\int_{x=}\int_{y=} y(\ -y)\,dy\,dx \qquad \int_{x=} \frac{y\ \ y}{}\Big|\,dx$

$\qquad \left[---\right]=\left[\frac{-}{}\right]=-$

5. $\qquad\qquad \dfrac{d\ y}{dx}+\dfrac{dy}{dx}+\ y=$

$\qquad (\qquad\qquad C\quad C\,x)e^{\ x}$

$\therefore\ y() \qquad \Rightarrow\quad C$

$\quad y'() \qquad \Rightarrow\ (\quad C\,x)()\qquad C$

$C \qquad \Rightarrow\quad C$

$\quad (\qquad\qquad\qquad x\ )\quad e^{\ x}$

6. $\qquad\qquad xy\,dx\,(\quad x\quad y\ )dy$

$\qquad\qquad\qquad dx \qquad dy$

$\qquad\qquad\qquad\qquad xy \qquad y \qquad x$

$\dfrac{\partial}{\partial}=\ x \qquad \dfrac{\partial}{\partial x}\quad x$

$-\left(\dfrac{\partial}{\partial x}-\dfrac{\partial}{\partial y}\right)\quad \dfrac{-\ x}{xy}=\dfrac{-}{y}$

$e^{-\int\frac{}{y}\,dy}\qquad \dfrac{}{y}=y^{-}=y^{a}\Rightarrow a$

7. $\displaystyle\oint_{C}\vec{F}\ \overrightarrow{dr} \qquad \oint_{C} a\,y\,dx$

$\displaystyle\int_{\theta=}^{\pi} a\quad \theta\big(-\quad \theta\,d\theta\big) \qquad -a\int_{\theta=}^{\pi}\quad \theta\,d\theta$

$\qquad\qquad\qquad -\ a-\dfrac{\pi}{}=\pi$

$()$

$\Rightarrow \qquad\qquad a\pi\quad \pi\Rightarrow a$

8. $\vec{F}=(ax+y+a)i+j-(x+y)k$

$\vec{F}\quad \begin{vmatrix} i & j & k \\ \dfrac{\partial}{\partial x} & \dfrac{\partial}{\partial y} & \dfrac{\partial}{\partial z} \\ ax+y+a & & -(x+y) \end{vmatrix}$

$-i+j-k$

$$\Rightarrow \quad \vec{F} \quad \vec{F} \quad -ax - y - a + \ + x + y =$$
$$x(\quad a) \ (\qquad a)$$
$$x \neq \ \Rightarrow a$$

9. $\quad G$

$H \quad A \in G \ (\quad A)$

$A \quad A \in H \quad \Rightarrow (\quad A)(\qquad A)$

$(\qquad A A) \ (\quad A)(\quad A)$

i.e. H

$$\begin{bmatrix} \ \\ \ \end{bmatrix} \in H \qquad\qquad H$$

H

$A \in H \ \Rightarrow (\quad A)$

$XAX \qquad X \in G$

$(\quad XAX \ ) \ (\quad X)(\quad A)(\quad X \ )$

$(\quad X)(\quad X \ )$

$\Rightarrow \qquad XAX^{-1} \in H$

$\Rightarrow H \qquad\qquad G$

H

$H \quad A \in G \quad A$

H

$$\begin{bmatrix} \ \\ \ \end{bmatrix} \in H$$

H

$XAX \ \in H \qquad X \in G \qquad A \in H$

i.e. $H \qquad\qquad G$

i.e.

10. $\quad \dfrac{Z}{Z}$ $\qquad\qquad z$

$$\dfrac{Z}{Z}$$

i.e. $\qquad\qquad \dfrac{Z}{Z}$

$$\dfrac{Z}{Z}$$

---

i.e. $\quad \phi(n) \quad$ *i.e.* $\phi()$ $\qquad \left(-- \right)\left(-- \right)$

$$- \ - =$$

i.e. $\qquad\qquad \dfrac{Z}{Z}$

11. $\qquad A \ ($ $\qquad\qquad A)$

$(\qquad A) \qquad \Rightarrow$

A

A

i.e. $(A \quad I)$

i.e. $A \ I \quad A \ I \quad A \quad A \ I$

$\Rightarrow A \quad I \quad A \quad I$

$(\qquad A \quad I) \ (\qquad A \quad I)$

i.e. $\qquad\qquad A \quad I$

14. $\qquad\qquad \displaystyle\sum \dfrac{n}{(\ n+ \ )}\left(x- \ \right)^{n}$

i.e. $\quad u_n \quad \dfrac{n}{(\ n+ \ )}\left(x- \ \right)^{3n}$

$u_n \quad \dfrac{(n+ \ )}{(\ n+ \ )}\left(x- \ \right)^{(n+ \ )}$

$\dfrac{u_n}{u_{n+}} \quad \dfrac{n}{(\ n+ \ )} \dfrac{(\ n+ \ )}{(n+ \ )} \dfrac{ }{(x- \ )}$

$\dfrac{u_n}{\underset{n\to\infty}{u_{n+}}} \quad \underset{n\to\infty}{\dfrac{n}{(n+ \ )}} \dfrac{(\ n+ \ )}{(\ n+ \ )} \dfrac{ }{(x- \ )}$

$$\overline{(x- \ )}$$

$$\left| \dfrac{ }{(x- \ )} \right| >$$

$\Rightarrow \left| x- \ \right| < \quad \Rightarrow (\qquad x)$

$\Rightarrow \quad x$

i.e. $\quad x \in ()$

i.e. $\qquad x$

$$\sum \frac{n}{(\ n+\ )}(x-\ )^{\,n}$$

(i)e.

$$\lim_{n\to\infty} \frac{n}{(\ n+\ )}$$

x

x

$$\lim_{n\to\infty} \frac{n}{(\ n+\ )} \to$$

$$\lim_{n\to\infty} n\,\frac{n}{(\ n+\ )} \xrightarrow{\ \phi\ } -$$

i.e.

$x \in)$

15. $\mathbb{R}$

$E\quad \left\{ \dfrac{n}{n+}\ \ n\in\mathbb{N} \right\}\quad F\quad \left\{ \dfrac{}{-x}\ \ \le x< \right\}$

$E\quad \left\{ --- \quad \right\}$

i.e. E $-$

$\notin E$ *i.e.* E

E

$F\quad \left\{ \dfrac{}{-x}\ \ \le x< \right\}$

$$\lim_{x\to}\ \frac{}{-x} \to \infty$$

16. a_n a a a

$$\sum_{n=}^{\infty} a_n$$

$($

$)$

a_n

i.e. k_n

i.e. k k a_{kn}

S_n

—

Σa_n

i.e. $\sum a_{k_n}$

$f \qquad \to \mathbb{R}$

$f'(x) \le \qquad x \in ()$

$f()\qquad f()$

$f'(x)\quad \dfrac{f(\ )-f(\ )}{-}$

$x \in ()$

$f'(x)\quad \dfrac{-}{-} =$

i.e. $f'(x)\qquad\qquad 0$

$f'(x) \le \qquad 0$

$()\ ()$

f

$f'(x)$

$f(x)\quad x\quad c$

$f()\qquad \Rightarrow c$

$f(x)\quad x.$

17. $f'(a)\qquad f'(b)$

$f'(a)\qquad \Rightarrow f(x)\quad f(a)\ x\in\ a\ a\quad \delta$

$f'(b)\qquad \Rightarrow f(b)\quad f(x)\ x\in\ b\ \delta\ b$

$f(a)\quad f(x)\quad f(b)\ x\in\ a\ b$

i.e. $f(x)\qquad\qquad a\ b$

$a\ b$

$\exists\ c\in(a\ b)\qquad\qquad f(x)$

i.e. $\qquad f(c)\qquad f(x)$

$a \le x \le b$ **Proved.**

x

$$f'(x)\quad \lim_{h\to}\ \frac{f(x+h)-f(x)}{h}$$

$$\lim_{h\to}\ \frac{f(x+h)-f(x-h)-\ f(x)}{h}$$

$$\lim_{h\to}\ \frac{1}{h}\left[\frac{f(x+h)-f(x)}{h}-\frac{\big[f(x)-f(x-h)\big]}{h}\right]$$

$$\lim_{h\to}\ \frac{1}{h}\big[f'(x)-f'(x-h)\big]$$

$$\lim_{h\to}\ \frac{f'(x)-f'(x-h)}{h}\quad f''(x)$$

18. u_x $\qquad\Rightarrow\quad x\quad x\quad y$

$\Rightarrow\qquad\qquad x\quad x\quad y\qquad 0$

$u_y\qquad\Rightarrow\quad y\quad y\quad x$

$\Rightarrow\qquad\qquad y\quad y\quad x\qquad\qquad 0$

$(\ )\ (\ )\qquad\qquad\qquad\qquad x\quad y$

$\Rightarrow\qquad\qquad\qquad\qquad x\quad y$

$\qquad\qquad\qquad\qquad x=-\,y$

$(\ )$

$x\quad x\quad x\qquad\Rightarrow x(x\ )$

$\Rightarrow\qquad\qquad\qquad x\qquad \sqrt{\ }\,-\sqrt{\ }$

$(\ )$

$\left(\sqrt{\ }-\sqrt{\ }\right)\qquad\left(-\sqrt{\ }\ \sqrt{\ }\right)$

$\qquad\qquad u_{x_x}\quad x\ (\ )$

$\qquad\qquad u_{y_y}\quad y\ (\ )$

$\qquad\qquad u_{x_y}\ (\ )$

$(\ )$

i.e.

$(\ )\qquad\qquad\left(\sqrt{\ }-\sqrt{\ }\right)$

i.e. $\qquad\qquad\qquad\left(\sqrt{\ }-\sqrt{\ }\right)$

$\left(-\sqrt{\ }\ \sqrt{\ }\right)$

$\Rightarrow\qquad\qquad\qquad\left(-\sqrt{\ }\ \sqrt{\ }\right)$

19. $\qquad\qquad \phi\quad a\ b\ \to$

$\qquad\qquad\quad c\ d\qquad \phi(x)\quad a\le x\le b$

$f\quad c\ d\ \to$

$g\quad a\ b\ \to\qquad\qquad\qquad g(x)\quad \displaystyle\int_{c}^{\phi(x)} f(t)dt$

$\qquad\qquad\qquad \forall\ x\in\ a\ b$

$\qquad\qquad\qquad g(x)\quad \displaystyle\int_{c}^{\phi(x)} f(t)dt$

$\qquad\qquad\qquad g'(x)\quad f\big(\phi(x)\big)\phi'(x)-$

$\because\ c\ d\qquad \phi(x)\quad a\le x\quad b$

$g\ a\ b$

$\Rightarrow\qquad\qquad g'(x)\quad f(\phi(x)\ \phi'(x)$

$\qquad\qquad\quad \forall\ x\in\ a\ b$

$f\qquad\qquad\to\qquad\qquad \displaystyle\int^{x} f(t)dt$

$\qquad\qquad\qquad\qquad \dfrac{\sqrt{\ }}{\ }x$

$f\qquad\qquad\to\qquad \displaystyle\int^{x} f(t)dt\quad \dfrac{\sqrt{\ }}{\ }x$

$\qquad\qquad\qquad x\in$

i.e. $\qquad f(\ x)\quad x\quad \dfrac{\sqrt{\ }}{\ }$

$\qquad\qquad\qquad f(\ x)\quad \dfrac{\sqrt{\ }}{x}$

$x\quad \dfrac{\pi}{\ }\qquad\qquad x\in$

$\qquad\qquad f\!\left(\ \dfrac{\pi}{\ }\right)\quad \dfrac{\sqrt{\ }}{\dfrac{\pi}{\ }}$

$\qquad\qquad\qquad \dfrac{\sqrt{\ }}{\sqrt{\ }}=$

i.e. $\qquad\qquad f\!\left(-\right)=$

20. $\qquad\qquad\qquad\qquad dS$

$\qquad dS\quad \sqrt{K}\,dxdy$

$$k \quad +\left(\frac{\partial z}{\partial x}\right) \quad +\left(\frac{\partial z}{\partial y}\right)$$

$$z \qquad x \qquad y$$

$$\frac{\partial z}{\partial x} \qquad x \qquad \frac{\partial z}{\partial y} \qquad y$$

$$\Rightarrow \qquad k \qquad x \qquad y$$

i.e. $\qquad dS \quad \sqrt{+\ x\ +\ y}\ dx dy$

$$z \qquad -\sqrt{x\ +y}$$

$$\iint dS \qquad \iint_{x\ +y\ =} \sqrt{+\ x\ +\ y}\ dx\, dy$$

$$x \quad r \quad \theta \quad y \quad r \quad \theta$$

$$r$$

$$\int_{\theta=}^{\pi} \int_{r=} \sqrt{+\ r}\ r dr d\theta$$

$$S \quad \int_{\theta=}^{\pi} \int_{r=} \sqrt{+\ r}\ r dr d\theta$$

$$\int_{\theta=}^{\pi} d\theta \int_{r=} \sqrt{+\ r}\ r dr$$

$$\frac{\pi\left(+\ r\right)^{/}}{/}\Bigg|$$

$$\frac{\pi}{}\left[\left(+\ r\right)^{/}\right]$$

$$\frac{\pi}{}\left[\left(\ \right)^{/} -\ \right]$$

21.

$$y - x\frac{dy}{dx} = \frac{dy}{dx}\ y\ e^{y}$$

$$y dx\ (\quad x \quad y\ e^{y})dy \qquad\qquad 0$$

$$dx \qquad dy$$

$$y \quad (\qquad x \quad y\ e^{y})$$

$$\frac{\partial}{\partial y} = \frac{\partial}{\partial x}$$

$$-\left(\frac{\partial}{\partial x} - \frac{\partial}{\partial y}\right) \quad -\frac{}{y} = f(y)$$

(i.e. $\qquad\qquad y\,)$

$$(\ )$$

$$e^{-\int \frac{}{y} dy} \qquad \frac{}{y}$$

$$\frac{dx}{y} - \frac{x}{y}dy - e^{y}dy$$

$$\frac{x}{y} - e^{y} \qquad c \qquad x \qquad y(c \quad e^{y})$$

$$x \quad cy \quad ye^{y}.$$

$$\frac{dy}{dx} \quad \frac{x+\ y+}{x+y+} \qquad 0$$

$$x \qquad h \qquad y$$

$$\frac{dy}{dx} \quad \frac{d}{d}$$

$$(\ )$$

$$\frac{d}{d} \quad \frac{+h+\ +\ +}{+\ +h+\ +}$$

$$\frac{(\ +\ )+(h+\ +\ )}{(\ +\ )+(\ h+\ +\ )}$$

$$h \qquad k$$

$$h \quad k \qquad\qquad h \quad k$$

$$h \qquad k$$

i.e. $\quad \dfrac{d}{d} \quad \dfrac{+}{+}$

$$\frac{d}{d} \quad \frac{-+}{-+}$$

$$\frac{d}{d} \quad \frac{+}{+}$$

()

$$\frac{d}{d} \quad \frac{(\ +\ )}{(\ +\ )} -$$

$$\frac{+\ -\ -}{(\ +\ )} \qquad \frac{-}{(\ +\ )}$$

$$\frac{(\ +\ )}{(\ -\ )}d \qquad \frac{d}{}$$

$$\frac{+}{(\ -\ )} \qquad \overline{(\ -\ )}$$

$$()\ ()$$

$$(x \quad y) \qquad c(x \quad y)$$

22.

$$x\,\frac{d\ y}{dx}+\frac{xdy}{dx}+y$$

$$x \quad e^{z}$$

$$(\ ) \qquad\qquad y$$

$$\frac{d}{dz}$$

$$(\ )\quad y$$

$$\Rightarrow \qquad y \quad c \quad z \quad c \quad z$$

$$y \quad c\ (\quad x) \quad c\ (\quad x)$$

$$\because \qquad y()$$

$$\Rightarrow c\ () \qquad\qquad c\ ()$$

$$\Rightarrow \qquad c$$

$i.e.$
$$y \quad c\ (\quad x)$$

$$y(b)$$

$$\Rightarrow c\ (\quad b)$$

$$\Rightarrow \qquad b \quad n\pi \quad n$$

$$\Rightarrow \qquad b \quad e^{n\pi} \qquad n$$

$$b$$

$$\frac{d\ y}{dx}-\frac{dy}{dx}+\quad y(\quad x \quad x \quad x\ )e^{x}\ ()$$

$$y(x) \quad e^{x}\,v(x)\ ()$$

$$y \quad v\,e^{x} \quad v e^{x}$$

$$y \quad v\,e^{x} \quad v\,e^{x} \quad v e^{x}$$

$$y,\ y \qquad y\ ()$$

$$v\,e^{x} \quad v\ e^{x} \quad v e^{x} \quad v\,e^{x} \quad v e^{x}$$

$$v e^{x}(\quad x \quad x \quad x\ )e^{x}$$

$$e^{x}\,v \quad v \quad v \quad v \quad v \quad v$$

$$(\quad x \quad x \quad x\ )e^{x}$$

$$v\ (\quad x \quad x \quad x\ )$$

$i.e.$
$$\frac{d\ v}{dx} \quad x \quad x \quad x$$

$$x$$

$$v \quad c\ x+c \quad +\frac{x}{}+\frac{x}{}+\frac{x}{}$$

$$()$$

$$y \quad e^{x}\,v$$

$$e^{x}\!\left[c\ x+c \quad +\frac{x}{}+\frac{x}{}+\frac{x}{}\right]$$

$$c\ \left(xe^{x}\right)+c\ e^{x}+\left(\frac{x}{}+\frac{x}{}+\frac{x}{}\right)e^{x}$$

23.

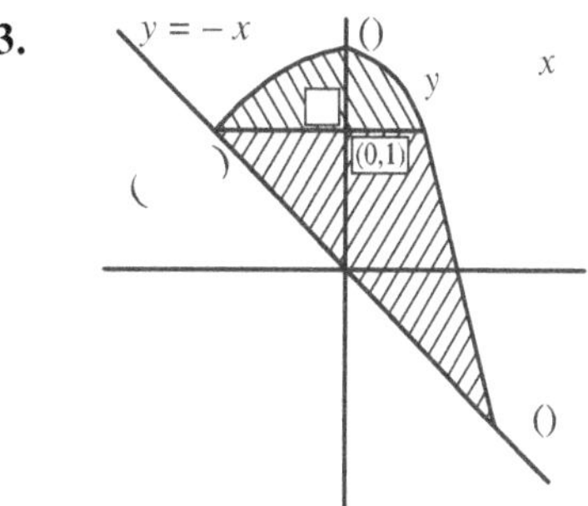

$$y \qquad x \qquad y \qquad x$$

$$x \qquad x$$

$$x \quad x$$

$$\Rightarrow \qquad (x)(\quad x)$$

$$\Rightarrow \qquad x$$

$i.e.\ (\ )\ (\ )$

$$\int_{-}^{}\left[\int_{-x}^{-x} f(x\ y)\,dy\right]dx$$

$$\int_{y=-}^{}\int_{-y}^{\sqrt{\ }\,y} f(x\ y)\,dx\,dy + \int\int^{\sqrt{\ }\,-y} f(x\ y)\,dx\,dy$$

$$\overline{} = (x^{} - xy)\,i + y^{}\,j$$

$$\oint_c \overline{}\cdot d\vec{r} = \oint (x^{} - xy)\,dx + y^{}\,dy$$

$$y = \sqrt{{} - x^{}}$$

S C

$$\oint {}\,dx + {}\,dy = \iint_S \left(\frac{\partial}{\partial x} - \frac{\partial}{\partial y}\right)dx\,dy$$

$$\iint_S x\,dx\,dy$$

$$\int x \int_{y=}^{\sqrt{{}-x}} dy\,dx = \int x\sqrt{{}-x^{}}\,dx$$

$$(i.e. \ x\sqrt{{}-x^{}}\ )$$

24.

$$\iint_S (\bar{\nabla}\times\overline{})\cdot n\,dS$$

$$\overline{F} = (x^{} + y - {})\,i + ({}xy)\,j + ({}xz + z^{})\,k$$

$$S: \ z = {} - \sqrt{x^{} + y^{}}$$

$$xy$$
$$S$$

$x \quad y \qquad xy$

$$\iint_S (\bar{\nabla}\times\overline{F})\cdot n\,dS = \oint_C \overline{F}\cdot d\vec{r}$$

C $x \quad y$

$$\Rightarrow \oint_C \overline{F}\cdot d\vec{r} = \oint (x^{} + y - {})\,dx + {}xy\,dy$$

$x \quad \theta \quad y \quad \theta$

$$\int^{\pi} ({}\theta + {}\theta - {})(-{}\theta)\,d\theta + {}\theta\,{}\theta\,{}\theta\,d\theta$$

$$\int^{\pi} ({}\theta - {}\theta + {}^2\theta\,{}\theta)\,d\theta$$

$$\int^{\pi} {}\theta\,d\theta$$

$(\ )$

$$\Rightarrow \quad {} - {} - \frac{\pi}{} \quad \pi$$

$$\sum \frac{x}{\sqrt{n}\left({} + n^p x\right)}$$

$$f_n(x) = \frac{x}{\sqrt{n}\left({} + n^p x\right)}$$

$$f_n'(x) = \frac{1}{\sqrt{n}}\left[\frac{({} + n^p x) - x\,n^p\,{}}{({} + n^p x)^{}}\right]$$

$$f_n'(x)$$

$$\Rightarrow \quad n^p x \quad n^p x \quad \Rightarrow n^p x$$

$$\Rightarrow \quad x \quad \frac{}{n^p}$$

$$f_n(x) = \frac{n^{p/}}{n^{/}[{} + {}]} = \frac{}{n^{\frac{p+}{}}}$$

$$\lim_{n\to\infty} f_n(x) = \lim_{n\to\infty} \frac{}{n^{\frac{p+}{}}} \to$$

p

25.

$$x \quad y \quad z$$
$$x \quad y \quad Cz$$
$$x \quad Cy \quad z$$

$$\left[\quad\quad\quad \right]$$

$$\to \qquad\qquad \to$$

$$\begin{bmatrix} & & - \\ & & \end{bmatrix}$$

$$\rightarrow \quad 0$$

$$\begin{bmatrix} & -(\ ) & \end{bmatrix}$$

00

00
$$\neq$$

$\Rightarrow$

$\Rightarrow$

$$\neq \quad \Rightarrow$$

V

$$W \quad \left\{ p \in \quad \int p(x)^{dx} = \right\}$$

$$\in W \quad \int \ dx \quad \in W$$

i.e. W

$$p\ (x)\ p\ (x) \in W$$

$$\int p\ (x)dx = \qquad \int p\ (x)dx =$$

$$\int \big(ap\ (x)+bp\ (x)\big)dx \qquad a\ b \in$$

$$a\!\int p\ (x)dx + b\!\int p\ (x)dx$$

$a \qquad b$

$$\Rightarrow ap\ (x)+bp\ (x) \in W \qquad p\ (x)\ p\ (x) \in W$$
$$W \qquad\qquad V$$

$$p \in W \qquad \int p(x)dx =$$

$$p(x) \quad a \quad a\,x \quad a\,x \quad \dots\ a_n x^n$$

$$\int p(x)dx \quad a \quad \frac{a}{\ } + a\ -+a\ -+a\ -$$

$$+\ a_n \frac{\ }{n+} =$$

$n \in N$

$$a \quad a \quad a \quad a \qquad a_n$$
$$W(\quad n) \qquad V$$

26.

$$adj$$
$$adj$$
$$\Rightarrow \quad 0(\qquad adj) \qquad \mathbb{A}\ |$$
$$0\ \ 00$$
$$0 \qquad\qquad n$$
$$(\qquad n \qquad\qquad\qquad n\ )$$
$$\Rightarrow \quad (\qquad\quad adj\,)$$
$$\Rightarrow \qquad (\quad adj\,) \qquad -=$$

28.

$$(\quad x\ y,\ t)(\ x'\ y'\ t')(\ x''\ y''\ t'') \in \mathbb{R}$$
$$(\quad x,\ y,\ t) \quad \{(x'\ y'\ t')\ (x''\ y''\ t'')\}$$
$$(\ x\ y\ t)$$

$$\left[\left[\left(x'+x''\ y'+y''\ t'+t''\ +-\big(x''y'-x'y''\big)\right)\right]\right]$$

$$\left(x+x'+x''\ y+y'+y''\ t+t'+t''\ +-\big(x''y'-x'y''\big)\right.$$
$$\left.+-\big(x'+x''\big)y-\big(y'+y''\big)x\right)$$

$$x \quad x' \quad x''\ y \quad y'+y''\ t \quad t'\quad t''$$

$$- \quad x'y \quad xy' \quad x''y \quad x''y \quad y''x \quad y''x$$

$$(\quad x\ y\ t)(\ x'\ y'\ t')(\ x''\ y''\ t'')$$

$$\left(x+x'\ y+y'\ t+t'\ +-\big(x'y-xy'\big)\right)(\ x''\ y''\ t'')$$

$$\left[x+x'+x''\ y+y'+y''\ t+t'+t''\ +-\right.$$
$$\left.\{x'y-xy'+x''y+x''y-y''x-y''x'\}\right]$$

i.e. $(\quad)$

$$(\qquad x'\ y'\ t')\ (\qquad\qquad\qquad x\ y\ t)$$
$$(\quad x\ y\ t)(\ x'\ y'\ t')(\ x\ y\ t)$$

$$\Rightarrow \left(x+x'\ y+y'\ t+t'\ +-\big(x'y-xy'\big)\right)(\ x\ y\ t)$$

$\Rightarrow \qquad\qquad x' \qquad y' \qquad t'$

$\Rightarrow () \ (\qquad\qquad\qquad\qquad x \quad y \quad t)$

$(\qquad\quad x \ y \ t)$

$(\qquad\quad) \qquad a$

$(\qquad z) \qquad \mathbb{R}$

$(\qquad x' \ y' \ t') \in z$

$(\qquad x' \ y' \ t')(\ x \ y \ t)(\ x \ y \ t)(\ x' \ y' \ t')$

$\forall (\ x \ y \ t) \in \mathbb{R}$

i.e. $\qquad -(x'y - xy') = -(xy' - x'y)$

$\Rightarrow \qquad\qquad x'y \quad xy' \quad xy' \quad x'y$

$\Rightarrow \qquad\qquad x'y \quad xy' \Rightarrow y' \quad \dfrac{y}{x} x'$

$\qquad\qquad\qquad \mathbb{R}$

$\left\{ \left(x' \ \dfrac{y}{x} x' \ t' \right) \ x' \ t' \ x \ y \in \right\}$

$kz \qquad\qquad k \quad k \quad k \ o, k, \ k, \ k, \ ...$

$\qquad\qquad kz$

$\qquad\qquad\qquad z \ kz \in kz$

$\qquad\qquad mz \qquad\qquad m \quad m \quad m \ o \ m \quad m$

$nz \qquad\qquad n \quad n \quad n \ o \ n \quad n$

$\qquad mz \cap nz \qquad\qquad p \quad p \quad p \ o, p, \ p \quad p$

$\qquad p \qquad\qquad\qquad\qquad\qquad m \qquad n.$

$pz \ (\quad p)$

$(\qquad p) \quad lcm(m \ n)$

29. $() \qquad\qquad\qquad p$

$\quad x \in \qquad\qquad y \in \qquad xy \quad yx$

i.e.

i.e. $\forall \ x \ y \in \qquad xy \quad yx.$

$()(\qquad\qquad Z) \quad \displaystyle\sum_{a \notin z} \dfrac{(\ )}{(\quad_a)}$

$(\quad_a)() \qquad\qquad a \notin z$

$() \qquad\qquad\qquad\qquad p^n (\qquad_a) \quad p^k$

$\qquad\qquad k \quad n$

$\therefore \qquad\qquad\qquad \dfrac{(\ )}{(\quad_a)} \qquad \dfrac{p^n}{p^k} = p^{n-k}$

$\Rightarrow p \qquad\qquad \dfrac{(\ )}{(\quad_a)} \qquad\qquad a \notin z$

$\Rightarrow p \qquad\qquad \displaystyle\sum_{a \notin z} \dfrac{(\ )}{(\quad_a)}$

$\qquad p \ () \qquad\qquad p^n$

ie. $p \ () \qquad\qquad p^n$

i.e. $p \qquad\qquad \left[(\ ) - \sum \dfrac{(\ )}{(\quad_a)} \right] (\qquad z)$

i.e. $p() \qquad \Rightarrow () \qquad ie. \ p$

$() \qquad\qquad\qquad p \ (ie. \ n)$

$() \qquad\qquad\qquad \Rightarrow () \qquad p \quad p$

Case-I $() \qquad\qquad\qquad p$

$()()() \qquad\qquad\qquad\qquad p$

$\Rightarrow$

$\Rightarrow$

$a \in \quad \Rightarrow a \in \quad \Rightarrow ax \quad xa \ \forall \ x \ a \in$

Case-II $() \qquad\qquad\qquad p$

$() \qquad\qquad p \quad p$

$\qquad\qquad\qquad\qquad a \in \qquad\qquad\qquad a \notin$

$\qquad\qquad_a \qquad x \in \qquad xa \quad ax$

$\qquad\qquad\qquad \subset \quad_a \quad a \in \quad_a \quad a \notin$

$(\qquad\qquad\qquad_a) () \qquad\qquad p$

$\quad (\qquad\qquad\qquad\qquad_a)$

$() \qquad p \ (\qquad_a) \quad p$

$\quad (\qquad\qquad\qquad_a) \quad p \Rightarrow (\quad_a)()$

$\Rightarrow \quad_a \qquad\qquad_a$

$\Rightarrow a \in \quad_a \ \forall \ x \in \quad \Rightarrow x \quad ax \ \forall \ x \in$

$\Rightarrow x \in ()$

$() \qquad\qquad\qquad p$

ie. $() \qquad p$

☆☆☆☆☆☆

PREVIOUS YEARS' PAPERS
(Solved)

IIT-JAM
JOINT ADMISSION TEST
FOR M.Sc. MATHEMATICS

IIT–JAM

JOINT ADMISSION TEST FOR
M.SC. (MATHEMATICS)-2010

1. Which of the following conditions does **not** ensure the convergence of a real sequence (a_n)?
   A. $|a_n - a_{n+}| \to$ as $n \to \infty$
   B. $\sum_{n=}^{\infty} |a_n - a_{n+}|$ is convergent
   C. $\sum_{n=}^{\infty} n\, a_n$ is convergent
   D. The sequences (a_{2n+1}), (a_{2n+1}) and (a_{3n}) are convergent

2. The value of $\iint_G \dfrac{(x+y)}{x+y}\, dx\, dy$, where $G = \{(x\ y) \in\ \ \le x+y \le e\}$, is
   A. π
   B. 2π
   C. 3π
   D. 4π

3. The number of elements of S_5 (the symmetric group on 5 letters) which are their own inverses equals
   A. 10
   B. 11
   C. 25
   D. 26

4. Let S be an infinite subset of R such that S $\cap$ Q = ϕ. Which of the following statements is true?
   A. S must have a limit point which belongs to Q
   B. S must have a limit point which belongs to R/Q
   C. S cannot be a closed set in R
   D. R/S must have a limit point which belongs to S

5. Let $f : (1,4) \to$ R be a uniformly continuous function and let (a_n) be a Cauchy sequence in $(1, 2)$. Let $x_n = a_n f(a_n)$ $y_n = \dfrac{}{+a_n} f(a_n)$ for all $n \in$ N. Which of the following statements is true?
   A. Both (x_n) and (y_n) must be Cauchy sequences in R
   B. (x_n) must be a Cauchy sequence in R but (y_n) need not be a Cauchy sequence in R
   C. (y_n) must be a Cauchy sequence in R but (x_n) need not be a Cauchy sequence in R
   D. Neither (x_n) nor (y_n) needs to be a Cauchy sequence in R

6. Let $\vec{} = xyz\, e^x\, i + z e^x\, j + y e^x\, k$ be the gradient of a scalar function. The value of $\int_L \vec{}\ dr$ along the oriented path L from $(0, 0, 0)$ to $(1, 0, 2)$ and then to $(1, 1, 2)$ is
   A. 0
   B. $2e$
   C. e
   D. e^2

7. Let $\vec{} = xyi + yj - yzk$ denote the force field on a particle traversing the path L from $(0, 0, 0)$ to $(1, 1, 1)$ along the curve of intersection of the cylinder $y = x^2$ and the plane $z = x$. The work done by $\vec{}$ is
   A. 0
   B. $-$
   C. $-$
   D. 1

8. Let R[X] be the ring of real polynomials in the variable X. the number of ideals in the quotient ring $R[X]/[X^2 - 3X + 2)$ is
   A. 2
   B. 3
   C. 4
   D. 6

9. Consider the differential equation

$$\frac{dy}{dx} = ay - by \quad a,\ b > 0 \ \text{ and } \ y(0) = y_0.$$ As $x \to +\infty$, the solution $y(x)$ tends to

A. 0   B. $\dfrac{a}{b}$

C. $\dfrac{b}{a}$ D. y_0

10. Consider the differential equation $(x + y + 1)\,dx + (2x + 2y + 1)\,dy = 0$. Which of the following statements is true?

A. The differential equation is linear
B. The differential equation is exact
C. e^{x+y} is an integrating factor of the differential equation
D. A suitable substitution transforms the differentiable equation to the variables separable form

11. Let $T : R^2 \to R^2$ be a linear transformation such that $T((1, 2)) = (2, 3)$ and $T((0, 1)) = (1, 4)$. Then $T((5, 6))$ is

A. $(6, -1)$ B. $(-6, 1)$
C. $(-1, 6)$ D. $(1 - 6)$

12. The number of 2×2 matrices over Z_3 (the field with three elements) with determinant 1 is

13. The radius of convergence of the power series

$$\sum_{n=}^{\infty} a_n z^n \quad \text{where } a_0 = 1,\ a_n = 3^{-n}\, a_{n-1} \text{ for}$$

$n \in N$, is

A. 0   B. $\sqrt{}$
C. 3   D. ∞

14. Let $T : \mathbf{R}^3 \to \mathbf{R}^3$ be the linear transformation whose matrix with respect to the standard basis

$$\begin{pmatrix} e & e & e \end{pmatrix} \quad \mathbf{R}^3 \qquad \begin{pmatrix} \ \\ \ \\ \ \end{pmatrix} \quad \text{Then } T$$

A. maps the subspace spanned by e_1 and e_2 into itself
B. has distinct eigen values
C. has eigen vectors that span $\mathbf{R}^3$
D. has a non-zero null space

15. Let $T : \mathbf{R}^3 \to \mathbf{R}^3$ be the linear transformation whose matrix with respect to the standard basis

of $\mathbf{R}^3$ is $\begin{pmatrix} a & b \\ -a & & c \\ -b & -c \end{pmatrix}$ where $a,\ b,\ c$ are real numbers not all zero. Then T

A. is one-to-one
B. is onto
C. does not map any line through the origin onto itself
D. has rank 1

16. A. Obtain the general solution of the following system of differential equations

$$\frac{dx}{dt} = x + y$$

$$\frac{dy}{dt} = x - y + e^{t}$$

B. Find the curve passing through $\left(- \ \right)$ and having slope at (x, y) given by the differential equation
$2(1 + y^2)\,dx + (2x - \tan^{-1} y)\,dy = 0$.

17. A. Find the volume of the region in the first octant bounded by the
$x = 0,\ y = x,\ y = 2 - x^2,\ z = 0$ and $z = x^2$.

B. Suppose $f : R \to R$ is a non-constant continuous function satisfying $f(x + y) = f(x)\,f(y)$ for all $x, y \in R$.
(i) Show that $f(x) \neq 0$ for all $x \in R$.
(ii) Show that $f(x) > 0$ for all $x \in R$.
(iii) Show that there exists $\beta \in R$ such that $f(x) = \beta^x$ for all $x \in R$.

18. A. Let $f(x)$ and $g(x)$ be real valued functions continuous in $[a, b]$, differentiable in (a, b) and let $g'(x) \neq 0$ for all $x \in (a, b)$. Show that there exists $c \in (a, b)$ such that

$$\frac{f(c) - f(a)}{g(b) - g(c)} = \frac{f'(c)}{g'(c)}$$

B. Let $0 < \lambda < 4$ and let (a_n) be a sequence of positive real numbers satisfying $a_{n+1} = \lambda a_2^1(1 - a_n)$ for $n \in N$. Prove that $\lim_{n \to \infty} a_n$ exists and determine this limit.

19. Let G be an open subset of R.

   A. If $0 \notin G$, then show that $H = \{xy : x, y \in G\}$ is an open subset of R.

   B. If $0 \in G$ and if $x + y \in G$ for all $x, y \in G$, then show that $G = R$.

20. Let $p(x)$ be a non-constant polynomial with real coefficients such that $p(x) \neq 0$ for all $x \in$

   Define $f(x) = \dfrac{1}{p(x)}$ for all $x \in R$. Prove that

   (i) for each $\varepsilon > 0$, there exists $\alpha > 0$ such that $|f(x)| < \varepsilon$ for all $x \in R$ satisfying $|x| > \alpha$, and

   (ii) $f : R \to R$ is a uniformly continuous function.

21. A. Let $M(k)$ and $m(k)$ denote respectively that absolute maximum and the absolute minimum values of $x^3 + 9x^2 - 21x + k$ in the closed interval $(-10, 2]$. Find all the real values of k for which $|M(k)| = |m(k)|$.

   B. Let $\alpha_1 = 0, \beta_1 = 1; \alpha_2 = 1, \beta_2 = 1$, and for $n \geq 3, \alpha_n = \alpha_{n-1} + 2\alpha_{n-2}, \beta_n = \beta_{n-1} + 2\beta_{n-2}$. Prove that, for $n \in N$

   (i) $\beta_n = 2\alpha_n + (-1)^{n-1}$

   (ii) $\alpha_n + \beta_n = 2^{n-1}$

   Deduce that $\dfrac{\alpha_n a + \beta_n b}{n-} \underset{n \to \infty}{=} \dfrac{a + b}{n-}$ for any a, $b \in R$.

22. A. Let $f(x, y) = \alpha x^2 + xy + \beta y^2, \alpha \neq 0, \beta \neq 0, 4\alpha\beta \neq 1$. Find sufficient conditions on α, β such that $(0, 0)$ is

   (i) a point of local maxima of $f(x, y)$

   (ii) a point of local minima of $f(x, y)$

   (iii) a saddle point of $f(x, y)$.

   B. Find the derivative of $f(x, y, z) = 7x^3 - x^2z - z^2 + 28y$ at the point $A = (1, -1, 0)$ along the unit vecor $-\left(i - j + k \right)$ What is the unit vector along which f decreases most rapidly at A? Also, find the rate of this decrease.

23. Using $x = e^u$, transform the differential equation

$$x\,\dfrac{d\,y}{dx} + x\dfrac{dy}{dx} + y = \qquad x \quad \text{to a second order}$$

differential equation with contant coefficients. Obtain the general solution of the transformed differential equation.

24. Let G be a group and let A(G) denote the set of all automorphisms of G, i.e., all one-to-one, onto, group homomorphisms from G to g. An automorphism $f : G \to G$ of the form $f(x) = axa^{-1}, x \in G$ (for some $a \in G$) is called an inner automorphism. Let I(G) denote the set of all inner automorphisms of G.

   A. Show that A(G) is a group under composition of functions and that I(G) is a normal subgroup A(G).

   B. Show that I(G) is isomorphic to G/Z(G), where $Z(G) = \{g \in G : xg = gx$ for all $x \in G\}$ is the center of G.

25. A. Give an example of a linear transformation $T : R^2 \to R^2$ such that $T^2(v) = -v$ for all $v \in R^2$.

   B. Let V be a real n-dimensional vector space and let $T : V \to V$ be a linear transformation satisfying $T^2(v) = -v$ for all $v \in V$.

   (i) Show that n is even.

   (ii) Use T to make V into a complex vector space such that the multiplication by complex numbers extends the multiplication by real numbers.

   (iii) Show that, with respect to the complex vector space structure on V obtained in (ii), $T : V \to V$ is a complex linear transformation.

26. Let W be the region bounded by the planes $x = 0, y = 0, y = 3, z = 0$ and $x + 2z = 6$. Let S be the boundary of this region. Using Gauss' diversgence theorem, evaluate $\iint\limits_{S} \vec{F}\, n\, dS$ where

$$\vec{} = xyi + yz\, j + xzk \quad \text{and} \quad n \quad \text{is the outward}$$

unit normal vector to S.

27. **A.** Using Stokes' theorem evaluate the line integral $\int_{L}\left(yi + zj + xk\right) d\vec{r}$ where L is the intersection of $x^2 + y^2 + z^2 = 1$ and $x + y = 0$ traversed in the clockwise direction when viewed from the point (1, 1, 0).

B. Change the order of integration in the integral $\int_{x-}^{} \int_{}^{\sqrt{-x}} f(x\ y)\,dy\,dx$

28. In a group G, $x \in$ G is said to be conjugate to $y \in$ G, written $x \sim y$, if there exists $z \in$ G such that $x = zyz^{-1}$.

A. Show that $\sim$ is an equivalence relation on G. Show that a subgroup N of G is a normal subgroup of G if and only if N is a union of equivalence classes of $\sim$

B. Consider the group of all non-singular 3 $\times$ 3 real matrices under matrix multiplication.

Show that 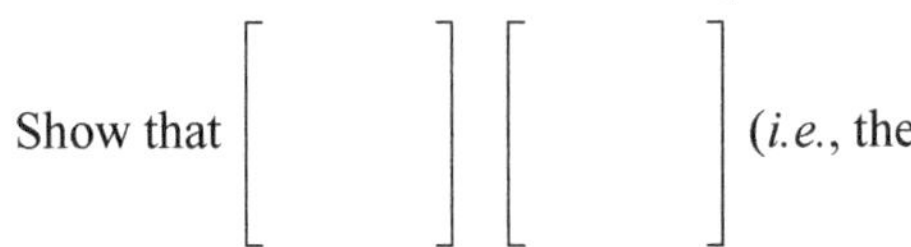 (*i.e.*, the two matrices are conjugate).

29. Let S denote the commutative ring of all continuous real valued functions on [0,1], under pointwise addition and multiplication. For $a \in$ [0, 1], let $M_a = |f \in$ S $| f(a) = 1]$.

A. Show that M_a is an ideal in S.

B. Show that M_a is a maximal ideal in S.

ANSWERS

1	2	3	4	5	6	7	8	9	10

11	12	13	14	15

SOME SELECTED EXPLANATORY ANSWERS

1. As if
$$a_n = \sqrt{n}$$
then
$$|a_n - a_{n+}| = |\sqrt{n} - \sqrt{n+}|$$
$$= \left|\frac{}{\sqrt{n} + \sqrt{n+}}\right| \rightarrow$$
However $a_n \rightarrow \infty$ as $n \rightarrow \infty$.

2. $\iint_{C} \frac{\left(x\ + y\ \right)}{x\ + y}\,dx\,dy \qquad 1 \le x^2 + y^2 \le e^2$

= Changing into polar co-ordinate by putting $x = r\cos\theta, y = r\sin\theta$, we get

$$= \int_{r=}^{e} \int_{\theta=}^{\pi} \frac{r}{r}\,r\,d\theta\,dr = \int_{r=}^{e} \frac{r}{r}\,dr \int_{\theta=}^{\pi} d\theta$$

$$= \left. \frac{(\ r)}{}\right|^{e} \pi = -\left[(\ e) - \quad \right]\pi$$

$$= 2\pi$$

3. Total no. of such elements $= 5c_2 + 1 = 11$.

As such elements satisfy $S^2 = I$ which will be possible if cycle length is equal to 2.

6. $\int_{L} \vec{dr} = \int_{AB} xyz\,e^x\,dx + ze^x\,dy + ye^x\,dz$

$$+ \int_{BC} xyz\,e^x\,dx + ze^x\,dy + ye^x\,dz \qquad (\ )$$

Equation of AB

$$\frac{x}{\ } = \frac{y}{\ } = \frac{z}{\ } \Rightarrow z = 2x$$

$$I_1 = \int xyz\, e^x\, dx + ze^x\, dy + ye^x\, dz = 0$$

$$[\because\ y = 0,\ dy = 0]$$

$$I_2 = \int xyz\, e^x\, dx + ze^x\, dy + ye^x\, dz.$$

Equation of BC

$$\frac{x-1}{0} = \frac{y}{1} = \frac{z-2}{0} = \int e\, dy = e$$

7. Work done

$$W = \int \vec{F}\cdot d\vec{r} = \int xy\,dx + y\,dy - yz\,dz$$

$$= \int x\, x\, dx + n\ \ x\,dx - x\ x\,dx = \int x\, dx$$

$$= \frac{x}{\ }\Bigg|\ = -\ .$$

9. $\dfrac{dy}{dx} = ay - by^2$

$$\Rightarrow \qquad \frac{dy}{ay - by} = dx$$

$$\Rightarrow \quad \frac{ }{a}\left(\frac{ }{y} + \frac{b}{a - by}\right) dy = dx$$

$$\Rightarrow \frac{ }{a}\left[\ \ y + b\ \frac{(a - by)}{-b}\right] = x + c$$

$$\Rightarrow \qquad \frac{y}{a - by} = a(x + c)$$

$$\Rightarrow \qquad \frac{a - by}{y} = e^{-a(x + c)}$$

$\Rightarrow$ Now as $x \to \infty$

$$\frac{a - by}{y} \to \quad \Rightarrow y \to \frac{a}{b}.$$

10. $(x + y + 1) + (2x + 2y + 1)\dfrac{dy}{dx} =$

put $\qquad\qquad x + y = z$

$$\Rightarrow \qquad \frac{dz}{dx} = \frac{dy}{dx} +$$

$$\Rightarrow (z + 1) + (2z + 1)\left(\frac{dz}{dx} - \ \right) = 0$$

$$\Rightarrow \qquad \frac{dz}{dx}\left(\ z + \ \right) = z$$

$$\Rightarrow \qquad \frac{z\, dx}{dz} = (2z + 1)$$

or, $\qquad\qquad dx = \left(\ \ + \frac{\ }{z}\right) dz,$

i.e. both variables reduced into separable form.

11.
$$T((1, 2)) = (2, 3)$$
$$T((0, 1)) = (1, 4)$$
$$T((5, 6)) = 5T((1, 2)) - 4T((0, 1))$$
$$= 5(2, 3) - 4(1, (4)$$
$$= (10, 15) - (4, 16)$$
$$= (6, -1).$$

12. 2×2 matrix can be written as

$$A = \begin{bmatrix} a & b \\ c & d \end{bmatrix}$$

where a, b, c, d can take three $(0, 1, 2)$ values.
Now from question $|ad - bc| = 1$.

$ad = 1$, $bc = 0$. Now $bc = 0$, is possible as
or $ad = 0$, $bc = 1$

$$\begin{array}{ll} b = 0, & c = 1 \\ b = 0, & c = 0 \\ b = 1, & c = 0 \\ b = 2, & c = 0 \\ b = 0, & c = 1 \end{array}$$

$ad = 1$
either through

$$a = 1,\ b = 1$$
$$a = 2,\ b = 2$$

$\Rightarrow$ Total no. of such matrix $= 2 \times 2 \times 5 = 20$

Also when $ad = 2$, $bc = 1$
or $ad = 1$, $bc = 2$
then $|ad - bc| = 1$
No. of such matrix $= 2 + 2 = 4$.

13. If R be the radius of convergence of the power series.

Then

$$\frac{\ }{\ } = \lim_{n \to \infty}\left|\frac{a_n}{a_{n+}}\right|$$

$$= \lim_{n\to\infty} \left| \frac{a_n}{-(n+\ )\, a_n} \right| = \lim_{n\to\infty} \overline{-(n+\ )}$$

$$\Rightarrow\ -\!\!-\to\infty \qquad \Rightarrow\ R\to 0.$$

14.
$$T = \begin{bmatrix} & & \\ & & \\ & & \end{bmatrix}$$

$$|T-\lambda I| = 0$$

$$\Rightarrow \begin{bmatrix} -\lambda & & \\ & -\lambda & \\ & & -\lambda \end{bmatrix}$$

$$\lambda^2(1-\lambda) + 1(\lambda-1) = 0$$
$$\Rightarrow \quad (\lambda-1)(1-\lambda^2) = 0 \ \Rightarrow\ \lambda = 1, 1, -1$$
$\Rightarrow$ T has only zero null space.

$$|T-I| = 0 \qquad \begin{bmatrix} - & & \\ & & \\ & & - \end{bmatrix}\begin{bmatrix} x \\ y \\ z \end{bmatrix} = \begin{bmatrix} \ \\ \ \\ \ \end{bmatrix}$$

$$\Rightarrow \qquad -x+z = 0$$

Then the eigen vector
$$[0,1,0] \ \& \ [1,0,1]$$

$$|T+I| = 0 \qquad \begin{bmatrix} & & \\ & & \\ & & \end{bmatrix}\begin{bmatrix} x \\ y \\ z \end{bmatrix} = \begin{bmatrix} \ \\ \ \\ \ \end{bmatrix}$$

$$x+z = 0 \quad y = 0$$

$\Rightarrow$ eigen vector $[1, 0, -1]$.
Clearly all are independent.
Hence, it span $\mathbf{R}^3$.

15. $T = \begin{bmatrix} & a & b \\ -a & & c \\ -b & -c & \end{bmatrix}$

Clearly T is a skew - symmetric matrix
$$|\,T\,| = -a[bc] + b.ac = 0$$
$\Rightarrow$ Rank(T) is less than 3.
Also it has a non-zero 2×2 co-factor
$$\Rightarrow \qquad \text{Rank}(T) = 2$$
$\Rightarrow$ T is not one-to-one.

Also from question
$$T(1,0,0) = (0,-a,-b)$$
$$T(0,1,0) = (a,0,-c)$$
$$T(0,0,1) = (b,c,0)$$
Now $\qquad T(x,y,z) = (x,y,z)$
$$(0,-ax,-bx) + (ay,0,-cy) + (bz,cz,0)$$
$$= (x,y,z)$$

$$\begin{aligned} ay+bz-x &= \\ -ax+cz-y &= \\ -bx-cy-z &= \end{aligned} \qquad \begin{bmatrix} - & a & b \\ -a & - & c \\ -b & -c & - \end{bmatrix}\begin{bmatrix} x \\ y \\ z \end{bmatrix} = \begin{bmatrix} \ \\ \ \\ \ \end{bmatrix}$$

Now $\begin{vmatrix} - & a & b \\ -a & - & c \\ -b & -c & - \end{vmatrix}$

$$= -1(1+c^2) - a(a+bc) + b(ac-b^2)$$
$$= -(a^2+b^2+c^2+1) \neq 0$$
i.e. $(x,y,z) = (0,0,0)$ only satisfy
$$T(x,y,z) = (x,y,z).$$

16. A. Given $\qquad \dfrac{dx}{dt} = x+2y$

and $\qquad \dfrac{dy}{dt} = 4x-y+e^{3t}$

$$\therefore \qquad \frac{d\,x}{dt} = \frac{dx}{dt} + \left(x-y+e^{\ t} \right)$$

$$\Rightarrow \qquad \frac{d\,x}{dt} = \frac{dx}{dt} + x + e^{\ t} + x - \frac{dx}{dt}$$

$$\Rightarrow \qquad \frac{d\,x}{dt} - x = 2e^{3t}$$

$$\text{C.F.} = C_1 e^{3t} + C_2 e^{-3t}$$

$$\text{P.I.} \ x = \frac{1}{D-\ } e^{\ t}$$

$$= \frac{te^{\ t}}{\ } = \frac{te^{\ t}}{\ }.$$

i.e. General solution is

$$x = \ e^{\ t} + \ e^{-\ t} + \frac{te^{\ t}}{\ }$$

Also from

$$2y = \frac{dx}{dt} - x$$

$$= e^{t} - \quad e^{-t} + -\left(e^{t} + te^{t}\right) - \quad e^{t} - \quad e^{-t} - \frac{te^{t}}{}$$

$$2y = \quad e^{t} - \quad e^{-t} + \frac{e^{t}}{} + -te^{t}$$

$$\therefore \; y = \quad e^{t} - \quad e^{-t} + \frac{e^{t}}{} + -te^{t}$$

$$x = \quad e^{t} + \quad e^{-t} + \frac{te^{t}}{}$$

$$y = \quad e^{t} - \quad e^{-t} + \frac{e^{t}}{} + \frac{t}{}e^{t}$$

B. The given differential equation is
$$2(1+y^2)dx + (2x - \tan^{-1} y)\, dy = 0$$

$$dx + \left(\; x - \quad \; y\right)\frac{dy}{+y}$$

put $z = \tan^{-1} y$ $\qquad \dfrac{dz}{dx} = \dfrac{dy}{+y\; dx}$

$$\Rightarrow \quad +\left(\; x - z\right)\frac{dz}{dx} = 0$$

$$\Rightarrow \qquad \frac{dx}{dz} + x = \frac{z}{}$$

$$\Rightarrow \qquad \text{I.F.} = e^{\int dz} = e^{z}$$

$$xe^{z} = -\int ze^{z} dz$$

$$\Rightarrow \qquad xe^{z} = \frac{(z-)}{} e^{z} + c$$

$$\Rightarrow \qquad x = \frac{(z-)}{} + ce^{-z}$$

or, $\qquad (2x - z + 1) = 2ce^{-z}$

as it passes $\left(- \quad \right)$

$$\Rightarrow \qquad (1 - 1 + 1) = 2c.1 \; \Rightarrow \; 2c = 1$$

$$\therefore \; (2x - \tan^{-1} y + 1) = e^{-\quad y}$$

$$\Rightarrow \qquad (2x + 1) = \left(e^{-\quad y} + \quad y\right).$$

17. A. Point of intersection of $y = x$ & $y = 2 - x^2$
$$\Rightarrow x = 2 - x^2 \quad x^2 + x - 2 = 0$$
$$\Rightarrow (x+2)(x-1) = 0 \;\Rightarrow\; x = -2, 1$$

i.e. $(1, 1)$ is the point of intersection in Ist octant.

Hence, volume of region in the first octant

$$V = \int\limits_{x=}^{} \int\limits_{x}^{-x} \int\limits_{}^{x} dz\, dy\, dx$$

$$= \int\limits_{}^{} \int\limits_{x}^{-x} z\Big|^{x}\, dy\, dx = \int x \left(\; -x\; -x\right)dx$$

$$= \left. \frac{x}{} - \frac{x}{} - \frac{x}{} \right| = \left(\frac{}{} - - - - -\right)$$

$$= \frac{- \quad -}{} = \frac{-}{} = \frac{}{}$$

B. Clearly $f(x) \neq 0$ for any $x \in R$

otherwise $\qquad f(x) = 0 \quad \forall\, x \in R$

$\Rightarrow f(x)$ is constant function.

Now put $\dfrac{x}{} \; \dfrac{x}{}$ in the equation

$$f(x+y) = f(x) . f(y)$$

we get $\qquad f(x) = \left\{ f\!\left(\dfrac{x}{}\right) \right\}$

$\Rightarrow \qquad f(x) > 0 \quad \forall\, x \in R$

$\therefore$ we can take the logarithm of $f(x)$

define $\qquad g(x) = \ln_e f(x)$

then $\qquad g(x+y) = \ln_e f(x+y)$
$$= \ln_e \{ f(x) . f(y) \}$$
$$\Rightarrow \qquad g(x+y) = \ln_e f(x) + \ln_e f(y)$$
$$= g(x) + g(y) \; \forall\, x, y \in R$$

i.e. $\qquad g(x+y) = g(x) + g(y)$

$\Rightarrow \qquad g(0) = 0$

& $\qquad g(-x) = -g(x) \quad \forall\, x \in R.$

Again, for each positive integer n, we have, by induction on n

$$g(nx) = ng(x), \text{ for all } x \in R$$

Replacing x by $\dfrac{x}{n}$ in above, we obtain

$$\Rightarrow \qquad g\!\left(\frac{x}{n}\right) = \frac{}{n} g(x) \; \forall x \in$$

$\therefore$ for any pair of integers p, q (q being +ive), we have

$$\therefore \qquad g\left(\frac{p}{q}x\right) = \frac{p}{q}g(x) \qquad \forall\, x \in R.$$

i.e. $\qquad g(rx) = rg(x) \qquad \forall\, x \in R.$

If we put $x = 1$, then $g(r) = rg(1)$

$\Rightarrow \qquad g(r) = cr$ where $g(1) = c$

i.e. $\qquad g(r) = cr$

Also g is continuous, then a sequence $\{r_n\}$ of rational numbers, converging to ξ.

$$\Rightarrow \qquad (r_n) = \xi$$

$$\therefore \quad {}_{n\to\infty}\, g(r_n) \to g(\xi)$$

$$[\because\ g \text{ is a continuous function}]$$

$$\therefore \qquad g(\xi) = {}_{n\to\infty}\, g(r_n) = {}_{n\to\infty}\, cr_n = c\xi$$

$$\therefore \qquad g(\xi) = c\xi$$

$$\Rightarrow \qquad g(x) = xg(1) \qquad \forall\, x \in R.$$

$$\Rightarrow \qquad \ln_e f(x) = x \ln_e f(1)$$

$$\Rightarrow \qquad f(x) = e^{x\ln_e f(1)} = \beta^x \text{ Proved.}$$

18. Let define a function

$$\phi(x) = f(x)\,g(x) - f(x)\,g(a)$$
$$- f(x)\,g(b)$$

then $\qquad \phi(a) = -f(a)\,g(b).$

$\Rightarrow \qquad \phi(a) = \phi(b)$

and $\qquad \phi(b) = -g(b)\,f(a).$

Also ϕ is continuous in $[a, b]$

and ϕ is differentiable in (a, b).

$\therefore$ By Rolle's Theorem,

$\quad \exists\ c\ a < c < b$ such that $\phi'(c) = 0$

$\quad \phi'(x) = f'(x)\,g(x) + f(x)\,g'(x)$
$$- g'(x)\,f(a) - f'(x)\,g(b)$$

Now $\qquad \phi'(c) = 0$

$\Rightarrow f'(c)\,g(c) + f(c)\,g'(c) - g'(c)\,f(a)$
$$- f'(c)\,g(b) = 0$$

$$f'(c)\{g(c) - g(b)\} = g'(c)\{f(a) - f(c)\}$$

$$\Rightarrow \qquad \frac{f(c) - f(a)}{g(b) - g(c)} = \frac{f'(c)}{g'(c)} \text{ Proved.}$$

20. $\therefore \qquad p(x) \neq 0$

i.e. there exist a positive δ such that

$$|p(x)| > \delta$$

$$\Rightarrow \qquad \left|\frac{1}{p(x)}\right| < \frac{1}{\delta}$$

or $\qquad |f(x)| = \frac{1}{\delta} \qquad \forall\, x \in R$

$\Rightarrow \qquad |f(x)| < \varepsilon \qquad \delta = \dfrac{1}{\varepsilon}$

i.e. $\qquad |f(x)| = \varepsilon \qquad \forall\, x \in R$

Now choose any $x, y\ \varepsilon\ R$ then

$$|f(x) - f(y)| < \varepsilon$$

i.e. ε does not depends on the choice of x and y.

Hence $f(x)$ is a uniformly continuous function.

21. A. Let $\qquad f(x) = x^3 + 9x^2 - 21x + k.$

$$f'(x) = 3x^2 + 18x - 21$$
$$f'(x) = 0$$

$\Rightarrow \quad (x + 7)(x - 1) = 0 \quad \Rightarrow x = -7, 1$

Sign scheme of $f'(x) = 0$

$$\vdash\!\!\!\!-\!\!\!\!-\!\!\!\!-\!\!\!\!+\!\!\!\!-\!\!\!\!-\!\!\!\!+\!\!\!\!-\!\!\!\!-\!\!\!\!-\!\!\!\!\dashv$$

$()$

$\Rightarrow f(1)$ is minium

$\quad f(-7)\ \&\ f(2)$ is maximum

$\quad f(1)$ is minimum

$$f(-7) = -343 + 441 + 147 + k$$
$$= 245 + k$$
$$f(2) = 8 + 36 - 42 + k = k + 2$$
$$f(1) = 1 + 9 - 21 + k = k - 11$$

Now $\qquad |f(-7)| = |f(1)|$

$\Rightarrow \qquad |k + 2| = |k - 11| \Rightarrow k + 2 = 11 - k$

$$2k = 9 \ \ k = 9/2$$
$$|f(-7)| = f(1)$$
$$|245 + k| = |k - 11|$$
$$245 + k = 11 - k \quad 2k = -234$$

$\Rightarrow \qquad k = -117$

i.e. $\qquad k = --\qquad .$

B. From question,

$$\alpha_n = \alpha_{n-1} + 2\alpha_{n-2} \text{ for } n \geq 3$$
$$\beta_n = \beta_{n-1} + 2\beta_{n-2}$$

Now we have to prove

$$\beta_n = 2\alpha_n + (-1)^{n-1}$$

We can prove it by induction

Now for $n = 1$

$$\beta_1 = 2\alpha_1 + (-1)^{1-1} = 1, \quad \beta_1 = 1$$

i.e. $\qquad \beta_2 = 2\alpha_2 + (-1)^{2-1} = 2 - 1,$

$$\beta_2 = 2$$

P(1) & P(2) are true $\hspace{3cm}$ ...(i)

let P(m) is true

then $\qquad \beta_m = 2\alpha_m + (-1)^{m-1}$

& $\qquad \beta_{m-1} = 2\alpha_{m-1} + (-1)^{m-2}$

Now $\qquad \beta_{m+1} = \beta_m + 2\beta_{m-1}$

$$= 2\alpha_m + (-1)^{m-1}$$
$$+ 2[2\alpha_{m-1} + (-1)^{m-2}]$$
$$= 2(\alpha_m + 2\alpha_{m-1}) + (-1)^{m-2}[2-1]$$
$$= 2\alpha_{m+1} + (-1)^{m-2}(-1)^2$$
$$= 2\alpha_{m+1} + (-1)^m$$

i.e. $\beta(m+1)$ is also true $\hspace{2.5cm}$ ...(ii)

i.e. from (i) & (ii)

$\qquad$ P(n) is true for $n \in N$

$\Rightarrow \qquad \beta_n = 2\alpha_n + (-1)^{n-1}$

Again $\qquad \alpha_n + \beta_n = 2^{n-1}$

for $\qquad n = 1 \quad \alpha_1 = 0 \quad \beta_1 = 1$

$\Rightarrow \qquad \alpha_1 + \beta_1 = 1 = 2^0$

$\Rightarrow \qquad$ P(1) is true $\hspace{3cm}$ ...(i)

Now let P(m + 1) is true

i.e. $\qquad \alpha_{m+1} + \beta_{m+1}$

$$= \alpha_m + 2\alpha_{m-1} + \beta_m + 2\beta_{m-1}$$
$$= (\alpha_m + \beta_m) + 2(\alpha_{m-1} + \beta_{m-1})$$
$$= 2^{m-1} + 2.2^{m-2} = 2^m$$

i.e. $\quad \alpha_{m+1} + \beta_{m+1} = 2^{(m+1)-1}$

i.e. P(m + 1) is true while P(m) is true $\hspace{1cm}$ ...(ii)

i.e. from (i) & (ii)

$\qquad$ P(n) is true for all $n \in N$

i.e. $\qquad \alpha_n + \beta_n = 2^{n-1}$

consider $\qquad \dfrac{\alpha_n a + \beta_n b}{n-}$

then $\quad \dfrac{\alpha_n a + \beta_n b}{n-} = \dfrac{\alpha_n a + \left({}^{n-} - \alpha_n \right) b}{n-}$

$\Rightarrow \dfrac{\alpha_n(a-b)}{n-} + b \hspace{3cm}$ ...(i)

Also $\qquad \alpha_n + \beta_n = 2^{n-1}$

$\Rightarrow \alpha_n + 2\alpha_n + (-1)^{n-1} = 2^{n-1}$

$$3\alpha_n = 2^{n-1} - (-1)^{n-1}$$

$$\frac{\alpha_n}{n-} = - - \frac{(-)^{n-}}{n-}$$

taking $n \to \infty$

$\Rightarrow \qquad \displaystyle\lim_{n\to\infty} \frac{\alpha_n}{n-} = -$

i.e. $\quad \displaystyle\lim_{n\to\infty} \frac{\alpha_n a + \beta_n b}{n-} = \lim_{n\to\infty} \frac{d_n}{n-}(a-b) + b$

$$= -(a-b) + b$$

$$= \frac{(a+\,b)}{n-} \; \forall\, a\, b \in \; .$$

22. A. The given function is

$$f(x, y) = \alpha x^2 + xy + \beta y^2 \hspace{2cm} ...(i)$$

Necessary condition for $f(x\,y)$ to have extremum value

$f_x = 0 \quad \Rightarrow 2\alpha x + y = 0 \hspace{2cm}$ ...(i)

& $\qquad f_y = 0 \quad \Rightarrow x + 2\beta y = 0 \hspace{1.5cm}$ ...(ii)

Solving (i) & (ii)

$\quad -4\alpha\beta y + y = 0 \quad \Rightarrow y(1 - 4\alpha\beta) = 0$

$\Rightarrow \hspace{2cm} y = 0 \hspace{1.5cm} [\because \; 4\alpha\beta \neq 1]$

$\Rightarrow \hspace{2cm} x = 0$

i.e. $(0, 0)$ is a stationary point.

Now $\hspace{2cm} f_{xx} = 2\alpha$

$$f_{xy} = 1$$
$$f_{yy} = 2\beta$$

Now the function $f(x, y)$ gives extremum value if

$$f_{xx} f_{yy} - f_{xy} > 0$$

$\Rightarrow \hspace{1.5cm} 4\alpha\beta - 1 > 0 \quad \Rightarrow 4\alpha\beta > 1$

in such case

if $\hspace{2.5cm} f_{xx} = 2\alpha < 0$ leads to maximum.

& $\hspace{2.5cm} f_{xx} = 2\alpha > 0$ leads to minimum.

& if $\quad f_{xx} f_{yy} - f_{xy} < 0$

i.e. $\hspace{1.5cm} 4\alpha\beta - 1 < 0 \quad \Rightarrow 4\alpha\beta < 1$

gives saddle point

i.e. $4\alpha\beta > 1 \quad \alpha < 0 \quad \Rightarrow$ maxima at $(0, 0)$

$\qquad 4\alpha\beta > 1 \quad \alpha < 0 \quad \Rightarrow$ minima at $(0, 0)$

$\qquad 4\alpha\beta > 1 \hspace{2cm} \Rightarrow$ saddle point.

22. B.
$$f(x, y, z) = 7x^3 - x^2z - z^2 + 28y$$
$$\nabla f = (\ x\ -\ xz)i$$
$$+\ j + (-x\ -\ z)k$$
$$\nabla f\big|_{(\ -\ )} =\ i +\ j - k$$

i.e. directional derivative along the unit vector

$$-(\ i -\ j +\ k)$$

$$= -(\ i +\ j - k)(\ i -\ j +\ k)$$

$$= -(\ \ -\ \ -\ ) = -\ .$$

The decreases most rapidly along the $|\nabla f|$ direction and the unit vector along this direction

$$= \frac{i +\ j - k}{\sqrt{\ +\ +\ }} = \frac{i +\ j - k}{\sqrt{\ }}$$

and rate of this decrease $= \dfrac{i +\ j - k}{\sqrt{\ }}$

23. The given differential equation is

$$x\,\frac{d\ y}{dx} +\ x\frac{dy}{dx} +\ y = \cos x$$

put $\qquad\qquad x = e^u$

then above equation reduces to

$$[D_1(D_1 - 1) + 4D_1 + 2 + 2]y = \cos(e^u)$$

$$D_1 = \frac{d}{du}$$

$$(D_1^2 + 3D_1 + 2)y = \cos t\, e^u$$

C.F. is $\qquad\qquad y = c_1 e^{-u} + c_2 e^{-2u}$

$$= c\ \frac{-}{x} + c\ \frac{-}{x}$$

$$\text{P.I.} = \frac{}{(\ +\ )(\ +\ )}\ (e^u)$$

$$= \frac{}{(\ +\ )}\ \frac{-}{x}\int x^-\ \ x\,dx$$

$$= \frac{}{(\ +\ )}\,x^-\ \ x$$

$$= x^-\int x^-\ x^-\ \ x\,dx$$

$$= x^-\int\ x\,dx = -\frac{x}{x}\,.$$

Hence general solution of the differential equation is

$$y = \frac{c}{x} + \frac{c}{x} - \frac{x}{x}\,.$$

24. As $I \in A(G)$ *i.e.* $A(G) \neq \phi$

Now let $T \in A(G)$

Then T is $1 - 1$ onto from G to G.

let $T_1, T_2 \in A(G)$

Then $\quad (T_1 T_2)(xy) = T_1(T_2(xy))$
$$= T_1(T_2(x)T_2(y))$$

as T_2 is homomorphism
$$= T_1(T_2(x))\, T_1(T_2(y))$$

as T_1 is homomorphism
$$= (T_1 T_2)(x)(T_1 T_2)(y)$$

for all $x, y \in G$.

$\therefore\ T_1 T_2$ is a homomorphism from G into G.

Again $\quad (T_1 T_2)(x) = (T_1 T_2)(y)$

$\Rightarrow \qquad\qquad T_1(T_2(x)) = T_1(T_2(y))$

$\Rightarrow \qquad\qquad T_2(x) = T_2(y)$ as T_1 is $1 - 1$

$\Rightarrow \qquad\qquad x = y$ as T_2 is $1 - 1$

$\therefore\ T_1 T_2$ is $1 - 1$

let $x \in G$.

Since $T : G \to G$ is onto $\Rightarrow \exists\, y \in G$

such that $T_1(y) = x$.

Again $T_2 : G \to G$ is onto, $\exists\, z \in G$ such that
$$y = T_2(z).$$

Then $\quad T_{g1}\, T_{g2}(x) = T_{g1}(g_2 x g_2^{-1})$
$$= g_1 g_2 x\, g_2^{-1} g_1^{-1}$$
$$= (g_1 g_2)x\, (g_1 g_2)^{-1}$$
$$= T_{g1g2}(x) \text{ for all } x \in G$$

$\therefore \qquad\qquad T_{g1}\, T_{g2} = T_{g1g2} \in I(G)$

let $\qquad\qquad T_g \in I(G)$

Then $\qquad\qquad T_g T_g^{-1} = T_e = 1$

as $\qquad\qquad T_e(x) = exe^{-1} = x\ \forall\ x \in G$

and $\qquad\qquad T_g^{-1} T_g = I$

$\therefore \qquad\qquad T_g^{-1} = (T_g)^{-1}\ \Rightarrow (I_g)^{-1} \in I(G)$

$\therefore\ I(G)$ is a subgroup.

Now to prove $I(G)$ is normal, we've to prove
$$T_0 T g^0 T^{-1} \in I(G) \; \forall \; T \in A(G) \, \& \, Tg \in I(G)$$
let $x \in G$ be arbitrary. Then
$$(T_0 T g^0 T^{-1})(x) = (T_0 Tg) \, T^{-1}(x)$$
$$= (T_0 Tg)(y)$$
where $\quad y = T^{-1}(x) \in G$
$$= T(Tg(y)) = T(gyg^{-1})$$
$$T(g) \, T(y) \, T(g^{-1}) = T(g) \, TT^{-1}(x) \, T(g^{-1})$$
$$= T(g) \, x \, [T(g)]^{-1}$$
$$= g_1 \, x g_1^{-1} = Tg_1(x) \in I(G)$$
$$\text{where } g_1 = T(g)$$

Hence $I(G)$ is normal.

B.
$$\overline{} \cong I(G)$$

Define $\theta : \dfrac{}{(\ )} \to I(G)$ such that
$$\theta(gz) = T_g$$
Clearly θ is well defined as
$$g_1 \, Z(G) = g_2 Z(G)$$
$$\Rightarrow \quad g^- g \in (\ )$$
$$\Rightarrow \qquad g^- g \, x = x g^- g \quad \forall x \in$$
$$\Rightarrow \qquad (T_1(T_2(z))) = x \Rightarrow (T_1 T_2)(z) = x$$
$\therefore \; T_1 T_2$ is also onto
$\Rightarrow T_1 T_2 \in A(G)$
Again let $T \in A(G)$ Then T is $1-1$ onto
$\Rightarrow T$ is invertible and
$$T^{-1} : G \to G \text{ such that } T^{-1}(x) = y \Leftrightarrow T(y) = x$$
$$TT^{-1} = I = T^{-1}T$$
T^{-1} is $1-1$ as $T^{-1}(x_1) = T^{-1}(x_2)$
$$\Rightarrow \qquad TT^{-1}(x_1) = TT^{-1}(x_2)$$
$$\Rightarrow \qquad I(x_1) = I(x_2)$$
$$\Rightarrow \qquad x_1 = x_2$$
Let $x \in G$ then $\quad y = T(x) \in G$
$$\therefore \qquad T^{-1}(y) = T^{-1}T(x) = (T^{-1}T)(x) = x$$
$\therefore \; T^{-1}$ is onto
Let $\qquad T^{-1}(xy) = z$ then $T(z) = xy$
Let $\qquad T^{-1}(x) = x_1, \quad T^{-1}(y) = y_1$
Then $\qquad x = T(x_1), \quad y = T(y_1)$
$$\Rightarrow \qquad T(z) = xy = T(x_1) \, T(y_1) = T(x_1 y_1)$$

as T is a homomorphism
$$\therefore \qquad z = x_1 \, y_1 \text{ as } T \text{ is } 1-1$$
So $T^{-1}(xy) = z = x_1 y_1 = T^{-1}(x) \, T^{-1}(y)$
for all $\quad x, y \in G$
$\Rightarrow T^{-1}$ is a homomorphism
Thus $T^{-1} \in A(G)$
Hence $A(G)$ is a subgroup
2nd part
$$T_e = exe^{-1} = x \in G$$
$\Rightarrow T_e \in I(G)$
$i.e. \qquad\qquad I(G) \neq \phi$
let $\qquad T_{g1}, \, T_{g2} \in I(G)$
$$\Rightarrow \qquad T_{g1}(x) = T_{g2}(x) \quad \forall \, x \in G$$
$$\Rightarrow \qquad g_1 z(G) = g_2 z(G)$$
θ is onto as $T_g \in I(G) \quad \Rightarrow g \in G$

and $\qquad gz(G) \in \overline{\dfrac{}{(\ )}}$ such that
$$\theta(gz(G)) = T_g$$
Also $\theta(g_1 z(G) \, g_2 z(G)) = \theta(g_1 g_2 z(G))$
$$= T_{g1g2} = T_{g1} T_{g2}$$
$$= \theta(g_1 z(G) \, \theta(g_2 z(G))$$
$\therefore \; \theta$ is homomorphism and hence an isomorphism.

25. A. $T : R^2 \to \mathbf{R}^2$ such that $T^2(v) = -v$ for all $v \in \mathbf{R}^2$
$$\Rightarrow \qquad \begin{pmatrix} x \\ y \end{pmatrix} = \begin{pmatrix} -x \\ -y \end{pmatrix}$$
$$\Rightarrow \qquad T^2 = \begin{bmatrix} - & \\ & - \end{bmatrix} \Rightarrow T^2(v) = -v$$
Let $\qquad T = \begin{bmatrix} a & b \\ c & d \end{bmatrix}$
$$\Rightarrow \qquad T^2 = \begin{bmatrix} a^+ bc & ab + bd \\ ac + cd & bc + d \end{bmatrix} = \begin{bmatrix} - & \\ & - \end{bmatrix}$$
$$\Rightarrow \qquad a^2 + bc = -1 \quad (a+d)b = 0$$
$$c(a+d) = 0 \qquad bc + d^2 = -1$$
Let $\qquad b = c = 0$ then $a^2 = -1$
$$\Rightarrow \qquad a = \pm i \quad d^2 = -1 \quad b = \pm i$$
$$\Rightarrow \qquad T = \begin{bmatrix} i & \\ & i \end{bmatrix} \quad \begin{bmatrix} -i & \\ & -i \end{bmatrix}$$
Also when $a + d = 0 \Rightarrow a = -d.$
Then such matrix is written as

$$T = \begin{bmatrix} & -\sqrt{} \\ -\sqrt{} & - \end{bmatrix}$$

then $$T^2 = \begin{bmatrix} - & \\ & - \end{bmatrix}$$

i.e. T over real field is given as $T = \begin{bmatrix} & \sqrt{} \\ -\sqrt{} & - \end{bmatrix}$.

26. From Gauss's divergence theorem

$$\iint n\, ds = \iiint (\bar{\nabla}\ ^-)\, dV$$
$$= \iiint (y+z +x)\, dx\, dy\, dz$$
$$= \int\limits_{y=} \int\limits_{x=} \int\limits_{z=}^{-(-x)} (y+z +x)\, dz\, dx\, dy$$
$$= \int\limits_{y=} \int\limits_{x=} \left. yz + \frac{z}{}+ xz \right|_{z=}^{-(-x)} dx\, dy$$
$$= \int\limits_{y=} \int\limits_{x=} \left\{ y(-x)+ \frac{}{}(-x) + \frac{x}{}(-x) \right\} dx\, dy$$
$$= \int\limits_{y=} \left. y\left(x - \frac{x}{}\right) + \frac{(-x)}{(-)} + - \left(x - \frac{x}{}\right) \right| dy$$
$$= \int\limits_{y=} y(\ -\ ) + \frac{}{} + -(\ -\ ) \} dy$$
$$\int\left(y + \ + \frac{}{}\right) dy = \frac{y}{} + \left. \frac{}{} y \right|$$

$$= \ + \frac{}{} = \ + \ = \ .$$

27. A. From Stoke's Theorem

$$\int_c \ d\bar{r} = \iint (\bar{\nabla}\times\ ^-)\, n\, ds$$
$$= \int_c \left(yi + zj + xk \right) d\bar{r}$$
$$= \iint -\left(i + j + k \right) n\, ds$$

$$\therefore \quad \bar{\nabla}\times\ ^- = \begin{vmatrix} i & j & k \\ \dfrac{\partial}{\partial x} & \dfrac{\partial}{\partial y} & \dfrac{\partial}{\partial z} \\ y & z & x \end{vmatrix} = -\left(i + j + k \right)$$

$$n = \frac{\nabla(x+y=)}{|\nabla(x+y)|} = -\frac{(i+j)}{\sqrt{}}$$

$$\therefore \quad \int \ d\bar{r} = \iiint \frac{+}{\sqrt{}}\, ds$$
$$= \sqrt{}\iint ds .$$

Now here S is great circle whose radius is 1.

hence $\iint ds = \pi$

$$\therefore \quad \int \ d\bar{r} = \sqrt{}\,\pi .$$

B. $$I = \int\limits_{}\int\limits_{x-}^{\sqrt{+x}} f(x\ y)\, dy\, dx$$

shaded area is domain of integration

$$\therefore \quad I = \int\limits_{}\int\limits_{x-}^{\sqrt{-x}} f(x\ y)\, dy\, dx \quad ()$$
$$= \int\limits_{}\int\limits_{}^{\sqrt{-y}} f(x\ y)\, dx\, dy$$
$$= \int\limits_{-}\int\limits_{}^{+y} f(x\ y)\, dx\, dy$$

i.e. $$\int\limits_{x-}\int\limits_{}^{\sqrt{-x}} f(x\ y)\, dx\, dy$$
$$= \int\limits_{-}\int\limits_{}^{\sqrt{-y}} f(x\ y)\, dx\, dy + \int\limits_{}\int\limits_{}^{+y} f(x\ y)\, dx\, dy .$$

28. A. $x \sim y$ if there exist $z \in$ G such that
$$x = zyz^{-1}$$
Now clearly $\quad x \sim x$
as $\quad x = exe^{-1}$ where $e \in$ G.
i.e. It is symmetric.
Also when $x \sim y \quad \Rightarrow x = zyz^{-1} \Rightarrow y = z^{-1} xz.$
$$= (z^{-1})x\,(z^{-1}) \Rightarrow y \sim x$$
i.e. It is reflexive.
Again let $x \sim y$ & $y \sim w$
$\Rightarrow$ there exist z & $v \in$ G such that
$$x = zyz^{-1} \ \& \ y = vwv^{-1}$$
then $\quad x = zvwv^{-1}z^{-1}$
$\Rightarrow \quad x = zvw(vz)^{-1}$
Clearly $zv \in$ G
i.e. $\quad x \sim w$

i.e. $x \sim y$ & $y \sim w \Rightarrow x \sim w$

i.e. It is transitive

Hence $\sim$ is an equivalence relation.

B. To show that $\begin{bmatrix} & & \\ & & \\ & & \end{bmatrix} \begin{bmatrix} & & \\ & & \\ & & \end{bmatrix}$

We have to show that there exist a non-singular matrix P such that

$$\begin{bmatrix} & & \\ & & \\ & & \end{bmatrix} \sim P^{-1} \begin{bmatrix} & & \\ & & \\ & & \end{bmatrix}$$

Clearly $(3, 0, 0)(0, 1, 0)$ & $(4, 0, 1)$ are independent

let $(a, b, c) \in$

then $\forall \, x, y, z \in$ R such that

$$(a, b, c) = x(3, 0, 0) + y(0, 1, 0) + z(4, 0, 1)$$
$$\Rightarrow \quad (a, b, c) = (3x + 4z, y, z)$$
$$\Rightarrow \quad z = c \;\; y = b \quad \& \quad x = \left(\frac{a - c}{} \right)$$

i.e. $(a, b, c) = \left(\dfrac{a - c}{} \right)(\quad)b(\quad) + c(4, 0, 1)$

$$\therefore \quad (1, 1, 1) = (-1)(3, 0, 0) + 1(0, 1, 0) + 1(4, 0, 1)$$

$$(0, 3, 2) = --(\quad) + (\quad) + 2(4, 0, 1)$$

$$(0, 0, 1) = --(\quad) + (\quad) + (\quad)$$

$$\Rightarrow \quad P = \begin{bmatrix} - & -- & -- \\ & & \\ & & \end{bmatrix}$$

then we can check now
$$|P| \neq 0$$

& $\begin{bmatrix} & & \\ & & \\ & & \end{bmatrix} = - \begin{bmatrix} & & \\ & & \\ & & \end{bmatrix}$

i.e. They are conjugate.

29. Let g be a function such that $g(x) = 0 \; \forall \, x \in (0, 1)$

then $\qquad g(a) = 0$

for $\qquad a \in (0, 1)$

i.e. M_a is not empty

Now let $f, g, \in M_a$

then $\qquad f(a) = 0$ & $g(a)$

Now $\quad (f - g)(a) = f(a) - g(a) = 0 \Rightarrow fg \in M_a$

Further $f \in M_a$ & $h \in$ S
$$fh(a) = f(a) \; h(a) = 0$$
$$\Rightarrow \qquad fh \in M_a$$
$$\Rightarrow M_a \text{ is an ideal of R.}$$

B. Now define a function $\theta: S \to R \mid$

such that $\quad \theta(x) = 1 \; \forall \, x \in (0, 1)$

then $\qquad \theta(a) = 1 \neq 0$
$$\Rightarrow \qquad 1 \notin M_a$$

also for any function $\theta \; \lambda \in S$
$$\lambda \theta(x) = \lambda(x)$$

i.e. θ is unity of S.

Now if possible let
$$M_a \subseteq I \subseteq S$$

then $\quad \exists \, \lambda \in I \mid \lambda \in M_a$

i.e. $\qquad \lambda(a) \neq 0$

let $\qquad \lambda(a) = c$ where $c \neq 0$

Now consider
$$\beta : S \to R \mid \beta(x) = C \; \forall \, x \in (0, 1)$$

then $\qquad \psi = \beta - \lambda$

then $\qquad \psi(a) = \beta(a) - \lambda(a) = c - c = 0$
$$\Rightarrow \qquad \psi \in M_a \Rightarrow \psi \in I$$
$$\Rightarrow \qquad \beta \in I \qquad [\because \; I \text{ is ideal}]$$

Again define
$$\gamma : S \to R \mid \gamma(x) = \frac{-c}{c} = \quad \forall \, x \in (\quad)$$

then $\gamma . \beta(x) = \gamma(x) . \beta(x) = \dfrac{1}{c} . c = 1 \; \forall x \in (0, 1)$

i.e. $\qquad \gamma\beta = \theta \in I$

i.e. I is ideal containing unity
$$\Rightarrow \qquad I = S$$

i.e. $\quad M_a \subset I \subset S \Rightarrow I = S$

$\therefore \; M_a$ is a maximal ideal.

IIT–JAM

JOINT ADMISSION TEST FOR
M.SC. (MATHEMATICS)-2009

1. Let V be the vector space of all 6×6 real matrices over the field R. Then the dimension of the subspace of V consisting of all symmetric matrices is:
   A. 15
   B. 18
   C. 21
   D. 35

2. Let R be the ring of all functions from R to R under point-wise addition and multiplication. Let $I = \{f : R \to R \mid f$ is a bounded function$\}$, $J = \{f : R \to R \mid f(3) = 0$. Then
   A. J is an ideal of R but I is not an ideal of R
   B. I is an ideal of R but J is not an ideal of R
   C. both I and J are ideals of R
   D. neither I nor J is an ideal of R

3. Which of the following sequences of functions is uniformly convergent on $(0, 1)$?
   A. x^n
   B. $\dfrac{n}{nx +}$
   C. $\dfrac{x}{nx +}$
   D. $\dfrac{}{nx +}$

4. Let $T : R^4 \to R^4$ be linear transformation satisfying $T^3 + 3\,T^2 = 4\,I$, where I is the identity transformation. Then the linear transformation $S = T^4 + 3T^3 - 4I$ is
   A. one-one but not onto
   B. onto but not one-one
   C. invertible
   D. non-invertible

5. The number of all subgroups of the group $(Z_{60}, +)$ of integers modulo 60 is
   A. 2
   B. 10
   C. 12
   D. 60

6. Let $a_n = \begin{cases} \dfrac{}{n} \quad n \\[2ex] \dfrac{}{n} \quad n \end{cases}$

Then the radius of convergence of the power series $\displaystyle\sum_{n=}^{\infty} a_n x^n$ is
   A. 4
   B. 3
   C. $-$
   D. $-$

7. The set of all limit points of the sequence
$$1, - - - - - - - - - - - - - -$$ is
   A. $[0, 1]$
   B. $(0, 1]$
   C. the set of all rational numbers in $[0, 1]$
   D. the set of all rational numbers in $[0, 1]$ of the form $\dfrac{m}{n}$ where m and n are integers

8. Let $F : R \to R$ be a continuous function and $a > 0$. Then the integral $\displaystyle\int^{a} \left[\int^{x} F(y)dy \right] dx$ equals
   A. $\displaystyle\int^{a} y\,F(y)dy$
   B. $\displaystyle\int^{a} (a - y)\,F(y)dy$
   C. $\displaystyle\int^{a} (y - a)\,F(y)dy$
   D. $\displaystyle\int_{a} y\,F(y)dy$

9. The set of all positive values of a for which the series $\displaystyle\sum_{n=}^{\infty}\left(\dfrac{}{n} - - \left(\dfrac{}{n}\right)\right)^{a}$ converges, is
   A. $\left(\quad - \right]$
   B. $\left(\quad - \right)$
   C. $\left[- \infty \right)$
   D. $\left(- \infty \right)$

10. Let a be a non-zero real number. Then

$$\lim_{x \to} \frac{}{x - a} \int_a^x (\quad)t \; dt \text{ equals}$$

A. $\dfrac{}{a}(\quad)a$

B. $\dfrac{}{a}(\quad)a$

C. $-\dfrac{}{a}(\quad)a$

D. $-\dfrac{}{a}(\quad)a$

11. Let $T(x, y, z) = xy^2 + 2z - x^2 z^2$ be the temperature at the point (x, y, z). The unit vector in the direction in which the temperature decreases most rapidly at $(1, 0, -1)$ is

A. $-\dfrac{}{\sqrt{}}i + \dfrac{}{\sqrt{}}k$

B. $\dfrac{}{\sqrt{}}i - \dfrac{}{\sqrt{}}k$

C. $\dfrac{}{\sqrt{}}i + \dfrac{}{\sqrt{}}j + \dfrac{}{\sqrt{}}k$

D. $-\left(\dfrac{}{\sqrt{}}i + \dfrac{}{\sqrt{}}j + \dfrac{}{\sqrt{}}k\right)$

12. Consider the differential equation $2 \cos(y^2) \; dx - xy \sin(y^2) \; dy = 0$. Then
A. e^x is an integrating factor
B. e^{-x} is an integrating factor
C. $3x$ is an integrating factor
D. x^3 is an integrating factor

13. Suppose $\vec{V} = p(x, y)i + q(x, y)j$ is a continuously differentiable vector field defined in a domain D in R^2. Which one of the following statements is NOT equivalent to be remaining ones?
A. There exists a function $\phi(x, y)$ such that

$$\frac{\partial \phi}{\partial x} = p(x, y) \quad \text{and} \quad \frac{\partial \phi}{\partial y} = q(x, y) \quad \text{for all}$$

$(x, y) \in D$

B. $\dfrac{\partial q}{\partial x} = \dfrac{\partial p}{\partial y}$ holds at all points of D

C. $\oint_C \vec{V} \cdot d\vec{r} = \quad$ for every piecewise smooth

closed curve C in D
D. The differential $p \; dx + q \; dy$ is exact in D

14. Let $f, g : [-1, 1] \to R, f(x) = x^3, g(x) = x^2|x|$. Then

A. f and g are linearly independent on $[-1, 1]$
B. f and g are linearly dependent on $[-1, 1]$
C. $f(x) \, g'(x) - f'(x)g(x)$ is NOT identically zero on $[-1, 1]$
D. there exist continuous functions $p(x)$ and $q(x)$ such that f and g satisfy $y'' + py' + qy = 0$ on $[-1, 1]$

15. The value of c for which there exists a twice differentiable vector field $\vec{F}$ with curl $\vec{F} = xi - yj + czk$ is

A. 0   B. 2
C. 5   D. 7

16. Container A contains 100 cc of milk and container B contains 100 cc of water. 5 cc of the liquid in A is transferred to B, the mixture is thoroughly stirred and 5 cc of the mixture in B is transferred back into A. Each such two-way transfer is called a dilution. Let a_n be the percentage of water in container A after n such dilutions, with the understanding that $a_0 = 0$.

A. Prove that $a = \dfrac{}{}$ and that, in general,

$$a_n = \frac{}{} + \frac{}{} a_{n-} \quad \text{for } n = 1, 2, 3,...$$

B. Using (a) prove that $a_n = \left[\; - \left(\dfrac{}{}\right)^n \right]$

for $n = 1, 2, 3, ...$

Find $\lim_{n \to \infty} a_n$ and explain why the answer is intuitively obvious.

17. A. Let $f : N \times N \to R$ be a non-negative function. Assume that for every $m \in N$, the

series $\displaystyle\sum_{n=}^{\infty} f(m, n)$ is convergent and has

sum a_m and further that the series $\displaystyle\sum_{m=}^{\infty} a_m$ is also convergent and has sum L. Prove

that for every n, the series $\displaystyle\sum_{m=}^{\infty} f(m, n)$ is

convergent and if we denote its sum by b_n

then the series $\displaystyle\sum_{n=}^{\infty} b_n$ is also convergent

and has sum L.

B. Define $f : \mathrm{N} \times \mathrm{N} \to \mathrm{R}$ by

$$f(m, n) = \begin{cases} & n > m \\ \dfrac{-}{m-n} & n < m \\ & n = m \end{cases}$$

Show that $\displaystyle\sum_{m=}^{\infty}\sum_{n=}^{\infty} f(m, n) = \quad$ and

$$\sum_{n=}^{\infty}\sum_{m=}^{\infty} f(m, n) =$$

18. A. Evaluate $\displaystyle\iint_{R} \left(\left\{ x \quad y \middle/ \right\} \right) dx\, dy$

where $R = [0, 1] \times [0, 1]$.

Let $S = \sqrt{\ } + \sqrt{\ } + \sqrt{\ } + \ + \sqrt{\quad}$ and I

$$= \int \sqrt{x}\, dx \quad \text{Show that } I \le S \le I + 100.$$

19. Let $D = \{(x, y) : x \ge 0, y \ge 0\}$. Let $f(x, y) = (x^2 + y^2)\, e^{-x-y}$ for $(x, y) \in D$. Prove that f attains its maximum on D at two boundary points.

Deduce that $\dfrac{x + y}{} \le e^{x+y-}$ for all $x \ge 0, y \ge 0$.

20. A. Let $a_1, b_1, a_2, b_2 \in \mathrm{R}$. Show that the condition $a_2\, b_1 > 0$ is sufficient but not necessary for the system

$$\frac{dx}{dt} = a\, x + b\, y$$

$$\frac{dy}{dt} = a\, x + b\, y$$

to have two linearly independent solutions of the form $x = c\, e^{\lambda t}$ $y = d\, e^{\lambda t}$ and $x = c\, e^{\lambda t}$ $y = d\, e^{\lambda t}$ with $c_1, d_1, c_2, d_2, \lambda_1, \lambda_2 \in \mathrm{R}$.

B. Show that the differential equation representing the family of all straight lines which have an intercept of constant length L between the coordinate axes is

$$x\frac{dy}{dx} - y = \frac{L\dfrac{dy}{dx}}{\sqrt{+\left(\dfrac{dy}{dx}\right)}}$$

21. Let $A, B, k > 0$. Solve the initial value problem

$$\frac{dy}{dx} - Ay + By = \quad x > 0 \ y \quad = k$$

Also show that

A. If $k < \sqrt{\dfrac{A}{B}}$, then the solution $y(x)$ is monotonically increasing on $(0, \infty)$ and tends to $\sqrt{\dfrac{A}{B}}$ as $x \to \infty$;

B. If $k > \sqrt{\dfrac{A}{B}}$, then the solution $y(x)$ is monotonically decreasing on $(0, \infty)$ and tends to $\sqrt{\dfrac{A}{B}}$ as $x \to \infty$.

22. A. Evaluate

$$\int_{C} (\ y + \ ) \ dx(+ \ x) - \ z\ (y\, dy + \ )xz - \ y\ dz$$

$$()()$$

$$C$$

$$z \quad x \quad y \qquad z \quad y$$

$$x \quad y\ ()$$

$P,$

$$\vec{F}(x, y) = \frac{x}{y}i + \frac{y}{x}j \quad \text{Prove that there are two}$$

possible locations of P such that the work done by $\vec{F}$ is 1.

23. Verify Stokes's theorem for the hemisphere $x^2 + y^2 + z^2 = 9$, $z \ge 0$ and the vector field

$$\vec{F} = (z - y)i + (x - y)\ j + (\ xz - y)\ k$$

24. A. Let $T : \mathrm{R}^3 \to \mathrm{R}^2$ be the linear transformation defined by $T(x, y, z) = (x + 2y, x - z)$. Let $N(T)$ be the null space of T and

$$W = \left\{ \vec{v} \in \quad \vec{v}\ \vec{u} = \quad (\ ) \ \vec{u} \in N\ T \right\}$$

Find a linear transformation $S : \mathrm{R}^2 \to \mathrm{W}$

such that $TS = I$, where I is the identity transformation on $\mathbb{R}^2$.

   B. Suppose A is a real square matrix of odd order such that $A + A^T = 0$. Prove that A is singular.

25. A. Find all pairs (a, b) of real numbers for which the system of equations
$$x + 3y = 1$$
$$4x + ay + z = 0$$
$$2x + 3z = b$$
has (i) a unique solution, (ii) infinitely many solutions, (iii) no solution.

   B. Let A be an $n \times n$ matrix such that $A^n = 0$ and $A^{n-1} \neq 0$. Show that there exists a vector $v \in \mathbb{R}^n$ such that $\{v, Av, ..., A^{n-1} v\}$ forms a basis for $\mathbb{R}^n$.

26. A. In which of the following pairs are the two groups isomorphic to each other? Justify your answers.

    (i) R/Z and S^1, where R is the additive group of real numbers and $S^1 = \{z \in$ C $: |z| = 1\}$ under complex multiplication.

    (ii) (Z, +) and (Q, +).

   B. Prove or disprove that if G is a finite abelian group of order n, and k is a positive integer which divides n, then G has at most one subgroup of order k.

27. Let I and J be ideals of a ring R. Let IJ be the set of all possible sums $\sum_{i=}^{n} a_i b_i$ where $a_i \in I$, $b_i \in J$ for $i = 1, 2, ..., n$ and $n \in$ N.

   A. Prove that IJ is an ideal of R and $IJ \subseteq I \cap J$.

   B. Is it true that $IJ = I \cap J$? Justify your answer.

28. A sequence $\{f_n\}$ of functions defined on an interval I is said to be uniformly bounded on I if there exists some M such that $|f_n(x)| \leq M$ for all $x \in I$ and for all $n \in$ N.

   A. Prove that if a sequence of functions $\{f_n\}$ converges to a function f on I and $\{f_n\}$ is uniformly bounded on I, then f is bounded on I.

   B. Suppose the sequences $\{f_n\}$ and $\{g_n\}$ of functions converge uniformly to f and g respectively on I and both are uniformly bounded on I. Prove that the product sequence $\{f_n g_n\}$ converges to fg uniformly on I. Show by an example that this may fail if only one of $\{f_n\}$ and $\{g_n\}$ is uniformly bounded on I.

29. A. Prove that if f is a real-valued function which is uniformly continuous on an interval (a, b), then f is bounded on (a, b).

   B. Let f be a differentiable function on an interval (a, b). Assume that f' is bounded on (a, b). Prove that f is uniformly continuous on (a, b).

ANSWERS

1	2	3	4	5	6	7	8	9	10
11	12	13	14	15					

SOME SELECTED EXPLANATORY ANSWERS

1. In symmetric matrix $a_{ij} = a_{ji}$

   i.e., dimension of a 16×6 real matrix = No. of independent variable

   = No. of diagonal elements +

   ____

   $= \; + \!\!-\!\! =$

2. A. Give

   $I = \{f : \mathbb{R} \to \mathbb{R} \mid f \qquad \}$

   $J = \{f : \mathbb{R} \to \mathbb{R} \mid f() \; = \}$ is a ring of $f : \mathbb{R} \to \mathbb{R}$

   Infact product of a bounded function & an unbounded function not necessary a bounded function.

   i.e., if $f \in I$ & $g \in R$ then fg not necessarily belong to I.

However $f\ R \to R$ $f) \quad = \quad$ then
$$\forall\ g \in R \qquad gf(3) = 0.$$
[Hence J is ideal of R. Infact J is maximal ideal of IR]

3. In the given option only x^n converges uniformly to 0.

   On the other hand $\left\{\dfrac{n}{n^x +}\right\}$ is decreasing sequence with $f_n \to \infty$ at similarly.
   $\left\{\dfrac{x}{n^x +}\right\}$ is an increasing sequence.

4.. As T satisfy $T^3 + 3T^2 = 4I$
   i.e. it is satisfied by annihilating polynomial $\lambda^3 + 3\lambda^2 = 4$.
   Which is satisfied by $\lambda = 1$
   Now, $S = T^4 + 3T^3 - 4I = T(T^3 + 3T^2) - 4I = 4(T - I) = 0$
   i.e. $\lambda = 1$ satisfy $|T - \lambda I| = 0$
   i.e. $S = 0$. i.e. $\lambda = 0$ satisfy $|S - \lambda I| = 0$
   or $\lambda = 0$ is a root of eigen value of S.
   Hence S is non-invertible.

5. As $60 = 2^2 \times 5 \times 3$
   So, number of subgroups of $(Z_{60}, +)$ is
   $(2 + 1)(1 + 1)(1 + 1) = 12$

6. If r_1 be radius of convergence when n is prime
   then $\qquad r_1 = \lim\limits_{n \to \infty}\left[\dfrac{}{an}\right]^n =$
   Similarly $\qquad r_2 = \lim\limits_{n \to \infty}\left[\dfrac{}{an}\right]^n =$
   $\Rightarrow$ radius of convergence $\min(r_1, r_2) = 3$

7. By definition of limit point, the given sequence contains all the points of the interval [0,1].

8. The shaded area represent the integrand domain.

   Hence $\int\limits^a \left[\int\limits_{y=}^a F(y)dy\right]dx$

   on changing the order of integral.
   $$\int\limits_{y=}^a F(y)\int\limits_{x=y}^a x\,dy = \int\limits_{y=}^a (a-y)F(y)dy$$

9. The given series is
$$\sum_{n=}^{\infty}\left[\frac{}{n} - \left(\frac{}{n}\right)\right]^a$$
$$= a_n = \left[\frac{}{n} - \left(\frac{}{n}\right)\right]^a$$
$$= \left[\frac{}{n} - \left(\frac{}{n} + \frac{}{n} + \frac{}{n} + \frac{}{n} + \right)\right]^a$$
$$= \left[\frac{}{n}\ \frac{}{n}\ \frac{}{n}\ \frac{}{n}\right]^a$$
$$= \frac{(-)^a}{{}^a n^a}\left(+ \frac{}{n} + \frac{}{n} + \right)^a$$
Now the series will be convergent

if $\qquad 3a > 1 \Rightarrow a > -$

10. The given expression
$$\lim_{x \to a}\frac{}{x - a}\int\limits_a^x t\,dt \qquad \left[\frac{}{}\right]$$
By L'Hospital Rule $\lim\limits_{x \to a}\dfrac{}{x} = \dfrac{}{a} \quad a$

11. $\nabla T = (y - xz)i(xy)j + (- xz)k$
   $\nabla\big|_{(-)} = - i + k$
   If ∇T changes rapidly along the unit vector $\perp_r$ to T at that point (*i.e.* along ∇T).
   Hence if decreases rapidly along $(-\nabla T)$ direction
   Hence, unit vector along it $\dfrac{}{\sqrt{}}i - \dfrac{}{\sqrt{}}k$

12. The differential equation is
   $2\cos y^2 dx - xy\sin y^2 dy = 0$
   $M = 2\cos y^2, \qquad N = -xy\sin y^2$
   $$\Rightarrow \qquad \frac{\partial}{\partial y} = 4y\sin y^2, \quad \frac{\partial N}{\partial y} = -y\sin y^2$$
   $$-\left\{\frac{\partial}{\partial y} - \frac{\partial}{\partial x}\right\} = \frac{}{x} = f(x)$$
   i.e $\qquad$ I.F. $= -e^{\int \frac{-dx}{x}} = \dfrac{}{x}$

13. Except C, all statements are for the exactness of differential equation.

14. Given
$$f(x) = x^3 \quad -1 \le x \le 1$$
$$g(x) = -x^3 \quad -1 \le x \le 0$$
$$= x^3 \quad 0 \le x \le 1$$

Consider $\quad a\,f(x) + g(x) = 0$

$\Rightarrow \qquad ax^3 + bx^3 = 0 \quad 0 \le x \le 1$

and $\qquad ax^3 - bx^3 = 0 \quad -1 \le x \le 0$

which is true if $\quad a = b = 0 \quad \forall x \in [-1, 1]$

i.e. $f(x)$ and $g(x)$ are linear independent.

15. $$\bar{\nabla} \times \bar{} = xi - j + czk$$

Also $\quad \nabla\left(\bar{\nabla} \times \bar{}\right) = 0 \quad \Rightarrow 2 - 7 + C = 0$

$\therefore \qquad C = 5$

16. A. Amount of water in 'A' before dilution $= 0$

i.e. $\qquad q_0 = 0$

Amount of milk in 'A' after 1st dilution

$$= \quad + \frac{\ }{\ } \quad = \quad + \frac{\ }{\ }$$

Amount of water in 'A' $= \quad -\left(\quad + \frac{\ }{\ }\right)$

$$= \frac{\ }{\ } = a_1.$$

Now amount of water transferred from A to B in

2nd dilution $= \left(\frac{\ }{\ } - \frac{\ }{\ }\right)$

and amount of water transferred from B to A is

2nd dilution $= \left(\quad - \frac{\ }{\ }\right) \dfrac{\left(\ - \frac{\ }{\ } + \frac{\ }{\ }\right)}{\ } \times$

$$= \frac{\ }{\ } - \frac{\ }{\ }$$

i.e. amount of water in 'A' after 2nd dilution.

$$a_2 = \frac{\ }{\ } + \frac{\bar{\ }}{\ } + \frac{\ }{\ } = \frac{\ }{\ } + \frac{\ }{\ } - \frac{\ }{\ }$$

$$= \frac{\ }{\ } + \frac{\ }{\ }\left(\ - \frac{\ }{\ }\right) = \frac{\ }{\ } + \frac{\ }{\ }\left(\frac{\ }{\ }\right)$$

i.e. $a_2 = \frac{\ }{\ } + \frac{\ }{\ } a$

Hence, on recursion similarly $a = \frac{\ }{\ } + \frac{\ }{\ } a$

in general, $a_n = \frac{\ }{\ } - \frac{\ }{\ } a_{n-}$ for $n = 1, 2, 3 \ldots\ldots$

B. As $\qquad a_n = \frac{\ }{\ } + \frac{\ }{\ } a_{n-} \qquad \ldots(1)$

$$a_{n-1} = \frac{\ }{\ } + \frac{\ }{\ } a_{n-} \quad \ldots(2) \times \frac{\ }{\ }$$

$$\ldots\ldots\ldots\ldots\ldots\ldots\ldots\ldots\ldots\ldots \times \left(\frac{\ }{\ }\right)$$

$$\ldots\ldots\ldots\ldots\ldots\ldots\ldots\ldots\ldots$$
$$\ldots\ldots\ldots\ldots\ldots\ldots\ldots\ldots\ldots$$
$$\ldots\ldots\ldots\ldots\ldots\ldots\ldots\ldots\ldots$$

$$a_2 = \frac{\ }{\ } + \frac{\ }{\ } a \quad \ldots\ldots\ldots\ldots$$

$$a_1 = \frac{\ }{\ } \quad \ldots\ldots\ldots \left(\frac{\ }{\ }\right)^{n-} - (n)$$

Equation $(1) + (2) \times \frac{\ }{\ } + \quad \times \left(\frac{\ }{\ }\right)$

$$+ (n) \times \left(\frac{\ }{\ }\right)^{n-} \quad \text{given.}$$

$$a_n = \frac{\ }{\ }\left[\ + \frac{\ }{\ } + \left(\frac{\ }{\ }\right) + \left(\frac{\ }{\ }\right)^{n-}\right]$$

$$= \frac{\ }{\ }\left[\dfrac{\ - \left(\frac{\ }{\ }\right)^{n}}{\ - \frac{\ }{\ }}\right]$$

$$= \left[\ - \left(\frac{\ }{\ }\right)^{n}\right] \quad n = 1, 2, \ldots$$

$$\Rightarrow \quad \lim_{n\to\infty} a_n = \lim_{n\to\infty}\left[\ - \left(\frac{\ }{\ }\right)^{n}\right]$$

$$= 50(1 - 0) = 50.$$

Intuitively in the long run both container A and B have equal amount of milk and water.

17. A. Given $\sum\limits_{n=}^{\infty} f(m\ n) = a_m$ ...(i)

and $\sum\limits_{m=}^{\infty} a_m = L$ ...(ii)

$\Rightarrow \sum\limits_{m=}^{\infty}\sum\limits_{n=}^{\infty} f(m\ n) = L$ ...(iii)

As (i) and (ii) are convergent, so equation (iii) can be written as

$$\sum\limits_{n=}^{\infty}\sum\limits_{m=}^{\infty} f(m\ n) = L \;\Rightarrow\; \sum\limits_{n=}^{\infty} b_n = L.$$

i.e. $\sum\limits_{m=}^{\infty} f(m\ n)$ is convergent and $\sum\limits_{m=}^{\infty} b_n$ converges to L.

B. $\sum\limits_{m=}^{\infty}\sum\limits_{n=}^{\infty} f(m\ n) = \;+\left[\;--\;\right]+\left[\;=----\;\right]$

$+\left[\;------\;\right]+\;\; = +-+-+-+$

$$= \;\frac{-\ -}{-----}\; =$$

$$\sum\limits_{n=}^{\infty}\sum\limits_{m=}^{\infty} f(m\ n) = \left[\;------+\;\right]$$

$$+\left[\;------\;\right]+$$

$= [1-1]+[1-1]+\,...\,[1-1]+....=0$

18. By Green's Theorem

$$\iint\limits_{R} \left(\;\times\{x\ y\ \}\right)dxdy$$

$$= \oint\limits_{C}$$

Over contour which is perimeter of the above region.

$$= \int\limits_{x=}\; x\ dx + \int\limits_{y=}\; dy - \int\limits_{x=}\; dx - \int\limits_{y=}\; y\ dy$$

$$= \int\; dx + \int\limits_{x=}\left(\; x +\ x\ \right)dx$$

B. Now $\int \sqrt{x}\,dx = \mathrm{I}$ (let)

$$= \int \sqrt{x}\,dx + \int \sqrt{x}\,dx + \int \sqrt{x}\,dx$$

$\Rightarrow \int\; dx + \int \sqrt{\ }\; dx + \int \sqrt{\quad}\; dx \le$

$$\le \int\; dx + \int \sqrt{\ }\,dx + \int \sqrt{\quad}\; dx$$

$\Rightarrow \sqrt{\ } + \sqrt{\ } + \sqrt{\quad} \le$

$$\le \sqrt{\ } + \sqrt{\ } + \sqrt{\ } + \sqrt{\quad}$$

$\Rightarrow \qquad 1 \le S$ (1)

Also $\sqrt{\ } + \sqrt{\ } + \sqrt{\quad} + \sqrt{\quad} \le\ + \sqrt{\quad}$

$\Rightarrow \qquad b \le \mathrm{I} + 10000$ ...(2)

Hence (1) & (2) $\Rightarrow \mathrm{I} \le S \le \mathrm{I} + 100$ proved.

19. Given $f(x,y) = (x^2 + y^2)\,e^{-x-y}$

$\Rightarrow \quad f_x = 2xe^{-x-y} - (x^2+y^2)\,e^{-x-y}$

$\qquad\qquad = (2x - x^2 - y^2)\,e^{-x-y}$

$\qquad f_y = (2y - x^2 - y^2)e^{-x-y}$

At stationary point $f_x = f_y = 0$

$\Rightarrow \qquad 2x = x^2 + y^2 = 2y$

$\Rightarrow \qquad x = y \;\;\&\;\; 2x - 2x^2 = 0$

$\Rightarrow \qquad x = 0, 1$

i.e. extremum points are $(0,0)$ and $(1,1)$.

Also $\qquad f_{xx} = (2 - 4x + x^2 + y^2)e^{-x-y} < 0$

At $(1, 1)$

$\Rightarrow \; f(1, 1)$ corresponds to maxima.

i.e. $\qquad f(1, 1) \ge f(x, y)$

$\Rightarrow \qquad 2e^{-2} \ge (x^2 + y^2)\,e^{-x-y}$

or, $\qquad e^{x+y-2} \ge \dfrac{\left(x\ +y\ \right)}{\underline{\qquad}} \ge \dfrac{x\ +y}{\underline{\qquad}}$

$\Rightarrow \qquad \dfrac{x\ +y}{\underline{\qquad}} \le e^{x+y-2}$ proved.

20. A $\qquad \dfrac{dx}{dt} = a_1 x + b_1 y$

$\qquad\qquad \dfrac{dy}{dt} = a_2 x + b_2 y$

$$\Rightarrow \quad \frac{d\,x}{dt} = a\,\frac{dx}{dt} + b\,\frac{dy}{dt}$$

$$= a\,\frac{dx}{dt} + b\left[a\,x + b\,y\right]$$

$$= a\,\frac{dx}{dt} + b\left[a\,x + b\,\frac{\left(\frac{dx}{dt} - a\,x\right)}{b}\right]$$

$$\frac{d\,x}{dt} = \left(a + b\right)\frac{dx}{dt} + \left(ba - b\,a\right)x$$

$$\Rightarrow \quad \frac{d^2x}{dt^2} - \left(a_1 + b_2\right)\frac{dx}{dt} + \left(b_2a_1 - b_1a_2\right)x = 0$$

A.E. is $m^2 - (a_1 + b_2)\,m + (b_2a_1 - b_1a_2) = 0$

$$\Rightarrow \quad m = \frac{(a + b) \pm \sqrt{(a + b) - (b\,a - b\,a)}}{}$$

$$= \frac{(a + b) \pm \sqrt{(a - b) + a\,b}}{}$$

If $a_2b_1 > 0$ the two real roots are, *i.e.* it is sufficient. However m can be real even if $(a_1 - b_2)^2 + 4a_2b_1 > 0$. (*i.e.* $a_2b_1 > 0$ may not necessarily greater than zero in this case).

B. Consider a straight line $\dfrac{x}{a} + \dfrac{y}{b} =$ ...(1)

length of its intercept between co-ordinate axes

$$= \sqrt{a + b} = L\ (\text{say})$$

$$\Rightarrow \quad \frac{-}{a} + \frac{-}{b}\frac{dy}{dx} = 0 \quad \Rightarrow \quad \frac{-}{a} = -\frac{-}{b}\frac{dy}{dx}$$

or $\qquad\qquad b = -a\dfrac{dy}{dx}$

Also $\quad a^2 + b^2 = L^2 \Rightarrow a\left[+ \left(\dfrac{dy}{dx}\right)\right] =$

$$\Rightarrow a = \frac{-\left(\dfrac{dy}{dx}\right)}{\left[\left|\left(\dfrac{dy}{dx}\right)\right|\right]^{-}} \qquad b = \frac{-\left(\dfrac{dy}{dx}\right)}{\left[+\left|\left(\dfrac{dy}{dx}\right)\right|\right]^{-}}$$

Putting a & b in (1), we get

$$\Rightarrow \qquad \frac{xdy}{dx} - y = \frac{\dfrac{dy}{dx}}{\sqrt{\quad + \left|\dfrac{dy}{dx}\right|}}$$

21. $\dfrac{dy}{dx} - Ay + By = 0 \quad x > 0,\ y(0) = k$

This is in Bernauli form

$$\frac{-}{y}\frac{dy}{dx} - Ay = -B$$

put $\qquad y^{-2} = z \quad \Rightarrow \quad -y^{-}\frac{dy}{dx} = \frac{dz}{dx}$

$$\Rightarrow \quad \frac{-dz}{dx} - Az = -B \quad \Rightarrow \quad \frac{dz}{dx} + Az = 2B$$

$$\Rightarrow \qquad ze^{\int A dx} = \frac{B}{A}e^{Ax} + C$$

or, $\qquad \dfrac{e^{Ax}}{y} = \dfrac{B}{A}e^{Ax} + C$

or, $\qquad \dfrac{-}{y} = \dfrac{B}{A} + Ce^{-Ax}$

Now $y(0) = k \Rightarrow C = \dfrac{-}{k} - \dfrac{B}{A}$

$$\therefore \qquad \frac{-}{y} = \frac{B}{A} + \left[\frac{-}{k} - \frac{B}{A}\right]e^{-Ax}$$

Now if $k < \sqrt{\dfrac{A}{B}}$ then $\dfrac{-}{k} - \dfrac{B}{A} >$

Also e^{-2Ax} is monotonic decreasing function

i.e. $\left[\dfrac{-}{k} - \dfrac{B}{A}\right]e^{-Ax}$ is decreasing function

i.e. $\dfrac{-}{y}$ is decreasing & hence y is an increasing function

Also $\qquad \underset{x \to}{Lt}\ \dfrac{-}{y} = \dfrac{B}{A} \Rightarrow y = \sqrt{\dfrac{A}{B}}$

B. Also in case $k > \sqrt{\dfrac{A}{B}}$ y is decreasing function.

22. A. The given integral is

$$I = \int_C (y + z)\,dx + y(x - z)\,dy + (xz - y)\,dz$$

& the curves are

$$z^2 = x^2 + y^2, \quad \text{and } z = y + 1$$
$$\Rightarrow \quad (y+1)^2 = x^2 + y^2 \;\Rightarrow\; x^2 = 2y + 1$$

or $\quad y = \left(\dfrac{x\ -\ }{}\right) \quad \Rightarrow z = \left(\dfrac{x\ +\ }{}\right)$

Consider

$$I_1 = \int_C (y + z)\,dx$$

$$\Rightarrow \quad I_1 = \int\left[-(x -) + -(x +)\right]dx$$

$$= \int\left(-x - \dfrac{x}{} + -\right)dx$$

$$= -\dfrac{x}{} - \dfrac{x}{} + -x \,\Big|$$

$$= -(-) - -(-) + -(-)$$

$$= \dfrac{}{}$$

$$I_2 = \int_C y(x - z)\,dy$$

$$= \int y\sqrt{y+ }\,dy - \int y(y+)\,dy$$

$$= \left[\dfrac{y(y+)^{}}{} - \dfrac{(y+)^{}}{}\right] - \left[\dfrac{y}{} + \dfrac{y}{}\right]$$

$$= \left[\dfrac{}{} - (-)\right] - \left[\dfrac{}{} + \right]$$

$$= - \dfrac{}{}\, c$$

$$I_3 = \int_C (xz - y)\,dz$$

$$= \int z\sqrt{z- }\,dz - \int(z-)\,dz$$

$$= \left[\dfrac{z(z-)^{}}{} - \dfrac{(z-)^{}}{}\right] - \left[\dfrac{(z-)}{}\right]$$

$$= \left[\dfrac{(\times\ \ -)}{} - - (-)\right] - \left[\dfrac{}{}\right]$$

$$= \dfrac{}{} - \dfrac{}{} = \dfrac{}{}$$

$$\therefore \qquad I = I_1 + I_2 + I_3$$

$$= \dfrac{}{} - \dfrac{}{} + \dfrac{}{}$$

$$= \dfrac{- + }{}$$

$$= - \dfrac{}{} = -$$

22. B. The given curve is

$$\dfrac{x}{} + \dfrac{y}{} = 1$$

any general point on this curve $\left(\ \theta\ \sqrt{}\ \ \theta\right)$

Now, work done

$$W = \int \vec{dr} = \int_{(\ )} \left(\dfrac{x}{y}i + \dfrac{y}{x}j\right)(dx\,\bar{z} + dy\,\bar{j})$$

Converting into θ variable

$$\int_{\theta=}^{\theta} \left[\dfrac{\theta}{\sqrt{}\ \theta}(- \theta) + \dfrac{\sqrt{}\ \theta}{\theta}(\sqrt{}\ \theta)\right]d\theta$$

$$= \int_{\theta=}^{\theta} \left(\ \theta - \dfrac{\theta}{\sqrt{}}\right)d\theta$$

$$= -\ \theta - \dfrac{\theta}{\sqrt{}}\,\Big|_{\theta=}^{\theta}$$

$$= -\ \theta + \dfrac{\theta}{\sqrt{}} = \quad \text{(Given)}$$

$$\Rightarrow \sqrt{}\ \ \theta + \ \theta = \sqrt{}$$

or, $\qquad \sin\theta = \sqrt{3}\,(2 - 3\cos\theta)$

$$\sin^2\theta = 3(2 - 3\cos\theta)^2$$

$$1 - \cos^2\theta = 12 - 36\cos\theta + 27\cos^2\theta$$

or, $\qquad 28\cos^2\theta - 36\cos\theta + 11 = 0$

$$\therefore \qquad \cos\theta = \frac{\pm\sqrt{\qquad -\qquad}}{\qquad}$$

$$= \frac{\pm}{\qquad}$$

$$\therefore \qquad \cos\theta = \text{—} \quad \text{—}$$

And both of $\cos\theta$ value are possible

i.e. there exist two values of θ for which the work done is equal to 1.

i.e. $\qquad W = \{(a,\ a+b)\,|\,a,b \in R\}$

Now $\qquad TS = I$

$\Rightarrow \qquad TS(x,y) = (x,y)$

let $\qquad S(x,y) = a(1,2,0)+b(0,2,1)$

let $\qquad TS(x,y) = T(1a, 2a+2b+b)$

$\qquad\qquad = (5a+4b,\ a-b)$

Now $\qquad TS(x,y) = (5a+4b,\ a-b) = (x,y)$

$\Rightarrow \qquad 5a+4b = x$ and $a-b = y$

Solving we get

$$a = \frac{x+\ y}{\qquad} \quad b = \frac{x-\ y}{\qquad}$$

Thus $\quad S(x,y) = \frac{x+\ y}{\qquad}(\quad) + \frac{x-\ y}{\qquad}(\quad)$

$$S(x,y) = \left(\frac{x+\ y}{\qquad}\ \frac{x-\ y}{\qquad}\ \frac{x-\ y}{\qquad}\right)$$

23. The Stoke's Theorem

$$\iint_S (\bar\nabla \times {}^-)\, n\, dS = \oint_C {}^- \, d\bar r$$

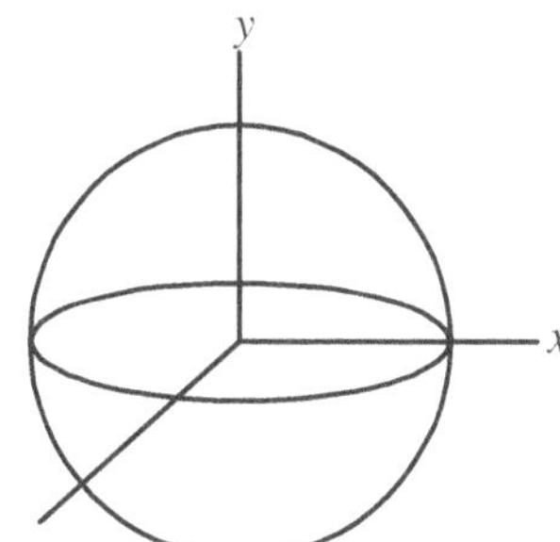

Here C = enclosing circle is $x^2 + y^2 + z^2 = 9$

$$z = 0$$

i.e. $\qquad x^2 + y^2 = 9$

0

$$\therefore \int {}^- d\bar r = \int\left[(z-y)i + (x-\ yz)j + (\ xz-y\ )k\right]$$

$$\left[dxi + dyj + \quad k\right]$$

$$= \int_C -ydx + xdy.$$

Converting into polar by putting

$$x = 3\cos\theta, \quad y = 3\sin\theta$$

$$\int_{\theta=}^{\pi} (\quad \theta + \quad \theta)\, a\theta = 18\pi$$

Now, As $\oiint(\bar\nabla \times {}^-)\, n\, dS = 0$

$$\Rightarrow \iint_S (\bar\nabla \times {}^-)\, n\, dS = -\iint_{S'}(\bar\nabla \times {}^-)\, n\, dS$$

(Refer to figure; S and S′ form closed surface)

$$\Rightarrow \iint_S (\bar\nabla \times {}^-)\, n\, dS = -\iint_{S'} -dx\,dy = \iint dx\,dy$$

$$= \iint dx\,dy = \quad \pi \quad = 18\pi$$

[Note : for S′ surface, $n = -k$]

Hence the Stoke's theorem verified.

24. A. Given $\ T(x,y,z) = (x+2y,\ x-z)$

$N(T) \ \Rightarrow\ T(x,y,z)=(0,0)$

$\Rightarrow \quad (x+2y, x-z) = (0,0) \ \Rightarrow\ x=z=-2y$

$\Rightarrow \quad N(T)$ is generated by $(-2, 1, -2)$

Now $\qquad\qquad W = \{v \in \quad |\ \bar v\, \bar u = \forall \bar u \in (\ )\}$

$\Rightarrow \quad -2x+y-2z = 0$

$\Rightarrow \quad W$ is generated $(1,2,0)$ and $(0,2,1)$.

(ii) For infinite solution, $3a-30=0$ & $b+10=0$

$\Rightarrow \qquad\qquad a = 10,\ b=-10$

(iii) For no solution $3a-30=0$ & $b+10\neq 0$

$\Rightarrow \qquad\qquad a = 10,\ b=-10$

24. B. Given $\quad A+A^T = 0$

or, $\qquad\qquad A = A^T$

Now $\qquad\qquad |A| = (-\ )^n |\quad|$

$\qquad\qquad n = \text{order of matrix A}$

$\Rightarrow \qquad |A| = -|A| \qquad [\because n = \text{odd}]$

$\Rightarrow \qquad |A| = 0 \ \Rightarrow\ A$ is singular.

25. A. Writing the given equation in Augmented matrix form

$$[A:B] = \begin{bmatrix} & & \\ & a & \\ & & b \end{bmatrix}$$

Apply $R_1 \rightarrow R_2 - 4R_1$ $\quad R_3 \rightarrow R_3 - 2R_1$

$$\begin{bmatrix} & & \\ & a - & & - \\ & - & & b - \end{bmatrix}$$

Apply $R_3 \rightarrow R_3 - 3R_2$

$$\begin{bmatrix} & & \\ & a - & & - \\ & - & a & b + \end{bmatrix}$$

Now for unique solution
$$30 - 3a \neq 0 \quad \Rightarrow \quad a \neq 10$$

26. A. from question $R = \{a \quad a \in \quad\}$

$\&$ $\qquad S' = \{z \in C \quad |z| = \quad\}$

define a function $f: R \rightarrow S'$ such that
$$f(r) = e^{i2\pi r}.$$
then f is homomorphic image.

Hence by fundamental theorem,
$$\frac{R}{K} \cong S'$$
where K is kernal of f.

Now if $R \in K$ then
$$f(k) = 1 \quad \Rightarrow \quad e^{i2\pi k} = 1$$
$$\Rightarrow \qquad 2\pi k = 2\pi n \Rightarrow 2 \leq k \qquad ...(1)$$
$$n = \text{an integer}$$

Also $\qquad z \in z.$

then $\qquad f(z) = 1 \quad \Rightarrow \quad k \leq z \qquad ...(2)$

from (1) and (2)
$$k = z$$

Hence $\dfrac{R}{K} \cong S' \quad \Rightarrow \quad \dfrac{R}{z} \quad S'$ are isomorphic

to each other.

(ii) $(z, +)$ and $(Q, +)$

Although both form of group.

But $(z, +)$ is also a subgroup of $(Q, +)$.

i.e. they are not isomorphic to each other.

(B) If $G = \{[\ ][\ ][\ ][\ ]\}_\times$ is abelian group of order 4. Also 2/4 and subgroup of order 2 are

$$\{[\ ][\ ]\}_\times \; ; \; \{[\ ][\ ]\}_\times \; \text{ and } \; \{[\ ][\ ]\}_\times \; .$$

i.e. statement has been disapproved.

27. A. As I & J both are ideal of R, $\Rightarrow 0 \in I \; \& \; 0 \in J$

$\Rightarrow \qquad 0.0 \in I.J \Rightarrow$ IJ is not empty

let $\qquad x, y \in IJ$

then $\qquad x = a_1 b_1 + ... a_n b_n$

$\&$ $\qquad y = \alpha_1 \beta_1 + ... \alpha_m \beta_m$

where $\qquad q_i \in \pi, \alpha_j \in I \; \& \; b_i \in J \; \& \; \beta_j \in J$

$\Rightarrow \qquad x - y = (a_1 b_1 + a_2 b_2 + ...a_n b_n)$
$$- (\alpha_1 \beta_1 + ... + \alpha_m \beta_m)$$
$$= (a_1 b_1 + ...) + (-\alpha_1)\beta_1 + ... (-\alpha_m)\beta_m \in IJ$$

Alos for $r \in R \; \& \; x \in IJ$
$$rx \in IJ$$

$\Rightarrow$ IJ is an ideal

Also I$\cap$J is an ideal

let $x \in IJ \quad \Rightarrow \quad x = a_1 b_1 + ... + a_n b_n.$

$\qquad a_i \in A, b_i \in B, \; 1 \leq i \leq n$

$\Rightarrow \quad a_1 b_1 + ... + a_n b_n \in A \quad \Rightarrow \quad x \in I$

Also $\qquad a_i \in R, b_i \in J$

$\Rightarrow \qquad a_i b_i \in J$
$$a_1 b_1 + ... + a_n b_n \in J$$

$\Rightarrow \qquad x \in I \cap J$

$\Rightarrow \qquad IJ \in I \cap J$

B. Infact $\qquad IJ \in I \cap J$

with $IJ = I \cap J$ holds only if $I + J = R$.

IIT–JAM

JOINT ADMISSION TEST FOR M.SC. (MATHEMATICS)-2008

1. The least positive integer n, such that

$$\begin{pmatrix} \dfrac{\pi}{} & \dfrac{\pi}{} \\ -\dfrac{}{} & \dfrac{\pi}{} \end{pmatrix}^{n}$$

is the identity matrix of order 2, is

A. 4
B. 8
C. 12
D. 16

2. Let $S = \{T : R^3 \to R^3 \mid T$ is a linear transformation with $T(1,0,1)=(1,2,3),\ T(1,2,3)=(1,0,1)\}$. Then S is

A. a singleton set
B. a finite set containing more than one element
C. a countably infinite set
D. an uncountable set

3. Let $s_n = \displaystyle\int \frac{nx^{n-}}{(\ +)x}\,dx$ for $n \geq 1$. Then as $n \to \infty$, the sequence $\{s_n\}$ tends to

A. 0
B. 1/2
C. 1
D. $+\infty$

4. The work done by the force $\vec{F} = yi - xyj + z\,k$ in moving a particle over the circular path $x^2 + y^2 = 1,\ z = 0$ from $(1, 0, 0)$ to $(0, 1, 0)$ is

A. $\pi + 1$
B. $\pi - 1$
C. $-\pi + 1$
D. $-\pi - 1$

5. The set of all boundary points Q in R is

A. R
B. R/Q
C. Q
D. $\varnothing$

6. Let $V = \left\{ (x\ y\ z) \in\quad -\leq x + y + z \leq \right\}$

and $\vec{F} = \dfrac{xi + yj + zk}{(x + y + z)}$ for $(x, y, z) \in V$.

Let n denote the outward unit normal vector to the boundary of V and S denote the part

$$\left\{ (x\ y\ z) \in R\quad x + y + z = - \right\}$$ of the

boundary of V. Then $\displaystyle\iint_{S} \vec{F}\, n\, dS$ is equal to

A. -8π
B. -4π
C. 4π
D. 8π

7. The set $U = \left\{ x \in\quad\quad x = - \right\}$ is

A. open
B. closed
C. both open and closed
D. neither open nor closed

8. Let $f(x) = \displaystyle\int^{x} (x - t\ )g(t)\,dt$ where g is a real valued continuous function on R. Then $f'(x)$ is equal to

A. 0
B. $x^3\, g(x)$
C. $\displaystyle\int^{x} g(t)\,dt$
D. $x\displaystyle\int^{x} g(\ )\ dt$

9. Let $y_1(x)$ and $y_2(x)$ be linearly independent solutions of the differential equation $y'' + P(x)y' + Q(x)y = 0$, where $P(x)$ and $Q(x)$ are continuous functions on an interval I. Then $y_3(x) = ay_1(x) + by_2(x)$ and $y_4(x) = cy_1(x) + dy_2(x)$ are linearly independent solutions of the given differential equation if

A. $ad = bc$
B. $ac = bd$
C. $ad \neq bc$
D. $ac \neq bd$

10. The set $R = \{f \mid f$ is a function from Z to R$\}$ under the binary operations $+$ and defined as $(f+g)(n) = f(n) + g(n)$ and $(fg)(n) = f(n)\,g(n)$ for all $n \in Z$ forms a ring.

Let $S_1 = \{ f \in R\quad f(-n) = f(n)\quad\quad n \in Z \}$

and $S_2 = \{f \in R \mid f() = \}$. Then
A. S_1 and S_2 are both ideals in R
B. S_1 is an ideal in R while S_2 is not
C. S_2 is an ideal in R while S_1 is not
D. neither S_1 nor S_2 is an ideal in R

11. Let $T: \mathbb{R}^3 \to \mathbb{R}^3$ be a linear transformation such that $T(1, 2, 3) = (1, 2, 3)$, $T(1, 5, 0) = (2, 10, 0)$ and $T(-1, 2, -1) = (-3, 6, -3)$. The dimension of the vector space spanned by all the eigenvectors of T is
A. 0   B. 1
C. 2   D. 3

12. Let $\{a_n\}$ and $\{b_n\}$ be sequences of real numbers defined as $a_1 = 1$ and for $n \geq 1$, $a_{n+1} = a_n + (-1)^n 2^{-n}$, $b_n = \dfrac{a_{n+} - a_n}{a_n}$ Then
A. $\{a_n\}$ converges to zero and $\{b_n\}$ is a Cauchy sequence
B. $\{a_n\}$ converges to a non-zero number and $\{b_n\}$ is a Cauchy sequence
C. $\{a_n\}$ converges to zero and $\{b_n\}$ is not a convergent sequence
D. $\{a_n\}$ converges to a non-zero number and $\{b_n\}$ is not a convergent sequence

13. Let $f: (-1, 1) \to \mathbb{R}$ be defined as $f(x) = \dfrac{x}{- x}$ for $x \neq 0$ and $f(0) = 2$. If $f(x) = \sum\limits_{n=}^{\infty} a_n x^n$ is the Taylor expansion of f for all x in $(-1, 1)$, then $\sum\limits_{n=}^{\infty} a_{n+}$ is
A. 0   B. 1/2
C. 1   D. 2

14. Let $y_1(x)$ and $y_2(x)$ be twice differentiable functions on an interval I satisfying the differential equations $\dfrac{dy}{dx} - y - y = e^x$ and $\dfrac{dy}{dx} + \dfrac{dy}{dx} - y = $ Then $y_1(x)$ is

A. $C e^{-x} + C e^{x} - -e^x$

B. $C e^{x} + C e^{-x} + -e^x$

C. $C e^{x} + C e^{-x} - -e^x$

D. $C e^{-x} + C e^{x} + -e^x$

15. Let G be a finite group and H be a normal subgroup of G of order 2. Then the order of the center G is
A. 0   B. 1
C. an even integer ≥ 2 D. an odd integer ≥ 3

16. A. Let f and g be continuous functions on $\mathbb{R}$ such that $f(x) = \int\limits_{x}^{x} g(t)\,dt$ and $g(x) = \int\limits_{x}^{x} f(t)\,dt +$ Prove that $(f(x))^2 + (g(x))^2 = 1$ for all $x \in \mathbb{R}$.
B. Let $f: \mathbb{R} \to \mathbb{R}$ be a function such that f' is continuous on $\mathbb{R}$. Show that the series $\sum\limits_{n=}^{\infty} \left(f\left(\dfrac{x}{n}\right) - f\left(\dfrac{x}{n+}\right) \right)$ converges uniformly on $[0, 1]$.

17. A. Find the maxima, minima and saddle points, if any, for the function $f(x, y) = (y - x^2)(y - 2x^2)$ on $\mathbb{R}^2$.
B. Let $P(x) = a_0 + a_1 x^2 + a_2 x^4 + \ldots + a_n x^{2n}$, where $n \geq 1$ and $a_k > 0$ for $k = 0, 1, \ldots, n$. Show that $P(x) - x\,P'(x) = 0$ has exactly two real roots.

18. A. Given that $y_1(x) = x$ is a solution of $(1 + x^2)y'' - 2xy' + 2y = 0$, $x > 0$, find a second linearly independent solution.
B. Solve—$x^2 y'' + xy' - y = 4x \log x$, $x > 0$.

19. A. Let ϕ be a differentiable function on $[0, 1]$ satisfying $\phi'(x) \leq 1 + 3\,\phi(x)$ for all $x \in [0, 1]$ with $\phi(0) = 0$. Show that $3\phi(x) \leq e^{3x} - 1$.
B. If $y_1(x) = x(1 - 2x)$, $y_2(x) = 2x(1 - x)$ and $y_3(x) = x(e^x - 2x)$ are three solutions of a non-homogeneous linear differential equation $y'' + P(x)y' + Q(x)y = R(x)$, where $P(x)$, $Q(x)$ and $R(x)$ are continuous functions on $[a, b]$ with $a > 0$, then find its general solution.

20. A. Evaluate $\iint\limits_{y}\int \dfrac{x}{\sqrt{z}}\,dx\,dy\,dz$

B. Find the surface area of the portion of the cone $z^2 = x^2 + y^2$ that is inside the cylinder $z^2 = 2y$.

21. A. Use Green's theorem to evaluate the integral

$$\oint_C x\, dx + (x + y\ )dy$$

where C is the closed curve given by $y = 0$, $y = x$ and $y^2 = 2 - x$ in the first quadrant, oriented counter clockwise.

B. Let $f : \mathrm{R} \to \mathrm{R}$ be a continuous function. Use change of variables to prove that

$$\iint_D f(x - y)dxdy = \int_- f(u)du$$

where $D = \left\{ (x\ y)\ \in R \quad x\ +\ y \le\ \right\}$

22. Using Gauss's divergence theorem, evaluate the integral $\iint_S \vec{F}\, n\, dS$ where $\vec{F} = xzi - y\ j + \ yzk$ S is the surface of the solid bounded by the sphere $x^2 + y^2 + z^2 = 10$ and the paraboloid $x^2 + y^2 = z - 2$, and n is the outward unit normal vector to S.

23. A. A square matrix M of order n with complex entries is called skew Hermitian if $M + \overline{M}^T = \quad$ where 0 is the zero matrix of order n.

    Determine whether $V = \{M \mid M$ is a 2×2 skew Hermitian matrix$\}$ is a vector space over (*i*) the field R and (*ii*) the field C with the usual operations of addition and scalar multiplication for matrices?

B. Let $V : \{P(x) \mid P(x)$ is a polynomial of degree $\le n$ with real coefficients$\}$ and $T : V \to \mathrm{R}^m$ be defined as $T(P(x)) = P(1), P(2), ..., P(m)$. Then show that T is linear and determine the Nullity of T.

24. Let G be the set of all 3×3 real matrices M such that $MM^T = M^T M = I_3$ and let $H = \{M \in G \mid \det M = 1\}$, where I_3 is the identity matrix of order 3. Then show that

A. G is a group under matrix multiplication

B. H is a normal subgroup of G.

C. $\phi : G \to \{-1,\ 1\}$ given by $\phi(M) = \det M$ is onto,

D. G/H is abelian.

25. A. Suppose that $(R,\ +,\ .)$ is a ring having the property $a.b = c.\ a \Rightarrow b = c$, when $a \ne 0$. Then prove that $(R,\ +,\ .)$ is a commutative ring.

B. Let R be a commutative ring with identity. For $a_1, a_2, ..., a_n \in R$, the ideal generated by $\{a_1, a_2, ..., an\}$ is given by

$$\langle a\ a \quad a_n \rangle =$$

$$\{ra + ra + \quad + r_n a_n \quad r \in R \quad \le i \le n\}$$

Let $Z[x]$ be the set of all polynomials with integer coefficients. Consider the ideal $I = \{f \in Z[x] \mid f(0)$ is an even integer$\}$. Prove that $I = \langle\ x \rangle$ and that it is a maximal ideal.

26. For a given positive integer $n > 1$, show that there exist subspaces $X_1, X_2, ..., X_n$, of R^m for some integer $m > n$ and a linear transformation $T : \mathrm{R}^m \to \mathrm{R}^m$ such that

— $\dim X_k = k$, $k = 1, 2 ..., n$,

— for $i \ne j$, $X_i \cap X_j = \left\{ \vec{}\ \right\}$, where $\vec{}$ is the zero vector of R^m,

— $T(X_k) = X_{k-1}$, $k = 1, 2, ..., n$, where $X_0 = \left\{ \vec{}\ \right\}$.

Also, find the rank of T.

27. Let $f : (0,\ \infty) \to (0,\ \infty)$ be a continuously differentiable function and let $z = \dfrac{xy}{f(x\ + y\ )}$ be defined for $xy \ne 0$.

A. Prove that $\dfrac{\partial z}{\partial x} + \dfrac{\partial z}{\partial y} = \dfrac{(x + y)}{f(x\ + y)}$

$$\left\{ f(x\ + y\ ) - xy f'(x\ + y)\ \right\}$$

B. Further, if f is homogeneous of degree $-$, then verify that $x\dfrac{\partial z}{\partial x} + y\dfrac{\partial z}{\partial y} = z$

28. Determine the interval of convergence of the power series $\displaystyle\sum_{n=} n(\ n +)\ x^{\,n}$ and show that its sum is $\dfrac{x\ (\ +\ x)}{(\ - x)}$ at any point x in its interval of convergence.

29. A. Let $f : \mathrm{R}^2 \to \mathrm{R}$ be defined as $f(x, y) = x^2 \cos (y/x)$ for $x \ne 0$ and $f(x, y) = 0$ for $x = 0$. Compute

$\dfrac{\partial f}{\partial x}$ at all points in R² and show that it is continuous at the origin.

B. Let $f:(0, 1) \to (0, \infty)$ be a uniformly continuous function. If $\{x_n\}$ is a Cauchy sequence in (0, 1), then prove that $\{f(x_n)\}$ is a Cauchy sequence in $(0, \infty)$. Hence deduce that for any two Cauchy sequences $\{x_n\}$ and $\{y_n\}$ in (0, 1), $\{|f(x_n) - f(y_n)|\}$ is a Cauchy sequence in $(0, \infty)$.

ANSWERS

1	2	3	4	5	6	7	8	9	10

11	12	13	14	15

SOME SELECTED EXPLANATORY ANSWERS

1. If $A = \begin{bmatrix} \theta & \theta \\ - \theta & \theta \end{bmatrix}$ then,

$$A^n = \begin{bmatrix} n\theta & n\theta \\ - n\theta & n\theta \end{bmatrix}$$

i.e. $A^n = \begin{bmatrix} & \\ & \end{bmatrix} \Rightarrow \cos n\theta = 1$

$\Rightarrow n\theta = 2m\pi \quad m = 0, 1, 2, ...$

$\Rightarrow n\dfrac{\pi}{} = m\pi \quad \Rightarrow n = 8m,$

i.e. $n = 8 < \text{minimum positive } m >$.

2. As one more vector independent of $(1, 0, 1)$ and $(1, 2, 3)$ is required to form a basis whose transformed value can be taken as any triad, so number of possible transformation are uncountable.

3. Important result

$$\int \frac{x^{a-}}{- x} dx \text{ is convergent if } 0 < a < 1 \text{ [Remember]}$$

i.e. $\displaystyle\int \frac{x^{n-}}{+ x} dx$ is divergent if $n \geq 1$.

Hence $\{S_n\}$ is divergent

or, $\qquad S_n = \displaystyle\int \frac{nx^{n-}}{+ x} dx$

put $x = \tan^2\theta \quad dx = 2\tan\theta \, \sec^2\theta \, d\theta$

$$S_n = \int^{\pi} n^{n-} \theta \, d\theta$$

$$= \int^{\pi} n^{n-} \theta\left(\theta - \right) dx$$

$$= n\left[\frac{}{n-} - \frac{}{n-} + \frac{}{n-} - \int^{\pi} \theta d\theta \right]$$

$$= n\left[\frac{}{n-} - \frac{}{n-} + \frac{}{n-} - \sqrt{} \right]$$

Clearly $S_n = nx$ some finite value $\Rightarrow S_n \to \infty$

i.e. S_n is divergent or $S_n \to \infty$

4. Work done $\qquad W = \displaystyle\int^{-} d\overline{r}$

$$= \int \left(y\overline{i} - xy\overline{j} + z\,\overline{k} \right) dx\overline{i} + dy\overline{j}$$

$$= \int_C y\,dx - xy\,dy$$

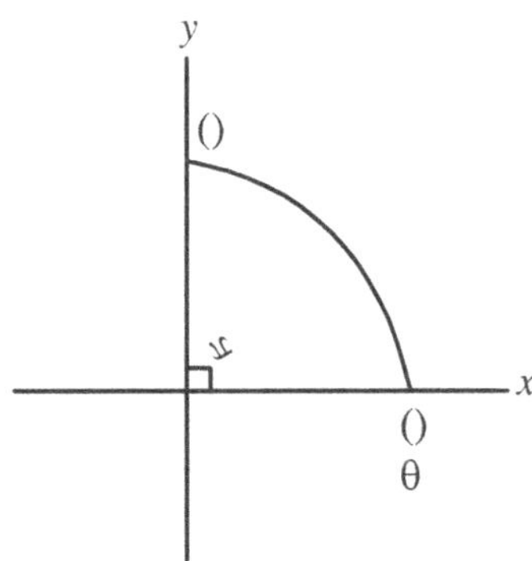

Change into polar co-ordinate by substitution $x = \cos\theta, y \sin\theta$

$$= \int^{\pi} \left(- \theta - \theta \; \theta \right) d\theta$$

$$= \int\limits^{\pi} \theta\, d\theta - \int\limits^{\pi} \theta \quad \theta\, d\theta$$

$$= - \;-\frac{\pi}{} + \left.\frac{\theta}{}\right|^{\pi} \quad = -\pi - 1 =$$

5. As neighbourhood of every real number contains some points of Q and some points of R – Q, so R is the set of boundary points of Q.

6. $\vec{F} = \dfrac{x\hat{i} + y\hat{j} + z\hat{k}}{(x^2 + y^2 + z^2)^2}$

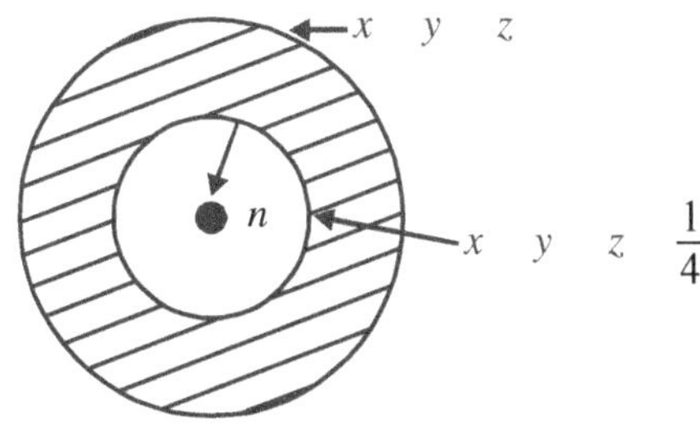

Now n on S is given by

$$= -\nabla f.$$

where $\qquad f = x^2 + y^2 + z^2 - 1/4.$

$$\Rightarrow \qquad n = \frac{\left(xi + yj + zk\right)}{\sqrt{x + y + z}}$$

$$\Rightarrow \qquad -n = -\frac{\left(x + y + z\right)}{\left(x + y + z\right)}$$

Now $\quad \displaystyle\iint \overline{F}.\hat{n}\, dS = -\iint\limits_{S} \frac{}{\left(x + y + z\right)}\, dS$

$$= -\iint\limits_{S} dS$$

$$= - \;\pi\left(-\right) \quad = -\pi$$

7. Clearly, $U = \left\{ \;\dfrac{-\pi}{}\;\dfrac{-7\pi}{}\;\dfrac{\pi}{}\;\dfrac{\pi}{}\;\dfrac{\pi}{}\;\dfrac{\pi}{} \;\right\}$

$\therefore$ Derived set of U i.e. $U' = \phi$

As $U' \subseteq U$, so U is closed.

No point of U is interior point, so U is not open.

8. Given $f(x) = \int_0^x (x^2 - t^2)g(t)dt$

then $\qquad f'(x) = \dfrac{\partial}{\partial x}\int\limits_0^x (x^2 - t^2)g(t)dt$

$$= 2x\int\limits_0^x g(t)dt - \left(x^2 - x^2\right)g(x) - 0$$

$$= x\int\limits^x g(t)dt.$$

9. $\quad y_3(x) = ay_1(x) + by_2(x)$ &
$\quad y_4(x) = cy_1(x) + dy_2(x)$

will be linearly independent if

$$\begin{vmatrix} a & b \\ c & d \end{vmatrix} \neq 0 \quad \Rightarrow \quad ad \neq bc.$$

10. $\quad S_1 = \{f \in R \mid f(-n) = f(n) \text{ for all } n \in Z\}$

Now, $f \in S$ & $g \in R$

then, $\qquad fg(-n) = f(-n)\,g(-n) = f(n)\,g(-n)$

Here $g(-n)$ may or may not be equal to $g(n)$

i.e., $fg \notin S_1$ is not an ideal.

Further $\qquad S_2 = \left\{f \in R \mid f(\;) = \;\right\}$

then $\qquad f, g \in S_2 \;\Rightarrow\; (f-g) \in S_2$

also $\qquad h \in R$

then $\qquad fh(0) = f(0).\,h(0) = 0$

$\Rightarrow \qquad fh \in S_2 \;\Rightarrow\; S_2$ is an ideal

11. Infact if $\qquad \alpha = (1, 2, 3), \;\; \beta = (1, 5, 0)$
and $\qquad \gamma = (-1, 2, -1)$
then, $\qquad T(\alpha) = \alpha\,; \quad T(\beta) = 2\beta,$
$\qquad\qquad T(\gamma) = 3\gamma$

i.e. Transformation matrix for $\{\alpha, \beta, \gamma\}$ as ordered basis will be

$$\begin{bmatrix} 1 & 0 & 0 \\ 0 & 2 & 0 \\ 0 & 0 & 3 \end{bmatrix}$$

i.e. eigen values of T are 1, 2, 3 which are distinct, and non-zero.

i.e. Its eigen vectors are linear independent.

Hence, dimension $= 3$.

12. $\qquad\qquad a_1 = 1,\; a_{n+1} = a_n + (-1)^n\, 2^{-n}$

$$a_1 = 1 - \frac{1}{2}; \qquad a_3 = 1 - \frac{1}{2} + \frac{1}{2^2}$$

$$a_n = 1 - \frac{1}{2} + \frac{1}{2^2} + ... + \left(-\frac{1}{2}\right)^{n-1}$$

$$\Rightarrow \qquad \underset{n\to\infty}{Lt}\ a_n = \frac{1}{1-\left(-\frac{1}{2}\right)} = \frac{2}{3}$$

Now $\qquad b_n = \dfrac{2a_{n+1} - a_n}{a_n}$

$$= \frac{\left[a_n + (-)^{n\ -n}\right] - a_n}{a_n}$$

$$= + \frac{}{a_n}\left(\frac{-}{}\right)^n$$

i.e. $\qquad b_n = + \dfrac{}{a_n}\left(\dfrac{-}{}\right)^n$

$\Rightarrow \qquad \underset{n\to\infty}{Lt}\ b_n = 1$

i.e. $\{b_n\} \to 1 \Rightarrow \{b_n\}$ is also convergent
$\Rightarrow \{b_n\}$ is a Cauchy sequence.

13. Given $f(x) = \dfrac{x^2}{1-\cos x} = \displaystyle\sum_{n=0}^{\infty} a_n x^n$

$\Rightarrow \dfrac{x^2}{1-\cos x} = a_0 + a_1 x + a_2 x^2 + a_3 x^3 + ...$

$\Rightarrow \dfrac{1}{1-\cos 1} = a_0 + a_1 + a_2 + ...$ ...(i)

(put $x = 1$)

$\Rightarrow \dfrac{(-1)^2}{1-\cos(-1)} = a_0 - a_1 + a_2 + ...$ ...(ii)

(put $x = -1$)

(i) and (ii)

$\Rightarrow \quad \displaystyle\sum_{n=}^{\infty} a_{n+} = 0 \qquad\qquad \displaystyle\sum_{n=}^{\infty} a_{n+} = \ .$

14. As $\dfrac{dy_1}{dx} - y_1 - y_2 = e^x$

$\Rightarrow \dfrac{d^2 y_1}{dx^2} - \dfrac{dy_1}{dx} - \dfrac{dy_2}{dx} = e^x$

$\Rightarrow \dfrac{d^2 y_1}{dx^2} - \dfrac{dy_1}{dx} - \left(6y_1 - 2\dfrac{dy_1}{dx}\right) = e^x$

$\Rightarrow \dfrac{d^2 y_1}{dx^2} + \dfrac{dy_1}{dx} - 6y_1 = e^x$

C.F. is $m^2 + m - 6 = 0$

$\Rightarrow (m+3)(m-2) = 0$

$\Rightarrow m = 2, -3$

So, $y = c_1 e^{2x} + c_2 e^{-3x}$

Also, P.I. is $\dfrac{1}{D^2 + D - 6} e^x = -\dfrac{1}{4} e^x$

$\Rightarrow y_1 = c_1 e^{2x} + c_2 e^{-3x} - \dfrac{1}{4} e^x.$

15. As centre of z is subgroup of $G \Rightarrow 0(z)|0(G)$
Also element of H belongs to $z \Rightarrow H \subseteq z$
i.e. $0(z) \geq 2$.
Also $0(H)$ is even
i.e. $0(G)$ is an even integer i.e. $0(G) \geq 2m$

16. A. Given $\qquad f(x) = \displaystyle\int_0^x g(t)dt$

$\Rightarrow \qquad f'(x) = g(x)$ ...(i)

Also $\qquad g(x) = \displaystyle\int_x^0 f(t)dt + 1$

$\Rightarrow \qquad g'(x) = -f(x)$ ...(ii)

$(1) \times f(x) + (2) \times g(x)$

$\Rightarrow f(x)f'(x) + g(x)g'(x) = 0$

$\Rightarrow [f(x)]^2 + [g(x)]^2 = c$

Also, $\qquad f(0) = 0$ & $g(0) = 1$

$\Rightarrow [f(0)]^2 + [g(0)]^2 = c \Rightarrow c = 1$

$\Rightarrow [f(x)]^2 + [g(x)]^2 = 1$ proved.

B. $\displaystyle\sum_{n=1}^{\infty}\left(f\left(\frac{x}{2n}\right) - f\left(\frac{x}{2n+1}\right)\right)$

$= \left[f\left(\dfrac{x}{2}\right) - f\left(\dfrac{x}{3}\right)\right] + \left[f\left(\dfrac{x}{4}\right) - f\left(\dfrac{x}{5}\right)\right] + ...$

$= \left[f\left(\dfrac{x}{2}\right) + f\left(\dfrac{x}{4}\right) + ...\right] - \left[f\left(\dfrac{x}{3}\right) + f\left(\dfrac{x}{5}\right) + ...\right]$

As f' is continouous so, above sum is going to be a finite value so, converges uniformly on $(0, 1)$
Also, by M_n test

$\underset{n\to\infty}{Lt}\ f\left(\dfrac{x}{2n}\right) - f\left(\dfrac{x}{2n+1}\right) = f(0) - f(0) = 0$

So, $\sup \left| f\left(\dfrac{x}{2n}\right) - f\left(\dfrac{x}{2n+1}\right) \right| \to 0$ as $n \to \infty$

hence convergence is uniform.

17. A. The given function is
$$f(x, y) = (y - x^2)(y - 2x^2) = y^2 - 3x^2y + 2x^4$$
$$\Rightarrow\ f_x = -6xy + 8x^3\ ;\ f_{xx} = -6y + 24x^2$$
$$f_y = 2y - 3x^2\ ;\ f_{yy} = 2\ ;\ f_{xy} = -6x$$
Now, $\qquad f_x = 0$
$$\Rightarrow\qquad 2x(4x^2 - 3y) = 0$$
$$\Rightarrow\ x = 0,\ y = \dfrac{4}{3}x^2$$
$$f_y = 0\ \Rightarrow\ y = \dfrac{3}{2}x^2$$
i.e. $(x, y) = (0, 0)$ is the only stationary point
Also at $(0,0)$
$$f_{xx} f_{yy} - \left(f_{xy}\right)^2 = 0$$
i.e., $(0, 0)$ is saddle point.

B. $P(x) = a_0 + a_1 x^2 + a_2 x^4 + \dots + a_n x^{2n}$
$$\Rightarrow P'(x) = 2a_1 x + 4a_2 x^3 + \dots + 2na_n x^{2n-1}$$
$$\Rightarrow P(x) - xP'(x) =$$
$$a_0 - a_1 x^2 - 3a_2 x^4 + \dots - (1 - 2n)a_n x^{2n}$$
Now Using Descarte's rule of sign.

$f(x) = P(x) - xP'(x) = 0$ has only one sign change.

i.e. $f(x)$ has at most positive roots.

Similarly

$f(-x) = 0$ has only one sign change

i.e. total no. of real roots = 2.

18. A. We know that

if $y = uv$ be the solution of
$$y_2 + py_1 + Q = 0 \text{ then} \qquad\qquad \dots(i)$$
this equation can be written into
$$\dfrac{d\,V}{dx} + \left(P + \dfrac{du}{u\,dx}\right)\dfrac{dV}{dx} + \dfrac{v}{u}\left[\dfrac{d\,u}{dx} + P\dfrac{du}{dx} + Qu\right] =$$
$$\dots(ii)$$
Now u is solution of (i) $\Rightarrow u_2 + Pu_1 + Qu = 0$

i.e. (2) reduces to

$$\dfrac{d\,V}{dx} + \left(P + \dfrac{du}{u\,dx}\right)\dfrac{dV}{dx} = \qquad\qquad \dots(iii)$$
Now the given equation is
$$y_2 - \dfrac{x}{+x}\,y + \dfrac{}{+x}\,y = \qquad\qquad \dots(iv)$$
Putting P and $u = x$ is (iii) we get
$$\Rightarrow\ \dfrac{d\,V}{dx} + \dfrac{dV}{x(\ +x\ )\,dx} = 0$$
$$\Rightarrow\ \dfrac{dq}{dx} + \dfrac{q}{x(\ +x\ )} = 0 \qquad \left[q = \dfrac{dV}{dx}\right]$$
$$\Rightarrow\ \dfrac{dq}{dx} + \dfrac{dx}{x(\ +x\ )} = 0\ \Rightarrow\ q = c\,\dfrac{(x\ +\ )}{x}$$
$$\Rightarrow\ \dfrac{dV}{dx} = c\left(\ +\dfrac{}{x}\right)$$
$$\Rightarrow\ v = c\left(x - \dfrac{}{x}\right) + c$$
i.e. $\quad y = uv = c_1(x^2 - 1) + c_2 x$

i.e. $\quad$ 2nd solution of (iv) is $(x^2 - 1)$.

B. The given equation is
$$x^2 y'' + xy' - y = 4x \log x, x > 0 \qquad\qquad \dots(i)$$
$$\text{(Euler-Cauchy form)}$$
Put $x = e^z$ then (i) reduces to
$$[D_1(D_1 - 1) + D_1 - 1]y = 4ze^z \qquad \left[D = \dfrac{d}{dz}\right]$$
$$\Rightarrow\ [D_1^2 - 1]y = 4ze^z$$
A.E. is $m^2 - 1 = 0\ \Rightarrow\ $C.F. $= c_1 e^z + c_2 e^{-z}$

P.I. $y = \dfrac{1}{\left(D_1^2 - 1\right)}4ze^z = 4e^z \cdot \dfrac{1}{D_1^2 + 2D_1}z$
$$= 4e^z \cdot \dfrac{1}{2D_1}\left(1 - \dfrac{D_1}{2} + \dfrac{D_1^2}{4}\dots\right)z$$
$$= 4e^z \dfrac{1}{2D_1}\left(z - \dfrac{1}{2}\right) = 2e^z\left(\dfrac{z^2}{2} - \dfrac{z}{2}\right)$$
i.e. complete solution
$$y = c_1 e^z + c_2 e^{-z} + e^z(z^2 - z)$$
$$= c_1 x + c_2 x^{-1} + x\left[(\ x) - (\ x)\right]$$

19. A. $\phi'(x) \le 1 + 3\phi(x)$

$\Rightarrow \phi'(x) - 3\phi(x) - 1 \le 0$ ...(i)

Consider $\phi'(x) - 3\phi(x) - 1 = 0$

or $\phi'(x) - 3\phi(x) = 1$

Integrating factor $e^{-\int dx} = e^{-x}$

$\Rightarrow \qquad e^{-3x}\,\phi(x) = -\dfrac{e^{-x}}{\quad} + c$

or, $\phi(x) = ce^{x} - -$

$\because \qquad\quad \phi(0) = 0 \Rightarrow c = \dfrac{1}{3}$

$i.e., \qquad\quad \phi(x) = \dfrac{1}{3}(e^{3x} - 1)$

Clearly $\phi(x)$ is an increasing function hence (i), can be satisfied if we put

$$\phi(x) \le -\left(e^{x} - \right)$$

or, $3\phi(x) \le e^{3x} - 1$. (proved)

B. We know that if y_1 and y_2 are two solution of linear differential equation

$(D^2 + PD + Q)y = 0$ ...(i)

then $y = ay_1 + by_2$

also satisfy (i)

where a, b are arbitrary constant.

Now given $y_1(x) = x - 2x^2$

$\qquad\qquad\qquad y_2(x) = 2x - 2x^2$

$\qquad\qquad\qquad y_3(x) = x(e^x - 2x)$

Using above result, we can say x and x^2 are C.F. of given equation where $y_3(x)$ is the particular integral.

Hence its general solution is

$$y = ax + bx^2 + x(e^x - 2x).$$

20. A. The given integral is

$$\iiint_y \frac{x}{\sqrt{z}}\, dx\,dy\,dz$$

By changing the order of integration

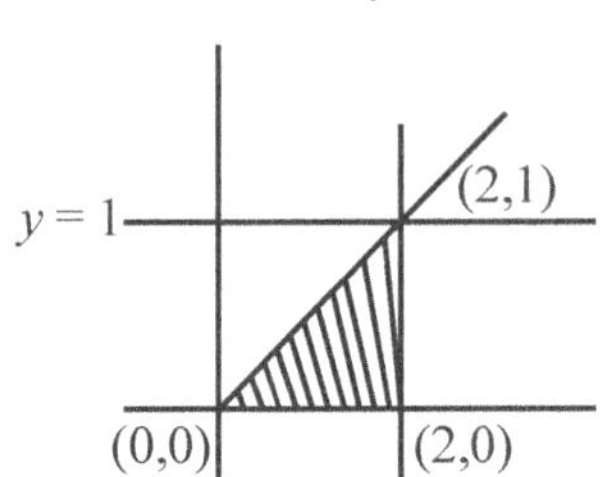

$$\iint\int^{x} \frac{x}{\sqrt{z}}\, dy\,dx\,dz = \iint \frac{x}{\ } \cdot \frac{x}{\sqrt{z}}\, dx\,dz$$

$$= \int - \quad x \left|\ \frac{dz}{\sqrt{z}}\ = \left(-\quad\right)\frac{z}{\ }\ \right|$$

$$= - \quad .$$

B. $z^2 = x^2 + y^2$ and $z^2 = 2y$

$\Rightarrow x^2 + y^2 = 2y$

$\Rightarrow x^2 + (y - 1)^2 = (1)^2$

     Here y takes values from 0 to 2

     Hence value of z^2 is from 0 to 4

     Thus z takes values from 0 to 2

     Elementary surface area will be

$$\pi(z + dz)\sqrt{2}(z + dz) - \pi z\sqrt{2}z$$

$$= \sqrt{2}\pi(2z\,dz + dz^2) \approx 2\sqrt{2}\pi z\,dz$$

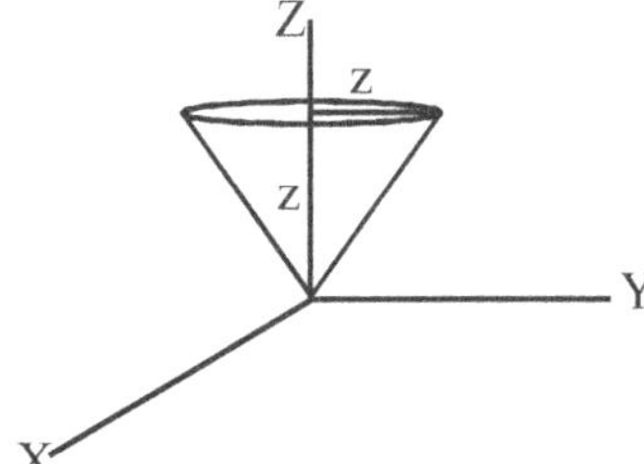

     Thus required surface area will be

$$\int_0^2 2\sqrt{2}\pi z\,dz = \sqrt{2}\pi z^2 \Big|_0^2 = 4\sqrt{2}\pi$$

21. A. Green's Theorem

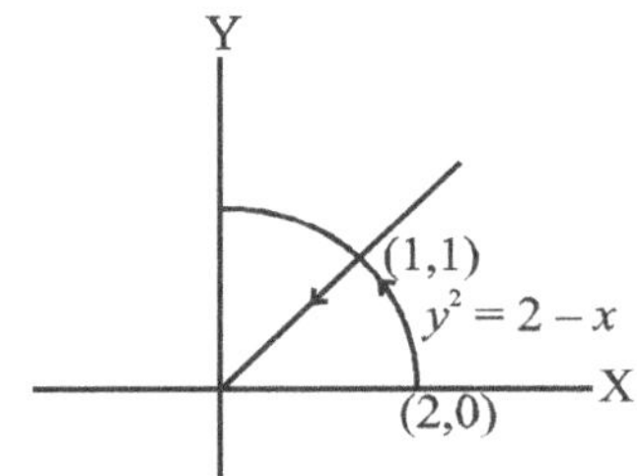

$$\oint_C Mdx + Ndy = \iint_R \left(\frac{\partial N}{\partial x} - \frac{\partial M}{\partial y} \right) dxdy$$

$$\therefore \ \oint_C x\,dx + (x + y)dy = \iint (\ - \ )dxdy$$

$$= \int\limits_{x=}^{x} \int\limits_{y=} dydx + \int\limits_{x=}^{\sqrt{\ -x}} \int\limits_{y=} dydx$$

$$= \int xdx + \int \sqrt{\ - x}\ dx$$

$$= \left. \frac{x}{\ } \right| + \left[-\frac{(\ - x)^{-}}{-} \right] = - + - = -$$

B. $\displaystyle\iint_D f(x - y)dxdy$

$$|x| + |y| \le 1$$

put $\qquad\qquad u = x - y; \ v = x + y$

then $\qquad\qquad x = \dfrac{u + v}{2}, \ y = \dfrac{v - u}{2}$

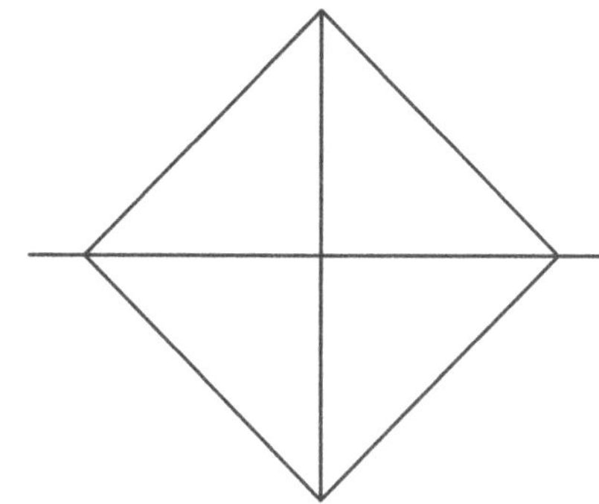

then $\qquad \dfrac{\partial(x\ y)}{\partial(u\ v)} = \begin{vmatrix} - & - \\ -- & - \end{vmatrix} = -$

$$\iint f(u) - dudv = \int\limits_{u=-} \int\limits_{v=-}^{1} f(u) - dudv$$

$$= \int\limits_{u=-} f(u)du \ .$$

22. Given $\vec{F} = 4xz\,\vec{i} - y^2\vec{j} + 4yz\vec{k}$
Region is bounded by

$x^2 + y^2 + z^2 = 10 \ \ \& \ \ x^2 + y^2 = z - 2$

Now $x^2 + y^2 + (x^2 + y^2 + 2)^2 = 10$

$\Rightarrow \quad (x^2 + y^2) + (x^2 + y^2)^2 + 4(x^2 + y^2) + 4 = 10$

$\Rightarrow \quad (x^2 + y^2 + 6)\,(x^2 + y^2 - 1) = 0$

$$[\because \ x^2 + y^2 + 6 \ne 0]$$

$\Rightarrow \qquad\qquad x^2 + y^2 = 1,$

Also when $x^2 + y^2 = 1, \ \ z = 3$

Also the intersection point common to both curves at z axis is given $x^2 + y^2 = 0 \Rightarrow z = 2$

Hence by the Gauss's divergence theorem

$$\Rightarrow \quad \iint (\overline{\nabla}.\overline{F})dV = \iint \overline{F}.\hat{n}ds$$

$$\int \vec{\ }\,n\,dS = \iiint (\ x - \ y)dx\,dy\,dz$$

$$= \int\limits_{z=} \int \int\limits_{-\sqrt{\ -y}}^{\sqrt{\ -y}} (\ z + \ y)dx\,dy\,dy$$

$$= \iint_{-} (\ z + \ y)\sqrt{\ - y}\ dydz$$

Using property of definite integral

$$= \int \ \times \ z \left\{ \frac{y\sqrt{\ - y}}{\ } + - \quad ^{-}\ y \right\}$$

$$= \int \ z\left\{ \frac{\pi}{\ } dz \right. = 10\,\pi$$

23. A. We know that if H is Skew-Hermitian then

$\qquad H^{-T} = -H \quad [H^{-T} = \text{conjugate transpose of H}]$

Now if α, β are Skew Hermitian matrix then

$$\alpha^{-T} = -\alpha \text{ and } \beta^{-T} = -\beta$$

consider $\overline{(a\alpha + \beta)}^{T}$ where $a, b \in R$

then $\quad a\alpha^{-T} + b\,\beta^{-T} = a(-\alpha) + b(-\beta)$

$$= -(a\alpha + b\beta)$$

i.e. $a\alpha + b\beta \in v$ provided $\alpha, \beta \in v$

Hence v is a vector space over R.

However this might not true if $a, b \in c$

as $\qquad\qquad A = \begin{bmatrix} 0 & i \\ -i & 0 \end{bmatrix} \in V$

but $\qquad\qquad iA = \begin{bmatrix} 0 & -i \\ 1 & 0 \end{bmatrix} \notin V.$

B. Given $\{p(x) \mid p(x)$ is polynomial of degree $\le n$ with real coefficient$\}$

i.e. the
$$P(x) = \sum_{i=0}^{n} a_i x^i \quad a_i \in R$$

the
$$T(P(x)) = [P(1), P(2), \dots P(m)]$$

where
$$P(k) = \sum_{i=0}^{n} a_i x^i$$

Now if $P, Q \in V$

then
$$P = \sum_{i=0}^{n} a_i x^i \ \& \ \sum_{i=0}^{n} b_i x^i \ a_i, b_i \in R$$

then
$$AP(x) + BQ(x) = \sum_{i=0}^{n} (Aa_i + Bb_i) x^i$$

$$\Rightarrow T[A(P(x) + BQ(x)] = T[S(Aa_i + Bb_i) x^i]$$
$$= AT(P(x)) + BTQ(x)$$

i.e. T is linear.

Now
$$T(P(x)) = 0$$
$$\Rightarrow (P(1), P(2), P(3), \dots P(m)) = (0, 0, \dots 0)$$
$$\Rightarrow (a_0 + a_1 + a_2 + \dots a_n, \ a_0 + 2a_1 + 2^2 a_2 + \dots 2^n a_n,$$
$$a_0 + 3a_1 + \dots 3^n a_n, \ a_0 + ma_1 + \dots m^n a_n)$$
$$= (0, 0, 0, \dots 0)$$

$$\Rightarrow \quad a_0 + a_1 + a_2 + \dots a_n = 0$$
$$a_0 + 2a_1 + 2^2 a_2 + \dots 2^n a_n = 0$$
$$a_0 + 3a_1 + \dots 3^n a_n = 0$$
$$\vdots$$
$$\vdots$$
$$a_0 + ma_1 + \dots m^n a_n = 0$$

or
$$\begin{bmatrix} 1 & 1 & 1 & 1 \dots & 1 \\ 1 & 2 & 2^2 & 2^3 \dots 2^n \\ \vdots & & & \\ \vdots & & & \\ 1 & m & m^2 & \dots \dots m^n \end{bmatrix} \begin{bmatrix} a_0 \\ a_1 \\ \vdots \\ \vdots \\ a_n \end{bmatrix} = 0$$

Clearly the above matrix is of $[m \times (n+1)]$ order

Hence rank $\leq \min(m, n+1)$

if $m \geq n+1$. then rank of matrix $= (n+1)$

also Nullity $(T) = \dim P - \text{sim}(\text{Imag} T)$
$$= n + 1 - n + 1 = 0$$
$$[\because \dim(\text{Null} T) + \dim(\text{Imag} T) = \dim(0)]$$

when $n + 1 > m$

then $N(T) = n + 1 - m$

24. From question,
$$G = \left\{ \ \Big| \quad = \quad = \ \right\}$$

Clearly $I_3 \in G \Rightarrow$ G is not emply

Suppose $M, N \in G \Rightarrow MM^T = M^T M = I_3$

&
$$NN^T = N^T N = I_3$$
Now consider $(MN^{-1})(MN^{-1})^T = MN^{-1}(N^{-1})^T M^T$
$$= M(NN^T)^{-1} M^T = I_3$$
$$\Rightarrow \quad MN^{-1} \in G$$
$$\Rightarrow \quad \text{G is group.}$$

$\because \ H = \{M \in G | \det(M) = I\}$

Now $M \in H \ \& \ N \in G$

then $\det(NMN^{-1}) = \det(N)\det(M)\det(N^{-1}) = 1$
$$\Rightarrow \quad NMN^{-1} \in H$$
$$\Rightarrow \quad \text{H is normal subgroup of G.}$$

as $\forall \ M \in G$ also $M^T M = I_3 \Rightarrow (\det M)^2 = 1$
$$\Rightarrow \quad \det(M) = \pm 1$$

i.e. we $\phi : G \to \{-1, -1\}$ is onto as $\det(N) = \pm 1$.

G/H is abelian

$A, B \in G \Rightarrow HA.HB$ are coset of G.

Now let $HA.HB = HB.HA$ [Ze G/H is abelian]
$$HAB = HBA \Rightarrow HABA^{-1}B^{-1} = H$$
or $ABA^{-1}B^{-1} \in H.$

Now we prove that $ABA^{-1}B^{-1} \in H$

as $\det(ABA^{-1}B^{-1}) = 1$
$$\Rightarrow \quad ABA^{-1}B^{-1} \in H$$
$$\Rightarrow \quad \text{G/H is abelian.}$$

25. A. Given $a \cdot b = c \cdot a \Rightarrow b = c$

Now ring follows distributive laws.
$$\Rightarrow x \cdot (yx) = (xy) \cdot x \quad [\because a \cdot b = c \cdot a \Rightarrow b = c]$$
Now as R satisfy cross cancellation
$$\Rightarrow xy = yx \Rightarrow \text{R is commutative.}$$

B.
$$z[x] = \left\{ \sum a_i x^i \Big| a_i \in z \right\}$$
Now $I = \{ f | f(0) \text{ is even integer}\}$

Let then $f(x)$ must be of form
$$2a_0 + x(a_1 + a_2 x + \dots) \Rightarrow f(0) = 2a_0$$
Now I is ideal

as $f, g \in I \Rightarrow f - g \in I$

Also, $h \in z[x], f \in I \Rightarrow fh \in I$

$\because \qquad f(x) = 2a_0 + x(a_1 + a_2 x + \dots)$
$$\Rightarrow \qquad f \in \ <2, x>$$
Also $(2, x) = 2f(x) + xg(x) \in \ <1>$

If possible let
$$\Rightarrow \qquad <2, x> C U C I$$
then constant term in element of U must be odd.

Let $(2a_0 + 1) + a_1 x + a_2 x^2 + \dots \in U$

$\Rightarrow \qquad (2a_0 + a_1 x + a_2 x^2 + ...) + 1$

$\therefore \qquad (2a_0 + a_1 x + a_2 x^2 + ... \in \, <2, x>$

$\Rightarrow \qquad 2a_0 + a_1 x + ... \in U$

$\Rightarrow \qquad\quad 2 \in I \;\Rightarrow\; U = z[x]$

$\Rightarrow \qquad <2, x> \text{ is maximal.}$

$$\sum t_n \; = \; -\frac{}{+a} + \frac{}{+a} - \frac{}{(\;+a\;)(\;+a\;)} +$$

$$= \; -\frac{}{(\;+a\;)(\;+a\;)\;(\;+a_n\;)} \; = \; -$$

$$(\because \Sigma a_\text{n} \text{ is divergent}).$$

B. Let P(x, y) be the required point then

$$\text{AP}^2 + \text{PB}^2 + \text{PC}^2$$

$$\text{L}^2\text{Q}^2 = (x - x_1)^2 + (y - y_1)^2$$
$$+ (x - x_2)^2 + (y - y_2)^2$$

Now for minima or maxima

$$\frac{\partial L}{\partial x} = \quad \& \quad \frac{\partial L}{\partial y} =$$

$$\Rightarrow \; x - x_1 + x - x_2 + x - x_3 = 0$$

$$\Rightarrow \; x = -(x \; + x \; + x \;)$$

$$y - y_1 + y - y_2 + y - y_3 = 0$$

$$\Rightarrow \; y = -(y \; + y \; + y \;)$$

i.e. $\quad \equiv \left(\dfrac{\Sigma x_i}{} \;\; \dfrac{\Sigma y_i}{} \right)$ which is centroid of the triangle.

26. Subspaces spanned by following vectors.

$X_1 = \{(1, 0, 0, -, 0)\}$

$X_2 = \{(1, 1, 0, -, 0), (0, 1, 0, -, 0)\}$

$X_3 = \{(1, 1, 1, -, 0), (0, 1, 1, -, 0),$
$\quad (0, 0, 1, 0, -, 0)\}$

$$\vdots$$

$X_k = \{(1, 1, 1, 1, +, 0), (1, 1, 1, +, 0), ...,$
$\quad (0, 0, ..., 1, 0, -, 0)\}$

$$\vdots$$

$X_n = \{(1, 1, 1, ..., 1, 0, ..., 0), (1, 1, 1, ..., 1, 0,$
$\quad 0, ..., 0\}, ...,$

$\quad (0, 0, ..., 0, 1, 0, ..., 0)\}$

Here dimension of $X_k = K$

Also, for $i \neq j\, X_i \cap X_j = \{\vec{0}\,\}$

If X_k is generated by

$\{\alpha_1, \alpha_2, ..., \alpha_k\}$, then

$$T(X_k) = T(a_1 \alpha_1 + a_2 \alpha_2 + ... + a_k \alpha_k)$$
$$= a_1 T(\alpha_1) + a_2 T(\alpha_2) + ... + a_k T(\alpha_k)$$
$$= a_1(\alpha_1 - \alpha_k) + a_2 (\alpha_2 - \alpha_k) + ...$$
$$+ a_{k-1}(\alpha_{k-1} - \alpha_k) \in X_{k-1}$$

Rank of transformation

$= \text{Rank of } X_{n-1} = n - 1$

27. A. Given $z = \dfrac{xy}{f(x^2 + y^2)}$

$$\Rightarrow \frac{\partial z}{\partial x} = \frac{y}{f(x^2 + y^2)} + xy \left[-\frac{2xf\,'(x^2 + y^2)}{\{f(x^2 + y^2)\}^2} \right]$$

$$\& \frac{\partial z}{\partial y} = \frac{x}{f(x^2 + y^2)} + xy \left[\frac{-2yf\,'(x^2 + y^2)}{\{f(x^2 + y^2)^2\}} \right]$$

$$\Rightarrow \frac{\partial z}{\partial x} + \frac{\partial z}{\partial y} = \frac{(x + y)}{f(x^2 + y^2)} - \frac{2xy(x + y)f\,'(x^2 + y^2)}{\{f(x^2 + y^2)\}^2}$$

$$= \frac{(x + y)}{[f(x^2 + y^2)]^2} \{f(x^2 + y^2) - 2xyf\,'(x^2 + y^2)\}$$

Proved.

B. For, $\quad z = \dfrac{xy}{\sqrt{x^2 + y^2}}$

and using above equations, we get by putting

$$f(x^2 + y^2) = \sqrt{x^2 + y^2}$$

and $f'(x^2 + y^2) = \dfrac{1}{2\sqrt{x^2 + y^2}}$

$$x\frac{\partial z}{\partial x} + y\frac{\partial z}{\partial y} = \frac{xy^3}{\left(x^2 + y^2\right)^{\frac{3}{2}}} + \frac{yx^3}{\left(x^2 + y^2\right)^{\frac{3}{2}}}$$

$$= \frac{xy\left(x^2 + y^2\right)}{\left(x^2 + y^2\right)^{\frac{3}{2}}} = \frac{xy}{\sqrt{x^2 + y^2}} = z$$

Thus $\quad x\dfrac{\partial z}{\partial x} + y\dfrac{\partial z}{\partial y} = z$

28. $\displaystyle\sum_{n=1}^{\infty} n(2n-1)x^{2n}$

$u_n = n(2n-1)x^{2n}$

$$Lt\,\frac{u_{n+1}}{u_n} = Lt\,\frac{(n+1)(2n+1)x^{2n+2}}{(n)(2n-1)x^{2n}} = x^2$$

$|x^2| < 1 \quad\Rightarrow\quad -1 < x < 1$

Interval of convergence is $(-1, 1)$

Also, $P(x) = 1 \cdot x^2 + 2 \cdot 3x^4 + 3 \cdot 5x^6 + \dots$

$$\Rightarrow \text{As } \sum_{n=1}^{\infty} x^{2n} = \frac{x^2}{(1-x^2)}$$

$$\Rightarrow \sum_{n=1}^{\infty} 2nx^{2n-1} = \frac{2x(1-x^2)-x^2(-2x)}{(1-x^2)^2}$$

$$= \frac{2x}{(1-x^2)^2}$$

on differentiating both sides.

$$\Rightarrow \sum_{n=1}^{\infty} nx^{2n-1} = \frac{x}{(1-x^2)^2}$$

$$\Rightarrow \sum n(2n-1)x^{2n-2} = \frac{1}{(1-x^2)^2} - \frac{2x(-2x)}{(1-x^2)^3}$$

$$= \frac{1-x^2+4x^2}{(1-x^2)^3}$$

$$\Rightarrow \sum_{n=1}^{\infty} n(2n-1)x^{2n-2} = \frac{1+3x^2}{(1-x^2)^3}$$

$$\Rightarrow \sum_{n=1}^{\infty} n(2n-1)x^{2n} = \frac{x^2(1+3x^2)}{(1-x^2)^3}$$

29. A. $f(x, y) = x^2\cos(y/x)\,;\ x \neq 0$

$\qquad = 0 \quad ; \quad x = 0$

$$\frac{\partial f}{\partial x} = Lt_{h\to 0}\,\frac{f(x+h, y) - f(x, y)}{h}$$

$$= Lt_{h\to 0}\,\frac{(x+h)^2\cos(y/x+h) - x^2\cos y/x}{h}$$

$$= Lt_{h\to 0}\,2(x+h)\cos\left(\frac{y}{x+h}\right)$$

$$+(x+h)^2\left\{\frac{y}{(x+h)^2}\sin\left(\frac{y}{x+h}\right)\right\}$$

$$= 2x\cos\frac{y}{x} + y\sin\frac{y}{x}$$

$$\Rightarrow \frac{\partial f}{\partial x} = 2x\cos\frac{y}{x} + y\sin\frac{y}{x}$$

At origin, $\dfrac{\partial f}{\partial x} = Lt_{h\to 0}\,\dfrac{f(h,0) - f(0,0)}{h}$

$$= Lt_{h\to 0}\,\frac{h^2-0}{h} = 0 = f(x, y) \text{ at } x = 0$$

Thus $\dfrac{\partial f}{\partial x}$ is continuous at origin.

B. $\{x_n\}$ is a Cauchy sequence

$\Rightarrow$ there exist $m \in N$ for all

$\qquad \in\, > 0$, such that

$\qquad |x_{m+p} - x_m| < \in \forall\, n \geq m \wedge p \geq 1$

$\qquad$ As $f : (0, 1) \to (0, \infty)$

$\qquad$ so, $|f(x_{m+p}) - f(x_m)| < \in$ will be also true for certain

$\qquad m_1 \in N$ and $p \geq 1$.

$\qquad$ Thus $f(x_n)$ is a Cauchy sequence

$\qquad$ Also, If $\{x_n\}$ and $\{y_n\}$ are Cauchy sequences, then.

$$|f(x_{n+p}) - f(x_n)| < \frac{\in}{2}, \forall\, n \geq m_1$$

$$|f(y_{n+p}) - f(y_n)| < \frac{\in}{2}, \forall\, n \geq m_2$$

$$\Rightarrow |\{f(x_{n+p}) - f(y_{n+p})\} - \{f(x_n) - f(y_n)\}|$$

$$= |\{f(x_{n+p}) - f(x_n)\} + \{f(y_n) - f(y_{n+p})\}|$$

$$\leq |f(x_{n+p}) - f(x_n)| + |f(y_{n+p}) - f(y_n)|$$

$$< \frac{\in}{2} + \frac{\in}{2} = \in, \forall\, n \geq \max(m_1, m_2)$$

Thus $\{|f(x_n) - f(y_n)|\}$ is a Cauchy sequence.

IIT–JAM

JOINT ADMISSION TEST FOR
M.SC. (MATHEMATICS)-2007

1. Let $A(t)$ denote the area bounded by the curve $y = e^{-|x|}$, the x-axis and the straight lines $x = -t$ and $x = t$. Then $\lim_{t \to \infty} A(t)$ is equal to
   A. 2   B. 1
   C. 1/2   D. 0

2. If k is a constant such that $xy + k = e^{(x-)}$ satisfies the differential equation $x\dfrac{dy}{dx} = (x - x -) \, y + x +$ then k is equal to
   A. 1   B. 0
   C. –1   D. –2

3. Which of the following functions is uniformly continuous on the domain as stated?
   A. $f(x) = x^2, x \in \mathbb{R}$

   B. $f(x) = -\dfrac{}{x} \ \ x \in [1, \infty)$
   C. $f(x) = \tan x, \ x \in (-\pi/2, \pi/2)$
   D. $f(x) = [x], x \in [0, 1]$ ([x] is the greatest integer less than or equal to x)

4. Let R be the ring of polynomials over Z_2 and let I be the ideal of R generated by the polynomial $x^3 + x + 1$. Then the number of elements in the quotient ring R/I is
   A. 2   B. 4
   C. 8   D. 16

5. Which of the following sets is a basis for the subspace
$$W = \left\{ \begin{bmatrix} x & y \\ & t \end{bmatrix} \Big| \ x + \ y + t = \ \ y + t = \right\}$$
   of the vector space of all real 2×2 matrices?

   A. $\left\{ \begin{bmatrix} & \\ & \end{bmatrix} \begin{bmatrix} & \\ & \end{bmatrix} \begin{bmatrix} & \\ & \end{bmatrix} \right\}$

   B. $\left\{ \begin{bmatrix} & \\ - & \end{bmatrix} \begin{bmatrix} & - \\ & \end{bmatrix} \right\}$

   C. $\left\{ \begin{bmatrix} - & \\ & - \end{bmatrix} \right\}$ D. $\left\{ \begin{bmatrix} & - \\ & \end{bmatrix} \right\}$

6. Let G be an Abelian group of order 10. Let $S = \{g \in G : g^{-1} = g\}$. Then the number of non-identity elements in S is
   A. 5   B. 2
   C. 1   D. 0

7. Let (a_n) be an increasing sequence of positive real numbers such that the series $\sum\limits_{k=}^{\infty} a_k$ is divergent. Let $s_n = \sum\limits_{k=}^{n} a_k$ for $n = 1, 2, \ldots$ and
$$t_n = \sum_{k=}^{n} \frac{a_k}{s_{k-} \, s_k} \ \text{for } n = 2, 3, \ldots \ . \ \text{Then } \lim_{n \to \infty} t_n \text{ is}$$
   equal to
   A. $1/a_1$ B. 0
   C. $1/(a_1 + a_2)$ D. $a_1 + a_2$

8. For every function $f : [0, 1] \to \mathbb{R}$ which is twice differentiable and satisfies $f'(x) \geq 1$ for all $x \in [0, 1]$, we must have
   A. $f''(x) \geq 0$ for all $x \in [0, 1]$
   B. $f'(x) \geq x$ for all $x \in [0, 1]$
   C. $f(x_2) - x_2 \leq f(x_1) - x_1$ for all $x_1, x_2 \in [0, 1]$ with $x_2 \geq x_1$
   D. $f(x_2) - x_2 \geq f(x_1) - x_1$ for all $x_1, x_2 \in [0, 1]$ with $x_2 \geq x_1$

9. Let $f : \mathbb{R} \to \mathbb{R}$ be defined by
$$f(x, y) = \begin{cases} \dfrac{x\,y}{x + y} & (x,y) \neq \\ & (x, y) = \end{cases}$$
   Which of the following statements holds regarding the continuity and the existence of partial derivatives of f at $(0, 0)$?
   A. Both partial derivatives of f exist at $(0, 0)$ and f is continuous at $(0, 0)$

B. Both partial derivatives of f exist at $(0, 0)$ and f is NOT continuous at $(0, 0)$

C. One partial derivative of f does NOT exist at $(0, 0)$ and f is continuous at $(0, 0)$

D. One partial derivative of f does NOT exist at $(0, 0)$ and f is NOT continuous at $(0, 0)$

10. Suppose (c_n) is a sequence of real numbers such that $\lim\limits_{n \to \infty} |c_n|^n$ exists and is non-zero. If the radius of convergence of the power series $\sum\limits_{n=}^{\infty} c_n x^n$ is equal to r, then the radius of convergence of the power series $\sum\limits_{n=}^{\infty} n\, c_n x^n$ is

A. less than r B. greater than r

C. equal to r D. equal to 0

11. The rank of the matrix $\begin{bmatrix} & & \\ & & \\ & & \end{bmatrix}$ is

A. 3   B. 2

C. 1   D. 0

12. Let $f : R \to R$ be a continuous function. If
$$\int^{x} f(\,)\, dt = \frac{x}{\pi}(\quad)\pi x \quad \text{for all } x \in R, \text{ then } f(2) \text{ is}$$
equal to

A. -1 B. 0

C. 1   D. 2

13. Let $\vec{u} = (ae^x\quad y) \, x(i + \quad y)e^x \quad y\, j + azk$ where a is a constant. If the line integral $\oint\limits_{C} \vec{u}\, d\vec{r}$ over every closed curve C is zero, then a is equal to

A. -2 B. -1

C. 0   D. 1

14. One of the integrating factors of the differential equation $(y^2 - 3xy)dx + (x^2 - xy)\, dy = 0$ is

A. $1/(x^2 y^2)$ B. $1/(x^2 y)$

C. $1/(xy^2)$ D. $1/(xy)$

15. Let C denote the boundary of the semi-circular disk $D = \{(x, y) \in R^2 : x^2 + y^2 \le 1, y \ge 0\}$ and let $\varphi(x, y) = x^2 + y$ for $(x, y) \in D$. If n is the outward unit normal to C, then the integral $\oint\limits_{C} (\vec{\nabla}\varphi)\, nds$ evaluated counter-clockwise over C, is equal to

A. 0   B. $\pi - 2$

C. π D. $\pi + 2$

16. A. Let $M = \begin{bmatrix} +i & i & i+ \\ & -i & i \\ & & i \end{bmatrix}$. Determine the eigenvalues of the matrix $B = M^2 - 2M + I$.

B. Let N be a square matrix of order 2. If the determinant of N is equal to 9 and the sum of the diagonal entries of N is equal to 10, then determine the eigenvalues of N.

17. A. Using the method of variation of parameters, solve the differential equation
$$x\,\frac{d\,y}{dx} + x\frac{dy}{dx} - y = x$$
given that x and $\dfrac{-}{x}$ are two solutions of the corresponding homogeneous equation.

B. Find the real number α such that the differential equation
$$\frac{d\,y}{dx} + (\ \alpha\ )(\ \alpha)- \frac{dy}{dx} + \alpha - \ y =$$
has a solution $y(x) = a \cos(\beta x) + b \sin(\beta x)$ for some non-zero real numbers a, b, β.

18. A. Let a, b, c be non-zero real numbers such that $(a - b)^2 = 4ac$. Solve the differential equation
$$a\left(x + \sqrt{\ }\right)\frac{d\,y}{dx} + b\left(x + \sqrt{\ }\right)\frac{dy}{dx} + cy =$$

B. Solve the differential equation $dx + (e^{y\sin y} - x)\,(y \cos y + \sin y)\, dy = 0$.

19. Let $f(x, y) = x\,(x - 2y^2)$ for $(x, y) \in R$. Show that f has a local minimum at $(0, 0)$ on every straight line through $(0, 0)$. Is $(0, 0)$ a critical point of f? Find the discriminant of f at $(0, 0)$. Does f have a local minimum at $(0, 0)$? Justify your answers.

20. A. Find the finite volume enclosed by the paraboloids $z = 2 - x^2 - y^2$ and $z = x^2 + y^2$.

B. Let $f : [0, 3] \to R$ be a continuous function with $\int f(x)dx =$

Evaluate $\int x f(\,)\, + \int^{x} f(t)dt\ dx$

21. **A.** Let S be the surface $\{(x, y, z) \in R^3 : x^2 + y^2 + 2z = 2, z \geq 0\}$, and let n be the outward unit normal to S. If $\vec{F} = yi + xzj + (x + y)k$ then evaluate the integral $\iint_S \vec{F}\ ndS$

B. Let $\vec{r} = xi + yj + zk$ and $r = |\vec{r}|$ If a scalar field φ and a vector field $\vec{u}$ satisfy $\vec{\nabla}\varphi = \vec{\nabla} \times \vec{u} + f(r)\vec{r}$ where f is an arbitrary differentiable function, then show that $\nabla\ \varphi = rf'(r) + f)\ r$.

22. **A.** Let D be the region bounded by the concentric spheres $S_1 : x^2 + y^2 + z^2 = a^2$ and $S_2 : x^2 + y^2 + z^2 = b^2$, where $a < b$. Let n be the unit normal to S_1 directed away from the origin. If $\nabla^2 \varphi = 0$ in D and $\varphi = 0$ on S_2, then show that $\iiint_D |\vec{\nabla}\varphi|\ dV + \iint_S \varphi(\vec{\nabla}\varphi)\ ndS = $

B. Let C be the curve in R^3 given by $x^2 + y^2 = a^2$, $z = 0$ traced counter-clockwise, and let $\vec{F} = x\ y\ i + j + zk$ Using Stokes' theorem evaluate $\oint_C \vec{F}\ d\vec{r}$.

23. Let V be the subspace of R^4 spanned by the vectors $(1, 0, 1, 2), (2, 1, 3, 4)$ and $(3, 1, 4, 6)$. Let $T : V \to R^2$ be a linear transformation given by $T(x, y, z, t) = (x - y, z - t)$ for all $(x, y, z, t) \in V$. Find a basis for the null space of T and also a basis for the range space of T.

24. **A.** Compute the double integral $\iint_D (x + y)\ dx\,dy$ where D is the region in the xy-plane bounded by the straight lines $y = x + 3$, $y = x - 3$, $y = -2x + 4$ and $y = -2x - 2$.

B. Evaluate

$$\int_\pi^\pi \left[\int_\pi^\pi \frac{x}{x}\,dx\right]dy + \int_\pi^\pi \left[\int_y^\pi \frac{x}{x}\,dx\right]dy$$

25. **A.** Does the series $\sum_{k=}^\infty \frac{(-)^k k + x^k}{k}$ converge uniformly for $x \in [-1, 1]$? Justify.

B. Suppose (f_n) is a sequence of real-valued functions defined on R and f is a real-valued function defined on R such that $|f_n(x) - f(x)| \leq |a_n|$ for all $n \in$ N and $a_n \to 0$ as $n \to \infty$. Must the sequence (f_n) be uniformly convergent on R? Justify.

26. **A.** Suppose f is a real-valued thrice differentiable function defined on R such that $f'''(x) > 0$ for all $x \in$ R. Using Taylor's formula, show that

$$f(x) - f(x) > (x - x)f'\left(\frac{x + x}{}\right) \text{ for all}$$

x_1 and x_2 in R with $x_2 > x_1$.

B. Let (a_n) and (b_n) be sequences of real numbers such that $a_n \leq a_{n+1} \leq b_{n+1} \leq b_n$ for all $n \in$ N. Must there exist a real number x such that $a_n \leq x \leq b_n$ for all $n \in$ N? Justify your answer.

27. Let G be the group of all 2×2 matrices with real entries with respect to matrix multiplication. Let G_1 be the smallest subgroup of G containing

$$\begin{bmatrix} & \\ & \end{bmatrix} \text{ and } \begin{bmatrix} & - \\ - & \end{bmatrix}, \text{ and } G_2 \text{ be the smallest}$$

subgroup of G containing $\begin{bmatrix} & - \\ & \end{bmatrix}$ and

$\begin{bmatrix} & \\ - & \end{bmatrix}$. Determine all elements of G_1 and find their orders. Determine all elements of G_2 and find their orders. Does there exist a one-to-one homomorphism from G_1 onto G_2 ? Justify.

28. **A.** Let p be a prime number and let Z be the ring of integers. If an ideal J of Z contains the set pZ properly, then show that $J = Z$. (Here $pZ = \{px : x \in Z\}$.)

B. Consider the ring $R = \{a + ib : a, b \in Z\}$ with usual addition and multiplication. Find all invertible elements of R.

29. **A.** Suppose E is a non-empty subset of R which is bounded above, and let $\alpha = \sup E$. If E is closed, then show that $\alpha \in E$. If E is open, then show that $\alpha \notin E$.

B. Find all limit points of the set $E = \left\{n + \dfrac{}{m}\ n\ m \in\ \right\}$.

ANSWERS

1	2	3	4	5	6	7	8	9	10
11	12	13	14	15					

SOME SELECTED EXPLANATORY ANSWERS

1. $A(t) = \int_{-t}^{t} y\,dx = \int_{-t}^{t} e^{-|x|}\,dx$

$\qquad = 2\int_{0}^{t} e^{-x}\,dx \quad ;\quad$ as $e^{-|x|}$ is even function.

$\qquad = 2(-e^{-x})\Big|_{0}^{t}$

$\qquad = 2(1 - e^{-t})$

$\qquad \lim_{t\to\infty} A(t) = \lim_{t\to\infty} 2(1 - e^{-t}) = 2$

2. $xy + k = e^{(x-1)^2/2}$

$\qquad \Rightarrow\; y + x\dfrac{dy}{dx} = (x-1)e^{(x-1)^2/2}$

$\qquad \Rightarrow\; x\dfrac{dy}{dx} = -y + (x-1)e^{(x-1)^2/2}$

$\qquad\qquad = -y + (x-1)[xy + k]$

$\qquad\qquad = (x^2 - x - 1)y + k(x-1)$

$\qquad \Rightarrow\; k = 1$

3. $f(x) = \dfrac{1}{x}$ is uniformly continuous in $[1, \infty)$

4. $x^3 + x + 1$ is irreducible in z_2

$\qquad$ So, $\dfrac{R}{I} = 2\times 2\times 2 = 8$

5. $x + 2y + t = 0 \quad \&\quad y + t = 0$

$\qquad \Rightarrow y = -t\ \&\ x = t$

$\qquad$ Thus a basis is $\left\{ \begin{bmatrix} 1 & -1 \\ 0 & 1 \end{bmatrix} \right\}$

6. $\{[0], [1], [2], [3], [4], [5], [6], [7], [8], [9]\}_{+10}$
$\qquad$ is an abelian group of order 10.
$\qquad [0]^{-1} = [0]\ \&\ [5]^{-1} = [5]$

$\qquad [0]$ is identity and $[5]$ is non-identity element.

7. Let $a_k = k$

$\qquad \Rightarrow S_k = 1 + 2 + \dots + k = \dfrac{k(k+1)}{2}$

$\qquad \Rightarrow t_n = \sum_{k=2}^{n} \dfrac{a_k}{S_{k-1}S_k} = \sum_{k=2}^{n} \dfrac{4k}{k^2(k^2-1)}$

$\qquad = 2\sum_{k=2}^{n} \left(\dfrac{1}{k-1} - \dfrac{1}{k} \right) - \left(\dfrac{1}{k} - \dfrac{1}{k+1} \right)$

$\qquad = 2\left[\left(1 - \dfrac{1}{n} \right) - \left(\dfrac{1}{2} - \dfrac{1}{n+1} \right) \right]$

$\qquad \Rightarrow\; \lim_{n\to\infty} t_n = 2\left[1 - \dfrac{1}{2} \right] = 1$

$\qquad = \dfrac{1}{a_1}$

8. $f'(x) \geq 1 \Rightarrow f(x)$ is an increasing function.
$\qquad \Rightarrow f'(x) - 1 \geq 0$
$\qquad \Rightarrow f(x) - x \geq c$
$\qquad \Rightarrow f(x_2) - x_2 \geq f(x_1) - x_1$ for all $x_1, x_2 \in [0, 1]$
$\qquad$ with $x_2 \geq x_1$.

9. Also $\quad y = x^2$

$\qquad \lim_{(x,y)\to(0,0)} f(x,y) = \lim_{x\to 0} \dfrac{x^4}{x^4 + x^4} = \dfrac{1}{2}$

$\qquad$ so, f is not continuous at $(0, 0)$

$\qquad \dfrac{\partial f}{\partial x}\Big|_{(0,0)} = \lim_{x\to 0} \dfrac{0}{x^4} = 0$

$\qquad \dfrac{\partial f}{\partial y}\Big|_{(0,0)} = \lim_{y\to 0} \dfrac{0}{y^2} = 0$

$\qquad$ so, both partial derivatives exist.

10. $\lim_{n\to\infty} (n^2 C_n x^n)^{1/n}$

$\qquad = \lim_{n\to\infty} (n^{1/n})^2\ \lim_{n\to\infty} (C_n x^n)^{1/n}$

$\qquad = \lim_{n\to\infty} (C_n x^n)^{1/n}$

$\qquad$ so radius of convergence is same (r).

11.
$$\begin{bmatrix} 1 & 4 & 8 \\ 2 & 10 & 22 \\ 0 & 4 & 12 \end{bmatrix} \sim \begin{bmatrix} 1 & 4 & 8 \\ 0 & 2 & 6 \\ 0 & 4 & 12 \end{bmatrix}$$

By $R_2 \to R_2 - 2R_1$

$$\sim \begin{bmatrix} 1 & 4 & 8 \\ 0 & 2 & 6 \\ 0 & 0 & 0 \end{bmatrix}$$

By $R_3 \to R_3 - 2R_2$

Number of non-zero rows = 2 so rank = 2

12. $\int_0^x f(2t)\,dt = \dfrac{x}{\pi}\sin(\pi x)$

Differentiating both sides w.r.t. x, we get

$$f(2x) = \frac{1}{\pi}\sin \pi x + x\cos \pi x$$

Putting $x = 1$, we get
$f(2) = -1$

13. $\because \oint \vec{u}\,d\vec{r} = 0$

$\Rightarrow \qquad \vec{u} = \nabla\,\mathrm{grad}\,(V)$

$\Rightarrow \qquad \dfrac{\partial V}{\partial x} = ae^x \sin y - 4x$

$\Rightarrow \qquad V = ae^x \sin y - 2x^2 + f_1(y, z)$

$\qquad\qquad \dfrac{\partial V}{\partial y} = 2y + e^x \cos y$

$\Rightarrow \qquad V = y^2 - e^x \sin y + f_2(x, z)$

$\qquad\qquad \dfrac{\partial V}{\partial z} = az \Rightarrow V = \dfrac{az}{} + f\,(x\;y)$

all the above three represent same scalar function
hence $\qquad a = -1.$

14. $M = y^2 - 3xy$

$\qquad \& \; N = x^2 - xy$

As $Mdx + Ndy = 0$ is homogeneous.

An I.F. is $\dfrac{1}{Mx + Ny} = \dfrac{1}{(-2x^2 y)}$

so, $\dfrac{1}{x^2 y}$ is an I.F. by ignoring constant.

15. $\phi = x^2 + y \quad \Rightarrow \quad \vec{\nabla}\phi = 2x\hat{i} + \hat{j}$

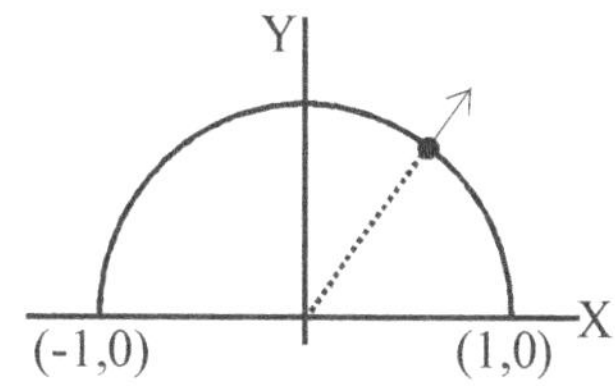

Outward unit normal $\hat{n}$ at $(x, y) = x\hat{i} + y\hat{j}$

$\Rightarrow \oint_C (\nabla\phi)\cdot\hat{n}\,dS = \oint_C (2x^2 + y)\,dS$

For $x^2 + y^2 = 1$, $\dfrac{dy}{dx} = \dfrac{-x}{y}$

$\Rightarrow dS = \sqrt{1 + \dfrac{x^2}{y^2}}\,dx = \dfrac{1}{y}\,dx$

Thus by putting these, we get the integral as
$\pi - 2.$

16. A. As M is upper triangular, so eigen values will be elements along principal diagonal, so eigen values of M are $1 + i$, $1 - i$ & i

As, $(1 + i)^2 - 2(1 + i) + 1 = -1$

$(1 - i)^2 - 2(1 - i) + 1 = -1$

$(i)^2 - 2i + 1 = -2i$

so eigen values of $M^2 - 2M + I$ will be $-1, -1$ and $-2i$

B. trace of N = sum of diagonal elements
$= 10 \mid N \mid = 9$

$\Rightarrow$ characteristic equation is
$\lambda^2 - 10\lambda + 9 = 0$

$\Rightarrow \lambda = 1, 9$

so eigen values are 1 and 9.

17. A. The given differential equation is

$$\frac{d\,y}{dx} + \frac{dy}{x\,dx} - \frac{y}{x} = \qquad\qquad \text{...(1)}$$

as $x - \dfrac{}{x}$ are the solution of above equation with
R.H.S. equal to zero

Hence solution of above is

$$y = \quad x + \quad \frac{}{x}$$

A, B are function of x

put a condition $\qquad x + \dfrac{}{x} = \qquad\qquad \text{...(2)}$

$\because y = \quad x + \dfrac{\ }{x} \Rightarrow y_1 = \quad -\dfrac{\ }{x}$

$y_2 = \quad -\dfrac{\ }{x} + \dfrac{\ }{x}$

put in equation (1), we get

$$-\dfrac{\ }{x} + \dfrac{\ }{x} + \dfrac{\ }{x} - \dfrac{\ }{x} - \dfrac{\ }{x} - \dfrac{\ }{x} = \phi$$

$$\Rightarrow \qquad -\dfrac{\ }{x} = b \qquad\qquad \ldots(3)$$

$$(2)\,\&\,(3) \;\Rightarrow\; 2A_1 = \phi \;\Rightarrow\; \dfrac{dA}{dx} = \dfrac{\phi}{\ }$$

$$\Rightarrow \qquad A = \dfrac{x}{2} + c_1 \;\Rightarrow\; B_1 \cdot \dfrac{1}{x} = -\dfrac{x}{2}$$

$$\Rightarrow \qquad B_1 = -\dfrac{x^2}{2} \quad \therefore\; B = c \quad -\dfrac{x}{\ }$$

$$\therefore\; y = \quad x + \dfrac{\ }{x} = c\,x + c \quad \dfrac{\ }{x} + \dfrac{x}{\ } - \dfrac{x}{\ }$$

$$= c\ x + c \quad -+\dfrac{x}{\ }$$

B. Auxiliary equation of the given D.E. is
$$m^2 + 2(\alpha - 1)(\alpha - 3)m + (\alpha - 2) = 0 \qquad \ldots(i)$$
For solution of the type
$$y(x) = a\cos(\beta x) + b\sin(\beta x)$$
roots of equation (i) should be purely imaginary, so
$$2(\alpha - 1)(\alpha - 3) = 0 \text{ and}$$
$$4[(\alpha - 1)(\alpha - 3)]^2 - 4(\alpha - 2) < 0$$
$$\Rightarrow \alpha = 3$$

18. A. $a\left(x + \sqrt{2}\right)^2 \dfrac{d^2 y}{dx^2} + b\left(x + \sqrt{2}\right)\dfrac{dy}{dx} + cy = 0$

$$\qquad\qquad\qquad\qquad\qquad \ldots(i)$$

Let $\left(x + \sqrt{2}\right) = e^z$ and $D = \dfrac{d}{dz}$

$\Rightarrow$ equation (i) is
$$(a\,D(D - 1) + bD + c)y = 0$$
A.E. is $am^2 + (b - a)m + c = 0$

$$\Rightarrow m = \dfrac{-(b - a) \pm \sqrt{(b - a)^2 - 4ac}}{2a}$$

$$\Rightarrow m = \dfrac{a - b}{2a}, \dfrac{a - b}{2a}$$

$\Rightarrow y = (c_1 + c_2 z)\, e^{(a - b)z/2a}$

$\Rightarrow y = [c_1 + c_2 \ln (x + \sqrt{2})]\,(x + \sqrt{2})^{(a - b)/2a}$

B. $\because$ Put $\qquad z = y \sin y$

$$dz = (y \cos y + \sin y)\, dy$$

$\Rightarrow$ d.e. becomes

$$dx + \left(e^z - x\right)dz = 0 \ \text{ or,}\ \ \dfrac{dx}{dz} - x = -e^z$$

$$\text{I.F.} = e^{-z}$$

$$\Rightarrow \qquad xe^{-z} = -z + c$$

or, $\qquad x = ce^z - ze^z$

or, $\qquad x = ce^{y \sin y} - (y \sin y)\, e^{y \sin y}.$

19. $f(x, y) = x(x - 2y^2)$

$$\begin{aligned}
f_x &= 2x - 2y^2 \\
f_y &= -4xy \\
f_{xx} &= 2 \\
f_{yy} &= -4x \\
f_{xy} &= -4y \\
f_x &= 0 \ \& \ f_y = 0
\end{aligned}$$

$$\Rightarrow x = y = 0$$

so, f has local minima at $(0, 0)$ along straight line through $(0, 0)$

$$f_{xx}f_{yy} - f(xy)^2 = -8x - 16y^2$$
$$= 0 \text{ at } (0, 0)$$

so further checking is required discriminant

$$(f_{xy})^2 - f_{xx}f_{yy}$$
$$= 8x + 16y^2$$

20. A. Volume enclosed $= \iiint dx\, dy\, dz$

$$z = x^2 + y^2 \ \& \ z = 2 - (x^2 + y^2)$$
$$\Rightarrow x^2 + y^2 = 1,\ z = 1$$

$$\text{volume} = \int_{-1}^{1}\int_{-\sqrt{1-x^2}}^{\sqrt{1-x^2}}\int_{x^2+y^2}^{2-(x^2+y^2)} dz\, dy\, dx$$

$$= \int_{-1}^{1}\int_{-\sqrt{1-x^2}}^{\sqrt{1-x^2}} 2(1 - (x^2 + y^2))dy\, dx$$

$$= \int_{-1}^{1} 4\sqrt{1 - x^2}\left[1 - x^2 - \dfrac{(1 - x^2)}{3}\right]dx$$

$$= \dfrac{16}{3}\int_{0}^{1}(1 - x^2)^{3/2}\, dx$$

Let $x = \sin\theta$

$$\Rightarrow dx = \cos\theta\, d\theta$$

$$= \frac{16}{3} \int_0^{\pi/2} \cos^4 \theta \, d\theta$$

$$= \frac{16}{3} \times \frac{3 \cdot 1}{4 \cdot 2} \times \frac{\pi}{2} = \pi$$

B. $\quad \int \left[x\, f(x) + \int^x f(t)\, dt \right] dx$

$$= \int x f(x)\, dx + \int \int^x f(t)\, dt\, dx$$

Changing the order of integration in second integration,

$$= \int x f(x)\, dx + \int f(t) \int_t dx\, dt$$

$$= \int x f(x)\, dx + \int f(t)\{\ -t\}\, dt \ = \ \int f(t)\, dt$$

$$= 3 \times 3 = 9.$$

21. A. $\because \qquad \phi = x^2 + y^2 + 2z - 2$

$$\Rightarrow \qquad n = \frac{\nabla \phi}{|\nabla \phi|} \Rightarrow n = \frac{xi + yj + k}{\sqrt{x + y +}}$$

Now $\displaystyle \iint_S {}^{-} n\, dS = \iint_S \left[xy + xyz + \left(x + y \right) \right] dS$

$$= \iint_S \{ xy + xyz + (x + y) \} \frac{dx\, dy}{|n\, k|}$$

$$= \iint \left[\{ xy(+ z) + x + y \} \sqrt{x + y + } \right] dx\, dy$$

$\because \quad x^2 + y^2 + 2z = 2 \ \Rightarrow \ 2z = 2 - (x^2 + y^2)$

$$(1 + z) = \ - \frac{\left(x + y \right)}{}$$

$$= \iint_{x+y \le} \left[dy \left\{ -\frac{\left(x + y \right)}{} \right\} + (x + y) \sqrt{x + y +} \right] dx\, dy$$

Changing into polar co-ordinate,

$$\int \int^{\pi} \left\{ r \quad \theta \quad \theta \left(-\frac{r}{} \right) + r \right\} \sqrt{r + } \ r\, dr\, d\theta$$

$$= \int^r r \left(-\frac{r}{} \right) \sqrt{r + } \ dr \int^{\pi} \quad \theta \quad \theta\, d\theta$$

$$+ \int^{\pi} d\theta \int^{\sqrt{}} r \ \sqrt{r + } \ dr$$

$$= \ + \ \pi \int \left(r + - \right) \sqrt{r + } \ r\, dr$$

put $\qquad r^2 + 1 = z^2 \ \Rightarrow \ r\, dr = z\, dz$

$$= \ \pi \int^{\sqrt{}} \left(z - \right) z\, dz = \ \pi \int \left(z - z \right) dz$$

$$= \ \pi \left[\frac{z}{} - \frac{z}{} \right]^{\sqrt{}}$$

$$= \ \pi \left[\left(- - - \right) - \left(- - - \right) \right] = \ \pi .$$

B. $\quad \because \qquad \bar{\nabla} \phi = \bar{\nabla} \times \bar{u} + f(r) \bar{r}$

Now $\quad \nabla \ \phi = \bar{\nabla} \left(\nabla \phi \right)$

$$= \bar{\nabla} \left[\bar{\nabla} \times \bar{u} + F(r) \bar{r} \right]$$

$$= \bar{\nabla} . \left(\bar{\nabla} \times \bar{u} \right) + \bar{\nabla} . \left(F(r) \bar{r} \right)$$

$$= \ + \bar{\nabla} \left(f(r) \right) \bar{r}$$

$$= f(r) \left(\bar{\nabla} \ \bar{r} \right) + \left\{ \nabla f(r) \right\} \ \bar{r}$$

$$= f(r) + f'(r) \frac{\bar{r}}{|r|} \ \bar{r}$$

$$= f(r) + r f'(r)$$

22. A. Consider

$$\iiint_D \bar{\nabla} \left(\phi \nabla \phi \right) dV$$

$$= \iiint_D \left\{ \left(\nabla \phi \right) \nabla \phi + \phi \nabla \left(\nabla \phi \right) \right\} dV$$

$$= \iiint_D \left[|\nabla \phi| + \phi \nabla \ \phi \right] dV$$

$$= \iint_S \left\{ \phi \nabla \phi \right\} d\vec{S} \qquad \text{[Stoke's Theorem]}$$

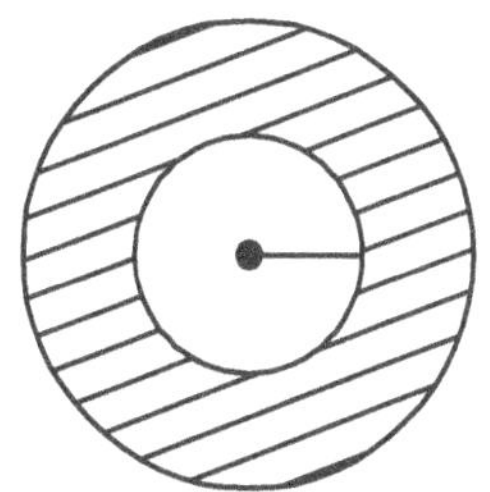

S is the shaded portion

$$= \iint\limits_{S} (\phi \nabla \phi)\, n\, dS - \iint\limits_{S} (\phi \nabla \phi)\, n\, dS$$

or, $$\iiint\limits_{D} |\nabla \phi|\, dV + \iint\limits_{S} (\phi \nabla \phi)\, n\, dS$$

$$= \iint\limits_{S} \{\phi(\nabla \phi)\}\, n\, dS = 0$$

$$[\because \ \phi = 0 \text{ on } S_2 \quad \& \quad \nabla^2 \phi = 0 \text{ on D}]$$

$$\Rightarrow \iiint\limits_{D} |\nabla \phi|\, dV + \iint\limits_{S} (\phi \nabla \phi)\, n\, dS = \ \ .$$

B. $\vec{F} = x^2 y^3 \hat{i} + \hat{j} + z\hat{k}$

$$\oint\limits_{C} \vec{F} \cdot dr = \iint\limits_{S} (\nabla \times \vec{F}) \cdot n\, dS\ ;$$

By Stoke's theorem.

$$\nabla \times F = \begin{vmatrix} i & j & k \\ \dfrac{\partial}{\partial x} & \dfrac{\partial}{\partial y} & \dfrac{\partial}{\partial z} \\ x^2 y^3 & 1 & z \end{vmatrix}$$

$$= -3x^2 y^2 k . n dS$$
$$= (-3x^2 y^2) k \cdot n dS$$
$$= -3x^2 y^2 dx dy$$

$$\Rightarrow I = \oint\limits_{C} \vec{F} \cdot d\vec{r} = 4 \int_0^a \int_0^{\sqrt{a^2 - x^2}} -3x^2 y^2\, dy\, dx$$

$$= -4 \int_0^a \left[(a^2 - x^2)\sqrt{(a^2 - x^2)} \right] x^2\, dx$$

Let $x = a \sin \theta$
$$\Rightarrow dx = a \cos \theta\, d\theta$$

$$\Rightarrow I = -4 \int_0^{\pi/2} a^2 \cos^2 \theta\, a \cos \theta\, a^2 \sin^2 \theta\, a \cos \theta\, d\theta$$

$$= -4a^6 \int_0^{\pi/2} \sin^2 \theta \cos^4 \theta\, d\theta$$

$$= -4a^6 \, \frac{3 \cdot 1}{6 \cdot 4 \cdot 2} \times \frac{\pi}{2} = -\frac{\pi a^6}{8} .$$

23. $T(x, y, z, t) = (x - y, z - t)$

$T(x, y, z, t) = (0, 0)$

$$\Rightarrow x - y = 0 = z - t$$

$$\Rightarrow x = y \text{ and } z = t$$

Thus null space will be

$N(T) = \{(a, a, b, b) \mid a, b \in R\}$

Thus a basis for null space is $\{(1, 1, 0, 0),$

$(0, 0, 1, 1)\}$

Now $T(1, 0, 1, 2) = (1, -1)$

$T(2, 1, 3, 4) = (1, -1)$

$T(3, 1, 4, 6) = (2, -2)$

Thus range space is generated by $(1, -1)$ only

So, Basis for range space of T is $\{(1, -1)\}$

Note : Rank $(T) = 1$ & Nullity $(T) = 2$.

24. A. The Region D is given as
$$-3 \le y - x \le 3$$
$$-2 \le y + 2x \le 4$$

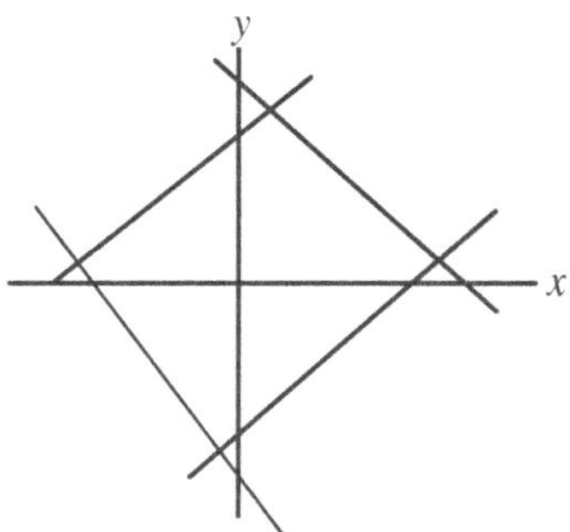

let $\qquad y - x = u \quad$ and $\quad y + 2x = v$

then $\qquad 3x = v - u \quad$ or $\quad x = -(v - u)$

& $\qquad y = v - -(v - u) = -(v + u)$

Also $\quad \dfrac{\partial(x\ y)}{\partial(u\ v)} = \begin{vmatrix} -- & - \\ - & - \end{vmatrix} = --$

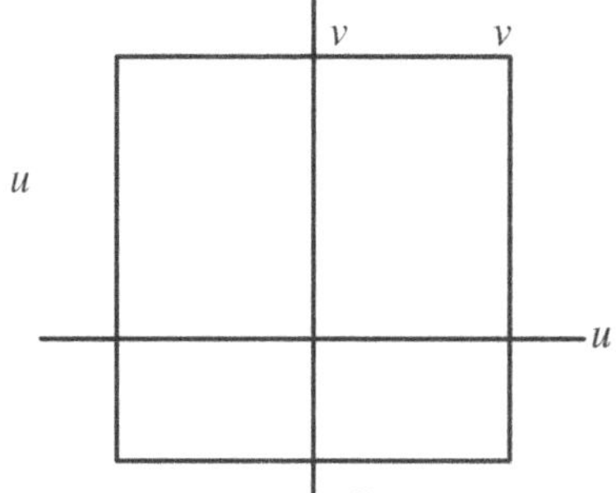

$$\therefore \iint (x + y)\, dx\, du = \iint (v + u)\left(-- \right) du\, dv$$

$$= -- \int\limits_{v=-}^{} \int\limits_{=-}^{} (v+u)\,du\,dv = -- \int\limits_{-}^{} v\,dv$$

$$= -- \left[\quad - \quad \right] = -12.$$

B. The given integral is

$$\int\limits_{\pi}^{\pi} \int\limits_{\pi}^{} \left[\frac{x}{x}\,dx \right] dy + \int\limits_{\pi}^{\pi} \left[\int\limits_{y}^{} \frac{x}{x}\,dx \right] dy$$

Changing the order of integration of 2nd integral

$$= \int\limits_{}^{\pi} \left\{ \int\limits_{\pi}^{\pi} \frac{x}{x}\,dx \right\} dy + \int\limits_{\pi}^{\pi} \left\{ \int\limits_{\pi}^{x} \frac{x}{x}\,dy \right\} dx$$

$$= \int\limits_{}^{\pi} \left[\int\limits_{\pi}^{\pi} \frac{x}{x}\,dx \right] dy + \int\limits_{\pi}^{\pi} \frac{x}{x}\left(x - \frac{\pi}{} \right) dx$$

$$= \frac{\pi}{} \int\limits_{\pi}^{\pi} \frac{x}{x}\,dx + \int\limits_{\pi}^{\pi} x\,dx - \frac{\pi}{} \int\limits_{\pi}^{\pi} \frac{x}{x}\,dx =$$

25. A. $\displaystyle \sum \frac{(-1)^k k}{k^2} = \sum \frac{(-1)^k}{k}$

is conditionally convergent series.

$\displaystyle \sum \frac{x^k}{k^2}$ is also convergent.

Both does not have uniform convergence in $[-1, 1]$

so, $\displaystyle \sum_{k=1}^{\infty} \frac{(-1)^k k + x^k}{k^2}$

converges uniformly is not true.

B. $|f_n(x) - f(x)| \le |a_n|$

As $a_n \to 0$ as $n \to \infty$

$\Rightarrow$ supremum of $|f_n(x) - f(x)|$

$\to 0$ as $n \to \infty$

so convergence is uniform.

26. A. By Taylor's theorem

$$f(x_2) = f(x_1) + (x_2 - x_1) f'(x_1) +$$

$$\frac{(x_2 - x_1)^2}{2!} f''(x) + \frac{(x_2 - x_1)^3}{3!} f'''(x) + \dots$$

$$\Rightarrow \frac{f(x_2) - f(x_1)}{(x_2 - x_1)} = f'(x_1) + \frac{(x_2 - x_1)}{2} f''(x) + \dots$$

As $f'''(x) > 0$

so, $\displaystyle f'\left(\frac{x_1 + x_2}{2} \right) < \frac{f(x_2) - f(x_1)}{(x_2 - x_1)}$

As $\dfrac{x_1 + x_2}{2}$ is midpoint of x_1 & x_2

$$\Rightarrow f(x_2) - f(x_1) > (x_2 - x_1)\, f'\left(\frac{x_1 + x_2}{2} \right)$$

B. As $a_n \le x \le b_n$

so x is not satisfied for all $n \in N$ because as $n \to \infty$, a_{n+1} & b_{n+1} becomes such that they are either equal or converges to a limit.

From the given inequality

$$a_1 \le a_2 \le a_3 \le \dots a_n \le b_n \le b_{n-1} \le \dots \le b_2 \le b_1$$

Thus both are convergent hence $a_n \le x \le b_n$ is true for each x.

27. For G_1: $\begin{bmatrix} 0 & 1 \\ 1 & 0 \end{bmatrix}^2 = \begin{bmatrix} 1 & 0 \\ 0 & 1 \end{bmatrix}$

$$\begin{bmatrix} -1 & 0 \\ 0 & -1 \end{bmatrix}^2 = \begin{bmatrix} 1 & 0 \\ 0 & 1 \end{bmatrix}$$

$$\begin{bmatrix} 0 & 1 \\ 1 & 0 \end{bmatrix}\begin{bmatrix} -1 & 0 \\ 0 & -1 \end{bmatrix} = \begin{bmatrix} 0 & -1 \\ -1 & 0 \end{bmatrix}$$

$$\begin{bmatrix} 0 & -1 \\ -1 & 0 \end{bmatrix}^2 = \begin{bmatrix} 1 & 0 \\ 0 & 1 \end{bmatrix}$$

Thus there are 4 elements.

$$\begin{bmatrix} 0 & 1 \\ 1 & 0 \end{bmatrix}, \begin{bmatrix} 0 & -1 \\ -1 & 0 \end{bmatrix}, \begin{bmatrix} -1 & 0 \\ 0 & -1 \end{bmatrix} \text{ and}$$

$$\begin{bmatrix} 1 & 0 \\ 0 & 1 \end{bmatrix} \text{ in the group.}$$

order of $\begin{bmatrix} 1 & 0 \\ 0 & 1 \end{bmatrix} = 1.$

order of $\begin{bmatrix} 0 & 1 \\ 1 & 0 \end{bmatrix}$ is 2.

order of $\begin{bmatrix} 0 & -1 \\ -1 & 0 \end{bmatrix}$ is 2.

order of $\begin{bmatrix} -1 & 0 \\ 0 & -1 \end{bmatrix}$ is 2.

Also, order of G_1 is 4.

For G_2 : $\begin{bmatrix} 0 & -1 \\ 1 & 0 \end{bmatrix}^2 = \begin{bmatrix} -1 & 0 \\ 0 & -1 \end{bmatrix}$

$\begin{bmatrix} 0 & -1 \\ 1 & 0 \end{bmatrix}^3 = \begin{bmatrix} 0 & 1 \\ -1 & 0 \end{bmatrix}$

$\begin{bmatrix} 0 & -1 \\ 1 & 0 \end{bmatrix}^4 = \begin{bmatrix} 1 & 0 \\ 0 & 1 \end{bmatrix}$

$\begin{bmatrix} 0 & 1 \\ -1 & 0 \end{bmatrix}^2 = \begin{bmatrix} -1 & 0 \\ 0 & -1 \end{bmatrix}$

$\begin{bmatrix} 0 & 1 \\ -1 & 0 \end{bmatrix}^3 = \begin{bmatrix} 0 & -1 \\ 1 & 0 \end{bmatrix}$

$\begin{bmatrix} 0 & 1 \\ -1 & 0 \end{bmatrix}^4 = \begin{bmatrix} 1 & 0 \\ 0 & 1 \end{bmatrix}$

Thus in G_2 there are 4 elements.

$\begin{bmatrix} 0 & -1 \\ 1 & 0 \end{bmatrix}, \begin{bmatrix} 0 & 1 \\ -1 & 0 \end{bmatrix}, \begin{bmatrix} -1 & 0 \\ 0 & -1 \end{bmatrix}$ and $\begin{bmatrix} 1 & 0 \\ 0 & 1 \end{bmatrix}$

so, $0(G_2) = 4$ and

order of $\begin{bmatrix} 1 & 0 \\ 0 & 1 \end{bmatrix}$ is 1

order of $\begin{bmatrix} -1 & 0 \\ 0 & -1 \end{bmatrix}$ is 2

order of $\begin{bmatrix} 0 & -1 \\ 1 & 0 \end{bmatrix}$ is 4

order of $\begin{bmatrix} 0 & 1 \\ -1 & 0 \end{bmatrix}$ is 4

As $0(G_1) = 0(G_2) = 4$

so, there exist one - one homomorphism from G_1 onto G_2.

28. A. As J is an ideal of z

$pz = \{px : x \in z\}$

$\Rightarrow pz = \{0, \pm p, \pm 2p, \pm 3p, ...\}$

If pz is contained properly in J, then $\exists\ a \in J$ such that

$a \neq M(p)$

Now $ap, a2p, a3p, ...$ will give integers which with respect to modulo p will go in all classes $[0], [1], ... , [p-1]$

Hence $J = z$

B. $R = \{a + ib : a, b \in Z\}$

For $a + ib$, $c + id$ will be inverse if

$(a + ib)(c + id) = 1 + i0$

$\Rightarrow (ac - bd) + i(ad + bc) = 1 + i0$

$\Rightarrow ac - bd = 1$ and $ad + bc = 0$

$\Rightarrow a = c = 1; b = d = 0\ \&\ a = c = -1, b = d = 0$

$a = c = 0, b = 1, d = -1 ; a = c = 0, b = -1, d = 1$

so, inverse of 4 elements $+1, -1, +i\ \&\ -i$ exists only.

29. A. If E is a closed set then all it's limit points belongs to it. As, sup E will be a limit point of the set, so for $\alpha = \sup.E$

$\alpha \in E$ if E is closed.

If E is open then interior points of E will be contained in it and it's boundary point which will be supremum is not contained in it.

Hence $\quad \alpha = \sup E \notin E$

B. Limit points of the set

$$E = \left\{ n + \frac{1}{2m} ; n, m \in N \right\} \text{ will be,}$$

$E' = \{1, 2, 3, ...\}$

i.e. all the natural numbers as, for $n = 1$, members of set are

$$1 + \frac{1}{2}, 1 + \frac{1}{4}, 1 + \frac{1}{6}, ...$$

whose limit point is 1 and so on.

IIT–JAM

JOINT ADMISSION TEST FOR
M.SC. (MATHEMATICS)-2006

1. $\lim\limits_{n\to\infty} \dfrac{n+\;\;+\;n+}{n\;+\;n}$ equals
   A. 3 B. 2
   C. 1 D. 0

2. Let $f(x) = (x-2)^{17}(x+5)^{24}$. Then
   A. f does not have a critical point at 2
   B. f has a minimum at 2
   C. f has a maximum at 2
   D. f has neither a minimum nor a maximum at 2

3. Let $f(x, y) = x^5 y^2 \;-\; \left(\dfrac{y}{x}\right)$ Then $x\dfrac{\partial f}{\partial x} + y\dfrac{\partial f}{\partial y}$ equals
   A. $2f$ B. $3f$
   C. $5f$ D. $7f$

4. Let G be the set of all irrational numbers. The interior and the closure of G are denoted by G^0 and $\overline{G}$, respectively (when ψ is the set of all real number). Then
   A. $G^0 = \phi,\ \overline{G} = G$ B. $G^0 = \psi,\ \overline{G} = \psi$
   C. $G^0 = \phi,\ \overline{G} = \psi$ D. $G^0 = G,\ \overline{G} = \psi$

5. Let $f(x) = \int\limits_{x}^{x} e^{-t}\, dt$ Then $f'(\pi/4)$ equals
   A. $\sqrt{e}$ B. $-\sqrt{e}$
   C. $\sqrt{e}$ D. $-\sqrt{e}$

6. Let C be the circle $x^2 + y^2 = 1$ taken in the anti-clockwise sense. Then the value of the integral
   $\int\limits_{C}\left[(\;xy\;+y\;dx + \;xy\;+)\;x\;dy\right]$ equals
   A. 1 B. $\pi/2$
   C. π D. 0

7. Let r be the distance of a point $P(x, y, z)$ from the origin O. Then ∇r is a vector
   A. orthogonal to
   B. normal to the level surface of r at P
   C. normal to the surface of revolution generated by OP about x-axis
   D. normal to the surface of revolution generated by OP about y-axis

8. Let $T : \psi^3 \to \psi^3$ be defined by (ψ–The set of all real numbers)
   $T(x\;x\;x) = (x - x\;x - x)$
   If $N(T)$ and $R(T)$ denote the null space and the range space of T respectively, then
   A. $\dim N(T) = 2$ B. $\dim R(T) = 2$
   C. $R(T) = N(T)$ D. $N(T) \subset R(T)$

9. Let S be a closed surface for which $\iint\limits_{S} \bar{r}\, nd\sigma =$ Then the volume enclosed by the surface is
   A. 1 B. 1/3
   C. 2/3 D. 3

10. If $(c_1 + c_2 \ln x)/x$ is the general solution of the differential equation
    $$x\frac{d^2 y}{dx^2} + kx\frac{dy}{dx} + y = \qquad x >$$
    then k equals
    A. 3 B. –3
    C. 2 D. –1

11. If A and B are 3×3 real matrices such that $rank(AB) = 1$, then $rank(BA)$ cannot be
    A. 0 B. 1
    C. 2 D. 3

12. The differential equation representing the family of circles touching y-axis at the origin is
    A. linear and of first order
    B. linear and of second order
    C. nonlinear and of first order
    D. nonlinear and of second order

13. Let G be a group of order 7 and $\phi(x) = x^4, x \in G$. Then ϕ is
    A. not one-one B. not onto
    C. not a homomorphism
    D. one-one, onto and a homomorphism

14. Let R be the ring of all 2×2 matrices with integer entries. Which of the following subsets of R is an integral domain? (**Z**–The set of all integers)

A. $\left\{ \begin{pmatrix} & x \\ y & \end{pmatrix} \; x \; y \in \mathbf{Z} \right\}$ B. $\left\{ \begin{pmatrix} x & \\ & y \end{pmatrix} \; x \; y \in \mathbf{Z} \right\}$

C. $\left\{ \begin{pmatrix} x & \\ & x \end{pmatrix} \; x \in \mathbf{Z} \right\}$ D. $\left\{ \begin{pmatrix} x & y \\ y & z \end{pmatrix} \; x \; y \; z \in \mathbf{Z} \right\}$

15. Let $f_n(x) = n \sin^{2n+1} x \cos x$. Then the value of

$$\lim_{n\to\infty} \int_0^{\pi} (f_n) \, x \, dx - \int_0^{\pi} \left(\lim_{n\to\infty} f_n \, x \right) dx \text{ is}$$

A. 1/2   B. 0
C. –1/2   D. $-\infty$

16. A. Test the convergence of the series

$$\sum_{n=}^{\infty} \frac{n^n}{n^{n}}$$

B. Show that

$$(\quad) \quad x \le \quad -\frac{x}{}$$

for $0 \le x \le \pi/2$.

17. Find the critical points of the function

$$f(x \; y) = x \; + y \; - \quad x - \; y +$$

Test each of these for maximum and minimum.

18. A. Evaluate $\iint_R x e^y \, dx \, dy$ where R is the region bounded by the lines $x = 0$, $y = 1$ and the parabola $y = x^2$.

B. Find the volume of the solid bounded above by the surface $z = 1 - x^2 - y^2$ and below by the plane $z = 0$.

19. Evaluate the surface integral

$$\iint_S x(\quad y - y \; + z \quad d\sigma$$

where the surface S is represented in the form $z = y^2$, $0 \le x \le 1$, $0 \le y \le 1$

20. Using the change of variables, evaluate $\iint_R xy \, dx \, dy$ where the region R is bounded by the curves $xy = 1$, $xy = 3$, $y = 3x$ and $y = 5x$ in the first quadrant.

21. A. Let u and v be the eigenvectors of A corresponding to the eigenvalues 1 and 3 respectively. Prove that $u + v$ is not an eigenvector of A.

B. Let A and B be real matrices such that the sum of each row of A is 1 and the sum of each row of B is 2. Then show that 2 is an eigenvalue of AB.

22. Suppose W_1 and W_2 are subspaces of ψ^4 spanned by $\{(1, 2, 3, 4), (2, 1, 1, 2)\}$ and $\{(1, 0, 1, 0), (3, 0, 1, 0)\}$ respectively. Find a basis of $W_1 \cap W_2$. Also find a basis of $W_1 + W_2$ containing $\{(1, 0, 1, 0), (3, 0, 1, 0)\}$. ($\psi$–The set of all real numbers)

23. Determine y_0 such that the solution of the differential equation

$$y' - y = 1 - e^{-x}, \; y(0) = y_0$$

has a finite limit as $x \to \infty$.

24. Let $\phi(x, y, z) = e^x \sin y$. Evaluate the surface integral $\iint_S \frac{\partial \phi}{\partial n} d\sigma$ where S is the surface of the cube $0 \le x \le 1$, $0 \le y \le 1$, $0 \le z \le 1$ and $\frac{\partial \phi}{\partial n}$ is the directional derivative of ϕ in the direction of the unit outward normal to S. Verify the divergence theorem.

25. Let $y = f(x)$ be a twice continuously differentiable function on $(0, \infty)$ satisfying

$$f(1) = 1 \text{ and } f'(x) = -f\left(\frac{}{x}\right) \quad x >$$

Form the second order differential equation satisfied by $y = f(x)$, and obtain its solution satisfying the given conditions.

26. Let $G = \left\{ \begin{pmatrix} a & b \\ c & d \end{pmatrix} \; a \; b \; c \; d \in \mathbf{Z} \right\}$ be the group under matrix addition and H be the subgroup of G consisting of matrices with even entries. Find the order of the quotient group G/H. (**Z**–The set of all integers)

27. Let

$$f(x) = \begin{cases} x & \le x \le \\ \sqrt{x} & x > \end{cases}$$

Show that f is uniformly continuous on $[0, \infty)$.

28. Find $M_n = \displaystyle\max_{x \geq} \left\{ \dfrac{x}{n(\ +nx)} \right\}$ and hence prove that the series

$$\sum_{n=}^{\infty} \frac{x}{n(\ +nx)}$$

is uniformly convergent on $[0, \infty)$.

29. Let R be the ring of polynomials with real coefficients under polynomial addition and polynomial multiplication. Suppose $I = \{p \in R : \text{sum of the coefficients of } p \text{ is zero}\}$. Prove that I is a maximal ideal of R.

ANSWERS

1	2	3	4	5	6	7	8	9	10
11	12	13	14	15					

SOME SELECTED EXPLANATORY ANSWERS

1. $\displaystyle\lim_{n\to\infty} \frac{2^{n+1}+3^{n+1}}{2^n+3^n}$

$= \displaystyle\lim_{n\to\infty} \frac{2\left(\dfrac{2}{3}\right)^n + 3}{\left(\dfrac{2}{3}\right)^n + 1}$

$= \dfrac{2\cdot 0 + 3}{0 + 1} = 3$

2. $f(x) = (x-2)^{17}(x+5)^{24}$

$\Rightarrow$ for $x < 2, f'(x) < 0$ and for $x > 2$

$f'(x) > 0$

so, $x = 2$ is neither maxima nor minima point.

3. $f(x,y) = x\, y\ ^{\ -\left(\frac{y}{x}\right)}$

$= x\left[\left(\dfrac{y}{x}\right)^{\ } - \left(\dfrac{y}{x}\right)^{\ }\right]$

$f(x,y) = x^{\ } \left(\dfrac{y}{x}\right)$

Hence by Euler Theorem,

$x\dfrac{\partial f}{\partial x} + y\dfrac{\partial f}{\partial y} = nf$

$[n = \text{order of homogeneous equation}]$

$= 7f.$

4. No point is interior as every neighbourhood contains rational numbers.

So, $G^0 = \phi$

Also each real number is a limit point as nbd of real number contains infinite irrationals.

$\Rightarrow \bar{G} = R$

5. $f(x) = \displaystyle\int_{\sin x}^{\cos x} e^{-t^2}\, dt$

$\Rightarrow f'(x) = -\sin x\, e^{-\cos^2 x} - \cos x\, e^{-\sin^2 x}$

$\Rightarrow f'(\pi/4) = -\dfrac{1}{\sqrt{2}} e^{-1/2} - \dfrac{1}{\sqrt{2}} e^{-1/2}$

$= -\sqrt{2}\, e^{-1/2} = -\sqrt{2/e}$

6. By Green's theorem

$\displaystyle\oint_C P\,dx + Q\,dy = \iint_S \left(\frac{\partial Q}{\partial x} - \frac{\partial P}{\partial y} \right) dx\,dy$

$\Rightarrow \displaystyle\int\left[(2xy^3 + y)dx + (3x^2 y^2 + 2x)dy \right]$

$= 4\displaystyle\int_0^1 \int_0^{\sqrt{1-x^2}} [(6xy^2 + 2) - (6xy^2 + 1)]dy\,dx$

$= 4\displaystyle\int_0^1 \int_0^{\sqrt{1-x^2}} dy\,dx = 4\int_0^1 \sqrt{1-x^2}\,dx$

$= 4\cdot\left[\dfrac{x\sqrt{1-x^2}}{2} + \dfrac{1}{2}\sin^{-1} x \right]_0^1$

$= 4\cdot\dfrac{1}{2}\cdot\dfrac{\pi}{2} = \pi$

7. $P(x,y,z)$ gives $\overrightarrow{OP} = x\hat{i} + y\hat{j} + z\hat{k}$

$r = \sqrt{x^2 + y^2 + z^2}$

$$\Rightarrow \nabla r = \frac{x}{r}\hat{i} + \frac{y}{r}\hat{j} + \frac{z}{r}\hat{k}$$

which is normal to the level surface of r at P.

8. $T(x_1, x_2, x_3) = (0, 0, 0)$
$\Rightarrow (x_1 - x_2, x_1 - x_2, 0) = (0, 0, 0)$
$\Rightarrow x_1 - x_2 = 0$
$\Rightarrow x_1 = x_2$
$\Rightarrow N(T) = \{(a_1\ a\ c)\,|\,a_1\ c \in R\}$
so, $\qquad\qquad \dim N(T) = 2$

9. $\displaystyle\iint_S \vec{r} \cdot \vec{n}\, d\sigma = 1$

$\Rightarrow 3\displaystyle\iiint_V dx\, dy\, dz = 1$

$\Rightarrow \displaystyle\iiint_V dx\, dy\, dz = 1/3$

10. By putting $x = e^z$ and taking $D = \dfrac{d}{dz}$, we get

$(D(D-1) + kD + 1)y = 0$

$\Rightarrow [D^2 + (k-1)D + 1]y = 0 \qquad \ldots(i)$

for $(c_1 + c_2 \ln x)/x$ to be solution discriminant of (i) should be zero.

i.e. $(k-1)2 - 4 = 0$

$\Rightarrow k - 1 = \pm 2$

$\Rightarrow k = -1, 3$

so, $k = 3$ is valid.

11. rank $(AB) = 1$

$\Rightarrow A$ and B both are not non-singular, so rank$(BA) \neq 3$.

12.

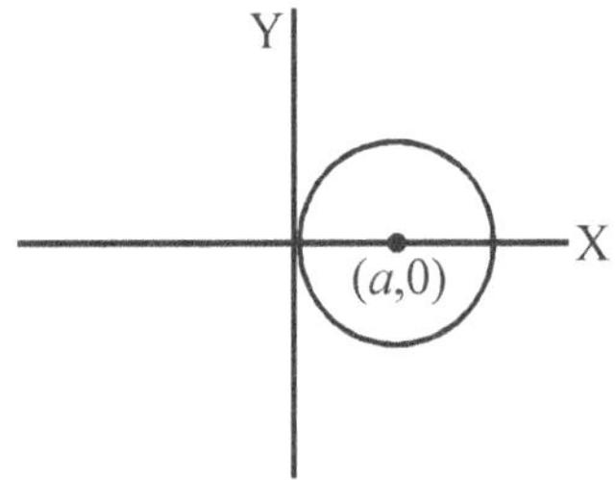

The equation of circle will be

$(x - a)^2 + y^2 = a^2$

$\Rightarrow x^2 + y^2 - 2ax = 0$

$\Rightarrow 2x + 2y\dfrac{dy}{dx} - 2a = 0$

$\Rightarrow a = x + y\dfrac{dy}{dx}$

$\Rightarrow x^2 + y^2 - 2x\left[x + y\dfrac{dy}{dx}\right] = 0$

$\Rightarrow 2xy\dfrac{dy}{dx} = y^2 - x^2$

$\Rightarrow \dfrac{dy}{dx} = \dfrac{y}{2x} - \dfrac{x}{2y}$

which is non linear of order one.

13. $\phi(x) = x^4$ for modulo 7 with addition is

$\Rightarrow \phi(0) = 0$
$\phi(1) = 4$
$\phi(2) = 1$
$\phi(3) = 5$
$\phi(4) = 2$
$\phi(5) = 6$
$\phi(6) = 3$

so, ϕ is one-one, onto and a homomorphism.

14. $\begin{pmatrix} x & 0 \\ 0 & x \end{pmatrix}\begin{pmatrix} y & 0 \\ 0 & y \end{pmatrix} = \begin{pmatrix} y & 0 \\ 0 & y \end{pmatrix}\begin{pmatrix} x & 0 \\ 0 & x \end{pmatrix}$

i.e. commutative.

$\begin{pmatrix} x & 0 \\ 0 & x \end{pmatrix}\begin{pmatrix} y & 0 \\ 0 & y \end{pmatrix} = \begin{pmatrix} 0 & 0 \\ 0 & 0 \end{pmatrix}$

$\Rightarrow x = 0$ or $y = 0$

$\Rightarrow$ No divisors of zero.

For $x = 1$ identity element exists.

so it is integral domain.

15. $\displaystyle\lim_{n\to\infty} f_n(x) = \lim_{n\to\infty} n\sin^{2n+1} x \cos x$

$= \displaystyle\lim_{n\to\infty} \frac{\sin^{2n+1} x \cos x}{1/n}$

$$\left[\frac{0}{0} \text{ case for } x \in (0, \pi/2)\right]$$

$= \displaystyle\lim_{n\to\infty} \frac{(2n+1)\sin^{2n} x \cos^2 x - \sin^{2n+2} x}{\dfrac{-1}{n^2}}$

$= \displaystyle\lim_{n\to\infty} \frac{-2(n+1)\sin^{2(n+1)} x + (2n+1)\sin^{2n} x}{\dfrac{-1}{n^2}} \to 0$

$\displaystyle\int_0^{\pi/2} f_n(x)\,dx = \int_0^{\pi/2} n\sin^{2n+1} x \cos x\, dx$

$= \dfrac{n \cdot 2n : (2n-2)(2n-4)\ldots}{2(n+1)\cdot 2n \cdot (2n-4)\ldots}$ by Walli's theorem

$$= \frac{1}{2} \cdot \frac{n}{n+1}$$

$$\Rightarrow \lim_{n \to \infty} \int_0^{\pi/2} f_n(x)\,dx \; \lim_{n \to \infty} \frac{1}{2} \cdot \frac{n}{n+1} = \frac{1}{2}$$

$\Rightarrow$ Required integral = 1/2

16. **A.** $\displaystyle\sum_{n=1}^{\infty} \frac{n^n}{n!3^n}$ is the series with

$$u_n = \frac{n^n}{n!3^n}$$

$$\Rightarrow u_{n+1} = \frac{(n+1)^{n+1}}{(n+1)!3^{n+1}}$$

$$\lim_{n \to \infty} \frac{u_{n+1}}{u_n} = \lim_{n \to \infty} \frac{1}{3}\left(1+\frac{1}{n}\right)^n = \frac{e}{3} < 1$$

so, given series is convergent.

B. Let $f(x) = \ln(1 + \cos x) + \dfrac{x^2}{4}$

$$\Rightarrow f'(x) = \frac{-\sin x}{1 + \cos x} + \frac{x}{2}$$

$$= -\tan\frac{x}{2} + \frac{x}{2}$$

$\Rightarrow f'(x) \le 0 \,; \forall\, 0 \le x \le \pi/2$

so, $f(x) \le f(0) \,; \forall\, 0 \le x \le \pi/2$

$$\Rightarrow \ln(1 + \cos x) + \frac{x^2}{4} \le \ln 2$$

$$\Rightarrow \ln(1 + \cos x) \le \ln 2 - \frac{x^2}{4}$$

17. $f(x, y) = x^3 + y^3 - 12x - 6y + 40$

$\Rightarrow f_x = 3x^2 - 12 \,; f_x = 0 \quad \Rightarrow x = -2, 2$

$\quad f_y = 2y - 6 \,; f_y = 0$

$\Rightarrow y = 3$

so, critical points are $(-2, 3)$ & $(2, 3)$

$f_{xx} = 6x \,; f_{yy} = 2 \,; f_{xy} = 0$

$f_{xx}f_{yy} - f_{xy}^2 = 12x$

At $(-2, 3) \,; f_{xx}f_{yy} - f_{xy}^2 = -24$

so, $(-2, 3)$ is neither maxima nor minima point.

At $(2, 3) \,; f_{xx}f_{yy} - f_{xy}^2 = 24$

and $f_{xx} = 12 > 0$

so $(2, 3)$ is minima point.

Minimum value $= 8 + 9 - 24 - 18 + 40 = 15$

18. **A.**

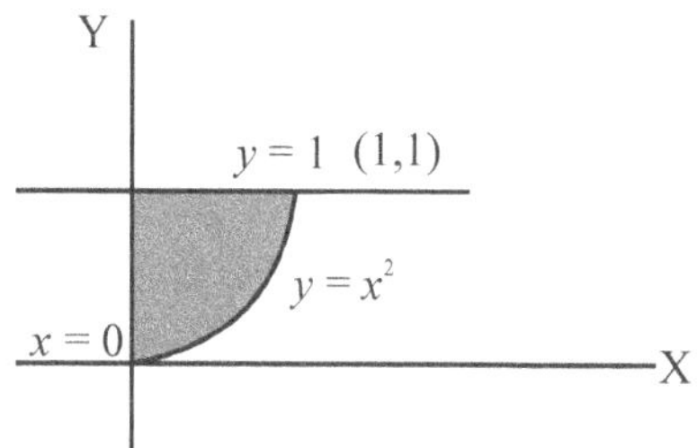

Region bounded is shaded one.

$$\iint_R xe^{y^2}\,dx\,dy$$

$$= \int_0^1 \int_0^{\sqrt{y}} xe^{y^2}\,dx\,dy = \int_0^1 \frac{y}{2}e^{y^2}\,dy = \frac{1}{4}e^{y^2}\Big|_0^1$$

$$= \frac{1}{4}(e-1)$$

B. $z = 1 - x^2 - y^2$

$\Rightarrow x^2 + y^2 = 1 - z$

Required volume is

$$V = 4\int_0^1 \int_0^{\sqrt{1-z}} \int_0^{\sqrt{1-z-y^2}} dx\,dy\,dz$$

$$= 4\int_0^1 \int_0^{\sqrt{1-z}} \sqrt{(1-z) - y^2}\,dy\,dz$$

$$= 4\int_0^1 \left[\frac{y}{2}\sqrt{(1-z) - y^2} + \frac{(1-z)}{2}\sin^{-1}\frac{y}{\sqrt{1-z}}\right]_0^{\sqrt{1-z}} dz$$

$$= 4\int_0^1 \frac{\pi}{4}(1-z)\,dz$$

$$= \pi\left[z - \frac{z^2}{2}\right]_0^1 = \frac{\pi}{2}$$

19. $\displaystyle\iint_S x(12y - y^4 + z^2)\,d\sigma$

over $z = y^2, \, 0 \le x \le 1, \, 0 \le y \le 1$ is

$$\int_0^1 \int_0^1 x(12y - y^4 + y^4)\,dx\,dy$$

$$= \int_0^1 \int_0^1 12xy\,dx\,dy$$

$$= 12\int_0^1 x\,dx \int_0^1 y\,dy = 12\left(\frac{1}{2}\right)\left(\frac{1}{2}\right) = 3$$

20. Put $\qquad xy = u, \quad \dfrac{y}{x} = v$

then $\qquad\qquad y = (uv)^{-}$

$$x = \left(\frac{u}{v}\right)^{-}$$

Also, $\dfrac{\partial(x\ y)}{\partial(u\ v)} = \begin{vmatrix} \dfrac{}{\sqrt{uv}} & --\left(\dfrac{u}{\sqrt{}}\right)^{-} \\[3mm] \dfrac{}{\sqrt{uv}} & -\left(\dfrac{u}{v}\right)^{-} \end{vmatrix}$

$$= \frac{}{v} + \frac{}{v} = \frac{}{v}$$

Also the new region of integration is $1 \le u \le 3$
$$3 \le v \le 5$$

$\therefore \quad \displaystyle\iint_R xy\,dx\,dy = \iint_R u\,\frac{}{v}\,du\,dv$

$$= \int\limits_{u=}\int\limits_{v=} \frac{u}{v}\,du\,dv$$

$$= \quad -- = \quad ---.$$

21. A. As u and v are eigen vectors corresponding to eigen values 1 and 3, so
$Au = 1 \cdot u$; $Av = 3 \cdot v = 3v$
$\Rightarrow A(u+v) = u + 3v$
   As R.H.S. is not multiple of $u + v$, so $u + v$ cannot be an eigen vector.

B. $A = \begin{bmatrix} 1/2 & 1/2 \\ 1/2 & 1/2 \end{bmatrix}$; $B = \begin{bmatrix} 1 & 1 \\ 1 & 1 \end{bmatrix}$

$\Rightarrow AB = \begin{bmatrix} 1 & 1 \\ 1 & 1 \end{bmatrix}$

$|AB - \lambda I| = (1-\lambda)^2 - 1 = 0$
$\Rightarrow 1 - \lambda = \pm 1 \Rightarrow \lambda = 2, 0$
   So, 2 is an eigen value of AB.

22.
$$W_1 = \{(1,2,3,4,),(2,1,1,2)\}$$
$$W_2 = \{1,0,1,0),(3,0,1,0)\}$$
Now, we'll calculate the dim $(W_1 \cup W_2)$ which is equal to number of independent row in

$$\begin{bmatrix} \\ \\ \\ \\ \end{bmatrix} = 4$$

Now dim $(W_1 \cup W_2) = \dim W_1$
$$\qquad\qquad + \dim W_2 - \dim(W_1 \cap W_2)$$
$\Rightarrow \dim(W_1 \cap W_2) = 0$
i.e. basis of $(W_1 \cap W_2) = \{(0,0,0,0)\}$
$\Rightarrow \qquad\qquad \psi^4 = W_1 \oplus W_2$
$\Rightarrow$ basis of W_2 can be extended to form basis of $W_1 + W_2$ which is given by
$= \{(1,0,1,0),(3,0,1,0),(0,1,0,0),(0,0,0,1)\}$.

23. $y' - y = 1 - e^{-x}$
A.E. is $(D-1) = 0$
$\Rightarrow D = 1$
$\Rightarrow$ C.F. is $y = c_1 e^x$

P.I. is $\dfrac{1}{(D-1)}(1 - e^{-x})$

$\Rightarrow y = c_1 e^x - 1 + \dfrac{e^{-x}}{2}$

$y(0) = y_0 \Rightarrow y_0 = c_1 - 1$
$\Rightarrow c_1 = y_0 + 1$

$\Rightarrow y = (1 + y_0)\,e^x - 1 + \dfrac{e^{-x}}{2}$

As $x \to \infty$ limit is finite if
$1 + y_0 = 0 \Rightarrow y_0 = -1$

24. From question
$$\phi(x, y, z) = e^x \sin y$$

Now $\displaystyle\iint \left(\frac{\partial \phi}{\partial n}\right) \partial\sigma = \iint_S (\nabla\phi)\, n\, dS$

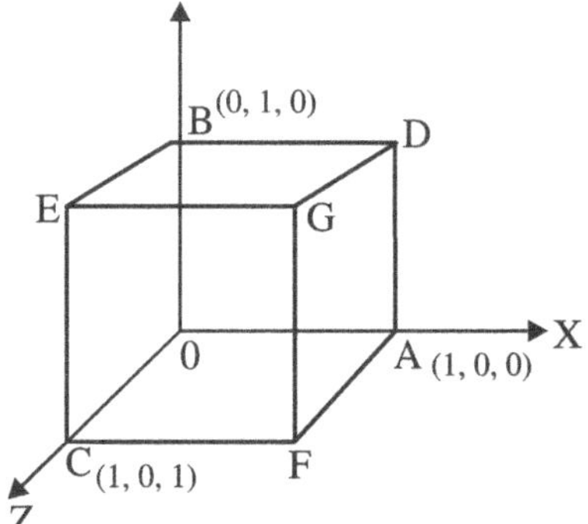

Now $\qquad\qquad \phi = \left(e^x \quad yi + e^x \quad yj\right)$

Now $\iint\left(\dfrac{\partial\phi}{\partial n}\right)\partial e = \iint\limits_{S}(\nabla\phi)\, n\, dS$

$= \iint (\nabla\phi)\, n\, dS + \iint (\nabla\phi)\, n\, dS$

$\qquad + \iint (\nabla\phi)\, n\, dS + \iint (\nabla\phi)\, n\, dS$

$\qquad + \iint (\nabla\phi)\, n\, dS + \iint (\nabla\phi)\, n\, dS$

$= + -\int\limits_{z=}\int\limits_{y=} e \quad y\,dy\,dz + \int\limits_{z=}\int\limits_{y=} e \quad y\,dy\,dz$

$\qquad -\int\limits_{z=}\int\limits_{x=} e^x\, dx\,dz + \int\limits_{z=}\int\limits_{x=} e^x \quad dx\,dz$

$= -(1-\cos 1) + e(1-\cos 1) - (e-1)$

$\qquad\qquad + \cos 1(e-1) = 0$

$u\iint\left(\dfrac{\partial\phi}{\partial n}\right)\partial\sigma = \iint\limits_{S}(\nabla\phi)\, n\, dS =$

By Guass divergence theorem

$$\iint\limits_{S}(\nabla\phi)\, n\, dS = \iiint \bar\nabla(\nabla\phi)\,dV = \iiint(\nabla\,\phi)\,dV$$

$$= \iiint\left(e^x \quad y - e^x \quad y\right)dV = 0$$

$\Rightarrow$ divergence theorem is verified.

25. $f'(x) = \dfrac{1}{2}f\left(\dfrac{1}{x}\right)$ ...(i)

$\Rightarrow f''(x) = \dfrac{1}{2}\left[-\dfrac{1}{x^2}f'\left(\dfrac{1}{x}\right)\right]$

$\qquad = -\dfrac{1}{2x^2}f'\left(\dfrac{1}{x}\right) = -\dfrac{1}{2x^2}\times\dfrac{1}{2}f(x)$

$\Rightarrow f''(x) + \dfrac{f(x)}{4x^2} = 0$

$\Rightarrow 4x^2\dfrac{d^2 y}{dx^2} + y = 0; \quad$ By $y = f(x)$

Let $x = e^z$, and $D = \dfrac{d}{dz}$

$\Rightarrow [4D(D-1) + 1]y = 0$

$\Rightarrow [4D^2 - 4D + 1]y = 0$

$\Rightarrow (2D-1)^2 y = 0$

$\Rightarrow y = (c_1 + c_2 z)\, e^{\frac{1}{2}z}$

$\Rightarrow y = (c_1 + c_2 \ln x)\, x^{\frac{1}{2}}$

As $f(1) = 1$

$f'(1) = \dfrac{1}{2}f(1) = \dfrac{1}{2}$

$\Rightarrow y' = \left(\dfrac{c_2}{x}\right)x^{\frac{1}{2}} + \dfrac{1}{2}x^{\frac{1}{2}}(c_1 + c_2 \ln x)$

$\Rightarrow c_1 = 1\ \&\ c_2 + \dfrac{c_1}{2} = \dfrac{1}{2} \quad \Rightarrow \quad c_2 = 0$

$\Rightarrow y = x^{\frac{1}{2}}$

26. In $G = \left\{\begin{pmatrix} a & b \\ c & d \end{pmatrix} : a,b,c,d \in z\right\}$

$H = \left\{\begin{pmatrix} e & f \\ g & h \end{pmatrix} : e,f,g,h \in \text{ even } z\right\}$

As, z/z_2 is of order 2, so as 2×2 matrix is of dimension 4.

$O(G/H) = O\left(\dfrac{z\times z\times z\times z}{z_2 \times z_2 \times z_2 \times z_2}\right)$

$= 2\times 2\times 2\times 2 = 16$

27. $f(x) = \begin{cases} x^2 & ; 0\le x \le 1 \\ \sqrt{x} & ; x > 1 \end{cases}$

For $0 \le x \le 1$

$|f(x_1) - f(x_2)| = |x_1^2 - x_2^2|$

$= |x_1 - x_2|\,|x_1 + x_2|$

$|f(x_1) - f(x_2)| < \in$

$\Rightarrow |x_1 - x_2|\,|x_1 + x_2| < \in$

$\Rightarrow |x_1 - x_2| < \dfrac{\in}{|x_1 + x_2|} < \dfrac{\in}{2}\ \forall\, x_1; x_2 \text{ in } [0,1]$

$\Rightarrow \delta = \dfrac{\in}{2}$ independent of x_1, x_2

For $x > 1$.

$|f(x_1) - f(x_2)| < \in$

$\Rightarrow \left|\sqrt{x_1} - \sqrt{x_2}\right| < \in$

$\Rightarrow |x_1 - x_2| < \in\left|\sqrt{x_1} + \sqrt{x_2}\right|$

$\Rightarrow$ least possible value of R.H.S. $= 2\in$

so δ independent of $\in$ is found.

Thus $f(x)$ is uniformly convergent on $[0, \infty)$

28. $M_n = \max\limits_{x \geq 0} \left\{ \dfrac{x}{n(1+nx^3)} \right\}$

$f(x) = \dfrac{x}{n(1+nx^3)}$

$\Rightarrow f'(x) = \dfrac{1}{n(1+nx^3)} + \dfrac{x}{n}\left[-\dfrac{3nx^2}{(1+nx^3)^2} \right]$

$= \dfrac{(1+nx^3) - 3nx^3}{n(1+nx^3)^2} = \dfrac{1-2nx^3}{n(1+nx^3)^2}$

$f'(x) = 0$

$\Rightarrow 1 - 2nx^3 = 0$

$\Rightarrow x^3 = \dfrac{1}{2n}$

$\Rightarrow x = \left(\dfrac{1}{2n}\right)^{1/3}$

$\Rightarrow M_n = \dfrac{1}{\left(\dfrac{3}{2}\right)n(2n)^{1/3}} = \dfrac{2}{3(2)^{1/3}\, n^{4/3}}$

$\displaystyle\sum_{n=1}^{\infty} \dfrac{x}{n(1+nx^3)} \leq \sum_{n=1}^{\infty} M_n \leq \sum \dfrac{2}{3(2)^{1/3}} \times \dfrac{1}{(n)^{4/3}}$

As $\displaystyle\sum_{n=1}^{\infty} \dfrac{1}{(n)^{4/3}}$ is a convergent series, so

given series converges uniformly on $[0, \infty)$

29. From question

$$R = \left\{a + a\,x + a\,x + \ \big|\ a_i \in R\right\}$$

from question $\quad I = \left\{p \in R \,\big|\, \Sigma q_i = \ \right\}$

Clearly $O \in I \ \Rightarrow$ I is not empty

if $p_1, p_2 \in I$ then $(p_1 - p_2) \in I$

Also let $\Sigma q_i\, x^i \in R$ and $\Sigma p_r x^i \in I$

then $\qquad\qquad \Sigma p_i = 0$

Now $\qquad (\Sigma q_r x^i)(\Sigma p_r x^i) =$

Sum of coefficient of above expression

$\qquad\qquad\qquad = (\Sigma q_i)(\Sigma p_i) = 0 \quad [\because \Sigma p_i = 0]$

$i.e.$ I is an ideal of R

let $I \subseteq \cup \subseteq R$

Now let there exist $q \in \cup$ such that $q \notin I$

then $\qquad\qquad \Sigma q_i \neq 0$

$\Rightarrow q(x) - \lambda \in I \ \Rightarrow q(l) - \lambda \in \cup$

$\Rightarrow \qquad\qquad \lambda \in \cup$

Also λ is non-zero $\Rightarrow \dfrac{\ }{\lambda} \qquad\qquad [\because \lambda$ is real$]$

$\Rightarrow \lambda \dfrac{\ }{\lambda} \in \cup \ \Rightarrow 1 \in \cup \ \Rightarrow \cup = R$

Hence, is maximal ideal of R.

IIT–JAM

Joint Admission Test for
M.Sc. (Mathematics)-2005

1. Let $\{a_n\}$, $\{b_n\}$ and $\{c_n\}$ be sequences of real numbers such that $b_n = a_{2n}$ and $c_n = a_{2n+1}$. Then $\{a_n\}$ is convergent
   A. implies $\{b_n\}$ is convergent but $\{c_n\}$ need not be convergent
   B. implies $\{c_n\}$ is convergent but $\{b_n\}$ need not be convergent
   C. implies both $\{b_n\}$ and $\{c_n\}$ are convergent
   D. if both $\{b_n\}$ and $\{c_n\}$ are convergent

2. An integrating factor of $x\dfrac{dy}{dx} + (x+)\,y = xe^{-x}$ is
   A. $x\,e^{3x}$
   B. $3x\,e^x$
   C. $x\,e^x$
   D. $x^3\,e^x$

3. The general solution of $x\dfrac{d\,y}{dx} - x\dfrac{dy}{dx} + 9y = 0$ is
   A. $(c_1 + c_2 x)\,e^{3x}$
   B. $(c_1 + c_2 \ln x)\,x^3$
   C. $(c_1 + c_2 x)\,x^3$
   D. $(c_1 + c_2 \ln x)\,e^x$
   (Here c_1 and c_2 are arbitrary constants.)

4. Let $\vec{r} = xi + yj + zk$ If $\phi(x, y, z)$ is a solution of the Laplace equation then the vector field $\left(\vec{\nabla}\phi + \vec{r}\right)$ is
   A. neither solenoidal nor irrotational
   B. solenoidal but not irrotational
   C. both solenoidal and irrotational
   D. irrotational but not solenoidal

5. Let $\vec{F} = xi + yj + zk$ S be the surface of the sphere $x^2 + y^2 + z^2 = 1$ and n be the inward unit normal vector to S. Then $\iint\limits_{S} \vec{F}\,n\,dS$ is equal to
   A. 4π
   B. -4π
   C. 8π
   D. -8π

6. Let A be a 3×3 matrix with eigenvalues $1, -1$ and 3. Then
   A. $A^2 + A$ is non-singular
   B. $A^2 - A$ is non-singular
   C. $A^2 + 3A$ is non-singular
   D. $A^2 - 3A$ is non-singular

7. Let $T : \mathrm{R}^3 \to \mathrm{R}^3$ be a linear transformation and I be the identity transformation of R^3. If there is a scalar c and a non-zero vector $x \in \mathrm{R}^3$ such that $T(x) = cx$, then rank $(T - cI)$
   A. cannot be 0
   B. cannot be 1
   C. cannot be 2
   D. cannot be 3

8. In the group $\{1, 2, ..., 16\}$ under the operation of multiplication modulo 17, the order of the element 3 is
   A. 4
   B. 8
   C. 12
   D. 16

9. A ring R has maximal ideals
   A. if R is infinite
   B. if R is finite
   C. if R is finite with at least 2 elements
   D. only if R is finite

10. The integral $\displaystyle\int\left[\int^{-z}\left(\int dx\right)dy\right]dz$ is equal to
   A. $\displaystyle\int\left[\int^{-y}\left(\int dx\right)dz\right]dy$
   B. $\displaystyle\int\left[\int^{-y}\left(\int dx\right)dz\right]dy$
   C. $\displaystyle\int\left[\int\left(\int^{-z}dx\right)dz\right]dy$
   D. $\displaystyle\int\left[\int\left(\int^{-y}dx\right)dz\right]dy$

11. Let $f : \mathrm{R} \to \mathrm{R}$ be continuous and $g, h : \mathrm{R}^2 \to \mathrm{R}$ be differentiable. Let $F(u, v) = \displaystyle\int_{v}^{u} f(t)\,dt$, where

$u = g(x, y)$ and $v = h(x, y)$. Then $\dfrac{\partial F}{\partial x} + \dfrac{\partial F}{\partial y} =$

A. $f(g(x, y)) \left[\dfrac{\partial g}{\partial x} + \dfrac{\partial g}{\partial y} \right] - f(h(x, y)) \left[\dfrac{\partial h}{\partial x} + \dfrac{\partial h}{\partial y} \right]$

B. $f(h(x, y)) \left[\dfrac{\partial g}{\partial x} + \dfrac{\partial g}{\partial y} \right] - f(g(x, y)) \left[\dfrac{\partial h}{\partial x} - \dfrac{\partial h}{\partial y} \right]$

C. $f(h(x, y)) \left[\dfrac{\partial g}{\partial x} + \dfrac{\partial g}{\partial y} \right] + f(g(x, y)) \left[\dfrac{\partial h}{\partial x} - \dfrac{\partial h}{\partial y} \right]$

D. $f(g(x, y)) \left[\dfrac{\partial g}{\partial x} - \dfrac{\partial g}{\partial y} \right] + f(g(x, y)) \left[\dfrac{\partial h}{\partial x} - \dfrac{\partial h}{\partial y} \right]$

12. Let $y = f(x)$ be a smooth curve such that $0 < f(x) < K$ for all $x \in [a, b]$. Let
 L = length of the curve between $x = a$ and $x = b$
 A = area bounded by the curve, x-axis, and the lines $x = a$ and $x = b$
 S = area of the surface generated by revolving the curve about x-axis between $x = a$ and $x = b$
 Then
 A. $2\pi KL < S < 2\pi A$ B. $S \le 2\pi A < 2\pi KL$
 C. $2\pi A \le S < 2\pi KL$ D. $2\pi A < 2\pi KL < S$

13. Let $f : R \to R$ be defined by $f(t) = t^2$ and let U be any non-empty open subset of R.
 Then
 A. $f(U)$ is open B. $f^{-1}(U)$ is open
 C. $f(U)$ is closed D. $f^{-1}(U)$ is closed

14. Let $f : (-1, 1) \to R$ be such that $f^{(n)}(x)$ exists and $|f^{(n)}(x)| \le 1$ for every $n \ge 1$ and for every $x \in (-1, 1)$. Then f has a convergent power series expansion in a neighbourhood of
 A. every $x \in (-1, 1)$

 B. every $x \in \left(\dfrac{-}{-} \right)$ only

 C. no $x \in (-1, 1)$

 D. every $x \in \left(\dfrac{}{-} \right)$ only

15. Let $a > 1$ and $f, g, h : [-a, a] \to R$ be twice differentiable functions such that for some c with $0 < c < 1 < a$,
 $f(x) = 0$ only for $x = -a, 0, a$;
 $f'(x) = 0 = g(x)$ only $x = -1, 0, 1$;
 $g'(x) = 0 = h(x)$ only for $x = -c, c$.
 The possible relations between f, g, h are
 A. $f = g'$ and $h = f'$ B. $f' = g$ and $g' = h$
 C. $f = -g'$ and $h' = g$ D. $f = -g'$ and $h' = f$

16. A. Solve the initial value problem

 $$\frac{d\,y}{dx} - y = x(\quad x +)e^x \quad y(0) = y'(0) = 1$$

 B. Solve the differential equation
 $(2y \sin x + 3y^4 \sin x \cos x)\, dx - (4y^3 \cos^2 x + \cos x)\, dy = 0$

17. Let G be a finite abelian group of order n with identity e. If for all $a \in G$, $a^3 = e$ then, by induction on n, show that $n = 3^k$ for some non-negative integer k.

18. A. Let $f : [a, b] \to R$ be a differentiable function. Show that there exist points $c_1, c_2 \in (a, b)$ such that

 $$f(c)\,f'(c) = f'(c)\,(f)a + (f)b$$

 B. Let $f(x, y) =$

 $$\begin{cases} (x\ +y\ )(\quad x\ +y\quad +(\quad)\quad (x,\ y \ne \\ \alpha \qquad\qquad\qquad\qquad (\quad x,\ y() = \end{cases}$$

 Find a suitable value for α such that f is continuous. For this value of α, is f differentiable at $(0, 0)$? Justify your claim.

19. A. Let S be the surface $x^2 + y^2 + z^2 = 1, z \ge 0$. Use Stoke's theorem to evaluate

 $$\int_C (\quad x -)y\, dx - y\,dy - z\,dz$$

 where C is the circle $x^2 + y^2 = 1, z = 0$, oriented anticlockwise.

 B. Show that the vector field

 $$\vec{F} = (\quad xy - y\ +)\, i + (x\ -\ xy)\, j \qquad \text{is}$$

 conservative. Find its potential and also the work done in moving a particle from $(1, 0)$ to $(2, 1)$ along some curve.

20. Let $T : R^3 \to R^3$ be defined by $T(x, y, z) = (y + z, z, 0)$. Show that T is a linear transformation. If $v \in R^3$ is such that $T^2(v) \ne 0$, then show that $B = \{v, T(v), T^2(v)\}$ forms a basis of R^3. Compute the matrix of T with respect to B. Also find a $v \in R^3$ such that $T^2(v) \ne 0$.

21. A. For each $n \in N$, define $f_n : [-1, 1] \to R$ by

$$f_n(x) = \begin{cases} n\,x & x \in \left[\ \dfrac{}{n}\right) \\ -\,n\left(x - \dfrac{}{n}\right) & x \in \left[\dfrac{}{n}\ \dfrac{}{n}\right) \\ & x \in \left[\dfrac{}{n}\ \right) \end{cases}$$

Compute $\int f_n(x)\,dx$ for each n. Analyse pointwise and uniform convergence of the sequence of functions $\{f_n\}$.

B. Let $f : R \to R$ be a continuous function with $|f(x) - f(y)| \ge |x - y|$ for every $x, y \in R$. Is f one-one? Show that there cannot exist three points $a, b, c \in R$ with $a < b < c$ such that $f(a) < f(c) < f(b)$.

22. Find the volume of the cylinder with base as the disk of unit radius in the xy-plane centred at $(1, 1, 0)$ and the top being the surface $z = [(x-1)^2 + (y-1)^2]^{3/2}$.

23. A. Bag A contains 3 white and 4 red balls, and bag B contains 6 white and 3 red balls. A biased coin, twice as likely to come up heads as tails, is tossed once. If it shows head, a ball is drawn from bag A, otherwise, from bag B. Given that a white ball was drawn, what is the probability that the coin came up tail?

B. Let the random variables X and Y have the joint probability density function $f(x, y)$ given by

$$f(x\ y) = \begin{cases} y\,e^{-(\ x)} & x \ge \quad y \ge \end{cases}$$

Are the random variables X and Y independent? Justify your answer.

24. A. Let $X_1, X_2, \dots, X_n$ be independently identically distributed random variables (rv's) with common probability density function (pdf)

$$f_x(x\ \theta) = \dfrac{}{\theta}e^{-x\ \theta} \qquad x > 0,\ \theta > 0.$$ Obtain the moment generating function (mgf) of

$$\overline{X} = \dfrac{}{n}\sum_{i=}^{n} X_i$$ Also find the mgf of the rv $Y = n\overline{X}\ \theta\,.$

B. Let $X_1, X_2, \dots, X_9$ be independent random sample from $N(2, 4)$ and Y_1, Y_2, Y_3, Y_4, be an independent random sample from $N(1, 1)$. Find $P(\overline{X} > \overline{Y})$ where $\overline{X}$ and $\overline{Y}$ are sample means. [Given $P(Z > 1.2) = 0.1151$, where $Z \sim N(0, 1)$]

25. A. Let $X_1, X_2, \dots, X_n$ be a random sample from a distribution having pdf

$$f(x\ x\ \alpha) = \begin{cases} \dfrac{\alpha\,x^{\alpha}}{x^{\alpha+}} & x > x \end{cases}$$

where $x_0 > 0$, $\alpha > 0$. Find the maximum likelihood estimator of α if x_0 is known.

B. Let $X_1, X_2, \dots, X_5$ be a random sample from the standard normal population. Determine the constant c such that the random variable

$$Y = \dfrac{c(X\ +X\ )}{\sqrt{X\ +X\ +X}}$$

will have a t-distribution.

26. A. A random sample of size $n = 1$ is drawn from

$$\text{pdf}\,f_x(x, \theta) = \dfrac{}{\theta}e^{-x\ \theta} \quad x > \theta > 0.$$ It is decided to test $H_0 : \theta = 5$ against $H_1 : \theta = 7$ based on the criterion: reject H_0 if the observed value is greater than 10. Obtain the probabilities of type I and type II errors.

B. Let $X_1, X_2, \dots, X_n$ be a random sample from a normal population $N(\mu, \sigma^2)$. Find the best test for testing $H_0 : \mu = 0, \sigma^2 = 1$ against $H_1 : \mu = 1$, $\sigma^2 = 4$.

27. A. Let $f, g : R \to R$ be such that for $x, y \in R$,

$$\phi(x + iy) = e^x\ f(\ y)\ + ig(\ y)$$

is an analytic function. Find a differential equation of order 2 satisfied by f.

B. Compute $\int_{|z+\ |=}(\ z\ )\ e^{(\sqrt{\ }+)\,z}\,dz$

28. A. Let $f(z)$ be analytic in the whole complex plane such that for all $r > 0$,

$$\int_{}^{\pi} \left|f(re^{i\theta})\right|\,d\theta \le \sqrt{r}$$

Find $\dfrac{f^{(n)}()}{n}$ for all $n \ge 0$.

B. Find all values of $\alpha \in C$ such that $f(z) = (z + \bar{z}) + \alpha|z| + \alpha\, \bar{z}$ is analytic at some point z having non-zero real part.

29. A hemispherical bowl of radius 12 cm is fixed such that its rim is horizontal. A light rod of length 20 cm with weights w and W attached to its two ends is placed inside the bowl. In equilibrium, the weight w is just touching the rim of the bowl. Find the ratio w : W.

30. A uniform ladder of length $2a$ and mass m lies in a vertical plane with one end against a smooth wall, the other end being supported on a horizontal floor. The ladder is released from rest when inclined at an angle α to the horizontal. Find the inclination of the ladder to the horizontal when it ceases to touch the wall.

31. A. Estimate the error in evaluating the integral
$$\int (+ x)\, e^{-x}\,dx$$
by Simpson's $-$ rule with spacing $h = 0.25$.

   B. Using Newton-Raphson method, compute the point of intersection of the curves $y = x^3$ and $y = 8x + 4$ near the point $x = 3$, correct up to 2 decimal places. [Round-off the first iteration up to 2 decimal places for further computation].

32. The polynomial $p_3(x) = x^3 + x^2 - 2$ interpolates the function $f(x)$ at the points $x = -1, 0, 1$ and 2. If the data $f(3) = -14$ is added, find the new interpolating polynomial by using Newton's forward difference formula. Also find $f(2.5)$ by using Newton's backward difference formula with pivot value 3. Justify whether the value obtained will be the same if pivot value 2 is taken.

$$\boxed{\textbf{ANSWERS}}$$

1	2	3	4	5	6	7	8	9	10

11	12	13	14	15

$$\boxed{\textbf{SOME SELECTED EXPLANATORY ANSWERS}}$$

1. $\{a_n\}$ is convergent implies both it's odd numbered term (subsequence) and even numbered term (subsequence) converges individually.

2. $x\dfrac{dy}{dx} + (3x+1)y = xe^{-2x}$

   $\Rightarrow \dfrac{dy}{dx} + \dfrac{(3x+1)}{x}y = e^{-2x}$ is linear D.E.

   so, Integrating factor is
   $$e^{\int\left(\frac{3x+1}{x}\right)dx} = e^{\int\left(3+\frac{1}{x}\right)dx} = e^{3x+\ln x}$$
   $$= e^{3x}\, e^{\ln x} = xe^{3x}$$

3. $x^2\dfrac{d^2 y}{dx^2} - 5x\dfrac{dy}{dx} + 9y = 0 \qquad ...(i)$

   Let $z = \ln x \Rightarrow x = e^z$

   $\Rightarrow D = \dfrac{d}{dz}$

   so, equation (i) becomes
   $$[D(D-1) - 5D + 9]y = 0$$
   $$\Rightarrow [D^2 - 6D + 9]y = 0$$
   $$\Rightarrow (D-3)^2 y = 0$$
   $$\Rightarrow D = 3, 3$$
   $$\Rightarrow y = (C_1 + C_2 z)e^{3z}$$
   $$= (C_1 + C_2 \ln x)\, x^3$$

4. $\vec{r} = x\hat{i} + y\hat{j} + z\hat{k}$

   As $\phi(x, y, z)$ is a solution of laplace equation,

   so, $\dfrac{\partial^2 \phi}{\partial x^2} + \dfrac{\partial^2 \phi}{\partial y^2} + \dfrac{\partial^2 \phi}{\partial z^2} = 0 = \nabla^2\phi$

   Now, $\vec{\nabla}\cdot(\vec{\nabla}\phi + \vec{r})$
   $$= \nabla^2\phi + \vec{\nabla}\cdot\vec{r} = 0 + 3$$
   $$\Rightarrow \vec{\nabla}\phi + \vec{r} \text{ is not solenoidal.}$$

   Also, $\vec{\nabla}\times(\vec{\nabla}\phi + \vec{r})$
   $$= \vec{\nabla}\times\vec{\nabla}\phi + \vec{\nabla}\times\vec{r}$$

$$= 0 + \begin{vmatrix} \hat{i} & \hat{j} & \hat{k} \\ \dfrac{\partial}{\partial x} & \dfrac{\partial}{\partial y} & \dfrac{\partial}{\partial z} \\ x & y & z \end{vmatrix} = 0 + 0 = 0$$

$\Rightarrow \vec{\nabla}\phi + \vec{r}$ is irrotational.

5. $\vec{F} = x\hat{i} + 2y\hat{j} + 3z\hat{k}$

By Divergence theorem.

$$\iint_S \vec{F} \cdot \hat{n}\, ds = -\iiint_V (\nabla \cdot \vec{F})\, dx\, dy\, dz$$

$$= -\iiint_V 6\, dx\, dy\, dz = -6\left(\frac{4}{3}\pi(1)^3\right)$$

As volume of given sphere is $\dfrac{4}{3}\pi(1)^3$

$$= -6\left(\frac{4}{3}\pi\right) = -8\pi$$

6. Eigen values of A is $1, -1, 3$
so, eigen values of A^2 is $1, 1, 9$
$\Rightarrow$ eigen values of $A^2 + 3A$ is
$1 + 3 \cdot 1, 1 + 3(-1), 9 + 3(3)$
i.e. $4, -2$ and 18
As no eigen values is 0, so
$A^2 + 3A$ is non-singular.

7. $(T - CI)x = T(x) - CI(x)$
$= Cx - Cx = 0$
$\Rightarrow |T - CI| = 0$
$\Rightarrow r(T - CI) \neq 3$

8. $[3]^4_{\times_{17}} = [13]_{\times_{17}}$

$[13]^2_{\times_{17}} = [16]_{\times_{17}}$

$[16]^2_{\times_{17}} = [1]_{\times_{17}}$

$\Rightarrow [3]^{16}_{\times_{17}} = [1]$

$\Rightarrow$ order of 3 is 16.

10. $y = 0$ to $1 - z$ and $z = 0, 1$

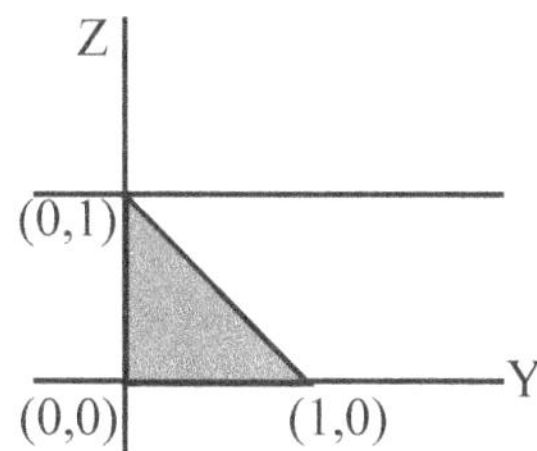

$\Rightarrow z = 0$ to $1 - y$ and $y = 0$ to 1
Given integral is

$$\int_0^1 \left[\int_0^{1-y} \left(\int_0^2 dx \right) dz \right] dy$$

11. $F(u, v) = \int_v^u f(t)\, dt$

$\Rightarrow \dfrac{\partial F}{\partial u} = f(u)$ and $\dfrac{\partial F}{\partial v} = -f(v)$

$$\frac{\partial F}{\partial x} = \frac{\partial F}{\partial u} \cdot \frac{\partial u}{\partial x} + \frac{\partial F}{\partial v} \cdot \frac{\partial v}{\partial x}$$

$$= f(g(x, y)) \cdot \frac{\partial g}{\partial x} + (-f(h(x, y))) \frac{\partial h}{\partial x}$$

$$\frac{\partial F}{\partial y} = \frac{\partial F}{\partial u} \cdot \frac{\partial u}{\partial y} + \frac{\partial F}{\partial v} \frac{\partial v}{\partial y}$$

$$= f(g(x, y)) \cdot \frac{\partial g}{\partial y} + [-f(h(x, y))] \frac{\partial h}{\partial y}$$

$$\frac{\partial F}{\partial x} + \frac{\partial F}{\partial y} = f(g(x, y)) \left[\frac{\partial g}{\partial x} + \frac{\partial g}{\partial y} \right]$$

$$-f(h(x, y)) \left[\frac{\partial h}{\partial x} + \frac{\partial h}{\partial y} \right]$$

12.
$$L = \int_a^b \sqrt{+\left(\frac{dy}{dx}\right)}\, dx$$

$$A = \int_a^b f(x)\, dx$$

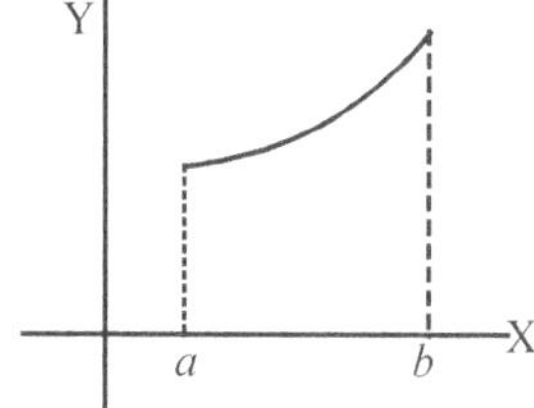

$$S = \int_a^b \pi y \sqrt{+\left(\frac{dy}{dx}\right)^2}\, dx$$

$$< \int \pi k \sqrt{+\left(\frac{dy}{dx}\right)}\, dx = 2\pi\, KL$$

$\Rightarrow \qquad S < 2\pi\, KL \qquad \qquad ...(1)$

Also $\qquad S \geq \int_a^b \pi\, dx = \pi \int_a^b y\, dx \quad \pi$

i.e. $\qquad S \geq 2\pi A \qquad \qquad ...(2)$

from (1) and (2) $2\pi A \leq S < 2\pi KL.$

13. $U \in \,]a, b[$

$\Rightarrow f(U) \in \,]a^2, b^2[$ is not necessarily true.

As $U \in \,]{-5}, 5[$

$\Rightarrow f(U) \in [0, 25[$

If $f(U)$ is invertible, $f^{-1}(U)$ is open.

14. As $|f^n(x)| \leq 1 \; \forall \, n \geq 1$

so, $x \in (-1, 1) \; f$ has a convergent power series expansion.

15. From the given relation

$f' = g$ and $g' = h.$

16. A. $\dfrac{d^2 y}{dx^2} - y = x(\sin x + e^x) \; ; y(0) = y'(0) = 1$

A.E. is $m^2 - 1 = 0$

$\Rightarrow m = \pm 1$

C.F. is $y = C_1 e^x + C_2 e^{-x}.$ $\qquad ...(i)$

P.I. is $y = \dfrac{1}{D^2 - 1} x \sin x + x e^x$

$= \left[x - \dfrac{2D}{D^2 - 1} \right] \dfrac{1}{D^2 - 1} (\sin x) + e^x \cdot \dfrac{1}{(D+1)^2 - 1} x$

$= \left[x - \dfrac{2D}{D^2 - 1} \right] \left[\dfrac{-\sin x}{2} \right] + e^x \cdot \dfrac{1}{(D^2 + 2D)} x$

$= \dfrac{-x \sin x}{2} + \dfrac{2D(\sin x)}{(-2)(2)} + e^x \cdot \dfrac{\left(1 + \dfrac{D}{2}\right)^{-1} x}{2D}$

$= \dfrac{-x \sin x}{2} - \dfrac{\cos x}{2} + e^x \dfrac{\left[1 - \dfrac{D}{2} + ...\right] x}{2D}$

$= \dfrac{-x \sin x - \cos x}{2} + e^x \cdot \dfrac{1}{2D}\left(x - \dfrac{1}{2}\right)$

$= \dfrac{-x \sin x - \cos x}{2} + \dfrac{e^x}{2}\left(\dfrac{x^2}{2} - \dfrac{x}{2}\right)$

$\Rightarrow$ complete solution is

$y = C_1 e^x + C_2 e^{-x} - \dfrac{x \sin x + \cos x}{2} + \dfrac{e^x}{2}\left(\dfrac{x^2 - x}{2}\right)$

$\Rightarrow y' = C_1 e^x + C_2 e^{-x} - \dfrac{1}{2}[-x \cos x]$

$\qquad \qquad + \dfrac{1}{4}[e^x(x^2 - x + 2x - 1)]$

$y(0) = 1 \Rightarrow C_1 + C_2 - \dfrac{1}{2} = 1$

$y'(0) = 1 \Rightarrow C_1 - C_2 - \dfrac{1}{4} = 1$

$\Rightarrow C_2 = \dfrac{1}{8}$ and $C_1 = \dfrac{11}{8}$

$\Rightarrow y = \dfrac{11}{8} e^x + \dfrac{1}{8} e^{-x} - \dfrac{x \sin x + \cos x}{2} + \dfrac{e^x}{4}(x^2 - x)$

B. $(2y \sin x + 3y^4 \sin x \cos x)$

$dx - (4y^3 \cos^2 x + \cos x) dy = 0$

$M = 2y \sin x + 3y^4 \sin x \cos x$

$N = -(4y^3 \cos^2 x + \cos x)$

$\dfrac{\partial M}{\partial y} = 2 \sin x + 12 y^3 \sin x \cos x$

$\dfrac{\partial N}{\partial x} = 4y^3 (2 \cos x \sin x) + \sin x$

$\dfrac{\dfrac{\partial M}{\partial y} - \dfrac{\partial N}{\partial x}}{N} = \dfrac{4y^3 \cos x \sin x + \sin x}{-(4y^3 \cos^2 x + \cos x)}$

$= -\dfrac{\sin x}{\cos x} = -\tan x$

so, $e^{\int -\tan x\, dx} = e^{\ln \cos x} = \cos x$

is an Integrating factor

$\Rightarrow [2y \sin x \cos x + 3y^4 \cos^2 x \sin x]\, dx$

$\qquad -[4y^3 \cos^3 x + \cos^2 x]\, dy = 0$ is exact D.E.

$\Rightarrow 2y \dfrac{\sin^2 x}{2} + 3y^4 \left(-\dfrac{\cos^3 x}{3}\right) = C$

is the solution.

$\Rightarrow$ solution is $y \sin^2 x - y^4 \cos^3 x = C$

17. $a^3 = e$

$\Rightarrow \{a, a^2, e\}$ are three elements of G

so, 3^k is true for $k = 1$

If b is not power of a, then

b, b^2 are distinct elements, so $ab, ab^2, a^2 b$

and $a^2 b^2$ will be four more elements.

So number of elements $= 9 = 3^2$

Let $\alpha(G) = 3^{k-1}$

then one element 'C' other than in $0(G)$, we have group G' with elements $C \cdot G$, $C^2 \cdot G$ and $e \cdot G$ as the elements of new group with each element satisfying $C^3 = e$
$$\Rightarrow |G_1| = 3|G| = 3 \cdot 3^{k-1} = 3^k$$

18. A. As $f(x)$ is differentiable, so it will be continuous. So range of $f(x)$ includes all points from $f(a)$ to $f(a)$

Let $f(C_1) = \dfrac{f(b) + f(a)}{2}$ ...(i)

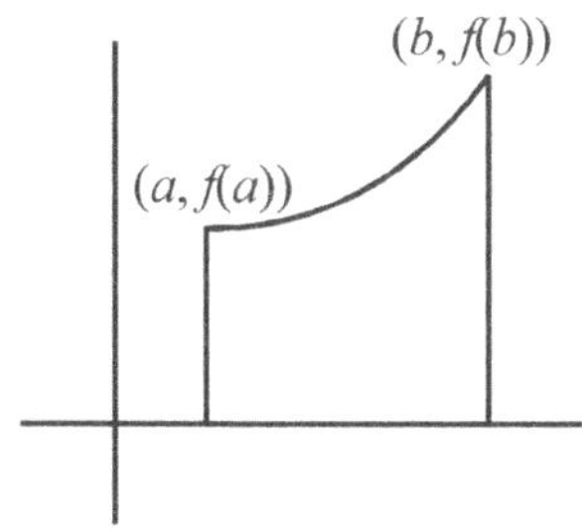

and $f'(C_1) = f'(C_2)$ ...(ii)

equation (i) × equation (ii) gives

$$f(C_1) f'(C_1) = f'(C_2) \frac{[f(b) + f(a)]}{2}$$
$$\Rightarrow 2f(C_1) f'(C_1) = f'(C_2)[f(a) + f(b)]$$

B. $\underset{(x,y)\to(0,0)}{Lt} (x^2 + y^2)[\ln(x^2 + y^2) + 1]$

$= \underset{x\to 0}{Lt}\ x^2(1 + m^2)[\ln x^2(1 + m^2) + 1] = 0$

[along line, $y = mx$]

so, $\alpha = 0$, for continuity.

19. A. $\int_C [(2x - y)dx - ydy - zdz]$
$$\Rightarrow A = (2x - y)\hat{i} - y\hat{j} - z\hat{k}$$
$$\Rightarrow \nabla \times A = \begin{vmatrix} \hat{i} & \hat{j} & \hat{k} \\ \dfrac{\partial}{\partial x} & \dfrac{\partial}{\partial y} & \dfrac{\partial}{\partial z} \\ 2x - y & -y & -z \end{vmatrix} = \hat{k}$$

so, by Stoke's theorem, we get integral as
$$\iint_S (\nabla \times A) \cdot n\, dS = \iint_S (+\hat{k}) \cdot \hat{n}\, dS$$
$$= +\iint_S dx\, dy = -4 \int_0^1 \int_0^{\sqrt{1-x^2}} dy\, dx$$

$= +4\int_0^1 \sqrt{1 - x^2}\, dx$

$= +4\left[\dfrac{x}{2}\sqrt{1 - x^2} + \dfrac{1}{2}\sin^{-1} x \right]_0^1$

$= \pi$

B. $\vec{F} = (2xy - y^4 + 3)\hat{i} + (x^2 - 4xy^3)\hat{j}$

$$\vec{\nabla} \times \vec{F} = \left(\frac{\partial}{\partial x}\hat{i} + \frac{\partial}{\partial y}\hat{j} \right) \times \vec{F}$$
$$= \{[2x - 4y^3] - [2x - 4y^3]\}\,\hat{k}$$
$$= 0\hat{k}$$
$\Rightarrow \vec{F}$ is conservative.

Also, $(2xy - y^4 + 3)\, dx + (x^2 - 4xy^3)dy = 0$

As, $\dfrac{\partial M}{\partial y} = \dfrac{\partial N}{\partial x}$

So, $x^2 y - xy^4 + 3x = C$

So, potential, $\phi = x^2 y - xy^4 + 3x$

Work done in moving a particle from $(1, 0)$ to $(2, 1)$ is $\phi(2, 1) - \phi(1, 0) = 8 - 3 = 5$.

20. $T(x, y, z) = (y + z, z, 0)$

Let $\alpha = (x_1, y_1, z_1)$

and $\beta = (x_2, y_2, z_2)$

As, $T(a\alpha + \beta) = aT(\alpha) + T(\beta)$

so, T is linear.

Let $V = (1, 1, 1)$

$T(V) = (2, 1, 0)$

$T^2(V) = (1, 0, 0)$

As, $a(1, 1, 1) + b(2, 1, 0) + c(1, 0, 0) = (0, 0, 0)$

$\Rightarrow a + 2b + c = 0$

$a + b = 0$

$\&\ a = 0$

$\Rightarrow a = 0,\ b = 0,\ c = 0$

So, $B = \{V, T(V), T^2(V)\}$ is L.I. and also as $|B| = 3$, so B is a basis.

21. A. $\displaystyle\int_0^1 f_n(x)dx = \int_0^{1/2n} 4n^2 x\, dx$

$+ \displaystyle\int_{1/2n}^{1/n} -4n^2\left(x - \frac{1}{n} \right)dx + \int_{1/n}^1 0\, dx$

$= 4n^2 \left. \dfrac{x^2}{2} \right|_0^{1/2n} - 4n^2 \left. \left(\dfrac{x^2}{2} - \dfrac{x}{n} \right) \right|_{1/2n}^{1/n} + 0$

$$= \frac{1}{2} - 4n^2 \left[-\left(\frac{1}{8n^2} - \frac{1}{2n^2} \right) + \left(\frac{1}{2n^2} - \frac{1}{n^2} \right) \right]$$

$$= \frac{1}{2} + \frac{1}{2} = 1$$

Also for $\lim_{n\to\infty} f_n(x)$

gives $\lim_{n\to\infty} \frac{1}{2n} = \lim_{n\to\infty} \frac{1}{n} = 0$

$\Rightarrow \lim_{n\to\infty} f_n(x) = f(x_1) = 0 \quad ; \quad x \in [0, 1]$

Thus $f_n(x)$ is pointwise convergent in $[0, 1]$ convergence is also uniform as

$\lim_{n\to\infty} |f_n(x) - f(x)|$

$= \lim_{n\to\infty} |0 - 0| = 0.$

B. $\because \qquad\qquad f : R = R$

Such that $|f(x) - f(y)| \geq |x - y|$

or, $\quad \left| \dfrac{f(x) - f(y)}{(x - y)} \right| \geq 0 \quad \forall\, x, y \in R$

$\Rightarrow \left| \dfrac{f(y + h) - f(y)}{h} \right| \geq 0 \quad \Rightarrow |f'(y)| \geq 0$

$\Rightarrow f$ is either an increasing or decreasing function

$\Rightarrow \quad \forall\, a < b < c \quad \Rightarrow \quad f(a) < f(b) < f(c)$

or, $\quad a > b > c \qquad \Rightarrow \quad f(a) < f(b) < f(c)$

i.e. $\quad a < b < c \qquad\qquad f(a) < f(c) < f(b)$

22. $\qquad\qquad Z = \left[(x -)\ + (y -) \right]^{-}$

$$V = \iiint dx\,dy\,dz = \int\limits_{z=} \iint dx\,dy\,dz$$

$$= \iint dx\,dy$$

put $\qquad x = 1 + \cos t, \quad y = 1 + \sin t$

$$= 1.[\pi.1] = \pi.$$

23. A. Let $W =$ White ball was drawn and $T =$ Tail come up.

$$P(T \mid W) = \frac{P(T \cap B)}{P(W)}$$

$$= \frac{\dfrac{1}{3} \times \dfrac{6}{9}}{\dfrac{1}{3} \times \dfrac{6}{9} + \dfrac{2}{3} \times \dfrac{3}{7}}$$

$$= \frac{\dfrac{2}{9}}{\dfrac{2}{9} + \dfrac{2}{7}} = \frac{7}{16}$$

B. $f(x, y) = \begin{cases} y^2 e^{-y(x+1)} & x \geq 0 \\ 0 \qquad \text{otherwise} & y \geq 0 \end{cases}$

$\Rightarrow$ Marginal p.d.f. of X,

$$f(x) = \int_0^\infty y^2 e^{-y(x+1)}\,dy$$

Let $y(x + 1) = t$

$\Rightarrow (x + 1)dy = dt$

$$\Rightarrow f(x) = \int_0^\infty \frac{t^2}{(x+1)^2} e^{-t} \cdot \frac{1}{(x+1)}\,dt$$

$$= \frac{1}{(x+1)^3} \int_0^\infty t^2 e^{-t}\,dt$$

$$= \frac{1}{(x+1)^3} \Gamma(3) = \frac{2}{(x+1)^3} \quad ; \quad x \geq 0$$

$$f(y) = \int_0^\infty y^2 e^{-y(x+1)}\,dx$$

$$= \frac{y^2}{-y} \cdot e^{-(y)(x+1)} \Big|_0^\infty$$

$$= y e^{-y} \quad ; \quad y \geq 0$$

As $f(x, y) \neq f(x) f(y)$

so X and Y are not independent.

24. A. $\bar{X} = \dfrac{1}{n} \sum_{i=1}^{n} X_i$

$$M_{\bar{X}}(t) = E[e^{t\bar{X}}] = \Sigma e^{t\bar{x}} p(\bar{X} = \bar{x})$$

$$= \frac{1}{\theta} \int_0^\infty e^{tx} e^{-x/\theta}\,dx$$

$$= \frac{1}{\theta} \int_0^\infty e^{-\left(\frac{1}{\theta} - \frac{1}{t} \right) x}\,dx$$

$$= \frac{1}{\theta} \frac{e^{-\left(\frac{1}{\theta}-t\right)x}}{-\left(\frac{1}{\theta}-t\right)}\bigg|_0^\infty$$

$$= \frac{1}{\theta} \frac{1}{\frac{1}{\theta}-t} = \frac{\theta}{\theta(1-t\theta)} = \frac{1}{1-t\theta}$$

M.G.F. of $Y = E[e^{tY}]$

$$= E[e^{t2n\bar{X}/\theta}]$$

$$= \frac{1}{\theta} \int_0^\infty e^{2n+x/\theta} e^{-x/\theta}$$

$$= \frac{1}{\theta} \int_0^\infty e^{-\left(\frac{1}{\theta}-\frac{2nt}{\theta}\right)x} dx$$

$$= \frac{1}{\theta} \cdot \frac{e^{-\left(\frac{1}{\theta}-\frac{2nt}{\theta}\right)x}}{-\left(\frac{1}{\theta}-\frac{2nt}{\theta}\right)}\bigg|_0^\infty = \frac{1}{1-2nt}$$

B. $\bar{X} = \dfrac{X_1 + X_2 + ... + X_9}{9}$

$$\bar{Y} = \frac{Y_1 + Y_2 + Y_3 + Y_4}{4}$$

$$E(\bar{X}) = 2;\, E(\bar{Y}) = 1$$

$$V(\bar{X}) = \frac{9 \times 4}{9 \times 9} = \frac{4}{9}$$

$$V(\bar{Y}) = \frac{4 \times 1}{4 \times 4} = \frac{1}{4}$$

$$P(\bar{X} > \bar{Y}) = P(Z > 1 \cdot 2) = 0.1151$$

25. A. Likelihood function, $L(x, \alpha)$ of

$$f(x, \alpha) = \Pi \frac{\alpha x_0^\alpha}{x_i^{\alpha+1}}$$

$$\Rightarrow L(x, \alpha) = \frac{\alpha^n x_0^{\alpha n}}{x_1^{(\alpha+1)} x_2^{\alpha+1} ... x_n^{\alpha+1}}$$

$$\Rightarrow \log L = n \log \alpha + \alpha n \log x_0 - (\alpha + 1) \Sigma x_i$$

$$\Rightarrow \frac{1}{L} \times \frac{\partial L}{\partial \alpha} = \frac{n}{\alpha} + n \ln x_0 - \Sigma x_i \quad \frac{\partial L}{\partial \alpha} = 0$$

$$\Rightarrow \frac{n}{\alpha} + n \ln x_0 = \Sigma x_i$$

$$\Rightarrow \alpha^{-1} = \frac{\Sigma x_i}{n} - \ln x_0$$

$$\Rightarrow \alpha = \frac{1}{\dfrac{\Sigma x_i}{n} - \ln x_0}$$

Thus M.L.E. of α is

$$\alpha^n = \frac{1}{\dfrac{\Sigma x_i}{n} - \ln x_0}$$

B. For t - distribution

$$Y = \frac{\dfrac{X_1 + X_2}{2}}{\sqrt{\dfrac{X_1^2 + X_2^2 + X_3^2}{(3-1)}}}$$

$$= \frac{\dfrac{1}{\sqrt{2}}(X_1 + X_2)}{\sqrt{X_1^2 + X_2^2 + X_3^2}} \quad \Rightarrow \quad c = \frac{1}{\sqrt{2}}$$

26. A. Type I error $= P(H_1 \text{ is true} \mid H_0 \text{ is true})$

$$= \int_{10}^\infty \frac{1}{5} e^{-x/5} dx$$

$$= -e^{-x/5}\bigg|_{10}^\infty = e^{-2} = \frac{1}{e^2}$$

Type II error $= P(H_0 \text{ is true} \mid H_1 \text{ is true})$

$$= \int_0^{10} \frac{1}{7} e^{-x/7}$$

$$= -e^{-x/7}\bigg|_0^{10}$$

$$= 1 - e^{-10/7}$$

B. The best test for testing
$H_0 : \mu = 0, \sigma^2 = 1$ against
$H_1 : \mu = 1, \sigma^2 = 4$ will be
two tailed test and
x^2 will suit it.

27. Given $\phi(x + iy) = e^x f(y) + i\, e^x g(y)$

As it is an analytic function

$$\Rightarrow \frac{\partial \left(e^x f(y)\right)}{\partial x} = \frac{\partial}{\partial y}\left(e^x g(y)\right)$$

$$\Rightarrow \quad e^x f(y) = e^x g'(y) \ \& \ e^x f'(y) = -e^x g(y)$$
$$\Rightarrow \quad e^x f''(y) = -e^x g'(y) = -e^x f(y)$$
$$\Rightarrow e^x [f''(y) + f(y)] = 0 \quad \Rightarrow f''(y) + f(y) = 0$$

which is required *d.e.* of 2nd order.

B. $\displaystyle \int_{|z+1|=2}(2z+1)e^{\left(\sqrt{2}+\frac{1}{z}\right)}dz$

$$= \int_{|z+1|=2} e^{\sqrt{2}}\,(2z+1)e^{1/z}\,dz$$

$$= \int_{|z+1|=2} e^{\sqrt{2}}\,(2z+1)\left(1+\frac{1}{z}+\frac{1}{2!z^2}+...\right)dz$$

As $z = 0$ is singular point in the region,
so integral $= 2\pi i$ (residue at $z = 0$)

$$= 2\pi i e^{\sqrt{2}}\left[\frac{2}{2!}+1\right] = 4\pi i e^{\sqrt{2}}$$

28. A. $z = re^{i\theta}$

$$\Rightarrow dz = rie^{i\theta}\,d\theta \quad \Rightarrow \quad d\theta = \frac{dz}{iz}$$

$$\Rightarrow \int_0^{2\pi}|f(re^{i\theta})|\,d\theta$$

$$= \int_{|z|=1}\frac{|f(z)|}{iz}dz = 2\pi\,|f(0)|$$

Now $f^{(n)}(0) = \dfrac{n!}{2\pi i}\displaystyle\int\frac{f(z)}{z^{n+1}}dz$

$$\Rightarrow f^{(n)}(0) = \frac{1}{2\pi i}\oint_{|z|=1}\frac{f(z)}{z^{n+1}}dz$$

for all $n \geq 0$

B. $f(z) = (z+\overline{z})^2 + 2\alpha\,|z|^2 + \alpha(\overline{z})^2$

$$= z^2 + 2z\overline{z} + (\overline{z})^2 + 2\alpha\,|z|^2 + \alpha(\overline{z})^2$$
$$= z^2 + 2(1+\alpha)|z|^2 + (1+\alpha)(\overline{z})^2$$

Thus for $f(z)$ to be analytic coefficient of both $|z|^2$ and $(\overline{z})^2$ should be zero.

so, $1 + \alpha = 0$
$$\Rightarrow \alpha = -1$$

29.

for equilibrium,
$$w \times 12 = (20-12)w$$

$$\Rightarrow \frac{w}{W} = \frac{8}{12}$$

$$\Rightarrow w:W::2:3$$

30.

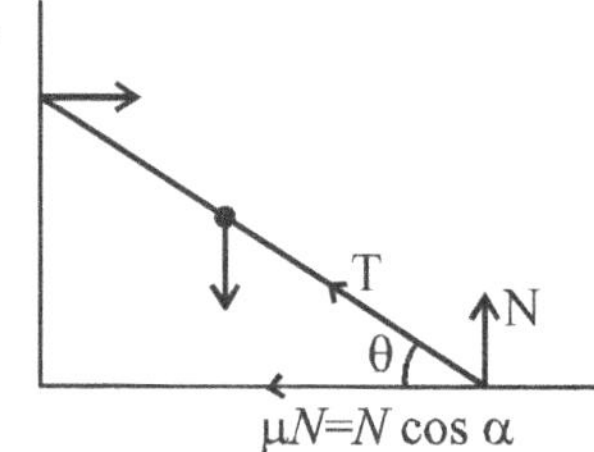

At the time ladder ceases to touch the wall at angle is θ.
$$T\cos\theta = mg\cos\alpha$$
$$T\sin\theta = mg$$
$$\Rightarrow \tan\theta = \cos\alpha$$
$$\Rightarrow \theta = \tan^{-1}(\cos\alpha)$$

31. A. $\displaystyle\int_0^8(1+x^2)e^{-x}dx = -(1+x^2)e^{-x}+\int 2xe^{-x}dx$

$$= -(1+x^2)e^{-x} - 2xe^{-x} + \int 2e^{-x}dx$$

$$= -(1+x^2)e^{-x} - 2xe^{-x} - 2e^{-x}\Big|_0^8$$

$$= 2 - [83e^{-8}] = \left[\frac{2e^8 - 83}{e^8}\right]$$

By simpson's $\dfrac{1}{3}rd$ rule.

$$\int_0^8(1+x^2)e^{-x}dx$$

$$= \frac{h}{3}\left[y_0 + 4(y_1 + y_3 + ... + y_{n-1})\right.$$
$$\left. + 2(y_2 + y_4 + ... + y_{n-2}) + y_n\right]$$

where $h = 0.25$
and $y_k = y(0 + 0.25k) = [1 + (0.25k)^2]e^{-0.25k}$

Error is evaluated when subtracted by integrated value.

B. Point of intersection of $y = x^3$ and $y = 8x + 4$ will be solution of

$$f(x) = x^3 - 8x - 4 = 0$$

$$\Rightarrow f'(x) = 3x^2 - 8$$

$$x - \frac{f(x)}{f'(x)} = x - \frac{x^3 - 8x - 4}{3x^2 - 8} = \frac{2x^3 + 4}{3x^2 - 8}$$

so, iterative formula for Newton-Raphson method is

$$x_{n+1} = \frac{2x_n^3 + 4}{3x_n^2 - 8} \quad ; \quad n = 0, 1, 2, \ldots$$

and $x_0 = 3$

$$\Rightarrow x_1 = \frac{2(3^3) + 4}{3(3^2) - 8} = \frac{58}{19} = 3.05$$

$$x_2 = \frac{2(3.05)^2 + 4}{3(3.05)^2 - 8} = \frac{60.74525}{19.9075} = 3.05$$

Thus $x = 3.05$ is the required solution.

32.

x	y	Δ	Δ^2	Δ^3	Δ^4
-1	-2				
0	-2		2		
		2	6		
1	0		8		-48
		10		-42	
2	10		-34		
		-24			
3	-14				

$$x = x_0 + ph \quad \Rightarrow \quad x = -1 + p$$
$$\Rightarrow p = x + 1$$
$$y(x) = y_0 + p\Delta y_0$$

$$+ \frac{p(p-1)}{2!}\Delta^2 y_0 + \frac{p(p-1)(p-2)}{3!}\Delta^3 y_0$$
$$+ \frac{p(p-1)(p-2)(p-3)}{4!}\Delta^4 y_0$$

$$\Rightarrow y(x) = -2 + \frac{2(x+1)x}{2!} + \frac{6(x+1)x(x-1)}{3!}$$
$$- \frac{48(x+1)x(x-1)(x-2)}{4!}$$

$$\Rightarrow y(x) = -2 + x(x+1) + x(x^2 - 1)$$
$$- 2x(x-2)(x^2 - 1)$$

By Newton's forward difference formula.

By Newton's backward formula

$$x = x_n + ph \quad \Rightarrow \quad x = 3 + p$$
$$\Rightarrow p = x - 3$$
$$\Rightarrow y(2.5) = -14 + (2.5 - 3)(-24)$$
$$+ \frac{(2.5 - 3(2.5 - 2)}{2!}(-34)$$
$$+ \frac{(2.5 - 3(2.5 - 2)(2.5 - 1)(2.5 - 0)}{4!}(-48)$$

$$= -14 + 12 + \frac{17}{4} + \frac{21}{8} + \frac{15}{8}$$

$$= -2 + 4.25 + 4.5 = 6.75$$

By pivot as 2 polynomial of third degree will be generated and hence different value will be obtained as it will be an extrapolation.

Test Papers (Solved)

IIT-JAM

Joint Admission Test
for M.Sc. Mathematics

TEST PAPER - 1

PART - A

1. Consider the function
   $$f(x) = x(x + 3)\ e^{-x/2}$$
   How many values of x exist in $[-3, 0]$ for which $f'(x)$ vanishes ?
   A. None
   B. One
   C. Two
   D. Three

2. The value of
   $$\lim_{n \to \infty} \left[\frac{\pi}{n} \cdot \frac{\pi}{n} \cdots \frac{n\pi}{n} \right]^n \text{ is}$$
   A. e
   B. e^{-1}
   C. ∞
   D. 1

3. The least possible number of positive roots of the equation $2x^7 - x^4 + 4x^3 - 5 = 0$ is
   A. 2
   B. 4
   C. 6
   D. none of the above

4. The rank of the matrix :
   $$\begin{bmatrix} a & b & c \\ a & b & c \end{bmatrix}$$
   a, b, c being all real, is 3 if
   A. a, b, c are all different and $a + b + c \neq 0$
   B. $a = b = c$
   C. a, b, c are all different but $a + b + c = 0$
   D. Two of the numbers a, b, c are equal but are different from the third.

5. Assuming that the petrol burnt (per hour) in driving a motor boat varies inversely as the cube of its velocity, the most economical speed when going against a current of 10 km/hr is
   A. 15 km/hr
   B. 20 km/hr
   C. 25 km/hr
   D. 30 km/hr

6. The series : $x + x^{1+1/2} + x^{1+1/2+1/3} + \ldots\ldots$ is convergent if
   A. $x > e$
   B. $x < e$
   C. $x < 1/e$
   D. $x > 1/e$

7. The area of the region enclosed by the curve $y(x^2 + 2) = 3x$ and $4y = x^2$ is given by
   A. $\displaystyle\int\int_{y=}^{x} dx\,dy$
   B. $\displaystyle\int\int_{y=}^{x(x+)} dx\,dy$
   C. $\displaystyle\int\int_{y=x}^{x(x+)} dx\,dy$
   D. $\displaystyle\int\int_{y=x}^{x(x+)} dx\,dy$

8. The function $f(x) = x^{1/x}$ has a minimum value at
   A. $x = e$
   B. $x = e^{-1}$
   C. $x = e^2$
   D. $x = 0$

9. The maximum number of different possible non-zero entries in a skew symmetric matrix of order n is
   A. $-(n - n)$
   B. $-(n + n)$
   C. n^2
   D. none of the above

10. The vectors
    $$\vec{i} + 2p\,\vec{j} + 4q\,\vec{k} \text{ and } \vec{i} + 4p\,\vec{j} + 2q\,\vec{k} \text{ are}$$
    A. Orthogonal if $p = q$
    B. Orthogonal if $p = -q$
    C. Orthogonal if $p^2 = q^2 = -1$
    D. Never orthogonal

11. Let V be a vector space and let $L(S)$ denote the set of all linear combinations of members of S. Then which of the following statements is incorrect ?
    A. $L(S)$ is a subspace of V
    B. $A \subset B \Rightarrow L(A)$ is a subspace of $L(B)$
    C. S is a subspace of V iff $L(S) = S$
    D. $A \neq B \Rightarrow L(A) \neq L(B)$

12. The values of a, b, c for which the function

$$f(x) = \begin{cases} \dfrac{(\ \ a\ )\ \ x + \ \ x}{x} & x < \\ c & x = \\ \dfrac{(x + bx\ ) \ \ - x}{bx} & x > \end{cases}$$

is continuous at $x = 0$, are

A. $a = -\ \ b = -\ -\ \ c = -$

B. $a = -\ -\ \ c = -\ \ b$ is arbitrary non-zero real

C. $a = -\ -\ \ b = -\ -\ \ c = -$

D. None of the above

13. If ω is the cube root of unity, then the inverse

of $A = \begin{bmatrix} \omega & \omega \\ \omega & \omega \end{bmatrix}$ is

A. $\begin{bmatrix} \omega & \omega \\ \omega & \omega \end{bmatrix}$

B. $-\begin{bmatrix} \omega & \omega \\ \omega & \omega \end{bmatrix}$

C. $-\begin{bmatrix} \omega & \omega \\ \omega & \omega \end{bmatrix}$

D. $-\begin{bmatrix} \omega & \omega \\ \omega & \omega \end{bmatrix}$

14. The entire length of the given curve $x^{2/3} + y^{2/3} = a^{2/3}$ is given by

A. $8\ a$ B. $6\ a$

C. $\sqrt{8ay}$ D. $4\sqrt{3a}$

15. The multiple points on the curve $x^4 - 2ay^3 - 3a^2y^2 - 2a^2x^2 + a^4 = 0$ are

A. $(0, 0)$, $(0, -a)$ and $(a, 0)$

B. $(0, -a)$, $(a, 0)$ and $(a, -a)$

C. $(a, 0)$, $(a, -a)$ and $(-a, -a)$

D. $(a, 0)$, $(-a, 0)$ and $(0, -a)$

PART - B

16. A. Maximize $z = x^{0.8}\ y^{0.2}$ subject to $5x + 3y = 75$.

    B. An object is heated to 300°F and allowed to cool in a room whose air temperature is 80°F. If after 10 min. the temperature of the body is 250°F, what will be its temperature after 20 min.?

17. A. Prove that the least perimeter of an isosceles triangle in which a circle of radius r can be inscribed is $6r\sqrt{3}$

    B. For the infinite series given by

$$\frac{1}{2} + 1 + \frac{1}{8} + \frac{1}{4} + \frac{1}{32} + \frac{1}{16} + \frac{1}{128} + \frac{1}{64} + \ \dots$$

    find :

    (i) $\lim\sup\limits_{n \to \theta} \dfrac{a_{n+1}}{a_n}$ (ii) $\lim\inf\limits_{n \to \theta} \dfrac{a_{n+1}}{a_n}$

18. A. A heavy ladder of length 21 rests in limiting equilibrium against a smooth vertical wall and a rough horizontal floor. If μ be the coefficient of friction between the ladder and the floor, then find the angle of inclination θ to the horizontal.

    B. Find the area of the triangle formed by the points whose position vectors are

$$3\vec{i} + \vec{j};\ 5\vec{i} + 2\vec{j} + \vec{k};\ \vec{i} - 2\vec{j} + 3\vec{k}.$$

19. A. Find the triple intergral of the function $f(x, y, z) = x^2$ over the region V enclosed by the planes $x = 0$, $y = z = 0$ and $x + y + z = a$

    B. Prove that

$$\int_0^\pi \frac{x\,dx}{1 + e\sin x} = \frac{\pi \cos^{-1} e}{\sqrt{1 - e^2}}\ (e^2 < 1)$$

20. A. Find the limiting value,

when n → ∞ of $\dfrac{(n!)^{1/n}}{n}$

B. Find the general solution of the equation $y'' + y' = 4\cos x$.

21. A. Show that the radius of curvature at any point of the astroid $x = a\cos^3\theta$, $y = a\sin^3\theta$ is equal to three times the length of the perpendicular from the origin to the tangent.

B. Let $\vec{a}, \vec{b}, \vec{c}$ be the position vectors of A, B, C respectively. Find the vector area of $\triangle ABC$.

22. A. For what differentiable functions f, g, h is the equation
$f(x + y) = g(x) + h(y)$ true for all real numbers x and y?

B. $\displaystyle\lim_{x\to 0}\dfrac{x^3\sin^3 x}{(1-\cos\sqrt{x})^6}$

23. A. If $y = v(x)$ is solution of the differential equation $[D^2 + P(x)D + Q(x)]\,y = 0$, then find the general solution of the equation $[D^2 + P(x) + Q(x)]y = R(x)$.

B. Find the condition for which the curves $ax^2 + by^2 = 1$ and $a_1x^2 + b_1y^2 = 1$ shall cut orthogonally.

24. A. A and B are $n \times n$ real matrices and A is invertible. Then show AB and BA have the same characteristic polynomial.

B. Find $\displaystyle\lim_{n\to\infty}\dfrac{\dfrac{1}{2}+\dfrac{2}{3}+\dfrac{3}{4}+...+\dfrac{n}{n+1}}{n}$

25. A. Show that for every real number x.

$$\dfrac{1}{5}\le\dfrac{x^2-4x+9}{x^2+4x+9}\le 5.$$

B. Find the shortest distance from the point $(-1, -1)$ to the graph of $9x^2 - 16y^2 + 36x - 32y = 124$.

26. A. If $f(x) = \displaystyle\sum_{n=1}^{\infty}\dfrac{\sin nx}{n^3}$, then show that $\displaystyle\int_0^{\pi} f(x)dx$ will be $2\displaystyle\sum_{n=1}^{\infty}\dfrac{1}{(2n-1)^4}$

B. Show that the power series
$$1+\dfrac{a.b}{1.c}x+\dfrac{a(a+1).b(b+1)}{1.2c(c+1)}x^2+\cdots$$
has radius of convergence 1.

27. For the distribution with density
$$f(x) = \dfrac{1}{\pi}\dfrac{1}{(1+x^2)}, -\infty < x < \infty$$
Find mean, mode, median, variance, first and third quartiles and distribution function.

28. $y(x) \quad xe^x$

$y(x) \quad x + \quad {}^x (x-t)y(t)dt$

29.

ANSWERS

1	2	3	4	5	6	7	8	9	10
11	12	13	14	15					

PART - A

1. The given function is
$$\Rightarrow \qquad f(x) = x\,(x+3)\,e^{-x/2}$$

$$\Rightarrow \qquad f'(x) = \left[x + \frac{x}{} - \frac{x}{} \right] e^{-x}$$

$$\Rightarrow \qquad f'(x) = \left[\frac{x}{} + - \frac{x}{} \right] e^{-x}$$

$$= (6 + x - x^2)\,e^{-x/2}$$

$$\Rightarrow \qquad f'(x) = 0 \;\Rightarrow\; 6 + x - x^2 = 0$$

$$\Rightarrow \qquad x = +3, -2.$$

is given interval, only -2 lie.

2. By Cauchy Theorem,

if $\displaystyle\lim_{n\to\infty} a_n \to l$ then $\displaystyle\lim_{n\to\infty} \left(a\,a\;\cdots\;a_n \right)^{\frac{1}{n}} \to l$

Using this theorem

$\displaystyle\lim_{n\to\infty} \frac{n\pi}{n} \to \infty$ hence the given expression also tend to ∞.

3. The given equation is
$$2x^7 - x^4 + 4x^3 - 5 = 0$$

as the sign of maximum and minimum power are opposite.

Hence the above equation has at least one positive roots.

Further, By Descarte rule of sign change.

$f(x) = 0$ for $x > 0$ changes sign as $+\;-\;+\;-$
   i.e. thrice

i.e. $f(x) = 0$ has at most three positive roots.

Hence $f(x) = 0$ has at most three positive roots.

4. The given matrix is

$$\begin{bmatrix} a & b & c \\ a & b & c \end{bmatrix} \sim \begin{bmatrix} b-a & c-a \\ b-a & c-a \end{bmatrix}$$

$R_2 \to R_2 - aR_1$
$R_3 \to R_3 - a^3 R_1$

Rank in this case 1.

The rank is 3.

if $\qquad\qquad \Delta \neq 0$

$\Rightarrow (b-a)\,(c-a)\,[c^2 + ca + a^2 - b^2 - ab - a^2]$

$\qquad (b-a)\,(c-a)\,(c-b)\,[c + b + a] \neq 0$

i.e. $\qquad a \neq b \neq c \;\;\&\;\; a + b + c \neq 0.$

5. If speed of motor boat = V

then actual velocity = (V $-$ 10)

hence consumption of petrol (P) = $\dfrac{(\;-\;)}{}$

Now $\qquad\qquad$ P = $\dfrac{}{} - \dfrac{}{}$

$\therefore \qquad \dfrac{d}{d} = \dfrac{-}{} = \dfrac{-}{} + \dfrac{}{} =$

$\Rightarrow \qquad\qquad$ V = 15 km/hr.

i.e. most economical speed = 15 km/hr.

6. $\qquad \dfrac{n}{n+} = \dfrac{}{x^{\overline{n+}}}$

$\Rightarrow \qquad \dfrac{n}{n+} = -\dfrac{}{n+} \quad x = -\dfrac{}{n+} \quad x$

By Logrithmic test for convergence

$\displaystyle\lim_{n\to\infty} n\,\dfrac{u_n}{u_{n+}} < 1$

$\Rightarrow \displaystyle \lim_{n\to\infty} n\left(-\dfrac{}{n+} \quad x \right) < 1 \quad$ or, $\;-\log x < 1$

or, $\quad \dfrac{-}{x} > \quad$ or, $\;\dfrac{-}{x} > e \quad$ or $\;x < \dfrac{-}{e}.$

7. The point of intersection of the curve
$$y(x^2 + 2) = 3x \;\; \text{and} \;\; 4y = x^2 \;\text{is equal to}$$

$\dfrac{x}{x\;+} = \dfrac{x}{} \quad$ or, $\;12x = x^2(x^2 + 2)$

$\Rightarrow x(x^3 + 2x - 12) = 0$

$\Rightarrow x(x-2)\,(x^2 + 2x + 6) = 0 \;\Rightarrow\; x = 0, 2$

Hence the area of region is given by

$$\int\limits_{y=x}^{} \int\limits^{x\;x\;+} dx\,dy \, .$$

8. $\because \qquad f(x) = x^{1/x}$

$\Rightarrow \qquad \ln f(x) = \dfrac{}{x}\ \ x$

$\Rightarrow \qquad \dfrac{}{y}\dfrac{dy}{dx} = -\dfrac{}{x}\ \ x + \dfrac{}{x}$

$\Rightarrow \qquad \dfrac{dy}{dx} = x^{\overline{x}}\left[\dfrac{\left(\ -\ x\right)}{x}\right] = 0$

$\therefore \qquad 1 - \log x = 0 \ \Rightarrow\ \ln x = 1 \ \therefore\ x = e.$

9. In skew symmetric matrix $a_{ij} = -a_{ji}$

$\Rightarrow \qquad a_{ii} = -a_{ii} \ \Rightarrow\ a_{ii} = 0$

i.e. diagonal elements are always zero

Hence maximum number of non-zero elements

$$= -\left(n\ - n\right).$$

10. If $\overrightarrow{}\ \ \overrightarrow{}$ are orthogonal then $\overrightarrow{}\cdot\overrightarrow{} =$

Now, $\left(\vec{i} + p\vec{j} + q\vec{k}\right)\left(\vec{i} + p\vec{j} + q\vec{k}\right) =$

$\Rightarrow 8p^2 + 8q^2 + 1 = 0$

Not possible for real p and q.

12. $\displaystyle\lim_{x\to\ ^-} f(x) = \lim_{x\to\ ^-}\dfrac{\left(a + \ \right)x + \ x}{x}$

$\qquad\qquad = (a+1) + 1 = (a+2)$

$\displaystyle\lim_{x\to\ ^+} f(x) = \dfrac{\left(x + bx\ \right)^{\overline{}} - x^{\overline{}}}{bx^{\overline{}}}$

$\qquad\qquad = \dfrac{\sqrt{\ + bx\ } - }{b} = \quad \text{if } b \neq 0$

Also $\qquad f(0) = c$

$f(x)$ is continuous at $x = 0 \ \Rightarrow\ a + 2 = c = 0$

$\Rightarrow a = -2, c = 0 \ \ \&\ \ b \neq 0.$

13. $\qquad A^{-1} = \dfrac{}{|\ |}adj(\ )$

$\because \qquad A = \begin{bmatrix} & \omega & \omega \\ & \omega & \omega \end{bmatrix}$

$\Rightarrow \qquad |A| = \begin{bmatrix} & \omega & \omega \\ & \omega & \omega \end{bmatrix}$

$[\text{using } 1 + \omega + \omega^2 = 0]$

$\Rightarrow \qquad |A| = 3(\omega^2 - \omega).$

$$adj\,A = \begin{bmatrix} \omega\ -\omega & \omega\ -\omega & \omega\ -\omega \\ \omega\ -\omega & \omega\ - & -\omega \\ \omega\ -\omega & -\omega & \omega\ - \end{bmatrix}$$

$\Rightarrow \qquad A^{-1} = \dfrac{}{|\ |}adj\ = -\begin{bmatrix} \omega & \omega \\ \omega & \omega \end{bmatrix}$

14. The curve is symmetric about x and y axis

as $\quad x\ + y\ = a \qquad\qquad\qquad\qquad …(1)$

any general point on curve (i) is given

$$x = a\cos^3\theta,\ y = a\sin^3\theta$$

$$\int_{x=}^{a}\sqrt{\ + \left(\dfrac{dy}{dx}\right)}\ dx = \int_{\theta=\frac{\pi}{}}\ \theta\left(-a\ \ \theta\ \ \theta\right)d\theta$$

$$= a\int^{\frac{\pi}{}}\ \theta\ \ \theta\, d\theta$$

$$= a\left[\dfrac{\theta}{}\right]^{\frac{\pi}{}} = 6a.$$

15. At multiple points of $f(x, y) = 0$

$$\dfrac{\partial f}{\partial x} = \ = \dfrac{\partial f}{\partial y}$$

$$\dfrac{\partial f}{\partial x} = \ x\ - a\ x = \left(\ x\ x\ -\right)a\ =$$

$\Rightarrow \quad x = 0,\ a, -a$

$$\dfrac{\partial f}{\partial y} = \ \Rightarrow\ -6ay^2 - 6a^2y = 0$$

$\Rightarrow -6ay\,(y + a) = 0 \ \Rightarrow\ y = 0, -a$

$\therefore$ The combination of these which satisfy $f = 0$ are

$(a, 0)\,(-a, 0)\ \&\ (0, -a).$

PART - B

16. A. $\because \quad 5x + 3y = 75$

$\Rightarrow \qquad y = \dfrac{\ - x}{}$

Also $\qquad z = x^{0.8}\, y^{0.2}$

$\qquad\qquad z = x^{0.8}\ -\left(\dfrac{\ - x}{}\right)$

for maxima or minima $\dfrac{dz}{dx} = 0$

Now $\quad \dfrac{dz}{dx} = (0.8)\,x^{-0.2}\left(\dfrac{\quad - x}{\quad}\right)$

$\qquad\qquad + 0.2\,x^{0.8}\left(\dfrac{\quad - x}{\quad}\right)^{-}\left(\dfrac{}{\quad}\right)$

$= \dfrac{x^{-}}{\left(\dfrac{\quad - x}{\quad}\right)}\left[\dfrac{(\quad - x)}{\quad} - - x\right]$

$\Rightarrow \dfrac{dz}{dx} = \quad \Rightarrow x^{-0.2}(5x - 60) = 0$

$\Rightarrow x = 0 \quad$ or $\quad x = 12$

$x = 0$ leads to minima

At $x = 12$, z is maxima and at $x = 12$ $y = 5$

Hence $\quad z_{\max} = 12^{0.8}\,5^{0.2}$.

B. By Newton's law of cooling

$$\dfrac{\theta}{\quad} = - \ (\theta - \theta\ )$$

where $\qquad \theta =$ Temperature of body

$\qquad\qquad \theta_0 =$ Temperature of surroundings

$\Rightarrow \qquad \dfrac{d\theta}{\theta - \theta} = -k\,dt \Rightarrow \displaystyle\int \dfrac{d\theta}{\theta -} = -k\int dt$

$\Rightarrow \qquad \ln \dfrac{}{\quad} = 10k \quad$ or, $\ k = \dfrac{}{\quad}\left(\dfrac{}{\quad}\right)$

Now $\displaystyle\int \dfrac{d\theta}{\theta -} = - \dfrac{}{\quad} \ - \int dt$

$\Rightarrow \qquad \dfrac{\theta -}{\quad} = - \ \dfrac{}{\quad}$

or, $\qquad \dfrac{}{\theta -} = \dfrac{}{\quad} \Rightarrow \theta - 80 = \dfrac{}{\quad}$

$\therefore \qquad\qquad \theta = \dfrac{}{\quad} + \ = 211.36^{\circ}\text{F}.$

Perimeter $= 2r \tan\theta + 4r \cot\dfrac{\theta}{2}$

$$\text{P} = 2r \tan\theta + 4r \cot\dfrac{\theta}{2}$$

$\therefore \ \dfrac{dP}{d\theta} = 2r \sec^2\theta - 4\dfrac{r}{2}\cosec^2\dfrac{\theta}{2} = 0$

or, $\cos^2\theta = \sin^2\dfrac{\theta}{2}$

$$\left(1 - 2\sin^2\dfrac{\theta}{2}\right)^2 = \sin^2\dfrac{\theta}{2}$$

put $\sin^2\dfrac{\theta}{2} = x$

$\Rightarrow (1 - 2x)^2 = x \ \Rightarrow \ 4x^2 - 5x + 1 = 0$

$\therefore \ x = \dfrac{5 \pm \sqrt{25 - 16}}{8} = \dfrac{5 \pm 3}{8} = 1, \dfrac{1}{4}$

Now $\sin^2\dfrac{\theta}{2} = 1 \ \Rightarrow \ \dfrac{\theta}{2} = \dfrac{\pi}{2}$

$\Rightarrow \theta = \pi$ (Not acceptable)

as $\qquad\qquad \theta < \dfrac{\pi}{\quad}$

$\sin^2\dfrac{\theta}{2} = \dfrac{1}{4} \ \Rightarrow \ \dfrac{\theta}{\quad} = - \qquad (\because \theta$ is acute$)$

$\Rightarrow \theta = \dfrac{\pi}{3}$

$\therefore \ \text{P} = 2r \tan\theta + 4r \cot\dfrac{\theta}{\quad}$

$\qquad = 2r\sqrt{3} + 4r\sqrt{3} = \quad \sqrt{\quad}.$

B. The given series is

$$- + \ + - + - + - + - + - + - + - +$$

$$\dfrac{a_{n+}}{a_n} = \left\{\quad - \quad - \quad - \quad - \quad - \quad\right\}$$

$$\dfrac{}{\quad}\underset{\to\infty}{+} = \quad \text{and} \quad \lim_{n\to\infty}\dfrac{a_{n+}}{a_n} = -$$

18. A.

17.A.

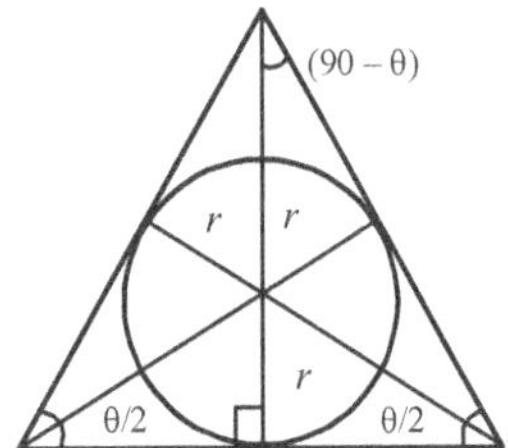

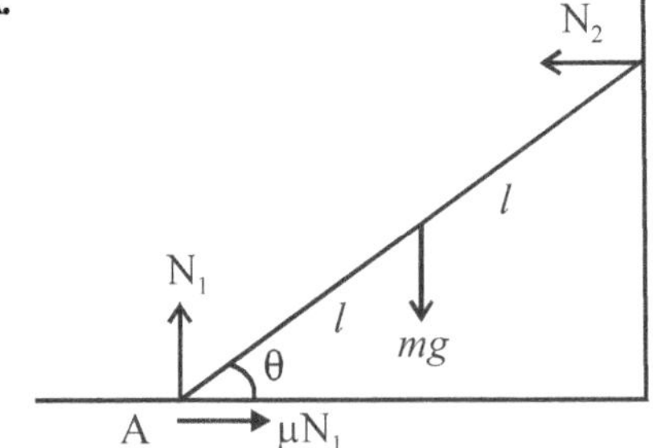

In equilibrium,
$$N_1 = mg \quad ...(i) \qquad N_2 = \mu N_1 \qquad ...(ii)$$

Also taking moment about A
$$= mg\, \ell \cos\theta - N_1 . 2\ell \sin\theta = 0$$

$$\Rightarrow \qquad \tan\theta = \left(\frac{1}{\mu}\right)$$

$$\therefore \qquad \theta = \ ^{-}\left(\frac{}{\mu}\right).$$

B. $(3, 1.0); (5, 2, 1); (1, -2, 3)$

$$\Delta_z = \begin{vmatrix} 3 & 1 & 1 \\ 5 & 2 & 1 \\ 1 & -2 & 1 \end{vmatrix} = (-4)$$

$$\Delta_y = \begin{vmatrix} & & \\ & & \\ & & \end{vmatrix} = (-8)$$

$$\Delta_x = \begin{vmatrix} 1 & 1 & 0 \\ 1 & 2 & 1 \\ 1 & -2 & 3 \end{vmatrix} = (6)$$

$$\therefore \qquad \Delta = \frac{1}{2}\sqrt{\Delta_x^2 + \Delta_y^2 + \Delta_z^2}$$

$$= \sqrt{\ }\ .$$

19. A. $\displaystyle \int\limits_{x=0}^{a} \int\limits_{y=0}^{a-x} \int\limits_{z=0}^{(a-x-y)} x^2\, dx\, dy\, dz$

$$= \int\limits_{0}^{a} \int\limits_{0}^{a-x} x^2\,(a - x - y)\, dx\, dy$$

$$= \int^{a} \left[x\ (a\ )\ y\ \frac{x\ y}{} \right]^{(a\ )}\, dx$$

$$= \int^{a} \left[x\ (a\ x)\ \frac{x\ (a\ x)}{} \right] dx$$

$$= -\int\left(x \qquad ax\ + a\ x\ \right) dx$$

$$= \frac{1}{2}\left[\frac{x^5}{5} - \frac{2ax^4}{4} + \frac{a^2 x^3}{3} \right]_{0}^{a}$$

$$= \frac{1}{2}\left[\frac{a^5}{5} - \frac{2a^5}{4} + \frac{a^5}{3} \right]$$

$$= \frac{17a^5}{120}\ .$$

B. Let $\displaystyle I = \int_{0}^{\pi} \frac{x\, dx}{1 + e\sin x} = \int_{0}^{\pi} \frac{(\pi - x)\, dx}{1 + e\sin x}$

$$\Rightarrow \quad 2I = \pi \int^{\pi} \frac{\pi dx}{+ e \quad x}$$

$$\Rightarrow \quad 2I = \pi \int^{\pi} \frac{dx}{\dfrac{x}{} + \quad \dfrac{x}{} + e \quad \dfrac{x}{} \quad \dfrac{x}{}}$$

$$= \pi \int^{\frac{\pi}{}} \frac{dx}{\dfrac{x}{} + \quad \dfrac{x}{} + e \quad \dfrac{x}{} \quad \dfrac{x}{}}$$

$$= 2\pi \int_{0}^{\frac{\pi}{2}} \frac{\sec^2 \dfrac{x}{2}\, dx}{1 + \tan^2 \dfrac{x}{2} + 2e \tan \dfrac{x}{2}}$$

$$= 2\pi \int_{0}^{\frac{\pi}{2}} \frac{\sec^2 \dfrac{x}{2}\, dx}{\left(\tan \dfrac{x}{2} + e\right)^2 + \left(1 - e^2\right)}\ ;$$

put $\quad e + \tan \dfrac{x}{2} = z$

$$\Rightarrow \frac{1}{2}\sec^2 \frac{x}{2}\, dx = dz$$

$$\Rightarrow 2I = 2\pi \int_{e}^{e+1} \frac{2dz}{z^2 + \left(\sqrt{1 - e^2}\right)^2}$$

$$\Rightarrow I = \ \pi \int_{e}^{+e} = \frac{dz}{z^2 + \left(\sqrt{\ - e}\right)}$$

$$= \left. \frac{\pi}{\sqrt{\ - e}} \quad \frac{z}{\sqrt{\ - e}} \right|_{e}^{+e}$$

$$I = \frac{2\pi}{\sqrt{1 - e^2}} \left[\tan^{-1} \frac{1 + e}{\sqrt{1 - e^2}} - \tan^{-1} \frac{e}{\sqrt{1 - e^2}} \right]$$

$$= \frac{2\pi}{\sqrt{1-e^2}} \left[\tan^{-1} \frac{1/\sqrt{1-e^2}}{1+e\dfrac{(1+e^2)}{1-e^2}} \right]$$

$$I = \frac{2\pi}{\sqrt{1-e^2}} \tan^{-1}\left(\frac{\sqrt{1-e^2}}{1+e} \right)$$

$$\because\ \frac{2\pi}{\sqrt{1-e^2}} \cos^{-1} \frac{1+e}{\sqrt{2(1+e)}}$$

$$\Rightarrow I = \frac{2\pi}{\sqrt{1-e^2}} \cos^{-1}\left(\sqrt{\frac{(1+e)}{2}} \right)$$

$$= \frac{2\pi}{\sqrt{1-e^2}} \left(\cos^{-1} \sqrt{\frac{(1+e)}{2}} \right)$$

$$= \frac{\pi}{\sqrt{1-e^2}} \cos^{-1}\left[2\frac{(1+e)}{2} - 1 \right] \frac{\pi \cos^{-1} e}{\sqrt{1-e^2}}$$

$$[\because\ 2\cos^{-1} x = \cos^{-1}(2x^2-1)]$$

$$i.e.\ I = \int_0^{\pi} \frac{x\, dx}{+e\ x} = \frac{\pi}{\sqrt{-e}}.$$

20. A. Let $a_n = \dfrac{n}{n^n}$ then $a_{n+1} = \dfrac{n+}{(n+)^{n+}}$

then by Cauchy's Theorem

$$\lim_{n\to\infty} (a_n)^{\frac{1}{n}} = \lim_{n\to\infty} \frac{a_{n+}}{a_n} = \lim_{n\to\infty} \frac{(n+)}{(n+)^{n+}} \frac{n^n}{n}$$

$$= \lim_{n\to\infty} \frac{1}{\left(1+\dfrac{1}{n}\right)^n} = \frac{1}{e}$$

or, $\quad \lim_{n\to\infty} \dfrac{(n)^{\frac{1}{n}}}{n} \to \dfrac{1}{e}$

B. $\because (D^2+D)y = 4\cos x$;

A.E. is $m^2 + m = 0 \Rightarrow m = 0, -1$

$\Rightarrow$ C.F. $= c_1 + c_2 e^{-x}$

P.I. $= \dfrac{}{D^2+D}\ x = \dfrac{x}{+D} = \dfrac{x}{(D-)}$

$$= \frac{(D+)}{(D\ )}\ x = -2(-\sin x + \cos x)$$

$= 2\sin x - 2\cos x.$

∴ General solution is

$y = c_1 + c_2 e^{-x} + 2\sin x - 2\cos x.$

21. A. Parameteric equation of astroid is

$x = a\cos^3\theta; y = a\sin^3\theta$

As radius of curvature at point 'θ' is given by

$$\rho = \frac{\left[x^2 + y^2 \right]^{-}}{x\ y - x\ y}$$

Now $\qquad x_1 = -3a\cos^2\theta\sin\theta$

$\Rightarrow \qquad x_{11} = -3a[\cos^3\theta - 2\cos\theta\sin^2\theta]$

$\qquad\qquad y_1 = 3a\sin^2\theta\cos\theta$

$\Rightarrow \qquad y_{11} = 3a[-\sin^3\theta + 2\sin\theta\cos^2\theta]$

$\qquad x^2 + y^2 = 9a^2\cos^2\theta\sin^2\theta(\cos^2\theta+\sin^2\theta)$

$\qquad x_1 y_{11} - x_{11} y_1 = -9a^2\cos^2\theta\sin^2\theta$
$\qquad\qquad [-\sin^2\theta + 2\cos^2\theta - \cos^2\theta + 2\sin^2\theta]$
$\qquad\qquad = -9a^2\cos^2\theta\sin^2\theta$

∴ $\qquad \rho = \dfrac{a\ \theta\ \theta}{-a\ \theta\ \theta}$

$\qquad\qquad = -3a\sin\theta\cos\theta$

∴ $\qquad |\rho| = |3a\sin\theta\cos\theta|$

Also equation of tangent at 'θ'

$\qquad y - a\sin^3\theta = -\tan\theta(x - a\cos^3\theta)$

$\Rightarrow \qquad \tan\theta\, x + y = a\sin\theta \qquad\qquad ...(i)$

∴ length of perpendicular from origin to (i) is given by

$$p = \frac{|a\ \theta|}{\sqrt{+\ \theta}} = \alpha\sin\theta\cos\theta$$

Clearly $\quad p = \dfrac{e}{}.$

B. From figure

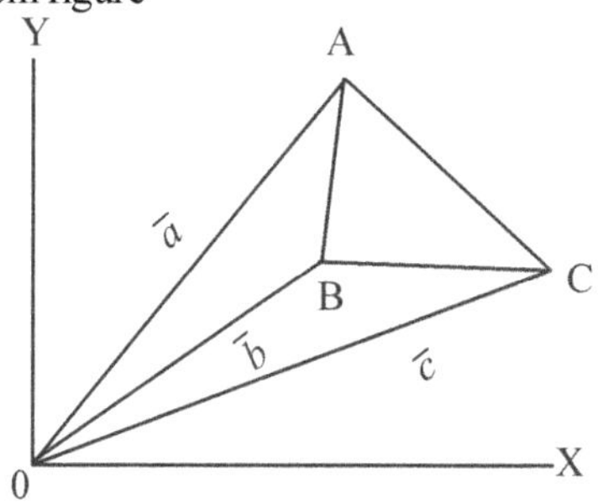

$$\overrightarrow{BA} = \vec{a} - \vec{b} \quad \text{and} \quad \overrightarrow{BC} = \vec{c} - \vec{b}$$

Vector area of $\triangle ABC$ is

$$\frac{1}{2}\left(\overrightarrow{BC} \times \overrightarrow{BA}\right) = \frac{1}{2}\left[\left(\vec{c} - \vec{b}\right) \times \left(\vec{a} - \vec{b}\right)\right]$$

$$= \frac{1}{2}\left[\vec{c} \times \vec{a} - \vec{c} \times \vec{b} - \vec{b} \times \vec{a} + \vec{b} \times \vec{b}\right]$$

$$= \frac{1}{2}\left[\vec{a} \times \vec{b} + \vec{b} \times \vec{c} + \vec{c} \times \vec{a}\right].$$

22. A. $\because f(x+y) = g(x) + h(y)$

$\Rightarrow f(x) = g(x) + h(0)\,;\, f(0+x) = g(0) + h(x)$

$\Rightarrow g(x) - h(x) = g(0) - h(0) = c\,(\text{say})$

i.e. $g(x)$ & $h(x)$ are differed by only a constant.

$\Rightarrow f(x+x) = g(x) + h(x) = 2g(x) + c = 2h(x) - c$

i.e. $f(2x) = 2g(x) + c = 2h(x) - c$ for all x

$\Rightarrow f(x), g(x)$ and $h(x)$ are linear function of x.

23. A. Let $y = uv$

$$\Rightarrow \frac{dy}{dx} = u\frac{dv}{dx} + v\frac{du}{dx}$$

$$\Rightarrow \frac{d^2y}{dx^2} = u\frac{d^2v}{dx^2} + v\frac{d^2u}{dx^2} + 2\frac{du}{dx}\frac{dv}{dx}$$

So the given eq. $(D^2 + PD + Q)\,y = R$ becomes

$$v\frac{d^2u}{dx^2} + \left(2\frac{dv}{dx} + Pv\right)\frac{du}{dx}$$

$$+ \left(Pu\frac{dv}{dx} + u\frac{d^2v}{dx^2} + Quv\right) = R$$

$$\Rightarrow v\frac{d^2u}{dx^2} + \left(2\frac{dv}{dx} + Pv\right)\frac{du}{dx}$$

$$+ u\left(P\frac{dv}{dx} + \frac{d^2v}{dx^2} + Qv\right) = R \qquad ....(i)$$

But v is the solution of the given equation so eq.(i) is

$$v\frac{d^2u}{dx^2} + p'\frac{du}{dx} = R\ ; p' = \left(2\frac{dv}{dx} + Pv\right) ....(ii)$$

Now $\qquad$ let $\dfrac{du}{dx} = w$

$$\Rightarrow \qquad \frac{d^2u}{dx^2} = \frac{dw}{dx},$$

So now (ii) becomes $v\dfrac{dw}{dx} + p'w = R$

which is a L.E. in w so,

$$w\left(e^{\int \frac{p'}{v}dx}\right) = \int e^{\int \frac{p'}{v}dx}\frac{R}{v}dx + c$$

by virtue of which we get

$$w = f(x) \Rightarrow \frac{du}{dx} = f(x) \text{ from which } u \text{ is}$$

obtained.

B. Given curves are $ax^2 + by^2 = 1$

and $\quad a_1x^2 + b_1y^2 = 1$

$$\left(\frac{dy}{dx}\right)_1 = \frac{-ax}{by}; \left(\frac{dy}{dx}\right)_2 = \frac{-a_1x}{b_1y} \qquad ...(i)$$

At their point of intersection is

$$ax^2 + by^2 = a_1x^2 + b_1y^2$$

or $(a - a_1)\dfrac{x^2}{y^2} = (b_1 - b) \Rightarrow \dfrac{x}{y} = \left[\dfrac{b_1 - b}{a - a_1}\right]^{1/2}$

$$\Rightarrow \left(\frac{dy}{dx}\right)_1 = \frac{-a}{b}\left[\frac{b_1 - b}{a - a_1}\right]^{1/2}$$

$$\left(\frac{dy}{dx}\right)_2 = \frac{-a_1}{b_1}\left(\frac{b_1 - b}{a - a_1}\right)^{1/2} \quad \text{from } (i)$$

They will be orthogonal if $\left(\dfrac{dy}{dx}\right)_1\left(\dfrac{dy}{dx}\right)_2 = -1$

$$\Rightarrow \frac{aa_1}{bb_1}\left(\frac{b_1 - b}{a - a_1}\right) = -1$$

$$\Rightarrow aa_1(b_1 - b) = -bb_1(a - a_1)$$

or $aa_1(b_1 - b) + bb_1(a - a_1) = 0.$

24. A. As A is invertible $\Rightarrow A^{-1}$ exists.

$$I - AB = A[I - BA]A^{-1}$$

$\Rightarrow$ put $\dfrac{1}{\lambda}$ in place of B we get

$$- \frac{\;}{\lambda} = \left[-\frac{\;}{\lambda} \right]^{-}$$

$\Rightarrow \quad [\lambda I - AB] = A[\lambda I - BA]A^{-1}$

$\Rightarrow \det[\lambda I - AB] = \left\{ (\lambda - \;)^{-} \right\}$

$\Rightarrow \det(AB - \lambda I) = \det(BA - \lambda I)$

$\Rightarrow$ AB & BA have same eigen values.

B. $\displaystyle \lim_{n \to \infty} \frac{\left[1 - \dfrac{1}{2}\right] + \left[1 - \dfrac{1}{3}\right] + \ldots\ldots \left[1 - \dfrac{1}{n+1}\right]}{n}$

$\displaystyle = 1 - \lim_{n \to \infty} \frac{1}{n} \sum_{r=1}^{n} \frac{1}{r+1}$

As $\displaystyle \lim_{n \to \infty} \frac{u_1 + u_2 + u_3 + \ldots\ldots u_n}{n} = \lim_{n \to \infty} u_n$

(By Cauchy's first theorem)

$\displaystyle = \lim_{n \to \infty} \frac{n}{n+1} = 1$

25. A. Let $y = \dfrac{x^2 - 4x + 9}{x^2 + 4x + 9}$

$\Rightarrow x^2(y-1) + 4x(y+1) + 9(y-1) = 0$

x is real if $[4(y+1)]^2 - (4)(9)(y-1)^2 \geq 0$

i.e. $-20y^2 + 104y - 20 \geq 0$

$\Rightarrow -5y^2 + 26y - 5 \geq 0$

i.e. $(5y - 1)(y - 5) \leq 0$

$$\xleftarrow{\qquad +\qquad \Big|\;-\;\Big|\qquad +\qquad}$$
$$\qquad 1/5 \qquad\qquad 5$$

$\Rightarrow \dfrac{1}{5} \leq y \leq 5$

B. $9(x+2)^2 - 16(y+1)^2 = 144$

$\Rightarrow \dfrac{(x+2)^2}{(4)^2} - \dfrac{(y+1)^2}{(3)^2} = 1$

Any point on it is $(4\sec\phi - 2,\ 3\tan\phi - 1)$ Its distance from $(-1, -1)$ will be D, where

$D^2 = (4\sec\phi - 1)^2 + (3\tan\phi)^2$

$\dfrac{d(D)^2}{d\phi} = 2(4\sec\phi - 1)\, 4\sec\phi\tan\phi$

$\qquad\qquad\qquad + 2(3\tan\phi)\, 3\sec^2\phi = 0$

$\Rightarrow 25\sec\phi = 4$ or $\tan\phi = 0$ or $\sec\phi = 0$

but $\sec\phi \neq 0$ and $\sec\phi \neq \dfrac{4}{25}$ so $\phi = 0$

$\therefore D^2_{min} = (4-1)^2 + 0 \Rightarrow D_{min} = 3$

26. A. $\left| \dfrac{nx}{n} \right| \leq \dfrac{\;}{n} \quad \forall x$

$$\pi \qquad\qquad x \qquad\qquad \leq x \leq$$

$$\int^{\pi}_{\;} f(x)\,dx \qquad \int^{\pi}_{\;} \left(\sum_{n=}^{\infty} \frac{nx}{n} \right) dx$$

$$\sum_{n=}^{\infty} \int^{\pi}_{\;} \frac{nx}{n}\,dx \qquad \sum_{n=}^{\infty} \left(\frac{-\;}{n}\; n\pi \right)$$

$$\left(\frac{\;}{\;} + \frac{\;}{\;} + \frac{\;}{\;} + \right) \qquad \sum_{n=}^{\infty} \frac{\;}{(\;n-\;)}$$

B.

$$a_n \qquad \frac{a(a+\;)(a+\;)\;(a+n-\;)\,b(b+\;)\;(b+n-\;)}{n\,c(c+\;)(c+\;)\;(c+n-\;)}$$

$$a_n \qquad \frac{a(a+\;)(a+\;)\;(a+n)\,b(b+\;)\;(b+n)}{(n+\;)c(c+\;)(c+\;)\;(c+n)}$$

$$\therefore \qquad \lim_{n \to \infty} \left| \frac{a_n}{a_{n+}} \right| \qquad \lim_{n \to \infty} \frac{(n+\;)(c+n)}{(a+n)(b+n)}$$

$$\lim_{n \to \infty} \frac{\left(\dfrac{\;}{\;} + \dfrac{\;}{n} \right)\left(\dfrac{\;}{\;} + \dfrac{c}{n} \right)}{\left(\dfrac{\;}{\;} + \dfrac{a}{n} \right)\left(\dfrac{\;}{\;} + \dfrac{b}{n} \right)}$$

27. $F'(x) = f(x) \Rightarrow F(x) = \dfrac{\;}{\pi} \displaystyle\int^{x}_{-\infty} \frac{dx}{\;+x\;}$

$$\frac{\;}{\pi} \qquad \;^{-}\; x + \frac{\pi}{\;}$$

$$\frac{\;}{\pi} \qquad \;^{-}\; x + \;-\;$$

$$(\quad\quad x) \quad -\; \Rightarrow \quad x \quad \Rightarrow x$$

$$(\quad\quad x) \quad -\; \Rightarrow \frac{\;}{\pi} \quad x \quad -\;-\;$$

$$\Rightarrow \quad x \quad -\frac{\pi}{\;} \Rightarrow x =$$

$$(\quad\quad x) \quad -\; \Rightarrow \frac{\;}{\pi} \quad x \quad -\;-\;$$

$$x \quad \frac{\pi}{\;} \Rightarrow x$$

$$\frac{}{\pi}\int_{-\infty}^{\infty}\frac{x}{+x}\,dx \qquad\qquad \frac{x}{+x}$$

odd

$$\mu \quad \frac{}{\pi}\int_{-\infty}^{x}\frac{x}{+x}\,dx \quad \frac{}{\pi}\int^{\infty}\left(+\frac{-}{+x}\right)dx$$

$$\frac{}{\pi}\left[\,|x|^{\infty}-\frac{\pi}{}\,\right]$$

$$x\quad '(x)\qquad \Rightarrow \frac{}{\pi}\frac{-x}{\left(+x\right)}$$

$$\Rightarrow x$$
$$\therefore$$

28. Substituting $y(x)=xe^{x}$ in the R.H.S. of *(i)*, we

have $\quad x+\int^{x}(x-t)\,te^{t}\,dt$

$$x+ \quad \int^{x} x\, t\, e^{t}\ t\,dt + \int^{x} x\, te^{t}\ t\,dt$$

$$(\,)$$

$$x+\quad x - \left| t\,e^{t}(\ t+\ t)\right|^{x}$$

$$-- \int^{x} e^{t}(\ t)+\ t\,dt + \quad x$$

$$-\left| t\,e^{t}(\ t)-\ t\right|^{x} -- \int^{x} e^{t}(\ t+\ t)\,dt$$
$$x \quad xe^{x}(\quad x \quad x \quad x \quad x$$
$$x \quad x)- \quad x\,\int^{x} e^{t}(\ t+\ t)\,dt$$
$$- \quad x\,\int^{x} t(\ t-\ t)\,dt$$

$$x+xe^{x}- \quad x\left| e^{t}\ t\right|^{x} + \quad x\left| e^{t}\ t\right|^{x}$$
$$x \quad xe^{x}-e^{x} \quad x \quad x\ e^{t} \quad x \quad x$$
$$\qquad\qquad\qquad\qquad\qquad x\quad xe^{x}$$
$$y(x)\quad xe^{x}$$
$$(i)$$

29. Consider the arc OPA of the curve which rotates
about the *x*-axis as shown in Fig.

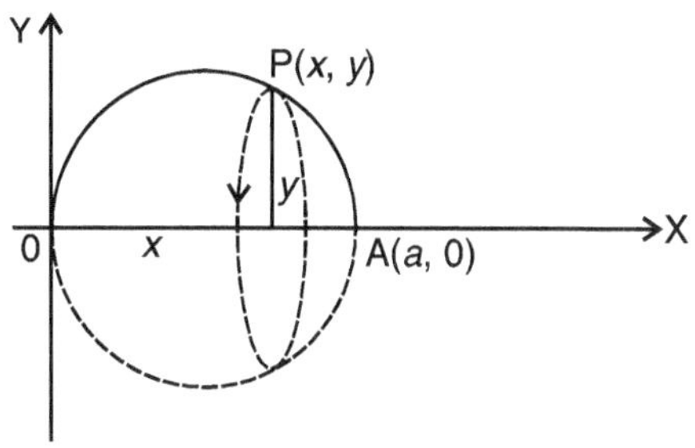

$$\int_{x=}^{a} \pi y\,ds$$

$$\int^{a} \pi y\sqrt{(\ +y'\ )}\,dx$$

$$\int^{a} \pi y\ dx$$

$$f\quad \pi y \qquad g\quad \pi y\sqrt{(\ y')}$$
$$f\quad \lambda g\quad \pi y\quad \pi\lambda y\,\sqrt{(\quad)}$$

$$x$$

$$\therefore\quad -y'\frac{\partial}{\partial y'}\qquad\qquad c$$

$$i.e.\ \pi y\ +\ \pi\lambda y\sqrt{(\ +y'\ )}-y'\ \pi\lambda y\frac{y'}{\sqrt{(\ +y'\ )}}$$

$$c\quad \pi y\ +\frac{\pi\lambda y}{\sqrt{(\ +y'\ )}}\quad c \qquad\qquad (i)$$

$$y\quad (i)\qquad c$$
$$\therefore y \quad \lambda\ \sqrt{(\ y')}$$

$$y'\quad y'\left(=\frac{dy}{dx}\right)\qquad \frac{\sqrt{(\ \lambda\ -y\ )}}{y}$$

$$\int dx \quad \int\frac{y\,dy}{\sqrt{(\ \lambda\ -y\ )}}+k$$

$$x\quad k\quad \sqrt{(\ \lambda\quad y\ )} \qquad\qquad (ii)$$
$$x\quad y\quad \therefore k\quad \lambda$$

$$\therefore\ (ii)(\qquad x\quad \lambda)\quad y\,(\quad \lambda)$$
$$(\qquad\qquad \lambda)\qquad\qquad \lambda$$

TEST PAPER - 2

PART - A

1. The equation of the plane passing through three points A, B and C with position vectors

$$\vec{i} + \vec{j}, \ \vec{j} + \vec{k}, \ \vec{k} + \vec{i} \ \text{ is}$$

$$\vec{r} \cdot (\vec{i} + \vec{j} + \vec{k}) = 0 \qquad \vec{r} \cdot (\vec{i} + \vec{j} + \vec{k}) = 1$$

$$\vec{r} \cdot (\vec{i} + \vec{j} + \vec{k}) = 2 \qquad \vec{r} \cdot (\vec{i} + \vec{j} + \vec{k}) = 3$$

2. The integrating factor of the differential equation $\sin x \dfrac{dy}{dx} + 3y = \cos x$ is calculated as

$$e^{\tan 3x/2}$$

$$\frac{x}{2} \qquad\qquad \frac{x}{2}$$

3. If $u = \tan^{-1}\left(\dfrac{x^3 + y^3}{x - y}\right)$ the value of

$$x\,\frac{\partial u}{\partial x} + xy\frac{\partial u}{\partial x\,\partial y} + y\,\frac{\partial u}{\partial y} \ \text{ is}$$

$$u \qquad u \qquad u$$
$$u\,(\qquad\qquad u)$$
$$u\,(\qquad u \qquad u)$$
$$u\,(\qquad u)$$

4. The value/values of k such that the following system

$$kx + y + z = 1$$
$$x + ky + z = 1$$

$x + y + kz = 1$, in unknowns x, y and z has a unique solution.

$$k \qquad\qquad\qquad k$$
$$k \neq \qquad k \neq \qquad\qquad k$$

5. A steel girder 27 ft. long is moved horizontally along a passage way 8 ft. wide and into a corridor at right angles to passage way. How wide the corridor at least must be so that the girder may go around the corner? (Neglect the horizontal width of the girder)

A. $4\sqrt{3}$ ft. B. $5\sqrt{5}$ ft.

C. $6\sqrt{2}$ ft. D. None of these

6. The area of an equilateral triangle with base lying on the line $px + qy + r = 0$ and vertex $(0, 0)$ is

A. $\dfrac{r^2}{\sqrt{3}\sqrt{p^2 + q^2}}$ B. $\sqrt{\dfrac{3r^2}{p^2 + q^2}}$

C. $\dfrac{r^2}{\sqrt{3}(p^2 + q^2)}$ D. $\dfrac{\sqrt{3}}{2}\dfrac{r^2}{(p^2 + q^2)}$

7. Study the following assertions about a square matrix :

(*i*) The sum of the eigenvalues of A is equal to its trace

(*ii*) The product of the eigenvalues of A is equal to the determinant of A

(*iii*) All eigenvalues of A are non-zero if and only if A is non-singular.

(*iv*) If A^{-1} exists, then the eigenvalues of A^{-1} are equal to the reciprocal of the eigen values of A.

Which among the following is correct with respect to above assertions?

A. Only (*iii*) and (*iv*) are true

B. Only (*i*) and (*ii*) are true

C. Only (*ii*), (*iii*) and (*iv*) are true

D. (*i*), (*ii*), (*iii*) and (*iv*) are all true

8. The direct sum $F_1 \oplus F_2$ of two fields under the usual operations of componentwise addition and multiplication is

A. a field

B. a division ring but not a field

C. an integral domain but not a division ring
D. a commutatitve ring but not an integral domain

9. A hole of radius 'r' is bored symmetrically through a sphere of radius $2r$. The volume of the solid that remains is

A. $4\sqrt{3}\pi r^3$

B. $\dfrac{2}{3}\sqrt{2}\pi r^2$

C. $\dfrac{3\sqrt{3}}{2}\pi r^2$

D. $4\sqrt{2}\pi r^2$

10. The hypotenuse of a right triangle is 10 inches but the lengths of the two legs are variable. The triangle is rotated about its hypotenuse, thus generating a top shaped solid consisting of two cones with a common base and with altitudes whose sum is 10 inches. The maximum possible volume of this solid is

A. $\dfrac{250}{3}\pi$ in^3

B. $\dfrac{160}{3}\pi$ in^3

C. $\dfrac{325}{3}\pi$ in^3

D. None of these

11. The boundary value problem

$$\dfrac{d^2 y}{dx^2} + y = 0, x \in [0, \pi], y(0), y(\pi) = 0 \quad \text{has}$$

A. a unique solution
B. no solution
C. more than one but finitely many solutions
D. infinitely many solutions

12. What is the limit of the sequence $\{a_n\}_{n \geq 1}$ where $a_n = \dfrac{n!}{n^n}$?

A. 0

B. 1

C. ∞

D. $\dfrac{1}{\ln 2}$

13. What is the value of $\lim\limits_{x \to \infty} xe^{-x^2} \cdot \int_0^x e^{t^2} dt$?

A. 0

B. $\dfrac{1}{2}$

C. $\dfrac{1}{e+1}$

D. ∞

14. **Assertion (P) :** $\sin|x|$ is differentiable at $x = 0$.
Reason (Q) : $\sin x$ is continuous at $x = 0$.
Which of the following is true ?
A. Both P and Q are true and Q is the correct explanation for P.
B. Both P and Q are true but Q is not the correct explanation
C. P is true but Q is false.
D. P is false but Q is true.

15. The base of solid is the triangle $\left\{\begin{array}{l} (x, y) \leq x \leq 1, \\ 0 \leq y \leq x \end{array}\right\}$ in the xy plane and each cross-section perpendicular to the x-axis is a square. The volume of the solid is

A. 2/9

B. 2/3

C. $\dfrac{4}{9}$

D. $\dfrac{1}{3}$

PART - B

16. A. Evaluate:

$$\int_0^{\pi/2} \dfrac{d\theta}{(x^2 \cos^2\theta + y^2 \sin^2\theta)^2}.$$

B. A solid of revolution is obtained by rotating a square about an axis lying in its plane and passing through one of its corners. Determine the maximum volume of the solid.

17. A. Find the sum

$$\sum_{n=1}^{\infty} \dfrac{a_n}{(1+a_1)(1+a_2)....(1+a_n)}.$$

Given that $a_n > 0$ and $\sum\limits_{n=1}^{\infty} a_n$ divergent.

B. Sum the series:
$$e^x + 2e^{-2x} + 3e^{-3x} + ... + ne^{-nx} + ...$$

18. A. Show that the family of tangent lines to the family of solutions of the linear differential equation $y + P(x) = Q(x)$ at the points corresponding to $x = K$ (K any constant) are concurrent.

B. A 200 gallon open top tank contains initially 100 gallons of solution in which 50 lbs. of salt are dissolved. A solution containing 2 lbs/gal. of salt is pumped into the tank at the rate of 3 gal/min. The thoroughly stirred mixture is allowed to flow out at the rate of 1 gal/min. How much salt is in the tank after 20 minutes?

19. A. Show:

$$\frac{d^n}{dt^n}\int_{-t}^{t} f(x+t)dx = 2^n f^{(n-1)}(2t), n \geq 1$$

where $f^{(n-1)}$ $(2t)$ is the $(n-1)$th derivative.

B. Prove:

$$.5 < \int_{0}^{\frac{1}{2}} \frac{dx}{\sqrt{1-x^n}} \leq .586$$

for each integer $n > 1$.

20. A. Find the general solution of the differential equation given by

$$\begin{vmatrix} y & F(x) & G(x) \\ y' & F'(x) & G'(x) \\ y'' & F''(x) & G''(x) \end{vmatrix} = 0.$$

B. Water is flowing into a tank in the form of right circular cylinder at the rate of $\frac{4\pi}{5}$ ft^3/min. The tank is stretching in such a way that even though it remains cylindrical, its radius is increasing at the rate of 0.002 ft/min. How fast is the depth of the water rising when the radius is 2 ft and the volume of water in the tank is 20π ft^3 ?

21. What are the dimensions of the right circular cone of maximum volume which may be inscribed in a sphere of radius r?

22. "If $a < b < c < d$, then the roots of the equation $(x-a)(x-c) + 2(x-b)(x-d) = 0$ are real and distinct". Prove.

23. If $f(x) = \dfrac{x}{x}$, then find the value of $f'(x)$ at $x = e$.

24. Find the sum of the series $\displaystyle\sum_{n=1}^{\infty} \frac{(n-1)^1}{(n+p)^1}$. If you think the series is convergent. If you think it is divergent, then give reason.

25. Find the value of

$$\int_{0}^{2a} \frac{f(x)}{f(x)+f(2a-x)}dx.$$

26. A.

$$\frac{x}{a}+\frac{y}{b} =$$

B. (

$$\begin{matrix} & & e & & e \\ & & \alpha & \beta & \gamma) \end{matrix}$$

$$\frac{x}{a}+\frac{y}{b}$$

$$\frac{\alpha}{(x-\alpha)} - \frac{\beta}{(y-\beta)} + \frac{(a-b)}{(z-\gamma)}$$

27. A particle of mass m moves in a smooth circular tube of radius a, under the action of a force, equal to $m\mu\, x$ distance, to a point inside the tube at a distance c from its centre; if the particle be placed very nearly at its greatest distance from the centre of force, show that it will describe the quadrant ending at its least distance in time

$$\sqrt{\frac{a}{\mu c}}\, log\left(\sqrt{} + \right)$$

28. $F = (\ x\ -) z\, i - \ xyj - \ xk$

$$\iiint_V \bar{V}\ FdV$$

$$\begin{matrix} & & x & y & z \\ x & y & z & & \end{matrix}$$

Also Evaluate $\displaystyle\iiint_V \nabla \times FdV$

29. $\displaystyle\int_{0}^{a/2} x^m \qquad c^n\ x\ dx \qquad iff$

$n < (m + 1).$

$$\frac{\partial \rho}{\partial t} + \frac{}{r}\frac{\partial}{\partial \theta}(\rho \upsilon\ ) + \frac{\partial}{\partial z}(\rho \upsilon_z) =$$

$$\upsilon \ \ and \ \upsilon_z$$

$$z$$

0

$$\boxed{\textbf{ANSWERS}}$$

1	2	3	4	5	6	7	8	9	10
11	12	13	14	15					

$$\boxed{\textbf{SOME SELECTED EXPLANATORY ANSWERS}}$$

$$\boxed{\textbf{PART - A}}$$

1. $\vec{A} = \vec{i} + \vec{j}, \ \vec{B} = \vec{j} + \vec{k}, \ \vec{C} = \vec{k} + \vec{i}$

Now a plane vector I_r to the plane ABC is given by

$$\left| \overrightarrow{} \times \overrightarrow{} \right| = \left| \left(\vec{k} - \vec{i} \right) \times \left(\vec{k} - \vec{j} \right) \right|$$
$$= \left(\vec{i} + \vec{j} + \vec{k} \right)$$

If $\vec{r}$ be any point on the plane ABC then using geometry

$$\Rightarrow \left(\vec{r} - \overrightarrow{OA} \right) . \left(\vec{i} + \vec{j} + \vec{k} \right) = 0$$
$$\Rightarrow \vec{r} . \left(\vec{i} + \vec{j} + \vec{k} \right) - 2 = 0$$
$$\Rightarrow \vec{r} \left(\vec{i} + \vec{j} + \vec{k} \right) = 2.$$

2. $\dfrac{dy}{dx} + 3 \operatorname{cosec} xy = \cot x$

$$e^{\int P dx} = e^{3 \operatorname{cosec} x . dx} = e^{-3 \ln (\operatorname{cosec} x + \cot x)}$$
$$= (\operatorname{cosec} x + \cot x)^{-3}$$

$$\dfrac{\overline{}}{\left(\dfrac{+ \quad x}{x} \right)} = \dfrac{x}{(\ + \ ) \ x}$$

$$= \left(\dfrac{\dfrac{x}{} \quad \dfrac{x}{}}{\dfrac{x}{}} \right) = \quad \dfrac{x}{}.$$

3. $z = \tan u = \dfrac{x^3 + y^3}{x - y}$ homogeneous function of degree 2

$$\Rightarrow x \frac{\partial z}{\partial x} + y \frac{\partial z}{\partial y} = nz \quad \text{(Euler Theorem)}$$

$$\Rightarrow x \qquad u \frac{\partial u}{\partial x} + y \qquad u \frac{\partial u}{\partial y} = \qquad u$$

$$\Rightarrow x \frac{\partial u}{\partial x} + y \frac{\partial u}{\partial y} = 2 \sin u \cos u = \sin 2u \quad ...(i)$$

Taking p.d. of both sides w.r.t. x and y we get

$$x \frac{\partial^2 u}{\partial x^2} + \frac{\partial u}{\partial x} + \frac{\partial^2 u}{\partial x \partial y} y = 2 \cos 2u \frac{\partial u}{\partial x} \quad ...(ii)$$

$$x \frac{\partial^2 u}{\partial x \partial y} + y \frac{\partial^2 u}{\partial y^2} + \frac{\partial u}{\partial y} = 2 \cos 2u \frac{\partial u}{\partial y} \quad ...(iii)$$

$(2) \times (x) + (3) \times (y)$

$$\Rightarrow R + \left(x \frac{\partial u}{\partial x} + y \frac{\partial u}{\partial y} \right) = 2 \cos 2u \left(x \frac{\partial u}{\partial x} + y \frac{\partial u}{\partial y} \right)$$

$$\Rightarrow R = (2 \cos 2u - 1) \sin 2u$$
$$= \sin 2u \left(1 - 4 \sin^2 u \right)$$

4. $R_1 \to R_1 + R_2 + R_3$

$$\Rightarrow k + 2 \begin{vmatrix} & k & \\ & & \\ & & k \end{vmatrix} \neq$$

$R_1 \to R_1 - R_3$

$$\Rightarrow (k + 2) \begin{vmatrix} & & -k \\ & k & \\ & & k \end{vmatrix} \neq$$

$$\Rightarrow (k + 2) (1 - k)^2 \neq 0$$
$$\Rightarrow k \neq -2 \ \text{ and } \ k \neq -1.$$

5.

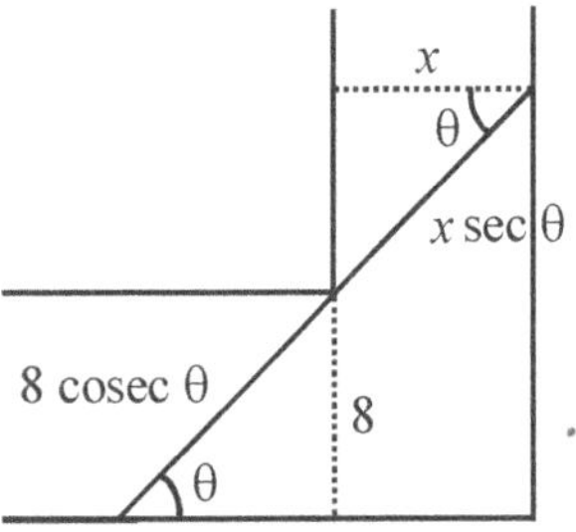

$$\Rightarrow x \sec \theta + 8 \cosec \theta = 27$$

$$\Rightarrow x = \frac{27 - 8\cosec\theta}{\sec\theta} = 27\cos\theta - 8\cot\theta$$

$$\Rightarrow \frac{dx}{d\theta} = -27\sin\theta + 8\cosec^2\theta = 0$$

$$\Rightarrow \sin^3\theta = \frac{8}{27}$$

$$\Rightarrow \sin\theta = \frac{2}{3}$$

$$\Rightarrow x^{\min} = \frac{27 - 8.\dfrac{3}{2}}{\dfrac{3}{\sqrt{5}}} = \frac{15\sqrt{5}}{3} = 5\sqrt{5}$$

6.

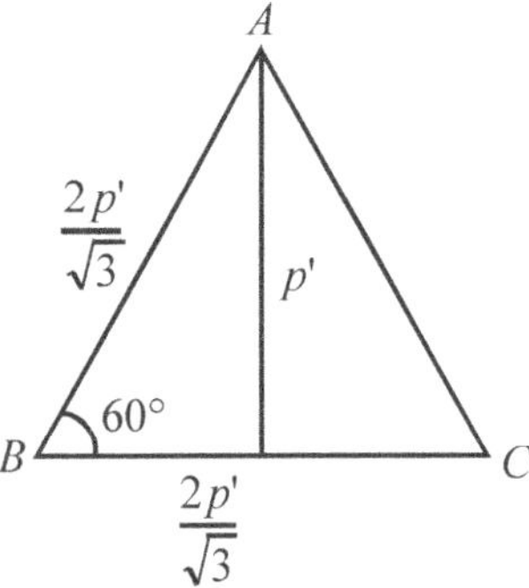

$$\Rightarrow \text{Area} = \frac{1}{2}.p'.\frac{2p'}{\sqrt{3}} = \frac{p'^2}{\sqrt{3}}$$

Now, $p' = \dfrac{r}{\sqrt{p^2 + q^2}}$

$$\Rightarrow \Delta = \frac{r^2}{\sqrt{3}\left(p^2 + q^2\right)}$$

0

7. The sum of the eigenvalues of A is equal to its trace

The product of the eigenvalues of A is equal to its $|A|$

All eigen values of A are non-zero if $|A| \neq 0$

If A^{-1} exists, then the eigenvalues of A^{-1} are equal to reciprocal of the eigen values of A.

8. Field.

9.

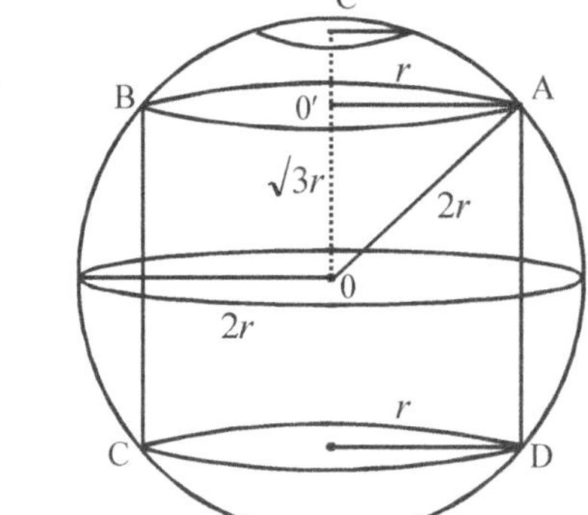

The volume of sphere $V = \dfrac{4}{3}\pi.8r^3$

$$\Rightarrow V = \frac{32}{3}\pi r^3$$

volume of excavated portion

$$V' = \pi r^2\left(2\sqrt{3}r\right) + 2.\int_{\sqrt{3}r}^{2r} \pi x^3\, dy$$

$$= 2\sqrt{3}\pi r^3 + 2\pi \int_{\sqrt{3}r}^{2r}\left(4r^2 - y^2\right)dy$$

$$= 2\sqrt{3}\pi r^3 + 2\pi\left[4r^2 y - \frac{y^3}{3}\right]_{\sqrt{3}r}^{2r}$$

$$= 2\sqrt{3}\pi r^3 + \frac{2\pi y}{3}\left(12r^2 - y^2\right)\Big|_{\sqrt{3}r}^{2r}$$

$$= 2\sqrt{3}\pi r^3 + \frac{2\pi}{3}\left\{16r^3 - 9\sqrt{3}r^3\right\}$$

$$= \frac{32}{3}\pi r^3 - 4\sqrt{3}\pi r^3$$

Hence volume of remaining portion

$$V - V' = 4\sqrt{3}\pi r^3.$$

10.

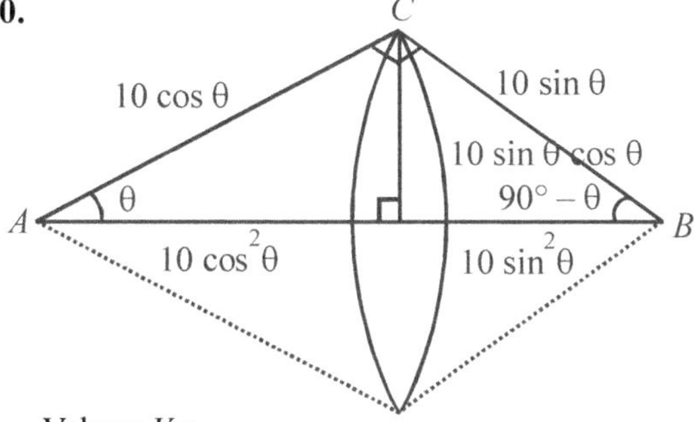

Volume $V =$

$$\frac{1}{3}\pi \cdot 100 \sin^2\theta \cos^2\theta [10\cos^2\theta + 10\sin^2\theta]$$

$$= \frac{1000\pi}{3}\sin^2\theta \cos^2\theta \qquad \qquad ...(i)$$

$$\frac{dV}{d\theta} = 0 \Rightarrow 2\sin\theta \cos^3\theta - 2\cos\theta \sin^3\theta = 0$$

$$\Rightarrow \sin\theta \cos\theta(\cos^2\theta - \sin^2\theta) = 0$$

$$\Rightarrow \theta = 0, \frac{\pi}{2}, \frac{\pi}{4}$$

V is max^m at $\theta = \dfrac{\pi}{4}$

$$\therefore \quad V^{max} = \frac{1000\pi}{3} \cdot \frac{1}{4} = \frac{250\pi}{3}$$

11.

$$\frac{d^2 y}{dx^2} + y = 0$$

$$\Rightarrow y = A\cos x + B\sin x$$

$$y(0) = 0$$

$$\Rightarrow A = 0 \text{ and } y(\pi) = 0$$

$$\Rightarrow A = 0$$

$\Rightarrow y = B\sin x$ where B is any arbitrary constant

$\Rightarrow$ infinitely many solutions.

12.

$$\lim_{h\to\infty} \frac{n!}{n^n} = 0 .$$

13.

$$\lim_{x\to\infty} xe^{-x^2}\int_0^x e^{t^2}\,dt = \lim_{x\to\infty} \frac{\displaystyle\int_0^x e^{t^2}\,dt}{\dfrac{e^{x^2}}{x}}\left(\frac{\infty}{\infty}\,\text{case}\right)$$

Applying L' Hospital's rule.

$$= \frac{e^{x^2}}{\dfrac{xe^{x^2}(2x) - e^{x^2}}{x^2}} = \frac{1}{\dfrac{2x^2 - 1}{x^2}} = \frac{1}{2} .$$

15.

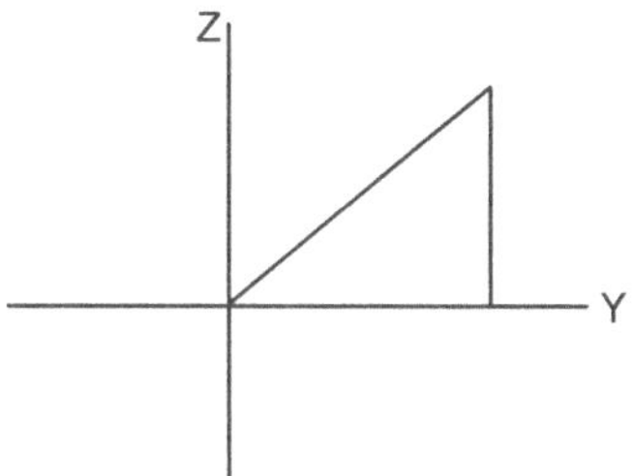

Cross section $\perp^r$ to x-axis is $(y - z)$ plane *i.e.*

figure in the yz plane is a square subject to the given condition so the required volume is

$$V = \int_{x=0}^{1}\int_{y=0}^{x}\int_{z=0}^{x} dx\,dy\,dz = \frac{1}{3}$$

$$\boxed{\textbf{PART - B}}$$

16. A. Let $I = \displaystyle\int_0^{\frac{\pi}{2}} \frac{d\theta}{x^2\cos^2 + y^2\sin^2\theta}$

$$= \int_0^{\frac{\pi}{2}} \frac{d\theta}{x^2 + (y^2 - x^2)\sin^2\theta}$$

$$= \int_0^{\frac{\pi}{2}} \frac{d\theta}{a + b\sin^2\theta} \quad \begin{cases} a = (x^2) \\ b = (y^2 - x^2) \end{cases}$$

$$= \int_0^{\frac{\pi}{2}} \frac{\sec^2 d\theta}{a + (b+a)\tan^2\theta}$$

$$= \int_0^{\infty} \frac{dz}{a + (b+a)z^2} \quad z = \tan\theta$$

$$= \frac{1}{(b+a)}\int_0^{\infty} \frac{dz}{\left(\dfrac{a}{a+b}\right) + z^2}$$

$$= \frac{1}{b+a} \cdot \frac{1}{\sqrt{\dfrac{a}{a+b}}} \tan^{-1} \frac{z}{\sqrt{\dfrac{a}{a+b}}}\Bigg|_0^{\infty}$$

$$= \frac{1}{\sqrt{a(a+b)}} \cdot \frac{\pi}{2}$$

$$\Rightarrow I = \int_0^{\frac{\pi}{2}} \frac{d\theta}{a + b\sin^2\theta} = \frac{1}{\sqrt{a(a+b)}}$$

$$\Rightarrow \quad \frac{\partial I}{\partial a} = \int_0^{\frac{\pi}{2}} \frac{-d\theta}{(a+b\sin^2\theta)^2}$$

$$= \frac{-(2a+b)}{2\left[(a)(a+b)\right]^{\frac{3}{2}}}$$

$$\Rightarrow \int_0^{\frac{\pi}{2}} \frac{d\theta}{(a+b\sin^2\theta)^2} = \frac{2a+b}{2\left[a(a+b)\right]^{\frac{3}{2}}}$$

$$\Rightarrow \int_0^{\frac{\pi}{2}} \frac{d\theta}{(x^2\cos^2\theta + y^2\sin^2\theta)^2}$$

$$= \frac{x^2+y^2}{2\left(x^2 y^2\right)^{\frac{3}{2}}} = \frac{x^2+y^2}{2(xy)^3}$$

B.

$a/\sqrt{2}$

a

$\pi/4$

$$V^{Max} = 2\pi \frac{a}{\sqrt{2}}(a)^2 = \sqrt{2}\pi a^3$$

17. A.
$$\sum_{n=1}^{\infty} \frac{(1+a_n)-1}{(1+a_1)(1+a_2)\ldots(1+a_n)}$$

$$\sum_{n=1}^{\infty} \frac{1+a_n}{(1+a_1)(1+a_2)\ldots(1+a_n)} -$$

$$\sum_{n=1}^{\infty} \frac{1}{(1+a_1)(1+a_2)\ldots(1+a_n)}$$

$$= \sum_{n=1}^{\infty} \frac{1}{(1+a_1)\ldots(1+a_{n-1})}$$

$$- \frac{1}{(1+a_1)+(1+a_2)+\ldots+(1+a_n)}$$

$$= \left(1-\frac{1}{1+a_1}\right) + \left(\frac{1}{1+a_1} - \frac{1}{(1+a_1)(1+a_2)}\right) + \ldots$$

$$= 1 - \frac{1}{(1+a_1)(1+a_2)\ldots(1+a_n)} = 1-0 = 1$$

B.
$$S = 1.e^{-x} + 2.e^{-2x} + 3e^{-3x} + \ldots \qquad \ldots(i)$$

$$e^{-x}.S = 1.e^{-2x} + 2.e^{-3x} + \ldots \qquad \ldots(ii)$$

Subtracting equation (*ii*) from equation (*i*), we get

$$S(1-e^{-x}) = e^{-x} + e^{-2x} + e^{-3x} + \ldots$$

$$S(1-e^{-x}) = e^{-x}(1+e^{-x} + e^{-2x} + \ldots)$$

$$S(1-e^{-x}) = \frac{e^{-x}}{(1-e^{-x})}$$

$$S = \frac{e^{-x}}{(1-e^{-x})^2}$$

18. A. $y' + py = Q$

$$\Rightarrow \quad ye^{\int Pdx} = \int e^{\int Pdx} Q\,dx + c \qquad \ldots(i)$$

Now, *(i)* is the family of solutions of the given L.D.E.

Now for the family of curve $y' = Q - Py$

Let at $x = k$; $y = k'$ then

$$\left(\frac{dy}{dx}\right)_{(k_1 k')} = Q(k) - P(k)k' = c'$$

(a constant)

$\Rightarrow$ family of tangent lines is $(y - K') = c\,(x - K')$ which are equations of concurrent lines through (K, K') (K, K') being point of consequency where $K' = y_{(x=K)}$.

B. Amount of salt at time $t = 50 + 6t$

Amount of water at time $t = 100 + 3t$

Amount of salt per gallon $= \dfrac{50+6t}{100+3t}$

Volume of salt flown out of tank as a function of time is

$$\frac{ds}{dt} = \frac{50+6t}{100+3t}$$

or,
$$\int dS = \int_{t=0}^{20} \frac{50+6t}{100+3t}\,dt$$

$$= 2\left[\int_0^{20} dt - 75\int \frac{1}{100+3t}\,dt\right]$$

$$\Rightarrow \qquad S = 40 - \frac{150}{3}\ln\left(100 + 3t\right)\Big|_0^{20}$$
$$= 16.49 \ \text{lbs} = 16.48$$

Also, amount of salt accumulated in tank
$$= 50 + 6 \times 20 = 170 \ \text{lbs}.$$
Hence, amount of salt remained in tank
$$= (170 - 16.49) \ \text{lbs.} = 153.5 \ \text{lbs.}$$

19. A. $\dfrac{d^n}{dt^n}\displaystyle\int_{-t}^{t} f(x+t)\,dx = 2^n f^{(n-1)}(2t), n \geq t$

$$\frac{d}{dt}\int_{-t}^{t} f(x+t)\,dx$$

$$= \int_{-t}^{t} \frac{\partial}{\partial t} f(x+t)\,dx + f(2t) - f(0)$$

$$= f(x+t)\Big|_{-t}^{t} + f(2t) - f(0)$$

$$= 2f(t) - 2f(0)$$

Now, $\dfrac{d^n}{dt^n}\displaystyle\int_{-t}^{t} f(x+t)\,dx = \dfrac{d^{n-1}}{dt^{n-1}}\left(\dfrac{d}{dt}\int_{-t}^{t} f(x+t)\,dx\right)$

$$= \frac{d^{n-1}}{dt^{n-1}}[2f(2t) - 2f(0)]$$

$$= 2^n f^{n-1}(2t)$$

B. $\dfrac{1}{\sqrt{1-x^n}} > 1$ and $\dfrac{1}{\sqrt{1-x^n}} \leq \dfrac{1}{\sqrt{1-x^2}}$

$$\Rightarrow \int_0^{\frac{1}{2}} dx < \int_0^{\frac{1}{2}} \frac{1}{\sqrt{1-x^n}}\,dx$$

$$\leq \int_0^{\frac{1}{2}} \frac{1}{\sqrt{1-x^2}}\,dx = \sin^{-1} x\Big|_0^{\frac{1}{2}} = \frac{\pi}{6}$$

$$\Rightarrow \frac{1}{2} < \int_0^{\frac{1}{2}} \frac{1}{\sqrt{1-x^n}}\,dx \leq \frac{\pi}{6}$$

20. A. $y = c_1 F(x) + c_2 G(x)$ where c_1 and c_2 are any arbitrary constants.

B. $V = \pi r^2 h$ at $V = 20\pi$, $r = 2$; $h = 5$

$$\frac{dV}{dt} = 2\pi r h \frac{dr}{dt} + \pi r^2 \frac{dh}{dt}$$

$$\Rightarrow \frac{4\pi}{5} = 2\pi(2)(5)\left(\frac{2}{1000}\right) + \pi(2)^2 \cdot \frac{dh}{dt}$$

$$\Rightarrow \frac{dh}{dt} + \frac{1}{100} = \frac{1}{5}$$

$$\Rightarrow \frac{dh}{dt} = \frac{19}{100} = 0.19 \ \textit{ft}/\text{min}.$$

21.

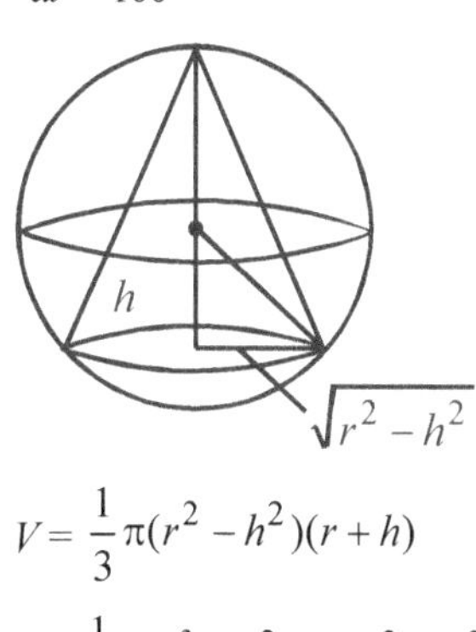

$$V = \frac{1}{3}\pi(r^2 - h^2)(r + h)$$

$$= \frac{1}{3}\pi(r^3 + r^2 h - rh^2 - h^3)$$

$$\frac{dV}{dh} = \frac{1}{3}\pi(r^2 - 2hr - 3h^2) = 0$$

$$\Rightarrow 3h^2 + 2hr - r^2 = 0$$

$$\Rightarrow (3h - r)(h + r) = 0$$

$$\Rightarrow h = \frac{r}{3}, -r$$

$$\Rightarrow h = \frac{r}{3};$$

$$r_c = \sqrt{r^2 - \frac{r^2}{9}} = \frac{2\sqrt{2}}{3}r$$

$$\therefore \ \text{radius} = \frac{2\sqrt{2}}{3}r \ \text{ and}$$

$$\text{height} = r + \frac{r}{3} = \frac{4r}{3}$$

22. $(x - a)(x - c) + 2(x - b)(x - d) = 0$
$$a < b < c < d$$

$$\begin{array}{ccccc} + & + & - & - & + \end{array}$$

$$\begin{array}{ccccc} a & & b & & c & & d \end{array}$$

fA. (+)ve fB. ($-$)ve $\qquad\qquad a < \alpha < b$

fC. ($-$)ve fD. ($-$)ve $\qquad\qquad c < \beta < d$

23. $f(x) = \dfrac{\ln \ln x}{\ln x}$

$$\Rightarrow f'(x) = \dfrac{\dfrac{1}{x} - \dfrac{1}{x}(\ln \ln x)}{(\ln x)^2}$$

$$\Rightarrow f'(e) = \dfrac{1}{e}$$

24. $I_n = \displaystyle\sum_{n=1}^{\infty} \dfrac{(n-1)}{(n+p)}$

$$u_n = \dfrac{n-1}{n+p}$$

$$\lim_{n\to\infty} u_n = \lim_{n\to\infty} \dfrac{n-1}{n+p}$$

$$= \lim_{n\to\infty} \dfrac{1 - \dfrac{1}{n}}{1 + \dfrac{p}{n}} = 1 \ne 0$$

So, the series is divergent because for a series to be convergent it is necessary that $\lim\limits_{n\to\infty} u_n = 0$.

25.
$$I = \int_0^{2a} \dfrac{f(x)}{f(x) + f(2a-x)}\, dx$$

$$= \int_0^{2a} \dfrac{f(2a-x)}{f(2a-x) + f(x)}\, dx$$

$$2I = \int_0^{2a} 1\, dx = x\Big|_0^{2a} = 2a$$

$$\Rightarrow \qquad I = a$$

26. A. Let LS′L′ is one latus rectum of ellipse whose co-ordinates of ends L and L′ are $\left(ae\ \dfrac{b}{a}\right)$

and $\left(ae\ \dfrac{b}{a}\right)$ respectively.

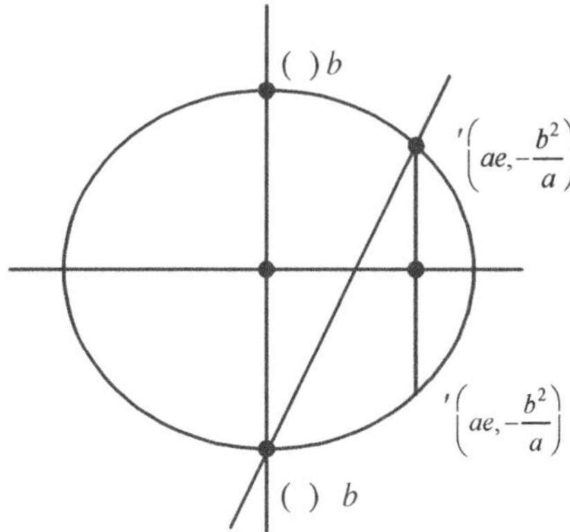

$$\therefore \qquad\qquad\qquad\qquad i.$$

$$e\ \left(ae\ \dfrac{b}{a}\right)$$

$$\dfrac{x\ ae}{\left(\dfrac{ae}{a}\right)} = \dfrac{y\ \left(\dfrac{b}{a}\right)}{\left[\left(\dfrac{b}{a}\right)\ b\right]}$$

$$\dfrac{a(x\ ae)}{e} = (ay\ b)$$

$$ax\ aey\ e(a\ b\ )\qquad\qquad 0$$

$$()\qquad\qquad\qquad '(\ -b)$$

$$a\quad ae(\ b)\ e(a\ b\ )$$
$$abe\ ea\ eb$$
$$a\ ab\ b\qquad\qquad 0$$

$$a\quad a\,a\ \sqrt{(\ e\ }\quad a(\ e\ )$$

$$\because b\ = a(\ )e$$

$$a\ e = a\ \sqrt{(\ e\ )}$$

$$e\ = \sqrt{(\ e\ )}$$

$$e\qquad e$$
$$e\quad e$$

B. The normal at a point (x', y', z') of the paraboloid

$$\dfrac{x}{a} + \dfrac{y}{b} = 2z \text{ is given by}$$

$$\frac{(x - x')}{(x'\ a)} \quad \frac{(y - y')}{(y'\ b)} \quad \frac{(z - z')}{-}$$

$$(\alpha\ \beta\ \gamma)$$

$$\frac{(\alpha - x')}{(x'\ a)} \quad \frac{(\beta - y')}{(y'\ b)} \quad \frac{(\gamma - z')}{-} \quad \lambda()$$

$$x'\ \frac{a\ \alpha}{(a + \lambda)} \quad y'\ \frac{b\ \beta}{(b + \lambda)} \quad z'\ \gamma\ \lambda \qquad (\ i)$$
$$l\ m\ n$$

$$\frac{(x - \alpha)}{l} \quad \frac{(y - \beta)}{m} \quad \frac{(z - \gamma)}{n} \qquad (\ ii)$$

$$\frac{l}{(x'\ a)} \quad \frac{m}{(y'\ b)} \quad \frac{n}{-}$$
$$()$$

$$\frac{l}{\alpha(\ a + \lambda)} \quad \frac{m}{\beta(\ b + \lambda)} \quad \frac{n}{-}$$

$$\frac{(a + \lambda)l}{\alpha} \quad \frac{(b + \lambda)m}{\beta} \quad \frac{n}{-}$$

$$a\ \lambda\ \frac{-n\alpha}{-l} \quad b\ \lambda\ \frac{-n\beta}{m}$$

$$a\ b \quad n\left(\frac{\alpha}{l} - \frac{\beta}{m}\right)$$

$$\frac{\alpha}{l} - \frac{\beta}{m} + \frac{(a - b)}{n} \qquad (\ iii)$$
$$l\ m\ n\,()$$
$$()$$

$$\frac{\alpha}{(x\ \alpha} \quad \frac{\beta}{(\ y)\beta} + \frac{(a\ b)}{(z\ y)} =$$

27. A. *C* is the centre of force, *A* the starting point, *P* the position of the particle at any instant, where $\angle AOP = \theta$.

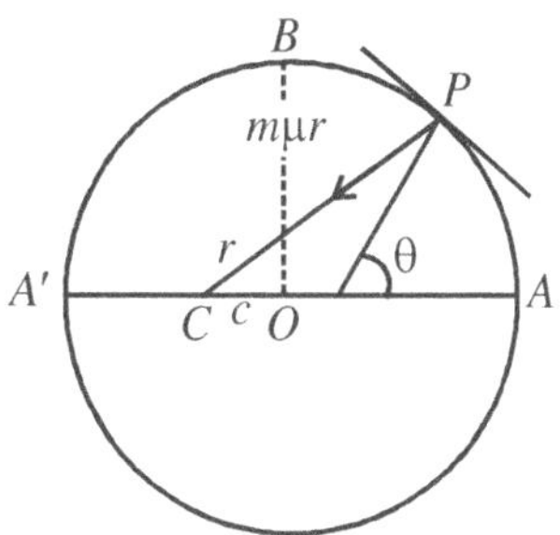

$$-mv = \int_A^P m\mu r\, dr$$

$$i\,e \quad -a\ \theta = \int_{a+c}^r \mu r\, dr = \frac{\mu}{}r\ \Big]_{a+c}^r$$

$$= \frac{\mu}{}\Big[r(\ a + c\ )\Big]$$

$$= \frac{\mu}{}\Big[a + c \quad a\ c \quad \theta \quad a+c\ \Big]$$

$$= \mu ac \quad \theta$$

$$\therefore\ \theta = \sqrt{\frac{\mu c}{a}} \quad \theta$$
$$B\quad A'$$

$$\sqrt{\frac{\mu c}{a}}\,t = \int_\pi^\pi \frac{d\theta}{\theta} = \quad \theta\ \Big]_\pi^\pi$$

$$\frac{\pi}{\pi} = \quad \frac{\pi}{} = \quad \frac{\pi}{\pi}$$

$$= \quad \frac{\pi}{\pi} = \quad \frac{+\ \pi}{\pi} = \quad \frac{\sqrt{+}}{\sqrt{}}$$

$$= \quad \left(\sqrt{\ }+\right) = \quad \left(\sqrt{\ }+\right)$$

$$t = \sqrt{\frac{a}{\mu c}} \quad \left(\sqrt{\ }+\right)$$

28. $$\vec{F} = (\ x\ -)z\,i - xy\,j - xk$$

$$\nabla\ \vec{F} = \left(i\frac{\partial}{\partial x} + j\frac{\partial}{\partial y} + k\frac{\partial}{\partial z}\right)\Big[(\ x\ )z\,i - xy\,j - xk\Big]$$

$$=\frac{\partial}{\partial x}(x-)z+\frac{\partial}{\partial y}(-)xy+\left(\frac{\partial}{\partial z}\right)-x=x-x=x$$

$$\therefore \iiint_V \vec{\nabla}\,\vec{F}\,dV=\iiint_V x\,dx\,dy\,dz$$

$$\left[\because dV=dx\,dy\,dz\right]$$

$$=\int_{x=}\int_{y=}^{-x}\int_{z=}^{-x-y} x\,dx\,dy\,dz$$

$$\therefore \iiint_V \vec{\nabla}\,\vec{F}\,dV=\int_{x=}\int_{y=}^{-x}x\,[z]_{z=}^{-x-y}\,dx\,dy$$

$$=\int_{x=}\int_{y=}^{-x}(x-x)-y\,dx\,dy$$

$$\int_{x=}\left[xy-xy-xy\right]_{y=}^{-x}dx$$

$$=\int\left[(x-)x+(x)-(x-)x-x\right]dx$$

$$=\int\left[x-x+x\right]dx$$

$$=\left[-x--x+x\right]=\left[--+\right]=-$$

Second part,

$$\vec{\nabla}\times\vec{F}=\begin{vmatrix} i & j & k \\ \dfrac{\partial}{\partial x} & \dfrac{\partial}{\partial y} & \dfrac{\partial}{\partial z} \\ x-z & -xy & -x \end{vmatrix}$$

$$=\left[\frac{\partial}{\partial y}(-x)-\frac{\partial}{\partial z}(-xy)\right]i$$

$$-\left[\frac{\partial}{\partial x}(-x)-\frac{\partial}{\partial z}(x+z)\right]j$$

$$+\left[\frac{\partial}{\partial x}(-xy)-\frac{\partial}{\partial y}(x+z)\right]k$$

$$=i(-)+(j+)-y\,k=j-yk$$

$$\therefore \iiint_V \vec{\nabla}\times\vec{F}\,dV=\iiint_V (j-yk)\,dx\,dy\,dz$$

$$=\int_{x=}\int_{y=}^{-x}\int_{z=}^{-x-y}(j-yk)\,dx\,dy\,dz$$

$$=\int_{x=}\int_{y=}^{-x}(j-yk)(-x)-y\,dx\,dy$$

$$=\int_{x=}\left[j(y-xy-y)-k\left(y-xy--y\right)_{y=}^{-x}\right]dx$$

$$=\int_{x=}\left[\begin{array}{c}j(-)(-x-)+(-)(-x)\\ \{-x-(+)x\}\end{array}\right]dx$$

$$=\int\left[(-)j-(+)x\right]dx$$

$$=\int\left[(x-)j+(x-)k\right]dx$$

$$=\left[\frac{(x-)}{}\right]j+\left[\frac{(-x)-}{}\right]k$$

$$=-j--k=-(j-k)$$

29. A. We have

$$f(x)=x^m=\frac{n\,x\,x^m}{\sin^n x}=\left(\frac{x}{\sin x}\right)^n x^{m-n}$$

$$f(x)=\left(\frac{x}{\sin x}\right)^n \frac{1}{x^{n-m}}$$

$$\therefore \lim_{x\to 0^+} f(x) \begin{cases} 1.\ \ 0=0 & \text{if } n-m<0,\\ 1.\ \ 1=1 & \text{if } n-m=0,\\ \infty & \text{if } n-m>0.\end{cases}$$

$$n-m\le 0$$

$$n-m>0 \ i.e.,\ n>m.$$

$$g(x)=\frac{1}{x^{n-m}}(n-m).$$

$$\lim_{x\to 0^+}\frac{f(x)}{g(x)}=\lim_{x\to 0^+}\left(\frac{x}{\sin x}\right)^n=1.$$

$$\int_0^{\pi/2} g(x)dx \text{ and } \int_0^{\pi/2} g(x)dx$$

$$\int_0^{\pi/2} g(x)dx = \int_0^{\pi/2} \frac{dx}{x^{n-m}} \qquad n$$

m

$n \quad m$

$n \quad m$

B. Consider a point P in the fluid having cylindrical coordinates (r, θ, z).

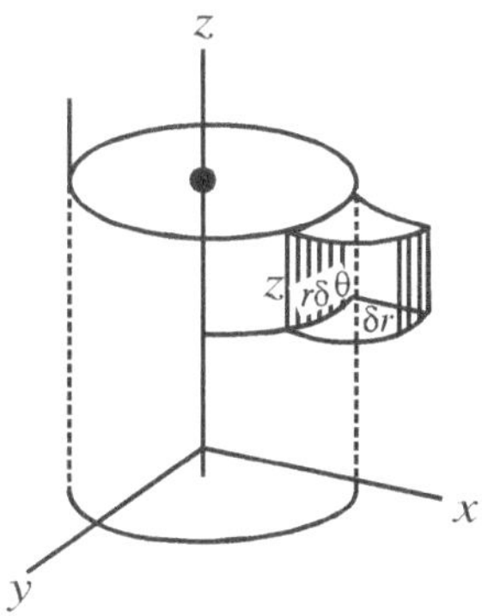

$$PA = r\,\delta\theta \quad PB = \delta r \qquad PC = \delta z$$

0

PB

PA

$$= -r\,\delta\theta\,\frac{\partial}{r\partial\theta}(\rho\upsilon\;\delta r\;\delta z)$$

PC

$$= -\delta z\,\frac{\partial}{\partial z}\,\rho\upsilon_z\,\delta r\,r\,\delta\theta$$

PB

$$= \rho r\,\delta\theta\;\delta r\;\delta z$$

$$= \frac{\partial}{\partial t}\,\rho r\,\delta\theta\,\delta r\,\delta z = r\,\delta\theta\,\delta r\,\delta z\,\frac{\partial\rho}{\partial t}$$

$\therefore$

$$(r\,\delta\theta\,\delta r\,\delta z)\frac{\partial\rho}{\partial t} = -r\delta\theta\,\frac{\partial}{r\,\partial\theta}\,\rho\upsilon\;\delta r\,\delta z$$

$$-\delta z\,\frac{\partial}{\partial z}\,\rho\upsilon_z\,\delta r\,r\,\delta\theta$$

i.e. $\dfrac{\partial\rho}{\partial t} + \dfrac{1}{r}\dfrac{\partial}{\partial\theta}(\rho\upsilon) + \dfrac{\partial}{\partial z}(\rho\upsilon_z) =$

TEST PAPER - 3

PART - A

1. The radius of convergence of the power series

$$\sum_{n=}^{\infty} \frac{n}{n^n} x^n \text{ is}$$

   x x

   x e

2. The sum to infinity of the series

   $$\frac{2}{1.2.3} + \frac{3}{3.4.5} + \frac{4}{5.6.7} + . \;\ldots.. \text{ is equal to}$$

   A. $\sqrt{\pi}$ B. $\log 2 - \dfrac{1}{6}$

   C. $e - \dfrac{1}{2}$ D. None of the above

3. The point on $y^2 = 4ax$ nearest to the focus has its abscissa
   A. $x = -a$ B. $x = a$
   C. $x = 0$ D. None of these

4. Infimum and supremum of the following set of real numbers S = {x : ($x - a$) ($x - b$) ($x - c$) ($x - d$) < 0} where $a < b < c < d$ are
   A. $-\infty, +\infty$ B. $-\infty, + a$
   C. $d, +\infty$ D. None of the above

5. The statements 1, 2 and 3 marked below are associated with $f(x) = x^3 - 3x^2 - 9x - 2$
   (i) $f(x)$ x x
   (ii) $f(x)$ x x
   (iii) $f(x)$ x x

   (i)
   (i) (iii)

6. Let $h(x) = 1 + x,$

   $g(x) = \sqrt{} x \;\; f(x) = x \, (k) x = \sqrt{} x$

Two lists 1 and 2 are given below with respect to these functions :

List 1	List 2
(Points of differentiability)	*(Function)*
(i)	
(ii)	
(iii)	
(iv)	

Identify the correct matching of the list 1 with list 2.

   i)   (ii)   (iii)   (iv)

7. Let G be a group and let A, B be subgroups of G. Which one of the following statements is false?

   A B
   AB BA
   A B
   $\cap$ e e G
       ab ba a A b B
   A B B
           G A
     G

8. For a given matrix A of order n, identify the false statement

                   $p(x)$
   $p() \neq$ $p(1)$
       A
   $f()$
   $f(1)$
     A n

9. Suppose $\phi\,(.)$ is a differentiable function. If $\phi(x + y) = \phi(x)\,\phi(y)$ for all x, y and $\phi(5) = 2$, $\phi'(0) = 3$ then $\phi'(5)$ is
A. 6
B. 3
C. 0
D. None of the above

10. For $n \geq 2$, let $u_n = a^{-\left(1 + \frac{1}{2} + \frac{1}{3} - + \frac{1}{n-1}\right)}$ where a is a positive number. Then the series $\displaystyle\sum_{n=2}^{\infty} u_n$
A. diverges
B. converges for $a < 1$ and diverges for $a > 1$
C. converges for $a > e$ and diverges for $a < e$
D. None of the above

11. Identify the false statement : A finite group G is abelian if
A. $(ab)^2 = a^2\,b^2$ for all a, b in G
B. the order of G is less than or equal to 4
C. the order of G is 11
D. None of the above

12. Let A be the 4×4 real matrix

$$A = \begin{bmatrix} & & & \\ & & & \\ & & & \\ & & & \end{bmatrix}$$

Then the characteristic polynomial for A is
A. $x^2\,(x - 1)^2$
B. $(x - 1)^2\,(x + 1)^2$
C. $x^2\,(x + 1)^2$
D. None of the above

13. The sum of the series :

$$1 + \frac{5}{3} + \frac{5}{3}\cdot\frac{7}{6} + \frac{5}{3}\cdot\frac{7}{6}\cdot\frac{9}{9} + \dots \text{ is equal to}$$

A. $3\sqrt{2}$
C. $9\sqrt{3}$
$5\sqrt{7}$

14. Let A be a square matrix. Among the following statements, identify the one :

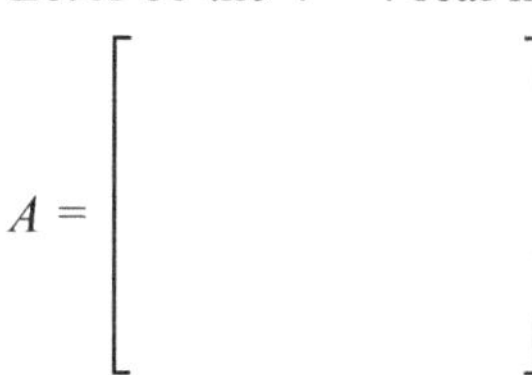

15. The solution of the differential equation

$$(x - y)\,\frac{dy}{dx} = (x + y) \text{ is equal to}$$

A. $\sin^{-1}\left(\dfrac{y}{x}\right) = \log_e\left(C\sqrt{x^2 + y^2}\right)$

B. $\cos^{-1}\left(\dfrac{y}{x}\right) = \log_e\left(C\sqrt{x^2 + y^2}\right)$

C. $\tan^{-1}\left(\dfrac{y}{x}\right) = \log_e\left(C\sqrt{x^2 + y^2}\right)$

D. None of the above
where C is a constant.

PART - B

16. A. Let G be a group and N and M be two normal subgroups of G such that $(|N|, |M|) = 1$, where $|N|.,\ |M|$ are the orders of N and M respectively. Prove that G is abelian if G/N and G/M are both abelian.
   B. Determine the range of values of a for which the equation $3x^4 - 8x^3 - 6x^2 + 24x + a = 0$ has four real unequal roots.

17. Show that

$$x \qquad \frac{1+x}{1-x} < 2x + \frac{2}{3}$$
$$\frac{x^3}{1-x^2} \qquad x$$

$$e < \left(+ \frac{}{n}\right)^{n+} \quad < e\ e^{\overline{n(n+\ )}}$$
$$n$$

18. A. Find the two tangent planes to the sphere $(x - 1)^2 + (y + 4)^2 + (z - 2)^2 = 9$ that are perpendicular to the vector $[\,1, -5, 2\,]$?
   B. Let $x^2 + y^2 + z^2 - 2xyz - 1 = 0$. Show that

$$\frac{dx}{\sqrt{1 - x^2}} + \frac{dy}{\sqrt{1 - y^2}} + \frac{dz}{\sqrt{1 - z^2}} = 0$$

19. Use the solution to $y' + P(x)\,y = Q(x)$ to show $y'' + (P^1 - P^2)\,y = Q' - PQ$.

20. Solve the differential equation

$$x^3 \frac{d^3 y}{dx^3} - 4x^2 \frac{d^2 y}{dx^2} + 8x \frac{dy}{dx} - 8y = 4 \ \ln x,$$

for $x > 0$.

21. A. Show that $\{(1, 1), (-1, 1)\}$ is basis for R^2 over R.

B. Find the extreme points of the function

$$f(x_1 x_2) = x + x + x + x +$$

22. A. Find the dimensions of a cylindrical tin (with top and bottom) made up of sheet metal to maximize its volume such that the total surface area is equal to $A_0 = 24\pi$.

B. Determine the curve such that the part of the tangent line intercepted between the co-ordinate axes is bisected at the point of tangency.

23. A. A particle starts at rest and ends at rest after traversing one foot is one second along a straight. Assuming same magnitude of acceleration and deceleration. Show that it is equal to 4ft/sec².

B. Given $\begin{vmatrix} y & F(x) & G(x) \\ y' & F'(x) & G'(x) \\ y'' & F''(x) & G''(x) \end{vmatrix} = 0,$

Find the general solution.

24. Given that $a_r > 0$, for all $i = 1, 2 \ .... $ and Σa_i is divergent. Find the sum, if possible, of the infinite series,

$$\frac{a}{(+a)} + \frac{a}{(+a)(+a)} + \frac{a}{(+a)(+a)(+a)} + \ .$$

25. A. A solid of revolution is obtained by rotating a square about an axis lying in its plane and passing through one of its corners. What is the maximum volume of the solid?

B. Find the point within a given triangle for which sum of square of its distances from vertices of triangle is least.

26. A particle slides down the smooth curve $y = a \sinh \dfrac{x}{a}$ the axis of x being horizontal and the axis of y downwards, starting from rest at the point where the tangent is inclined at α to the horizon; show that it will leave the curve when it has fallen through a vertical distance $a \sec \alpha$.

27.

$$\frac{x}{a} + \frac{y}{b} + \frac{z}{c} =$$

$$(\qquad \pi d\ )$$

28. $u \quad v$

$$\left(e^{\,y} + e^{-\,y} - \qquad x \right)$$

$$f(z) \quad u \quad iv$$

29. A.

$$\begin{matrix} & ax & by & z \\ & u \equiv lx & my \\ nz \quad p & u' \equiv l'x & m'y & n'z \quad p \end{matrix}$$

$$u\left(\frac{l'}{a} + \frac{m'}{b} + n'p'\right) \quad uu'\left(\frac{ll'}{a} + \frac{mm'}{b} + np' + n'p\right)$$

$$+ u'\left(\frac{l}{a} + \frac{m}{b} + np\right) =$$

B.

$$\frac{x}{a} + \frac{y}{b} + \frac{z}{c}$$

$$l \quad my \quad nz \qquad \frac{\pi abc}{p} \qquad p$$

ANSWERS

1	2	3	4	5	6	7	8	9	10
11	12	13	14	15					

SOME SELECTED EXPLANATORY ANSWERS

PART - A

1.
$$\left| \lim_{n \to p} \frac{U_{n+1}}{U_n} \right| = \left| \lim_{n \to \infty} \frac{(n+1)\,(n)^n}{(n+1)^{n+1}}\, x \right|$$

$$= \left| \lim_{n \to \infty} \frac{x}{\left(1 + \dfrac{1}{n}\right)^n} \right| = \left| \frac{x}{e} \right| < 1$$

$\Rightarrow |x| < e \Rightarrow -e < x < e$

At $x = -e$ $e^n \Sigma(-1)^n\, n!/n^n$ is divergent

At $x = e$ $\Sigma n!/n^n\, e^n$ is divergent

So $|x| < e$

2. The given series is

$$\sum \frac{(n+1)}{(2n-1)\,2n\,(2n+1)}$$

$$= \sum \frac{2n+1-n}{(2n-1)\,2n\,(2n+1)}$$

$$= \sum \frac{1}{(2n-1)\,(2n)} - \frac{1}{2} \sum \frac{1}{(2n-1)\,(2n+1)}$$

$$= \sum \frac{1}{2n(2n-1)} - \frac{1}{2} \sum \frac{1}{(2n-1)\,(2n+1)}$$

$$= \sum \left(\frac{}{(\ n-\ )} - \frac{}{n} \right) - - \left(\sum \frac{}{n-} - \frac{}{n+} \right)$$

$$= \left(1 - \frac{1}{2} + \frac{1}{3} - \frac{1}{4} + \ldots \right) - - \left(\ - - + - - - + \ \right)$$

$$= \left(\log 2 - \frac{1}{4} \right)$$

3. Any point on parabola $y^2 = 4ax$ is $(at^2,\ 2at)$

Its distance from the focus is

$$= \sqrt{\left(a - at^2\right)^2 + 4a^2 t^2}$$
$$= a(1 + t^2)$$

Now this is minimum for $t = 0$

i.e. abscissa of minimum distance $x = at^2 = 0$
$$x = 0$$

4. The solution set of S is

$$\overset{+\quad\ -\quad\ +\quad\ -\quad\ +}{\underset{a\quad\ b\quad\ c\quad\ d}{\rule{6cm}{0.4pt}}}$$

$$W = \left\{ (a, b) \cup (c, d) \right\}$$

$\therefore$ Infimum of W $= a$

  Supremum of W $= d$.

5. $\therefore \qquad f(x) = x^3 - 3x^2 - 9x - 2$

$\qquad\qquad f'(x) = 3x^2 - 6x - 9$

$\Rightarrow x^2 - 2x - 3 = 0$

$\Rightarrow (x - 3)\,(x + 1) = 0$

$\Rightarrow x = -1,\ 3$

$$\overset{\textstyle +ve \qquad\qquad -ve \qquad\qquad +ve}{\longleftarrow\!\!\rule{10cm}{0.4pt}\!\!\longrightarrow}$$

i.e. $f(x)$ is monotinic increasing

& $f(x)$ is monotonic decreasing for $x \in (-1,\ 3)$

6. $f(x) = 1 - x;\quad k(x) = \sqrt{1 - x}\ ;\ g = \sqrt{1 + x}\ ;$

$\qquad h = 1 + x$

1. $kf(x) = \sqrt{x} \qquad\qquad\qquad x > 0\ (iv)$

2. $gh = \sqrt{2+x}$ $x > -2$ (iii)

3. $gf = \sqrt{2-x}$ $x < 2$ (ii)

4. $hg = 1 + \sqrt{1+x}$ $x > -1$ (i)

9. $\phi(x+y) = \phi(x)\,\phi(y)$

$\Rightarrow \phi(5+0) = \phi(5)\,\phi(0)$

$\Rightarrow \phi(5)\,[\phi(0) - 1] = 0$

$\Rightarrow \qquad \phi(0) = 1$ $[\because \phi(5) \neq 0]$

Now, $\phi'(5) = \lim\limits_{h \to 0} \dfrac{\phi(5+h) - \phi(5)}{h}$

$\qquad\qquad = \lim\limits_{h \to} \dfrac{\phi(\ )\phi(h) - \phi(\ )}{h}$

$\qquad\qquad = \phi(5)\,\phi'(0) = 2.3 = 6$

10. $\because u_n = a^{-\left(1 + \frac{1}{2} + \dots \frac{1}{n-1}\right)}$

$\Rightarrow \quad u_{n+1} = a^{-\left(1 + \frac{1}{2} + \dots \frac{1}{n}\right)}$

$\Rightarrow \quad \dfrac{u_n}{u_{n+1}} = a^{\frac{1}{n}}$

By Logarithmic test, series converges if

$$\lim\limits_{n \to \infty} n\left(\log \dfrac{u_n}{u_{n+1}} \right) > 1$$

$\Rightarrow a > 1$ and diverges $a < 1$

Also $a = 1$ series diverges

i.e. Σu_n convergent if $a > 1$

$\qquad\qquad\quad$ divergent if $a \leq 1$.

12. The characteristic polynomial is

$\quad |A - xI| = 0$

$\Rightarrow \quad = \begin{vmatrix} 1-x & 1 & 0 & 0 \\ -1 & -1-x & 0 & 0 \\ -2 & -2 & 2-x & 1 \\ 1 & 1 & -1 & -x \end{vmatrix} = 0$

$\quad (x-1)^2 \, [x^2 - 1 + 1] = 0$

$\Rightarrow x^2 \, (x-1)^2 = 0$.

13. Given $S = 1 + \dfrac{5}{3} + \dfrac{5}{3}\cdot\dfrac{7}{6} + \dfrac{5}{3}\cdot\dfrac{7}{6}\cdot\dfrac{9}{9}$

   We know for $n < 0$

$$(1+x)^n = 1 + nx + \dfrac{n(n-1)}{2!}x^2 + \dots.$$

$\qquad\qquad$ [Binomial expansion]

Comparing we get, $rx = \dfrac{5}{3}$

$\dfrac{nx.(n-1)x}{2} = \dfrac{5}{3}\cdot\dfrac{7}{6} \Rightarrow nx - x = \dfrac{7}{3}$

$\Rightarrow \qquad x = -\dfrac{2}{3} \quad \therefore \ n = -\dfrac{5}{2}$

$\therefore \qquad S = \left(1 - \dfrac{2}{3}\right)^{-\frac{5}{2}} = 3^{\frac{5}{2}} = 9\sqrt{3}\ .$

15. $\because \qquad \dfrac{dy}{dx} = \dfrac{x+y}{x-y}$ ...(i)

put $y = vx$

then (i) reduces to

$\Rightarrow v + x\dfrac{dv}{dx} = \dfrac{1+v}{1-v}$

$\Rightarrow \dfrac{-v}{+v}\,dv = \dfrac{dx}{x}$

$\Rightarrow \quad \ ^{-}v - \left(\quad \right) + v \quad = \ln x + \ln c$

$\Rightarrow \tan^{-1}\dfrac{y}{x} = \ln c\,\sqrt{x^2 + y^2}\ .$

$$\boxed{\textbf{PART - B}}$$

16. **A.** $\because \dfrac{G}{N}$ and $\dfrac{G}{M}$ are abelian.

Also, $\dfrac{G}{N} = \{Na \mid a \in G\};$

$\qquad\qquad \dfrac{G}{M} = \{Ma \mid a \in G\}$

Now $\dfrac{G}{N}$ is abelian,

$\Rightarrow Na.Nb = Nb.Na \quad \forall\ a, b \in G$

$\Rightarrow Nab = Nba.$ $[\because N$ is Normal$]$

$\Rightarrow (ab)\,(ba)^{-1} \in N$

$\Rightarrow aba^{-1}b^{-1} \in N.$

Similarly $\dfrac{G}{M}$ is abelian $\Rightarrow aba^{-1}b^{-1} \in M$

$\Rightarrow aba^{-1}b^{-1} \in M \cap N.$

However, $(|M|\,|N|) = 1$

$\Rightarrow \qquad aba^{-1} = e$

$\Rightarrow \qquad\qquad ab = ba \;\; \nabla\; a,\, b \in G$

$i.e.$ G is abelian.

B. $-13 < a < -8$

$\qquad f(x) = 3x^4 - 8x^3 - 6x^2 + 24\,x + a = 0$

$\qquad f'(x) = 12\,(x^3 - 2x^2 - x + 2) = 0$

$\Rightarrow 12\,(x-2)\,(x-1)\,(x+1)$

$\qquad f'(x) = 0 \underset{\;-1\qquad 1\qquad 2}{\overline{\quad-\quad|\quad+\quad|\quad-\quad|\quad+\quad}}$

$\Rightarrow f(-1) < 0;$

$\qquad f(1) > 0;\; f(2) < 0$

17. **A.** Let $S = \left[\dfrac{+\,x}{-x}\right] = \log(1+x) - \log(1-x)$

$\Rightarrow S = \left[\,x - \dfrac{x}{\;} + \dfrac{x}{\;} - \;\right] - \left[\,-x - \dfrac{x}{\;} - \dfrac{x}{\;} - \;\right]$

$\Rightarrow S = 2\left[\,x + \dfrac{x^3}{3} + \dfrac{x^5}{5} + ...\right]$

$\therefore\; S = 2x + \dfrac{2}{3}x^3\left(1 + \dfrac{3}{5}x^2 + \dfrac{3}{7}x^4 + ...\right)$

$\Rightarrow 2x < S < 2x + \dfrac{2}{3}x^3\left(1 + x^2 + x^4 + ...\right)$

$\Rightarrow 2x < S < 2x + \dfrac{2}{3}\dfrac{x^3}{1-x^2}.$

B. $e < \left(\;+\dfrac{}{n}\right)^{n+-} < e\; e^{\overline{\;n(n+\;)\;}}$

Taking log of both sides w.r.t. base e

$1 < \left(n + -\right)\left(\;+\dfrac{}{n}\right) < \;+\dfrac{}{n(n+\;)}$

Let $\qquad S = \left(n + -\right).$

---

18. **A.** Equation of plane perpendicular to $(1, -5, 2)$ vector is given by

$\qquad x - 5y + 2z + d = 0$

Now if it is a tangent plane to given sphere then

$$\dfrac{\left|\;+\quad+\;+d\right|}{\sqrt{\;}} = 3$$

$\Rightarrow \quad |d + 30| = 3\sqrt{30}$

$\Rightarrow \qquad\qquad d = -\quad \pm\; \sqrt{\;}$

$i.e.$ two tangent planes are $x - 5y + 2z - 30 \pm 3\sqrt{30} = 0.$

B. $\because\; x^2 + y^2 + z^2 - 2xyz - 1 = 0 \qquad\qquad ...(i)$

$\Rightarrow x^2 - 2xyz + y^2z^2 = y^2z^2 + 1 - y^2 - z^2$

$\Rightarrow (x - yz)^2 = (1 - y^2)\,(1 - z^2)$

$\Rightarrow (x - yz) = \sqrt{\left(1 - y^2\right)\left(1 - z^2\right)}$

Similarly $(y - zx) = \sqrt{\left(1 - x^2\right)\left(1 - z^2\right)}$

and $(z - xy) = \sqrt{\left(1 - x^2\right)\left(1 - y^2\right)}$

Now differentiating (i) we get

$\qquad (x - yz)\,dx + (y - zx)\,dy + (z - xy)\,dz = 0$

Using above relation & then divided by

$\sqrt{\left(1 - x^2\right)\left(1 - y^2\right)\left(1 - z^2\right)}$ we get

$$\dfrac{dx}{\sqrt{1 - x^2}} + \dfrac{dy}{\sqrt{1 - y^2}} + \dfrac{dz}{\sqrt{1 - z^2}} = 0.$$

19. $\because\quad y' + Py = Q$

$\Rightarrow \qquad\qquad y' = Q - Py$

$\Rightarrow \qquad\qquad y'' = Q' - Py' - P'y$

$\qquad\qquad\qquad = Q' - P(Q - Py) - P'y$

$\qquad\qquad\qquad = Q' + P^2y - P'y - PQ$

Now $\qquad y'' = (P' - P^2)y$

$\qquad = Q' + P^2y - P'y - PQ + (P' - P^2)y$

$\qquad = Q' - PQ.$

20. $\because \qquad\qquad x > 0 \quad$ let $x = e^z$

Then $\qquad x\dfrac{d}{dx} \equiv \dfrac{d}{dz} \quad x\mathrm{D} \equiv \mathrm{D}_1$

Similarly $x^2 D^2 = D_1 (D_1 - 1)$

$$x^3 D^3 = D_1(D_1 - 1)(D_1 - 2)$$

Hence differential equation becomes

$$= [D_1(D_1 - 1)(D_1 - 2) - 4D_1(D_1 - 1)$$
$$+ 8D_1 - 8]y = 4z$$

$$\Rightarrow \left[D_1^3 - 3D_1^2 + 2D_1 - 4D_1^2 + 4D_1 + 8D_1 - 8 \right] y = 4z$$

$$\Rightarrow (D_1 - 1)\left(D_1^2 - 6D_1 + 8 \right) y = 4z$$

$$\Rightarrow (D_1 - 1)(D_1 - 2)(D_1 - 4) = 4z$$

C.F. is $y = C_1 e^z + c_2 e^{2z} + c_3 e^{4z}$

Particulae integral is $\dfrac{1}{\left(D_1^3 - 7D_1^2 + 4D_1 - 8 \right)} 4z$

$$= -\frac{1}{8}\left(1 - \frac{7}{4}D_1 + \frac{8}{7}D_1^2 - \frac{D_1^3}{8} \right)^{-1} 4z$$

$$= -\frac{1}{8}\left[1 - \frac{7}{4}D_1 - \frac{8}{7}D_1^2 ..... \right] 4z$$

$$= -\frac{1}{8}[4z + 7] = -\frac{z}{2} - \frac{7}{8}$$

Hence general solution is

$$y = C_1 e^z + c_2 e^{2z} + c_3 e^{4z} - \frac{z}{2} - \frac{7}{8}$$

$$= c_1.x + c_2 x^2 + c_3 x^4 - \frac{\ln x}{2} - \frac{7}{8}.$$

21. A. To show $\{(1, 1), (-1, 1)\}$ is a basis.
It is sufficient to show that they are linear independent.
If possible let $\alpha(1, 1) + \beta(-1, 1) = (0, 0)$
$\Rightarrow (\alpha - \beta, \alpha + \beta) = (0, 0)$
$\Rightarrow \qquad \alpha - \beta = 0, \ \alpha + \beta = 0$
$\Rightarrow \qquad \alpha = 0, \ \beta = 0$
Hence both are L.I. $\Rightarrow$ They form a basis of $\mathbb{R}^2$.

B. $f(x_1, x_2) = x_1^3 + x_2^3 + 2x_1^2 + 4x_2^2 + 6$

$$\frac{\partial f}{\partial x_1} = 3x_1^2 + 4x_1 = 0 \quad \Rightarrow \quad x_1 = 0, -\frac{4}{3} \ ;$$

$$\frac{\partial f}{\partial x_2} = 3x_2^2 + 8x_2 = 0 \quad \Rightarrow \quad x_2 = 0, -\frac{8}{3}$$

Hence stationary points are

$$(0,0)\left(0, -\frac{8}{3} \right), \left(-\frac{4}{3}, 0 \right), \left(-\frac{4}{3}, -\frac{8}{3} \right)$$

Now, $\dfrac{\partial^2 f}{\partial x_1^{\,2}} = 6x_1 + 4; \quad \dfrac{\partial^2 f}{\partial x_2^{\,2}} = 6x_2 + 8;$

& $\dfrac{\partial^2 f}{\partial x_1 \partial x_2} = 0$

Now for $(0,0)$ & $\left(\dfrac{-4}{3}, \dfrac{-8}{3} \right)$;

$$\left(\frac{\partial f}{\partial x} \right)\left(\frac{\partial f}{\partial x} \right) \ \left(\frac{\partial f}{\partial x \ \partial x} \right) > 0$$

$\Rightarrow (0, 0)$ & $\left(\dfrac{-4}{3}, \dfrac{-8}{3} \right)$ are extreme points.

Also for $\left(\ - \ \right)$ & $\left(- \ \right)$;

$$\left(\frac{\partial f}{\partial x} \right)\left(\frac{\partial f}{\partial x} \right) \ \left(\frac{\partial f}{\partial x \ \partial x} \right) > 0$$

$\Rightarrow \left(\ - \ \right), \left(- \ \right)$ are saddle points.

Further $\dfrac{\partial^2 f}{\partial x_1^2} > 0$ at $(0, 0)$

$\Rightarrow f(0, 0)$ is minimum

$$\frac{\partial^2 f}{\partial x_1^2} < 0 \ \text{ at } \left(-\frac{4}{3}, -\frac{8}{3} \right)$$

$\Rightarrow f\left(-\dfrac{4}{3}, -\dfrac{8}{3} \right)$ is maximum.

22. A. Total surface area $= 2\pi rh + 2\pi r^2 = 24\pi$

$$\Rightarrow \qquad h = \frac{\left(12 - r^2 \right)}{r}$$

Now volume 'V' $= \pi r^2 h$

$$= \pi r^2 \frac{\left(12 - r^2 \right)}{r}$$

$$= \pi(12r - r^3)$$

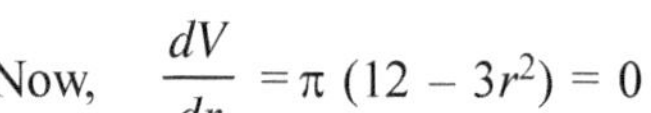

Now, $\dfrac{dV}{dr} = \pi(12 - 3r^2) = 0$

$\Rightarrow \qquad r = 2 \quad \Rightarrow h = 4$

Hence $V^{\text{Max}} = \pi(2)^2 \cdot 4 = 16\pi$

at $\qquad r = 2$ and $h = 4$.

B. Let $P(x, y)$ be any point on curve c,
then equation of tangent AB is bisected at P.
$\Rightarrow$ *i.e.* $\quad$ A $\equiv (2x, 0)$ $\quad$ B $\equiv (0, 2y)$

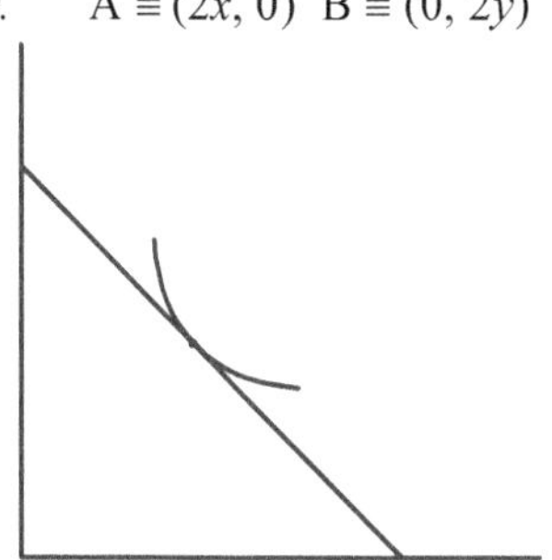

Also, $\dfrac{dy}{dx}\bigg|_{at(x,y)}$ $=$ Slope of AB $= -\dfrac{2y}{2x} = -\dfrac{y}{x}$

$\Rightarrow \qquad \dfrac{dy}{dx} = -\dfrac{y}{x}$ $\quad$ or, $xy = c$ [hyperbola].

23. A. From the V-t graph

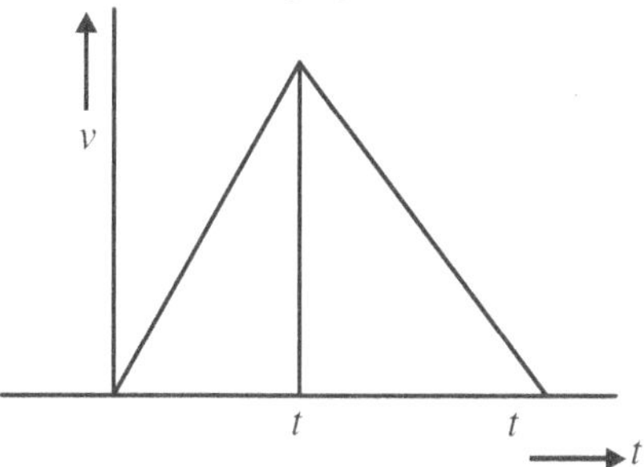

distance covered S $= \dfrac{1}{2}.v.t$

$\Rightarrow \qquad v = 2$

Now by symmetry, acceleration

time = deceleration $\Rightarrow t = \dfrac{1}{2}$

$\because\ v = at\ \Rightarrow\ 2 = a.\dfrac{1}{2}\ \Rightarrow\ a + 4\text{ft/sec}^2.$

B. $\begin{vmatrix} y & F(x) & G(x) \\ y' & F'(x) & G'(x) \\ y'' & F'(x) & G''(x) \end{vmatrix} = 0$

It is a 2nd order linear differential equation.
Also $y = F(x)$ and $y = G(x)$ satisfy above differential equation
Hence by properties
$\qquad y = C_1F(x) + C_2G(x)$ is a general solution.

24. The nth term of the series

$$t_n = \frac{a_n}{(1+a_1)(1+a_2)....(1+a_n)}$$

$$= \frac{(1+a_n)-1}{(1+a_1)(1+a_2)....(1+a_n)}$$

$$= \frac{1}{(1+a_1)(1+a_2)....(1+a_{n-1})}$$

$$- \frac{1}{(1+a_1)(1+a_2)....(1+a_n)}$$

$$\Rightarrow t_n = \frac{1}{(1+a_1)(1+a_2)....(1+a_{n-1})}$$

$$- \frac{1}{(1+a_1)(1+a_2)....(1+a_n)}$$

25. A. By Papu's theorem volume will be maximum if centre of gravity is farthest from the axis of rotation. Hence centre of gravity will be maximum if inclination of sides to the axis is $\pi/4$.

Hence $\quad V^{max} = \sqrt{2}\,\pi\,a^3;$

$\qquad\qquad a =$ side of square.

B. Let $a_i\,x + b_i\,y + c_i = 0$; $i = 1,2,3$ be the sides, so sum of square of $\perp^r$ distances from (x, y) is $\sum (a_i\,x + b_i\,y + c_i)^2 / a_i^2 + b_i^2$

$\dfrac{\partial\Sigma}{\partial x} = \qquad \dfrac{\partial\Sigma}{\partial y} = \quad$ gives the value of (x, y)

26. $\qquad P$

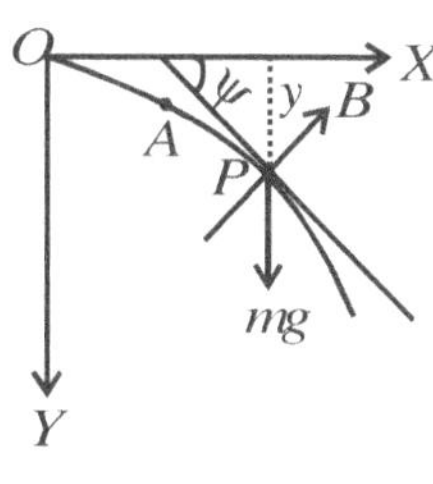

v

energy gives v $\qquad g\,(y\ y\,)$

$$\frac{mv}{\rho} = mg \quad \Psi \quad R$$

$$v = g\rho \quad \Psi.$$

$$R \quad 0$$

$$y \quad a \quad \frac{x}{a}$$

$$\therefore \quad \Psi = \frac{dy}{dx} = \quad \frac{x}{a}$$

$$\frac{d^2 y}{dx^2} = \frac{x}{a} \cdot \frac{x}{a}$$

$$\therefore \quad \rho = \frac{\left(+ \dfrac{x}{a}\right)^-}{\dfrac{x}{a} \cdot \dfrac{x}{a}}$$

$$\therefore \quad \rho \quad \Psi = \frac{\left(+ \dfrac{x}{a}\right)^-}{\dfrac{x}{a} \cdot \dfrac{x}{a}} \times \frac{1}{\left(+ \dfrac{x}{a}\right)^-}$$

$$= \frac{+ \dfrac{x}{a}}{\dfrac{x}{a} \cdot \dfrac{x}{a}} = \frac{+ \dfrac{x}{a}}{\dfrac{x}{a} \cdot \dfrac{x}{a}}$$

$$= \frac{+ \dfrac{y}{a}}{\dfrac{y}{a}} = \frac{a + y}{y}$$

$$\therefore \quad g(y \quad y) \quad g\rho \quad \Psi$$

$$(y \quad y) = \frac{a + y}{y}$$

$$y \quad yy \quad a \quad y \quad y \quad yy \quad a$$
$$(y \quad y) \quad a \quad y$$

$$\Psi = \frac{x}{a} = \sqrt{ + \frac{x}{a}}$$

$$= \frac{\sqrt{a + y}}{a}$$

$$\therefore \quad \alpha = \frac{\sqrt{a + y}}{a} \quad a + v = a \quad \alpha$$

$$(\quad y \quad y) \quad a \quad a \quad \alpha \quad a \quad \alpha$$
$$\therefore \quad y \quad y \quad a \quad \alpha$$

27. $(\quad \alpha, \beta, \gamma)$

$(\quad\quad\quad\quad \alpha, \beta, \gamma)$

$$\frac{ax}{a} + \frac{\beta y}{b} + \frac{\gamma z}{c} = \frac{\alpha}{a} + \frac{\beta}{b} + \frac{\gamma}{c} \qquad (\ i)$$

()

$$p = \frac{\alpha\ /a\ + \beta\ /b\ + \gamma\ /c}{\sqrt{\alpha\ /a\ + \beta\ /b\ + \gamma\ /c}}$$

()

$$\frac{\alpha x}{a} + \frac{\beta y}{b} + \frac{\gamma z}{c} = \sqrt{\frac{a\ \alpha}{a} + \frac{b\ \beta}{b} + \frac{c\ \gamma}{c}}$$

$$p = \frac{\sqrt{\alpha\ /a\ + \beta\ /b\ + \gamma\ /c}}{\sqrt{\alpha\ /a\ + \beta\ /b\ + \gamma\ /c}}$$

$$k = \frac{p}{p} = \left(\frac{\alpha}{a} + \frac{\beta}{b} + \frac{\gamma}{c} \right)$$

$$\frac{x}{a} + \frac{y}{b} + \frac{z}{c} = \quad lx \quad my \quad nz \quad p$$

$$\pi k \quad abc \frac{\sqrt{l\ + m\ + n}}{\sqrt{a\ l\ + b\ m\ + c\ n}}$$

$$k \quad \frac{p}{p}$$

$$\frac{\pi\ abc \left\{ \left(\dfrac{\alpha}{a} + \dfrac{\beta}{b} + \dfrac{\gamma}{c} \right) \right\} \sqrt{\dfrac{\alpha}{a} + \dfrac{\beta}{b} + \dfrac{\gamma}{c}}}{\sqrt{a\ \dfrac{\alpha}{a} + b\ \dfrac{\beta}{b} + c\ \dfrac{\gamma}{c}}}$$

πd ()

$$a \ b \ c \left(\dfrac{\alpha}{a} \ \dfrac{\beta}{b} \ \dfrac{\gamma}{c} \right) \left(\dfrac{\alpha}{a} + \dfrac{\beta}{b} + \dfrac{\gamma}{c} \right)$$

$$= d \left(\dfrac{\alpha}{a} + \dfrac{\beta}{b} + \dfrac{\gamma}{c} \right)$$

$$(\qquad\qquad \alpha, \beta, \gamma)$$

$$a \ b \ c \left(\dfrac{x}{a} \ \dfrac{y}{b} \ \dfrac{z}{c} \right) \left(\dfrac{x}{a} + \dfrac{y}{b} + \dfrac{z}{c} \right)$$

28. $(\quad i)\ f(z)(\ u \quad v) \quad i(u \quad v)$
$\qquad iV$

$(\quad i)\ f'(z) \quad \dfrac{\partial}{\partial x} + \dfrac{i\partial}{\partial x} \qquad \dfrac{\partial}{\partial y} + i\dfrac{\partial}{\partial x}$

$\downarrow \ \downarrow$

$\phi\ (x\ y)\phi\ (x\ y)$

$$\phi\ (x\ y) \quad \dfrac{\partial}{\partial y} \quad \dfrac{-\quad x\left(e^{\,y} - e^{-\,y} \right)}{\left(e^{\,y} + e^{-\,y} - \quad x \right)}$$

$$\phi\ (x\ y) \quad \dfrac{\partial}{\partial x}$$

$$\left[\dfrac{x\left(e^{\,y} + e^{-\,y} - \quad x \right) - \qquad x}{\left(e^{\,y} + e^{-\,y} - \quad x \right)} \right]$$

$$\left[\dfrac{x \quad e^{\,y} + e^{-\,y} \quad -}{\left(e^{\,y} + e^{-\,y} - \quad x \right)} \right]$$

$$(\ )$$

$(\quad i)\ f(z) \quad \left[\phi\ (z\ ) + i\ \phi\ (z\ ) \right] dz + c$

$$\left[+ i \dfrac{(\qquad z - \ )}{(\ - \qquad z)} \right] dz + c$$

$$i \quad \dfrac{dz}{z - } + c$$

$$-i \qquad z\ dz + c$$

$$i \quad z \quad c$$

$$\therefore\ f(z) \quad \dfrac{i}{+i} \qquad z + \dfrac{c}{+i}$$

$$-(\ +i) \qquad z + \alpha$$

29. A. $\qquad\qquad\qquad\qquad u \qquad u'$

$()\ u \quad \lambda u'$

$\qquad lx \quad my \quad nz \quad p \quad \lambda(\ l'x \quad m'y$
$\qquad\qquad\qquad\qquad\qquad\qquad n'z \quad p)$

$()(\ l \quad \lambda l')x(\ m \quad \lambda m')y(\ n \quad \lambda n')\ z$
$\qquad p \quad \lambda p'$

$()$

$$\dfrac{(l+\lambda l')}{a} + \dfrac{(m+\lambda m')}{b} + (\ n+\lambda n')(\ p+\lambda p' =$$

$$() \quad \lambda \left(\dfrac{l'}{a} + \dfrac{m'}{b} + \ n'p' \right) + \lambda \left(\dfrac{ll'}{a} + \dfrac{mm'}{b} + n'\,p + np' \right)$$

$$+ \dfrac{l}{a} + \dfrac{m}{b} + \ np =$$

$$\lambda \quad \dfrac{u}{u'}\ ()\ ()$$

$$u \left(\dfrac{l'}{a} + \dfrac{m'}{b} + \ n'\,p' \right) \quad uu' \left(\dfrac{ll'}{a} + \dfrac{mm'}{b} + n'p + np' \right)$$

$$+ u' \left(\dfrac{l}{a} + \dfrac{m}{b} + \ np \right) =$$

$$u \qquad u'$$

B. $\qquad\qquad\qquad\qquad \dfrac{x}{a} + \dfrac{y}{b} + \dfrac{z}{c}$
$\qquad\qquad\qquad\qquad\qquad\qquad x$

$\qquad y \quad z \quad r$

$$\dfrac{x}{a} + \dfrac{y}{b} + \dfrac{z}{c} \qquad \dfrac{(x\ + y\ + z\ )}{r}$$

$$x\left(\frac{1}{a}-\frac{1}{r}\right)+y\left(\frac{1}{b}-\frac{1}{r}\right)+$$

$$z\left(\frac{1}{c}-\frac{1}{r}\right)$$

$$l\left(\frac{1}{a}-\frac{1}{r}\right)+m\left(\frac{1}{b}-\frac{1}{r}\right)+$$

$$n\left(\frac{1}{c}-\frac{1}{r}\right)$$

$$\frac{al}{(r-a)}+\frac{bm}{(r-b)}+\frac{cn}{(r-c)}$$

$$al(r-b)(r-c)+bm(r-a)$$
$$(r-c)+cn(r-a)(r-b)$$
$$r(al+bm+cn)-ra(b+c)$$
$$-bm(c+a)-cn(a+b)$$
$$abc(l+m+n)$$

$$r \qquad r$$

$$r-r=abc\,\frac{(l+m+n)}{(al+bm+cn)}$$

$$lx \quad my \quad nz \quad \frac{\sqrt{(al+bm+cn)}}{p}$$

$$p\;\frac{\sqrt{(al+bm+cn)}}{\sqrt{(l+m+n)}}$$

$$A$$

$$A \quad \pi \qquad \pi\,abc\;\frac{\sqrt{(l+m+n)}}{\sqrt{(al+bm+cn)}}$$

$$\frac{\pi abc}{p}$$

TEST PAPER - 4

PART - A

1. The function $f(x)$ defined on R by
$f(x) = x$ when x is irrational $-x$ when x is rational
is continuous

2. x

$$x, \quad \int_0^3 [x]\, dx$$

$-$

3. The unit vector parallel to $a = 3i + 4j - 2k$ is

$$\sqrt{29}\,(3i + 4j - 2k)$$

$$\frac{1}{\sqrt{29}}\,(3i + 4j - 2k)$$

$$(\quad i \quad j \quad k)$$

$$\frac{1}{29}\,(3i + 4j - 2k)$$

4. In a determinant A of order 3, a_{ij} denotes the element in i^{th} row and jth column. $i = 1, 2, 3$, and $j = 1, 2, 3$. If $a_{ij} = a_{ji}$ for all i and j then the elements in principal diagonal are necessary

5. The angle between the tangents drawn from the origin to the parabola $y^2 = 4a\,(x - a)$ is

6. The volume of a spherical soap bubble of radius r increases

πr

πr

πr

7. The vector $-i + j - k$ bisects the angle between the vectors c and $3i + 4j$ the unit vector along c is

$$\frac{1}{15}\,(11i + 10j + 2k)$$

$$\frac{15}{2}\,(-11i + 10j - 2k)$$

$$\frac{.1}{15}\,(-11i + 10j - jk)$$

8. If $\displaystyle\int_0^{\pi/2} \frac{d\theta}{4\cos^2\theta + 9\sin^2\theta} = k\pi$, then k equals

$$\frac{1}{3} \qquad \frac{1}{6}$$

$$\frac{1}{12}$$

9. The set of all points when the function

$$f(x) = \frac{x}{(1 + |x|)}$$ is differentiable is

$(\quad \infty \quad \infty) \qquad (\quad \quad \infty)$

$(\quad \infty \quad 0) \cup (\quad \quad \infty) \ (\quad \quad \infty)$

10. If $\log_{0.3}(x - 1) < \log_{.09}(x - 1)$ then x lies in the interval

$(\quad \infty) \qquad\qquad ()$

$() \qquad ()$

11. The series $x + \dfrac{x}{\ \ } + \dfrac{x}{\ \ } + \ ......$ is

$$x \qquad\qquad x\_$$

$$x\_ \qquad\qquad x$$

12. Which of the following transformations reduces the given differential equation $\dfrac{dy}{dx} = \dfrac{x - y + 1}{x + 2y - 3}$ into homogeneous one?

$x = X + \quad , \; y = Y -$

13. The area common to the curves $y^2 = x$ and $x^2 = y$ is

14. Evaluate $\displaystyle\lim_{x \to 0} \dfrac{e^{1/x}}{e^{1/x} + 1}$

15. Two sides of a triangle are formed by the vectors $a = 3i + 6j - 2k$ and $b = 4i - j + 3k$. One of the angle of the triangle is given by

  A. $\cos^{-1} \dfrac{7}{\sqrt{75}}$ B. $\cos^{-1} \dfrac{3}{\sqrt{15}}$

  C. $\cos^{-1} \dfrac{2}{3}$ D. none of the above

PART - B

16. A.

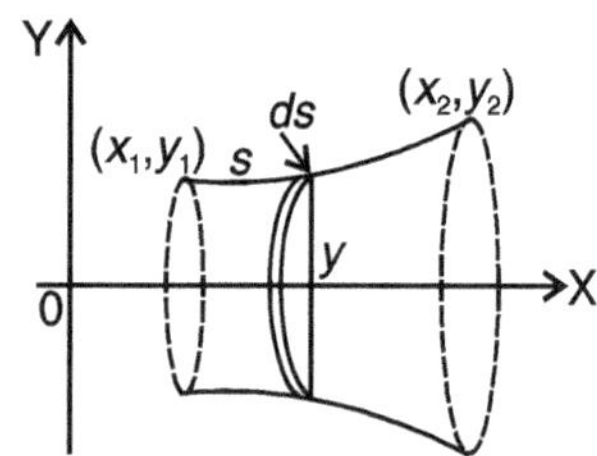

B. The radius 'r' of a cylinder is increasing at the rate of 0.25 cm/min, and its height 'h' is increasing at the rate of 0.2 cm. per min. How many cubic cm/min. is the volume of cylinder increasing when $r = 5$ cm and $h = 6$ cm.

17. A. Let $z = \log\left[\dfrac{x + y}{x + y}\right]$. Determine the value of $x\dfrac{\partial z}{\partial x} + y\dfrac{\partial z}{\partial y}$.

B. An element a of ring R is nilpotent if $a^n = 0$ for some positive integer n. Show that if a and b are nilpotent element of a commutative ring then $a + b$ is also nilpotent.

18. Let $T : V \to W$ be a linear map between two vector spaces V and W over some field F. If T is one-to-one and if $\alpha_1, \alpha_2, \ldots \alpha_k$, are linearly independent in V then show that $T(\alpha_1), T(\alpha_2) \ldots, T(\alpha_k)$ are linearly independent in W.

19. The volume of the tetrahedron whose vertices are the points with position vectors $i - 6j + 10k$, $-i - 3j + 7k$, $5i - j + \lambda k$ and $7i - 4j + 7k$ is 11 cubic units if the value of λ is?

20. For $f(x) = (1 + \sin x)\cos x$, where $0 \le x < 2\pi$, which of the following statements is true?

  (i) $f(x)$ has a local maxima at $x = \dfrac{\pi}{}$ $(0 < \text{at } x = \dfrac{\pi}{})$

    or

  (ii) $f(x)$ has a local maxima at $x = \dfrac{\pi}{}$ $(0 \le \text{at } x = \dfrac{\pi}{})$

21. Let W be the subspace spanned by $(2i, 0, 1, 2i)$, $(0, 2i - 2, i - 3, 0), (-i, 1, 0, i)$ and $(1, 1, 1, 1)$ in $\mathbb{C}^4$ over $\mathbb{C}$. The dimension of W over $\mathbb{C}$ is

22. The value of the integral $\displaystyle\int_0^\infty \int_x^\infty \dfrac{e^{-y}}{y}\, dy\, dx$ is

23. A. The function $f(x, y) = x^3 + 3xy^2 - 4y^3 - 15x$ has a local maxima at point.

B. The orthogonal trajectories of the curves $y = 3x^3 + x + c$ are

24. A. If $y_1'(x) = 3y_1(x) + 4y_2(x)$ and $y_2'(x) = 4y_1(x) + 3y_2(x)$, then $y_1(x)$ is

B. Let G be a group of order 8 generated by a and b such that $a^4 = b^2 = 1$ and $ba = a^3b$. The order of the centre of G is

25. The general solution of the differential equation

$$(x + y - 3)\, dx - (2x + 2y + 1)\, dy = 0$$

26.

$$y''(x) \quad \lambda y(x) \quad y() \quad y()$$

27.

$$f(x) \qquad \pi$$

$$- \qquad -\pi \leq x <$$

$$f(x) \qquad x =$$

$$\leq x \leq \pi$$

28.

$$\frac{\pi}{}\qquad --+---+-$$

$$a, b, c$$

$$\frac{x}{a} + \frac{y}{b} + \frac{z}{c}$$

29.

$$\pi$$

$$xy + \left(\frac{dx}{dt}\right) + \left(\frac{dy}{dt}\right)\, dt \qquad x()$$

$$x(\pi) \qquad y() \qquad y(\pi)$$

$$x \qquad t \ y \qquad t$$

ANSWERS

1	2	3	4	5	6	7	8	9	10

11	12	13	14	15

SOME SELECTED EXPLANATORY ANSWERS

PART - A

1. As in any interval there is infinite number of rationals and well as irrational numbers, hence for continuity

$$f(x) = x = -x$$
$$\Rightarrow \quad 2x = 0 \quad \Rightarrow \quad x = 0$$
so $\quad f(x)$ is continuous at $x = 0$

2.
$$\int_0^3 [x]\, dx = \int_0^1 0\, dx + \int_1^2 1\, dx + \int_2^3 2\, dx$$
$$= 0 + x\big|_1^2 + 2x\big|_2^3 = 0 + 1 + 2 = 3$$

3. $a = 3i + 4j - 2k$

$\Rightarrow \quad$ Unit vector parallel to $\vec{a}, \hat{a}$

$$= \frac{3i + 4j - 2k}{|3i + 4j - 2k|} = \frac{3i + 4j - 2k}{\sqrt{9 + 16 + 4}}$$

$$= \frac{1}{\sqrt{29}}(3i + 4j - 2k)$$

4. $a_{ij} = a_{ji} \Rightarrow a_{ii} = a_{ii}$

By putting $i = j$; so it is an identity, hence any value is possible.

5. Pair of tangents drawn from origin $(0, 0)$ on the parabola

$$y^2 = 4a\,(x - a) \text{ i.e., } y^2 - 4a\,(x - a) = 0$$
is $SS_1 = T^2$ i.e.,
$$[0 - 4a\,(-a)]\,[y^2 - 4a(x - a)]$$
$$= [0.y - 2a(x + 0) + 4a^2]^2$$
$$\Rightarrow \quad 4a^2\,[y^2 - 4a(x - a)] = 4a^2\,(x - 2a)^2$$
$$\Rightarrow \quad y^2 - 4ax + 4a^2 = x^2 - 4ax + 4a^2$$
$$\Rightarrow \quad y^2 - x^2 = 0 \Rightarrow y = \pm x$$

Coefficient of x^2 plus coefficient of $y^2 = 0$ so angle is $90°$

6.

$$\frac{4}{3}\pi r^3$$

Rate of increase $\dfrac{dV}{dr} = 4\pi r^2$

7. Let C be $xi + yj + zk$

$\Rightarrow \quad$ Bisector of C and $3i + 4j$

$$= \frac{C + 3i + 4j}{2} = -i + j - k$$

$$\Rightarrow \quad (x + 3)i + (y + 4)j + zk = -2i + 2j - 2k$$

$\Rightarrow \quad x + 3 = -2 ; y + 4 = 2 ; z = -2$

$\Rightarrow \quad x = -5, y = -2, z = -2$

$\Rightarrow \quad$ unit vector along $\vec{C} = \dfrac{-5\vec{i} - 2\vec{j} - 2\vec{k}}{\sqrt{33}}$

$\Rightarrow \quad C = -5i - 2j - 2k.$

8. $\quad I = \displaystyle\int_0^{\frac{\pi}{2}} \dfrac{d\theta}{4\cos^2\theta + 9\sin^2\theta} = k\pi$

$\Rightarrow \quad I = \dfrac{1}{9}\displaystyle\int_0^{\frac{\pi}{2}} \dfrac{\sec^2\theta \, d\theta}{\tan^2\theta + \left(\dfrac{2}{3}\right)^2} d\theta$

Let $\tan\theta = x \Rightarrow \sec^2\theta \, d\theta = dx$

At $\quad \theta = 0 ; x = 0$, At $\theta = \dfrac{\pi}{2} ; x = \infty$

$\Rightarrow \quad I = \dfrac{1}{9}\displaystyle\int_0^{\infty} \dfrac{dx}{\left(\dfrac{2}{3}\right)^2 + x^2}$

$= \dfrac{1}{9} \cdot \dfrac{1}{\left(\dfrac{2}{3}\right)} \tan^{-1} \dfrac{3x}{2} \Big|_0^{\infty} = \dfrac{\pi}{12}$

$\Rightarrow \quad k = \dfrac{1}{12}$

9. $\quad f(x) = \dfrac{x}{1 + |x|}$

$\Rightarrow \quad f(x) = \dfrac{x}{1 + x} \quad$ if $x \geq 0$

$\qquad\quad = \dfrac{x}{1 - x} \quad$ if $x \leq 0$

suspicious point is $x = 0$

$\Rightarrow \quad f'(x) = \dfrac{x}{(1 + x)^2} \quad$ if $x \geq 0$

$\qquad\quad = \dfrac{x}{(1 - x)^2} \quad$ if $x \leq 0$

At $\quad x = 0$ both gives same value so it is differentiable in $(-\infty, \infty)$

10. $\quad \log_{0.3}(x - 1) < \log_{0.09}(x - 1)$

$\Rightarrow \quad \log_{0.09}(x - 1)^2 < \log_{0.09}(x - 1) \qquad ...(i)$

(by squaring both base value and argument of logarithm)

$\Rightarrow \quad (x - 1)^2 > (x - 1)$ (As base is less than 1 So inequallity changes)

$\Rightarrow \quad (x - 1)(x - 2) > 0$

$\Rightarrow \quad x > 2$ or $x < 1$; when $x < 1$ log is not defined

so $x > 2$ i.e. $x \in (2, \infty)$

11. $\quad s = x + \dfrac{x^3}{3} + \dfrac{x^5}{5} + ... = \displaystyle\sum_{n=1}^{\infty} \dfrac{x^{2n-1}}{2n-1} = \sum u_n$

$\displaystyle\lim_{n\to\infty} \dfrac{u_{n+1}}{u_n} = \lim_{n\to\infty} \dfrac{2n-1}{2n+1} x^2 = x^2$

$\Rightarrow x^2 < 1 \Rightarrow$ (convergent) ; $x^2 > 1$

$\Rightarrow$ divergent.

At $\quad x = 1$, series is $\displaystyle\sum \dfrac{1}{2n-1} \Rightarrow$ divergent.

so for $x^2 < 1$ convergent and
for $x^2 > 1$ divergent
No answer is given in terms of x^2, so 4 is the answer.

12. $\quad \dfrac{dy}{dx} = \dfrac{x - y + 1}{x + 2y - 3}$

If $x = X + h$ and $y = Y + k$ is taken, then
$h - k + 1 = 0$ and $h + 2k - 3 = 0$

$\Rightarrow \quad h = 1/3 ; k = \dfrac{4}{3} \Rightarrow x = X + 1/3 ; y = Y + \dfrac{4}{3}$

13. $\quad y^2 = x$ and $x^2 = y$ intersects at $x^4 = x$

$\Rightarrow \quad x(x^3 - 1) = 0 \Rightarrow x = 0, 1,$

so, common area $= \displaystyle\int_0^1 (y_1 - y_2) dx$

$= \displaystyle\int_0^1 (\sqrt{x} - x^2) dx = 2\dfrac{x^{3/2}}{3} - \dfrac{x^3}{3} \Big|_0^1 = \dfrac{1}{3}.$

14. $\quad \displaystyle\lim_{x\to 0} \dfrac{e^{1/x}}{e^{1/x} + 1}$

L.H.S. $= \displaystyle\lim_{x\to 0^-} \dfrac{e^{1/x}}{e^{1/x} + 1} = \dfrac{0}{0 + 1} = 0$

R.H.S. $= \lim_{x\to 0^+} \dfrac{e^{1/x}}{e^{1/x}+1} = \lim_{x\to 0^+} \dfrac{1}{1+\dfrac{1}{e^{1/x}}}$

$= \dfrac{1}{1+0} = 1$

L.H.S. $\neq$ R.H.S.

$\Rightarrow$ limit does not exist.

15. $a = 3i+6j-2k\,;\ b = 4i-j+3k$
Third side c is $a-b = -i+7j-5k$
If θ is angle between a and c, then
$$\vec{a}\cdot\vec{c} = |\vec{a}||\vec{c}|\cos\theta$$
$\Rightarrow\quad -3+42+10 = 7\sqrt{75}\cos\theta$

$\Rightarrow\quad \cos\theta = \dfrac{7}{\sqrt{75}} \qquad \Rightarrow\quad \theta = \cos^{-1}\dfrac{7}{\sqrt{75}}$

$$\boxed{\textbf{PART - B}}$$

16. **A.** The surface area is given by $= \displaystyle\int_x^x \pi y\, ds$

$\pi \displaystyle\int_x^x y\sqrt{(\,+y')}\, dx$

$f\quad y\sqrt{(\quad y')}\qquad\qquad x$

$f - y'\dfrac{\partial f}{\partial y'}\qquad\qquad c$

$\therefore\ y\sqrt{(\,+y'\,)} - y'\dfrac{\partial}{\partial y'}\,y\sqrt{(\,+y'\,)}\qquad c$

$\Rightarrow y\sqrt{(\,+y'\,)} - y'\,\dfrac{y}{}(\,+y'\,)^{-/}\ y'\qquad c$

$\Rightarrow\ y\sqrt{(\quad y')}\ c\ y'\ \dfrac{dy}{dx}\ \dfrac{\sqrt{(y\ -c\,)}}{c}$

$\dfrac{dy}{\sqrt{(y\ -c\,)}}\qquad \dfrac{dx}{c}+c'\qquad h^{-}\left(\dfrac{y}{c}\right)$

$\dfrac{x+a}{c}$

$(\ )$

$\Rightarrow\quad y\quad c\quad h\!\left(\dfrac{x+a}{c}\right)$

$catenary \qquad\qquad a\qquad c$

$(\qquad\qquad\qquad x\quad y\,)$

$(x\quad y\,)$

B. $v = \pi r^2 h \Rightarrow \dfrac{dv}{dt} = 2\pi r\dfrac{dr}{dt}\,h + \pi r^2\dfrac{dh}{dt}$
(use it for desired result)

17. **A.** $f = e^z = \dfrac{x+y}{x+y} =$ eq. of order 1

$\Rightarrow\quad x\dfrac{\partial f}{\partial x} + y\dfrac{\partial f}{\partial y} = 1.$

$\Rightarrow\quad e^z\left[x\dfrac{\partial z}{\partial x} + y\dfrac{\partial z}{\partial y}\right] = e^z \Rightarrow x\dfrac{\partial z}{\partial x} + y\dfrac{\partial z}{\partial y} = 1$

B. a and b are nilpotent element
$\Rightarrow\quad a^n = 0$ and $b^m = 0$
$\Rightarrow\quad (a+b)^{m+n} = a^{m+n} + (m+n)\,c\,a^{m+n-1}\,b$
$+\ \dots\ m+n\,c_n\,a^m b^n + {}^{m+n}c_{n+1}\,a^{m-1}\,b^{n+1}$
$+\ \dots\ = 0+0+0+\ \dots\ = 0$
$\Rightarrow\quad (a+b)^{m+n} = 0$ $i.e.$ $a+b$ is also nilpotent.

18. $\alpha_1, \alpha_2, \dots\dots \alpha_n$ and L.I. in V
i.e. $c_1\alpha_1 + c_2\alpha_2 + \dots + c_n\alpha_n = 0$
$\Rightarrow\quad c_1 = c_2 = \dots.. = c_n = 0$
Now $T[\,c_1\alpha_1 + c_2\alpha_2 + \dots\dots c_n a_n\,] = T(0)$
$\Rightarrow\quad c_1 T(\alpha_1) + c_2 T(\alpha_2) + \dots\dots c_n T(\alpha_n) = 0$
but $c_1 = c_2 = \dots\dots c_n = 0$
$\Rightarrow\quad T(\alpha_1), T(\alpha_2), \dots\dots T(\alpha_n)$
are L.I. in W.

19. Volume of the tetrahedron with given vertices will be

$$\frac{1}{6}\begin{vmatrix} 1 & -6 & 10 & 1\\ -1 & -3 & 7 & 1\\ 5 & -1 & \lambda & 1\\ 7 & -4 & 7 & 1\end{vmatrix} = 11$$

$$\Rightarrow\quad \frac{1}{6}\begin{vmatrix} 1 & -6 & 10 & 1\\ -2 & 3 & -3 & 0\\ 4 & 5 & \lambda-10 & 0\\ 6 & 2 & -3 & 0\end{vmatrix} = 11$$

$$\begin{bmatrix} BY & R_2 \to R_2 - R_1; \\ & R_3 \to R_3 - R_1; \\ & R_4 \to R_4 - R_1 \end{bmatrix}$$

$$\Rightarrow \quad -\frac{1}{6}\begin{vmatrix} -2 & 3 & -3 \\ 4 & 5 & \lambda - 10 \\ 6 & 2 & -3 \end{vmatrix} = 11$$

$$= -\frac{1}{6}\begin{vmatrix} -2 & 3 & -3 \\ 0 & 11 & \lambda - 16 \\ 0 & 11 & -12 \end{vmatrix} = 11$$

$$\begin{bmatrix} BY & R_2 \to R_2 + 2R_1 \\ and & R_3 \to R_3 + 3R_1 \end{bmatrix}$$

$$\Rightarrow \quad \frac{1}{3} \times 11(4 - \lambda) = 11$$

$$\Rightarrow \quad \lambda = 1$$

20. $f(x) = (1 + \sin x)\cos x$

$$\Rightarrow \quad f'(x) = \cos^2 x - \sin x\,(1 + \sin x)$$

$$= 1 - 2\sin^2 x - \sin x$$

$$f'(x) = 0 \Rightarrow 2\sin^2 x + \sin x - 1 = 0$$

$$\Rightarrow \quad \sin x = \frac{-1 \pm \sqrt{1 + 8}}{4}$$

$$= \frac{-1 \pm 3}{4} = \frac{1}{2}, -1$$

$$\Rightarrow \quad x = \frac{\pi}{6} \ \text{ or } \ \frac{3\pi}{2}$$

Now $f''(x) = -4\sin x \cos x - \cos x$

$$< 0 \ at \ x = \frac{\pi}{6}$$

So $f(x)$ has a local maxima at $x = \dfrac{\pi}{6}$.

21. $W = \{(2i, 0, 1, 2i), (0, 2i - 2, i - 3, 0), (-i, 1, 0, i), (1, 1, 1, 1)\}$

Dimension of W is the rank of matrix

$$\begin{bmatrix} 2i & 0 & 1 & 2i \\ 0 & 2i-2 & i-3 & 0 \\ -i & 1 & 0 & i \\ 1 & 1 & 1 & 1 \end{bmatrix} \sim \begin{bmatrix} 0 & 2 & 1 & 2i \\ 0 & 2i-2 & i-3 & 0 \\ 0 & 1+i & i & 2i \\ 1 & 1 & 1 & 1 \end{bmatrix}$$

By $R_1 \to R_1 + 2R_3 \, ; \, R_3 \to R_3 + iR_4$

Its determinant is non-zero, so rank = 4

22. $\quad I = \displaystyle\int_x^\infty \int^\infty \frac{e^{-y}}{y}\, dy\, dx$

By changing the order of integration

$$I = \int_0^\infty \int^y \frac{e^{-y}}{y}\, dx\, dy$$

$$= \int_0^\infty \frac{e^{-y}}{y}\, x \Big|_0^y \, dy$$

$$= \int_0^\infty e^{-y}\, dy = -e^{-y}\Big|_0^\infty$$

$$= 0 - (-1) = 1$$

23. A. $\quad f(x, y) = x^3 + 3xy^2 - 4y^3 - 15x \qquad ...(i)$

for local extreme points

$$\frac{\partial f}{\partial x} = 0 \, ; \, \frac{\partial f}{\partial y} = 0$$

$$\Rightarrow \quad \frac{\partial f}{\partial x} = 3x^2 + 3y^2 - 15 = 0$$

$$\frac{\partial f}{\partial y} = 6xy - 12y^2 = 0$$

$$\Rightarrow \quad 6y\,(x - 2y) = 0$$

$$\Rightarrow \quad y = 0 \quad \text{or} \quad x = 2y$$

At $\quad y = 0 \quad 3x^2 = 15$

$$\Rightarrow \quad x = \pm\sqrt{5}$$

So $\left(\sqrt{5}, 0\right), \left(-\sqrt{5}, 0\right)$ are the points under scan.

$$\frac{\partial^2 f}{\partial x^2} = 6x; \ \frac{\partial^2 f}{\partial x^2} \ \text{ at } (x, y) = \left(-\sqrt{5}, 0\right)$$

$$-6\sqrt{5} < 0 \qquad \left(-\sqrt{5}, 0\right)$$

B. $\quad (9y + 3\tan^{-1} 3x = k)$

$$y = 3x^3 + x + c$$

$$\Rightarrow \quad \frac{dy}{dx} = 9x^2 + 1 \qquad ...(i)$$

Its orthogonal trajectory is

$$-\frac{1}{\dfrac{dy}{dx}} = 9x^2 + 1$$

$$\Rightarrow \quad \frac{dx}{x^2 + \left(\dfrac{1}{3}\right)^2} = -9\,dy$$

$$\Rightarrow \quad \frac{1}{\dfrac{1}{3}} \tan^{-1} \frac{x}{\dfrac{1}{3}} = -9y + k'$$

$$\Rightarrow \quad 9y + 3\tan^{-1} 3x = k$$

24. A.

$$\frac{dy_1}{dx} = 3y_1 + 4y_2 \qquad \qquad \ldots(i)$$

$$\frac{dy_2}{dx} = 4y_1 + 3y_2 \qquad \qquad \ldots(ii)$$

From (i)

$$\frac{d^{\,}y}{dx} = \frac{3dy_1}{dx} + \frac{4dy_2}{dx}$$

$$= \frac{3dy_1}{dx} + 16y_1 + 12y_2$$

$$= \frac{3dy_1}{dx} + 16y_1 + 3\left(\frac{dy_1}{dx} - 3y_1\right)$$

$$\Rightarrow \quad \frac{d^2 y_1}{dx^2} - 6\frac{dy_1}{dx} - 7y_1 = 0$$

$$\Rightarrow \quad m^2 - 6m - 7 = 0$$

$$\Rightarrow \quad (m-7)(m+1) = 0$$

$$\Rightarrow \quad m = 7, -1$$

$$\Rightarrow \quad y_1 = c_1 e^{-x} + c_2 e^{7x}$$

B.

$$O(G) = 8 = 2^3$$

From class equation

$$O(G) = O(z) + \sum_{a \notin z} O\!\left(\frac{G}{Na}\right)$$

$$\Rightarrow \quad O(z) = O(G) - \sum_{a \notin z} O\!\left(\frac{G}{Na}\right)$$

$$\because \quad O(G) = 2^3 \ \& \ \frac{2}{O\!\left(\dfrac{G}{Na}\right)}$$

$$\Rightarrow \quad 2 \mid O(z) \quad \Rightarrow \quad O(z) > 1 \quad \Rightarrow \quad O(z) = 2, 4, 8$$

Also when $O(z) = 8$ G is abelian.

$$\Rightarrow \quad ab = ba = a^3 b \ \Rightarrow \ a^2 = 1 \ (\text{ contradiction})$$

when $O(z) = 4$, then

$$O\!\left(\frac{G}{Na}\right) = 8 \ \Rightarrow \ a \in z \ (\text{contradiction})$$

$$\Rightarrow \quad O(z) = 2.$$

25. $(x + y - 3)\,dx - (2x + 2y + 1)\,dy = 0$

$$\Rightarrow \quad \frac{dy}{dx} = \frac{x + y - 3}{2(x + y) + 1} \qquad \qquad \ldots(i)$$

Let $\ x + y = u$

$$\Rightarrow \quad 1 + \frac{dy}{dx} = \frac{du}{dx}$$

$$\Rightarrow \quad \frac{du}{dx} - 1 = \frac{u - 3}{2u + 1}$$

$$\Rightarrow \quad \frac{du}{dx} = \frac{u - 3}{2u + 1} + 1 = \frac{3u - 2}{2u + 1}$$

$$\Rightarrow \quad \frac{2u + 1}{3u - 2}\,du = dx$$

$$\Rightarrow \quad \frac{\dfrac{2}{3}(3u - 2) + \dfrac{7}{3}}{(3u - 2)}\,du = dx$$

$$\Rightarrow \quad \frac{2}{3} + \frac{7}{3(3u - 2)}\,du = dx + c$$

$$\Rightarrow \quad -u + - (\quad u -) \ = x + c$$

$$\Rightarrow \quad 6u + 7\ln(3u - 2) = 9x + k$$

$$\Rightarrow \quad 7\ln(3x + 3y - z) + 6y - 3x = k$$

26. Integrating both sides of the given differential equation w.r.t. x over $(0, x)$, we get

$$y'(x) - y'(\ ) + \lambda \int^{x} y(x)\,dx$$

$$y'(x) \quad c - \lambda \int^{x} y(x)\,dx \qquad \qquad y'() \quad c \quad (i)$$

$$(i) \qquad x(\qquad x)$$

$$y(x) \quad y() \quad cx - \lambda \int^{x}\int^{x} y(x)\,dx$$

$$y(x) \quad cx - \lambda \int^{x}(x - t)\,y(t)\,dt \qquad \qquad (ii)$$

(i)

x (ii)

$$y() \quad c - \lambda \int (\ -t)y(t)dt \qquad \because y()$$

$$\therefore \quad c = \lambda \int (\ -t)y(t)dt \qquad (iii)$$

$$c \qquad (iii) \quad (ii)$$

$$y(x) \quad \lambda x \int (\ -t)y(t)dt - \lambda \int^x (x-t)y(t)dt$$

$$\lambda x \int (\ -t)y(t)dt + \int_x (\ -t)y(t)dt\ -$$

$$\lambda \int^x (x-t)y(t)dt$$

$$\lambda \int^x t(\ -x)y(t)dt + \lambda \int (\ -t)y(t)dt$$

$$\lambda \int^x (x\ t)y(t)dt + \int_x (x\ t)y(t)dt$$

$$(\qquad x\ t) \quad \begin{cases} t(\ -x) & t < x \\ x(\ -t) & t > x \end{cases}$$

$$y(x) \quad \lambda \int (x\ t)y(t)dt$$

$$(\qquad\qquad x\ t)$$

27. $a \quad \dfrac{}{\pi} \int_{-\pi}^{\pi} f(x)dx$

$$\dfrac{}{\pi} \int_{-\pi} (-\ )dx + \dfrac{}{\pi} \int^{\pi} (\ )dx$$

$$\dfrac{}{\pi}\big[-x\big]_{-\pi} + \dfrac{}{\pi}\big[x\big]^{\pi}$$

$$\dfrac{}{\pi}(-\pi + \pi)$$

$$a_n \quad \dfrac{}{\pi} \int_{-\pi}^{\pi} f(x)\ nx\,dx$$

$$\dfrac{}{\pi} \int_{-\pi} (-\ )\ nx\,dx + \dfrac{}{\pi} \int^{\pi} (\ )\ nx\,dx$$

$$\dfrac{}{\pi}\left[-\dfrac{nx}{n}\right]_{-\pi} + \dfrac{}{\pi}\left[\dfrac{nx}{\pi}\right]^{\pi}$$

$nx \qquad x \quad \pi \quad \pi \qquad n$

$$b_n \quad \dfrac{}{\pi} \int_{-\pi}^{\pi} f(x)\ nx\,dx$$

$$\dfrac{}{\pi} \int_{-\pi} (-\ )\ nx\,dx + \dfrac{}{\pi} \int^{\pi} (\ )\ nx\,dx$$

$$\dfrac{}{\pi}\left[\dfrac{nx}{n}\right]_{-\pi} + \dfrac{}{\pi}\left[-\dfrac{nx}{n}\right]^{\pi}$$

$(\quad x) \qquad x$

$$b_n \quad \dfrac{}{n\pi}(\ -\ n\pi) + \dfrac{}{n\pi}(-\ n\pi +)$$

$$\dfrac{}{n\pi}(\ -\ n\pi) \qquad /n\pi \qquad \begin{matrix} n \\ n \end{matrix}$$

$\therefore$

$$f(x) \quad \sum_{n=}^{\infty} b_n \quad nx$$

$$\dfrac{}{\pi}\left[\dfrac{x}{} + \dfrac{x}{} + \dfrac{x}{} + \right]$$

Second part :

$x \quad \pi \qquad\qquad x \quad \pi$

$f(\pi)$

$$\dfrac{}{\pi}\left(\dfrac{\pi}{} + - \dfrac{\pi}{} + - \dfrac{\pi}{} + \right)$$

$$\dfrac{\pi}{} \qquad - - + - - - + -$$

28. $\qquad\qquad\qquad\qquad\qquad\qquad a,\ b,\ c$

$x,\ y$

$a,\ b \qquad c$

$x \qquad y$

$$\dfrac{x}{a} + \dfrac{z}{c}\dfrac{\partial z}{\partial x} \qquad \dfrac{y}{b} + \dfrac{z}{c}\dfrac{\partial z}{\partial y}$$

$$\therefore \quad c\ x + a\ z\dfrac{\partial z}{\partial x} \qquad \dfrac{c}{a} \quad -\dfrac{z}{x}\dfrac{\partial z}{\partial x} \qquad (i)$$

$$c\ y + b\ y\frac{\partial z}{\partial y} \qquad \frac{c}{b} \qquad -\frac{z}{y}\frac{\partial z}{\partial y} \qquad (ii)$$

$$\qquad\qquad (i) \qquad\qquad x \quad (ii)$$
$$y$$

$$c\ +a\left(\frac{\partial z}{\partial x}\right) + a\ y\frac{\partial\ z}{\partial x}$$

$$\frac{c}{a} \qquad -\left(\frac{\partial z}{\partial x}\right) - z\frac{\partial\ z}{\partial x} \qquad (iii)$$

$$c\ +b\left(\frac{\partial z}{\partial y}\right) + b\ z\frac{\partial\ z}{\partial y}$$

$$\frac{c}{b} \qquad -\left(\frac{\partial z}{\partial x}\right) - z\frac{\partial\ z}{\partial y} \qquad (iv)$$

$$(i) \qquad (iii)$$

$$-z\frac{\partial z}{\partial x} + x\left(\frac{\partial z}{\partial x}\right) + xz\frac{\partial\ z}{\partial x} \qquad (v)$$

$$(ii) \qquad (iv)$$

$$-z\frac{\partial z}{\partial y} + y\left(\frac{\partial z}{\partial y}\right) + yz\frac{\partial\ z}{\partial y} \qquad (vi)$$

$$(v) \qquad (vi)$$

29.
$$\frac{\partial f}{\partial x} - \frac{d}{dt}\left(\frac{\partial f}{\partial x'}\right) \qquad (i)$$

$$\frac{\partial f}{\partial y} - \frac{d}{dt}\left(\frac{\partial f}{\partial y'}\right) \qquad (ii)$$

$$\Rightarrow \quad f \quad xy \quad x' \quad y' \quad \therefore \frac{\partial f}{\partial x} \quad y\frac{\partial f}{\partial x'} \quad x'$$

$$\frac{\partial f}{\partial y} \qquad x \quad \frac{\partial f}{\partial y'} \qquad y'$$

$$(i) \qquad\qquad y - \frac{d}{dt}\left(\ x'\right)$$

$$i.e. \quad y - \frac{d\ x}{dt} \qquad \frac{d\ x}{dt} \quad y \qquad (iii)$$

$$(ii) \qquad\qquad x - \frac{d}{dt}\left(\ y'\right)$$

$$i.e. \quad x - \frac{d\ y}{dt} \qquad \frac{d\ y}{dt} \quad x \qquad (iv)$$

$$(iii)$$

$$\frac{d\ x}{dt} \quad \frac{d\ y}{dt} \quad x \qquad (iv)$$
$$(\quad) \quad x$$

$$x \quad c\ e^x \quad c\ e^{\ x} \quad c \quad x \quad c \quad x$$
$$(v)$$
$$(iii)\ y \quad x'' \quad c\ e^x \quad c\ e^{-x} \quad c \quad x \quad c \quad x$$
$$(vi)$$
$$x \qquad t \quad \therefore \quad c \quad c \quad c \quad (vii)$$
$$y \qquad t \quad \therefore \quad c \quad c \quad c \quad (viii)$$
$$x \qquad t \quad \pi$$
$$\therefore \quad c\ e^\pi \quad c\ e^{\ \pi} \quad c \qquad (ix)$$
$$y \qquad t \quad \pi \quad \therefore \quad c\ e^\pi \quad c\ e^{\ \pi} \quad c \quad (x)$$
$$(vii) \quad (viii)\ c \quad c$$
$$(ix) \quad (x)\ c\ e^\pi \quad c\ e^{\ \pi}$$
$$c \quad c$$
$$(viii),\ c \quad c \quad c \qquad (ix)\ c$$
$$(v) \quad x \qquad x \qquad (vi)$$
$$y \quad x$$

TEST PAPER - 5

PART - A

1. $\int \dfrac{\log x^2}{x}\, dx$ is equal to

  A. $\dfrac{(\log x)^2}{2} + c$ B. $\dfrac{(\log x)^2}{3} + c$

  C. $\dfrac{(\log x)^2}{4} + c$ D. $\dfrac{(\log x^2)^2}{4} + c$

2. $\int x \tan^{-1} x\, dx$ is equal to

  A. $\dfrac{(x^2+1)\tan^{-1} x}{2} - x + c$

  B. $\dfrac{(x^2+1)\tan^{-1} x - x}{2} + c$

  C. $\dfrac{-(x^2+1)\tan^{-1} x + x}{2} + c$

  D. none of the above

3. If $d = \lambda(\vec{a} \times \vec{b}) + \mu(\vec{b} \times \vec{c}) + \eta(\vec{c} \times \vec{a})$ and $[a\ b\ c] = 1/8$, then $\lambda + \mu + \eta$ is equal to

  A. $(a + b + c)$ B. $(a \cdot b \times c)$

  C. $(a \times b \times c)$ D. none of the above

4. $\lim\limits_{x \to 1} \dfrac{\sum\limits_{r=1}^{n} x^r - n}{x - 1}$ is equal to

  A. $n/2$ B. $n(n+1)/2$

  C. 1   D. none of the above

5. The area included between the parabola $y^2 = 4ax$ and $x^2 = 4ay$ is equal to

  A. $8a^2/3$ B. $16a^2/3$

  C. $4a^2/3$ D. none of the above

6. Let a, b and c be three non-zero vectors such that

  $a + b + c = 0$ and $|a| = 3$, $|b| = 5$ and $|c| = 7$. Then the angle between a and b is

  A. 15^0 B. 30^0

  C. 45^0 D. 60^0

7. The order of 2 in the field $\mathbb{Z}_{29}$ is

8. If $\vec{u}(t) = u_1(t)\mathbf{i} + u_2(t)\,j + u_3(t)\mathbf{k}$ is a unit vector and $\dfrac{d\vec{u}}{dt} \neq 0$, then the angle between $\vec{u}(t)$ and $\dfrac{d\vec{u}}{dt}$ is

     $\dfrac{\pi}{4}$

  $\dfrac{\pi}{3}$ $\dfrac{\pi}{2}$

9. The differential equation
$2y\,dx - (3y - 2x)\,dy = 0$ is

10. The surface area of the solid generated by revolving the line segment $y = x + 2$ for $0 \le x \le 1$ about the line $y = 2$ is

  $\sqrt{2}\pi$ π

  $2\sqrt{2}\pi$ π

11. Let $f(x) = x^2 + 1$, $g(x) = x^3 + x^2 + 1$ and $h(x) = x^4 + x^2 + 1$. Then

  $f(x)$ $g(x)$ $\mathbb{Z}_2$

  $g(x)$ $h(x)$ $\mathbb{Z}_2$

  $f(x)$ $h(x)$ $\mathbb{Z}_2$

  $f(x)\ g(x)$ $h(x)$ $\mathbb{Z}_2$

12. The general solution of the differential equation
$y''(x) - 4y'(x) + 8y(x) = 10e^x \cos x$ is

$$e^{2x}(k_1 \cos 2x + k_2 \sin 2x) + e^x (2 \cos x + \sin x)$$

$$e^{2x}(k_1 \cos 2x + k_2 \sin 2x) + e^x (2 \cos x - \sin x)$$

$$e^{-2x}(k_1 \cos 2x + k_2 \sin 2x) - e^x (2 \cos x - \sin x)$$

$$e^{-2x}(k_1 \cos 2x + k_2 \sin 2x) + e^x (2 \cos x + \sin x)$$

13. Let $\sigma = \begin{pmatrix} 1 & 2 & 3 & 4 & 5 & 6 & 7 & 8 & 9 & 10 & 11 & 12 \\ 2 & 10 & 8 & 5 & 9 & 3 & 6 & 11 & 4 & 12 & 1 & 7 \end{pmatrix}$.

the cardinalty of the orbit of 2 under σ is

14. Let $f(x, y) = \ell n \sqrt{x + y}$ and $g(x, y) = \sqrt{x + y}$.

Then the value of $\nabla^2 (fg)$ at $(1, 0)$ is

$$-\frac{1}{2}$$

$$\frac{1}{2}$$

15. Let F be a field. Given below are six statements about F.

F

F

F

F

F

F

In which of the following options all the statements are correct?

PART - B

16. A. The general solution of the differential equation

$$\left(6x^2 - e^{-y^2}\right) dx + 2xye^{-y^2}\, dy = 0 \text{ is}$$

B. If $f(x, y) = \begin{cases} \dfrac{x^3}{x^2 + y^2}, & (x, y) \neq (0,0) \\ 0, & \text{otherwise} \end{cases}$

then at $(0,0)$, show that it is not differentiable.

17. A. The function $f(x) = \begin{cases} x^a \sin\dfrac{1}{x}, & x \neq 0 \\ 0, & x = 0 \end{cases}$

is differentiable at $x = 0$ for all a in the interval

B. The work done by the force $\vec{p} = 3i - 2j + 4k$ acting on a particle, if the particle is displaced from $A(8, -2, -3)$ to $B(-2, 0, 6)$ along the line segment AB, is

18. A. If $8x - y = 15$ is a tangent at $(2, 1)$ to the curve $y = x^3 + ax^2 + b$, then (a, b) is

B. The entire area bounded by the curve $r^2 = a \cos 2\theta$ is

19. A. Find the inverse of the matrix

$$\begin{bmatrix} & \\ & \end{bmatrix}$$

B. $\displaystyle \int_{1}^{2} \int_{x}^{2x} f(x,y)\,dy\,dx$

$x = u(\quad v)\ y$

uv

20. A. Expand $f(z) = \dfrac{z+}{\left(z - z - \right)z}$ in powers of z. In region

 $(i)\ |z| < 1$ $(ii)\ 1\ |z|\ 2$ $(iii)\ |z| > 2.$

B. The area bounded by the curve $y = (x + 1)^2$, its tangent at $(1, 4)$ and the x-axis is

21. A. Let V and W be vector spaces over a field F with $dim_F V = m$ and $dim_F W = n$, where m and n both are finite. then $dim_F Hom(V, W)$ is

B. Find a unit normal vector to surface $z = xy$ at $P(2, -1, -1)$.

22. A. The nullity of the matrix

$$\begin{pmatrix} 1 - i & 0 & i & i - 1 \\ 0 & 2 - i & -2 & 2 \\ -2 & -4 & 3 - i & -3 \\ 1 + i & 2 + i & -1 & 2 - i \end{pmatrix} \text{ is}$$

B. Arc length of the curve $y = x^{3/2}$, $z = 0$ from $(0, 0, 0)$ to $(4, 8, 0)$ is

23. A.
$$\int_{1}^{\infty} \frac{dx}{x^2(1 + e^x)}$$

B. The order of the quotient group

$$\mathbb{Z}_8 \times \mathbb{Z}_9 \times \mathbb{Z}_{18} / \langle (2, 2, 2) \rangle \text{ is}$$

24. The volume of the smaller part of the sphere $x^2 + y^2 + z^2 = 1$ when cut off by the plane

$$z = \frac{1}{2} \text{ is}$$

25. A. Let $\quad M = \begin{pmatrix} 1 & 1+i & 2-i \\ 1-i & 2 & 3+i \\ 2+i & 3-i & 3 \end{pmatrix}$.

If $B = \begin{pmatrix} x_1 & y_1 & z_1 \\ x_2 & y_2 & z_2 \\ x_3 & y_3 & z_3 \end{pmatrix}$, where $\begin{pmatrix} x_1 \\ x_2 \\ x_3 \end{pmatrix}$, $\begin{pmatrix} y_1 \\ y_2 \\ y_3 \end{pmatrix}$

and $\begin{pmatrix} z_1 \\ z_2 \\ z_3 \end{pmatrix}$ are linearly independent eigen vectors of M, then the main diagonal of the matrix $B^{-1}MB$ has

B. The number of values of λ for which the system of equations

$$\lambda x + (\lambda + 3) y = 10z$$
$$(\lambda - 1) x + (\lambda - 2)y = 5z$$
$$2x + (\lambda + 4) y = \lambda z$$

has infinitely many solutions, is

26.
$$\int_{a}^{b} x^2 \, dx$$

27. A.
$$y \qquad ax$$

B.
$$y \qquad\qquad y \qquad y \qquad xy$$

28. A.
$$()$$
$$\int \frac{\sqrt{x}}{x} dx$$

B.

29. A.
$$U \; i$$

$$v = \frac{UV}{\sqrt{U + V}}$$

$$\frac{V}{g}\left[\tan\left(\frac{U}{V}\right) + \tanh\left(\frac{v}{V}\right)\right]$$

B.
$$x \qquad y \qquad z \qquad yz$$
$$zx \qquad xy$$

ANSWERS

1	2	3	4	5	6	7	8	9	10
11	12	13	14	15					

SOME SELECTED EXPLANATORY ANSWERS

PART - A

1. $I = \int \dfrac{\log x^2}{x} dx = \int 2\dfrac{\log x}{x} dx$

Let $\log x = y \Rightarrow \dfrac{1}{x}dx = dy$

$\Rightarrow \quad I = \int 2y\, dy = y^2 + c = (\log x)^2 + c$

$\qquad = \dfrac{(\log x^2)^2}{4} + c$

2. $I = \int x \tan^{-1} x \, dx$

$\qquad = (\tan^{-1}x)\dfrac{x^2}{2} - \int \dfrac{x^2}{2(1 + x^2)} dx$

$$= \frac{x^2 \tan^{-1} x}{2} - \frac{1}{2} \int \left(1 - \frac{1}{1+x^2}\right) dx$$

$$= \frac{x^2 \tan^{-1} x}{2} - \frac{1}{2} x + \frac{1}{2} \tan^{-1} x + c$$

$$= \frac{(x^2 + 1) \tan^{-1} x - x}{2} + c$$

3. $\because \quad d = \lambda(\vec{a} \times \vec{b}) + \mu(\vec{b} \times \vec{c}) + \eta(\vec{c} \times \vec{a})$

$$\Rightarrow \quad \vec{c}.\vec{d} = \lambda \, \vec{c}.\left(\vec{a} \times \vec{b}\right) \Rightarrow \vec{c}.\vec{d} = \frac{\lambda}{8}$$

$$\Rightarrow \quad \lambda = 8 \vec{c}.\vec{d}$$

Again $\vec{a}.\vec{d} = \frac{1}{8}\mu \quad \Rightarrow \mu = 8\vec{a}.\vec{d}$

Also $\vec{b}.\vec{d} = \frac{1}{8}\eta \quad \Rightarrow \eta = 8\vec{b}.\vec{d}$

$$\therefore \quad \lambda + \mu + \eta = 8\left(\vec{a} + \vec{b} + \vec{c}\right).\vec{d}$$

4. $L = \lim\limits_{x \to 1} \dfrac{\sum\limits_{r=1}^{n} x^r - n}{x-1} \left[\dfrac{0}{0} \text{case}\right]$

By L Hospital's rule

$$L = \lim_{x \to 1} \sum_{r=1}^{n} r x^{r-1} = \sum_{r=1}^{n} r = \frac{n(n+1)}{2}$$

5. $y^2 = 4ax$ and $x^2 = 4ay$ have point of intersection as

$$x^4 = 16a^2 y^2 = 16a^2 (4ax)$$
$$\Rightarrow \quad x(x^3 - 64a^3) = 0$$
$$\Rightarrow \quad x = 0, 4a$$

So, area included between them will be.

$$\int_0^{4a} (y_1 - y_2) dx = \int_0^{4a} \left(\sqrt{4ax} - \frac{x^2}{4a}\right) dx$$

$$= 2\sqrt{a} \left.\frac{x^{3/2}}{3/2} - \frac{x^3}{12a}\right|_0^{4a}$$

$$= \frac{4\sqrt{a}}{3} (4a)^{3/2} - \frac{64a^3}{12a} = \frac{32}{3} a^2 - \frac{16}{3} a^2$$

$$= \frac{16a^2}{3}$$

6. $a + b + c = 0 \quad \Rightarrow \quad a + b = -c$
$$\Rightarrow \quad (a+b)(a+b) = c \cdot c$$
$$\Rightarrow \quad |a|^2 + |b|^2 + 2ab = |c|^2$$

()

$$\Rightarrow \quad 9 + 25 + 2|a||b|\cos\theta = 49$$
$[\theta$ is angle between a and $b]$
$$\Rightarrow \quad 34 + 30\cos\theta = 49$$
$$\Rightarrow \quad \cos\theta = 1/2 \Rightarrow \theta = 60^0$$

7. Z_{29} field means modulo 29 field

Here $[2] + [2] + ... + [2]$ at least 29 times will make it zero, so order of 2 is 29.

8. As $\vec{u}.\vec{u} = |\vec{u}|^2 \qquad \qquad ...(1)$

So differentiating both sides with respect to 't'

$$2\left(\vec{u}.\frac{d\vec{u}}{dt}\right) = 0$$

$$\Rightarrow \quad \vec{u} \text{ and } \frac{d\vec{u}}{dt} \text{ are perpendicular to each other.}$$

9. $2ydx + (2x - 3y) dy = 0 \qquad ...(1)$

It is Homogeneous
$$M = 2y$$
$$\Rightarrow \quad \frac{\partial M}{\partial y} = 2$$
$$N = 2x - 3y$$
$$\Rightarrow \quad \frac{\partial N}{\partial x} = 2$$

As $\dfrac{\partial M}{\partial y} = \dfrac{\partial N}{\partial x}$ so it is exact

(1) can be written as

$$\frac{dy}{dx} = \frac{2y}{2x - 3y}$$

$\Rightarrow \quad$ it is not linear

10.

The required solid is a cone with $r = 1$ and height, $h = 1$

Slant height $l = \sqrt{1+1} = \sqrt{2}$

Surface Area $= \pi r l = \sqrt{2}\pi$

11. Let $f(x) = x^2 + 1 = (x + a)(x + b)$

$\Rightarrow$ $a + b = 0$; $ab = 1$ ...(1)

$a = [1]$ and $b = [1]$ is the solution of 1 in z_2

i.e., modulo 2 field.

so $f(x)$ is reducible.

$g(x) = x^3 + x^2 + 1 = (x + a)(x^2 + bx + c)$

$\Rightarrow$ $a + b = 1$; $ab + c = 0$; $ac = 1$ ...(2)

equation (2) is not satisfied by any choice so it is not reducible.

$h(x) = x^4 + x^2 + 1 = (x + 1)(x^3 + ax^2 + bx + 1)$

$\Rightarrow$ $a + 1 = 0$; $a + b = 1$; $b + 1 = 0$ ...(3)

$\Rightarrow$ (3) is not satisfied, but

$x^4 + x^2 + 1 = (x^2 + ax + 1)(x^2 + bx + 1)$

$\Rightarrow$ $a + b = 0$; $1 + 1 + ab = 1$

$\Rightarrow$ $[a] = [b] = 1$ is satisfied

$\Rightarrow h(x)$ is reducible

12. $y''(x) - 4y'(x) + 8y(x) = 10e^x \cos x$

$\Rightarrow$ $(D^2 - 4D + 8)y = 10e^x \cos x$

$\Rightarrow$ $[(D - 2)^2 + 4]y = 10e^x \cos x$

Auxiliary equation is

$(m - 2)^2 + 4 = 0$ $\Rightarrow$ $m = 2 \pm 2i$

So, complementary function is

$y = e^{2x}[k_1 \cos 2x + k_2 \sin 2x]$ ...(1)

Particular Integral is

$$\frac{1}{(D - 2)^2 + 4} 10e^x \cos x$$

$$= 10e^x \frac{1}{(D + 1 - 2)^2 + 4} \cos x$$

$$= 10e^x \left[\frac{1}{D^2 - 2D + 5} \cos x\right]$$

$$= 10e^x \left[\frac{1}{-1 - 2D + 5}(\cos x)\right]$$

$$= 10e^x \frac{4 + 2D}{16 - 4D^2} \cos x$$

$$= \frac{e^x}{2}(4 \cos x - 2 \sin x)$$

$$= e^x(2 \cos x - \sin x) \qquad ...(2)$$

Solution is $y = $ C.F. + P.I.

$\Rightarrow$ $y = e^{2x}(k_1 \cos 2x + k_2 \sin 2x) + e^x(2 \cos x - \sin x)$

13. orbit of 2 is $(2, 10, 12, 7, 6, 3, 8, 11, 1)$ whose cardinality is 9.

14. $f(x, y) = \ln \sqrt{x + y}$

$g(x, y) = \sqrt{x + y}$

$\Rightarrow$ $fg = \sqrt{x + y} \ln \sqrt{x + y}$

$$\nabla^2 fg = \frac{\partial}{\partial x}(fg) + \frac{\partial}{\partial y}(fg) \qquad ...(1)$$

$$\frac{\partial^2}{\partial x^2}(fg) = \frac{\partial}{\partial x}\left(\frac{1}{2\sqrt{x + y}} \ln \sqrt{x + y} + \sqrt{x + y} \frac{1}{\sqrt{x + y}} \cdot \frac{1}{2\sqrt{x + y}}\right)$$

$$= \frac{\partial}{\partial x}\left[\frac{1}{2\sqrt{x + y}}\left(1 + \ln \sqrt{x + y}\right)\right]$$

$$= \frac{-}{(x + y)}\left(+ \sqrt{x + y}\right)$$

$$+ \frac{}{\sqrt{x + y}} \quad \frac{}{\sqrt{x + y}} \quad \frac{}{\sqrt{x + y}}$$

$$= \frac{}{(x + y)}\left[- - \sqrt{x + y}\right]$$

$$= \frac{- \sqrt{x + y}}{(x + y}$$

Similarly $\dfrac{\partial \, fg}{\partial y} = - \dfrac{\sqrt{x + y}}{(x + y)}$

$\Rightarrow$ $(\nabla^2 fg)_{(0\,1)} = - \dfrac{\sqrt{ + }}{} - \dfrac{\sqrt{ + }}{} = 0.$

15. Integral domain has no zero divisors.

$$\boxed{\textbf{PART - B}}$$

16. A. $\left(6x^2 - e^{-y^2}\right) dx + 2xye^{-y^2} \, dy$ ...(1)

$\Rightarrow$ $M = 6x^2 - e^{-y^2}$

$$\Rightarrow \quad \frac{\partial M}{\partial y} = 2ye^{-y^2}$$

$$N = 2xye^{-y^2}$$

$$\Rightarrow \quad \frac{\partial N}{\partial x} = 2ye^{-y^2}$$

As, $\dfrac{\partial M}{\partial y} = \dfrac{\partial N}{\partial x}$,

so differential equation (1) is exact,
so its solution is

$$2x^3 - xe^{-y^2} = C$$

$$\Rightarrow \quad x\left(2x^2 - e^{-y^2}\right) = C$$

B. $\quad \dfrac{\partial f}{\partial x}\bigg|_{(0,0)} = \underset{h \to 0}{Lt} \ \dfrac{\dfrac{h^3}{h^2 + 0} - 0}{h} = 1$

$\quad \dfrac{\partial f}{\partial y}\bigg|_{(0,0)} = \underset{k \to o}{Lt} \ \dfrac{\dfrac{0}{0 + k} - 0}{k} = 0$

$\Rightarrow \quad \dfrac{\partial f}{\partial x}$ and $\dfrac{\partial f}{\partial y}$ exist but are not equal.

Hence f is not differentiable at $(0, 0)$.

17. A. $\quad f'(0) = \underset{h \to 0}{Lt} \ \dfrac{h^a \sin \dfrac{1}{h}}{h}$

$$= \underset{h \to 0}{Lt} \ h^{a-1} \sin\left(\dfrac{1}{h}\right)$$

It exist $a - 1 > 0$ *i.e.,* $a > 1$
so $a \in (1, \infty)$

B. Displacement is from $A(8, -2, -3)$ to $B(-2, 0, 6)$, so displacement vector is

$$\vec{d} = -10\,i + 2j + 9k$$

force is $\vec{p} = 3i - 2j + 4k$

Work done $= \vec{p} \cdot \vec{d}$

$$= -30 - 4 + 36$$

$$= 2$$

18. A. $\quad y = x^3 + ax^2 + b \qquad\qquad ...(1)$

$\Rightarrow \quad \dfrac{dy}{dx} = 3x^2 + 2ax \qquad\qquad ...(2)$

Tangent at $(2, 1)$ is $8x - y = 15$

i.e., $\quad y = 8x - 15$

By equation (1) and (2) putting the point and slope of tangent, we get

$$1 = 8 + 4a + b \qquad\qquad ...(3)$$
$$8 = 12 + 4a \qquad\qquad ...(4)$$

$\Rightarrow \quad a = -1, b = -3$

B. $\quad$ Area $= \dfrac{1}{2} r^2 \, d\theta$

$$= \int^{\pi} -a \qquad \theta \, d\theta$$

$$= 2 \cdot \dfrac{1}{2} a \int_0^{\pi/2} \cos 2\theta \, d\theta$$

$$= a \cdot 2 \int_0^{\pi/4} \cos 2\theta \, d\theta$$

$$= 2a \ \dfrac{\sin 2\theta}{2}\bigg|_0^{\pi/4} = a$$

19. A. $\quad A = \begin{bmatrix} & \\ & \end{bmatrix}$

$$= \int_{\frac{1}{2}}^{\frac{2}{3}} \int_{\frac{1}{(1-v)}}^{\frac{2}{(1-v)}} f(u-uv,\, uv)\, u \, du \, dv$$

20. A. (*i*) within the unit circle about the origin.

$$f(z) = -\frac{\ }{z} + \frac{\ }{(z+\ )} + \frac{\ }{(z-\ )}$$

$$|z|$$

$$= -\frac{\ }{z} + -(\ +z)^{-} - -\left(\ -\frac{z}{\ }\right)^{-}$$

$$= -\frac{\ }{z} + -\big[\ -z+z\ -z+\ \big]$$

$$= --\left[\ +\frac{z}{\ }+\frac{z}{\ }+\frac{z}{\ }\right]$$

(*ii*)

$$|z|$$

$$f(z) = -\frac{\ }{z} + -\frac{\ }{z}\left(\ +\frac{\ }{z}\right)^{-} - -\left(\ -\frac{z}{\ }\right)^{-}$$

(*iii*)

i.e. $|z|$

$$f(z) = -\frac{\ }{z} + -\frac{\ }{z}\left(\ +\frac{\ }{z}\right)^{-} + -\frac{\ }{z}\left(\ --\frac{\ }{z}\right)^{-}$$

B.

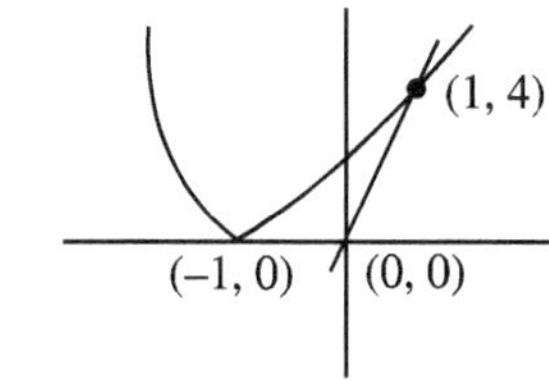

$$y = (x+1)^2$$

$$\Rightarrow \quad \frac{dy}{dx} = 2(x+1)$$

$$\left.\frac{dy}{dx}\right|_{(1,4)} = 4$$

$$\Rightarrow \quad (y-4) = 4(x-1) \text{ is the tangent}$$

Area enclosed

$$= \int_{-1}^{1} f(x)\, dx - \int_{0}^{1} 4x \, dx$$

B. $x = u(1-v),\ \ y = uv$

$$J = \frac{\partial(x,y)}{\partial(u,v)} = \begin{vmatrix} \dfrac{\partial x}{\partial u} & \dfrac{\partial x}{\partial v} \\[2mm] \dfrac{\partial y}{\partial u} & \dfrac{\partial y}{\partial v} \end{vmatrix}$$

$$= \begin{vmatrix} 1-v & -u \\ v & u \end{vmatrix} = u$$

$$x = u(1-v)$$

$\Rightarrow \quad 1 = u(1-v)$ at $x=1$

$\Rightarrow \quad 2 = u(1-v)$ at $x=2$

$$\Rightarrow \quad u = \frac{1}{(1-v)} \text{ to } u = \frac{2}{(1-v)}$$

$$y = x \ \Rightarrow \ uv = u(1-v) \ \Rightarrow \ v = \frac{1}{2}$$

$$y = 2x \ \Rightarrow \ uv = 2u(1-v) \ \Rightarrow \ v = \frac{2}{3}$$

$$\int_{1}^{2}\int_{x}^{2x} f(x,y)\, dy\, dx = \int \int f(u,\, v)\, J\, du\, dv$$

$$\Rightarrow \quad \int_{-1}^{1}(x+1)^2\,dx - \int_{0}^{1}4x\,dx$$

$$= \left.\frac{(x+1)^3}{3}\right|_{-1}^{1} - 2x^2\Big|_{0}^{1} = \frac{8}{3} - 2 = \frac{2}{3}$$

21. **A.** $\dim_F \mathrm{Hom}\,(U,V) = \dim(U)\,.\,\dim V = mn$

B. $f(x,y,z) = z - xy$

$$\Rightarrow \frac{\partial f}{\partial x} = -y\,;\ \frac{\partial f}{\partial y} = -x\,;\ \frac{\partial f}{\partial z} = 1$$

Normal is $\dfrac{\partial f}{\partial x}\hat{i} + \dfrac{\partial f}{\partial y}\hat{j} + \dfrac{\partial f}{\partial z}\hat{k}$

$$= -y\hat{i} - x\hat{j} + \hat{k}$$

At $(2,-1,-1)$ normal is

$$\hat{i} - \hat{j} + \hat{k}$$

unit normal is $\dfrac{i - 2j + k}{\sqrt{6}}$

22. **A.** (rank is 4; nullity is 0)

$$A = \begin{pmatrix} 1-i & 0 & i & i-1 \\ 0 & 2-i & -2 & 2 \\ -2 & -4 & 3-i & -3 \\ 1+i & 2+i & -1 & 2-i \end{pmatrix}$$

$$= \begin{pmatrix} 2 & 0 & i-1 & -2 \\ 0 & 2-i & -2 & 2 \\ -2 & -4 & 3-i & -3 \\ 2 & 3-i & -i+i & 1-3i \end{pmatrix}$$

$$R \to R \times (\ +i)$$
$$R \to R \times (\ -i)$$

$$= \begin{pmatrix} 2 & 0 & i-1 & -2 \\ 0 & 2-i & -2 & 2 \\ 0 & -4 & 2 & -5 \\ 0 & 3-i & 0 & -1-3i \end{pmatrix}$$

$$R \to R + R$$
$$R \to R - R$$

$$= \begin{pmatrix} 2 & 0 & i-1 & -2 \\ 0 & 2-i & -2 & 2 \\ 0 & -2-i & 0 & -5 \\ 0 & 3-i & 0 & -1-3i \end{pmatrix}$$

$$R_3 \to R_3 + R_2$$

clearly determinant of matrix is non-zero,
so its rank is 4

so nullity $= 4 - 4 = 0$

B. $y = x^{3/2} \Rightarrow \dfrac{dy}{dx} = \dfrac{3}{2}x^{1/2}$

Arc length $= \displaystyle\int_{0}^{4}\sqrt{1 + \left(\frac{dy}{dx}\right)^2}\,dx$

$$= \int_{0}^{4}\sqrt{1 + \frac{9x}{4}}\,dx$$

$$= \left.\frac{\left(1+\dfrac{9x}{4}\right)^{\frac{3}{2}}}{\dfrac{3}{2}\times\dfrac{9}{4}}\right|_{0}^{4} = \frac{8}{27}\left(10^{\frac{3}{2}} - 1\right)$$

23. **A.** $\dfrac{1}{x^2(1+e^x)} < \dfrac{1}{x^2}$ when $1 \le x < \infty$

So $\displaystyle\int_{1}^{\infty}\frac{1}{x^2(1+e^x)}\,dx < \int_{1}^{\infty}\frac{1}{x^2}\,dx < \left.\frac{-1}{x}\right|_{1}^{\infty} < 1$

B. order of 2 in $Z_8 = \dfrac{8}{G.C.D.\,(2,8)} = 4$

Order of 2 in $Z_9 = \dfrac{9}{G.C.D.\,(2,9)} = 9$

Order of 2 in $Z_{18} = \dfrac{18}{G.C.D.\,(2,18)} = 9$

L.C.M. of $(4,9,9)$ is order of quotient group
$Z_8 \times Z_9 \times Z_{18} / (2,2,2) = 36$

24. $V = \displaystyle\int_{1/2}^{1}\int_{\sqrt{1-z^2}}^{\sqrt{1-z^2}}\int_{-\sqrt{1-z^2-x^2}}^{\sqrt{1-z^2-x^2}} dy\,dx\,dz$

$$= 2\int_{1/2}^{1}\int_{-\sqrt{1-z^2}}^{\sqrt{1-z^2}}\sqrt{1-z^2-x^2}\,dx\,dz$$

$$= 4\int_{1/2}^{1}\int_{0}^{\sqrt{1-z^2}}\sqrt{1-z^2-x^2}\,dx\,dz$$

$$= 4\int_{1/2}^{1}\left[\frac{x\sqrt{1-z^2-x^2}}{2}+\frac{\left(1-z^2\right)}{2}\sin^{-1}\frac{x}{\sqrt{1-z^2}}\right]_{0}^{\sqrt{1-z^2}}dz$$

$$\left[\because \int\sqrt{a^2-x^2}\,dx=\frac{x\sqrt{a^2-x^2}}{2}+\frac{a^2}{2}\sin^{-1}\frac{x}{a}\right]$$

$$= 4\int_{1/2}^{1}\frac{1-z^2}{2}\cdot\frac{\pi}{2}\,dz\;=\;\pi\int_{1/2}^{1}\left(1-z^2\right)dz$$

$$= \pi\left[z-\frac{z^3}{3}\right]_{1/2}^{1}$$

$$= 4\left[\left(1-\frac{1}{3}\right)-\left(\frac{1}{2}-\frac{1}{24}\right)\right]=\frac{5\pi}{24}.$$

25. A.
$$M=\begin{pmatrix}1 & 1+i & 2-i\\ 1-i & 2 & 3+i\\ 2+i & 3-i & 3\end{pmatrix}$$

conjugate transpose of M

i.e., $M^{\theta}=M$

$\Rightarrow$ M is hermitian matrix

$\Rightarrow$ All its roots (eigen values) are real

So $B^{-1}MB$ will have entries in Main diagonal as all three real entries.

B. For infinitely many solutions of homogeneous equation determinant of coefficient matrix will be zero

$$\Rightarrow\quad\begin{vmatrix}\lambda & (\lambda+3) & -10\\ \lambda-1 & (\lambda-2) & -5\\ 2 & (\lambda+4) & -\lambda\end{vmatrix}=0$$

$$\Rightarrow\quad \lambda\left(-\lambda^2+2\lambda+5\lambda+20\right)$$
$$-(\lambda-1)\left(-\lambda^2-3\lambda+10\lambda+40\right)$$
$$+2(-5\lambda-15+10\lambda-20)=0$$

$$\Rightarrow\quad \lambda(-\lambda^2+7\lambda+20)-(\lambda-1)$$
$$(-\lambda^2+7\lambda+40)+2(5\lambda-35)=0$$

$$\Rightarrow\quad -\lambda^3+7\lambda^2+20\lambda-$$
$$\left[-\lambda^3+7\lambda^2+40\lambda+\lambda^2-7\lambda-40\right]$$
$$+10\lambda-70=0$$

$$\Rightarrow\quad \lambda^2-3\lambda-30=0$$

$$\Rightarrow\quad \lambda=\frac{3\pm\sqrt{9+120}}{2}\quad\textit{i.e.,}\text{ two values.}$$

26.
$$\int_{a}^{b} x\;dx$$

$$\lim_{\substack{n\to\infty\\h\to}} h\left[f(a)\,(+f(a)+h\,(+f(a+)\;h+\cdots+f(a+(n-\;)h)\right]$$

$$\lim_{\substack{n\to\infty\\h\to}} h\left[na\;+\;ah\;+\;+\;+\;(+n)\right.$$
$$\left.+h\;\;+\;\;+\;\;+(\;+n)-\right]$$

$$\lim_{\substack{n\to\infty\\h\to}} h\left[na\;+\frac{n(n-\;)}{}\;ah\right.$$
$$\left.+\frac{n(n-\;)(\;n-\;)}{}\;h\right]$$

$$\lim_{\substack{n\to\infty\\h\to}} h\left[na\;+anh(n-\;)+\frac{nh\;(n-\;)(\;n-\;)}{}\right]$$

$$\lim_{\substack{n\to\infty\\h\to}} h\left[nha\;+anh(nh-h)+\frac{nh(nh-h)(\;nh-h)}{}\right]$$

$$nh=b-a$$

$$\left[a\;(b-a)+a\,(b-a)\;+\frac{(b-a)}{}\right]$$

$$\Rightarrow\quad (b-a)\left[a\;+ab-a\;+\frac{b\;-\;ab+a}{}\right]$$

$$\Rightarrow\quad \frac{(b-a)}{}\left[a\;+b\;+ab\right]\;\frac{b\;-a}{}$$

27. A.
$$y\qquad ax$$

$$\therefore\quad y\frac{dy}{dx}\qquad a$$

$$\frac{dy}{dx}\qquad \frac{a}{y}=\frac{a}{\sqrt{ax}}=\sqrt{\left(\frac{a}{x}\right)}$$

$$\frac{dx}{dy} = \frac{\sqrt{x}}{a}$$

an extremity of the latus rectum arc x

$x = a$

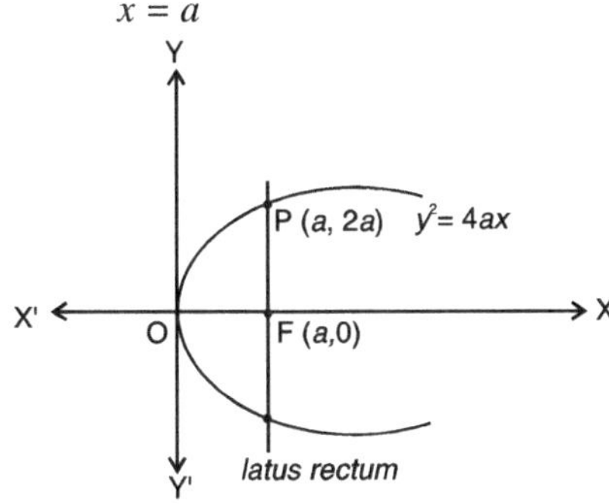

$\therefore$ i.e.,

$$\int^{a} \sqrt{ + \left(\frac{dy}{dx}\right)}\; dy \qquad \int^{a} \sqrt{\frac{+x}{a}}\; dy$$

$$\int^{a} \sqrt{ + \frac{y}{a}}\, dy \qquad \frac{}{a} \int^{a} \sqrt{y + a}\; dy$$

$$\frac{}{a}\left[y\frac{\sqrt{y+a}}{} + a \quad \left(y + \sqrt{y+a} \right)\right]^{a}$$

$$\frac{}{a}\left[\frac{a\,\sqrt{a}}{} + a \quad \left(a + \sqrt{a} \right) - a \quad a \right]$$

$$\frac{}{a}\left[\sqrt{a} + a \quad \left(+\sqrt{} \right) \right]$$

$$a\left[\sqrt{2} + \log\left(1 + \sqrt{2} \right) \right]$$

B. xy $x = \dfrac{}{y}$

y x

$-$

y $y \in [\quad]$

$\therefore$ $g(y)\, dy \quad \dfrac{}{y}\, dy \; [\quad y]$

Note : xy

     $x \qquad y$

28. A. $()\quad z \qquad z$

$\therefore$ $z \quad \pm\sqrt{}\, i$

$\therefore e^{iz} \quad \left(\pm\sqrt{} \right) i$

$(i)\; e^{iz} \quad \left(+\sqrt{} \right) i$

$\Rightarrow z \quad -i \quad \left(+\sqrt{} \right) i$

$$-i\left[\quad \left(+\sqrt{} \right) + \left(n\pi + \frac{\pi}{} \right) i \right]$$

$$\left(n\pi + \frac{\pi}{} \right) - i \quad \left(+\sqrt{} \right)$$

$$n\pi + \frac{\pi}{} - i \quad \left(+\sqrt{} \right)$$

$(ii)\; e^{iz} \quad \left(-\sqrt{} \right) i$

$\Rightarrow z \quad -i \quad \left(-\sqrt{} \right) i$

$$-i\left[\quad \left(-\sqrt{} \right) + \left(n\pi + \frac{\pi}{} \right) i \right]$$

$$\left(n\pi + \frac{\pi}{} \right) - i \quad \left(-\sqrt{} \right)$$

$$(n +)\pi - \frac{\pi}{} - i \quad \left(+\sqrt{} \right)$$

$\therefore$ $()\quad \pi + (-)^{n}\, \dfrac{\pi}{} - i \quad \left(+\sqrt{} \right)$

$\therefore$ $()\quad \dfrac{\pi}{} - i \quad \left(+\sqrt{} \right)$

B.

$$f(x) = \frac{\sqrt{x}}{x} \qquad g(x) = \frac{}{x-}$$

$$\lim_{x\to} \frac{f(x)}{g(x)} = \lim_{x\to^+} \frac{(x-)\ \sqrt{x}}{x}\left(-\right)$$

$$\lim_{x\to^+} \frac{-x \quad --x^-}{x}$$

$$\lim_{x\to^+} \left(-x \quad --x\right) =$$

$$\int g(x)\,dx = \int \frac{dx}{(x-)}$$

$$(\therefore n)$$

$$\int f(x)\,dx = \int \frac{\sqrt{x}}{x}$$

29. A. h

$$h = \frac{V}{g} \quad \frac{V+U}{V}$$

$$\frac{V+U}{V} = e^{\frac{gh}{V}}$$

$$v = V\left(e^{\frac{gh}{V}} \right)$$

$$= V\left(\frac{V}{V+U} \right)$$

$$= \frac{U\ V}{V+U}$$

t

$$t = \frac{V}{g} \quad \frac{U}{V}$$

$$= \frac{V}{g} \quad \frac{v}{V}$$

$$\therefore \quad = \frac{V}{g}\left[\frac{U}{V} + \frac{v}{V} \right]$$

B.

$$a \quad b \quad c \quad f \ -- \ g \quad h \ --$$
$$d$$

$$\lambda \quad \lambda\,0 \qquad \lambda(\qquad - \qquad -\,)$$

$$\left(-- \right)0 \quad \left(-- \right) \quad \left(-- \right)$$

$$0 \qquad \left(-- \right)$$

$$\lambda \quad \lambda \quad \frac{\lambda}{\ } \qquad - \qquad -$$

$$\lambda \quad \lambda \quad \frac{\lambda}{\ }$$

$$\lambda \quad 1\ \lambda \qquad \lambda$$
$$\lambda \quad \lambda \qquad \lambda \qquad \lambda\ \lambda$$
$$\lambda\,(\ \lambda) \qquad \lambda(\lambda)(\qquad \lambda)$$
$$(\quad \lambda)(\quad \lambda \qquad \lambda)$$

$$\lambda \qquad \left(\frac{\pm\ \sqrt{\ }}{\ } \right)$$

$$\lambda$$

$$\lambda$$

$$x \quad y \quad z \quad yz \quad zx \quad xy \ (\quad x \quad y \quad z \ )$$
$$(\quad x \quad y \quad z \quad yz \quad zx \quad xy)$$
$$(\quad x \quad z) \quad y(x \quad z) \quad y$$
$$(\quad x \quad y \quad z)(\quad x \quad z \quad y)$$

$$x \quad y \quad z \qquad x \quad y \quad z$$